Macworld
FreeHand 4
Bible

Macworld
FreeHand 4
Bible

by Deke McClelland

IDG Books Worldwide, Inc.
An International Data Group Company

San Mateo, California ✦ Indianapolis, Indiana ✦ Boston, Massachusetts

Macworld FreeHand 4 Bible

Published by
IDG Books Worldwide, Inc.
An International Data Group Company
155 Bovet Road, Suite 310
San Mateo, CA 94402

Library of Congress Catalog Card No.: 94-75904

ISBN 1-56884-170-1

Printed in the United States of America

10 9 8 7 6 5 4 3 2 1

1C/0V/RV/ZU

Distributed in the United States by IDG Books Worldwide, Inc.

Distributed in Canada by Macmillan of Canada, a Division of Canada Publishing Corporation; by Computer and Technical Books in Miami, Florida, for South America and the Caribbean; by Longman Singapore in Singapore, Malaysia, Thailand, and Korea; by Toppan Co. Ltd. in Japan; by Asia Computerworld in Hong Kong; by Woodslane Pty. Ltd. in Australia and New Zealand; and by Transword Publishers Ltd. in the U.K. and Europe.

For general information on IDG Books in the U.S., including information on discounts and premiums, contact IDG Books at 800-762-2974 or 415-312-0650

For information on where to purchase IDG Books outside the U.S., contact Christina Turner at 415-312-0633.

For information on translations, contact Marc Jeffrey Mikulich, Foreign Rights Manager, at IDG Books Worldwide; FAX NUMBER 415-358-1260.

For sales inquiries and special prices for bulk quantities, write to the address above or call IDG Books Worldwide at 415-312-0650.

 is a registered trademark of IDG Books Worldwide, Inc.

 The text in this book is printed on recycled paper.

About the Author

Deke McClelland, best-selling author of IDG Books' *Macworld Photoshop 2.5 Bible,* has written 25 books about desktop publishing and graphics. He's a contributing editor to IDG's *Macworld* magazine and also writes for *Publish* and *PC World.* He received the Ben Franklin Best Computer Book Award in 1989 and won the prestigious Computer Press Award in 1990 and again in 1992.

Credits

Publisher
David Solomon

Managing Editor
Mary Bednarek

Acquisitions Editor
Janna Custer

Production Director
Beth Jenkins

Senior Editors
Tracy L. Barr
Sandra Blackthorn
Diane Graves Steele

Production Coordinator
Cindy L. Phipps

Associate Acquisitions Editor
Megg Bonar

Project Editor
Julie A. King

Editorial Assistant
Darlene Cunningham

Technical Reviewer
Arne Hurty

Production Staff
Tony Augsburger
Valery Bourke
Mary Breidenbach
Chris Collins
Sherry Gomoll
Drew Moore
Kathie Schnorr
Gina Scott

Cover Design
Kavish + Kavish

Cover Illustrator
Don Baker

Proofreader
Betty Kish

Indexer
Steve Rath

Book Design
Beth Jenkins

About IDG Books Worldwide

Welcome to the world of IDG Books Worldwide.

IDG Books Worldwide, Inc., is a subsidiary of International Data Group, the world's largest publisher of computer-related information and the leading global provider of information services on information technology. International Data Group publishes over 200 computer publications in 63 countries. Forty million people read one or more International Data Group publications each month.

If you use personal computers, IDG Books is committed to publishing quality books that meet your needs. We rely on our extensive network of publications, including such leading periodicals as *Macworld*, *InfoWorld*, *PC World*, *Computerworld*, *Publish*, *Network World*, and *SunWorld*, to help us make informed and timely decisions in creating useful computer books that meet your needs.

Every IDG book strives to bring extra value and skill-building instructions to the reader. Our books are written by experts, with the backing of IDG periodicals, and with careful thought devoted to issues such as audience, interior design, use of icons, and illustrations. Our editorial staff is a careful mix of high-tech journalists and experienced book people. Our close contact with the makers of computer products helps ensure accuracy and thorough coverage. Our heavy use of personal computers at every step in production means we can deliver books in the most timely manner.

We are delivering books of high quality at competitive prices on topics customers want. At IDG, we believe in quality, and we have been delivering quality for over 25 years. You'll find no better book on a subject than an IDG book.

John Kilcullen
President and CEO
IDG Books Worldwide, Inc.

IDG Books Worldwide, Inc. is a subsidiary of International Data Group. The officers are Patrick J. McGovern, Founder and Board Chairman; Walter Boyd, President. International Data Group's publications include: **ARGENTINA'S** Computerworld Argentina, Infoworld Argentina; **AUSTRALIA'S** Computerworld Australia, Australian PC World, Australian Macworld, Network World, Mobile Business Australia, Reseller, IDG Sources; **AUSTRIA'S** Computerwelt Oesterreich, PC Test; **BRAZIL'S** Computerworld, Gamepro, Game Power, Mundo IBM, Mundo Unix, PC World, Super Game; **BELGIUM'S** Data News (CW) **BULGARIA'S** Computerworld Bulgaria, Ediworld, PC & Mac World Bulgaria, Network World Bulgaria; **CANADA'S** CIO Canada, Computerworld Canada, Graduate Computerworld, InfoCanada, Network World Canada; **CHILE'S** Computerworld Chile, Informatica; **COLOMBIA'S** Computerworld Colombia, PC World; **CZECH REPUBLIC'S** Computerworld, Elektronika, PC World; **DENMARK'S** Communications World, Computerworld Danmark, Macintosh Produktkatalog, Macworld Danmark, PC World Danmark, PC World Produktguide, Tech World, Windows World; **ECUADOR'S** PC World Ecuador; **EGYPT'S** Computerworld (CW) Middle East, PC World Middle East; **FINLAND'S** MikroPC, Tietoviikko, Tietoverkko; **FRANCE'S** Distributique, GOLDEN MAC, InfoPC, Languages & Systems, Le Guide du Monde Informatique, Le Monde Informatique, Telecoms & Reseaux; **GERMANY'S** Computerwoche, Computerwoche Focus, Computerwoche Extra, Computerwoche Karriere, Information Management, Macwelt, Netzwelt, PC Welt, PC Woche, Publish, Unit; **GREECE'S** Infoworld, PC Games; **HUNGARY'S** Computerworld SZT, PC World; **HONG KONG'S** Computerworld Hong Kong, PC World Hong Kong; **INDIA'S** Computers & Communications; **IRELAND'S** ComputerScope; **ISRAEL'S** Computerworld Israel, PC World Israel; **ITALY'S** Computerworld Italia, Lotus Magazine, Macworld Italia, Networking Italia, PC Shopping, PC World Italia; **JAPAN'S** Computerworld Today, Information Systems World, Macworld Japan, Nikkei Personal Computing, SunWorld Japan, Windows World; **KENYA'S** East African Computer News; **KOREA'S** Computerworld Korea, Macworld Korea, PC World Korea; **MEXICO'S** Compu Edicion, Compu Manufactura, Computacion/Punto de Venta, Computerworld Mexico, MacWorld, Mundo Unix, PC World, Windows; **THE NETHERLANDS'** Computer! Totaal, Computable (CW), LAN Magazine, MacWorld, Totaal "Windows"; **NEW ZEALAND'S** Computer Listings, Computerworld New Zealand, New Zealand PC World, Network World; **NIGERIA'S** PC World Africa; **NORWAY'S** Computerworld Norge, C/World, Lotusworld Norge, Macworld Norge, Networld, PC World Ekspress, PC World Norge, PC World's Produktguide, Publish & Multimedia World, Student Data, Unix World, Windowsworld; IDG Direct Response; **PAKISTAN'S** PC World Pakistan; **PANAMA'S** PC World Panama; **PERU'S** Computerworld Peru, PC World; **PEOPLE'S REPUBLIC OF CHINA'S** China Computerworld, China Infoworld, Electronics Today/Multimedia World, Electronics International, Electronic Product World, China Network World, PC and Communications Magazine, PC World China, Software World Magazine, Telecom Product World; IDG HIGH TECH BEIJING'S New Product World; IDG SHENZHEN'S Computer News Digest; **PHILIPPINES'** Computerworld Philippines, PC Digest (PCW); **POLAND'S** Computerworld Poland, PC World/Komputer; **PORTUGAL'S** Cerebro/PC World, Correio Informatico/Computerworld, Informatica & Comunicacoes Catalogo, MacIn, Nacional de Produtos; **ROMANIA'S** Computerworld, PC World; **RUSSIA'S** Computerworld-Moscow, Mir - PC, Sety; **SINGAPORE'S** Computerworld Southeast Asia, PC World Singapore; **SLOVENIA'S** Monitor Magazine; **SOUTH AFRICA'S** Computer Mail (CIO), Computing S.A., Network World S.A., Software World; **SPAIN'S** Advanced Systems, Amiga World, Computerworld Espana, Communicaciones World, Macworld Espana, NeXTWORLD, Super Juegos Magazine (GamePro), PC World Espana, Publish; **SWEDEN'S** Attack, ComputerSweden, Corporate Computing, Natverk & Kommunikation, Macworld, Mikrodatorn, PC World, Publishing & Design (CAP), DataIngenjoren, Maxi Data, Windows World; **SWITZERLAND'S** Computerworld Schweiz, Macworld Schweiz, PC Tip; **TAIWAN'S** Computerworld Taiwan, PC World Taiwan; **THAILAND'S** Thai Computerworld; **TURKEY'S** Computerworld Monitor, Macworld Turkiye, PC World Turkiye; **UKRAINE'S** Computerworld; **UNITED KINGDOM'S** Computing /Computerworld, Connexion/Network World, Lotus Magazine, Macworld, Open Computing/Sunworld; **UNITED STATES'** Advanced Systems, AmigaWorld, Cable in the Classroom, CD Review, CIO, Computerworld, Digital Video, DOS Resource Guide, Electronic Entertainment Magazine, Federal Computer Week, Federal Integrator, GamePro, IDG Books, Infoworld, Infoworld Direct, Laser Event, Macworld, Multimedia World, Network World, PC Letter, PC World, PlayRight, Power PC World, Publish, SWATPro, Video Event; **VENEZUELA'S** Computerworld Venezuela, PC World; **VIETNAM'S** PC World Vietnam

Acknowledgments

Thanks to the folks who helped make this book possible, including first and foremost, Ted Nace, who recognized that he already had one of the finest FreeHand books on the market, and Janna Custer and David Solomon, for inserting this book into their schedules at the last possible minute.

Thank you to Diane Steele for being her usual awesome self and for making everyone's life except mine miserable by negotiating and renegotiating production deadlines for this book. Thank you to Beth Jenkins and the rest of the production crew for doing such a fine job of labeling and processing the figures and fitting them on the right pages. And all under deadline pressures that would have made crews at other publishing houses whine like there was no tomorrow.

This book would be a pale imitation of itself without the invaluable assistance, suggestions, and flat-out rewriting of Julie King. Her name belongs on the cover of this book, but I'm too egocentric to allow that to occur. Especially since she's still not too clear on Bézier-curve theory. Just the same, she reads minds and clarifies sentences like you wouldn't believe. What an editor!

Many thanks to Arne Hurty for coming in at the last minute and making sure that the book wasn't hopelessly off base. And thanks to Galen Gruman, Carol Person, Marjorie Baer, and Jim Martin for pushing my deadlines around and putting up with my excuses. (Actually, I had only one excuse — this book.)

And, of course, Elizabeth, who's so incredibly great that she wakes up at 3 in the morning for days on end to talk with me.

(The publisher would like to give special thanks to Patrick J. McGovern, without whom this book would not have been possible.)

Contents at a Glance

Introduction 1

Part I: Taking the Fear Out of FreeHand 11

Chapter 1: FreeHand Wants to Be Your Friend 13

Chapter 2: Welcome to Macintosh 23

Chapter 3: Touring the FreeHand Neighborhood 65

Part II: Drawing in FreeHand 113

Chapter 4: Approaching Drawing Software 115

Chapter 5: Constructing Paths 145

Chapter 6: Tracing an Imported Template 187

Chapter 7: Reshaping and Combining Paths 213

Chapter 8: The Regimental Approach 269

Part III: Adding Text 305

Chapter 9: Entering and Editing Text 307

Chapter 10: Formatting and Copyfitting 343

Chapter 11: Special Text Effects 393

Part IV: Applying Color and Form 421

Chapter 12: Defining Colors and Styles 423

Chapter 13: Flat Fills and Gradations 449

Chapter 14: Assigning Strokes 495

Part V: Special Effects 529

Chapter 15: The Five Transformations 531

Chapter 16: Duplicating Objects and Effects 565

Chapter 17: Blends, Masks, and Composite Paths 579

Part VI: Desktop Publishing 611

Chapter 18: Importing and Exporting Graphics 613

Chapter 19: Setting Up Documents 633

Chapter 20: Printing from FreeHand 649

Index 681

Reader Response Card .... Back of Book

Table of Contents

Introduction **1**

How Is This One Different from the Rest? 2

Will the Wolf Survive? 3

How This Book Is Organized 3

    Part I: Taking the Fear out of FreeHand 4

    Part II: Drawing in FreeHand 4

    Part III: Adding Text 5

    Part IV: Applying Color and Form 5

    Part V: Special Effects 6

    Part VI: Desktop Publishing 7

Conventions 7

    Vocabulary 7

    Commands and options 8

    Version numbers 8

    Icons 9

How to Bug Me 10

Part I: Taking the Fear Out of FreeHand **11**

Chapter 1: FreeHand Wants to be Your Friend **13**

    In This Chapter 13

What Is FreeHand? 13

Pardon Me, Senator, What Is FreeHand? 14

Is FreeHand the Right Program for You? 14

    The top ten Illustrator tasks 15

    The top ten FreeHand tasks 16

    FreeHand's final advantage 18

Drawing Theory 18

    FreeHand vs. Photoshop 18

    The relative benefits of drawing 19

    The relative drawbacks of painting 20

    When to use FreeHand 21

    When to use Photoshop instead 21

Summary 22

Chapter 2: Welcome to Macintosh 23

In This Chapter 23
Teaching Your Computer to Heel 23
Computer Anatomy 25
  Computer brains 25
    The CPU 25
    The FPU 26
    The PowerPC 26
    Memory 27
    Disk space 28
    Disk space is not memory 28
    How digital space is measured 28
  Computer sensory organs 29
    Keyboard techniques 29
    Mouse techniques 30
    Keyboard and mouse, together at last 31
Using Your System Software 31
  How system software is organized 31
    Powering up 32
    The bits and pieces of the system 33
  Meet the Finder desktop 34
  Parts of the window 37
System Software Elements 39
  Menus and submenus 39
  Dialog boxes and options 39
  Navigating by dialog box 42
    The folder bar 42
    The scrolling list 43
    The navigation buttons 43
    Variations on the save 44
Working with Programs 45
  Starting an application 45
  Assigning application RAM 47
  Using the Get Info command 47
  Understanding memory fragmentation 50
  Managing multiple applications 51
    Switching between running applications 52
    Printing in the background 53
    Background screen refresh 54
    Hiding and showing running applications 55

Using the Clipboard 56
   Application Clipboards 57
   Using the Scrapbook 58
Using Fonts 59
   Installing PostScript screen fonts 59
   Installing PostScript printer fonts 61
   Using SuperATM 62
   Installing TrueType fonts 62
Summary 63

Chapter 3: Touring the FreeHand Neighborhood 65

In This Chapter 65
Getting Started with FreeHand 65
Installing FreeHand 66
   Contents of the FreeHand disks 66
   Installation advice 68
      Adding StuffIt Expander 69
      Deleting TeachText 70
   Network copy protection 70
Your First Look at FreeHand 71
   The FreeHand desktop 72
      Tools 74
      Cursors 76
      Floating palettes 77
   Working in the illustration window 80
      View size 81
      The zoom tool 82
      Dragging the scroll box 84
      Using the grabber hand 85
      Display modes 85
      Canceling the screen redraw 86
Shortcuts 87
   Selecting tools 91
   Navigating palettes 92
   Keys that produce different effects in Version 4.0 94
Customizing the Interface 94
   The FreeHand Preferences file 95
      The text inside the file 95
      Editing hidden preferences 96
   The Aldus FreeHand Defaults file 100

xvi

The File ➪ Preferences command 102
    The Display panel 102
    The Editing panel 106
    The Exporting panel 109
    The Sounds panel 110
Summary 112

Part II: Drawing in FreeHand 113

Chapter 4: Approaching Drawing Software 115

In This Chapter 115
Childhood Preparations 115
Drawing with Objects 116
    Lines vs. shapes 116
    Properties of lines and shapes 118
    Determining a path 119
The Infamous Groucho Scenario 120
    Step 1: Making a rough sketch 121
    Step 2: Creating the eyes 122
        Drawing the first oval 122
        Cloning the oval 124
        Drawing the crescent-shaped wrinkle 124
        Filling the shapes 125
        Cloning and transforming the right eye 126
    Step 3: Drawing the eyebrows 127
    Step 4: Building the cigar 129
        Deleting and adding points 129
        Layering the shapes 131
        Pasting the end of the cigar 132
    Step 5: Drawing the nose and mustache 132
        Changing eyebrow into mustache 133
        Adding a second nose 136
    Step 6: Finishing the face 137
    Step 7: Making the collar 140
    Step 8: Drawing smoke from the cigar 142
    The completed Groucho 143
Summary 144

Chapter 5: Constructing Paths 145

In This Chapter 145
Venturing Down the Garden Path 145

Geometric Shapes 146
  Drawing a rectangle 146
  Drawing a rectangle with rounded corners 148
  Drawing an ellipse 149
  Drawing a polygon 150
  Sides and stars 152
  Geometric shapes at an angle 153
Straight and Free-Form Paths 154
  Drawing straight segments 154
  Drawing freehand lines 155
    Freehand curve fit 157
    Erasing with the freehand tool 159
    Drawing free-form polygons 159
    Extending a line 161
    Sketching complicated paths 161
  Drawing calligraphic lines 162
    Pressure-sensitive input 163
    Pressure without the tablet 164
    The Calligraphic Pen option 165
The Subterranean World of Bézier Curves 166
  The math of the Béziers 166
  Using the bézigon and pen tools 167
  Moving points as you create them 170
  Test-driving the bézigon tool 170
    Drawing perpendicular segments 173
    Drawing curved segments 173
    Creating smooth transitions 174
  The versatile pen tool 176
    Creating cusps 177
    Three cusp point vignettes 178
    Why the pen tool is so great 184
Summary 186

Chapter 6: Tracing an Imported Template 187

In This Chapter 187
It Pays to Cheat 187
  A trace of tradition 188
  Why trace a bitmap? 189
Importing Tracing Templates 191
  Kinds of tracing templates 192
  Placing a template file 193
  Pasting a template file 195

Automated Tracing 196
    The trace tool 196
    Trace curve fit 199
    Image size 200
    Tracing layer control 201
Tracing Comparisons 202
Tracing Grayscale Images 204
Summary 211

Chapter 7: Reshaping and Combining Paths 213

In This Chapter 213
The Forgiving Medium 213
Selecting and Deselecting 214
    Selecting paths 215
    Selecting points 216
    Selecting everything 218
    Deselecting objects 218
    Deselecting specific points and paths 219
Reshaping Rectangles and Ellipses 219
    Using handles 220
    Handle coordinates 220
    Ungrouping geometric shapes 222
Moving Elements 223
    Moving points 223
    Constrained movements 225
    Snapping 226
    Using arrow keys 228
    Stretching segments 228
    Dragging Bézier control handles 230
        The way of the Bézier 230
        Rules of the Bézier road 233
Adding, Deleting, and Converting 235
    Adding points and other elements 235
        Appending endpoints 235
        Adding points inside a path 236
        Adding Bézier control handles 240
    Deleting points and other elements 241
        Removing a segment 242
        Deleting a whole path 243
        Retracting Bézier control handles 243
    Converting points 244
    Automatic curvature 246

Free-Form Path Info 248
Combining and Splitting Paths 250
  Joining open paths 250
    Fusing endpoints from separate paths 251
    Joining two lines with a straight segment 252
    Auto joining...253
  Combining path outlines 254
    Intersect 255
    Punch 257
    Union 259
  Splitting and slicing 260
  Reneging the past 264
  Undo 265
  Multiple undos 265
  Redo 266
  Revert 266
Summary...268

Chapter 8: The Regimental Approach 269
In This Chapter 269
FreeHand Eliminates Drafting Nightmares 269
Controlling Movements 271
  Using the rulers 271
    Changing the unit of measure 272
    Tracking lines 273
    Changing the ruler origin 274
  Using grids 276
  Creating guidelines 278
  Using the information bar 279
Alignment and Distribution 282
  Aligning selected objects to each other 282
  Spacing objects evenly 286
Grouping and Protecting Objects 287
  Making many objects into one 288
    General grouping facts 288
    Transforming as a unit 289
    Selecting elements within groups 291
    Ungrouping 292
    Distinguishing groups from composite paths 293
  Avoiding accidental alterations.....................................293
    Locking objects 293
    Unlocking objects 295

Layering Objects 295
   Working with drawing layers 296
      Assigning objects to layers 297
      Creating and naming a new layer 297
      Reordering layers 298
      Showing and hiding layers 299
      Protecting layers 299
      Deleting an existing layer 300
   Changing the stacking order within layers 300
      Forward and backward 301
      Paste in back 302
   The effect of grouping and joining on layering 302
Summary 303

Part III: Adding Text 305

Chapter 9: Entering and Editing Text 307

In This Chapter 307
Text Is a Drawing's Best Friend 307
   Isn't this a job for PageMaker? 308
   Come on, FreeHand can't do everything 308
Introducing Text Objects 309
   Creating a text block 309
      The mysteries of the text block 311
      Pressing keys to enter text 312
      Special characters and keyboard options 313
      Fixed spaces 314
   Creating a free-form text object 315
      Hiding the path outline 316
      Separating text and path 317
Importing Stories 317
   Preparing text 318
   Using the Place command 320
Adjusting Text Objects 321
   Manipulating text block handles 321
      Enlarging or reducing a text block 321
      The deactivated text block 323
      Spacing out your text 324
      Scaling text on the fly 326
   Reshaping geometric and free-form text objects 326
      Changing the dimensions of a free-form text object 330
      Using Inset values 332

Flowing text from one block to another 333

Reflowing a story 336

Separating a text block from a story 338

Breaking the link between text blocks 339

Selecting and Replacing Text 339

Summary 341

Chapter 10: Formatting and Copyfitting 343

In This Chapter 343

My Newest Office Caper 343

This Will Help Me Use FreeHand, Will It? 344

What is formatting? 345

What is copyfitting? 347

Character-Level Formatting 347

All about fonts 347

Type styles and families 348

Applying typeface and type style 348

Using the Type palette option boxes 349

Enlarging and reducing type 350

Changing the type size 351

Horizontal scale 351

Vertical and horizontal spacing 353

Increasing and decreasing leading 354

Pair and range kerning 355

Baseline shift 357

Stylistic effects 358

The inline effect 359

The shadow effect 360

The zoom effect 361

And lest we forget 362

Paragraph-Level Formatting 362

Tabs and indents 363

Why tabs are so great 363

Positioning tab stops 367

Paragraph indents 369

Types of indents 370

Changing the alignment 371

Paragraph spacing 372

Spacing letters and words 374

Hyphenating words 375

Automatic hyphenation controls 377

Manual hyphenation controls 378

Creating paragraph rules 378

Block-Level Formatting 380
   Columns and rows 381
   Wrapping order 383
Copyfitting 383
   Balancing columns 385
   Automatic size and leading adjustments 388
   First-line leading and initial caps 388
Summary 391

Chapter 11: Special Text Effects 393

In This Chapter 393
Aren't We Done with Text Yet? 393
Binding Text to a Path 394
   Reshaping a path of bound text 397
      Dragging and converting elements 398
      Other reshaping options and limitations 400
   Vertical alignment 402
   Type on an ellipse 405
   Changing the orientation 406
   How formatting affects bound text 408
   Horizontal alignment and direction 410
Wrapping Text Around Graphics 412
   Alignment and spacing 415
   Establishing a standoff dummy 416
   Unwrapping text blocks 416
Converting Type to Paths 417
Summary 419

Part IV: Applying Color and Form 421

Chapter 12: Defining Colors and Styles 423

In This Chapter 423
A Question of Color 423
Displaying Colors On-Screen 424
   Bit depths 425
   Third-party video boards 425
   Preparing your color monitor 426
      Monitor calibration 427
      Using the Apple Color Picker options 428
Creating and Organizing Colors 430
   Using the Color List palette 430
   Dragging (and dropping) colors 432

Mixing colors 435
    Using the CMYK color model 436
    Using the RGB color model 437
    Using the HLS color model 438
Process colors, spot colors, and tints 439
    Using pre-mixed spot colors 439
    Creating tints 441
Using color libraries 441
Using Attribute Styles 443
Creating and manipulating styles 444
    Redefining styles 445
    The effect of style changes on tagged objects ... 445
Duplicating attribute styles 446
Cutting and copying 447
Summary 447

Chapter 13: Flat Fills and Gradations 449

In This Chapter 449
The Benefits of Fill 449
How fill affects objects 450
How fill affects text 452
Assigning Flat Fills 453
Transparent fills 454
Single-color fills 454
    Overprinting colors 455
    Lifting the color of a fill 457
Applying Gradient Fills 458
Directional gradations 459
Radial gradations 463
Applying and Editing Patterns 465
Bitmapped patterns 466
Object-oriented tile patterns 467
    Creating and assigning a tile pattern 468
    Transforming a tile pattern independently of a path ... 475
    Tile pattern considerations 476
PostScript Fill Effects 477
The Custom fill effects 478
    Black & White Noise 479
    Bricks 479
    Circles 480
    Hatch 482
    Noise 484
    Random Grass 485

Random leaves 485

Squares 486

Tiger teeth 487

Top Noise 489

Transparent Fill Routines 489

PostScript textures 491

Summary 493

Chapter 14: Assigning Strokes 495

In This Chapter 495

Every Good Object Deserves Strokes 495

How stroke affects objects 496

How stroke affects text 497

Assigning a Stroke 499

Single-color strokes 500

Line weight 501

Line caps 502

Line joins 504

Cutting short overly long miter joins 506

Dash patterns 507

Arrowheads 509

Custom PostScript strokes 513

The Neon effect 516

Other patterned strokes 516

Mixing Stroke Attributes 517

Stacking strokes 517

Dash patterns and line caps 521

Stacking dash patterns and line caps 522

Converting a Stroked Line to a Filled Shape 523

Expanding the stroke 524

Creating an inset path 526

Summary 527

Part V: Special Effects 529

Chapter 15: The Five Transformations 531

In This Chapter 531

The Miracle of FreeHand's Transformations 531

Transforming objects in Version 4.0 532

The pasteboard error 535

Moving Whole Objects 535

Manual movements 536

Moving by the numbers 537
    Moving in direct distances 538
    Other things you should know 540
Scale, Reflect, Rotate, and Skew 541
   Enlarging and reducing objects 542
    Constrained scaling 547
    Scaling partial paths 548
    Using the Scale panel options 550
   Flipping objects 551
    Flipping partial paths 552
    Using the Reflect panel options 553
   Rotating objects 554
    Rotating partial paths 557
    Using the Rotate panel options 558
   Slanting objects 559
    Slanting partial paths 562
    Using the Skew panel 562
Summary..564

Chapter 16: Duplicating Objects and Effects 565

In This Chapter 565
Clones to the Rescue 565
Duplicating Objects and Type 566
   Cloning objects 567
   Cloning partial objects 568
Repeating Transformations 569
Series Duplication 571
Summary..577

Chapter 17: Blends, Masks, and Composite Paths........579

In This Chapter 579
The Most Special of Special Effects 579
Blending Paths 580
   Applying the Blend command 581
    Adjusting values in the Blend panel 582
    Specifying steps and range 583
   Selecting points in a blend 587
   Blending multiple paths 589
   Creating custom gradations 590
    Blending between gradations 593
    Avoiding banding 594
   Editing a blend 595
   Ungrouping a blend 595

All About Clipping Paths 596
  Creating a clipping path 596
  Adjusting masked elements 599
Creating and Using Composite Paths 600
  Poking holes 601
  Composite masking 605
    Filling across multiple shapes 607
    Composite paths and text 607
Summary 609

Part VI: Desktop Publishing 611

Chapter 18: Importing and Exporting Graphics 613

In This Chapter 613
FreeHand Publishes 613
Importing Graphics 614
  Placing a graphic file 616
  Pasting a graphic file 619
Manipulating Imported Graphics 619
  Scaling the graphic 620
  Editing a grayscale image 621
    Image mapping 623
    Preset mapping icons 625
  Cropping imported graphics 627
  Linking graphic files 627
Exporting an Illustration 628
  Exporting an EPS or PICT file 628
  Drawing an export boundary 631
Summary 632

Chapter 19: Setting Up Documents 633

In This Chapter 633
FreeHand Does Small Documents 633
Examining the Printed Page 635
  The pasteboard 636
  Creating multipage documents 637
    Moving pages in the pasteboard 638
    Navigating between pages 640
  Editing pages 643
    Printing differently sized pages 644
    Bleed size 645
Summary 646

Chapter 20: Printing from FreeHand 649

In This Chapter 649

Getting Your Work on Paper 649

Outputting Pages 650

    Choosing the printer driver 651

    Setting up the page 653

    Printing pages 655

    Adjusting print options 659

        Pages and margin notes 660

        Printing color separations 663

    Initiating printing 667

Printing to Disk 667

Special Printing Considerations 669

    Halftone screens 669

    Using downloadable fonts 674

    Splitting long paths 676

    Printing pattern tiles 678

Summary 679

Introduction

This book — or at least some version of it — has been around as long as FreeHand. Soon after Adobe Illustrator first hit the shelves in March 1987, my partner, still fulfilling the seemingly slight demands of his senior year of college, informed me that he and I would soon write a book about a piece of illustration software from a little startup company in Richardson, Texas, called Altsys. He assured me that the program would be every bit the equal of Illustrator, if not better. It was called Masterpiece, so naturally we would call the book *Mastering Masterpiece*. The program wouldn't sell all that well — how could these folks located out in the industry equivalent of Pago Pago hope to compete with Adobe? — so we wouldn't sell that many books, either. But at least we could get our feet in the computer publishing door.

Things change quickly in the computer industry, however. By the time we met with the programmers in November, the still unreleased product had become such a hot property that Altsys had signed a licensing agreement with the first name in desktop publishing, Aldus, maker of PageMaker. Altsys had hit the jackpot. Now that it had the support of a major software vendor, the product suddenly had a chance of competing with Illustrator. Never mind that Aldus changed the name of the program to FreeHand and ruined our infinitesimally clever title. FreeHand had major backing and so, by default, did we.

Seven years later, FreeHand is going strong. And, happily, so is this book. Now in its fourth incarnation, it's been the best-selling title on FreeHand since its original publication in 1988, despite considerable and — in some cases — praiseworthy competition.

If you've seen or purchased an earlier edition of this book, you should be aware that this one is substantially different. First of all, it's brought to you by a new publisher, IDG Books Worldwide. And with the considerable help and talent of IDG's editorial and design team, I've torn the book apart, thrown whole chapters away, reassembled what was left, and rewritten the rest. As a result, fully half of this book is composed of entirely new text and graphics. I think that readers of previous editions will be pleasantly surprised by the transformation.

How Is This One Different from the Rest?

Although you can find many solid books on FreeHand in your bookstore, this one is a little different from the rest. Actually, it's a lot different. Here are some of the features that set *Macworld FreeHand 4 Bible* apart:

- **Fundamental drawing issues:** Regardless of how powerful an illustration package is, it won't do you any good if you can't draw with it. That's why this book devotes more space than competing titles — nearly 200 pages — to the fundamental issues of drawing and editing FreeHand's amazingly deft but equally complex Bézier curves. Understanding these concepts is essential to creating successful drawings in FreeHand — or in any drawing program, for that matter. Yet many books don't explain them thoroughly or even adequately, leaving you to flail about on your own or, worse, give up in frustration.

- **No stone left unturned:** You'll also find a wealth of information not included in the Altsys software manual. Granted, the manual includes interesting and useful tips for drawing perspective illustrations, printing gradations without banding, and creating translucent objects. But strangely, its coverage of basic information is either abrupt or nonexistent. By contrast, this book was written so that any user, regardless of experience level, can understand not only the basics but also the advanced techniques that are covered.

- **Clarifying the new interface:** Although they may be amazed by FreeHand 4.0's new features, many long-time users find the program's new interface confusing and inefficient. I explain why things are the way they are, provide tips for remembering new and seemingly arbitrary keyboard equivalents, and even try to make you laugh at the new interface instead of curse it.

- **Technical accuracy:** This book is the only one reviewed for technical and artistic accuracy by one of the foremost FreeHand illustrators in the industry. Arne Hurty, the artist responsible for *Macworld* magazine's sophisticated informational graphics and winner of the first FreeHand illustration contest sponsored by Aldus, agreed to read my scribblings and let me have it when I missed important details. The result is a richer and more factual account of FreeHand's capabilities than would otherwise have been possible.

I know, I know — this all sounds like a sales pitch. Forgive me — like any parent, I'm a little too proud of my baby. But I honestly believe that these elements will make it easier for you to fully exploit FreeHand's capabilities.

Will the Wolf Survive?

Every time I tell one of my graphics artist buddies that I'm putting the finishing touches on the ultimate book about Aldus FreeHand, I hear the same response. "Gee whiz, Deke, how do you get that swelled head of yours through the door?" Then after I explain that at least I *hope* it's the ultimate book on FreeHand — I mean, I'm trying to do the best job possible here — they come back with, "Well, you'd better hurry up with it. At the rate things are going, there may not be a FreeHand much longer."

I know that they're just trying to make me feel better, but it's getting to be an old joke. Now that Aldus has agreed to merge with Adobe — makers of Illustrator, FreeHand's number-one nemesis — many FreeHand users are worried about what the future holds for their favorite product. Will FreeHand and Illustrator likewise merge into a single FrillHater or IlluFrand? Or will Adobe gobble up FreeHand's best features, stick them in Illustrator, and toss FreeHand away, a plundered and useless husk?

The answer is, neither. The only part of FreeHand that Aldus owns is its name and the documentation. Altsys, the little company from Texas, writes the software and owns the code. So regardless of what changes Adobe makes to the rest of the products it purchases from Aldus, it can't change the course of FreeHand. As I write this, Altsys has gone so far as to file a lawsuit against Aldus to regain the marketing rights to the program, which would potentially allow them to distribute FreeHand through another large software vendor. Quark, perhaps? The rumors abound.

Whatever happens, a software that racks up estimated annual sales in the neighborhood of $30 million isn't likely to disappear off the face of the map. Some company is going to keep it alive and well, and Altsys will continue to develop the product and build on its amazing suite of capabilities. You can rely on FreeHand to remain a dynamic competitor for years to come.

How This Book Is Organized

Here's a quick look at what topics are covered in each chapter and how the different parts of the book are organized.

Part I: Taking the Fear out of FreeHand

If you're new to the Mac, you've never used FreeHand, or you don't know the first thing about creating computer graphics, here's your chance to get acquainted. Each chapter assumes no previous knowledge, but even knowledgeable types may be surprised at how much they learn.

Chapter 1, FreeHand Wants to be Your Friend, explains how FreeHand measures up against arch-rival Adobe Illustrator, how it compares with image editors such as Adobe Photoshop, and how it fits into the larger experience of using the Mac to produce printed illustrations.

Chapter 2, Welcome to Macintosh, explores a range of topics that are fundamental to using a Macintosh computer. Get ready to familiarize yourself with CPUs, Power PCs, system software, random-access memory, fonts, and a bunch of other mystifying topics.

Chapter 3, Touring the FreeHand Neighborhood, explains how to install FreeHand onto your computer's hard drive, introduces you to the program's working environment, and examines FreeHand's plethora of tools, palettes, and preference settings.

Part II: Drawing in FreeHand

Bézier curves can be as intimidating as they are powerful. These chapters show you how to approach and execute an illustration, draw lines and shapes using a variety of tools, and make use of FreeHand's precision editing capabilities.

Chapter 4, Approaching Drawing Software, explains what it means to work inside an object-oriented drawing application. I introduce you to FreeHand's building blocks and show you how to create and combine them to create a sample illustration.

Chapter 5, Constructing Paths, examines FreeHand's capable drawing tools, including the new polygon and bézigon tools. You'll also learn how to use FreeHand's most powerful tool, the pen tool, to draw precise and versatile Bézier curves one point at a time.

Chapter 6, Tracing an Imported Template, explains how to import tracing templates and convert them to Bézier curves automatically using the trace tool. Drawing from scratch is all very well and good, but even advanced artists can benefit from tracing templates and the techniques discussed in these pages.

Chapter 7, Reshaping and Combining Paths, probes the innermost recesses of Bézier curves, showing how to edit paths by adding and deleting points, adjusting Bézier control handles, and joining and splitting paths. It also explains how to use FreeHand's new path operations to combine simple geometric shapes to create more complex objects. This is the longest and one of the most essential chapters in the book.

Chapter 8, The Regimental Approach, shows how to use rulers, guides, the grid, and FreeHand's updated information bar to establish a precise working environment, perfect for drafting and creating schematic artwork. In addition, it explains how to align and distribute objects.

Part III: Adding Text

Text is FreeHand 4.0's new and grandest frontier. The program offers more text creation and formatting functions than dedicated text wranglers PageMaker and QuarkXPress. These chapters show how to get the most out of these features.

Chapter 9, Entering and Editing Text, explains how to use Version 4.0's revamped text tool to draw text blocks. You'll also learn how to create text inside free-form outlines, import text from a word processor, and link a story across multiple text blocks.

Chapter 10, Formatting and Copyfitting, explores eight palettes and panels worth of editing options. You can hyphenate words automatically, insert space between paragraphs, kern text on the fly, control the length of lines of type in a flush left paragraph, set and move tabs, establish independent rows and columns, and instruct FreeHand to fit type inside a text block.

Chapter 11, Special Text Effects, tops off the two preceding chapters with the dessert of text-editing functions. Experienced FreeHand users will discover new ways to create and edit text on a path. I also explain how to wrap text around graphics and convert characters to editable outlines.

Part IV: Applying Color and Form

Without fill and stroke, the shapes and lines you draw in FreeHand are empty and meaningless skeletons. These chapters show how you can apply colors, gradations, custom patterns, and other special decorations to the interiors and outlines of graphic objects and text.

Chapter 12, Defining Colors and Styles, covers the fundamentals of editing colors on a computer screen. It explains how to manipulate common color models to achieve predictable results. It also examines the differences between spot colors, process colors, and tints, and explains how to define and apply custom attribute styles.

Chapter 13, Flat Fills and Gradations, shows how to overprint colors on different separations, create directional and radial gradations, manage and modify bitmapped and object-oriented patterns, and make use of FreeHand's extensive library of PostScript fill routines.

Chapter 14, Assigning Strokes, explores ways to change the appearance of the outline of a shape. You'll learn how to apply color and line weight to a stroke, specify the appearance of endpoints and corners using caps and joins, and create custom dash patterns. I also examine Version 4.0's new arrowhead editor and walk you through the creation of a few unusual stroking effects.

Part V: Special Effects

Learning how to make manual artistic enhancements to your drawing is important. But if time and energy are precious to you, you also need to know how to take advantage of FreeHand's automated features. These chapters show ways to manipulate text blocks and graphic objects using automated operations.

Chapter 15, The Five Transformations, introduces FreeHand's new Transform palette, which makes a range of manipulations available from a central location. You can move, scale, flip, rotate, and slant objects to any extent imaginable, as long as they don't exceed FreeHand's 20-square-foot working space.

Chapter 16, Duplicating Objects and Effects, describes the differences between copying objects, cloning them, and replicating effects. A substantial sample project shows how to combine duplication and transformation techniques to create a grand perspective effect.

Chapter 17, Blends, Masks, Composite Paths, is perhaps the most exciting chapter in the book. Here I investigate the Blend panel, which lets you "morph" between two selected objects. You can create custom gradations or even blend between paths filled with gradations to create more complex effects. You can then paste the blend inside another object to establish a mask and cut holes into the mask to create a composite path.

Part VI: Desktop Publishing

FreeHand 4.0 is the best program for creating small documents in all the world, and you can quote me on that. In addition to supplying the wealth of text-editing functions described back in Part III, FreeHand offers sophisticated import and export features, a unique ability to scale and orient pages independently within a document, and power-house printing functions. These chapters explain how to get full use out of these capabilities.

Chapter 18, Importing and Exporting Graphics, explains why FreeHand is one of the best graphics programs at handling file formats. You can import and edit imported Illustrator files, edit grayscale TIFF images, and export multiple EPS illustrations at once.

Chapter 19, Setting up Documents, delves into FreeHand's new page-layout capabilities. I define the pasteboard and explain its purpose, show how to add pages to a document and move them around, and briefly touch on special printing issues related to multipage documents.

Chapter 20, Printing from FreeHand, explains how to print illustrations and other documents in FreeHand. It introduces the new LaserWriter 8 PostScript print driver, shows how to select and use PPD files, and explores the printing of black-and-white composites and color separations. I also examine how to define custom halftone patterns, download printer fonts, and resolve a few printing errors.

Conventions

In an effort to avoid as much confusion as possible, I try to write the same way from one book to the next. I don't always use the exact same terms as the FreeHand manual, subscribing instead to more universal terminology whenever possible. This way, if you should ever venture beyond FreeHand, you'll be prepared to address the full gamut of the real world.

Vocabulary

As soon as the English-first folks get done making us all speak a common language, no doubt they'll get to work making doctors, lawyers, and propeller-heads like me shape up and stop using industry jargon. But whether they do or not, I can't explain the Mac or FreeHand in graphic and gruesome detail without reverting to the specialized language of the trade. However, to help you keep up, I have italicized vocabulary words (as in *random-access memory*) with which you may not be familiar or which I use in an unusual context. An italicized term is followed by a definition.

If you come across a strange word that is *not* italicized (that bit of italics was for emphasis), look it up in the index to find the first reference to the word in the book.

Commands and options

To distinguish the literal names of commands, dialog boxes, buttons, and so on, I capitalize the first letter in each word (for example, *click on the Cancel button*). The only exceptions are option names, which can be six or seven words long and filled with prepositions like *to* and *of*. Traditionally, prepositions and articles *(a, an, the)* don't appear in initial caps, and this book follows that time-honored rule, too.

When discussing menus and commands, I use an arrow symbol to indicate hierarchy. For example, *Choose File ⇨ Open* means to choose the Open command from the File menu. If you have to display a submenu to reach a command, I list the command used to display the submenu between the menu name and the final command. *Choose Arrange ⇨ Path Operations ⇨ Blend* means to choose the Path Operations command from the Arrange menu and then choose the Blend command from the Path Operations submenu. (If this doesn't quite make sense to you now, don't worry. Future chapters will make it abundantly clear.)

 For an introduction to menu commands and the like, check out the "System Software Elements" section in Chapter 2. For an introduction to Photoshop's tools, see "The FreeHand desktop" section of Chapter 3.

Version numbers

It's absolutely impossible to keep up with version numbers. Programmers are constantly updating their software to keep it current or to make sure they're one step ahead of the Joneses. FreeHand has already updated to Version 4.0a, which fixes a few bugs that existed in the previous version. By the time you read this, the version number may be even higher. So be aware that when I write *FreeHand 4.0*, I mean any version of FreeHand short of 5.0.

Similarly, when I write *FreeHand 3.0*, I mean both Version 3.0 and its successor, Version 3.1. The same goes for references to Version 2.0 and 1.0.

The term *System 7* includes Versions 7.0, 7.01, 7.1, and any other version that begins with a *7. Illustrator 3.0* incorporates all versions up to and including 3.2.3. *Illustrator 5.0* includes every version of Illustrator short of 6.0. Illustrator 4.0 was released only for Microsoft Windows; Illustrator 88 was the successor to Version 1.1 and the predecessor to Version 3.0.

I'm sure that there are other examples, but you get the idea. Instead of cluttering the book with a lot of references to *FreeHand 4.0 and 4.0a* or, worse yet, *FreeHand 4.x*, I've tried to keep things as simple as possible by referring to the significant version only. In those few instances that I cite a specific minor update, such as *FreeHand 3.1* or *System 7.1*, I am talking about that specific version only.

Icons

Okay, I admit it, icons are overused. But not in this book. Here, I use the icons sparingly, just frequently enough to focus your eyeballs smack dab on important information. The icons make it easy for you to skim through the book and touch on information that's either new to Version 4.0 or just new to you. They serve as little insurance policies against short attention spans. On the whole, they're pretty self-explanatory, but I'll explain them anyway.

 The Caution icon warns you that a step you're about to take may produce disastrous results. Well, perhaps "disastrous" is an exaggeration. Inconvenient, then. Uncomfortable. For heaven's sake, use caution.

 The Note icon highlights some little tidbit of information related to the topic at hand.

 The Background icon is like the Note icon, except that it includes specific background information required to understand intermediate and advanced topics. Sometimes I also throw in a modicum of history. I tell you how an option came into existence, why a feature is implemented the way it is, or how things used to be better back in the old days.

 The FreeHand 4.0 icon calls your attention to a brand new feature or one that works differently than it used to. If you've made the switch from an earlier version of the program to Version 4.0, the information presented by these icons will help you master this vast and significant upgrade. You folks who refuse to stop using Version 3.1 should pay particular attention to these icons.

As I write this, FreeHand 4.0 isn't yet available for Microsoft Windows users. But word has it that it will be soon. In the meantime, users of FreeHand for Windows Version 3.1 should take note of these icons, which highlight features and shortcuts that work differently under Windows than they do on the Mac.

 This book is bursting with tips and techniques. If I were to highlight every one of them, whole pages would be gray with little icons popping out all over the place. The Operations Tip icon calls attention to shortcuts and techniques that are specifically applicable to FreeHand. For the bigger, more useful power tips, I'm afraid you'll have to actually read the text.

 The biggest hardware news in 1994 is the emergence of the PowerPC, the fastest personal computer on the market. The PowerPC icon highlights the occasional differences between the old-model, 68,000 (sometimes pronounced *68-kay*) Macintoshes and the new RISC-based PowerPCs.

 The Cross-Reference icon tells you where to go for information related to the current topic. I included one a few pages back and you probably read it without thinking twice. That means you're either sharp as a tack or an experienced computer-book user. Either way, you won't have any trouble with this icon.

How to Bug Me

Even with all these great editors and technical reviewers at my disposal, you may still manage to locate a few errors and oversights. If you notice those kinds of things and you have a few spare moments, please let me know what you think.

You can contact me via America Online at DekeMc. If you subscribe to CompuServe, you can also reach me at 70640,670. Don't fret if you don't hear from me for a few days, or months, or ever. I read every letter and try to implement nearly every idea anyone bothers to send me.

Now that I've gotten all of this important introductory information out of the way, on to the good stuff. Turn the page and dive right in, and rest assured that even if FreeHand seems a little intimidating to you at first, with a little time and patience, you'll soon be able to enjoy amazing success. In fact, I think that you'll be just as happy as I am that those folks from Richardson, Texas, put their heads together way back when and came up with this gem of a program.

Taking the Fear Out of FreeHand

Chapter 1:
FreeHand Wants to Be Your Friend

Chapter 2:
Welcome to Macintosh

Chapter 3:
Touring the FreeHand Neighborhood

PART

I

FreeHand Wants to be Your Friend

CHAPTER

In This Chapter

- ➡ An introduction to FreeHand
- ➡ How FreeHand measures up to arch-rival Adobe Illustrator
- ➡ The difference between drawing and painting programs

What Is FreeHand?

Every time I start writing a new book, I embark down the inevitable road of completely trashing out my office. I mean, I just finished cleaning it up a couple of days ago, and I've already managed to surround myself with books, open software boxes, Post-it notes, and all the other trappings of what is sometimes laughingly called computer journalism. Pretty soon I'll be ignoring my mail, throwing my magazines in unread piles, misplacing cold slices of pizza, and topping it all off with spilt coffee.

Now, no doubt I'll get another complaint letter from a reader saying, "Can't you stick to the subject? The first paragraph of Chapter 1 has nothing whatsoever to do with FreeHand. Must we put up with the author's diatribes on his personal life? Doesn't anyone edit these books?" Well, you may as well know right now, I get to rambling every once in a while. It can't be helped. Top behavioral scientists and dog breeders have worked on me to no avail.

To quote the sweet potato, "I yam what I yam."

Pardon Me, Senator, What Is FreeHand?

FreeHand is a top-selling drawing application with a passionate and loyal following. (*Application,* incidentally, is just another word for a computer program.) Folks swear by FreeHand, and rightly so. Quite simply, it is more powerful and more reliable than just about any other drawing program for any brand of personal computer.

In fact, FreeHand currently has only one serious competitor: Adobe Illustrator. The rivalry between Illustrator and FreeHand dates back to the last year of the Reagan administration. Despite the fact that Illustrator had the field all to itself for nine months during the nostalgic days of the Iran-Contra hearings, FreeHand made such a power entry that roughly half of Illustrator's users — some say Ollie North was among them — jumped ship and never went back. To this day — two administrations and a half dozen nanny scandals later — the two programs split the market right down the middle.

Is FreeHand the Right Program for You?

As someone who has used both products since before their official introductions, I've tried to avoid being a fan of either FreeHand or Illustrator, though at times it has been tough. I've been accused of harboring a secret preference for Illustrator because of certain criticisms I made about FreeHand Versions 3.0 and 3.1. But on another occasion, I delivered equally frank statements against Illustrator 88 and in favor of FreeHand 2.0. It's just that back then, I didn't write for a major magazine, so nobody gave a darn what I said.

These days, FreeHand 4.0 and Illustrator 5.0 are so evenly matched and such marked improvements over their predecessors that it's impossible — at least for me — to pick a clear winner between the two. Oh sure, you'll come across portions of the book in which I make fun of the way some FreeHand function is implemented, but that's just to keep things lively. I don't want you to fall asleep because I'm being too reverent.

FreeHand and Illustrator are more alike than different — so much so that most users will be happy with either product. But though small in number, the handful of differences between the two programs may be important enough to sway you in one direction or the other. So before I venture any further into the wonderful world of FreeHand, let's make sure that you're using the right program.

The top ten Illustrator tasks

In a court of law, the plaintiff gets to go first, so I'll start by describing the benefits of arch-rival Adobe Illustrator. The following list examines ten tasks that Illustrator handles better than FreeHand, discussed in order from least important to most. If you anticipate performing these tasks on a regular basis, Illustrator may be the better program for you.

 If you saw the June 1994 issue of *Macworld* magazine and happened to read my article comparing FreeHand and Illustrator, you'll recognize this list and the one that follows. But they so clearly spell out the differences between the two programs that I couldn't bear the thought of letting you folks who didn't read the June issue miss out (though how in gravy's name you missed an issue of *Macworld,* I'll never know).

- **Creating graphs:** Illustrator may not be the first program you think of when you want to create a bar graph. But its dedicated graphing tools make it one of the best if you're interested in turning stagnant facts and figures into dynamic info art.

- **Swapping text with other programs:** Because Illustrator supports the Claris XTND system, you can import and export several common text formats, including Microsoft Word, MacWrite, WordPerfect, and WriteNow. FreeHand only supports RTF.

- **Selecting objects:** In addition to a slightly more flexible selection model that better accommodates simple shapes and masked elements, Illustrator provides filters for selecting objects automatically based on fill, stroke, or line weight. You can even select all masks or stray points in a document.

- **Formatting characters:** Illustrator allows you to change font, type size, leading, baseline shift, and other character-level formatting attributes without once moving your hands from the keyboard. FreeHand makes it more complicated to activate options in the Type palette from the keyboard and lacks keyboard equivalents for leading and justification adjustments. If productivity matters to you, Illustrator's formatting features are a big plus.

- **Combining paths:** Illustrator's Pathfinder functions are faster, more numerous, and generally more flexible than their equivalents in FreeHand. As long as your computer is equipped with a math coprocessor, you're in business.

- **Scaling and rotating:** When it comes to scaling and rotating, Illustrator can't be beat. You can reuse a single origin over and over, scale or rotate with respect to multiple independent origins, and transform and clone in a single operation. Meanwhile, FreeHand 4.0's Transformation palette represents a decline in functionality.

⊷ **Experimenting with automated effects:** Illustrator's new plug-in filters allow you to experiment with special effects in ways not permitted by FreeHand. Granted, the filters are randomly organized and sometimes strangely implemented, but they nonetheless provide access to a variety of useful options.

⊷ **Masking objects and images:** Only in Illustrator can you edit the contents of a mask without first taking the mask apart. You can also add paths to an existing mask in any order you please. Even text — real, editable text, not text converted to paths — can serve as a mask in Illustrator. FreeHand's cut-and-paste model is arguably easier to use, but significantly less flexible.

⊷ **Creating gradient fills:** Gradations are Illustrator's forte. With 32 colors at your disposal, complete midpoint control, and the ability to precisely position beginning and ending colors inside objects, how could you go wrong?

⊷ **Drawing complex paths:** Illustrator's pen tool is smooth as silk. You can't help but create artistic stuff when the tool itself is such a work of art. Custom guidelines, point-alignment functions, and a first-rate information palette make the process even dreamier.

The top ten FreeHand tasks

So much for the opening statement from the prosecution. But wait — before you throw down this book and go rushing out to purchase Illustrator, you need to hear the argument for the defense. If you've used FreeHand in the past, you'll probably find the following top ten tasks — again listed in order of least important to most — sufficiently compelling to keep you from flying the coop.

⊷ **Designing arrowheads:** FreeHand 4.0's new arrowhead editor may be the program's best-kept secret. Unlike Illustrator 5.0, which requires you to select from a handful of predefined Dingbat-like arrowheads and then scale them to size, Freehand gives you the absolute freedom to draw your own arrowheads. You have access to the pen tool, the full suite of transformation tools, and limited zooming and scrolling functions.

⊷ **Tracing imported images:** The automatic tracing tools included in FreeHand and Illustrator are mediocre at best. But when it comes to tracing bitmapped images by hand, FreeHand's template controls leave Illustrator's in the dust. You can import 24-bit color images stored in the PICT or TIFF format, dim the images on a background layer, and transform the images any way you please.

⊷ **Printing custom halftone patterns:** Only FreeHand allows you to change the frequency and angle of halftone patterns assigned to selected objects. You can even select from predefined halftone styles, such as elliptical dots and line screens.

- **Assigning colors to objects:** FreeHand 4.0 lets you drag and drop colors to change a stroke or fill, adjust the direction of a gradient fill, or reposition the center of a radial fill, all without so much as selecting the affected object. The feature is diminished by FreeHand's reliance on several different color palettes, which makes some tasks more of a chore than they should be, but we can't all be perfect.

- **Importing and manipulating TIFF images:** To Illustrator, TIFF is just another four-letter word. But to thousands of Macintosh artists, TIFF is the foremost lossless file format for saving and swapping images. FreeHand satisfies TIFF fans by enabling them not only to import TIFF images, but also to control on-screen image resolution, adjust brightness levels, and colorize grayscale and black-and-white artwork.

- **Schematic drawing:** Despite the improvements Illustrator made in recent versions, FreeHand is still the better program for precisely positioning points and objects. You can specify the location of points by entering numerical coordinates, distribute whole objects according to their widths, and align to locked objects. Most essential, FreeHand provides a grid; Illustrator does not.

- **Creating tables:** FreeHand's new text capabilities make tables a breeze. Besides supplying an unusually wide array of tab-stop options, FreeHand enables you to divide a text block into rows and columns, making it one of the most flexible table-making products on the market.

- **Designing multipage documents:** Except for spell-checking and automatic page numbers, FreeHand has everything it takes to create small, graphic-intensive documents. You can add pages, move pages and their contents, and scroll from one page to the next using page icons. You can even mix page sizes and orientations within a single document, something you can't do in either Aldus PageMaker or QuarkXPress.

- **Blending objects:** FreeHand continues to offer the only editable blends in the business. After blending between two objects, you can edit one or the other, and Freehand automatically recalculates the blend. In Illustrator, you have to delete the blended shapes and start over again.

- **Navigating in the preview mode:** When it comes to redrawing objects in the preview mode, FreeHand is the significantly faster product. As if that weren't enough, you can scroll in single-pixel increments and zoom to precise view sizes — ideal ingredients for getting around.

FreeHand's final advantage

FreeHand has one additional benefit: It lets you open and edit Illustrator files. This means that even if every other artist you know uses Illustrator, and you're the only maverick on your block to buck the status quo in favor of FreeHand, you'll still be able to work in perfect harmony with your colleagues. Illustrator, by contrast, wouldn't know a FreeHand document if it stepped in it.

So there it is. You decide. If you opt to use Illustrator, I wrote a book about that program too, though I can't mention its name because it's from a different publisher (but it involves the words *The, Illustrator,* and *Book* in no particular order). I just didn't want you to think that because you decided to use a different program, you had to miss out on my personal philosophy on the subject. In the name of fairness, IDG Books World-wide, the publisher of this book, also has an Illustrator title that you may want to take a look at.

Drawing Theory

You may have noticed the complete lack of information I've included so far on the subject of Adobe Photoshop, one of the most powerful and popular graphics programs ever written. If it's so great, how come I didn't compare it to FreeHand and Illustrator? The answer is that Photoshop isn't in the same category of software. FreeHand and Photoshop are both two-dimensional graphics programs, but that's where the similarities end.

FreeHand vs. Photoshop

Like any *drawing program,* FreeHand enables you to draw pristine line art and smooth-as-silk technical drawings. Tasks that used to be exceedingly nerve-wracking or down-right unlikely 10 or 20 years ago — like getting two thick pen lines to meet and form a perfectly sharp corner — are a breeze in FreeHand. With very little effort and not much more in the way of experience, you'll be churning out stuff in Freehand that would have made you bleed, sweat, and cry — to turn an old phrase — if you approached the task using traditional drawing tools. Better still, there's no mess. Unlike pens, which can clog; ink, which can dry up; brushes, which can harden; paint, which can stain your clothes; and paper, which you can rip and soil; FreeHand offers all the advantages of a tool that exists exclusively in your computer's imagination. Until you print your draw-ing, there's nothing real or physical about it. And if you rip or soil your final artwork, you just print another copy.

FreeHand works its precision magic by looking at artwork in terms of *objects,* which are independent, mathematically defined lines and shapes. For this reason, drawing programs are sometimes said to be *object-oriented.* Some folks prefer the term *vector-based,* but I reckon FreeHand is complicated enough without making it sound like an experiment at a science fair.

By contrast, Photoshop is an *image editor,* which means that it enables you to alter photographs and other scanned artwork. You can retouch a photograph, apply special effects, and swap details between photos — all functions that FreeHand can't match. Image editors fall into the larger software category of *painting programs.* In a painting program, you draw a line and the application converts it, then and there, to tiny square dots called *pixels.* The painting itself is called a *bitmapped image,* but *bitmap* or *image* on its own is equally acceptable.

Other examples of drawing programs include Canvas, MacDraw Pro, and the upcoming ClarisDraw on the Macintosh, as well as Windows Draw and CorelDraw on the PC. Painting programs include Fractal Design Painter, PixelPaint Pro, Color It, and the Mac's first program, MacPaint.

The relative benefits of drawing

Some artists shy away from FreeHand because it features tools that have no real-world counterparts. The process of drawing may be more aptly termed *constructing,* because you actually build lines and shapes point-by-point and stack them on top of each other to create a finished image. Each object is independently editable — one of the few structural advantages of an object-oriented approach — but you're still faced with the task of building your artwork one chunk at a time.

For an introduction to the object-oriented drawing process, read Chapter 4, "Approaching Drawing Software." If you're having problems adapting your knowledge of traditional drawing techniques to FreeHand's curve-construction options, this chapter is a must.

Nevertheless, because a drawing program defines lines, shapes, and text as mathematical equations, these objects automatically conform to the full resolution of the *output device,* whether it's a laser printer, imagesetter, or film recorder. The drawing program sends the math to the printer, and the printer *renders* the math to paper or film. In other words, the printer converts the drawing program's equations to printer pixels. And because your printer offers far more pixels than your screen — a 300 dot-per-inch laser printer, for example, offers 300 pixels per inch — the printed drawing appears smooth and sharply focused regardless of the size at which you print it, as shown in Figure 1-1.

Figure 1-1:
No matter how large or small you print your FreeHand drawing, it retains smooth edges and sharp contrast.

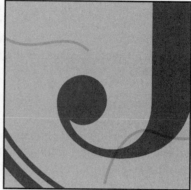

Furthermore, drawings take up relatively little room on disk. The file size of a drawing depends on the quantity and complexity of the objects the drawing contains. Thus, file size has almost nothing to do with the physical size of the printed image. A thumbnail drawing of a garden that contains hundreds of leaves and petals consumes several times more disk space than a poster-sized drawing that contains three rectangles.

The relative drawbacks of painting

Painting programs are indisputably easier to use than drawing programs. For example, although many of Photoshop's features are complex — *exceedingly* complex on occasion — its core painting tools are as straightforward as a pencil. You alternately draw and erase until you reach a desired effect, just like you've been doing since grade school.

The drawback of a painting program is that it limits your *resolution* options. Because bitmaps contain a fixed number of pixels, the resolution of an image — the number of pixels per inch — is dependent upon the size at which the image is printed, as demonstrated in Figure 1-2. Print the image small, and the pixels become tiny, which increases resolution; print the image large, and the pixels grow, which decreases resolution. An image that fills up a standard 13-inch screen (480×640 pixels) prints with smooth color transitions when reduced to, say, half the size of a postcard. But if you print that same image without reducing it, you may be able to distinguish individual pixels, which means that you can see jagged edges and blocky transitions. The only way to remedy this problem is to increase the number of pixels in the image, which dramatically increases the size of the file on disk.

Figure 1-2:
Paintings
appear
smooth or
jagged in
direct
relation to
the size at
which they
are printed.

 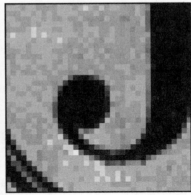

When to use FreeHand

Thanks to their specialized methods, drawing and painting programs fulfill distinct and divergent purposes. FreeHand and other drawing programs are best suited to the kinds of artwork listed below:

- Poster art and other high-contrast graphics that heighten the appearance of reality

- Architectural plans, product designs, or other precise line drawings

- Business graphics, charts, and "infographics" that reflect data or show how things work

- Traditional logos and text effects that require crisp, ultra-smooth edges. (Drawing programs are unique in allowing you to edit character outlines to create custom letters and symbols.)

- Brochures, flyers, and other single-page documents that mix artwork, logos, and standard-sized text (like the text you're reading now)

When to use Photoshop instead

However, you're better off using Photoshop or some other painting program if you're interested in creating or editing more naturalistic artwork, such as the items listed below:

- Scanned photos, including photographic collages and embellishments that originate from scans

☞ Realistic artwork that relies on the play between naturalistic highlights, midranges, and shadows

☞ Impressionistic-type artwork and other images created for purely personal or aesthetic purposes

☞ Logos and other display type that feature soft edges, reflections, or tapering shadows

☞ Special effects that require the use of filters and color enhancements you simply can't achieve in a drawing program

If you're serious about computer graphics, you should own at least one painting program and one drawing program. FreeHand and Photoshop are ideal candidates for any artist's software library.

Summary

●➤ FreeHand offers several advantages over Illustrator, including a better arrowhead editor, more versatile halftoning options, support for TIFF images, a flexible blend function, and a suite of small-document creation tools.

●➤ FreeHand and other drawing programs express all lines and shapes in a document as independent, mathematically defined objects.

●➤ Painting programs such as Photoshop define an image as a network of differently colored pixels.

●➤ Use FreeHand to create high-contrast or stylized graphics; use Photoshop to edit scanned images or to paint free-form artwork that features transitional colors.

Welcome to Macintosh

In This Chapter

- The anatomy of a Macintosh computer
- How the system software lets you communicate with your Mac
- An introduction to the PowerPC
- A first look at the Finder desktop
- Guidelines for using menus, dialog boxes, and options
- How to start programs and assign RAM space
- Installing PostScript and TrueType fonts

Teaching Your Computer to Heel

Computers can be as exasperating as they are amazing. When I first started using the Macintosh to do production work, I found more to curse than to praise. The computer was forever crashing or presenting me with errors that made no sense; I squandered hours of productivity reimplementing unsaved changes and recreating corrupted documents; and my software never seemed to work with my hardware as advertised. To make matters worse, I had actually spent money on this quagmire of frustration.

Nowadays, I have very few problems. I run my Mac for literally days at a time without a single crash; in fact, I don't think that I lost a total of one hour of work all last year. Programs perform more or less as I expect them to. And when I do encounter an error, I'm able to resolve it relatively quickly.

Much of this smooth sailing is due to better hardware and software. Compared to the stuff Macintosh vendors churned out in the mid-80s, today's computer solutions are works of artistic and engineering perfection, able to perform magic and perform it reliably.

But I also know what I'm doing — better than I used to, anyway. My IIci is nearly five years old and shows every day of it. The motherboard is half dead, the mouse stops working periodically, and the power supply is temperamental. Between you and me, the second I get some surplus cash, I'm going to replace this clunker with a PowerPC. But in the meantime, I've learned how to work around the big problems and solve the little ones. In return, my timeworn IIci performs like a champ, despite a few critical failings.

The point is, if you're new to the Mac and/or to computing, you may encounter some initial setbacks and irritation, as I did. So just keep in mind that your system will become easier to use and more reliable as you increase your knowledge of computers. With a little perseverance, you'll have half as many problems next year as you do this year, and even fewer the year after that. Ultimately, there's no substitute for experience — the more you use your computer, the faster you become adept — but you'll progress more expediently if you understand a few basics about how your Mac works.

The purpose of this chapter, then, is to show you the ropes. It's up to you to swing on them.

If you read my book *Macworld Photoshop 2.5 Bible* from cover to cover, you'll notice that this chapter is largely the same as Chapter 2 in that book. I wanted to warn you in case you decide to compare the two books side by side some night when you have nothing better to do. "Myrtle, will you look at . . . why, this whole chapter . . . it's just the same! By gum, all this guy did was search and replace *Photoshop* with *FreeHand*." Actually, I changed a few of the jokes and I rewrote the intro, so give me a break. More importantly, I added a few sections that you may want to look at, most notably "The PowerPC," "Background screen refresh," and "Application Clipboards."

Although this chapter is specifically geared toward Macintosh users, much of the information is equally applicable to any brand of personal computer. For example, all computers have CPUs, RAM, ROM, keyboards, and other essential elements, and these elements serve the same purposes no matter what type of system you have.

Computer Anatomy_____

Imagine your Macintosh computer as a person equipped with only a brain and sensory organs. No heart, no lungs. No hands or feet, either — which prevents the Mac from throttling you when you curse at it and eliminates any potential for it to wander away just when you need it most. You might also think of the power supply as the entrails because it takes in the computer nutrients, but we'll skip that for now.

Computer brains

Like real brains, computer brains aren't pretty. Okay, so they're not all gooey and wrinkly like real brains, but they're just as guaranteed to gross you out. Nearly every bit of computer gobbledygook you've ever heard — CPU, RISC, RAM, ROM — revolves around computer brains. But if you'll buck up and read the following couple of pages, you'll be able to keep up with the geekiest and most arrogant of computer store clerks. Better yet, you'll understand how your computer works and how to address problems later on down the line.

The CPU

The Mac's brain is the *motherboard* — also called the *logic board* — which is a big, green circuit board that contains a bunch of chips and rests on the bottom of the computer's housing. The main chip is the *central processing unit* (CPU). It does all the math and makes all the decisions required to create the images and noises that your computer produces. It also decides when and how to use memory and disk space — with your help, of course. Humans aren't completely out of the loop yet.

 CPU and the upcoming *FPU* are pronounced one syllable at a time, just like NFL or UPS. Other acronyms described in this chapter, such as CISC, RISC, RAM, and ROM, are pronounced like they're spelled: *sisk, risk, ram,* and *rom.* The general rule of thumb is: If you can pronounce the acronym as spelled, do so; if not, spell it out. One exception is SCSI, which is pronounced *scuzzy.*

The FPU

The *floating-point unit* (FPU) is a separate chip that processes math-intensive code more quickly than the CPU. Also called the *math coprocessor,* the FPU is capable of calculating decimal values (such as 31.2 or 165.783) rather than being limited to integers (such as 31 or 166). So although an FPU can process a complex equation in a single pass, the CPU might have to break it up into pieces, slowing down the processing time. In fact, the FPU can handle certain equations up to 100 times faster than the CPU.

Because a handful of popular computers don't include FPUs — including the Macintosh IIsi, LC, Color Classic, and Centris 610, as well as any DOS-based PC that ends in an SX — most programs, including FreeHand, don't look for an FPU chip and are therefore not accelerated by it. Functions that are accelerated by an FPU, including Adobe Illustrator's Pathfinder commands, don't work on machines without FPUs. However, when an FPU is present, Illustrator's Pathfinder commands operate at about 10 times the speed of FreeHand's comparable functions (found under the Arrange ➪ Path Operations submenu). This assumes that you're not using a PowerPC; for more on that subject, keep reading.

The PowerPC

 Macintoshes have always relied — and will continue to rely — on CPU chips manufactured by Motorola. DOS-based PCs rely on chips from Intel (famous for its "Intel Inside" media blitz). Roughly equivalent in capabilities, the previous generation of Motorola and Intel chips differed most notably in terms of naming conventions. In recent years, Motorola chips were numbered 68030 and 68040 for the Mac II and Quadra series, respectively; Intel chips were numbered 386 and 486. Higher numbers indicated faster and more sophisticated technology.

All these CPUs were CISC *(complex instruction set computer)* chips, which is an extremely technical way of saying that the chips spent a relatively long time processing intricate codes. Intel's latest CPU, the Pentium, is also a CISC chip and is widely regarded as having very nearly achieved the maximum performance permitted by the CISC architecture.

The limitations of the CISC architecture prompted Motorola to break with the past when creating the PowerPC, its revolutionary new breed of CPU. The PowerPC chip is a RISC *(reduced instruction set computer)* processor, meaning that it uses a smaller vocabulary of instructions. Although RISC chips necessarily use more words than their CISC counterparts to get across the same idea, they can process these words much more quickly, resulting in a net speed gain. As anyone who has used both Pentium and PowerPC computers will tell you, the PowerPC is quite obviously the faster machine.

Unfortunately, to take advantage of RISC-based speed gains, vendors must recompile their software using simplified code. Instead of saying, "The deciduous tree," for example, the new code might say, "The green tree that sheds its leaves in the winter." As a result, programs optimized for the PowerPC take up more room on disk.

But although the advent of the PowerPC means a lot of work for vendors, the transition should be fairly smooth and predictable for users. Most vendors are offering PowerPC-optimized software to their registered users for nominal upgrade fees. Industry analysts (you know, they're the ones wearing lab coats) predict that users will have fewer problems adapting to PowerPCs than they did to System 7 and 32-bit addressing.

 PowerPCs automatically include FPUs that can process data independently of the integer unit instead of having to constantly swap data back and forth between FPU and CPU — a limitation of older Macs. This setup accelerates decimal-point calculations; Apple estimates that decimal-point calculations will be 10 times as fast on the PowerPC as on a top-of-the-line Quadra, while integer calculations will be twice as fast. It also ensures that all RISC-optimized programs can take advantage of the FPU, universally accelerating math-intensive operations.

By the time you read this book, the PowerPC optimized version of FreeHand should be available. The commands under the Arrange ⇨ Path Operations submenu will be optimized to take advantage of the FPU, meaning that they will run 10 times as fast as they do on older model Macs and Windows machines. The rest of the program will run twice as fast. Sources at Aldus tell me that in FreeHand 5.0, all operations will be optimized for the FPU.

Memory

Like the CPU, *memory* is part of the motherboard, but it comprises many chips instead of just one. The first kind of memory is ROM *(read-only memory),* which can never be altered. ROM is like an animal's instinct; it's memory that your computer was born with. It is *hard-wired memory* — meaning that it can only be changed by replacing the chips — and contains portions of the system software, which I explain in the upcoming section, "Using Your System Software" (uncanny naming convention).

The second kind of memory is RAM *(random access memory),* which you can alter at will. When you open a program, the CPU copies it to RAM in order to access it more quickly. When you quit the program, the CPU deletes it from RAM. When you restart or turn off your machine, all data stored in RAM is lost. So RAM data is entirely temporary in nature.

Disk space

Disk space is separate from the motherboard. It acts as a collection of satellite brains that includes hard drives, floppy disks, and other *removable media devices,* such as SyQuest and Bernoulli cartridges, flopticals, magneto-optical drives, and tape-backup systems. Incidentally, *floppy disk* is just an informal name for those plastic disks that you insert into the front of your computer. Beneath their hard plastic exteriors are flexible round disks, hence the term *floppy.*

Disk space is not memory

Sometimes you may hear folks incorrectly refer to disk space as memory, but the two are very separate concepts. You can't store data permanently in RAM but you can store data permanently on disks. You can't change the data stored in ROM but you can change the data on disks. (The one exception to this rule is when you work with CD-ROMs.)

The main difference between memory and disk space is that the CPU controls the contents of memory and *you* control the contents of a disk. Although you can specify how RAM is divvied up among programs, you can't specify how a program makes use of that memory.

 A CD-ROM is disk space, but you can't alter or delete the data on it. In fact, it's just like a standard music CD. You can copy data to a CD-ROM only once, just as you can record music to a CD only once, and you need a special piece of professionally-priced hardware (meaning that it's mondo expensive) to do the job. Consumer CD-ROM drives only let you copy data, just as stereo CD decks only play music.

 For specific information on assigning RAM space to FreeHand, see the section "Assigning application RAM" later in this chapter.

How digital space is measured

Whether it's in memory or on disk, you measure digital space in terms of *bits* and *bytes.* A bit is the absolute smallest unit of measurement. It can be either 0 or 1, off or on. A byte is equal to eight bits.

To give you an idea of how small this is, every letter in a word processor consumes exactly one byte of disk or memory space. (This assumes a Roman alphabet. When you use a Japanese alphabet, which contains thousands of Katakana, Hiragana, and Kanji characters, each letter consumes two bytes.)

A *kilobyte* (K) is 1,024 bytes; a *megabyte* (MB) is 1,024K, which is more than a million bytes. Typically, disk space and memory are measured in megabytes. For example, if you see an ad for an 8/230 Macintosh Quadra, the computer is equipped with 8MB of RAM and 230MB of hard disk space. The next unit up is a *gigabyte,* which equals 1,024MB, or more than one billion bytes. No Mac user has this much RAM, and folks who have this much space on a single disk aren't likely to take time out to read this chapter. We're talking major bucks.

 All computers rely on a *binary counting system,* in which there are only two digits, 0 and 1. This means that your computer counts 0, 1, 10, 11, 100, 101, 110, 111, 1000, 1001, and so on. A bit is one digit long. A byte is eight digits long, meaning that it can accommodate up to 256 variations. How did I figure this out? Simple. Take the number 2 — as in 2 digits — and raise it to a power equal to the number of digits in the unit. In a byte, you have 2^8, which equals 256.

By no coincidence, the Macintosh alphabet contains 256 characters — including letters, numbers, foreign characters, and symbols — so one byte is enough to express one character of type. In Asian countries, including Japan, the system software permits 2 bytes per each character. Each 2-byte unit is 16 digits long, thus accommodating up to 2^{16} or 65,536 variations.

Computer sensory organs

With the exception of hard drives and removable media devices, everything that lies outside your computer's casing qualifies as a sensory organ. You communicate with your computer by typing on the keyboard and by moving the mouse. It responds to you by displaying images on the screen, printing images on paper, and producing beeps and other noises from its speaker. (Okay, the speaker is inside the casing, and so is the monitor on machines like the Color Classic, but you get the idea.) Your computer can even communicate with other computers by sending and receiving data over a modem or network.

Keyboard techniques

You can use the keyboard to produce text on-screen or to call up commands and options. For example, pressing Command-C implements the Copy command in all Macintosh programs. Such key combinations are called *keyboard equivalents* or simply *shortcuts.*

Mouse techniques

Moving the mouse changes the location of the on-screen cursor, which is typically an arrow that points up and to the left. (It's just another example of right-handers dominating the earth. As if we left-handers don't have a hard enough time in life trying to find a decent pair of scissors, now we have to put up with this.) The typical mouse features a single button on top that registers clicks and a trackball underneath that registers movement. If your mouse offers more than one button, you'll quickly discover that only the left button works with the Macintosh version of FreeHand. (More right-handed domination.)

In the Windows version of FreeHand, the right mouse button serves only one function: If you press the Control key and right click, you can select an object that is behind the previously selected object.

As in most graphic applications (remember, *application* is just another word for a computer program), the cursor changes appearance in FreeHand based on its function. For example, when you select the pen tool, the cursor looks like a little pen nib. For a complete guide to FreeHand's cursors and their meanings, check out the "Cursors" section in Chapter 3.

Here's a quick look at the terminology associated with using your mouse:

- ↝ To *move* your mouse is to move it without pressing the button.

- ↝ To *click* is to press the button and immediately release it without moving the mouse. Sometimes I tell you to *click on* a screen element, which means to position the cursor over the element and then click the mouse button. Other times I tell you to *click with* a tool, as in *click with the text tool.* This means to select the tool, position its cursor in the illustration window, and then click the mouse button.

- ↝ To *double-click* is to press and release the button twice in rapid succession without moving the mouse. For example, if you double-click on a word with the text tool, you select the entire word. If you *triple-click* — click three times in rapid succession — you select the entire paragraph.

- ↝ To *press and hold* (or *mouse down*) is to press the button and hold it down for a moment. I refer to this operation when an item remains on-screen only as long as the mouse button is pressed. For example, you press and hold on a menu name to display a list of commands.

- ↝ To *drag* is to press the button and hold it as you move the mouse. You then release the button to complete the operation. Sometimes I tell you to drag a screen element, as in *drag the title bar.* This instruction means to move the cursor over the title bar, press the mouse button and hold it down, move the mouse, and release the mouse button. Other times I say to *drag with* a tool, as in *drag with the freehand tool.* This means to select the freehand tool, position its cursor in the drawing area, and drag the mouse.

Keyboard and mouse, together at last

You can also use the keyboard and mouse in tandem. In FreeHand, for example, you can press the Shift key while dragging with the rectangle tool to draw a perfect square. To reduce the size of the drawing in the window, you can press Option while clicking with the zoom tool. Such actions are so common that you'll see key and mouse combinations joined into compound verbs, such as *Shift-dragging* or *Option-clicking*. (Still more abuse of the language.)

Using Your System Software _____

If the CPU, memory, and disk space represent the brain, and the mouse, keyboard, monitor, and so on are the sensory organs, then software represents knowledge. Software enables your computer to expand its range of capabilities. Adding a new piece of software to your hard drive is like enrolling your computer in night school. A single installation makes your computer smarter and more capable than its was before.

The *system software,* also referred to as the *operating system* or by its product name (System 6, System 7, etc.), provides your Mac with its most fundamental knowledge, which represents — in anthropomorphic terms — language and the capacity for learning. Other programs conform to the rules and regulations established by the system software and then go on to formulate their own.

How system software is organized

Some of the Mac's system software is stored in ROM. In effect the core of the operating system, this code handles the most fundamental operations of the Macintosh computer by managing memory, disk drives, screen display, and other internal and external hardware. The *Toolbox,* a special portion of the ROM-based operating system, offers a collection of graphic routines that allows any piece of software — including the system software itself — to quickly draw windows, create dialog boxes, handle fonts, and perform basic text editing functions.

 In case you ever wondered why zillions of manufacturers create IBM PC-compatible computers but Apple has a monopoly on the Mac, the ROM software is your answer. Apple refuses to license the ROM-based portion of its operating system to other vendors. By contrast, IBM's system software, whether it's DOS, OS/2, or Windows, is engineered and owned by Microsoft, which licenses it freely to Dell, NEC, Compaq, Zeos, AST, Gateway, Texas Instruments, Leading Edge, Zenith, Austin, Epson, Toshiba, Northgate, and anyone else who has a few bucks and a hand to shake.

Because you can't manipulate ROM-based data, the only way to update this portion of the system software is to physically replace the ROM chips on your computer's motherboard, an expensive and intricate proposition. For this reason, the majority of the system software is located on your hard drive, inside the aptly named *System Folder*. This setup enables Apple to easily distribute updates — System 7.0, System 7.1, System 7.5, and so on — until they're blue in the face.

Powering up

When you turn on your computer, the CPU inspects the ROM for the first few tidbits of system software. It then loads the remaining disk-based portion of the system into RAM. The entire system remains in RAM, available for use by other applications, until you turn off or restart your computer, at which point the motherboard interrupts the power supply to the RAM.

That split-second suspension of electricity erases the RAM, deleting the system software and all the weird little artifacts left over by other programs. This explains why restarting your computer can take care of so many problems. It makes a clean start of things by getting rid of the garbage that amassed in RAM and made a mess of the operating system. Next time you turn on your computer, the system software loading sequence begins anew.

You'll know when your Mac switches from ROM-based to disk-based system software by the appearance of the happy Mac icon, that grinning cherub that makes so many people think of the Mac as a hopelessly goofy toy. If a Mac with an inset question mark appears instead, the CPU can't find the system software on the hard drive. In that case, you need to insert a floppy disk that contains the system software. You should then use the Startup Disk control panel to select the icon for the hard drive that contains the system software, as demonstrated in Figure 2-1.

Figure 2-1:
Use the Startup Disk control panel to select the hard drive that contains the system software.

The bits and pieces of the system

The disk-based portion of the Macintosh operating system is more than a single file. In fact, it comprises an entire folder of files working in tandem. You can customize the performance of your system by adding, deleting, and altering specific files inside the System Folder. These files include the following:

- ☞ **System:** The System file is the first of the two key players that make up the disk-based portion of the Macintosh operating system. It contains the fundamental data required by other applications. It also contains various kinds of resources, most notably fonts and sounds. You can add and delete resources from your system to bolster the number of options available to other applications or save space on disk and in RAM.

- ☞ **Finder:** On its own, the System file communicates with applications and hardware, but it can't communicate with the user. That is the job of the System's mouthpiece, the Finder, which is actually an independent application, just like FreeHand. The *Finder desktop* is displayed immediately after your Mac finishes loading the system software. It acts as the home base from which you can launch applications, view the contents of disks and hard drives, and rename, organize, duplicate, and delete files. The upcoming section "Meet the Finder desktop" explains the Finder desktop in detail.

Both the System and Finder files are essential to using a Macintosh computer. The following files represent optional elements of the system software:

- ☞ **System extensions:** Also known as *INITs,* system extensions expand or modify the performance of the system software. They may also control some aspect of an external piece of hardware. The CPU loads system extensions into RAM along with the System and Finder files during the startup procedure. Many extensions display icons along the bottom of your screen as they load.

- ☞ **Control panels:** Like system extensions, control panels — also called *control panel devices,* or *cdevs* for short — slightly augment the capabilities of the System and Finder. Many control panels load into memory during the startup procedure. You can open a control panel to display a window of options that govern the performance of a feature or piece of hardware. For example, the General Controls cdev lets you change the time, date, and desktop pattern. To access a control panel, choose the Control Panels command — Control Panel (singular) under System 6 — from the Apple menu at the Finder desktop.

- ☞ **Desk accessories:** Desk accessories (DAs) are mini-applications — or *utilities* — that reside under the Apple menu at the Finder desktop. Under System 7, the only indispensable desk accessory is the Chooser, which provides access to printer and network drivers. Under System 6, the Control Panel DA is also essential because it provides access to cdevs. This DA was demoted to a folder under System 7. Unessential but equally common DAs include the Alarm Clock, Calculator, Key Caps (which shows the keyboard locations of characters in a specified font), and Scrapbook (which allows you to store copied text and images for easy retrieval).

 ∽ **Drivers:** Drivers, also called *Chooser extensions,* act as interpreters that allow your computer to communicate accurately with printers, networking systems such as AppleTalk and Ethernet, and other devices that require specialized communications. For example, the LaserWriter file is a printer driver that translates instructions from the QuickDraw screen format to the PostScript printer language. To access a driver, choose the Chooser command from the Apple menu at the Finder desktop.

 ∽ **Support files:** This catch-all term refers to any files that may be required to successfully operate a system extension, control panel, or desk accessory. These files may contain preference settings or essential data. The most common example of a support file is the *Clipboard,* which offers access to text or images copied using the Cut or Copy command.

Under System 7, optional system files are organized into one of several predefined subfolders within the System Folder. The Control Panels folder contains — you guessed it — control panels. The Extensions folder contains system extensions and drivers. The Apple Menu Items folder contains desk accessories, and the Preferences folder contains many, if not all, of the support files.

Meet the Finder desktop

The primary function of the Finder is to display and organize the contents of disks, whether they're floppy disks, hard drives, cartridges, CD-ROMs, tapes, optical drives, or volumes shared over a network. The Finder desktop facilitates this function by providing the elements shown in Figure 2-2.

 Figure 2-2 shows the Finder as it appears in System 7.0 and higher. If you're using an earlier version of the system software, upgrade immediately. There's no reason *not* to be using System 7 with FreeHand.

The elements of the Finder desktop work as follows:

 ∽ **Menu bar:** A single menu bar appears along the top of the desktop, a trait shared with all other Macintosh applications. Each word in the menu bar represents a menu, which contains a list of *commands* that you can use to manipulate selected files, change the way files are displayed in windows, and initiate other disk-management operations.

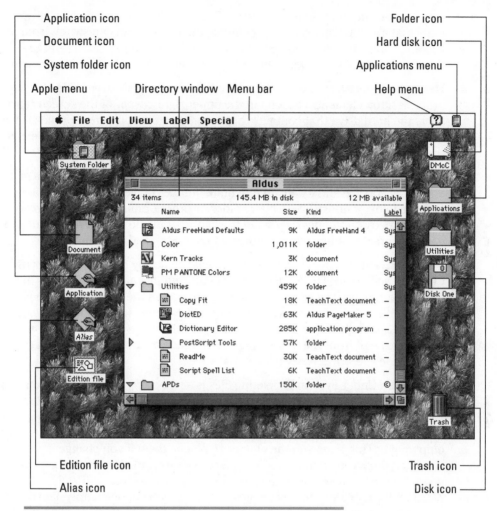

Figure 2-2: The Finder desktop as it might appear under System 7.

- **Apple menu:** The Apple menu contains a list of desk accessories. Under System 7, you can control the items that appear in the Apple menu by manipulating the contents of the Apple Menu Items folder in the System Folder.

- **Help menu:** Use the Help menu to activate System 7's *balloon help* feature, which displays a little text balloon filled with information about any desktop element you point to with your cursor. Just move your cursor around to find help on a range of topics. If you're new to the Mac, balloon help is a great way to get acquainted with your system software.

- **Applications menu:** Specific to System 7, the Applications menu lists all applications that are currently running, including the Finder. You can switch from one running application to another by choosing the application name from the menu. You can also hide windows from certain applications to eliminate screen clutter.

- **Hard disk icon:** An *icon* is a tiny picture that represents a disk, folder, file, or other desktop element. The icon in the upper right corner of the screen represents the hard drive that contains the current system software. Double-click on the hard drive icon to display its contents inside a directory window. (I explain the directory window in the next section.)

- **Folder icon:** Folders are optional organizational tools. You can create as many folders as you like and locate an indefinite number of files inside each folder. To create a folder, choose File ⇨ New Folder or press Command-N. You can create a folder directly on the desktop, as in the figure, or inside a directory window. You can even create folders within folders within folders, ad infinitum.

- **Disk icon:** A disk icon appears for each *mounted* floppy disk, SyQuest cartridge, CD-ROM, and so on. The Finder automatically mounts all available disks at the end of the startup procedure so that you can access their contents. The Finder also mounts a disk any time you insert one in its drive. (Special system extensions are generally required to mount removable media devices.) To dismount a disk and eject it from the drive, drag the disk icon to the Trash or select the icon and choose File ⇨ Put Away (Command-Y).

- **Trash icon:** Under System 7, deleting files is a two-step process. First, you drag the files to the Trash icon. Then you choose Special ⇨ Empty Trash. Press the Option key while choosing the Empty Trash command to bypass warnings and delete locked files. You can leave files in the Trash for as long as you like without emptying it. This gives you the chance to rescue them if you change your mind. However, after you choose the Empty Trash command, the files are gone for good. (Actually, some commercial utilities, such as Norton Utilities for Macintosh, enable you to rescue files even after you choose Empty Trash, but these utilities aren't 100 percent foolproof.) When in doubt, don't choose this command!

- **System Folder icon:** The System Folder contains all the files necessary to run your computer. I think that you've heard about as much on this topic as any human should have to withstand in one sitting.

- **Document icon:** A *document* is a file created with an application. Unlike applications, which can be executed independently of other programs (see the following paragraph), you have to use an application to open a document. The icon shown in Figure 2-2 is a generic document icon. Most applications assign special icons to their documents to provide a visual clue to their origin. You can open many document formats using a variety of applications, but some formats — called *native formats* — are exclusive to one brand of application only.

- **Application icon:** The application icon represents an *executable program;* that is, a file that runs and performs operations, offers its own desktop, opens other files, and so on. Under System 7, control panels and desk accessories also qualify as applications. To run an application, double-click on its icon. As with the document icon, the application icon shown in Figure 2-2 is a generic. Commercial programs such as FreeHand offer personalized icons to separate them from the crowd.

- **Alias icon:** Specific to System 7, an alias is a dummy file that references another file on disk. For example, if you create an alias for the FreeHand application, double-clicking on that alias runs FreeHand. Aliases are convenience tools, great for tossing into the Apple Menu Items folder and positioning on the desktop. The file name of an alias is italicized to distinguish it from other kinds of files. To create an alias, select the original document and choose File ⇨ Make Alias.

- **Edition file icon:** System 7's *publish and subscribe* feature permits you to save a portion of a document to disk as an *edition file.* When you import the edition into a different document, the application creates a live link between the imported element and the edition file on disk. Whenever you update the edition file, the application updates the imported element automatically.

- **Directory window:** Double-click on a disk or folder icon to display the contents of the disk or folder in a directory window. You can change the manner and order in which files appear in a window using commands from the View menu.

Parts of the window

The window is an especially important part of the Macintosh interface. At the Finder desktop, a window displays the contents of an open disk or folder. In other applications, a window displays the contents of a file. Whether displayed at the Finder desktop, within FreeHand, or in some other application, a window includes the following basic elements, as labeled in Figure 2-3:

- **Title bar:** At the Finder desktop, the title bar along the top of a directory window lists the name of the disk, folder, or file to which the window belongs. Inside other applications, the title bar lists the name of the open document. The *active* window is distinguished by the appearance of horizontal lines across the title bar. If you select an icon outside this window, you *deactivate* the window, making the close box, zoom box, size box, and scroll bars invisible. Drag the title bar to move an active window.

 Press the Command key and drag the title bar to move a background window without making it active. Command-dragging is a great method for shuffling around multiple windows inside FreeHand because it enables you to inspect details in a background document without bringing the document to the front and redrawing every object it contains.

✑ **Close box:** Click on the close box in the upper left corner of the title bar to close the active window. (Finally, some consideration for left-handers.) Press the Option key and click on the close box to close *all* directory windows on the desktop.

✑ **Zoom box:** Click on the zoom box in the upper right corner of the title bar to resize the active window to display as much of its contents as will fit on-screen. Click on the zoom box a second time to return the window to its previous size. Option-click on the zoom box to enlarge the window to full-screen size, regardless of its contents.

✑ **Size box:** Drag the size box in the lower right corner of the active window to resize the window manually.

✑ **Scroll bars:** Use the scroll bars along the right and bottom sides of the active window to display hidden contents of the window. If you click on a *scroll arrow,* you nudge the window slightly in that direction. Click in the gray area of a *scroll bar* to scroll the window more dramatically. Drag a *scroll box* to manually specify the distance scrolled. If all contents of a window are displayed, the scroll bars appear empty.

 If you use an *extended keyboard* — one that includes function keys along the top row — you can scroll the active window from the keyboard. Press the Page Down key to scroll down one screen, as if you had clicked in the gray area in the vertical scroll bar below the scroll box. Press Page Up to scroll up one screen. Press the End key to scroll all the way to the bottom of the active window. Press Home to scroll all the way to the top. The keyboard equivalents only work at the Finder desktop. They do *not* work inside FreeHand.

Figure 2-3:
Whether located at
the Finder desktop or
inside another
application, the
Macintosh window
comprises these
elements.

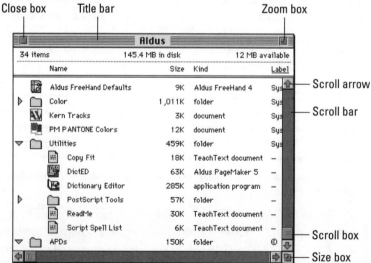

System Software Elements

Many elements provided by the system software are found throughout all Macintosh applications, including FreeHand. These elements make up the basic visual and logical composition of the Macintosh interface. They're so straightforward that explaining them is almost a waste of time, but each element provides a few clues that you may have overlooked. Hopefully, my explanations will help you predict the effect of unfamiliar functions throughout your future dealings with Macintosh software.

Menus and submenus

With the exception of a few applications that hide their menu bars, every Macintosh program features a series of menus across the top of the screen. Drag on a menu name to display a list of commands, each of which performs a specific function. If you choose a command followed by a right-pointing arrowhead, a *hierarchical submenu* (or just plain *submenu*) of related commands appears, as shown in Figure 2-4. Drag onto the submenu to choose the desired command.

Figure 2-4:
When you choose the Editions command inside FreeHand, a submenu appears.

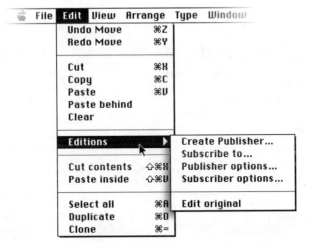

Dialog boxes and options

If a command is followed by an ellipsis (...), such as *Print...,* a *dialog box* appears when you choose the command, as shown in Figure 2-5. (Actually, Figure 2-5 shows two dialog boxes — Print Options and Screen Angle — but what's a little fudging between friends.) The dialog box is a way for the application or system software to request additional information from you before executing the command. It's not much of a dialog in the traditional sense — I mean, it's not like the software has any insights to share on the latest basketball game or the slightest interest in looking at your kid's photos — but it's a heck of a lot more sophisticated than any dialog you're likely to strike up with your toaster.

Dialog boxes request information by presenting a variety of options. Your response to each option determines the manner in which FreeHand eventually executes the command. The two closely related dialog boxes in Figure 2-5 show the five kinds of options that may appear:

⤷ **Radio button:** You can select only one round radio button from a set of radio buttons. To select a radio button, click on the button or on the option name that follows it. The selected radio button is filled with a black dot; all deselected radio buttons are hollow.

⤷ **Option box:** An option that allows you to enter a value or text is called an option box. Double-clicking on an option box highlights its contents. When the contents of an option box are highlighted, you can replace them by entering new characters from the keyboard. If a dialog box contains multiple option boxes, press the Tab key to advance from one option box to the next.

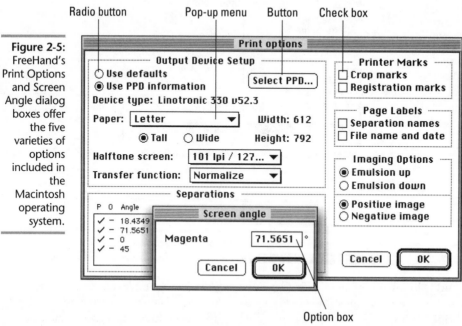

Figure 2-5: FreeHand's Print Options and Screen Angle dialog boxes offer the five varieties of options included in the Macintosh operating system.

Inside nearly all of FreeHand's dialog boxes, you can press Shift-Tab to return to the previous option box. (For some reason, the system software prevents this keyboard equivalent from working inside the Printer dialog box.)

- **Check box:** Although you can select only one radio button in a set of radio buttons, you can select any number of check boxes within a set of check boxes. To select a check box, click on the box or on the option name that follows it. Clicking on a selected check box deselects the option. A selected check box is filled with an X; a deselected check box is empty.

- **Pop-up menu:** To conserve space, some multiple-choice options appear as pop-up menus. Click and hold on the shadowed box to display a menu of option choices. Drag your mouse to highlight the desired option and release your mouse button to select it, just as if you were choosing a command from a standard menu.

- **Button:** Not to be confused with the radio button, a button enables you to close the current dialog box or display others. For example, click on the Cancel button to close the dialog box and cancel the current command. Click on the OK button to close the dialog box and execute the command according to the current settings. If the button name includes an ellipsis, as in the case of the Select PPD... button in Figure 2-5, the button takes you to another dialog box. If a button is surrounded by a heavy outline, you also can press the Return or Enter key to execute it.

 The *alert box*, a variation on the dialog box, displays an error message or warning. Most alert boxes include only buttons — OK, No, Cancel, I Hear Ya, Get Off My Case, whatever. The classic example is the Save Changes? alert box shown at the top of Figure 2-6, which appears when you try to close a document that you haven't yet saved.

Figure 2-6:
Two variations on the standard Save Changes? alert box.

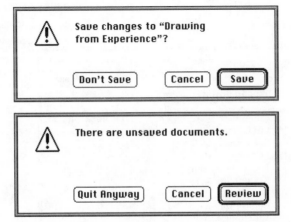

FreeHand provides a special alert box when you quit the software. As shown in the second example in Figure 2-6, this alert box asks whether you want to ignore the changes in all unsaved documents — a wonderful quick-escape option — or assess the changes in each document individually. If you click on the Review button, FreeHand displays the standard Save Changes? alert box for each unsaved document. You can cancel the Quit command from any one of these alert boxes.

Navigating by dialog box

Two operations — the opening and saving of documents — are standardized across all Macintosh programs. They provide a first look at the practical application of menu commands and dialog boxes. But more importantly, they enable you to navigate through disks and folders in ways that the Finder doesn't make possible.

 I've written the following discussions specifically with System 7 users in mind. Some features work slightly differently under System 6. For example, the Desktop button offered by System 7 is a Drive button under System 6.

The folder bar

Inside most programs, you choose File ➪ Open (Command-O) to display the Open dialog box, shown in Figure 2-7. The Open dialog box requests that you locate and select the document you want to open. Just above the scrolling list of documents is a *folder bar,* which tells you where you are inside the folder hierarchy. The name that appears in the bar reflects the current *folder.* Drag from the folder bar to relocate to a *parent folder;* that is, one of the folders that contains the current folder.

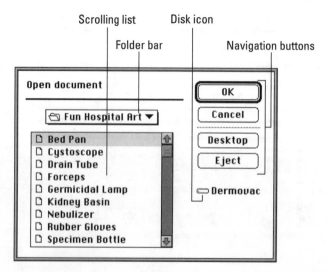

Figure 2-7:
The Open dialog box as it appears inside FreeHand.

The scrolling list

Below the folder bar, the Open dialog box provides a scrolling list that contains the names of all folders inside the current folder as well as all documents that you can open in the current application. Alias names appear italicized. You can use the scrolling list as follows:

- **Select a document or folder:** Click on the folder or document name.

- **Select by key entry:** To quickly locate a specific document or folder name, enter the first few letters of its name from the keyboard. The first item in alphabetical order whose name begins with these letters becomes selected.

- **Scroll through the list:** Press the up-arrow or down-arrow key to advance one name at a time through the scrolling list. On an extended keyboard, press the Page Up or Page Down key to scroll up or down several names at a time. Press the Home key to scroll all the way to the top of the list; press the End key to scroll all the way to the bottom.

- **Open an item:** Open a file or folder by double-clicking on its name or by selecting it and pressing the Return key.

- **Open a folder:** If a folder name is selected, press Command-down arrow to open that folder and display its contents.

- **Exit a folder:** To exit the current folder and display the contents of its parent folder, press Command-up arrow. You can also close the current folder by clicking on the disk icon below the Eject button.

The navigation buttons

To the right of the scrolling list is the name of the current disk. Above the disk name are four buttons. Each button has a keyboard equivalent, indicated in parentheses:

- **OK (Command-O):** Opens the selected document or folder. The fact that the OK button is surrounded by a heavy outline shows that you can also activate it by pressing the Return or Enter key.

- **Cancel (Command-period):** Cancels the Open command and returns to the application desktop.

- **Desktop (Command-D):** Exits the current folder and displays all documents and folders located at the Finder desktop.

- **Eject (Command-E):** Ejects the current disk from the disk drive. The disk remains mounted, enabling you to access it later. If the current disk is a hard drive, the Eject button appears dimmed.

Though the Desktop button replaces the System 6 Drive button, the functionality of the Drive button is not lost. Under System 7, you can switch from one drive to another from the keyboard. Press Command-right arrow to display the contents of the next disk; press Command-left arrow to display the contents of the previous disk.

Variations on the save

Choosing File ⇨ Save (Command-S) or File ⇨ Save As displays the Save dialog box (shown in Figure 2-8), which requires that you name the foreground document and specify its location. In many respects, the Save dialog box is identical to the Open dialog box, but there are a few interesting exceptions. For example, when you first display the Save dialog box, the option box in the lower left corner is active. In this option box, you enter the name under which you want to store the document.

If you click on the scrolling list or press the Tab key, you activate the scrolling list and deactivate the option box. A heavy line surrounds the scrolling list when it is active. You can now scroll through document and folder names by pressing keys from the keyboard, as described for the Open dialog box. To reactivate the option box, press Tab again.

The navigation buttons — OK, Cancel, Desktop, Eject — work identically to their counterparts in the Open dialog box. Many programs also offer a New Folder button that enables you to create a new folder inside the current one, but FreeHand 4.0 lacks this function. No doubt, by the time you read this book, Aldus will have come out with a revised version that includes a New Folder button, in which case, more power to them.

Figure 2-8: The Save dialog box as it appears inside FreeHand.

> **Save document**
>
> [🗁 Fun Hospital Art ▼]
>
> ☐ Bed Pan
> ☐ Cystoscope
> ☐ Drain Tube
> ☐ Forceps
> ☐ Germicidal Lamp
> ☐ Kidney Basin
> ☐ Nebulizer
>
> [Laparotomy Pack]
>
> **Format:** [FreeHand document ▼]
>
> [OK]
> [Cancel]
> [Desktop]
> [Eject]
> ⊂⊃ Dermovac

Working with Programs

Many folks believe that the Mac's most important contribution to personal computing was its graphical interface. But I think that it was the system software's ability to share information between applications. A running application could access any system element, most notably fonts, which is why the Mac quickly became synonymous with desktop publishing. But you could also trade data between documents or programs using the system's built-in Clipboard. To transfer text or images from Document 1 to Document 2, for example, you simply copied the items from Document 1, opened Document 2, and chose Edit ⇨ Paste. To transfer items between different programs, you had to quit one program before you launched the other one, but the system retained the contents of the Clipboard throughout.

Application management continues to be a hallmark of the Macintosh operating system. Only now, it's not limited to fonts and the Clipboard. You can run multiple programs at a time, assign chunks of RAM to each running program, and perform tasks in the background. I explain each of these options in the upcoming pages.

 Like System 7, Windows 3.1 on the PC provides *cooperative multitasking,* in which all running programs are on their honor to amicably share the computer's time and attention. This means that if one program messes up, it can bring down the entire system. The professional-level Windows NT offers *protected-mode multitasking,* a better solution that prevents bad applications from crashing good ones. If an application goes down, it bombs on its own and enables you to go about your business without restarting or losing important data.

Starting an application

Before you can use an application, you have to load it into RAM, thus making it available to the CPU. This is called *running, starting,* or *launching* a program. Of the three terms, I prefer the last because it suggests an air of romance that computing generally lacks. Can't you just see yourself launching FreeHand between refrains of "Rocket Man"? Maybe "Fly Me to the Moon"? How about "Twinkle Twinkle Little Star"? See, I knew that with a little effort, we could find common cultural ground. (Sorry — if you're one of those youngsters who's into Pearl Jam or Alice in Chains or some other alternative, primal experience, I can't help you.)

Unfortunately, whenever I say, "Go ahead and launch the program" (a phrase I constantly utter in day-to-day conversation), I get nothing but quizzical looks. "You want I should strap the disk to an Estes rocket and propel it into the stratosphere?" Well, okay, no one's ever actually asked me that, but you can tell that's exactly what people are thinking. "Does this software work by satellite or what?" So I'll stick with *run*. Or maybe *start*. They're boring terms but at least they don't require a countdown.

You can run a program from the Finder desktop by performing any of the following tasks:

- ☞ **Open the application directly:** Double-click on the application icon or select the icon and choose the Open command from the File menu (Command-O).

- ☞ **Open a document belonging to the application:** Double-click on a document icon or select the document and choose File ⇨ Open (Command-O). The system software locates the application in which the document was last saved, runs that application, and opens the selected document.

- ☞ **Drag a document icon onto the application icon:** Suppose that some pesky client has some artwork that she wants you to revise, but it was created in Adobe Illustrator 3.2 or earlier. Certainly, you can launch FreeHand and then open the Illustrator file. But under System 7, you can eliminate the middleman by dragging the Illustrator file icon directly onto the FreeHand application icon at the Finder desktop, as shown in Figure 2-9. This technique is called *drop-launching*. If the application supports the format of the document that you drag onto it, the system software highlights the application icon, as shown in the figure. If the format is not supported, the icon is not highlighted, and the application does not launch.

Figure 2-9:
Drag a document icon onto an application icon to open the selected document inside the highlighted application.

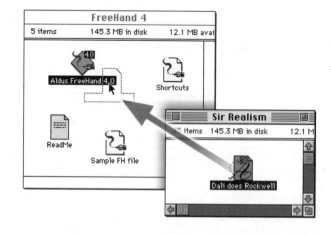

Assigning application RAM

Before running a program, you may want to specify the amount of space it will consume in RAM. This technique can prove useful when you want to conserve RAM space or, alternatively, to use as much as physically possible.

Suppose that you're trying to create a document in PageMaker that includes a drawing created in FreeHand and text created in Microsoft Word. You want to be able to run all three programs at once, but your Mac is equipped with only 8MB of RAM. By curtailing the amount of RAM available to each program, you can get all three to run at the same time.

The tradeoff is performance. When RAM is limited, a program may run slower, it may not be able to open large files, or both.

On the flip side, let's say that you want to work in FreeHand exclusively. By increasing the amount of RAM available to FreeHand, you can significantly speed up performance by permitting the program to keep complex documents entirely in memory instead of swapping bits and pieces with the disk drive.

However, when you're using FreeHand (or other drawing programs), there is a limit to how much memory you'll want to assign to the program. Unless you'll be juggling five or six documents at a time — or a document with five or six pages — more than 24MB of RAM is probably wasted on FreeHand and can be put to better use if freed up for other applications. Most folks won't even want to go that high, assigning somewhere in the neighborhood of 6MB to 16MB, depending on how much RAM is available. (Keep in mind that this is just a general rule of thumb. You'll of course want to experiment to determine the amount of memory that works best for you.)

Using the Get Info command

The amount of RAM set aside for use by a program is called the *application memory* or *application RAM.* You can adjust the amount of application memory that the system software assigns to a program by choosing the Get Info command from the File menu (Command-I).

Again, I'll use FreeHand as an example. (What the heck, it's a good program, and you can dance to it.) Before launching FreeHand, select its icon at the Finder desktop and choose File ⇨ Get Info to display the Info dialog box shown in Figure 2-10. System 7.1 provides three Memory Requirements values in the lower right corner of the dialog box, which work as follows:

☞ **Suggested Size:** The Suggested Size value indicates the minimum amount of RAM that the designers of this program recommend that you use. You cannot change this value. (Nor would you want to; it's just a reference number.)

☞ **Minimum Size:** Here's one you can change, but you probably shouldn't. The Minimum Size value represents the absolute smallest amount of RAM that the program needs to remain stable. As long as this much RAM is available, the system software starts the program. Lower this value, however, and you're flirting with disaster. If you assign far too little RAM, the program won't be able to fit into the space you've assigned to it and will quit on its own. If you give the program just enough RAM to get by, it will probably crash after a few moments of use. You may even have to restart your machine. The only advisable use for this option is to raise the value. For example, if you typically work on very complex drawings, you may want to boost the Minimum Size value to 6,000K. This way, FreeHand won't launch if less than 6MB is available in RAM, in which case you'll have to free some memory by quitting other programs.

Figure 2-10:
Adjust the amount of application memory assigned to the selected program by adjusting the spotlighted options.

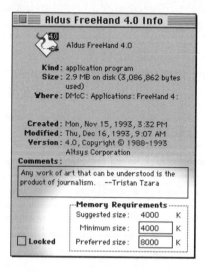

↦ **Preferred Size:** Now we're talking. You can change this option all you want. The Preferred Size value determines the amount of application RAM that the program will use if sufficient RAM is available. The value must be larger than the Minimum Size value, but otherwise there are no constraints. (So, provided that you don't go around lowering the Minimum Size value, you should always have enough RAM to launch the program.) If the amount of RAM available lies somewhere between the Minimum Size and Preferred Size values, the program ignores your recommendations and just consumes as much RAM as it can.

If you're using System 7.0, the Info dialog box offers only two memory values: Suggested Size and Current Size. The Current Size value serves the same purpose as the Preferred Size option provided by System 7.1.

The most important rule for managing digital space is to never completely fill it. Whether it's disk space or memory, try to leave no less than 10 percent of the space unused. This guideline is particularly important when it comes to RAM, because your system software always needs room to expand. You can check how much RAM is available by choosing the About This Macintosh command from the Apple menu at the Finder desktop. The dialog box shown in Figure 2-11 appears when you choose the command. The System Software value (last in list) includes the RAM space occupied by the Finder.

Figure 2-11:
Choose
Apple⇨About This
Macintosh to view
the way in which
running applications
make use of RAM.

About This Macintosh	
	System Software 7.1
Near-Dead Mac IIci	© Apple Computer, Inc. 1983–1992
Total Memory : 16,384K	**Largest Unused Block :** zero K
Adobe Photoshop	5,998K
Aldus FreeHand	4,000K
Calculator+	20K
DiskTop	20K
LW Font Utility	256K
Microsoft Word	2,048K
QuickDEX II	20K
Scrapbook	20K
System Software	3,978K

If the Largest Unused Block value (upper right) is zero K, as in Figure 2-11, you run an increased risk of encountering system problems. Symptoms include DAs and control panels quitting unexpectedly and the Finder refusing to open directory windows. To solve the problem, quit a running application, assign it a smaller Preferred Size value, and relaunch it.

Understanding memory fragmentation

If your Mac does not have a sufficiently large uninterrupted block of RAM to accommodate an application you're trying to run, an error message appears and prevents you from continuing. The only solution — other than decreasing the Minimum Size value — is to free up some memory by quitting one or more of the applications that are currently running.

Notice that I wrote *uninterrupted* memory. Just because your machine is equipped with 8MB of RAM, and you're only running one application besides the Finder doesn't mean that you'll also be able to run FreeHand. Memory can become *fragmented* — that is, subdivided into blocks too small to launch other applications.

Consider the example shown in Figure 2-12, which illustrates memory consumption on an 8MB machine. The white areas in the horizontal bars represent free RAM space. At startup, no application other than the Finder is running. The system software is very small, consuming only 1MB of RAM. This leaves 7MB free to run additional application software. Suppose that after startup, you run Microsoft Word, which requires at least 1MB in RAM. Then you run the communications software America Online, which consumes another 1MB. Finally, you run FreeHand, which you've set to take up 4MB. Only 1MB of RAM remains free.

Now suppose that you want to launch Microsoft Excel, which requires a minimum of 2MB to run. Before you can launch the program, you have to quit one or more applications to free up enough RAM space. Because 1MB of RAM is currently free, you reason that you need to free up another 1MB, so you quit America Online. But when you try to launch Excel, you find that you still don't have enough memory. Although you have 2MB of free RAM available, the memory is fragmented in 1MB chunks, as demonstrated in Figure 2-12. Like any Macintosh application, Excel requires uninterrupted RAM.

 Keep in mind that the 1MB figure for the system software suggested in Figure 2-12 is achievable but pretty darn unrealistic. Your system will grow based on the number of control panels and extensions that load during startup, the number of fonts and sounds you use, and a variety of other circumstances. My system tends to hover around 4MB, but I have all kinds of junk hooked up to this machine.

Figure 2-12: The white areas in the horizontal bars represent free RAM space. As shown in these five steps, running and quitting software can result in memory fragmentation.

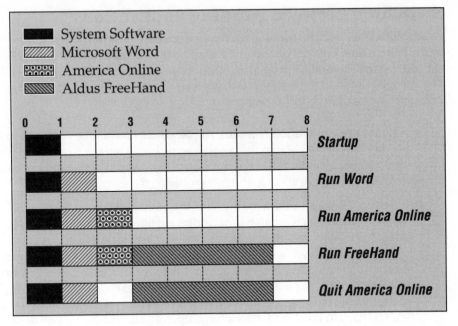

The only sure-fire way to avoid memory fragmentation is to quit applications in the *opposite* order that you launch them. Because few of us work that systematically, you may prefer to completely free up your RAM by quitting *all* applications and then rerunning the desired software.

Managing multiple applications

Being able to run multiple applications simultaneously vastly increases the number of tasks you can perform and reduces the amount of time it takes to complete those tasks. But you need to know a few things in order to take advantage of this capability. First, you need to be able to switch between running programs quickly and accurately. Second, you need to know how to control the actions of the background program when using another program in the foreground. And third, you need to remember to periodically clean up all that screen clutter so that you can see what the heck you're doing.

Switching between running applications

At any one time, only one running application resides in the *foreground*; the others run in the *background*. You can access the capabilities of an application only when it runs in the foreground. To bring a program to the foreground and send the previous foreground application to the background, you use a method called *switching*. Here are two different ways to switch to a new foreground application:

- ☞ **Choose the application from the Applications menu:** The Applications menu, located on the far right in the menu bar, provides access to every running application, including the Finder. Choose the desired application from the menu to bring that application to the foreground.

- ☞ **Click on a background window:** Like the Finder, every application offers its own desktop, including a menu bar, windows for open documents, and other elements (such as toolboxes, palettes, and floating rulers) that vary from application to application. Clicking on an open window or other visible element switches to the application to which the element belongs. For example, when working in FreeHand, you can click on a Finder window, a desktop icon, or the desktop pattern itself to bring the Finder to the foreground, as shown in Figure 2-13. To switch back to FreeHand, click on the open FreeHand document, as shown in Figure 2-14.

Figure 2-13: You can click on an open directory window to bring the Finder to the foreground.

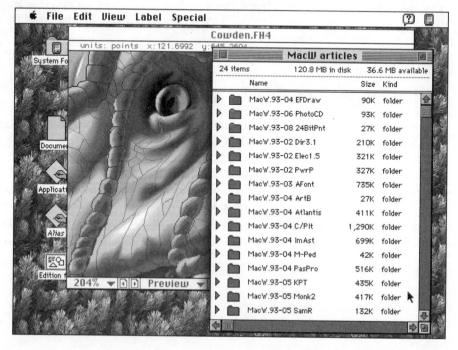

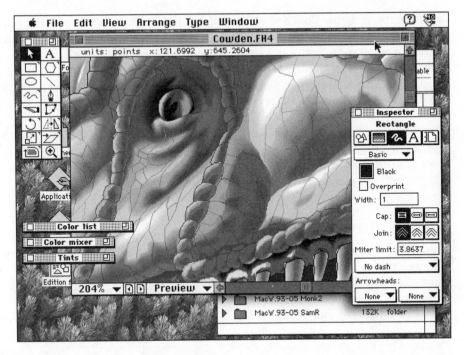

Figure 2-14:
If you click on
an open
application
window, you
bring that
application to
the fore-
ground.

In Figure 2-14, I clicked on the title bar of a FreeHand document to bring FreeHand
to the foreground. Note that this causes the toolbox and any open palettes to
appear. FreeHand hides both toolbox and palettes when it runs in the background.

If you haven't already done so, be sure to check out Portland-based Steve Cowden's
T-Rex drawing, called *Cowden.FH* in the Sample Illustrations folder on Disk 4.
Featured in Figures 2-13 and 2-14 (and page 18 of the FreeHand User Manual),
it's one of the best examples of object-oriented realism I've seen. Even if you are
sick of dinosaurs (personally, I can't get enough of them), it just goes to show
that you don't have to live in California or New York to create amazing art.

Printing in the background

Depending on your output device, you can also print FreeHand documents in the background, but this requires the use of a special System 7 capability called *background
printing*. Background printing only works with the Personal LaserWriter LS, the StyleWriter,
the LaserWriter SC series, or any model of printer that is equipped with PostScript.

Begin by choosing the Chooser from the list of desk accessories under the Apple menu. The Chooser window, shown in Figure 2-15, rears into view. Select the driver icon that corresponds to your printer model from the scrolling list on the left. If you own a PostScript printer, select the LaserWriter icon (preferably the LaserWriter 8.0 icon included with FreeHand). Then select On from the Background Printing options. Close the Chooser window, and you're ready to go.

If you can't get a document to print, try selecting Off from the Background Printing options and then reissuing the Print command. Or select a different printer driver. For complete information on printing, read Chapter 20, "Printing from FreeHand."

Background screen refresh

Unlike other varieties of graphics applications, drawing programs typically don't take hours on end to perform complex operations. In FreeHand, for example, only four operations are likely to take more than a minute to perform. The first three are printing a document, opening it, and saving it to disk. As I just mentioned, System 7 lets you print in the background. But FreeHand is incapable of opening or saving except in the foreground, so you just have to suffer while those operations take their sweet time. (You can try threats, jeers, and bribery, but your computer will most likely ignore you.)

The fourth time-consuming operation — the one that makes hundreds of other operations *seem* slow — is redrawing the document on-screen. Although I discuss this topic in more detail in the "Cancelling the screen redraw" section of Chapter 3, I want to warn you that FreeHand is capable of redrawing a document even when running in the background. This may sound like a benefit, but it is more frequently an inconvenience.

Figure 2-15: Turn on the Background Printing option to instruct System 7 to load a printed document into memory and send it to the printer in the background while you continue to work in the foreground.

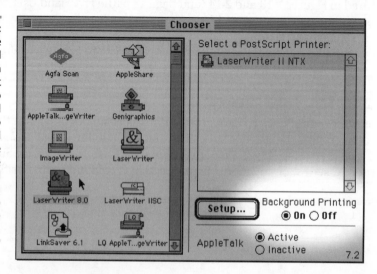

Suppose that you have some monumentally complex FreeHand drawing open, such as Mr. Cowden's T-Rex. You then bring Microsoft Word to the foreground and open a couple of documents, both of which partially obscure different portions of the extinct creature. If you close or move one of the Word documents in order to reveal a portion of the dinosaur, FreeHand sets about filling in the missing details. You won't be able to enter text or perform any other Word operations until FreeHand completes the redraw cycle.

Actually, you're not totally without options. If you don't want FreeHand to finish redrawing a background window, just press Command-period. Even though FreeHand is running in the background, it's smart enough to know who you're talking to. It immediately stops redrawing and relinquishes control to the foreground application.

Hiding and showing running applications

Normally, I'm one of those people who lives and works comfortably in a cluttered environment. But clutter on my computer screen is another matter entirely. Forget that it's unattractive; the problem is that on-screen clutter prevents you from being able to access important files, folders, disks, and data. For example, how do you get to a folder on the Finder desktop when a big FreeHand window is in your way?

The solution is to hide FreeHand from view. Hiding an application doesn't get rid of it or close any of its documents; it merely makes them temporarily invisible. You can hide and display one or more applications at a time using commands from the Applications menu.

- ∞ **Hide the foreground application:** Choose the first command from the Applications menu to hide the current foreground application. All windows and other miscellaneous screen debris associated with the current application disappear. The application running immediately behind the hidden application moves to the foreground.

Press the Option key and choose a program name from the Applications menu to bring that program to the foreground and hide the previous foreground application. You can also hide the foreground application by Option-clicking on a window or other element belonging to another running application.

- ∞ **Hide all background applications:** Choose the Hide Others command to hide all applications except the current foreground program. This command is especially useful when you are working at the Finder desktop, where windows from other applications can prove especially distracting.

- ∞ **Show a single application:** Icons in the Applications menu appear dimmed if they belong to hidden programs. To redisplay a running program that has a dimmed icon, just choose its name from the menu. The application simultaneously displays and moves to the foreground.

If you use a macro utility such as CE Software's QuicKeys to launch software, you can use the same macro to display a hidden program. For example, if you assign Command-Control-F to start FreeHand, and the FreeHand application is currently hidden, pressing Command-Control-F displays FreeHand and brings it to the foreground. You can likewise double-click on the application's icon at the Finder desktop.

  ∽ **Show all applications:** Choose the Show All command to redisplay all hidden applications without bringing them to the foreground. Keep in mind that if FreeHand is one of these hidden applications, it will busily set about redrawing its windows. Press Command-period to put a quick end to this process.

Using the Clipboard

Since the birth of the Mac, users have been able to swap data between documents and programs using the *Clipboard*, which is a section of RAM (called a *buffer*) set aside to hold a single collection of data. The Clipboard can hold three basic kinds of data: text, object-oriented graphics, and bitmapped images.

You can manipulate the contents of the Clipboard from inside just about any program by choosing commands from the Edit menu:

  ∽ **Cut (Command-X):** This command removes the selected data from the foreground document and places it in the Clipboard, thus replacing the Clipboard's previous contents.

  ∽ **Copy (Command-C):** The Copy command makes a copy of the selected data in the foreground document and places that copy in the Clipboard, thus replacing the Clipboard's previous contents.

  ∽ **Paste (Command-V):** This command makes a copy of the contents of the Clipboard and places it in the foreground document. Unlike Cut and Copy, the Paste command leaves the contents of the Clipboard unaltered.

 Many new users have trouble remembering the keyboard equivalents for the Clipboard commands. Command-C makes sense for Copy. Command-X is a stretch, but it sort of brings to mind Cut. But what does Command-V stand for? Guesses range anywhere from *vent* to *vomit*, but the answer resides at the bottom left corner of your keyboard. The keys read Z, X, C, and V. That's Undo (the first command in the Edit menu), Cut, Copy, and Paste.

The most common way to use the Clipboard is to cut or copy text or graphics from one document and paste them into another. You also can cut, copy, and paste within a single document, but you'll eventually learn to use this method only when creating masks (as explained in Chapter 17). Cloning, a technique discussed in Chapter 16, is a better way to duplicate objects in FreeHand.

Application Clipboards

Many applications have their own internal Clipboards, and FreeHand is no exception. These *application Clipboards* are distinct from but linked to the operating system's Clipboard. For example, if you copy an object inside one FreeHand document and then paste it into a different document, FreeHand stores the object in a special buffer, separate from the buffer that holds the system's Clipboard. Only when you switch applications does FreeHand convert the object to the Mac's native graphics format, PICT, and transfer it to the system's Clipboard. For this reason, you may get a delay when switching applications.

If the contents of the Clipboard are especially large, the system displays a Converting Clipboard message. If the conversion process takes too long, or if you simply don't want to transfer the contents of FreeHand's Clipboard, just press Command-period to cancel. This tells FreeHand to put the text string "Not enough memory to convert the items on the Clipboard" into the system's Clipboard. (You can even paste the string into a word processor and edit it, though admittedly there's no reason on earth you'd want to.)

You can copy FreeHand objects and paste them into many other applications. Photoshop, Word, and Excel are just a few of the popular applications that accept objects copied from FreeHand (though Photoshop converts the objects to a bitmapped image).

FreeHand is also talented at accepting text and graphics copied from other programs. Unlike Illustrator, which doesn't recognize the contents of any Clipboard except those of other Adobe products, FreeHand is usually smart enough to distinguish between objects, bitmapped images, and text. If you paste objects, FreeHand treats each object as both independent and editable. If you paste an image, FreeHand converts it to the TIFF format. And if you paste text, FreeHand automatically creates a new text block and places the text inside it with formatting intact.

Using the Scrapbook

You can use the Scrapbook desk accessory — included with all versions of the Macintosh system software — to hold data copied from various documents and programs. Unlike the Clipboard, which can hold no more than one chunk of data at a time, the Scrapbook adds a new page every time you paste text or graphics into it. Also, whereas the Clipboard resides in RAM and thus gets erased every time you restart or turn off your computer, the Scrapbook file resides on disk, ensuring that you can access it over and over again.

To transfer the contents of the Clipboard into the Scrapbook, choose the Scrapbook from the list of desk accessories under the Apple menu. Then choose Edit ⇨ Paste (Command-V). A new page appears, showing the pasted text or graphic. If the graphic is too large to fit inside the window, the Scrapbook displays it at a reduced size, as shown in Figure 2-16. In this example, the Scrapbook displays the graphic at 33 percent of its actual size so that you can see all of it in the page window.

To retrieve data from the Scrapbook, open the Scrapbook window and scroll to the page that contains the desired text or graphic. If you want to delete the current page of data from the Scrapbook, choose Edit ⇨ Cut (Command-X). You can also delete a page from the Scrapbook by pressing the Delete key. If you want to keep the data on hand for future use, choose Edit ⇨ Copy (Command-C).

Figure 2-16:
The dinosaur image,
copied from
FreeHand and pasted
into the Scrapbook
desk accessory.

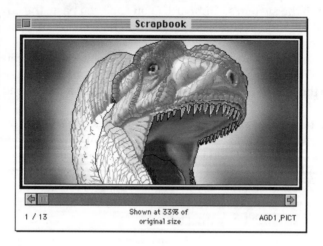

Using Fonts

When it comes to creating small brochures, reports, and other documents, FreeHand 4.0 may be the best program currently available for any personal computer. Its new text-handling capabilities, combined with features that enable you to create outrageous logos and other special treatments — the kind of stuff professional designers are always warning novices to use in moderation — put a heck of a lot of type potential in your hands. I, for one, don't care if you turn out pages and pages of wacky type; in fact, the more the merrier. I just want you to feel as though your options are unlimited, and to do that, I first need to tell you how to install and use *fonts* on a computer.

In case you don't know what I'm talking about, *fonts* are electronic descriptions of typefaces such as Helvetica, Times, and Courier. Regardless of the system software you use, you can access a wide variety of fonts from inside any application.

Electronic typography took off with the advent of PostScript printing technology in 1985, one year after the introduction of the Mac. PostScript *outline fonts* offer mathematical, character-by-character outline definitions that you can display on-screen or print to high-resolution output devices, including professional-quality typesetters. Nowadays, almost a decade after it was born, PostScript has become the accepted standard among typesetters, designers, and publishers.

If you use System 7, or System 6 with the TrueType system extension, you have access to two brands of outline font technology that can coexist harmoniously on your hard drive: PostScript and TrueType. You can scale outline fonts to absolutely any size, subject to the limitations of your software. Provided that you install Adobe Type Manager, your text will appear smooth and professional regardless of size.

Part 3, "Adding Text," comprises three chapters of instructions for creating and editing type inside FreeHand.

Installing PostScript screen fonts

Every PostScript font includes two parts: a bitmapped *screen font* and a mathematically-defined *printer font*. Technically, the screen font is designed to display characters on your monitor; the printer font contains the outline definitions used by the printer. However, if you use Adobe Type Manager, the printer font works with the screen font to smooth out the jagged edges once associated with on-screen type.

A screen font defines a single *type style* — plain, bold, italic, or other — when displayed at a single *type size*, measured in *points* — generally 9, 10, 12, 14, 18, or 24. (One point equals 1/72 inch.) Multiple screen fonts are packaged inside a special file called a *suitcase*, shown in Figure 2-17. A suitcase file can contain multiple screen fonts. A printer font file, on the other hand, describes only one typeface and style.

Figure 2-17:
A single suitcase file (top) can contain multiple screen fonts. Each printer font file (bottom) describes one typeface and style.

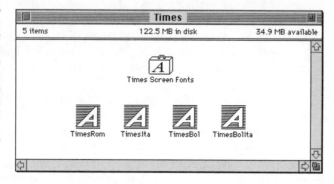

Before you can access a PostScript font in an application, you must install its screen font in your system software. How you accomplish this depends on the system you use:

- **System 6:** If you use System 6, you must copy screen fonts to the System file using Apple's Font/DA Mover utility. Upgrade to System 7, and you won't have to deal with this cumbersome, antiquated utility. (Sorry, but it's time you faced the tough facts.)

- **System 7.0:** Under System 7, you can open a suitcase at the Finder desktop merely by double-clicking on the suitcase icon as if it were a folder. (Doesn't that sound tempting, you System 6 users?) A directory window appears, displaying the contents of the suitcase, as shown in Figure 2-18. Each screen font icon looks like a folded page with a single letter *A* on it. Drag the screen font from the open suitcase window onto the System file icon to make it a part of the system software.

- **System 7.1 and later:** System 7.1 introduced the Fonts folder, which provides increased convenience by enabling you to install and delete whole suitcase files. Rather than opening the suitcase file and copying individual fonts, you can simply drag the suitcase icon into the Fonts folder.

The Fonts folder can accommodate up to 128 suitcase files. (There is no limit on the number of screen fonts inside the suitcases.) If your enthusiasm for fonts knows no bounds, you may have to combine two or more suitcases into one by opening one suitcase and dragging its contents into another suitcase. Keep in mind that each font you add increases the amount of RAM your system consumes and the amount of time it takes your computer to load the system software into memory when you first start your machine.

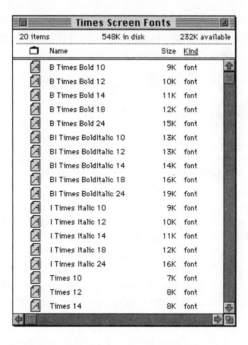

Figure 2-18:
The contents of a suitcase file viewed at the Finder desktop using System 7.

The system software does not allow you to delete screen fonts when any application but the Finder is open. However, you can add screen fonts at any time. In fact, FreeHand scans the Fonts folder periodically and adds any new typefaces that it finds to the Font submenu.

Installing PostScript printer fonts

To get the most out of FreeHand, you should also use Adobe Type Manager (ATM), which is a control panel sold separately by Adobe. (Who else would sell such a thing?) ATM displays PostScript fonts smoothly on-screen and renders them to non-PostScript printers. When using ATM, you need to install printer fonts for *all* typefaces you want to use with FreeHand — even if they're built into your printer. Use the following installation procedures:

- **System 6:** If you're still clinging to System 6, copy the printer fonts into the System Folder.

- **System 7.0:** Under System 7.0, you can copy the printer fonts either to the System Folder or to the Extensions folder inside the System Folder.

- **System 7.1 and later:** Assuming that you're using ATM 3.0 or later, copy the printer fonts to the Fonts folder inside the System Folder. Earlier versions of ATM look for fonts in the Extensions folder.

To make newly installed printer fonts available to an application, you have to restart your computer. ATM can only load printer fonts into RAM during the startup procedure. After that, the printer fonts it makes available to applications are set in stone.

Using SuperATM

Adobe sells two versions of ATM, regular and Super. In addition to rendering fonts smoothly on-screen, SuperATM lets you view Adobe-brand PostScript fonts on-screen and output those fonts at high resolutions, even when the corresponding printer fonts are unavailable.

Here's how it works: If SuperATM doesn't find a printer font, it consults a hefty 1.4MB database that contains *font metrics* — character size and spacing information — for 1,300 faces from the Adobe Type Library. After SuperATM locates the desired metrics, the program blends two *multiple master* fonts — one serif and the other sans serif — according to a recipe found inside the database. The result is a reasonable facsimile of the desired typeface. SuperATM can display the result on-screen and print it at full resolution to a PostScript or non-PostScript printer.

 Multiple master technology is a truly amazing invention. An application consults two related fonts that represent extremes in weight, width, *optical size* (meaning the design of characters as they relate to legibility at small and large sizes), and/or style. The application then mixes the fonts to create a unique variation that lies somewhere in between. Literally thousands of variations are possible.

What good is SuperATM? The product enables you to test out typeface variations quickly and conveniently. After selecting a screen font from the immense collection that SuperATM bundles on CD-ROM, you can try out the font inside FreeHand or any other application. It's no substitute for the real printer font definition, but it opens whole new avenues for experimentation.

Installing TrueType fonts

We now leave the action-packed world of PostScript for the less interesting but more straightforward world of TrueType. A TrueType font is made up of a single *variable-size font* file, which is used both to display the font on-screen at any size and to describe the font to the output device. Like PostScript screen fonts, multiple TrueType fonts are generally packaged in a suitcase file. Font manufacturers sometimes include separate screen fonts that provide better legibility at small sizes. These fonts are also packaged in the suitcase file.

You install TrueType fonts in the exact same way that you install PostScript screen fonts. I've been through it once already, but to quickly recap:

> ⮾ **System 6:** Use Apple's Font/DA Mover utility or upgrade to System 7.

> ⮾ **System 7.0:** Open a suitcase at the Finder desktop by double-clicking on the suitcase icon. Then drag the desired screen fonts from the open suitcase window onto the System file icon.

> ⮾ **System 7.1 and later:** Drag the suitcase icon into the Fonts folder. Beginning to sound familiar?

FreeHand is 100 percent compatible with both PostScript and TrueType fonts. You gain no inherent advantage by using one font format over the other, except that PostScript fonts are more plentiful and, thanks to SuperATM and multiple master technology, PostScript fonts have a wider range of applications.

Summary

> ⮞ Your computer's memory includes permanent data stored in ROM and temporary data stored in RAM. The CPU controls the contents of memory.

> ⮞ The FPU accelerates the calculation of complex mathematical equations, especially those that involve numbers with decimal points.

> ⮞ The PowerPC is the fastest personal computer available, easily outpacing top-of-the-line Pentium machines, which are currently the fastest machines that run DOS or Microsoft Windows.

> ⮞ You can use disk space to store system software, applications, and documents for later use. You can delete and update the contents of a disk at any time.

> ⮞ A bit is one of two digits, 0 or 1. A byte comprises eight bits; 1,024 bytes is 1K; 1,024K equals 1MB.

> ⮞ To get the most out of FreeHand, you should be using System 7.

> ⮞ Some of your Mac's system software is included in ROM; the rest is provided on disk to make it easy to upgrade.

> ⮞ The disk-based portion of the Macintosh operating system includes two main parts, the System and the Finder. The System defines the environment and offers up the resources required to run other programs; the Finder enables you to organize files on disk.

- Extensions and control panels increase the capabilities of your system software.

- The Open and Save dialog boxes allow you to navigate through disks and folders in ways that the Finder desktop does not.

- You can run an application by double-clicking on its icon at the Finder desktop or by dragging a document onto the application icon.

- Use the File ⇨ Get Info command to assign a minimum and maximum amount of application RAM to a program.

- If memory becomes fragmented to the point that you can't run a desired application, close all running applications and relaunch them.

- To switch between running programs, choose the desired program from the Applications menu or click on the program's window.

- You can cancel the redraw of a complex document by pressing Command-period, even when FreeHand is running in the background.

- The Scrapbook desk accessory serves as a holding cell for Clipboard data you want to save for later use.

- You can paste objects, images, and text copied from just about any application into FreeHand.

- Adobe Type Manager displays PostScript fonts on-screen and renders them to non-PostScript printers. The system software handles TrueType fonts internally.

- Computers respect experience. Over time, even your cantankerous machine will learn to behave.

Touring the FreeHand Neighborhood

In This Chapter

- Installing, decompressing, and deleting FreeHand files
- The contents of the eight FreeHand 4.0 disks
- A tour of the FreeHand desktop
- Brief introductions to FreeHand's tools, cursors, and palettes
- How to navigate using magnification and scrolling options
- News about the preview and keyline display modes
- FreeHand's hidden keyboard equivalents
- The wide world of preference settings

Getting Started with FreeHand

Remember when you were a newborn? (Of course you don't — only folks who believe that LaToya Jackson is one of the world's great thinkers and that unicorns really exist remember themselves as newborns — but go ahead and play along with me for a moment.) You do? Well, then you no doubt remember how you weren't exactly sure what to do with your tiny arms and legs, how your uncle's face scared you silly, and how hard it was to keep all that excess saliva in your mouth. Nowadays, your appendages are more familiar (if not always particularly coordinated), you've come to terms with your relatives (perhaps through counseling), and you don't drool nearly so often (only when a pillow is embedded in your face).

This, my friend, is the difference between being a novice at something and having become accustomed to it through experience. If FreeHand is new to you, you may find it somewhat intimidating. With time, of course, you'll be drawing and creating documents with the best of them, but in the meantime, you may live in abject fear of the program.

This chapter is designed to ease the transition from newness to familiarity. Rather than allowing you to look into the deepest recesses of FreeHand and freeze with terror like a fawn caught in the headlights, I'll walk you through the software one step at a time. By the chapter's end, you'll scoff at your early apprehensions about FreeHand.

Installing FreeHand

This part isn't scary. In fact, it's duller than stale bread. But the sad fact is, you can't use FreeHand until you install it on your computer's hard drive. Luckily, the process of installing FreeHand is well-documented (see the "Getting Started" guide included with FreeHand 4.0) and remarkably straightforward to boot. So rather than insulting your intelligence with the blow-by-blow, I'll just touch on the few topics that may prove useful.

 First, a quick warning: FreeHand 4.0 does not open FreeHand 1.0 documents. I know — it's not fair, but it's true. If you own FreeHand 3.0 or 3.1, keep that version's application file and FreeHand filters file on your hard disk. You can then open FreeHand 1.0 documents in FreeHand 3.0/3.1, save the documents in 3.0/3.1 format, and open the 3.0/3.1 formatted document in Version 4.0. So that the 3.0/3.1 files aren't overwritten when you install Version 4.0, copy the files to a separate location on your hard drive or to a removable media device such as a SyQuest cartridge.

Contents of the FreeHand disks

Back in the old days (sigh), programs shipped on one or two disks, each of which was labeled according to its exact contents. Nowadays (gnash teeth), software ships on a stack of disks, each of which sports an utterly meaningless label. FreeHand 4.0 is a case in point. The product ships on eight disks, which are labeled — what else? — Disk 1, Disk 2, and so on. Even power users may find themselves reduced to inserting Disk 1 and launching the Aldus Installer/Utility program to copy a single miscellaneous file such as a font or sample illustration.

Actually, it's relatively easy to bypass the intrusive installation procedure if you know what's on each disk (see Table 3-1). All you have to do is double-click on the file to instruct the Aldus Installer/Utility to transfer it to your hard drive.

To save space, most files on the eight-disk set were compressed using either Aldus Installer/Utility or StuffIt, the popular compression program from Aladdin. When you first run Installer/Utility to install FreeHand 4.0 (as documented in the "Getting Started" manual), Installer/Utility copies itself to the Aldus folder inside your System Folder. From then on, you can decompress and install any Installer/Utility documents — which look like pages with inset purple accordions — just by double-clicking on them. Installer/Utility asks you where to save the file and then quits automatically.

Table 3-1 lists the contents of all eight FreeHand 4.0 disks so that you don't have to stick disk after disk into your drive to see which one contains that special file. Better yet, you don't have to hunt around for files that don't even exist.

Bear in mind that Table 3-1 is specific to Version 4.0. Disks included with future versions of FreeHand will likely contain different files. Also note that the fonts on Disks 4 through 8 are compressed with StuffIt and cannot be opened by the Installer/Utility program. You have to use StuffIt Expander, included on either Disk 1 or 8, as explained in the "Adding StuffIt Expander" section later in this chapter.

Table 3-1	The Contents of the FreeHand 4.0 Disks	
Disk	**File or Folder**	**Description**
1	Aldus FreeHand 4.0.Pt2	The second half of the Installer/Utility archive containing the FreeHand application
	Additions	A folder containing a PageMaker 5.0 addition that allows PageMaker to import custom color palettes created in FreeHand
	Color	A folder of 12 commercial color collections from Pantone, Trumatch, and others
	Utilities	A folder containing Installer/Utility; a script file that tells Installer/Utility what to do; StuffIt Expander, to decompress StuffIt files; Apple's TeachText utility; and a ReadMe document
2	Aldus FreeHand 4.0.Pt1	The first half of the Installer/Utility archive containing the FreeHand application
	Aldus	A folder of dictionary files that FreeHand and PageMaker can share (FreeHand uses the dictionaries for hyphenation)
	Extensions	A folder containing Apple's QuickTime 1.6.1 system extension, used to display the Features at a Glance movies and previews of Aldus Fetch files

(continued)

Table 3-1 *(continued)*		

Disk	File or Folder	Description
3	Aldus	A folder containing files that keep track of FreeHand's preference settings, as well as a help document
	Extensions	A folder containing Version 8.0 of the LaserWriter driver plus several PostScript printer description files (PPDs)
	Features at a Glance	A folder of lame QuickTime movies that ostensibly demonstrate how various FreeHand 4.0 functions work
	Sample Illustrations	A folder of sample drawings that are protected by copyright — so you can't use them as clip-art
4	Shortcuts	A film by Robert Altman; or, in this case, a FreeHand document containing a list of keyboard equivalents
	Sample Illustrations	More sample FreeHand drawings, including that cool T-Rex graphic, Cowden.FH4
	Type 1 PostScript Fonts	A folder containing two variations on the text font Bodoni and a collection of special numerals and small caps called Stone Print Roman
5	Type 1 PostScript Fonts	Three more variations on Bodoni, a style of Futura, and an italic version of Stone Print Roman
6	Type 1 PostScript Fonts	One more Bodoni and four more Futuras
7	Type 1 PostScript Fonts	Yet another Bodoni and yet four more Futuras
8	Type 1 PostScript Fonts	One last Bodoni, three final Futuras, and another copy of StuffIt Expander to break up the monotony

Installation advice

After you launch the Aldus Installer/Utility, the Aldus Installer Main Window appears, as shown in Figure 3-1. If your hard drive is as vast and uninhabited as the great Wyoming plains, feel free to select every check box and install everything FreeHand has to offer. But if your hard drive more closely resembles a Tokyo subway station at rush hour, select only the Aldus FreeHand 4.0 check box. This installs everything except the sample illustrations, fonts, and Features at a Glance movies. The Installer program requires about 15MB of free disk space to install the necessary FreeHand files, but it will probably add fewer than 10MB of files to your hard drive.

After you click on the Install button, the utility periodically prompts you to remove one disk and insert another. Blindly and obediently do as instructed. (Isn't it great being bossed around by a machine? It's like something out of one of those Philip K. Dick androids-run-the-world novels.)

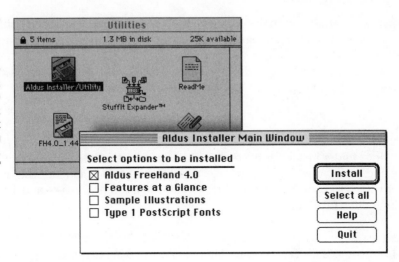

Figure 3-1:
To save hard drive space, select only the Aldus FreeHand 4.0 check box when first installing FreeHand.

When the utility finishes, it presents an alert box containing a single button, Restart. Why not a simple Quit button? Because FreeHand installs QuickTime 1.6.1, and to use QuickTime, you have to load it into your system — which requires that you restart your machine. Interestingly enough, QuickTime is *not* required to operate FreeHand; FreeHand doesn't even support QuickTime movies. The only reason QuickTime is installed is so that you can play the Features at a Glance movies and compress document previews intended for use with a fellow Aldus program, Fetch.

If your machine is already equipped with QuickTime, or if some other application is running and you don't want to risk losing changes, by all means do *not* click on the Restart button. Instead, press Command-Option-Escape, which *force quits* any running program. When you force quit, Installer/Utility abandons the Installer History document, which automatically keeps track of which files go where. But it's a small price to pay to avoid this random and largely senseless restarting of your computer.

Adding StuffIt Expander

How much would you pay for the installation advice you've read so far? Wait, there's more! Two more little tidbits, in fact.

First, Disks 1 and 8 include Aladdin's StuffIt Expander. However, the Installer/Utility never installs StuffIt Expander to your hard drive, regardless of which check boxes you select in the Aldus Installer Main Window. If you don't own StuffIt but you want to be able to selectively decompress the fonts on Disks 5 through 8 (the Installer/Utility program is only capable of installing *all* fonts), copy StuffIt Expander to your hard disk manually. I recommend copying it to the Utilities folder inside the Aldus folder, which is located in your System Folder. Then just double-click on a font file to decompress it.

StuffIt Expander enables you to decompress any file that was compressed using StuffIt. Such files generally end in an .SIT suffix. So from now on, if some friend of yours uses StuffIt, but you don't, you can receive a StuffIt file and open it on your machine. You cannot, however, use StuffIt Expander to *compress* a file. For that, you need the full working version of StuffIt (which, by the way, I heartily recommend).

Deleting TeachText

Open the Aldus folder inside the System Folder. Then locate the Utilities folder and open it. Inside, you should find the Installer/Utility program — evidence that it does indeed copy itself to your hard drive during the installation process — and TeachText, Apple's diminutive text editor.

FreeHand installs TeachText so that you can open the ReadMe file and edit the FreeHand Preferences file (as described in the "Customizing the Interface" section toward the end of this chapter). The problem is, nearly every major application automatically copies TeachText to your hard drive during its installation process, including System 7. This means that you probably already have at least one additional copy of TeachText lying around your hard drive.

At the Finder desktop under System 7, you can choose File ⇨ Find (Command-F) and File ⇨ Find Again (Command-G) to locate all occurrences of TeachText. If the Find Again command turns up any repeats, drag each one to the Trash.

FreeHand installs TeachText 1.2; System 7 installs the slightly improved TeachText 7.0. You can tell the difference between the two by their sizes (displayed in the directory window when you choose View ⇨ By Name). TeachText 1.2 takes up about 21K on disk; TeachText 7.0 takes up 36K. When trashing TeachTexts, you're better off keeping Version 7.0 and tossing Version 1.2.

Network copy protection

You may not have noticed, but FreeHand 4.0 is copy-protected. If you have two or more machines networked together, and both machines are equipped with versions of FreeHand with identical serial numbers, you can't run the two at the same time. In fact, if you launch one version of FreeHand on Machine A while it's already running on Machine B, the FreeHand on Machine B automatically quits. Be sure to press Command-S immediately, or you may lose some of your work.

The ReadMe file on Disk 1 explains, "Network administrators benefit from this feature, which helps them ensure that users on the network are operating Aldus FreeHand 4.0 within the legal rights granted by the Aldus Licensing Agreement." Oh, thank you, thank you, Aldus. We are eternally in your debt.

You want a workaround? Disconnect your network cabling *before* running FreeHand. This same technique works for Photoshop, PageMaker, and hundreds of other similarly protected programs. It's a royal inconvenience because it prevents you from accessing a network server or printing your artwork — and, in more structured offices, it may simply be impossible — but every blue moon, you may find that there's no other way to get that last-minute job out the door. Mind you, I don't condone this behavior; it's between you and your conscience. (Talk about walking an ethical tightrope — first I tell you how to blow up the roadrunner with dynamite and then I tell you that I abhor violence against roadrunners.)

Your First Look at FreeHand

After you install FreeHand, you can run the program by locating its icon at the Finder desktop and double-clicking on it. Shortly thereafter, the FreeHand *splash screen* appears. The splash screen features a graphic of a guy flinging his arms and legs about in a state of unqualified FreeHand glee along with some boring copyright information. What an auspicious beginning.

 You can bring up the splash screen at any time by choosing the About FreeHand command from the Apple menu. When you do, a list of credits scrolls in the bottom right corner of the screen. But here's the fun part: If you Option-click inside the graphic, you can create little animated worms that run around the screen, as demonstrated in Figure 3-2. Keep Option-clicking to create up to 15 worms. Why bother? Uh, you got me there . . . .

Figure 3-2:
The
FreeHand
splash
screen.

© 1988-1993 Altsys
Corporation. All rights reserved.
Portions © 1988-1993 Aldus
Corporation. All rights reserved.

Deke McClelland
Type & Graphics, Inc.
848400402841004878

1502348 bytes free
System Version 7.1.0

FreeHand Version 4.0

ALDUS. FREEHAND. 4.0

• Special Thanks: Brian Welter •

The FreeHand desktop

After the launch process completes and the splash screen disappears, the FreeHand desktop looms into view. Figure 3-3 shows the desktop as it might appear after a certain dinosaur drawing is opened.

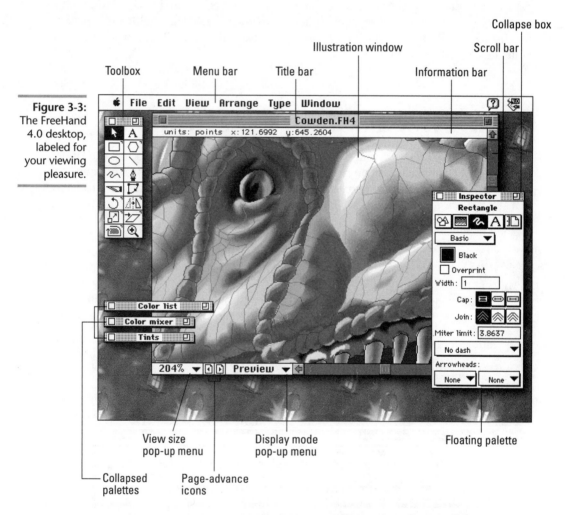

Figure 3-3: The FreeHand 4.0 desktop, labeled for your viewing pleasure.

If you read Chapter 2, many of the elements labeled in Figure 3-3 should be familiar to you. To make sure that you aren't falling behind the rest of the class, I think a quiz may be in order. Match the common desktop elements on the left with their definitions on the right.

1. Menu bar

   A. Your means of viewing hidden portions of a document

2. Title bar

   B. A literary-philosophic cult of nihilism and pessimism popularized by an exclusive clique of depressed French guys in the late 1940s

3. Scroll bars

   C. The top portion of the window; sports the name of the current document

4. Existentialism

   D. An enormous, purple creature who amuses very young children on PBS by singing syrupy ballads of love and family stability to the tune of "This Old Man"

5. Tyrannosaur

   E. A horizontal list of names that provide access to commands, which in turn bring up dialog boxes and perform operations

The answers will be printed in 4-point mirror-image Sanskrit along with next week's puzzler. In the meantime, there are a few elements of the FreeHand desktop that I haven't discussed, and they work as follows:

- **Illustration window:** You can open as many documents in FreeHand as memory permits. Each open document occupies its own independent window. The lower left corner of the window features a pair of *page-advance icons* bordered on either side by a pop-up menu. Click on a page-advance icon to advance from one page of a FreeHand document to the next. (Multiple-page documents are the subject of Chapter 19.) Press and hold on the *view size pop-up menu* to magnify or reduce the drawing inside the illustration window. Press and hold on the *display mode pop-up menu* to switch between the preview and keyline modes (as explained in the "Display modes" section later in this chapter).

- **Information bar:** The information bar displays a wealth of numerical data applicable to the current operation, including the coordinate location of the cursor, the angle of a drag, the extent of an enlargement, and so on. For complete information, read Chapter 8, "The Regimental Approach."

- **Toolbox:** The toolbox offers 16 *tool icons*, each of which represents a selection, navigation, drawing, text, or transformation tool. To select a tool, click on its icon. Then use the tool by clicking or dragging inside the illustration window.

- **Floating palettes:** FreeHand 4.0 offers ten floating palettes, not including the toolbox. The term *floating* refers to the fact that each palette is independent both of the image window and of other palettes. By clicking in the *collapse box* in the upper right corner of the palette, you can collapse the palette so that only the title bar remains visible, thus saving limited screen space. The floating palettes include Inspector, Color List, Color Mixer, Tints, Styles, Halftone, Type, Layers, Align, and Transform. You'll find a brief explanation of each in the "Floating palettes" section later in this chapter.

Tools

Figure 3-4 shows the FreeHand 4.0 toolbox complete with labels. The bottom portion of the figure sports an enlarged version of the freehand tool and shows off the *preference indicator*, which appears in the upper right corner of many tool icons. If a tool includes a preference indicator, you can double-click on its icon to display a dialog box of preference settings.

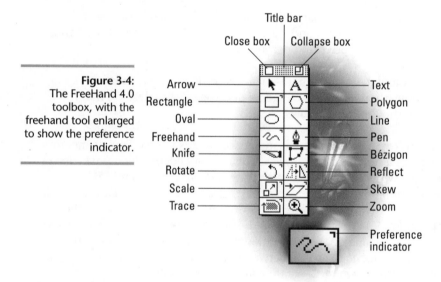

Figure 3-4:
The FreeHand 4.0 toolbox, with the freehand tool enlarged to show the preference indicator.

The following list explains how to use each tool. Unless I specify otherwise, you use the tool inside the illustration window. So if I say to *click*, you click with the tool in the illustration window; if I say to *click on the tool icon*, you click on the specified icon in the toolbox.

➤ **Arrow:** Click on an object with this tool to select the object. Shift-click to select multiple objects. Option-click to select an object inside a group. Drag one or more selected objects to move them.

➤ **Text:** Click with the text tool to create a new text block. Drag with the tool to define the size of the new text block. Drag inside an existing text block to select characters that you want to format or edit.

➤ **Rectangle:** Drag with this tool to create a rectangle. Shift-drag to draw a square. Double-click on the tool icon to draw a rectangle with rounded corners.

Polygon: Drag with the polygon tool to create a regular polygon or star. Double-click on the tool icon to specify the number of sides or points in the shape.

Oval: Drag with this tool to draw an oval. Shift-drag to draw a circle.

Line: Drag with the line tool to draw a straight line. Shift-drag to draw a line at a 45-degree angle.

Freehand: Drag with the freehand tool to draw a free-form line. Press the Command key while drawing to erase a portion of the line. Double-click on the tool icon to create calligraphic shapes and to make the tool compatible with a pressure-sensitive tablet.

Pen: Use the pen tool to create a line or shape one point at a time. Click to add a corner to the line or shape in progress; drag to add an arc. The pen tool is more precise than the bézigon tool because you can specify both the locations of points and the curvature of connecting segments.

Knife: Drag with this tool to slice through any selected line or shape that lies in your path.

Bézigon: Like the pen tool, the bézigon tool creates a line or shape one point at a time. Click to add a corner; Option-click to add an arc. Unlike the pen tool, the bézigon tool lets you specify the locations of the points only; FreeHand determines the curvature of the segments automatically.

Rotate: Drag with this tool to rotate one or more selected objects. The point at which you start dragging acts as the center of the rotation. Shift-drag to rotate the objects in 45-degree increments. Double-click on the tool icon to display the Rotate panel in the Transform palette.

Reflect: Drag with the reflect tool to flip selected objects. The angle of your drag defines the angle of the "mirror" about which the objects are reflected. Double-click on the tool icon to display the Reflect panel in the Transform palette.

Scale: Drag up and to the right to enlarge selected objects; drag down and to the left to reduce them. Shift-drag to scale the objects proportionally. Double-click on the tool icon to display the Scale panel in the Transform palette.

Skew: Drag with this tool to slant selected objects. More often, you'll want to Shift-drag to slant the objects horizontally or vertically. Double-click on the tool icon to display the Skew panel in the Transform palette.

Trace: Drag around some detail in a tracing template to automatically trace around its borders with an object-oriented line or shape. Double-click on the tool icon to adjust how the tool works.

Zoom: Click to magnify your document so that you can see small details more clearly. Option-click to step back from the image and take in a broader view. Drag to enclose the specific portion of the image that you want to magnify.

Keep in mind that the preceding list is merely the briefest of all possible introductions to FreeHand's tools. Figure 3-5 segregates the tools by category and indicates the chapter that contains complete and exhaustive information on each.

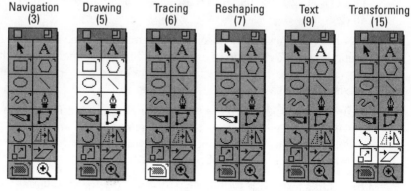

Figure 3-5:
FreeHand's tools
fall into the
categories listed
above the toolboxes.
The chapter in
which I discuss the
category appears in
parentheses.

Cursors

The one desktop element that I've neglected to mention — in this chapter, anyway — is the cursor. When it's outside the illustration window, the cursor looks like an arrow, just as it does at the Finder desktop and inside a million other Macintosh applications. But when you start using tools, the cursor changes to represent the current operation. Here's a list of the most common cursors and their meanings:

Arrow: The arrow cursor appears any time the cursor is outside of the illustration window or when you are using the arrow tool in the illustration window. You can select a tool, set palette options, choose a command, or select objects with this cursor. You can access the arrow cursor at any time by pressing and holding the Command key.

Hand: The grabber hand is the first of the navigational cursors. It appears when you press the spacebar inside the illustration window. When it is active, you can drag to scroll the page.

Zoom in: This cursor appears when you select the zoom tool or when you press Command-spacebar while some other tool is selected. Click to magnify the on-screen image.

Zoom out: This cursor appears when you press Option with the zoom tool or press Option-spacebar while some other tool is selected. Click with the zoom out cursor to reduce your view of the image.

Zoom limit: This cursor tells you that you're at the end of your zoom rope. You can't zoom in beyond 800 percent or out beyond 12 percent (1/8).

I **Text:** The common I-beam cursor indicates that the text tool is selected and ready to use. Feel free to create a new text block or edit an existing one.

+ **Draw:** The austere cross cursor appears any time you select a drawing tool, whether it's the rectangle, oval, polygon, freehand, pen, bézigon, or tracing tool. Drag in the illustration window and see what happens.

✛ **Move:** This cursor appears if you press and hold on a selected object and then drag it around. If you drag a selection without first mousing down for a moment, the cursor usually remains an arrow.

✳ **Transform:** This cheerful little star cursor appears when you use the rotate, scale, reflect, or skew tool to transform a selected object. Every one of these tools requires that you take a nice long drag. (But, please, refrain from smoking.)

⌐ **Place begin:** When you place artwork that was created in another program into FreeHand, as explained in far-off Chapter 18, this cursor appears. Click to import the artwork at the size you created it. Drag to scale the artwork as you import it.

⌐ **Place end:** If you drag with the place begin cursor, it changes to the place end cursor. Notice that the shapes of the place begin and place end icons assume that you're dragging down and to the right. More bias toward right-handers. I swear, there ought to be some quotas.

? **Help:** I don't really discuss the FreeHand help feature in this book. I don't particularly appreciate the competition. But this cursor forces the issue. If you press Command-Shift-slash (Shift plus the slash/question mark key), the question mark cursor appears. You know, as in ? for "Help." Now choose a command to get help on it. If you click on a tool or some other item, FreeHand just takes you to the main help window. Bogus, really.

⌚ **Watch:** You watch the watch cursor while you're waiting for FreeHand to complete some time-consuming task such as saving a file or opening one. Luckily, FreeHand doesn't make you wait too often, but when it does, there's no escaping it.

Floating palettes

One of the driving principles behind FreeHand 4.0 is that palettes are inherently superior to dialog boxes. The overwhelming majority of FreeHand's options are now found in palettes. For long-time FreeHand users like me, this setup is particularly frustrating. Options that used to be easily accessible are now buried in the recesses of an unfamiliar palette. In a couple of cases, there is even a loss of functionality.

But whatever your opinion on palettes, we're stuck with them. FreeHand 4.0 offers 11 palettes, including the toolbox. These palettes contain many standard dialog box elements — pop-up menus, option boxes, and so on — as well as a few elements normally associated with windows.

As shown in Figure 3-6, all palettes include close boxes, title bars, and collapse boxes. Click on the close box to hide the palette, drag the title bar to move the palette, and click on the collapse box to hide everything but the title bar, as demonstrated in the second example of Figure 3-6. To restore the entire palette, just click on the collapse box again.

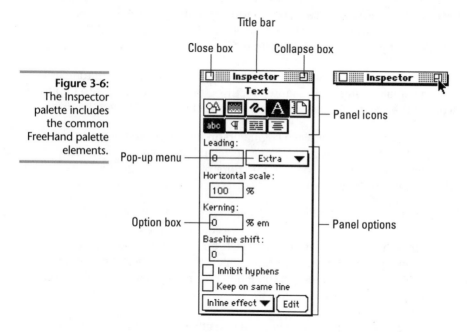

Figure 3-6:
The Inspector palette includes the common FreeHand palette elements.

Two palettes, Inspector and Transform, include *panel icons,* which enable you to access additional panels of options inside the palette. Just click on a panel icon to display a different panel. The Inspector palette is especially sprawling, offering two tiers of icons that access a total of 11 independent panels, which contain more than a hundred options, which in turn provide access to three additional dialog boxes. Meanwhile, FreeHand's simplest palette, Type, offers three pop-up menus and that's it.

The following list contains brief explanations of each of FreeHand's floating palettes.

     ⊸ **Inspector:** This mother of all palettes contains as many options as all the others put together. It's so rambling and inefficient, I like to think of it as the Inspector Clouseau palette (after the bumbling Peter Sellers character in the old *Pink Panther* movies, in case your cultural knowledge doesn't extend back any farther than *Star Wars* or Aerosmith). From left to right, the five main panel icons include the Object, Fill, Stroke, Text, and Document icons. The Text and Document icons offer access to second tiers of icons, which in turn display more panels. When a text block is selected, the Object icon produces a second tier of icons as well. Frankly, it's a mess.

 Just to give you an idea of how many different aspects of FreeHand are wrapped up in the Inspector palette, its various bits and pieces are covered in Chapters 7, 8, 9, 10, 11, 12, 13, 14, 19, and 20. Wowsers.

- **Color List:** While the Inspector palette is out there trying to be the one-stop center for all your editing needs, FreeHand's straightforward supply of color options spans four palettes (ignoring for a moment the vast Inspector itself). The first and most important among these is the Color List palette, which lists all colors you've created in the current document. The palette also displays the colors applied to a selected object.

- **Color Mixer:** In the Color Mixer palette, you define the colors in your document using one of three color models: CMYK (cyan, magenta, yellow, black); RGB (red, green, blue); and HLS (hue, lightness, saturation). You can also access Apple's Color Picker, which is built into the system software. After you define a color, just drag it into the Color List palette and give it a name.

- **Tints:** FreeHand lets you create shades of brand-name inks and other spot colors using the Tints palette. To create solid color, specify a tint value of 100 percent; any lesser value creates a lighter tint. After you define a tint, drag it into the Color List palette.

- **Styles:** FreeHand is unique in allowing you to define graphic styles. After applying the desired fill and stroke attributes to a selected object, choose New from the Styles palette's Options pop-up menu. Now you can apply those exact same attributes over and over to other objects in your drawing.

- **Halftone:** Look closely at any color image in a magazine or other publication, and you'll see patterns of tiny dots. Those dots are *halftone patterns*. In FreeHand, you can change the halftone pattern applied to a selected object by using the options in the Halftone palette. This is another area in which FreeHand makes mincemeat of Illustrator.

- **Type:** The Type palette is the only horizontal palette and the only one that lacks a title or a collapse box. The Type palette offers three pop-up menus that double as option boxes. You can enter the font, type style, and size of selected text or choose options from the pop-up menus.

- **Layers:** This palette lets you create independent drawing layers and assign objects to them. The Layers palette contains all options that affect layering and no miscellaneous junk. If all FreeHand palettes were as thoughtful or well organized, I wouldn't be able to have so much fun ridiculing them.

↪ **Align:** This palette lets you align objects and distribute them. These options are useful for creating schematic drawings and aligning text blocks. In order to use the options in the Align palette, you must first select two or more objects in the illustration window. To apply your settings to the selected objects, click on the Apply button or press the Return key.

↪ **Transform:** Like the Inspector palette, the Transform palette offers five panel icons. From left to right, the icons are Move, Rotate, Scale, Skew, and Reflect. These options let you transform selected objects numerically and are close cousins to the rotate, scale, skew, and reflect tools in the toolbox. At least one object must be selected in the illustration window before you can use these options. Click on the Apply button or press Return to apply your changes.

You display most palettes by choosing commands from the Window menu. The exceptions are Align and Transform, which you can access by choosing the identically named commands from the Arrange menu.

One of the big problems with using so many palettes is navigating between them. For example, to change the size and leading (the amount of space between lines) of a selected paragraph of type, you have to click inside the Size option box in the Type palette, enter a value, then click inside the Leading option box in the Inspector palette, and enter another value. Luckily, FreeHand lets you navigate between palettes from the keyboard.

Simply press Command-grave (`) — the key in the upper left corner of the keyboard, also marked with a tilde (~) — to activate the first option box in the next palette. Give it a try. As you press Command-grave, you hop from one palette to the next. When you get to the desired palette, you can advance to a different option by pressing Tab or Shift-Tab. (Both of these techniques only work with palettes that contain option boxes, which rules out the Color List, Styles, Layers, and Align palettes.)

Working in the illustration window

Like any Macintosh program worth its weight in dollar bills — which is about what these suckers cost — FreeHand provides a variety of navigational tools and functions that enable you to toodle around the illustration window. This section explains how to change the view size, scroll the document inside the illustration window, and switch between the preview and keyline display modes.

View size

FreeHand provides a nearly infinite supply of *view sizes*, which are levels of magnification at which the illustration appears on-screen. Magnified view sizes provide great detail but allow you to see only small portions of your drawing at a time. Reduced view sizes allow you to look at a large portion of your drawing but may provide insufficient detail for creating and manipulating objects. Because FreeHand makes it easy to change quickly between various view sizes, you can accurately edit your artwork and still maintain overall design consistency.

When you create a new illustration, FreeHand displays the document at *fit-in-window* size, which means that an entire page just barely fits inside the confines of the illustration window. The exact level of magnification required to pull off this feat depends on the size of the document and the size of your monitor. In the case of Figure 3-7, the T-Rex fits in the window at 44 percent, as indicated by the value in the view size pop-up menu in the lower left corner of the window.

Figure 3-7:
Despite his
enormous size,
even T-Rex fits in
the window.

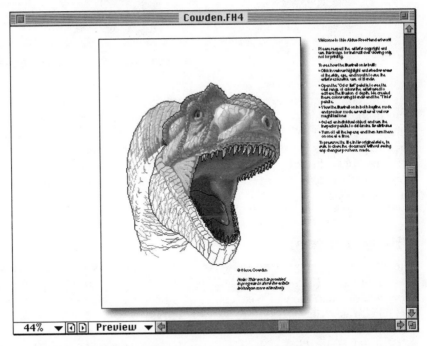

You can change the view size by choosing commands from the view size pop-up menu (new to FreeHand 4.0). In Figure 3-8, for example, I chose the 100% command to magnify T-Rex to *actual size*, which is the size at which the terrifying animal will print. This view size generally provides the most natural and reliable feedback concerning the progress of your artwork.

Figure 3-8:
The same
illustration
viewed at
actual size.

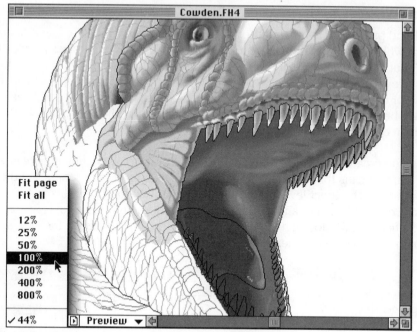

The nine commands in the view size pop-up menu also appear in the View ⇨ Magnification submenu. Unfortunately, although they are more accessible in the pop-up menu, only the submenu lists the keyboard equivalents. For example, to switch to actual size, you can just press Command-1. To fit the document in the window, press Command-W. Other useful keyboard equivalents are Command-5 for 50 percent (half actual size); Command-2 for 200 percent (twice actual size); and Command-4 for 400 percent (four times actual size).

The zoom tool

The other way to change view sizes is to use the *zoom tool*, the one that looks like a magnifying glass (located in the lower right corner of the toolbox). The zoom tool is more flexible than the view size commands because it enables you to access more than just nine preset view sizes. Here's how it works:

✎ Click in the illustration window with the zoom tool to magnify the drawing to twice the previous view size.

✎ Option-click with the zoom tool to reduce the drawing to half its previous view size.

↪ Drag a rectangular *marquee* (dotted line) around the portion of the drawing that you want to magnify. FreeHand magnifies the image so that the marqueed area just fits inside the image window. In the top example of Figure 3-9, I dragged with the zoom tool around the dinosaur's eye. FreeHand then magnified the marqueed area to 307 percent, as demonstrated in the bottom example.

Figure 3-9:
Drag with the zoom tool (top) to magnify the marqueed area so that it consumes the illustration window.

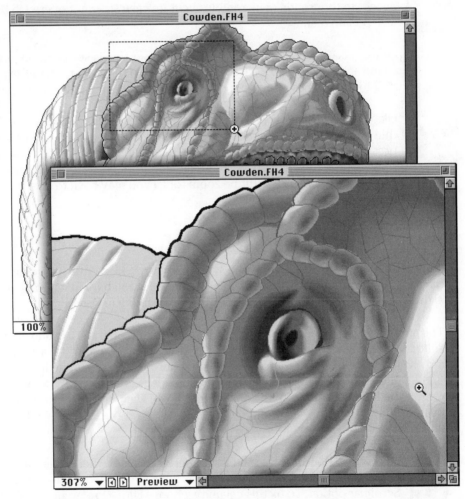

↪ If the horizontal and vertical proportions of the marquee do not match those of the illustration window — for example, if you draw a tall, thin marquee or a short, wide one — FreeHand favors the smaller of the two possible view sizes to avoid hiding any detail inside the marquee.

☞ Option-drag with the zoom tool to specify the space in which the windowed portion of the drawing should fit. In other words, when you Option-drag a marquee, FreeHand resizes the visible part of your drawing so that it fits inside your marquee.

 New to FreeHand 4.0, these dragging and Option-dragging features provide access to thousands of incredibly accurate view sizes not offered in the view size pop-up menu.

To temporarily access the zoom tool when some other tool is selected, press and hold the Command and spacebar keys. Release both keys to return control of the cursor to the selected tool. To access the zoom out cursor, press Command-Option-spacebar.

 Okay, if you've used FreeHand before, you know that. What you *don't* know is that you can magnify the view size to its absolute maximum, 800 percent, by pressing Command-Control-spacebar and clicking with the zoom tool. To reduce the view size to its absolute minimum, 12 percent, Command-Control-Option-spacebar-click with the zoom tool. (You may have to take off your shoes to make that one work!)

Dragging the scroll box

Back in Chapter 2, I explained how the scroll bars work. But for the most part, scroll bars are for screwballs. In particular, clicking on the scroll bar and clicking on a scroll arrow are unpredictable and slow methods for navigating in FreeHand.

The only scroll bar standout is the scroll box. In fact, FreeHand 4.0 is unusually well suited to tracking scroll box movements. Try pressing and holding on a scroll box and moving it around a bit. FreeHand responds to your movements immediately and predictably. Only after you release the scroll box does FreeHand take time out to redraw the hidden portions of the document. (If you want FreeHand to redraw continuously as you scroll, choose File ➪ Preferences and select the Redraw While Scrolling check box.)

 If FreeHand doesn't respond to your scroll box movements the way I say that it does, it's because some bonehead has gone and turned off the Dynamic Scrollbar option. To fix this calamity, choose File ➪ Preferences, select the Edit option from the pop-up menu, and select the Dynamic Scrollbar check box.

Using the grabber hand

An even better way to scroll is to use the *grabber hand*. And the only way to access the grabber hand is to press the spacebar. As long as a text block or option box is not active, pressing and holding the spacebar changes the cursor to a hand. Drag while pressing the spacebar to scroll the document. Releasing the spacebar returns control of the cursor to the selected tool.

 When a text block is active, or when the contents of an option box in a palette are selected, the spacebar works as you'd expect — it adds spaces. To access the grabber hand, press Command-Tab to deactivate the text block or option box. Then press the spacebar and drag as before.

Display modes

Look back at Figure 3-9. The drawing, like any created in FreeHand, is composed of many individual lines and shapes. In the case of this particular drawing, each shape is filled with a single, flat color. The shading you see is the result of hundreds of shapes piled on top of one another, each slightly lighter or darker than its immediate neighbor. Though you may never attempt anything so complex — few of us have the patience — your drawings will have fundamentally the same characteristics: one shape filled with one color stacked on top of another shape filled with a different color.

The drawing in Figure 3-9 is shown in the *preview mode*, which is one of two *display modes* offered by FreeHand. When the preview mode is active, FreeHand shows the document on-screen as closely as possible to the way it will look when printed. It shows all fills and all colors associated with the lines and shapes in your document. All this filling and coloring requires a lot of hard-core computing. In fact, the preview mode can be exasperatingly slow, especially when you're actually working on a drawing, not just looking at it.

To speed things up a little, you can instruct FreeHand to show only the skeletal framework of lines and shapes and bag the fills and colors. Figure 3-10 shows the drawing from Figure 3-9 in this minimalist display mode, called the *keyline mode*. Every shape gets a thin outline; its interior appears transparent. As you become more familiar with FreeHand and start creating more complicated artwork, you'll rely on the keyline mode more and more.

Figure 3-10:
An unbeliev-
ably intricate
network of
lines and
shapes is
exposed in
the keyline
mode.

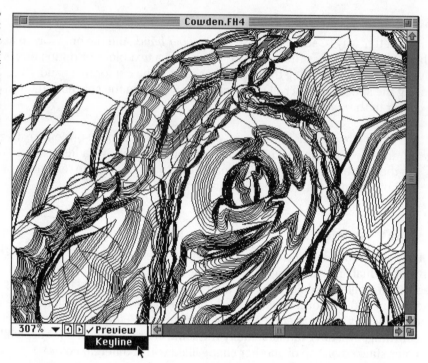

To access the keyline mode, choose the Keyline command from the display mode pop-up menu. It's located to the left of the horizontal scroll bar at the bottom of the window (as shown in Figure 3-10). You can also choose View ⇨ Preview to turn off the command (the check mark disappears) or, better yet, just press Command-K. This useful keyboard equivalent lets you toggle back and forth between the keyline and preview modes.

Canceling the screen redraw

You can press Command-period to cancel FreeHand's redraw, whether you're working in the preview or keyline mode. (I alluded to this in the previous chapter, but it bears repeating.) Note that if you press Command-period too quickly after scrolling or performing some other operation, FreeHand may think that you're trying to cancel the operation. For best results, wait for the screen redraw cycle to begin before pressing Command-period.

The great thing about canceling the screen redraw is that it allows you to view a specific detail and then move on. Suppose that you want to see how the back of the dinosaur's neck looks at a certain view size but you don't care about the face and other details. FreeHand redraws the document starting with the rearmost shapes and working its way toward the front, so that the neck is redrawn before forward items such as the eye and scales. After the neck comes into view, you can press Command-period to prevent the redraw from progressing any farther. This enables you to keep working with shorter interruptions. In time, you'll be pressing Command-period and Command-K on an almost continual basis.

 To reinitiate a screen redraw, change view sizes or click on the zoom box on the extreme right side of the title bar.

Shortcuts

Shortcuts enable you to access commands and other functions without resorting to the laborious task of choosing commands from menus or clicking on some fool icon until your arm falls off. Many shortcuts are fairly obvious. For example, FreeHand lists keyboard equivalents for its commands next to the command name in the menu. You can choose File ⇨ New by pressing Command-N, Edit ⇨ Undo by pressing Command-Z, View ⇨ Preview by pressing Command-K, and so on. But many of FreeHand's shortcuts are either hidden or can easily be overlooked. If you're a long-time user of FreeHand and you think you know all this, think again. Roughly half of the hidden shortcuts are new to FreeHand 4.0.

Table 3-2 lists my favorite FreeHand shortcuts. Some of these I've already mentioned, but they're worth repeating. Memorize them, photocopy them and tack them to a wall, write them on the backs of your hands, but whatever you do, use them. (Shortcuts marked with an asterisk are new to FreeHand 4.0.)

 Unless I indicate otherwise, whenever I say to press the Command key, Windows users should press Ctrl instead. And when I say to press Option, Windows users should press Alt.

Table 3-2   FreeHand's Most Extraordinary Hidden Shortcuts

Operation	Shortcut
Navigation tricks	
Scroll document with grabber hand	Press the spacebar and drag
Scroll document when editing text	Command-Shift-Tab and then press the spacebar and drag
Zoom in to next preset view size	Command-spacebar-click
Zoom out to previous preset view size	Command-Option-spacebar-click
Fit document in window	Command-W
View document at actual size	Command-1
Zoom in all the way (800%)*	Command-Control-spacebar-click or Command-8
Zoom out all the way (12%)*	Command-Control-Option-spacebar-click
Switch display modes	Command-K
Cancel the screen redraw	Command-period
Text tricks	
Select text tool	Shift-F9
Activate text block and select text tool simultaneously	Double-click on block with arrow tool
Draw text block outward from center	Option-drag with text tool
Select word	Double-click on word with text tool
Select paragraph	Triple-click in paragraph with text tool
Select all text across links blocks*	Command-A when a text block is active
Adjust column width	Drag corner handle of text block with arrow tool
Stretch or compress type	Option-drag corner handle of text block with arrow tool
Scale type proportionally	Shift-Option-drag corner handle of text block with arrow tool
Adjust leading	Drag top or bottom handle of text block with arrow tool
Adjust letter spacing	Drag side handle of text block with arrow tool
Adjust word spacing	Option-drag side handle of text block with arrow tool
Join selected type to selected line*	Command-Shift-Y
Flow selected type inside selected shape*	Command-Shift-U
Convert selected text to editable shapes*	Command-Shift-P
Deactivate text block	Command-Tab
Delete text block	Command-click on text block and press Delete

* New to Version 4.0

Table 3-2 *(continued)*

Operation	Shortcut
Special characters (text block must be active)	
Nonbreaking space	Option-spacebar (or Enter)
Em space	Command-Shift-M
En space	Command-Shift-N
Thin space	Command-Shift-T
Em dash	Shift-Option-hyphen
En dash	Option-hyphen
Discretionary hyphen	Command-hyphen
Line break	Shift-Return
Column break	Shift-Enter
Formatting text (one or more characters selected with text tool)	
Increase type size 1 point*	Command-Shift->
Decrease type size 1 point*	Command-Shift-<
Kern characters together 1% em	Option-left arrow (used to be Command-left arrow)*
Kern characters apart 1% em	Option-right arrow (used to be Command-right arrow)*
Kern characters together 10% em*	Shift-Option-left arrow
Kern characters apart 10% em*	Shift-Option-right arrow
Increase baseline shift 1 point*	Option-up arrow
Decrease baseline shift 1 point*	Option-down arrow
Drawing lines and shapes	
Draw oval outward from center	Option-drag with oval tool
Draw circle	Shift-drag with oval tool
Draw rectangle outward from center	Option-drag with rectangle tool
Draw square	Shift-drag with rectangle tool
Draw diagonal or perpendicular line	Shift-drag with line tool
Create a straight segment while drawing with freehand tool	Press and hold Option key
Erase while drawing with freehand tool	Press and hold Command key
Add a corner between straight segments	Click with pen or bézigon tool
Add a corner between curved segments	Press Option midway into dragging with pen tool
Add an arc	Drag with pen tool or Option-click with bézigon tool*
Provide a smooth transition between straight and curved segments*	Control-click with pen or bézigon tool

(continued)

Table 3-2 *(continued)*

Operation	Shortcut
Selecting objects (arrow tool active, all text blocks inactive)	
Select all objects in document	Command-A
Deselect all objects in document	Tab key
Deselect all points but leave shapes selected	Grave key (`)
Add object to selection	Shift-click on object
Select object behind current selection	Control-click on object
Add object behind selection to selection	Control-Shift-click with arrow tool
Select single object inside group	Option-click on object
Select points in grouped object	Option-drag around points
Select points in geometric shape	Click on shape, Command-U, click on point
Select group that contains selected object	Grave key (`)
Editing selected objects (arrow tool active)	
Move horizontally or vertically	Shift-drag with arrow tool
Move in predefined increments	Any arrow key
Rotate in 45-degree increments	Shift-drag with rotate tool
Flip horizontally or vertically	Shift-drag with reflect tool
Scale proportionally	Shift-drag with scale tool
Slant horizontally or vertically	Shift-drag with skew tool
Repeat the last transformation	Command-comma
Join two lines or shapes into one	Command-J
Slice objects into independent shapes*	Shift-F7, drag across shapes
Split composite path into independent shapes*	Command-Shift-J
Mask selected objects inside shape*	Command-X, click on shape, Command-Shift-V
Separate masked objects from a selected shape*	Command-Shift-X, Command-V
Coloring objects (drag from color swatch in Color List palette)	
Change color inside object	Drag color onto object
Change color of outline	Drag color onto outline
Change gradient fill to flat fill	Shift-drag color onto object
Change to linear gradient fill (or change angle of existing gradient fill)	Control-drag color onto object
Change to radial fill (or change center of existing radial fill)	Option-drag color onto object

* New to Version 4.0

Selecting tools

FreeHand is a rare program in that it allows you to select most of its tools from the keyboard, rather than having to click on an icon inside the toolbox. Pressing keys may not sound particularly more convenient than clicking on an icon, but as you delve deeper into the heart and soul of FreeHand wizardry, you'll discover that there are times when you want to switch tools without moving your cursor.

Suppose that you want to begin a rectangle at the exact spot where you just finished drawing a line with the freehand tool. Rather than moving the cursor and losing your place, you can simply press the 1 key and start drawing.

Figure 3-11 shows the keyboard equivalents required to select FreeHand's tools. Notice that many tools have more than one shortcut. To select one of the drawing tools, for example, you can either press a single number key or Shift plus a function key. Why use the latter when the former is so much easier? Because of text. If a text block is active, pressing a number key inserts a number into your text. By contrast, the Shift-function key combinations work regardless of what kind of object is active.

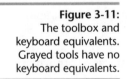

Figure 3-11:
The toolbox and keyboard equivalents. Grayed tools have no keyboard equivalents.

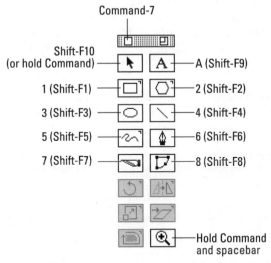

One note about the labels in Figure 3-11: If the label indicates that you hold a key, it means that the tool only remains active as long as the key is down. For example, you can either access the arrow tool temporarily by pressing and holding the Command key or select the arrow tool permanently by pressing Shift-F10.

To show or hide the toolbox, press Command-7. Why 7? Well, perhaps FreeHand's programmers were thinking of the toolbox as the program's Agent 007, ready for any emergency. Or perhaps the toolbox is a 7th heaven of functionality and potential. But more likely, it's because the toolbox is a veritable 7-11 of tools and gadgets, admittedly minus the Big Gulps and microwave burritos.

Navigating palettes

The final thing that you can do from the keyboard is display, hide, and navigate palettes, as listed in Table 3-3. FreeHand's Window menu displays many of these keyboard equivalents, which are nearly all new to FreeHand 4.0.

Incidentally, I segregated these keyboard equivalents from those in Table 3-2 primarily so that I could make fun of them. Although you stand at least a chance of memorizing the basically logical collection of keyboard shortcuts covered so far, those in Table 3-3 are almost nonsensical. If Command-Shift-C displays the Color Mixer palette, why doesn't Command-Shift-T — instead of Command-Shift-Z — display the Tints palette? And what's with Command-6 for the Layers palette? The Tints question I can't answer; Command-Shift-T currently isn't a shortcut for anything. As for the other shortcuts, many are leftovers from FreeHand 3.0. In addition to Command-6 for Layers, these include Command-3 for Color List, Command-9 for Styles, and Command-M for Transform.

Anyway, do your best to learn these shortcuts and try not to get all stressed out when you don't. By time you finally assign the last shortcut to memory, FreeHand 5.0 will probably come out and change everything anyway.

Table 3-3	Displaying, Hiding, and Navigating Palettes	
Operation	**Macintosh Shortcut**	**Windows Shortcut**
The Inspector palette		
Display/hide Inspector palette	Command-I (old Element Info shortcut)	Ctrl-I
Switch to Object panel	Command-Option-I	Alt-0
Switch to Object Dimensions & Inset panel	Command-Option-B	Alt-0, Alt-5
Switch to Object Column & Row panel	Command-Option-R	Alt-0, Alt-6

Table 3-3 *(continued)*

Operation	Macintosh Shortcut	Windows Shortcut
Switch to Object Copyfit panel	Command-Option-C	Alt-0, Alt-7
Switch to Fill panel	Command-Option-F	Alt-1
Switch to Stroke panel	Command-Option-L	Alt-2
Switch to Text Character panel	Command-Option-T	Alt-3, Alt-5
Switch to Text Paragraph panel	Command-Option-P	Alt-3, Alt-6
Switch to Text Spacing & Hyphenation panel	Command-Option-K	Alt-3, Alt-7
Switch to Text Alignment panel	Command-Option-A	Alt-3, Alt-8
Switch to Document Pages panel	Command-Option-D	Alt-4, Alt-6
Switch to Document Setup panel	None	Alt-4, Alt-7
All those other palettes		
Display Align palette	Command-Shift-A	Ctrl-Shift-A
Display/hide Color List palette	Command-9 (old Colors palette shortcut)	Ctrl-9
Display/hide Color Mixer palette	Command-Shift-C or double-click on a color in the Color list palette	Ctrl-Shift-C
Display/hide Halftone palette	Command-H	Ctrl-H
Display/hide Layers palette	Command-6	Ctrl-6
Display/hide Styles palette	Command-3	Ctrl-3
Display/hide Tints palette	Command-Shift-Z	Ctrl-Shift-Z
Display/hide Type palette	Command-T	Ctrl-T
Display Transform palette	Command-M	Ctrl-M
Activate first option box in next palette	Command-grave (`)	Ctrl-Tab
Activate next option box in same palette	Tab	Tab
Activate previous option box in same palette	Shift-Tab	Shift-Tab

 To bring an open panel in front of all others, press its keyboard equivalent twice in a row. The exceptions are the Transform and Align palettes, which only require that you press the keyboard equivalent once.

Keys that produce different effects in Version 4.0

 One of my minor frustrations with FreeHand 4.0 is how many keyboard equivalents have changed, however slightly, since Version 3.0. If you're frustrated with this phenomenon as well and you're interested in getting the lowdown on this subject, check out Table 3-4.

Table 3-4	The Old Shortcuts and Their New Functions		
Old Shortcut	**What It Used to Do**	**What It Does Now**	**New Method**
Command-E	Fill and stroke options	Export command	Command-Shift-F or Command-Shift-L
Command-I	Object information	Inspector palette	Command-Option-I
Command-J	Join text to a path	Join objects	Command-Shift-Y
Command-M	Move command	Transform palette	Command-M, click on Move icon
Command-/	Align command	nothing	Command-Shift-A
Command-Shift-V	Paste in back of selection	Paste inside mask	none
Command-Option-C	Copy object in PICT format	Copyfit panel	Command-C
Command-left arrow	Kern text together	Move back one word	Option-left arrow
Command-right arrow	Kern text apart	Move ahead one word	Option-right arrow
2, drag	Draw rounded rectangle	Polygon tool	Double-click on rectangle tool
8, click	Add curve point	Add corner point	8, Option-click
9, click	Add corner point	nothing	8, click
10, click	Add connector point	nothing	8, Control-click

Customizing the Interface

Everyone does not draw alike. For those who draw to a different drummer — in other words, all of us — FreeHand provides *preference settings*, which permit you to customize the interface. FreeHand ships with certain preference settings already in force, called *factory default settings*, but you can change the settings to reflect your own personal preferences.

You can change preference settings in two ways. You can make environmental adjustments by choosing File ⇨ Preferences and mucking about with the four panels of options inside the Preferences dialog box. Or you can change the operation of specific tools by double-clicking on a tool icon. FreeHand remembers all preference settings by saving them to a file called FreeHand Preferences, located in the Aldus folder inside the System Folder.

The FreeHand Preferences file

There are two interesting things about the FreeHand Preferences file. First, you can delete the file to restore FreeHand's factory default settings. Try this: When FreeHand is *not* running, drag the FreeHand Preferences file out of the Aldus folder and onto the Finder desktop. Then launch FreeHand. After the launch cycle completes, you'll notice that only the Inspector, Color List, and Color Mixer palettes are visible. These are the factory default palettes. The other palettes are hidden, whether or not you had them up last time you used the software. Tools and other settings have likewise reverted to their factory defaults.

Now quit the program. The last thing FreeHand does before quitting is update the FreeHand Preferences in the Aldus folder. Because no such file is available to update, FreeHand creates a new one.

Because FreeHand updates the FreeHand Preferences file only once per session — during the quit cycle — it cannot update the file if the program bombs or if your computer crashes. Just as you lose any unsaved changes to your document during a crash, you also lose all preference adjustments made throughout the session. When you restart FreeHand, it loads the preference settings from the previous session because those were the last settings saved.

After quitting FreeHand, drag the FreeHand Preferences file that you moved to the desktop back into the Aldus folder. The Finder asks whether you want to replace the new file that FreeHand just created. Respond positively by whacking that Return key. Now relaunch FreeHand and see how your old preference settings have been restored.

The text inside the file

The second thing that you should know about the FreeHand Preferences file is that you can edit it with a word processor. FreeHand saves the preference settings to an editable TeachText document, which means that you can open the document inside Microsoft Word, MacWrite, or whatever word processor it is you use. You can also double-click on the file at the Finder desktop to open and edit it in TeachText.

The contents of the FreeHand Preferences file are a little cryptic, but if you spend a little time with it, you'll begin to see the logic:

- ∞ First comes the header *% Aldus FreeHand Preferences File v4.0*, which tells FreeHand that it has the right file.

- ∞ The next 11 lines begin with *Modal* or *DataType*. These lines explain the locations of dialog boxes and what to do with imported file formats. Leave these items alone.

- ∞ The following 33 lines are all about palettes. Notice that the lines are grouped in 11 sets of three — three *XformSwitch* items, three *AlignMgr* items, and so on. Each set represents one palette. *XformSwitch* is the Transform palette; *AlignMgr* is Align; *HtoneEd* is Halftone; *StyleLP* is Styles; *TintMgr* is Tints; *FHLayerMgr* is Layers; *FontMgr* is Type; *ColorLP* is Color List; *ColorMaker* is Color Mixer; *InsMgr* is Inspector; and *ToolMgr* is the toolbox.

- ∞ The three lines in each palette set are *Zoom* (is the palette collapsed?); *Vis* (is it visible?); and *Pos* (what is the position?). *Zoom* and *Vis* are followed by a yes or no answer; *Pos* is followed by numerical coordinates. For example, the line *(XformSwitchZoom) (No)* means that the Transform palette is not collapsed, while *(XformSwitchVis) (Yes)* means that the palette is visible. If you change the last *Yes* to a *No*, the palette will be hidden the next time you launch FreeHand.

Following this, things get a little mixed together. Most items, such as *HiResTIFF* and *BufferedDrawing*, correspond directly to an option in the Preferences dialog box (which I explain later in this chapter). A few — *ExpandMiter* and *InsetWidth* among them — are based on settings from miscellaneous dialog boxes and palettes. Still others, such as *RectangleCornerRoundness* and *FHToolCalligraphic*, indicate adjustments made by double-clicking on tool icons.

But a select handful of items in the FreeHand Preferences file are *hidden preferences*, meaning that you can't access them from anywhere inside FreeHand. Quite frankly, these few items are the only reason to open the FreeHand Preferences file. I mean, what's the sense in editing a coded text file when you can simply change an option from inside FreeHand, right? The following section explains which items to edit and how to edit them.

Editing hidden preferences

Before I go any farther, I guess I should warn you to be careful. If you edit something incorrectly, it theoretically can cause FreeHand to crash or work strangely, though either of these scenarios is unlikely. However, if FreeHand does give you some trouble after you edit any of the items I explain below, just quit the program, throw away the FreeHand Preferences file, and restart the application.

Now that I've made that disclaimer, let me ease your fears a little. This isn't rocket science, so relax. If you follow the following rules, you won't get in trouble:

- Only edit the FreeHand Preferences file when FreeHand is *not* running. Otherwise, FreeHand overwrites your changes when you quit the program.

- Only change the word or value inside the second pair of parentheses. For example, in the item *(CrackPlacedEPS) (No)*, you can change the *No* to *Yes*, but don't change *CrackPlacedEPS* and don't add or delete parentheses or enter anything outside the parentheses.

- Use your head. If the value in the second parentheses is No, don't change it to *Yeah* or *Maybe* or *SureWhyNot* or *Banana*. If it isn't obvious what is or is not acceptable, I'll tell you.

The following items are found throughout the FreeHand Preferences file. Although I've listed them in the order that they appear, they may be separated by many other preference settings. You may want to use your word processor's Search function to locate these items.

- **(UseQTCompression) (No):** Set this value to Yes to compress Fetch previews using Apple's QuickTime system extension. The previews will take up less space on disk, but they will take longer to load because Fetch will have to decompress them. If you use Fetch, you may want to set this value to Yes. If not, leave it alone. Accompanying items *QTCompressType* and *QTCompressQuality* are strictly for QuickTime gearheads. Don't edit them unless you know what you're doing.

- **(SaveWindowSizeNLoc) (Yes):** When working on a document, you can change the size of the illustration window by dragging the size box in the lower right corner. You can also move the window by dragging the title bar. Normally, FreeHand saves the size and location of the illustration window along with the document so that the window appears in the same place when you next open the document. But if you set the *SaveWindowSizeNLoc* value to No, FreeHand doesn't save this information with the document. Files without this information open inside a window with the same dimensions and positioning as a new document. You'll probably want to leave this value unchanged.

- **(ViewingSetsActivePage) (Yes):** If that last explanation seemed like a lot of jabbering for nothing, this explanation will seem doubly so. Now that FreeHand supports multipage documents, it has to decide which page is active when more than one page is visible at a time. This item tells it to stick with the page that takes up the largest area of the screen. A close cousin, *ToolsSetActivePage*, makes a page active when you use a tool on it. My advice is to leave these poor items be.

- **(UserPSIncludeFile) (UserPrep):** If you're a PostScript whiz — which includes 2 or 3 folks out of FreeHand's total 9 billion users — you probably find yourself occasionally calling up PostScript-language routines from a separate text file on disk and downloading these routines to your printer. This file has traditionally been called *UserPrep*, as listed in this item. However, if you're such an intense power user that you have more than one file filled with PostScript routines, you can tell FreeHand which file to look for by entering the file's name inside the second pair of parentheses. Any filename is acceptable as long as the file exists inside the Aldus folder.

⥻ **(TiffModePrintOverride) (1):** Wow, we're really delving into TechnoDweeb city here. (You know, "Two brains for ev-ery boy.") But it's not my fault. I'm just covering these suckers in order. Okay, first, some background: The settings in the Output Options dialog box affect both how a FreeHand drawing is printed and how it's exported to the EPS format. One set of options, Image Data, controls how TIFF images are encoded. The default setting, Binary, is the most efficient. But if you select a different option, FreeHand changes the encoding when saving the EPS file. Your selection will *not*, however, affect the encoding that's used during printing, thanks to this item. When *TiffModePrintOverride* is set to 1, FreeHand prints using binary encoding regardless of what you tell it to do in the Output Options dialog box. If you have a specific reason for printing using some other encoding, set the value to –1 and then select the desired Image Data option. (A *TiffModePrintOverride* value of 0 always prints using slow-as-molasses ASCII encoding.)

⥻ **(StockLineWeights) (0.25 0.5 1 1.5 2 4 6 8 12):** Finally, we're to the good one. In fact, this one item makes this whole experience worthwhile. Do you suppose that I should try to snag the folks that have gotten bored and wandered off? Maybe shouting will work. *YOU! YEAH, YOU! STOP AND READ THIS PARAGRAPH!* There, that should do it. All right, now everyone calm down. New to FreeHand 4.0 is the Arrange ↷ Stroke Widths submenu, which includes nine preset line weights — the same line weights, in fact, that are listed in the *StockLineWeights* item. You can add as many line weights as you want inside the second set of parentheses, as long as each number is separated by a space. You can delete line weights you don't want as well. Keep in mind that these values are measured in points ($\frac{1}{72}$ inch). A value of 0.25 appears in the submenu as Hairline.

⥻ **(RememberDocumentView) (Yes):** Wasn't that a good one? Don't you feel vindicated for reading all this other junk? I hope so. Anyway, this next item affects the view size that FreeHand uses when opening a document. If *RememberDocumentView* is set to Yes, FreeHand opens the document so that you are looking at the exact same portion of the page at the exact same view size as you were when you saved the document. If you set this item to No, FreeHand opens all documents at the fit-in-window view size, just like FreeHand 3.0. Personally, I sort of like the No setting, but you may want to leave this item set to Yes.

- ✑ **(NewStylesTakeCurProps) (Yes):** This setting is another one of those leave-it-alone items. Normally, when you create a new graphic style in the Styles palette, FreeHand bases the style on the selected object. If you set the *NewStylesTakeCurProps* item to No, however, FreeHand just copies the default style, requiring you to manually change the new style later on down the line. The next item, *NewStylesAutoApply*, is equally silly. Leave both set to Yes.

- ✑ **(NewDocumentTemplate) (Aldus FreeHand Defaults):** Very soon, I'll be talking about something else, and when I do, it'll be the Aldus FreeHand Defaults file. This document, also found in the Aldus folder, controls the settings applied to each new document you create in FreeHand, including page size, unit of measure, and all that other stuff FreeHand 3.0 used to require you to specify before you created a new document. If you want to set up more than one kind of document template, save it to the Aldus folder and enter its name in the second pair of parentheses. See the next section for further details.

- ✑ **(CrackPlacedEPS) (No):** When you open an EPS graphic using File ➪ Open, FreeHand does its best to convert the graphic into an editable document. However, when you import the graphic using File ➪ Place, FreeHand imports it as static picture. Oh sure, you can transform the picture by moving it, rotating it, and so on, but you can't change the location of individual points and objects inside the graphic. If you want FreeHand to "crack" imported EPS graphics so that you can edit them, enter Yes for the *CrackPlacedEPS* item. (If FreeHand can't crack the graphic, as in the case of EPS documents created using previous versions of FreeHand, it simply imports it as a static picture.) I set this option to Yes so that I can combine and edit objects from different documents.

- ✑ **(AlwaysEmbedImports) (No):** To save space, FreeHand references imported TIFF and EPS artwork on disk rather than saving them in their entirety with the rest of the document. However, this means that you need access to the original TIFF and EPS files any time you open the FreeHand document. If you set the *AlwaysEmbedImports* item to Yes, FreeHand includes the full code from an imported EPS graphic with a saved document. The program also converts imported TIFF images to embedded EPS code. Your FreeHand files will be much larger, but you won't need access to the original EPS and TIFF files. Only set this item to Yes if you own a big hard drive with a lot of free space.

 The FreeHand Preferences file also includes some items left over from the programming and development cycle. These include *ThrashOMeter*, *IncludeEPSFonts*, and *DeleteEmptyTextContainers*. None of them has any affect on FreeHand's performance, even if you do set the value to *Banana*.

The Aldus FreeHand Defaults file

The other haven for preference settings is the Aldus FreeHand Defaults file, which resides in the Aldus folder inside the System Folder. This file determines the composition and contents of every new file you create in FreeHand. In fact, when you choose File ⇨ New, FreeHand actually opens the Aldus FreeHand Defaults file and puts it in a new window.

Every setting that is saved with the current document rather than with the FreeHand Preferences file can be stored in the Aldus FreeHand Defaults file. These settings include the following:

   ↪ **Document setup:** All settings from the Document Setup panel of the Inspector palette, shown on the left side of Figure 3-12. These options affect unit of measure, grid increments, the angle of the constraint axes, and printer resolution.

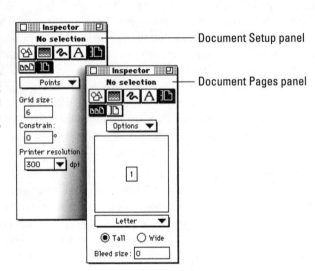

Figure 3-12:
The Aldus FreeHand Defaults file contains settings from the two Document panels in the Inspector palette.

Document Setup panel

Document Pages panel

   ↪ **Multipage settings:** All settings from the Document Pages panel of the Inspector palette, also featured in Figure 3-12. These options affect the number of pages in the document, the size and orientation of each page, the placement of the pages on the pasteboard, and the bleed size. To access this panel when the Inspector palette is displayed, press Command-Option-D.

   ↪ **Output options:** All settings from the Output Options dialog box, which you access by choosing File ⇨ Output Options or clicking on the Output button inside the Printer dialog box. As I mentioned in the preceding section, these options affect how a document is printed and exported in the EPS format.

✐ **Default formatting attributes:** Settings from the Type palette (accessed by pressing Command-T) and the various Text palettes inside the Inspector palette (Command-Option-T, P, K, and A). These default attributes include font, style, type size, leading, horizontal scale, kerning, baseline shift, paragraph spacing and indents, letter and word spacing, hyphenation (on or off), alignment, and a few more obscure options, such as effects, rules, and flush zone. In fact, all options shown in Figure 3-13 except the grayed-out hyphenation dictionary option are saved with the Aldus FreeHand Defaults file. (The hyphenation dictionary is saved with the FreeHand Preferences file.)

Figure 3-13:
All these formatting attributes are saved with the Aldus FreeHand Defaults file.

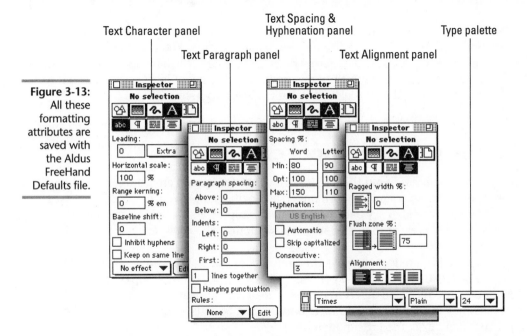

✐ **View menu settings:** All settings from the View menu, including the Preview, Rulers, Info Bar, Grid, Guides, Lock Guides, Snap to Point, Snap to Guides, and Snap to Grid commands. The selected view size is also saved.

✐ **Colors and layers:** All settings in the Color List, Halftone, Styles, and Layers palettes, as well as the Fill and Stroke panels of the Inspector palette.

✐ **Illustration window:** FreeHand also sizes and positions the new illustration window based on the size and position of the Aldus FreeHand Defaults document. If for no other reason, be sure to create your own Defaults document so that FreeHand doesn't constantly fill the entire screen with the illustration window.

You can also create objects that you want to appear in every new document. For example, if you want to include a copyright statement or logo inside each of your drawings, just add the necessary text blocks, lines, and shapes to the defaults file as you would add them to any drawing.

When the default settings and objects are in place, save your document inside the Aldus folder under the name Aldus FreeHand Defaults file. (If you use a different name, be sure to change the *NewDocumentTemplate* item in the FreeHand Preferences file. Regardless of name, the file must be inside the Aldus folder.) Also select the FreeHand Template option from the Format pop-up menu in the Save Document dialog box.

To restore FreeHand's factory default settings, quit FreeHand, throw away the Aldus FreeHand Defaults file, and relaunch FreeHand. FreeHand does not automatically create a new Aldus FreeHand Defaults file as it does the FreeHand Preferences file. If you want to customize the document-level settings, you have to make a new Aldus FreeHand Defaults file for yourself.

The File ⇨ Preferences command

Man, who would have thought that customizing your on-screen environment could be so complicated? Or so shamefully prolonged and exhausting? Well, we're not done yet. Now that I've discussed every back-door method I know for specifying preference settings, it's time to resort to the most obvious solution: the Preferences command.

Choosing File ⇨ Preferences displays the Preferences dialog box shown in Figure 3-14. The dialog box features a collection of check boxes topped off by a pop-up menu. The latter enables you to reveal different panels. The first to appear is the Display panel. You can display the others — Editing, Exporting, and Sounds — by choosing the like-named command from the pop-up menu.

The Display panel

The check boxes in the Display panel are designed to accelerate the pace at which FreeHand redraws objects in the preview mode. As a general rule of thumb, the fewer options you check, the faster the redraw speed and the lower the quality of screen representation. (The one exception is Buffered Drawing, which speeds up screen redraw when turned on.)

If you own a PowerPC, start off with all options in the Display panel — including Buffered Drawing — turned on. Don't worry — you have horsepower to handle it. If, over time, you find yourself working on extremely complicated drawings that bog down the screen redraw, deselect one or two options that you can do without.

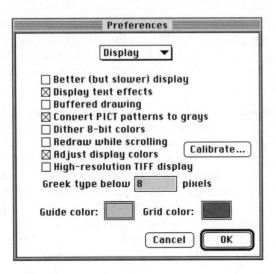

The options in the Display panel work as follows:

☞ **Better (But Slower) Display:** This option controls the display of linear, logarithmic, and radial gradations in the preview mode. When it is selected, gradations appear to contain up to 256 steps on a 24-bit monitor (see Figure 3-15) and 33 dithered steps on an 8-bit monitor or lower. If the option is deselected, only nine steps are assigned to a gradient fill, as the second example in Figure 3-15 illustrates. This option has no effect on blends, which always display at maximum quality.

Figure 3-15:
A radial gradation
as it appears on a
24-bit monitor
when the Better
(But Slower)
Display option is
selected (left) and
deselected
(right).

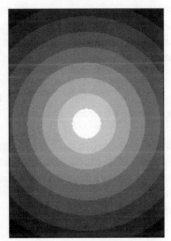

↬ **Display Text Effects:** When this option is turned on, FreeHand displays its predefined Inline, Shadow, and Zoom effects as closely as possible to the way they will print. When you turn the option off, text looks as if no effect is applied. In either case, the text prints accurately. Again, turn the option off to speed up screen display.

↬ **Buffered Drawing:** The opposite of the old Always Draw Object-by-Object option, this is one of the few options that control the manner in which the screen refreshes both in the preview and keyline display modes. When the option is turned off, objects appear one at a time in the drawing area, from the back of the drawing to the front, each time you change the view size or display mode or open a document. If you select this option, FreeHand redraws all objects off-screen and then displays the entire illustration at once when the redraw cycle is complete. This latter method is faster and results in smoother path drawing, but it requires more application RAM. If sufficient memory isn't available, FreeHand refreshes the screen as if the option were deselected.

↬ **Convert PICT Patterns to Grays:** MacDraw Pro and Canvas enable you to fill objects with bitmapped patterns (as does FreeHand). You can either import these drawings (via the PICT format) with patterns intact or you can convert the patterns to gray. This option has no effect on the exporting of bitmapped patterns or the speed at which the screen redraws. As a rule, bitmapped patterns are hideously ugly, so leave this option turned on.

↬ **Dither 8-Bit Colors:** If you work on an 8-bit monitor that displays a maximum of 256 colors, turn this option on. The speed you gain by turning the option off is slight and the decline in quality is unacceptable. Colors may be wildly inaccurate, particularly when you're using gradations. When selected, this option uses a technique called *dithering* to generate dot patterns that represent otherwise unattainable shades and color variations. When the option is turned off, FreeHand displays solid colors only.

 If your system supports 16-bit color (thousands of colors) or 24-bit color (millions of colors), leave the Dither 8-Bit Colors option off. You have plenty of solid colors to go around.

↬ **Redraw While Scrolling:** This option should be called the MTV-Generation Immediate Gratification option. When it is selected, FreeHand redraws the screen continuously as you drag a scroll box or drag the page with the grabber hand. Keep this option turned off for faster scrolling — assuming that you can stand the suspense.

↬ **Adjust Display Colors:** FreeHand offers what can only be termed dime-store-quality monitor calibration. If your screen colors appear vastly different from your printed colors — on-screen purple looks blue in the final output, for example — this option can be helpful. But don't expect precision adjustments out of it.

Here's how the option works: Select the Adjust Display Colors check box and then click on the Calibrate button. The Display Color Setup dialog box appears, sporting seven 100 percent combinations of cyan, magenta, and yellow ink. Assuming that you have a Pantone, Trumatch, or other color swatch book handy — or better yet, a test sheet from your regular commercial printer — compare the on-screen cyan to the printed cyan swatch, the on-screen yellow to the printed yellow, and so on. If the colors don't match — and this is pretty much a foregone conclusion — click on the offending color in the dialog box to display the Apple Color Picker. Then adjust it until you get the desired effect. (Don't knock yourself out too much; no matter what you do, the colors won't match exactly. The fact is, on-screen and printed colors occupy different ends of the visible color spectrum. Just do your best and call it a day.)

↪ **High-Resolution TIFF Display:** This option controls the on-screen appearance of imported TIFF images in the preview mode. When the option is selected, FreeHand displays TIFF images at their full resolution, as in the first example of Figure 3-16. When High-Resolution TIFF Display is turned off, FreeHand simplifies the TIFF image, displaying fewer pixels. The second example of Figure 3-16 illustrates the results. Turning the option off greatly speeds up screen redraw time but diminishes clarity and detail in the image.

Figure 3-16:
A TIFF image displayed with the High-Resolution TIFF Display option selected (top) and deselected (bottom).

❧ **Greek Type Below ___ Pixels:** This option controls the perceived type size at which FreeHand no longer tries to display type accurately on-screen and instead replaces lines of text with thin gray bars — a feature known as *greeking*. For example, if you enter a value of 8 for this option — the default setting — text set to 8-point or smaller appears gray at actual size; 16-point type and smaller appears gray at 50 percent view size; 32-point type and smaller appears gray at 25 percent view size; and so on. The benefit of greeking text is that FreeHand can display gray bars faster than it can generate individual characters. To turn off the greeking feature completely, enter a value of 0 for this option.

❧ **Guide Color/Grid Color:** To change the color of ruler guides or grid dots, click on the corresponding color swatch. After the Apple Color Picker surfaces, make the desired changes.

The Editing panel

The next panel in our breakneck tour of the Preferences dialog box is the Editing panel, which you access by selecting the Editing option from the pop-up menu. In fact, isn't that the Editing panel I see now in Figure 3-17? Dang, that means we have to keep our voices down so that it doesn't hear us talking about it. (*To be read out of the side of your mouth.*)

For the most part, options in this panel control the way you draw and edit objects. The only exception is the Dynamic Scrollbar check box — don't everybody look at once — which really belongs in the Display panel.

Figure 3-17: Select the Editing option from the pop-up menu to display the Editing panel.

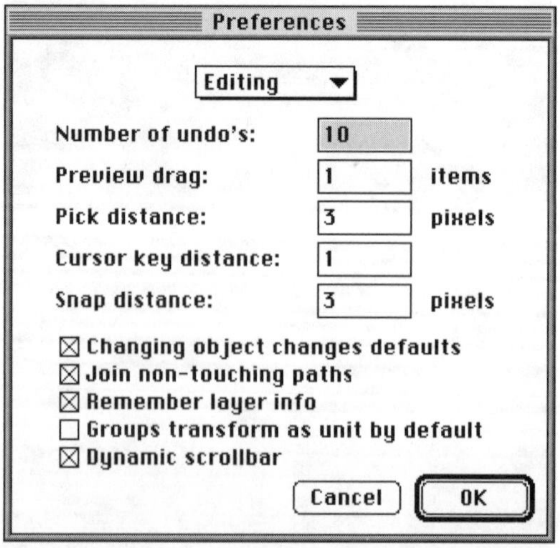

Preferences

Editing ▼

Number of undo's: 10

Preview drag: 1   items

Pick distance: 3   pixels

Cursor key distance: 1

Snap distance: 3   pixels

☒ Changing object changes defaults
☒ Join non-touching paths
☒ Remember layer info
☐ Groups transform as unit by default
☒ Dynamic scrollbar

Cancel   OK

The following items explain the Editing panel in muted but nevertheless shocking detail:

- **Number of Undo's:** FreeHand's versatile Undo command enables you to undo several consecutive operations. You can specify the maximum number of consecutive undo's by entering any value between 1 and 99 for this option. Keep in mind that by increasing this value, you decrease the amount of application RAM available to other FreeHand operations.

  The Number of Undo's option does not take effect until the next time you launch FreeHand. By quitting (as described later in this chapter) and restarting the program, you allow FreeHand to relegate the appropriate amount of space in the application RAM to remember the desired number of operations.

- **Preview Drag:** If you select and immediately drag an object in the illustration window, FreeHand shows you a rectangular dotted outline that demonstrates the boundaries of the object. By contrast, if you hold down your mouse button, pause for a second or two, and then begin dragging, FreeHand displays the object accurately throughout the drag. This is called a *drag preview.* By default, however, FreeHand dumps the drag preview when you drag more than one object, regardless of whether you pause or start dragging right away. FreeHand does this because it takes more time to animate multiple objects than to animate just one. By entering a higher number in the Preview Drag option (say, 6), you tell FreeHand to preview drags as long as that number (6) or fewer objects are selected.

 An even better alternative for previewing dragged objects is to press the Option key any time while dragging. Regardless of how many objects are selected or what the Preview Drag value is, pressing Option displays the objects in their entirety. So leave the Preview Drag value set to 1 and use the Option key to preview. This way, you get quick drags on a regular basis. When you want to be able to see what's going on, just press the Option key.

- **Pick Distance:** This option is just the thing for the sloppy selector. It lets you click outside an object and still select it, as long as your click falls within a specified range. For example, the default value of 3 ensures that as long as the arrow cursor is within 3 screen pixels of an object, clicking selects that object. If selecting isn't your forte, and you frequently find yourself missing objects, raise the value (5 is the maximum). However, if you're used to precise work and you anticipate creating complex artwork, lower the value to 2, which requires you to click more or less exactly on the objects you want to select.

 Don't lower the Pick Distance value to less than 2 or you'll have a heck of a time manipulating Bézier control handles (the levers that accompany points in a free-form line or shape). A Pick Distance value of 0 makes control handles downright impossible to select. (Too bad this option is a program-level preference instead of a document-level one. Otherwise, you could use it to keep other folks from editing your artwork.)

- **Cursor Key Distance:** FreeHand enables you to move any selected object by pressing one of the four arrow keys. Each keystroke moves the selection the distance entered in the Cursor Key Distance box, as measured in the units specified in the pop-up menu at the top of the Document Setup panel of the Inspector palette (refer back to Figure 3-12).

- **Snap Distance:** This option controls the distance at which a dragged object moves sharply toward — or *snaps to* — a stationary point, grid dot, or guide, as measured in screen pixels. For example, if the Snap Distance value is 3, a dragged object snaps to a guideline any time the object comes within 3 pixels of it. This option also affects how close endpoints must be to each other for you to fuse them together by choosing Arrange ⇨ Join Objects (Command-J) and how accurately you must click or drag to select and modify points and handles. In my opinion, the default setting is fine.

- **Changing Object Changes Defaults:** This option controls the default attributes assigned to all objects in the current illustration. When the option is selected, changing the formatting of text or the fill or stroke of an object also changes the default setting within the document, so that the next object you create is format-ted, filled, or stroked identically. If you deselect this option, the default attributes remain the same as those in the Aldus FreeHand Defaults file. (If you are trying to set up a new Defaults file, definitely select this option.)

- **Join Non-Touching Paths:** The Join Objects command joins lines in one of two ways. If two endpoints — one from each line — are close enough to each other, it fuses the two points into one. If the endpoints are separated by a greater number of pixels than specified in the Snap Distance option box (described above), the command draws a segment between the points — that is, as long as the Join Non-Touching Paths option is checked. If you turn the option off, the Join Objects command either fuses two endpoints into one or it ignores you. (Arrange ⇨ Join Objects also combines shapes into composite paths, an operation that has nothing to do with this option.)

- **Remember Layer Info:** When active, this option instructs FreeHand to include a tag with every object that tells which layer it comes from. Then, when you copy an object and paste it, FreeHand pastes it to the layer from which it was copied, not to the active layer. If you paste an object into a different document, and that document doesn't include the required layer, FreeHand adds the layer along with the object to the document. This option also affects groups and composite paths. When you group or join two shapes, FreeHand is forced to send them to the same layer. However, when you ungroup or separate them, FreeHand recalls the original layers assigned to the objects and sends them there.

  When the Remember Layer Info option is turned off, FreeHand doesn't tag objects. Regardless of where a cut or copied object was originally located, FreeHand pastes it onto the active layer. When you ungroup or separate a group or composite path, the individual objects stay on the same layer.

- **Groups Transform as Unit by Default:** The first time you use FreeHand, this check box is off; it ought to be on. When active, the option ensures that all objects in a group rotate, scale, slant, and otherwise transform as a single unit, as if they were all part of a collective being, like the Borg. (You know, from "Star Trek, The Next Generation?" Huh? Oh yeah? Well *you're* a nerd for *not* watching it.) By contrast, when you turn off this option, FreeHand transforms all objects independently. The result is usually fairly chaotic. For more information, read the "Grouping and Protecting Objects" section of Chapter 8.

- **Dynamic Scrollbar:** Remember back in the "Dragging the scroll box" section earlier in this chapter? I wrote that when you drag a scroll box, "FreeHand responds to your movements immediately and predictably." My exact words. If you deselect the Dynamic Scrollbar option, you make a liar out of me. The scroll box just moves without the illustration window updating one iota. So leave this option checked.

The Exporting panel

Only two more panels to go! Oh, right, you don't care. I forgot, you're reading this stuff out of order. You're fresh back from a game of golf or a particularly yummy lunch, and this is probably the first paragraph you've looked at all day. But *me*, I've been writing about preference settings for so long I'm starting to have dreams about them. More like bone-chilling nightmares, really. As in, quoth the raven, "Preference settings!" Dig?

But before they lock me up, let me quickly explain the Exporting panel, shown in Figure 3-18. It contains two options that affect the previews associated with EPS files.

Briefly, an EPS file is designed to be placed into a page-layout program such as PageMaker or QuarkXPress. The EPS file includes two parts: a PostScript definition of the drawing that gets downloaded to the printer; and a PICT preview that you can see on-screen inside the page-layout program.

 PICT is part of the QuickDraw screen-display language used by the Macintosh system software. DOS-based machines don't support PICT, so an EPS file for the Windows platform gets a TIFF preview, which is always bitmapped.

Here's how the options work:

- **Bitmap PICT Previews:** FreeHand 4.0 is the first version of this program that generates object-oriented PICT previews. This means that you can accurately view an EPS file at any view size in PageMaker or QuarkXPress. However, it also means that the artwork takes longer — sometimes much longer — to display. To speed things up, select the Bitmap PICT Preview option, which saves a static, bitmapped version of your drawing as it appears at actual size.

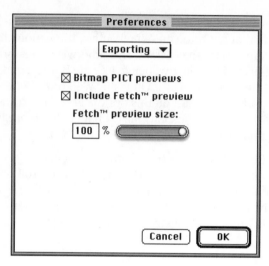

Figure 3-18:
The Exporting panel controls how FreeHand saves EPS files.

↪ **Include Fetch Preview:** If you'll be using your EPS file with Aldus Fetch, you may want to save a second preview especially for Fetch. For best results, leave the Fetch Preview Size value set at 100 percent. This way, Fetch accurately reports the file size.

The Sounds panel

FreeHand 3.1 introduced this hidden feature, which I like to call *sonic snapping*. The feature plays a sound whenever a point snaps to another point, grid dot, or guideline. In Version 3.1, you had to use ResEdit to get to sonic snapping. Now you can access it inside the Preferences dialog box by selecting the Sounds option from the pop-up menu — which is really great because it makes it easier to turn the feature off when you get sick of it.

Here's how it works. Go to the Sounds panel, shown in Figure 3-19. Select the sounds that you want to associate with each kind of snap from the pop-up menus. Each pop-up menu lists sounds loaded into your System file. Click on the Play button if you can't remember what a selected sound sounds like (or if you simply want to amuse yourself). Select the None option from the pop-up menu if you don't want to hear about a particular snap.

Then select one or both of these options:

↪ **Snap Sounds Enabled:** Select this option to instruct FreeHand to play the sounds. Now, every time a snap occurs, you'll hear a chirp, whistle, explosion, car crash, cult movie quote, or whatever sound you selected.

Figure 3-19:
The Sounds panel permits
FreeHand to sound off
during snaps.

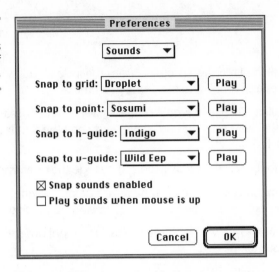

Figure 3-19:
The Sounds panel permits
FreeHand to sound off
during snaps.

- **Play Sounds When Mouse Is Up:** Only available when the Snap Sounds Enabled option is checked, this option allows you to hear sounds even when you're just moving your mouse around without dragging. What a nuisance! Leave this option off.

In fact, if you want my opinion, leave this entire feature off. As you'll quickly learn if you activate it, it turns your computer into a noise machine. If you spend any amount of time on the phone, talking to clients, listening to music or news, or just plain enjoying the little bit of silence left in the industrialized world, you'll go nuts within eight minutes — plus or minus 15 seconds — after you select Snap Sounds Enabled.

■ ■

Summary

- Only install the FreeHand program from the installer utility. Manually install the sample files and fonts as needed one at a time.

- After installing FreeHand, you'll probably want to trash TeachText (assuming that it's elsewhere on your hard drive) and copy the StuffIt Expander utility from Disk 1.

- You can double-click on many tools to change their behavior.

- Clicking on the collapse box on the right side of a palette's title bar hides all of the palette except the title bar, thereby freeing up precious screen space.

- Press Command-grave (the same key as ~) to highlight the first option box in the next palette.

- You can drag with the zoom tool to draw a marquee around the portion of the drawing you want to magnify. Option-drag to reduce the view size so that the visible portion of the drawing fits inside the marquee.

- Drag a scroll box or press the spacebar and drag the document with the grabber hand to move the document inside the illustration window.

- Though it provides substantially less detail, the keyline display mode is faster than the preview display mode.

- You can cancel the screen redraw at any time by pressing Command-period.

- You can access commands, select tools, and display and hide palettes by pressing keystroke combinations.

- FreeHand saves the settings in the Preferences dialog box, tool preferences, and other settings to the FreeHand Preferences file.

- To save document-level preferences — such as page setup options, formatting attributes, and the size and position of the illustration window — you have to create a template and name it Aldus FreeHand Defaults.

- Barney is the kind of lovable, huggable Tyrannosaur that makes other carnivores sick. I know for a fact that the sauropods openly mock him.

■ ■

Drawing in FreeHand

PART II

Chapter 4:
Approaching Drawing Software

Chapter 5:
Constructing Paths

Chapter 6:
Tracing an Imported Template

Chapter 7:
Reshaping and Combining Paths

Chapter 8:
The Regimental Approach

Approaching Drawing Software

- -

In This Chapter

- ➸ How points and paths work

- ➸ Definitions of fundamental terms such as *line, shape, stroke,* and *fill*

- ➸ A tour of the object-oriented drawing process

- -

Childhood Preparations

If this is your first venture into drawing software, be prepared for a modicum of frustration, particularly if you're a professional used to working with traditional tools. Though the artwork produced in FreeHand bears a striking resemblance to high-contrast line art produced with pen and ink, the approaches are as different as painting and sculpting.

In fact, if I had to craft an analogy to the FreeHand drawing process, it would be building an object with Tinker Toys. You know, those wooden spools, dowels, and little green cardboard flags that were never nearly so satisfying as Legos or Lincoln Logs because all you could build with them were frameworks. Perhaps the budding young engineers in the family were excited by the atomic-substructure quality of Tinker Toys, but the more results-oriented among us found them boring almost the moment we spilled them out on the floor. I mean, what good is a toy if all you can think about when you're playing with it is, "One day, Mom's gonna make me pick these up"?

Although FreeHand dramatically improves on the Tinker Toys model, it still requires you to build and adorn structures. The difference is that after sticking the dowels in the spools and even bending the dowels (you could do that with Tinker Toys, by the way — you just had to get the dowels nice and wet before warping them), you can wrap the structures in bright colors, festive gradations, and garish patterns.

Don't you wish you had known about FreeHand when you were six? Then, when your mom did eventually tell you to quit playing, clean things up, and get ready for bed, you could have stated with firm conviction, "Please, just another hour, Mom? Please, please, please? I'm preparing for my future here!"

 If you're already painfully familiar with the object-oriented drawing process, skip to Chapter 5, "Constructing Paths." There you'll find detailed descriptions of the pen and bézigon tools, both of which represent upgrades from their counterparts in Freehand 3.0.

Drawing with Objects

No matter what type of drawing you want to create in FreeHand, you produce it by combining two basic types of objects: lines and shapes. Every drawing, however complicated or straightforward, can be expressed as an interacting collection of lines and shapes.

Suppose that you want to create a collage. FreeHand provides an inexhaustible stack of lines and another stack of shapes. You can stretch, bend, and otherwise *reshape* each line and shape as if it were made of some impossibly flexible putty. You also can change the color of a line or shape. You then place these manipulated lines and shapes on your collage in any location and order.

Because it exists in the mind of a computer program, your collage is impermanent. You can pick up any line or shape and put it down in a new position, slip it between two other objects, or discard it altogether. You can duplicate an object, manipulate it in a new way, or leave it as is.

The trick to creating a drawing in FreeHand is to start simple and work toward complexity. You need to learn how to evaluate an illustration and break it down into its most basic parts. And the first step in learning to identify the parts of a prospective illustration is to learn about lines and shapes themselves.

Lines vs. shapes

Conceptually, *lines* in FreeHand are the same as lines you draw with a pencil on a piece of paper: A line starts at one location and ends at another. Lines can be any length. They can be mere scratch marks or they can stretch from the top of a page to the bottom and loop around like a roller coaster.

Lines in FreeHand are made up of basic building blocks called *points*. The simplest line is a connection between just two points, one at each end of the line. Anyone familiar with a little geometry will recognize this principle: two points make a line.

But in FreeHand, the concept of a line has been broadened to incorporate many points that are connected by *segments*. A segment can be straight, as if you drew it against the edge of a ruler. A straight segment flows directly from one point to another in any direction. A segment can also curve, like the outline of an oval. Curved segments connect two points in an indirect manner, bending inward or outward along the way. You can link segments together so that neighboring segments share a common point.

You might think of a line in FreeHand as a dot-to-dot puzzle. Each point represents a dot in the puzzle. You draw one segment from dot A to dot B, a second segment from dot B to dot C, a third segment from dot C to dot D, and so on. The completed dot-to-dot line is called a *path*. A path can consist of only one segment or several hundred. (If you're wondering why so many of my analogies have to do with childhood toys, it's because I' a firm believer in the phrase, "You're only young once, but you can be immature forever.")

Figure 4-1 shows two separate dot-to-dot paths used to draw a very happy fellow who is oblivious to the fact that he desperately needs a chin reduction. The dots are the points; the segments connect the dots.

The points of one path are numbered; the points of the other are labeled with letters. No segment connects a numbered point to a lettered point, or vice versa. The numbered and lettered paths are therefore *independent* of each other.

Figure 4-1:
Examples of a line (lettered) and a shape (numbered). Elements within both paths are labeled.

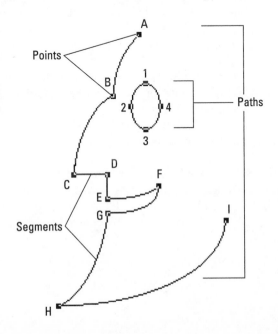

Obviously, the form of each straight and curved segment in a path determines the path's overall appearance. The appearance of a path is equally affected by the manner in which one segment meets another segment at a point.

Segments can meet at a point in two ways. First, the two segments can curve symmetrically on either side of a point. For example, each of the four segments in the numbered path in Figure 4-1 meets with its neighbor to form a seamless *arc* around their shared point.

Second, two segments can meet to form a *corner*. A straight segment can meet another straight segment to form a corner, as witnessed by point D in the figure; a straight segment and a curved segment can meet at a corner like the one at point E; two curved segments can meet to form a corner like those at points B and H.

The lettered path in Figure 4-1 is an example of an *open path*, because no segment connects its last point, I, to its first point, A. The numbered path is called a *closed path*, because a segment does connect its last point, 4, to its first point, 1. An open path in FreeHand is ordinarily called a *line;* a closed path is called a *shape*. Lines and shapes have various characteristics, as described in the following section.

Properties of lines and shapes

Unlike a line you draw with a pencil on paper, any path you draw in FreeHand is consistent in thickness, or *weight*. Of course, a line drawn with a very dull pencil will be heavier than one drawn with a newly sharpened pencil, but because a graphite pencil is an imprecise tool, the weight of the pencil line will fluctuate depending on how hard you press the tip to the page. This is not the case in FreeHand. Different lines can have different weights, but the weight of each line is always constant throughout its length.

Also, drawing a path in FreeHand is like having countless differently colored pencils at your disposal. A line can be black, as if you drew it with pen and ink, or it can be light gray or dark gray. It can also be red, or green, or blue, or any one of several million other colors. A line can even be white, transparent, or multicolored. It can also be intermittent (dashed), textured, or patterned.

Line weight and color combine to determine the *stroke* of a line or the outline of a shape. In addition, you can manipulate the area inside a path — called the *fill* — separately from the outline itself. Just like a line, the fill of a shape can be black or white, transparent or colored. It can even combine many colors interacting or fading into one another, as in a *gradation*.

Determining a path

Before creating a path in FreeHand, you should evaluate the segments that it will follow. You do this one point at a time. Each point indicates 1) where a corner occurs, 2) where a path begins to curve or stops curving, or 3) where a path changes its curve. One segment ends at a point and another segment begins.

To fully understand the function of points inside paths, imagine that you are driving on a winding mountain road. You see many yellow, diamond-shaped signs indicating what kind of path lies ahead of you. In Figure 4-2, the center sign indicates that the path of the road curves gradually to the right. The sign on the left indicates that the road turns dramatically to the left, forming a corner. The sign on the right indicates that the road curves all the way around so that your car will eventually face the opposite direction.

Figure 4-2:
Points guide segments in a path just as street signs guide drivers down a road.

There is one sign for each and every change in the path of the road. The signs serve the same purpose as points serve in a path. Just as the signs tell you which direction to go next, the points tell the path which way to go.

You will never see a sign like the one shown in Figure 4-3, except maybe in "Road Runner" cartoons and Coen brothers movies. If a road did actually follow the path pictured on the sign, the highway department wouldn't tell you about all the turns on one sign. You would be warned at every change in direction, one at a time. Similarly, you can't establish the course of a complex path using a single point. You have to place a point at every new twist and turn in the path.

Figure 4-3:
Too much information for
a single point.

Before I go any further, I want to note that I've used this road-sign analogy in other books that I've written about FreeHand, and it's received mixed reviews from readers. Some tell me that they absolutely love it, that they never understood how points worked until they thought of them in terms of highway road signs. But a few readers find the same analogy more confusing than it is helpful. If you fall in the latter camp, feel free to ignore the road sign thing completely — honest, you won't hurt my feelings. It's simply another way of looking at the issue at hand. Now if you'll excuse me, I think I'll go to the bedroom and cry myself to sleep.

The Infamous Groucho Scenario

The following example demonstrates how to draw a caricature of Groucho Marx from start to finish inside FreeHand. But unlike the step-by-step tutorials you typically see in software manuals, this one is not about using FreeHand's tools or commands. I am not going to demonstrate a new feature offered in Freehand 4.0, explain how to get the most out of a certain tool, or walk you through any dialog box. In fact, I don't so much as mention a single tool or command.

Instead, I concentrate on the pure object-oriented drawing process itself, largely independent of FreeHand's specific capabilities. The benefit is that after you understand how to create Groucho, you'll understand how to create artwork inside any drawing program, whether it's FreeHand, Illustrator, Canvas, or CorelDraw.

 If you're new to drawing programs — and I'm guessing that you are if you're bothering to read this chapter — you may not be totally familiar with some of the terms that you'll find in this demonstration. I'll try to offer brief explanations along the way so that you can get the gist of what's going on. But if you don't fully understand every term, don't worry; later chapters provide more in-depth information. My goal here is just to give you a broad overview of how to approach the drawing process. The specific how-tos and why-tos come later.

Step 1: Making a rough sketch

There's no two ways about it — it's easier to create free-form artwork in a painting program such as Photoshop than in a drawing program like FreeHand. Therefore, when approaching a new drawing, it's always a good idea to first sketch your idea in Photoshop or sketch it on a sheet of paper and then scan it into Photoshop. (If you don't have access to a scanner or a painting program, of course, you can always fall back on FreeHand's drawing tools and create from scratch. The approach I'm describing here, though, is much more efficient — so if you can't afford a scanner or painting program, perhaps you can convince your rich uncle to let you use his system for a day.)

After you rough in your preliminary sketch, import it into FreeHand and send it to a background layer. You can then use your sketch as a *tracing template* for your final drawing. (Chapter 6, "Tracing an Imported Template," explains this process in more detail.)

Figure 4-4 shows the sketch of Groucho Marx that I created in Photoshop. Granted, it looks like garbage. Although the general form and structure are okay, I sketched the image at such a low resolution that it appears riddled with lose pixels and jagged edges. As is, it's unacceptable for printing, unless you wanted to use it to line the bottom of a bird cage (assuming that the bird is an exceedingly generous and nonjudgmental creature). But as a tracing template, it will work just fine.

Step 2: Creating the eyes

After importing the sketch into FreeHand, I set about tracing it. The first element I wanted to sketch were Groucho's eyes. I began with the eyes not because they're the windows into the soul, but because they are easy to draw and are mirror images of each other.

Drawing the first oval

The first example of Figure 4-5 shows the left eye as it appears in FreeHand's maximum view size. The eye is grayed to show that it is part of the tracing template. In FreeHand, the template is an imported image that resides on the background layer. (Graying the template is FreeHand's way of showing that it is not a part of the actual drawing.)

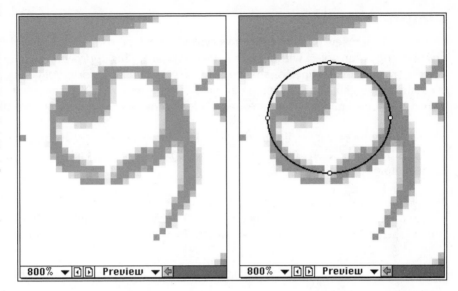

Figure 4-5:
The bitmapped tracing template unadorned (left) and traced with a simple object-oriented oval (right).

In the second example of Figure 4-5, I traced a perfect oval around the left eyeball. The oval and template are shown together to give you a perspective for the rest of the illustration and an idea of how the template and path look together.

Only Figures 4-5, 4-7, 4-14, and 4-19 show the underlying template. In FreeHand, you can show or hide a template at any time. I've hidden the template in the other figures to help avoid confusion and to present each portion of the drawing in sharp focus. Keep in mind, however, that the tracing template does exist, and that every line and shape I created was traced over some part of it.

To better examine the oval I created, I ungrouped it, which converts the shape from an absolute ellipse to a flexible free-form path composed of four points. Each of the four points helps to define the path that the outline of the oval follows. Because the oval is symmetrical, all four points are basically identical. Hearkening back to my points-are-street-signs discussion, suppose that the outline of the oval follows its path in a counterclockwise direction. Each point would then act like the street sign shown in Figure 4-6. As the outline progresses, the points tell the curve to continue to the left in a consistent manner.

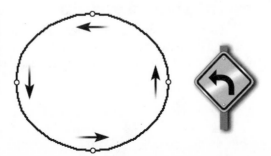

Figure 4-6:
The points in the oval tell the path to turn steadily in a counterclockwise direction.

Cloning the oval

I created the next few parts of Groucho's eye by *cloning* and *scaling* the first oval. Cloning creates a copy of an object without using the Clipboard. This approach is useful when you are tracing several lines or shapes that are very similar in form. All you need to do is create one original and then clone the similar forms from that. You can manipulate the cloned objects separately so that a reshaped clone only vaguely resembles the original.

After cloning the oval, I scaled the resulting shape to 85 percent of its original size. I then positioned the cloned shape so that the tops of both ovals met as shown in the first example of Figure 4-7.

Next, I cloned my newest oval and scaled its clone to 55 percent of the original. Then I cloned the third oval and scaled its clone to 75 percent. After I finished cloning, I moved each of the shapes to the positions shown in the second example of Figure 4-7.

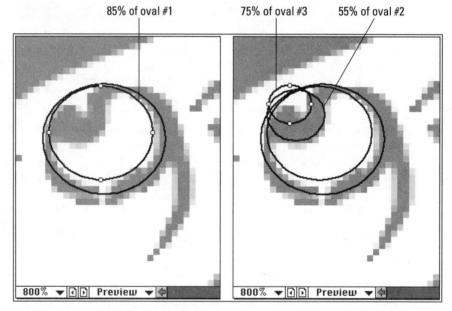

85% of oval #1   75% of oval #3   55% of oval #2

Figure 4-7:
I created a
series of
cloned ovals,
scaling each
one to a
different
percentage of
the original.

Drawing the crescent-shaped wrinkle

I now had all shapes required for the left eyeball. But before I could go on to the right eye, I needed to add the wrinkle beneath the eye. Figure 4-8 shows how to create this shape. Though slightly more difficult than the oval, the wrinkle is simply a long, thin crescent defined by four points.

Again, each point is analogous to a street sign, as the figure illustrates. Each sign is shown as if you were driving along the path in the direction indicated by the arrows. In this case, you're driving counterclockwise along the outline of the shape. You encounter four signs, two notifying you of gradual turns and two warning you of sharp corners in the path.

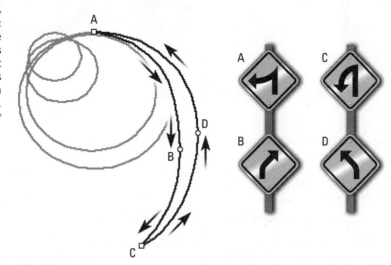

Figure 4-8: Each of the street signs on the right corresponds to a point in the crescent.

Filling the shapes

Every one of the objects I created so far was a shape, which meant that they all had the properties of both stroke and fill. All had very thin, black strokes and transparent fills — which I needed to change in order to get them to match my template.

To create Groucho's eye, I didn't need to apply any strokes — it could easily be created using fills only. Therefore, I made all of the strokes transparent. I then filled three shapes — the first and third ovals and the crescent-shaped wrinkle — with solid black. I filled the second and fourth ovals with white. The result is the eye on the right side of Figure 4-9.

New shapes cover up shapes that were created before them. On the left side of Figure 4-9, the five shapes are numbered 1 through 5, with 1 being the first shape created and 5 being the last. Each shape is shown as if were floating in space. This imaginary view demonstrates how FreeHand places the most recently created object in front and its predecessors in back. The five shapes are stacked upon each other so that they appear as one continuous black form.

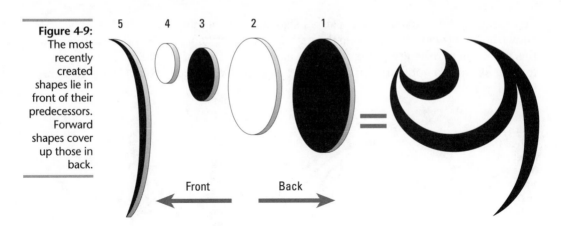

Figure 4-9:
The most recently created shapes lie in front of their predecessors. Forward shapes cover up those in back.

If I had painted this version of Groucho's eye on a canvas, it might have been a combination of three brush strokes. In FreeHand, it is five shapes. A computer can yield painterly results, but the approach has to be technical and carefully considered.

Cloning and transforming the right eye

After I created one of Groucho's eyes, it was very easy to create the other. First, I gathered my five shapes and grouped them so that they all became one object. In this way, I could clone and move the entire group of lines and shapes together instead of individually. FreeHand treats a grouped object as a single entity, protecting the size and relative placement of each line and shape.

Next, I cloned the group and reflected the clone around a –70 degree axis, as shown in the first example of Figure 4-10. To more fully understand this process, think of the axis as a double-sided mirror. Suppose that the mirror is mounted like an old cheval glass, so that it's free to tilt within a support. The mirror is normally situated horizontally, like a table top. But if you angled the mirror 70 degrees downward (–70 degrees or 290 degrees), it would produce the exact reflection shown in Figure 4-10. That is what is meant by *reflecting about an axis.* The axis is simply a mirror tilted at a prescribed angle.

Because the cartoon Groucho faces slightly away from the viewer, it's not appropriate for both eyes to be the same size. The right eye, which is farther away from the viewer, should be smaller to give the illusion of depth. Therefore, I needed to scale the eye.

However, to follow the template, I had to reduce the eye so that it was narrower than it was tall. This was no problem, because FreeHand allows for separate vertical and horizontal percentages when scaling. The second example of Figure 4-10 shows how I scaled the eye to 80 percent of its original width and 90 percent of its original height. The resulting eye matched my template almost perfectly.

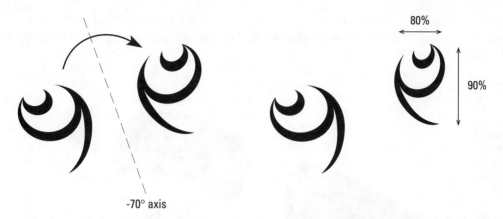

-70° axis

Figure 4-10: I cloned the five shapes that made up the left eye and reflected them about a -70 degree axis.

Step 3: Drawing the eyebrows

The next logical step was to create the eyebrows. I began with the left brow — a more difficult shape than any discussed so far. It involved eight points, labeled A through H in Figure 4-11. Each point is analogous to the street sign that bears the same letter. Keep in mind that, for the purpose of this example, you are seeing these street signs as if you were traveling counterclockwise on the path, as demonstrated by the arrows.

Figure 4-11: The left eyebrow is made up of eight points, each corresponding to one of the street signs shown above.

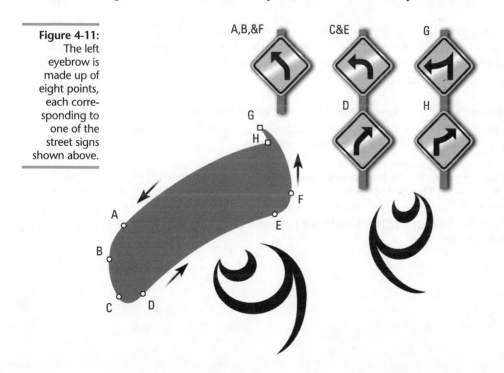

Once again, I made the stroke of this shape transparent and filled the shape with solid black. Then I cloned the eyebrow and reflected the clone about a -75 degree axis. Figure 4-12 shows the result.

Figure 4-12:
I cloned the
eyebrow
shape and
reflected it
across a -75
degree axis.

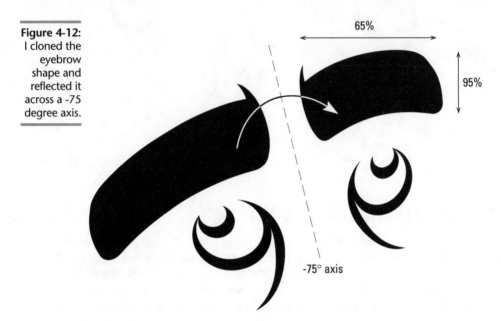

The newly reflected right eyebrow was not the correct size, nor did its path entirely conform to the shape of the right eyebrow in my template. To remedy the first problem, I scaled the brow to 65 percent of its original width and 95 percent of its original height, as shown in the second example of Figure 4-12.

To reshape the path of the eyebrow, I had to convert the identity of a few of its points. *Converting a point* is like posting a new street sign; it alters the direction of the path. Figure 4-13 shows which points I changed, and how.

Notice that the street sign for point E now curves to the right instead of to the left as it did in Figure 4-11. This is not because of any adjustment on my part but is instead the result of the recent reflection. When the shape was reflected, the identity of every point was also reflected, turning the path in the opposite direction, as demonstrated by the arrows the Figure 4-13.

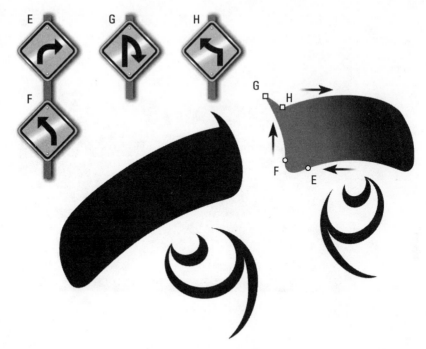

Figure 4-13: I reshaped the right eyebrow by converting points F, G, and H.

Now notice point F. Its street sign is identical to that shown in Figure 4-11. This means that it *has* been changed; otherwise, it would have been reflected like the others. Points G and H have also been changed. The result is an alteration in the path of the shape. You can see how the identity of each and every point directly influences the path.

Step 4: Building the cigar

Next, I worked on Groucho's prominent cigar. First, I traced an oval around the lighted ashes at the cigar's tip. Then I cloned this oval and reduced the clone so that I had two concentric ovals. I again cloned the larger oval and moved this clone about one-quarter inch to the left, as shown in Figure 4-14.

Deleting and adding points

Like an oval, my most recent shape comprised four more-or-less identical points, all telling the path to curve around in a continuous direction, as illustrated in Figure 4-15. I changed the path of this shape not by changing the identity of its points, but by deleting and adding points.

Figure 4-14:
Tracing the
tip of
Groucho's
cigar.

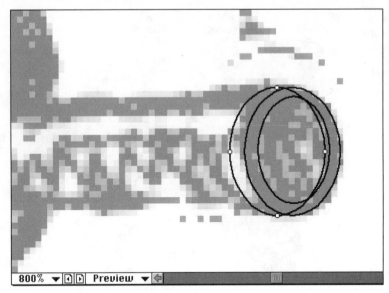

Figure 4-15:
I deleted point
D and changed
the identities of
points A and C,
resulting in a
straight
segment
between A and
C.

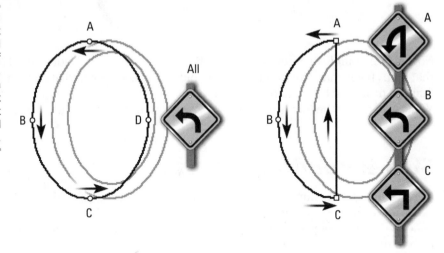

I deleted point D. Where there used to be two segments between A and C, there was now just one. I then changed the identities of points A and C to make the segment between them straight. The result is shown in the second example of Figure 4-15.

Next, I copied my most recent shape to the Clipboard so that I could recall this interim version of the object later in the drawing process.

I then added two points, D and E, to the vertical segment connecting points A and C, and moved the new points into the positions shown in Figure 4-16. The identities of points A and C changed to fit in with their new neighbors. Because point B is nestled between points A and C, its identity remained constant.

Figure 4-16:
Adding points D
and E further
alters the
identities of points
A and C.

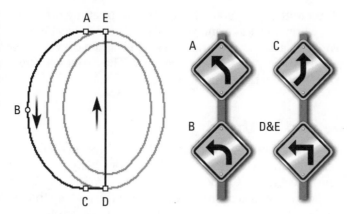

Layering the shapes

I now had the very tip of Groucho's cigar, though you could hardly recognize it. I still needed to define the stroke and fill of each of the three shapes. I made all strokes transparent; filled the first oval with a dark gray; and filled the second, smaller oval with a light gray. I filled my most recent shape with black. The result is shown in the first example of Figure 4-17.

Figure 4-17:
After filling the
shapes (left), I
pasted the
shape copied
earlier and
opened it
(right).

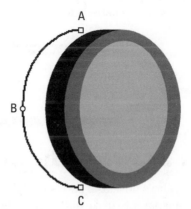

Unfortunately, my cigar tip had a problem: The black shape covered up both of the gray ovals. Because I created the black shape last, it was in front of both ovals. The solution was to send the black shape to the back. No matter when an object was created, you can send it to the back or bring it to the front.

By sending an object to the back, you tell FreeHand to treat the object as if it were the first one created. By bringing it to front, you tell FreeHand to treat it as the most recent object. After I sent the black shape to the back, the program drew the black shape first, then the dark gray oval, and then the light gray oval. The result was the cigar's end of glowing ashes, shown on the right side of Figure 4-17.

Pasting the end of the cigar

If you recall, a few paragraphs ago I mentioned that I copied an object to the Macintosh Clipboard. My next step was to retrieve that object. I did so by *pasting* the object, which takes a copy of the object in the Clipboard and places it on the drawing area. After I pasted the shape, I moved it into position and opened the path so that no segment linked points A and C, as shown in the second example of Figure 4-17.

By opening the pasted path, I converted the shape into a line. Then I added points to the line so that the path traces the form of the cigar as it goes into Groucho's mouth. As I created the last point in the line, I again closed the line to form a shape.

This time, I stroked the outline of the shape with a heavy, black line weight and filled the shape with white. Because I filled my shape with white rather than leaving it transparent, it will cover up any objects that I create and send to the back later in the drawing process. The finished cigar is shown in Figure 4-18.

Figure 4-18:
A heavy, black
stroke finishes
the cigar.

Step 5: Drawing the nose and mustache

I created Groucho's nose as a series of eight points, as shown in Figure 4-19. I then assigned a transparent stroke and a black fill. Looking at the finished nose in Figures 4-20 and later, you may wonder why I created it as a shape rather than as a line. It is, after all, very much a line in the traditional sense.

The problem is that the weight of this line in not uniform. In fact, it is downright calli-graphic — thin at the beginning, becoming fatter as it sweeps around, and then becom-ing thin again at its end. Lines in FreeHand can't have this property. As I said earlier, although the thickness of a stroke is determined by its line weight, the thickness of a fill is determined by the path that surrounds it. Therefore, to express a calligraphic line, you have to create a path that surrounds both sides of the "line" and then fill the resulting shape. This is what I did in the case of the nose and throughout the remainder of this illustration.

Figure 4-19:
Because the outline of the nose tapers at both ends, it must be expressed as a shape.

Changing eyebrow into mustache

In setting out to create Groucho's mustache, the first thing I noticed was how similar it was to his eyebrows. So I decided to clone the left eyebrow and move it into position between the nose and cigar.

To better match the eyebrow shape to the mustache, I reflected it about a 25-degree axis, as shown in Figure 4-20. This reflection is interesting because the axis runs directly through the shape, so that the shape actually reflects upon itself. A reflection axis can be angled in any way you want.

Figure 4-20:
I reflected
the eyebrow
clone about
a 25-degree
axis.

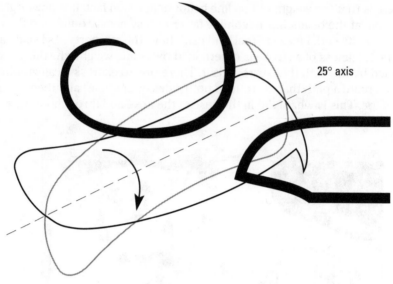

 Figure 4-20 shows the cloned eyebrow shape as having a black stroke and no fill even though the original eyebrow has no stroke and a black fill. I purposely changed the stroke and fill of this shape to make it stand out from the shapes around it.

The next step was to skew the shape so that it matched the angle of the mustache in the template. In this case, I wanted to skew it 25 degrees horizontally. Figure 4-21 shows how the skew is measured from the horizontal axis. Dotted lines show roughly the angle at which the shape sat before the skew and the resulting new angle of the shape.

Groucho's mustache is considerably larger than either of the eyebrows, so I enlarged it to 130 percent of its original size. But transformations are not enough to turn eyebrow into mustache. The basic form of the shape still wasn't what it should be, so I altered the path by converting points and adding new ones. The first example in Figure 4-22 shows the number and location of the points that existed before the alteration. The mustache has eight points, as did the eyebrow from which it was cloned.

The second example shows the points after alteration. Notice that there are now nine points, and all the points have been moved at least slightly. I moved some dramatically and changed the identities of several as well. Yet my alteration had just a subtle effect on the appearance of the path. Though I changed every point in some way, the outline of the shape in the second example of Figure 4-22 follows a path very similar to that of its predecessor in the first example. The subtleties of a path can make or break an illustration.

Figure 4-21:
I skewed the
eyebrow
clone 25
degrees
horizontally.

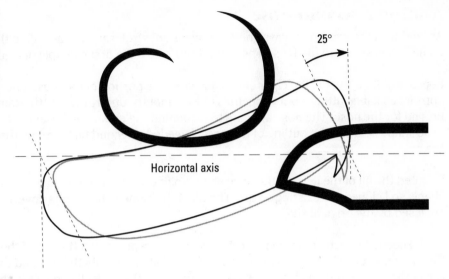

Figure 4-22:
Before reshaping, the
mustache has eight
points (top);
afterward (bottom), it
has nine points,
many of which differ
from their predeces-
sors.

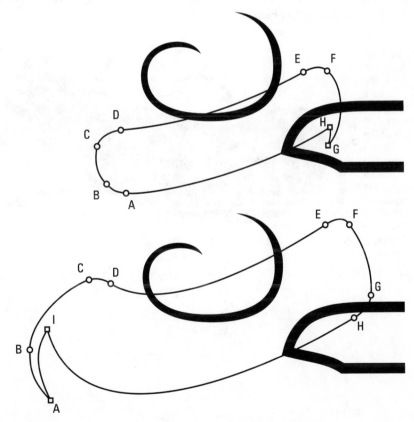

Adding a second nose

As I did with the eyebrows, I assigned a transparent stroke and a black fill to the mustache. I then sent it to the back. The result is shown in the first example of Figure 4-23.

Because of its white fill, the cigar effectively covers a portion of the mustache so that it appears as if it is jutting from Groucho's hidden mouth. Unfortunately, the same cannot be said for the nose. The nose appears to be behind the mustache because the fill of the nose shape acts like the outline of the nose. I needed a second fill to create the flesh of the nose.

I wanted the fill of the flesh-of-the-nose shape to fit exactly into the outline-of-the-nose shape, so I cloned the existing shape. The fill of the cloned shape then covers the area enclosed by the original shape.

Next, I needed a segment to connect the points that represented the top of the nose and the tip of the nostril. No problem. I simply deleted all the points that formed the outer rim of the nose and then closed the last two points in the path. The result is shown in the second example of Figure 4-23.

Figure 4-23:
Though in back, the black mustache obscures the shape of the nose (top). I needed to create a new shape to represent the flesh of the nose (bottom).

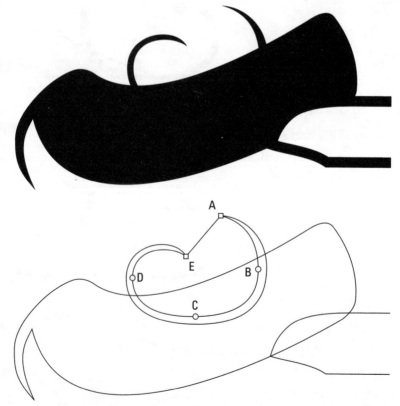

Notice that this second example shows shapes with no fills and thin strokes. Although the other figures in this chapter appear in the preview mode, this one is shown in the keyline mode. As I explained in Chapter 3, the keyline mode displays all lines and outlines with very thin, black strokes and all fills as transparent. By viewing the paths in this figure in the keyline mode, you can more clearly view the most recent developments.

To make it match the rest of Groucho's face, I filled the most recent shape with white. I then zoomed out from the illustration so that I could see the result of all my work so far, as shown in Figure 4-24. The picture looks about half finished, but looks can be deceiving. I was actually much closer than that.

Figure 4-24:
Although the nose now appears in front of the mustache, Groucho is no more than features in need of a face.

Step 6: Finishing the face

In Figure 4-24, many of Groucho's features are still missing — his glasses, the bridge of his nose, his ear, his hair, the outline of his face, and a few wrinkles. But, if you will recall my template (see Figure 4-4), all these features are less pronounced than those I created so far. The subtle features in a template are often harder to approach than their more obvious or outstanding counterparts. The best advice I can offer is to dive right in. (Big help, huh?) These incidental parts of an illustration round it out, giving it a more clearly defined appearance.

In Figure 4-25, I created a series of small shapes that act as calligraphic swashes. The majority of the shapes are made up of only two or three points each. The identity of each point causes one path segment to curve more than another, so that the fill creates a free-flowing stroke — simple but highly effective. The most complicated shape is constructed of only five points.

Figure 4-25: The wrinkles in the flesh and portions of the glasses are expressed as many small shapes, most comprising three points or fewer.

The next shape was very extensive, comprising 48 points, as shown in Figure 4-26. With one shape, I created the hair, most of Groucho's ear, lip, chin, neck, and part of his glasses. But the process itself was no more difficult than creating any of the shapes in Figure 4-25.

In fact, the most difficult part of something like this is probably recognizing that such a large portion of the template can be expressed as a single shape. This skill comes with practice. After you see the shape, you need only trace its outline point by point, carefully and patiently. But whatever you do, never be intimidated by a large shape. The only difference between a simple line with two points and a complex shape with one hundred points is that the latter takes longer to produce.

Figure 4-26:
Most of the outline of the face as well as several incidental features can be expressed as a single complex shape.

After filling the complex shape with solid black, I needed only two more shapes to finish Groucho's face: the remainder of the ear and the bridge of the nose. The ear required eleven points and the nose required six, as shown in Figure 4-27.

Always use points sparingly. If you find that you don't have enough points, you can always add more. But just one point too many means that someplace, there are two path segments where there should be only one. The result is a needlessly complicated object whose path may appear clumsy and malformed when printed.

Figure 4-27:
I finished
the face
with two
shapes, one
representing
the details
of the ear
and the
other the
bridge of
the nose.

Step 7: Making the collar

By now, you can probably imagine how I drew Groucho's collar. But there were a couple of stumbling blocks along the way.

The first example in Figure 4-28 shows the points required to create the jacket lapel and the shirt collar — four shapes altogether. Both lapel shapes get a transparent stroke and a black fill. The collars get a medium-weight black stroke and a white fill. The second example in the figure shows the results. Notice that I matched up the stroke of the collars exactly with the fill of the 48-point shape that wraps around to form the throat. Here is a case where the fill of a shape and the weight of a stroke are designed to be identical.

Figure 4-28:
The four
shapes
required to
create the
collar and
lapels (top)
and the three
shapes that
make up the
bow tie
(bottom).

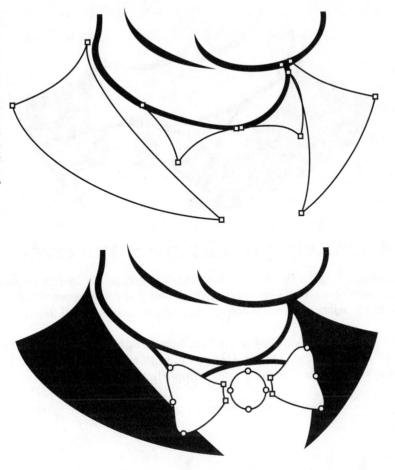

The second example in Figure 4-28 also shows the tie, which is made of three separate shapes. One is a simple oval and the other two have five points apiece.

If you look back at the original sketch in Figure 4-4, you can see that Groucho's tie covers his lapels in an unusual manner — there's a white line between the black of the tie and the black of the jacket. To recreate this effect, I had to consider the stroke as well as the fill of each shape. I used a medium-weight white stroke and a black fill for all three shapes of the tie. The white stroke provides the necessary definition between the tie and the jacket to distinguish the two as independent objects.

Finally, I brought both of the collar shapes from the top example of Figure 4-28 to the front of the drawing so that they covered the tie. The tie then appeared nestled between collar and lapels, as shown in Figure 4-29.

Step 8: Drawing smoke from the cigar

Often, a small finishing detail can sell a drawing. In this case, the last detail was to create the smoke rising from Groucho's cigar. Granted, the smoke wasn't absolutely necessary, but it balanced the drawing and gave the cartoon a small touch of realism.

I traced the smoke by drawing one shape containing 21 points, as shown in the first example of Figure 4-30. Then I assigned the shape a thin, light gray stroke with no fill. As shown in the second example, the shape is simple but entirely functional.

Figure 4-30:
The points
required to
express the cigar
smoke (left), and
the same path
when stroked
with a gray
outline (right).

The completed Groucho

Figure 4-31 shows the completed Groucho as he appeared when printed from FreeHand. Despite the large size, the resolution is far better than in the bitmapped Photoshop template. Every detail is crisp and accurate; the overall appearance is clean and smooth. All things said and done, the result is a highly professional product.

Figure 4-31:
The completed Groucho cartoon printed from FreeHand 4.0.

Although this example is more elementary than much of the artwork you may attempt in FreeHand, it lays the groundwork for creating almost any electronic illustration. The following chapters discuss the tools, commands, and dialog box options required to create this and other drawings in FreeHand 4.0.

Summary

- A path comprises numerous points joined by segments. The points direct the curvature of the segment, in effect telling the path where to go.

- An open path is a *line*. A closed path is a *shape*.

- The term *stroke* refers to the thickness and color of a path's outline. The *fill* is the color or colors assigned to the interior of a shape (closed path).

- To create an illustration in FreeHand, you layer paths one on top of another in collage formation.

- The easiest way to create artwork in FreeHand is to work from a bitmapped sketch captured by a scanner or created in Photoshop or a similar application.

- A filled path covers up a path that lies in back of it.

- When you need to create two similar shapes, create the first shape and then clone it to create the second shape.

- It's no more difficult to create a complicated path than a simple one; the complicated path just contains more points.

Constructing Paths

![marker dots]

In This Chapter

- ➺ Drawing simple geometric shapes like rectangles and ellipses
- ➺ Rounding off the corners of rectangles
- ➺ Using the polygon tool to draw multisided shapes and stars
- ➺ Drawing, erasing, and extending with the freehand tool
- ➺ Creating calligraphic shapes
- ➺ Mastering the strange ways of Bézier curves
- ➺ Constructing paths with the bézigon and pen tools
- ➺ Understanding corner, curve, and connector points

Venturing Down the Garden Path

Theory is all very well and good, and knowing how to draw Groucho Marx — as described in Chapter 4 — can be a real ice-breaker at parties. To get ahead in today's competitive, object-oriented marketplace, however, you need more than theoretical knowledge. You need to know how to use FreeHand's drawing tools. Staring at the screen and visualizing your drawing just won't work.

Fully half of FreeHand's tools are devoted to the mundane and sometimes unnerving task of drawing. I describe seven of these tools — rectangle, oval, polygon, line, freehand, pen, and bézigon — in this chapter. The lone holdout — the trace tool — is discussed in Chapter 6.

If you're familiar with previous versions of FreeHand, you know how most of the drawing tools work. But as you must be aware by now, an upgrade doesn't go by without some low-level (sometimes inexplicable) variations to the FreeHand drawing model. FreeHand 4.0 provides two new tools: the polygon tool, for drawing equilateral polygons and stars; and the hybrid bézigon tool, which takes the place of the old corner, curve, and connector tools that have been with FreeHand since its inception.

To keep things as straightforward as possible, I've divided this chapter into three major sections:

- **Geometric Shapes:** This first section discusses the prosaic rectangle and oval tools as well as the slightly more interesting polygon tool. Although most newborns could sit down and use these tools without my help, I feel duty-bound to explain them. However, one entry, "Geometric shapes at an angle," bears quick reading by one and all.

- **Straight and Free-Form Paths:** This section covers the line and freehand tools. The line tool takes all of three or four seconds to explain, but the freehand tool is remarkably capable and lends itself to a variety of drawing situations.

- **The Subterranean World of Bézier Curves:** If you're a beginner, you may want to skip this section for now. Although Bézier curves are incredibly powerful, you may find them somewhat bewildering at first. Like single-malt Scotch and Tom Waits, Bézier curves are an acquired taste. But once you learn to love them, you'll never go back.

Geometric Shapes

FreeHand offers three tools for creating geometric shapes: the rectangle, oval, and polygon tools. You operate each tool by dragging with it from one location to another. The points at which you begin and end the drag signify the boundaries of the rectangle, oval, or polygon. Although limited in utility, these geometric shapes are very easy to draw because they involve no planning and little guesswork.

Drawing a rectangle

Consider the rectangle tool, the second tool on the left side of the toolbox. After selecting this tool, drag inside the illustration window to create a rectangle. This process is the same one you use to create a rectangle in all graphics applications that run on the Mac and Windows.

One corner of the rectangle is determined by the point at which you begin to drag; the opposite corner occurs at the point at which you release (see Figure 5-1). The two remaining corners line up vertically and horizontally with their neighbors. A fifth point, called the *center point*, is created at the center of the shape. The center point of a rectangle is always visible in the keyline mode but is visible in the preview mode only when you are moving or transforming the shape.

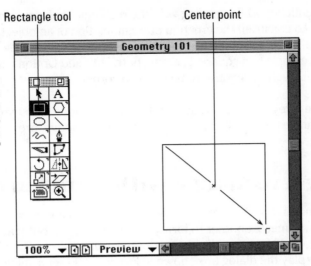

Rectangle tool   Center point

Figure 5-1:
Operate the rectangle tool by dragging from one corner to the opposite corner of the desired shape, as indicated by the arrow.

If you press the Option key while drawing with the rectangle tool, the beginning of your drag becomes the center point of the rectangle, as shown in Figure 5-2. As before, the release point becomes one of the rectangle's corners; it also determines the distance and direction from each of the remaining three corners to the center point.

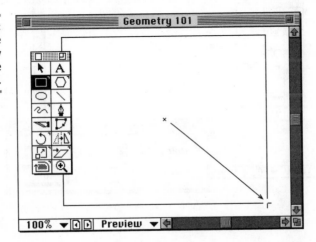

Figure 5-2:
Option-drag with the rectangle tool to draw a rectangle from the center outward.

Notice that the length of the drag in Figure 5-2 is the same as that in Figure 5-1, but because the Option key is pressed in Figure 5-2, the drag results in a rectangle that is twice as large as the one in Figure 5-1. So if you want to expend less mouse-moving energy when you're drawing, use an Option-drag instead of a plain old drag. This technique can come in handy when you're creating several rectangles at a time or when your wrist is starting to ache from overuse.

If you press the Shift key while drawing with the rectangle tool, you *constrain* the resulting shape. To constrain the creation or manipulation of an object is to attach certain guidelines to the effects of your mouse movements. In this case, pressing Shift constrains the rectangle to a square. Pressing both Shift and Option while drawing with the rectangle tool creates a square from center to corner.

 Press the 1 key — either in the standard key set or on the keypad — to select the rectangle tool. If a text block or option box is active, press Shift-F1 instead.

Drawing a rectangle with rounded corners

By default, rectangles drawn in FreeHand have perpendicular corners (which simply means that one side meets another to form a 90-degree angle). But you can also draw rectangles with rounded corners. To do so, double-click on the rectangle tool icon in the toolbox to display the dialog box shown in Figure 5-3. Enter a value into the Corner Radius option box (or drag the knob inside the slider bar) to specify the radius of the rounded corner.

Figure 5-3:
Double-click on the rectangle tool icon in the toolbox to round off the corners in a rectangle.

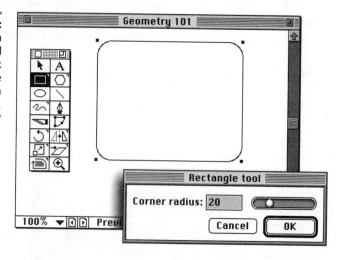

As you may recall from your junior-high geometry class, the *radius* is the distance from the center of a circle to any point on its outline. Think of a rounded corner as one-quarter of a circle, as shown in the first example of Figure 5-4. The arrows in the figure show the radius of the circle.

The size of the circle increases as the radius increases, so a large Corner Radius value rounds off the corners of a rectangle more dramatically than a smaller value. To demonstrate this idea, the second example of Figure 5-4 shows the result of increasing the radius. I superimposed a grayed version of the radius from the first example for comparison.

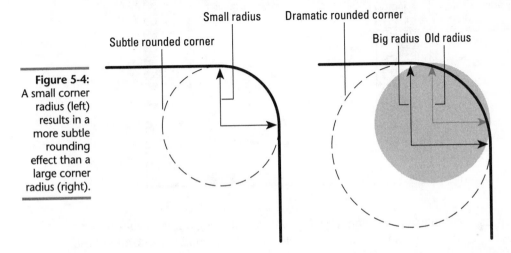

Figure 5-4:
A small corner radius (left) results in a more subtle rounding effect than a large corner radius (right).

By default, the Corner Radius value is measured in *points*. Not to be confused with points on a path, these points are very tiny increments of measure equal to 1/72 inch. (Because most Macintosh monitors display 72 screen pixels per inch, one point is equal to one screen pixel at actual size.) You can change the unit of measure by displaying the Document Setup panel in the Inspector palette and selecting a new option from the first pop-up menu. For more information, see the "Changing the unit of measure" section of Chapter 8.

Drawing an ellipse

You use the oval tool — the third tool on the left side of the toolbox — very much like the rectangle tool. One difference, of course, is that you use the oval tool to create ellipses and circles instead of rectangles and squares. Another difference is that the points at which you click and release with the oval tool do not reside on the path of the ellipse; they are merely reference points. An ellipse drawn with the oval tool fits inside the area of your drag.

To understand this concept, it helps to imagine an invisible bounding box forming as you drag with the oval tool, as illustrated in Figure 5-5. The ellipse exists entirely within the boundaries of this bounding box, as it does when you draw with an oval tool in most other Macintosh applications.

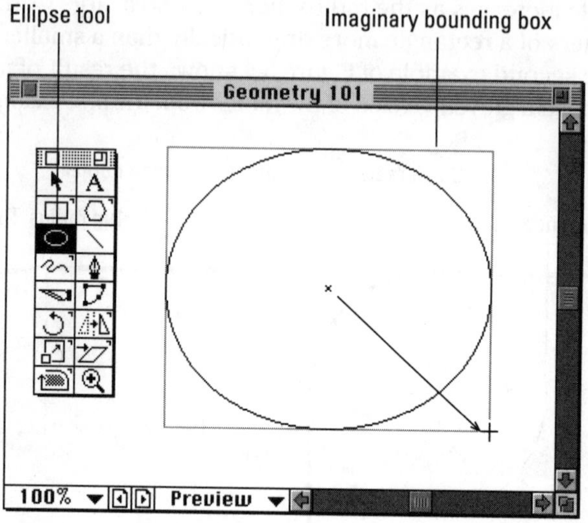

Ellipse tool   Imaginary bounding box

Figure 5-5:
An ellipse fits entirely
inside the area of your
drag.

If you press Option while drawing with the oval tool, the beginning of your drag becomes the center point of the ellipse. The release point becomes the corner of the bounding box, thereby determining the size and shape of the ellipse.

Press Shift and drag with the oval tool to create a perfect circle. Press both Shift and Option to draw a circle outward from the center point.

You can access the oval tool from the keyboard by pressing the 3 key in the standard key set or on the keypad. If a text block or option box is active, press Shift-F3.

Drawing a polygon

The polygon tool, the second tool from the top on the right side of the toolbox, is the first addition to FreeHand's suite of geometric shape tools since the product first shipped in 1988. When you drag with the polygon tool inside the illustration window, FreeHand draws an *equilateral polygon* — a shape with multiple straight sides, each of which are the same length and meet each other at a consistent angle. The hexagon in Figure 5-6 is an example of an equilateral polygon. Pentagons, octagons, and even squares are other examples.

Polygon tool

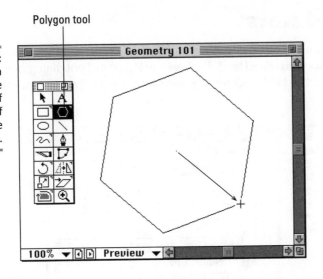

Figure 5-6:
Shapes drawn with
the polygon tool have
a set number of
straight sides, all of
which are the same
length.

As indicated by the arrow in Figure 5-6, the polygon tool *always* draws outward from the center; the Option key is not required, nor does it have any influence. It's also worth noting that FreeHand does not assign center points to polygons. This is because FreeHand doesn't treat polygons as special shapes as it does rectangles and ellipses. For example, you don't have to ungroup a polygon to edit it. In this sense, polygons are just like free-form paths drawn with the freehand and pen tools.

The other difference between the polygon tool and its geometric counterparts is the impact of the Shift key. When you press Shift while drawing with the rectangle or oval tool, FreeHand keeps the shape proportional. (Just thought I'd recap that little bit of information in case you plumb forgot.) But by definition, equilateral polygons are already proportional. So when you Shift-drag with the polygon tool, FreeHand limits your drag to four different angles for each side in the shape.

For example, if you set the polygon tool to draw a triangle, you can Shift-drag in 12 directions — 3 sides × 4 angles. There are 360 degrees in a circle, so you can drag in 30-degree increments — 360 degrees ÷ 12 directions. If you set the polygon tool to draw a hexagon, which has 6 sides, Shift-dragging constrains your movements to 24 different directions.

I realize that all this sounds a tad bit confusing, so let me oversimplify things a little: By pressing the Shift key, you can draw a shape with at least one side that is oriented horizontally, vertically, or diagonally. That's not the whole story, but it's close enough.

 To select the polygon tool, press the 2 key. If pressing 2 doesn't work because a text block or option box is active, press Shift-F2.

Sides and stars

To specify the number of sides you want in your polygon, double-click on the polygon tool icon in the toolbox. FreeHand displays the Polygon Tool dialog box shown in Figure 5-7. To add or subtract sides, enter any number between 3 and 20 into the Number of Sides option box.

Figure 5-7:
The Polygon Tool dialog box as it appears when the Polygon (top) and Star (bottom) options are selected.

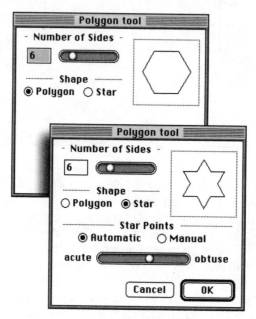

You can also create stars with the polygon tool. To do so, select the Star radio button in the Polygon Tool dialog box. The Star Points options appear, as shown in the lower dialog box in Figure 5-7. By default, the Automatic radio button is selected, which results in the kind of stars featured in the top row of Figure 5-8. The opposite arms of these stars are perfectly aligned with each other. For example, in the five-point star, the tops of the right and left arms form a horizontal line.

To override this option, you don't need to select the Manual radio button — just drag the knob inside the slider bar below the radio buttons, and FreeHand automatically selects the Manual radio button. Drag left (toward Acute) to reduce the angles at which the sides in a star meet; drag right (toward Obtuse) to enlarge the angles. Acute stars have sharp points; obtuse stars have dull ones. The bottom row of Figure 5-8 shows several acute stars inset inside their automatic companions. Notice that the arms of the acute stars — created with the manual option — do not align with each other.

Figure 5-8:
Three stars subject to the Automatic option (top), and the same three with acute stars inset (bottom).

Geometric shapes at an angle

In the course of drawing with one of the geometric shape tools, you may find that your path rotates at some odd angle, as demonstrated by the rectangle in Figure 5-9. Don't blame yourself — it's not happening because you're misusing the tool. It's happening because you — or someone else using your copy of FreeHand — altered the angle of the *constraint axes*. The constraint axes control the angle at which you can manipulate objects while pressing Shift. They also control the creation of geometric shapes.

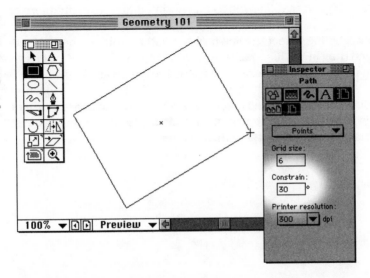

Figure 5-9:
Drawing a rectangle with the Constrain value set to 30 degrees.

You change the angle of the constraint axes by entering a value into the Constrain option in the Document Setup panel, located in the Inspector palette (spotlighted in the figure). If the Constrain value is anything but 0, rectangles and ellipses are rotated to that degree. The Constrain value also affects polygons that you create while pressing the Shift key.

For more information on the Constrain option, read the "Constrained movements" section of Chapter 7. This option can be very useful when you are reshaping and transforming objects.

Straight and Free-Form Paths

With the geometric shape tools, you can create simple shapes quickly and easily. However, FreeHand's true drawing prowess is rooted in its ability to define free-form paths. A free-form path can be simple, like a wedge or a crescent, or it can be an intricate polygon or naturalistic form that meets the most complex specifications.

Drawing straight segments

Because of its simplicity and limited utility, the straight line may seem more like a geometric path than a free-form path. But in FreeHand, the straight line shares more similarities with paths drawn with the freehand and pen tools than with rectangles or ellipses. Though a straight line is simple to create, you can manipulate it without first ungrouping it, just like a shape drawn with the polygon tool. But unlike polygons, straight lines are open, enabling you to quickly integrate them into more complex paths.

To draw a straight line, select the line tool — the third tool on the right side of the toolbox — and drag in the illustration window. (See Figure 5-10 if you're stumped.) The distance and direction of your drag determine the length and angle of the line. The beginning of your drag marks the first point in the line; the release location marks the final point. Both points are called *endpoints* because they appear at either end of the path and they are both associated with only one segment. Endpoints have special properties that are explored later in this chapter.

Line tool

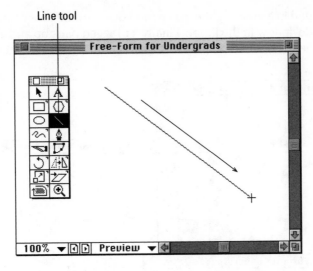

Figure 5-10:
Admit it, you'd
never understand
how to use the
line tool without
this figure.

If you press Shift and drag with the line tool, FreeHand constrains the line to a horizontal, vertical, or diagonal angle. Keep in mind that you can change the effect of pressing the Shift key by entering a value other than 0 into the Constrain option box in the Document Setup panel of the Inspector palette (deep breath), as described in the previous section.

 Pressing the 4 key selects the line tool. When it doesn't, press Shift-F4. If that doesn't work, beg, plead, and resort to bribery. Just because your computer doesn't respect you doesn't mean it won't pity you.

Drawing freehand lines

The fourth tool on the left side of toolbox, the freehand tool, is used for real-time drawing. After selecting this tool, you can click and drag as if you were drawing with a pencil on a sheet of paper. FreeHand tracks the exact movements of your mouse onscreen, creating a free-form line between the locations at which your drag begins and ends. After you release, FreeHand automatically determines the quantity and location of points and segments and creates the freehand path.

Consider the example of the apple shown in Figure 5-11. The figure shows the progression of the freehand tool cursor. I started by dragging with the tool from the upper left corner of the apple's stem down to the beginning of the leaf. I then dragged up and back down in two opposite arcs to create the leaf. After dragging downward to finish the stem, I swept around in a great rightward arc and down to the lower tip of the core, as shown in the third window in the figure. Finally, I dragged back up and around to the left, eventually meeting the first point in a single continuous movement.

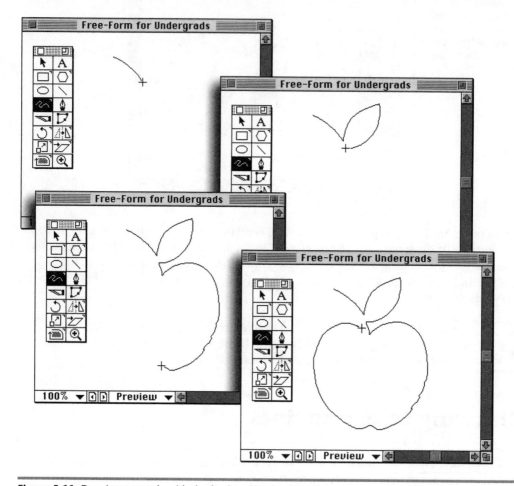

Figure 5-11: Drawing an apple with the freehand tool in four steps.

Notice that the apple in Figure 5-11 exhibits some jaggedness along its lower right side. This jagged area exists for two reasons. First, I drew this figure with a mouse. The mouse is not a precise drawing instrument. When you move a mouse, a ball within its chamber rolls about against the surface of the table or mouse pad. The ball in turn causes two internal tracking wheels to move, one vertically and one horizontally. Based on the activity of these two wheels, the mouse conveys movement information to the computer.

No matter how thoroughly you clean a mouse, there will be some interference between the ball and the wheels, even if it's only small particles of dust. For example, if you draw a 45-degree diagonal line, both the vertical and horizontal tracking wheels should move at exactly the same pace. If some interference comes between the ball and the horizontal wheel, causing the wheel to remain motionless for only a moment, the mouse sends purely vertical movement information to the computer until the interference has passed. The result is a momentary jag in an otherwise smooth diagonal line.

Second, most people — even skilled artists — are not very practiced at drawing with a mouse. It takes time to master this skill. You may find that your first drawing efforts look much different than you had planned — possibly far worse than Figure 5-11, for example. Luckily, the freehand tool is capable of smoothing out many imperfections.

Press the 5 key to access the freehand tool any time a text block or option box is not active. In the event that FreeHand treats the 5 as an everyday average character of text, press Shift-F5.

Freehand curve fit

After you complete the process of drawing a path and release your mouse button, FreeHand performs some calculations to determine how many points to assign to your path and where to locate those points. It bases these calculations on the following criteria:

- **Consistency:** FreeHand assigns a point to every location at which your drag changes direction. Thus, smooth, consistent mouse actions produce smooth, elegant paths; jerky or unsteady mouse actions produce overly complex lines.

- **Speed:** The speed at which you draw may also affect the appearance of a freehand path. If your mouse lingers at any location, FreeHand is more likely to assign a point there. However, if you draw too quickly, FreeHand ignores many of the subtle direction changes in your drag. A slow but steady technique is the most reliable.

- **Curve fit:** FreeHand enables you to control the sensitivity of the freehand tool by using the Tight Fit check box in the Freehand Tool dialog box. (To access this dialog box, double-click on the freehand tool icon in the toolbox.) Selecting this option instigates a tight *curve fit*, which results in a freehand path that more accurately matches your drag. Deselecting the option results in a looser curve fit, which instructs FreeHand to smooth over inaccuracies in your drag.

Figure 5-12 shows how FreeHand interprets my apple path depending on the selection of the Tight Fit option. The path on the left was created with Tight Fit on; the path on the right is the result of turning Tight Fit off. The two paths are similar, but a few differences are obvious. With Tight Fit off, FreeHand missed two key corners around the leaf. The stem is overly gooey, and the left side of the apple lacks sufficient definition. I recommend that you keep Tight Fit selected unless you consider yourself a total spaz with a mouse or have little confidence in your overall drawing ability.

Figure 5-12:
The points and segments assigned to the apple path when the Tight Fit option is selected (left) and dese-lected (right).

 You can't alter the curve fit for a path after the path is created, because FreeHand calculates the points for a path only once, after your release. For each of the two paths in Figure 5-12, therefore, I had to change the curve fit and then draw a new apple from scratch.

 However, you can give an existing path the appearance of a looser curve fit. To do this, select the path and then simplify it by choosing Arrange ⇨ Path Operations ⇨ Simplify. FreeHand automatically removes points that it considers excessive. The effect is similar to changing from a tight curve fit to a looser one.

Another option in the Freehand Tool dialog box, Draw Dotted Line, enables you to specify the manner in which FreeHand displays your freehand path while you're drawing it. When this option is off, which is the default setting, FreeHand displays your path as a solid line, as shown back in Figure 5-11.

If you want to draw more quickly, and FreeHand isn't keeping up with your mouse movements, turn this option on. FreeHand then displays your path as a broken dotted line, which takes less time to draw and track on-screen. The down side to this setting is that FreeHand barely provides you with enough visual feedback to figure out what you've drawn. Personally, I prefer to leave the Draw Dotted Line option deselected and draw carefully.

Erasing with the freehand tool

Normally, FreeHand tracks every movement you make with the freehand tool, creating a continuous path. If you press the Command key while drawing, however, you can erase a mistake. In the middle of a drag, press Command — don't release the mouse button! — and trace back over a portion of the path that you just drew. Be sure to trace your steps exactly. As you do, the path disappears in chunks. Each chunk represents a segment being deleted.

This technique enables you to fix mistakes as you go. You can draw a path with the freehand tool, immediately "undraw" part of it while pressing the Command key, and then release Command and continue drawing.

Drawing free-form polygons

Now, instead of Command-dragging back over your path, Command-drag away from it and then release the Command key and continue to draw. Notice that FreeHand does not display your path between the point where you pressed the Command key and the point where you released it. At the end of your drag, FreeHand calculates the quantity and position of the points necessary to represent your freehand path in the usual manner and displays the formerly invisible segment. The only difference is that any portion of your path that was created while the Command key was down is represented by a single segment.

This feature is a fluke, but it's a fun fluke. The official way to create a straight segment with the freehand tool is to press Option while dragging. FreeHand creates a straight segment between the points at which you press and release the Option key, just as it does when you press Command. However, when you press Option, you can see the straight segment between the two points as you draw. The following steps show how to use this powerful function.

STEPS: Drawing Straight Segments with the Freehand Tool

Step 1. Throughout these steps, keep the mouse button down. Begin by drawing a common, everyday, garden-variety squiggle.

Step 2. With the mouse button still down — don't you dare release it — press the Option key and drag to a different location. As illustrated in Figure 5-13, a straight segment follows the movements of your cursor.

Step 3. Release the Option key but don't release the mouse button. Then draw another squiggle. As shown in Figure 5-14, your movements are interpreted exactly as they were before you pressed Option.

Step 4. Release your mouse button. The completed path contains a single, straight segment between the points at which you pressed and released the Option key.

Press Option

Figure 5-13:
The freehand tool
draws a straight
segment as long as
the Option key is
pressed.

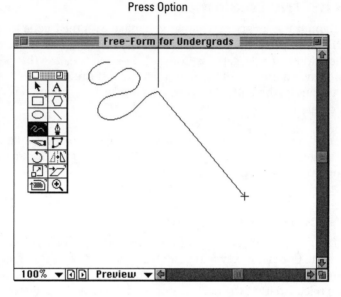

Release Option

Figure 5-14:
Continue drawing
after you release
the Option key.

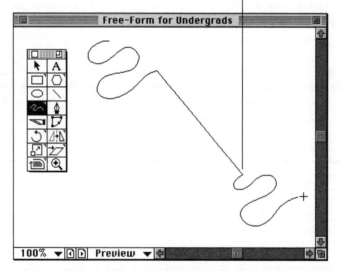

 In conjunction with the Option key, the freehand tool can serve as a polygon tool, similar to the one included in MacDraw. Press Option before beginning to drag with the freehand tool. When you're satisfied with your first segment, momentarily pause your freehand cursor. Then release and immediately repress the Option key and draw your next segment. Repeat this technique to create additional straight segments. After completing your final segment, release the mouse button and then release Option.

If you press Shift and Option together when dragging with the freehand tool, FreeHand constrains the straight segment to a 45-degree angle. Keep in mind that you can alter the effects of pressing the Shift key by rotating the constraint axes — which you accomplish by using the Constrain option, as described in the "Geometric shapes at an angle" section earlier in this chapter.

Extending a line

You can also use the freehand tool to extend an open path. Suppose that you drew a line with either the line tool or the freehand tool some time ago, but now you want to make the line longer or close the path. Select the path with the arrow tool and then drag from one of its endpoints with the freehand tool, as shown in Figure 5-15. FreeHand treats the line you create by dragging with the tool as an extension of the existing open path. To close the path, drag from one endpoint to the other.

Figure 5-15:
You can extend a selected straight line drawn with the line tool by dragging from its endpoint with the freehand tool.

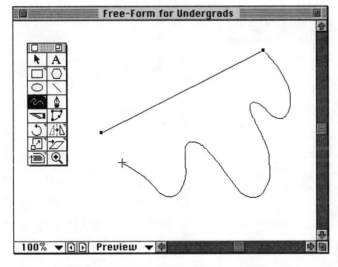

Sketching complicated paths

You can use the freehand tool to sketch complicated objects, especially line drawings. If you are skilled in drawing with the mouse or tablet, you may find the immediacy of producing high-resolution images in real time very appealing. Drawing with the freehand tool can soften the computer-produced appearance of an illustration and may convey a sense of informality and spontaneity to those who view your work.

However, regardless of your drawing ability or preferences, the freehand tool seldom results in paths that look just the way you want them to right off the bat. You'll need to manipulate most freehand paths to some degree or other in order for them to print acceptably. Like taking photographs with a Polaroid camera, drawing with the freehand tool provides immediate satisfaction. But you sacrifice accuracy and elegance. For this reason, I recommend that you use the tool primarily for sketching and prepare yourself to spend some time properly reshaping your paths (as described in Chapter 7, "Reshaping and Combining Paths").

Drawing calligraphic lines

 FreeHand 3.1 introduced the concept of a pressure-sensitive freehand tool that could create variable-weight paths as closed shapes. FreeHand 4.0 builds on this idea by offering both variable-weight and calligraphic options.

Double-click on the freehand tool icon in the toolbox to display the Freehand Tool dialog box. Then select either the Variable Stroke or Calligraphic Pen radio button. Figure 5-16 shows the options associated with each.

Figure 5-16:
By using the Variable Stroke and Calligraphic Pen options, you can create variable-weight paths as closed shapes.

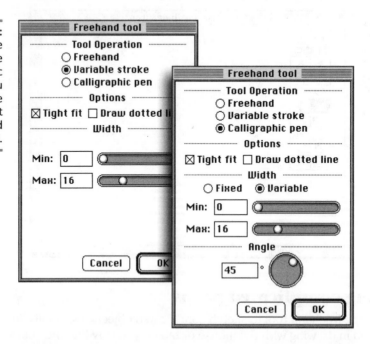

Pressure-sensitive input

The Variable Stroke option is designed to make the freehand tool compatible with pressure-sensitive drawing tablets such as the Wacom ArtZ, one of the most essential pieces of hardware available to computer artists.

The ArtZ includes a pen-like *stylus* that feels and behaves like a felt-tip pen. When the Variable Stroke option is active, FreeHand responds to the amount of pressure you apply to the stylus. As you bear down on the stylus while drawing with the freehand tool, FreeHand thickens the line; as you let up, the line becomes thinner. Figure 5-17 shows the freehand tool caught in the act of drawing a Japanese character using the Variable Stroke option.

The Variable Stroke
freehand icon

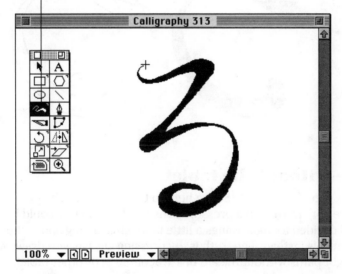

Figure 5-17:
When the Variable Stroke option is active, the freehand tool reacts dynamically to pressure-sensitive input.

The thickness of the line varies between the weights you enter into the Min and Max option boxes in the Freehand Tool dialog box. Any values between 0 and 72 are accepted. If you enter a value into the Min option box that is higher than the Max value, FreeHand is smart enough to simply reverse the values rather than irritating you with a bone-headed error message.

After you complete the line, FreeHand calculates the points required to express it as an object-oriented path. This is nothing out of the ordinary. What *is* unusual is that the path is automatically closed, because FreeHand has to trace around the line to produce the variable-weight effect. In doing so, FreeHand creates some strange overlapping areas that can interfere with reshaping.

For example, Figure 5-18 shows the path from the previous figure expressed as an object. In the second example, I've made the fill transparent so that you can more easily see its outline. Notice how the path wraps around the corners in the Japanese character? This wrapping ensures that the path follows the motion of your freehand cursor as closely as possible. However, it also makes the path very difficult to edit. To get rid of the overlaps, select the path and choose Arrange ⇨ Path Operations ⇨ Remove Overlap.

Figure 5-18:
Though my variable-weight path looks fine when filled (left), the outline of the path overlaps to express the corners in my drag (right).

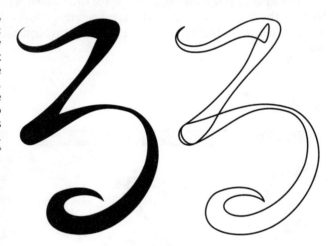

Pressure without the tablet

Confession is good for the soul. So I'm here to tell you, I lied. The paths from Figure 5-17 and 5-18 were *not* drawn with a pressure-sensitive tablet. They could have been, of course, but I decided to make things a little more challenging and test out FreeHand's keyboard controls instead. The truth is, by pressing keys as you draw, you can create variable-weight paths without the aid of a Wacom ArtZ or other tablet.

- ∽ To make the line thicker, press the right arrow key. If you sinned in a previous life and were therefore born right-handed, you'll probably prefer to use the 2 key, which serves the same purpose. You can also press the right-bracket key (just above Return), but why would you?

- ∽ To make the line thinner, press the left arrow key. Alternatively, you can press the left-bracket or 1 key.

These keyboard controls are fantastic. Each press of an arrow, number, or bracket key increases or decreases the thickness of the path by 1/8 of the difference between the Min and Max values in the Freehand Tool dialog box. For example, if the default Min and Max values are 0 and 16 respectively, each whack of a key changes the weight by 2 points. The only way to get a feel for this feature is to experiment. Have at it, and have a ball.

The Calligraphic Pen option

When you select the Calligraphic Pen radio button in the Freehand Tool dialog box, the freehand tool draws a path that looks like it was created with a broad-tipped pen. You specify the angle of the pen tip by entering a value into the Angle option box or by dragging the knob inside the circle just above the OK button (see Figure 5-16).

If the Fixed radio button is selected — it's located right there below the word *Width* — the calligraphic line conforms to a fixed weight. But if you select the Variable option, the freehand tool responds to pressure-sensitive input and keyboard controls just as it does when the Variable Stroke option is active. In my humble opinion, there's no reason *not* to select Variable.

The problem with the Calligraphic Pen option — and I'm talking opinion, not fact (though I'm generally pretty sure the two are identical) — is that it produces rather artificial results. Take the line in Figure 5-19 as an example. If I were to draw this character with a real flat-tipped pen, I could revolve the pen between my fingers to adjust the angle of the tip on the fly. But in FreeHand, the angle is fixed. Even if you had an iron grip and the steadiest hand on earth, you couldn't keep a pen tip this stationary. Only a machine could produce this line.

I'm not saying that FreeHand dropped the ball here — Illustrator offers a similar function that's equally inflexible — it's just that it doesn't measure up to the humanizing touch supplied by the Variable Stroke option and the freehand tool in general.

The Calligraphic Pen
freehand icon

Figure 5-19:
When the Calli-
graphic Pen option
is active, the
freehand tool draws
more or less like a
broad-tipped pen.

The Subterranean World of Bézier Curves

All right, so much for the easy stuff. If you've come this far, you're ready to get serious about drawing in FreeHand. The tools I've discussed up till now are laughably rudimentary and imprecise compared with the elemental machinery covered throughout the remainder of this chapter. Here's where you address the world of points and segments on an intimate basis. It's just you and your path, friend. Time to snuggle up. Armed with this knowledge, you'll be able to create absolutely any line or shape you need to begin or complete an illustration.

The math of the Béziers

Underneath the surface of each and every path you draw in FreeHand is a complex mathematical structure. As the story goes — and I tell you, it's an absorbing one — a French mathematician named Pierre Bézier (pronounced *bay-zee-ay*) discovered that you can define irregular curves by inventing two *control handles* (x_1,y_1 and x_2,y_2 for the algebra enthusiasts in the audience) for every fixed point (x,y) in a curve. In case you don't have the vaguest idea what I'm talking about, Figure 5-20 shows an aerial view.

These handles (our good buddies x_1,y_1 and x_2,y_2) act as levers. As a curve passes from one point (x,y) to another (Pierre was a little vague on this one, so I'll call it "Sam"), it is magnetically attracted to the control handles. One handle tells the curve how to enter the point; the other tells the curve how to exit the point. The fact is, these curves get bossed around a lot.

Figure 5-20:
The world according to Pierre Bézier.

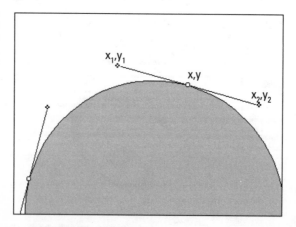

Now don't you feel newly educated? Can you sense your brains wanting to just bust out of your head? Kind of like the scarecrow after he stumbled on the Great and Powerful, huh? Pretty soon, you'll be spouting off Bézier theory at dinner parties and making your friends flee in terror.

Well, whatever your feelings, these so-called *Bézier curves* are at the heart of FreeHand's graphics capabilities, as well as those of the PostScript page-description language. Don't worry if you don't fully under the whole Bézier craze yet; I don't really expect you to. Throughout what remains of this chapter, I'll ease you into Bézier curves one limb at a time until, before you know it, you're fully immersed and wallowing around helplessly. It's the only way, trust me.

 Every time I rehash this introductory text, I try to find out a little something about Pierre Bézier, the man. What are his likes and dislikes? What makes him tick? Does he get a bang out of rock and roll, or do his preferences run more toward hip hop? As usual, I was unable to turn up anything this time. I don't even know if he's alive, dead, or in a cryogenic stupor. Oh, I could tell you volumes about Sir Henry Bessemer and Prince Otto Eduard Leopold von Bismark, but my exhaustive searches for Mr. Bézier have brought up nothing. So I ask you, the reader, to share any information you may have. If you've seen this mathematician, please, please call the Bézier hotline. We're all relying on *you*.

Using the bézigon and pen tools

FreeHand now offers two tools for drawing Bézier curves. One is the new bézigon tool, which incorporates the capabilities of the old corner, curve, and connector tools. And the other is the pen tool, which is slightly more difficult to use but provides you with more control.

The difference between the tools is slight. Continuing with my car-on-a-winding-road analogy from Chapter 4 — which, I'm happy to say, everyone but the Pope has lifted and used in a FreeHand book or article (the Pope prefers the analogy of the winding labyrinths of St. Peters) — the bézigon tool is like a '79 Volvo with an automatic transmission, and the pen tool is a brand new Hummer with a great big stick.

Regardless of which tool you use — or how vulgar your analogies may sound — you build a path by creating individual points. FreeHand automatically connects the points with *segments*. The following list explains the specific kinds of points and segments you can create in FreeHand and how to create them. Refer to Figure 5-21 for examples. Keep in mind that each of these techniques is described in more detail in an upcoming section.

- **Corner point:** Click with the bézigon or pen tool to create a *corner point*, which represents the corner between two straight segments in a path.

- **Straight segment:** Click at two different locations to create a straight segment between two corner points. Shift-click to draw a horizontal, vertical, or diagonal segment between the new corner point and its predecessor.

- **Curve point:** Option-click with the bézigon tool or drag with the pen tool to create a *curve point* with two symmetrical Bézier control handles. A curve point ensures that one segment meets with another in a continuous arc.

- **Curved segment:** Option-click (bézigon tool) or drag (pen tool) at two different locations to create a curved segment between two curve points.

- **Connector point:** After creating a corner point, Control-click with the bézigon tool or Control-drag with the pen tool to create a *connector* point with one control handle pointing away from the corner point. A straight segment joins the corner and connector points. Then Option-click (bézigon tool) or drag (pen tool) to create a curve point, which appends a curved segment to the connector point. The connector point ensures a perfectly smooth transition between this curved segment and the straight segment before it.

- **Straight segment followed by curved:** After creating a corner point, Option-drag at a new location with the pen tool to create another corner point with one control handle pointing away from its predecessor. A straight segment joins the two points. Then drag at a third location to append a curved segment to the end of the straight segment.

- **Curved segment followed by straight:** After creating a curve point, drag at a new location with the pen tool to create another curve point. Midway into the drag, press the Option key and move the control handle back to its point. Pressing Option converts the curve point to a corner point; dragging the handle back to its point deletes the handle. Then click again at a different location to append a straight segment to the end of the curved segment.

- **Cusp point:** After creating a curve point, drag at a new location with the pen tool to create another curve point. Midway into the drag, press the Option key — beginning to sound familiar? — only this time, move the control handle in some other direction of your choosing. Pressing Option converts the curve point to a corner point; dragging the handle without deleting it retains two independent handles. A corner point with two handles is sometimes called a *cusp point*. Finally, drag again at a new location to append a curved segment that proceeds in a different direction than the previous curved segment.

Figure 5-21:
The various kinds of
points and segments
you can draw with
the bézigon and pen
tools.

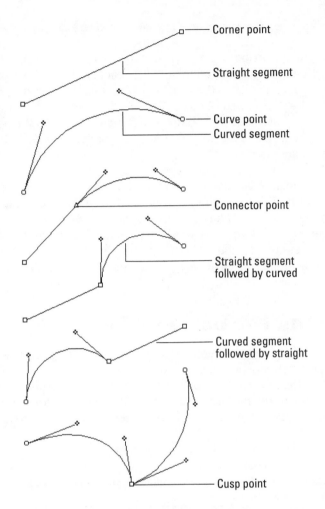

Corner point

Straight segment

Curve point
Curved segment

Connector point

Straight segment
follwed by curved

Curved segment
followed by straight

Cusp point

When using FreeHand for Windows, Alt-click with the bézigon tool to create a curve point. Press the Alt key and right click to create a connector point.

To complete your path, you can either close it to create a shape or leave it open to create a line. If you plan on eventually filling the path with a color or gradation, close the outline by clicking or dragging on the first point in the path. Every point will then have one segment coming into it and another segment exiting it.

To leave the path open, press the Tab key to deactivate it. Then click in the illustration window with either the bézigon or pen tool to begin a new path.

Moving points as you create them

Before I begin my long diatribe about the many ways to use the bézigon and pen tools, I want to tell you about a special function built into each. Both the bézigon and the pen tools let you move points while in the process of creating them. In the case of the bézigon tool, just drag with the tool rather than clicking. As you drag, the point moves around beneath your cursor. FreeHand draws a segment between the point in motion and its predecessor, giving you a feel for what the segment will look like subject to different point placements.

 To move a point while using the pen tool, press the Command key. For example, try this: Drag with the pen tool to create a curve point with two symmetrical Bézier control handles. The handles follow the motion of your cursor, while the point itself remains stationary. To move point and handles simultaneously, press the Command key as you continue to drag. As long as the key is pressed, the point moves. Release Command to fix the point in place.

Test-driving the bézigon tool

It's one thing to read and even understand a list of ways to use FreeHand's Bézier curve tools; it's another to actually put one of them to use. Because the bézigon tool is the most automated of the two, I'll demonstrate how to use it first. The following steps walk you through a simple bézigon tool scenario. You'll create a free-form polygon composed entirely of corner points. In later sections, you'll create curves and add connector points.

 To select the bézigon tool from the keyboard, press the 8 key or Shift-F8. As you become more familiar with these tools, you'll probably find yourself regularly switching back and forth between the bézigon and pen tools. To access the pen tool, press 6 or Shift-F6.

STEPS: Drawing a Straight-Sided Polygon

Step 1. Select the bézigon tool and click at some location in the illustration window to create a corner point, which will represent a sharp corner in your path. The corner point appears as a tiny hollow square to show that it is selected. It is also *open-ended*, meaning that it doesn't have both a segment coming into it and a segment going out from it. In fact, this new corner point — I'll call it point A — is associated with no segment whatsoever. It is a lone point, open-ended in two directions.

Step 2. Click at a new location in the illustration to create a new corner point — point B. FreeHand automatically draws a straight segment from point A to point B, as illustrated in Figure 5-22. Notice that point A now appears solid rather than hollow. This shows that point A is the member of a selected path but is itself deselected. Point B is selected and open-ended. FreeHand automatically selects a point immediately after you create it and deselects all other points.

Bézigon tool

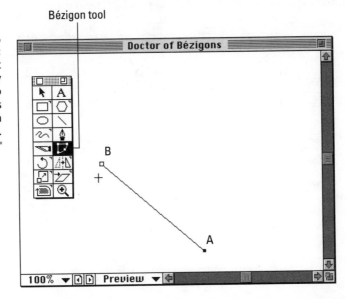

Figure 5-22:
Draw a straight segment by clicking at two separate locations with the bézigon tool.

Step 3.   Click a third time with the bézigon tool to create yet another corner point — point C. Because a point can be associated with no more than two segments, point B is no longer open-ended, as verified by Figure 5-23. Such a point is called an *interior point*.

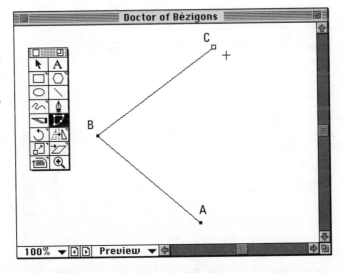

Figure 5-23:
Point B is now an interior point, incapable of receiving additional segments.

Step 4. You can keep adding points to a path one at a time for as long as you like. (Actually, FreeHand does limit you to about 1,000 points per path.) When finished, you can *close* the path by again clicking on point A, as shown in Figure 5-24. Since point A is open-ended, it willingly accepts the segment drawn between it and the previous point in the path.

Figure 5-24:
Clicking on the first point in a path closes the path and deactivates it. The next point you create begins a new path.

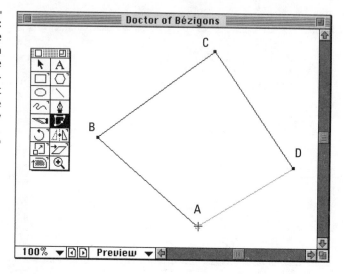

Step 5. All points in a closed path are interior points. Therefore, the path you just drew is no longer active, meaning that FreeHand will draw no segment between the next point you create and any point in the closed path. To verify this, click again with the bézigon tool. You create a new, independent point that is selected and open-ended in two directions, as shown in Figure 5-25. Meanwhile, the closed path becomes deselected. The path-creation process is begun anew.

Figure 5-25:
Creating a point E that is independent of the previous path deselects that path and begins a new one.

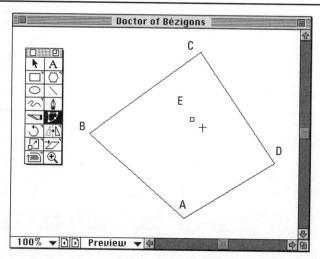

Drawing perpendicular segments

To constrain a point so that it is created at a multiple of 45 degrees from its predecessor, press Shift as you click with the bézigon tool. This technique allows you to create horizontal, vertical, and diagonal segments. In Figure 5-26, for example, I actually clicked at the location shown by the cross-shaped cursor. However, because I pressed the Shift key, point F was constrained to a 180-degree angle from point E, resulting in a horizontal segment.

You can alter the effect of pressing the Shift key by rotating the constraint axes. Just enter a value into the Constrain option box in the Document Setup panel of the Inspector palette, as described in "Geometric shapes at an angle," earlier in this chapter.

Figure 5-26:
Shift-click with the bézigon tool to create a horizontal, vertical, or diagonal segment.

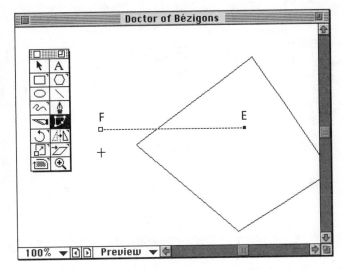

Drawing curved segments

When you Option-click with the bézigon tool, you create a curve point, which ensures a smooth arc between one curved segment and the next. A curve point sports two crosslike control handles. These handles act as levers, bending segments relative to the curve point itself.

Figure 5-27 shows a curve point bordered on either side by corner points. All three points are shown as they appear when selected. You can recognize the curve point because FreeHand displays it as a hollow circle, whereas the corner points are hollow squares. When not selected, both curve and corner points appear as black squares.

The small crosses are the Bézier control handles belonging to all three points. Each control handle is perched on the end of a lever. As you can see, the levers for the control handles associated with the curve point form a straight line. It is this alignment that forces the two segments on either side of the curve point to form an even, smooth arc.

Each of the corner points in Figure 5-27 also has a Bézier control handle. A curve point created with the bézigon tool always attaches a control handle to each of its neighboring points, regardless of their identity. This is a function of FreeHand's automatic curvature function, which is described in more detail in the "Why the pen tool is so great" section later in this chapter as well as the "Automatic curvature" section of Chapter 7.

Figure 5-27:
Option-clicking with the bézigon tool creates a curve point, which ensures a smooth arc between segments.

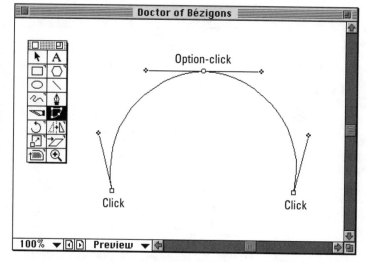

Curve points act no differently than corner points when it comes to building paths. You can easily combine curve and corner points in the same path by alternatively clicking and Option-clicking. If the first point in a path is a curve point, you can just click on it to close the path; you don't have to Option-click. If the first point is a corner point, Option-clicking on the point closes the path but does not convert the point from corner to curve. In other words, you can't change the identity of an existing point using the bézigon tool.

Creating smooth transitions

The connector point is a special point offered by FreeHand that ensures a smooth transition between straight and curved segments. As I mentioned earlier, you can create a connector point by Control-clicking with the bézigon tool.

Although some people will go their entire lives without once using these creatures (they don't even exist in competing applications such as Illustrator), connector points can be very useful in specific situations, as demonstrated in Figure 5-28.

Here, I created two archways, one of which features corner points near its base, and the other of which features connector points. (Connector points show up as hollow triangles when selected.) Each of the shapes in the archway features straight segments on the left and right sides of the base and curved segments near the top. When I positioned corner points at the intersections of the straight and curved segments, as in the rear example in the figure, FreeHand's automatic curvature routine caused the curves to bulge outward, resulting in definite corners. But when I redrew the archway using connector points, as in the forward example, I eliminated these corners.

Figure 5-28:
Corner points
result in corners
(left); connector
points ensure
smooth
transitions
between straight
and curved
segments (right).

Corner
points

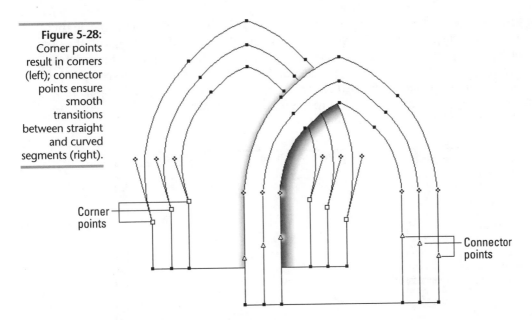

Connector
points

FreeHand ensures these smooth transitions by locking the Bézier control handle belonging to any connector point into alignment with the straight segment that precedes it. In the case of the archways, the straight segments associated with the connector points are vertically oriented, so the connector-point control handles are locked into vertical alignment. If I were to reshape these paths, I could move the connector point handles up and down, but not side to side.

Use connector points to create any straight path that ends in a rounded tip, such as a finger, bullet, or any other cylindrical object. Connector points can also be useful for creating rounded corners.

The versatile pen tool

Like the bézigon tool, the pen tool is capable of creating corner points, curve points, and connector points. But unlike the bézigon tool, it also enables you to precisely determine the placement and quantity of Bézier control handles. The pen tool offers less automatic software control and turns over more control to you. This means more freedom as well as more responsibility. It's just like growing up.

If you click with the pen tool, you create a corner point with no control handle. In this one respect, the pen tool works identically to the bézigon tool. If you drag with the pen tool, however, you create a curve point. The point at which you begin dragging determines the location of the curve point; the point at which you release becomes a Bézier control handle that affects the *next* segment you create. A second handle appears symmetrically about the curve point to the first. This handle determines the curvature of the most recent segment, as demonstrated in Figure 5-29.

Figure 5-29:
Drag with the pen tool to create a curve point flanked by two Bézier control handles.

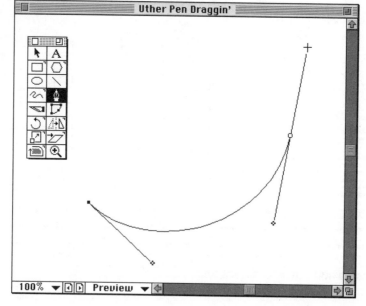

You might think of a curve point as if it were the center of a small seesaw, with the Bézier control handles acting as opposite ends. If you move one handle, the other handle moves in the opposite direction, and vice versa.

You can also create connector points by Control-dragging with the pen tool, but quite frankly, the bézigon tool is almost always better for this purpose. The problem with using the pen tool is that *you* have to do the work. *You* have to identify where the straight segment is and where the curved segment is going to be, or vice versa. *You* have to position the Bézier control handle. *You* have to make sure that you don't install the darn thing upside-down. *You're* in charge of everything. Because a connector point serves such a small and specific function, there's no sense in mucking around with it. Just Control-click with the bézigon tool and let FreeHand figure it out. Even super-advanced users will be glad they did.

Creating cusps

As I think I've mentioned a few times now — not sure, gettin' kinda senile — a curve point has two Bézier control handles, each positioned in an imaginary straight line with the point itself. A corner point, however, is much more versatile. It can have zero, one, or two handles.

To create a corner point that has one or two Bézier control handles — commonly called a *cusp* — press the Option key as you drag with the pen tool. If you press Option *before* dragging, you create a corner point with just one control handle that affects the next segment you create. If you press Option *after* you begin to drag but before you release the mouse button, you create a corner point with two independent control handles.

Suppose that you're dragging with the pen tool. As shown in the first example of Figure 5-30, the result is a curve point. The handle beneath your cursor controls the next segment that you create; the handle on the opposite side of the point controls the preceding segment. After correctly positioning the opposite handle — but before releasing the mouse button — you press the Option key. This changes the round curve point to a square corner point, as shown in the second example in Figure 5-30. While pressing Option, you can move the handle beneath your cursor independently of the handle for the preceding segment. This latter handle remains motionless as long as the Option key is pressed.

 If, while Option-dragging with the pen tool, you decide that you want to return the Bézier control handles to their original symmetrical configuration, simply release the Option key and continue dragging. The current corner point immediately changes back to a curve point.

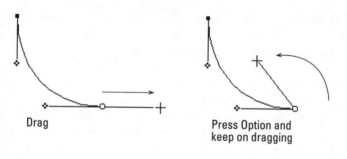

Figure 5-30:
Pressing Option while dragging with the pen tool changes the curve point (left) to a corner point with two independent Bézier control handles (right).

Three cusp point vignettes

To try out a few cusps on your own, check out the following steps, which provide three different examples of FreeHand's cusp-creation capabilities.

STEPS: Moving One Control Handle Independently of Another

Step 1.   Begin by drawing the path shown in Figure 5-31. You do so by dragging three times with the pen tool. First, drag downward from the right point (A). Then drag leftward from the bottom point (B). Finally, drag upward from the left point (C) — as shown in the figure — but do *not* release the mouse button.

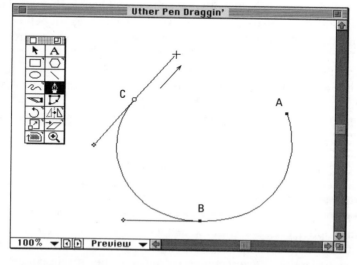

Figure 5-31:
Caught in the act of creating a curve point in a semicircular path with the pen tool.

Step 2. Suppose that you want to close the path with a concave top, resulting in a crescent shape (see Figure 5-34). All segments in this path are curved, and yet the upper segment meets with the lower segments to form two cusps. This means that you must change the two top curve points to corner points with two Bézier control handles apiece — one controlling the upper segment and one controlling a lower segment.

With the mouse button still down, press and hold the Option key. Now move your cursor downward, as indicated by the arrow in Figure 5-32, and release the mouse button and then the Option key. The handle affecting the next segment moves with your cursor while the other handle remains stationary. The result is a corner point with two control handles, each fully independent of the other.

Figure 5-32:
Press the
Option key and
continue your
drag downward
to convert the
curve point to a
cusp.

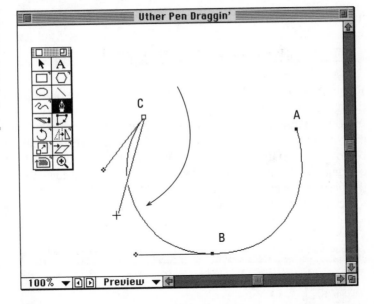

Step 3. Closing the path is a little bit tricky. In fact, what I'm about to show you is one of the least known and most useful tricks for closing a path. See, FreeHand's pen tool is generally very capable, except when it comes to closing paths. If you drag with the pen tool on the first point in the path, you're liable to make a mess of it. And if you only click on the first point, you sacrifice all control over the way in which the path closes. So don't do either. Instead of dragging on the first point, drag very near to it, at the location indicated by point D in Figure 5-33. As you drag upward, the control handle for the new segment moves downward, creating the concave portion of the segment. When your segment looks more or less like the one in the figure, pause your cursor but do *not* release the mouse button.

Figure 5-33:
Drag upward
from a location
near — but not
directly on —
the first point in
the path.

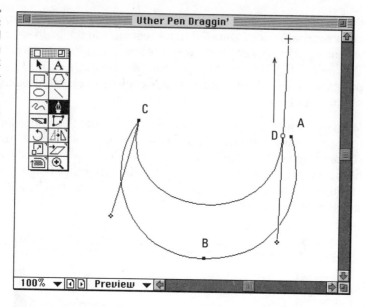

Step 4. Remember that tip a few pages back about moving a point by Command-dragging with the pen tool? Well, now's your chance to try it. With the mouse button still down, press and hold Command. Then move point D so that it exactly covers point A. As soon as the two points overlap, release the mouse button and then the Command key. Whenever two endpoints in the same path overlap, FreeHand automatically fuses the two into a single point and closes the path. In this case, fusing points A and D results in the conversion of point A to a cusp point with two independent control handles, as shown in Figure 5-34.

Figure 5-34:
Press the
Command key
and drop point
D onto point A
to close the
path.

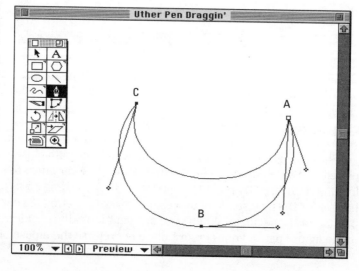

For more information on automatically joining endpoints in a path, see the "Auto joining" section of Chapter 7.

STEPS: Retracting a Curve Point Control Handle

Step 1. Begin again by drawing the path shown in Figure 5-31, as described in the first step of the preceding section.

Step 2. In these steps, you close the path with a flat top, resulting in a bowl shape (see Figure 5-36). Because curve points and Bézier control handles produce curved segments, you must convert points A and C to corner points and lop off one control handle from each point.

With the mouse button still down, press and hold the Option key. Then drag the control handle beneath the cursor back to point C, as shown in Figure 5-35, and release the mouse button and Option key. Notice that the Bézier control handle that would otherwise affect the next segment has disappeared. This technique is known as *retracting* a control handle.

If the control handle that you just tried to retract is still partially visible, press Command-Option-I to display the Object panel of the Inspector palette. Then click on the right-hand Curve Handles icon. This icon is highlighted and labeled in Figure 5-35.

Retract next control handle

Figure 5-35: Press Option and continue your drag back to point C, thereby retracting a control handle.

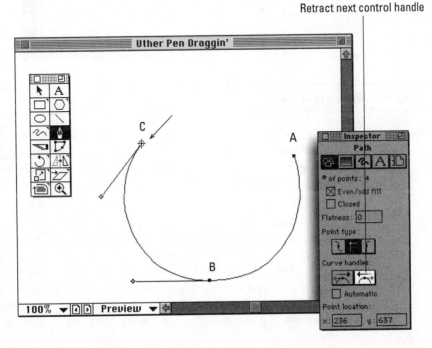

Step 3. Again, you'll be closing your path with the assistance of the Command key. Click and hold the mouse button at the location of point D in Figure 5-36. Do *not* move your mouse. With the mouse button still down, press and hold the Command key. Then drag point D onto point A and release the mouse button and then the Command key. FreeHand fuses points A and D into a single point, closing the shape. The new segment is flat, bordered on both sides by corner points with one Bézier control handle apiece.

Figure 5-36:
Press and hold
the mouse
button at point
D. Then press
the Command
key and drag
point D onto
point A.

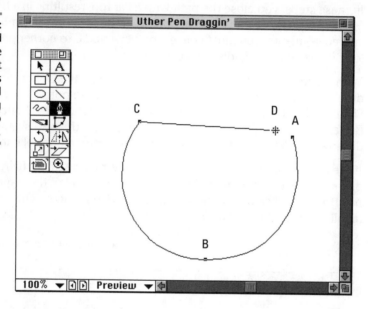

STEPS: Creating a Corner Point with One Handle

Step 1. This third exercise demonstrates how to create a corner point with only one Bézier control handle by pressing Option before dragging with the pen tool. Begin by creating a straight-sided path like the one shown in Figure 5-37. It doesn't matter how many points are in the path, just as long as they're all corner points.

Step 2. To prepare for the curved segment, press the Option key and drag to create a new corner point, like the selected point in Figure 5-37. Because the Option key is pressed, the pen tool automatically creates a corner point with only one Bézier control handle. The segment that connects the new point to its predecessor is straight because the control handle is positioned to affect the next segment you create. When you position the control handle where you want it, release the mouse button and then the Option key.

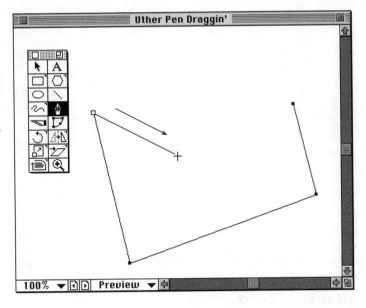

Figure 5-37: Option-drag to create a corner point with one control handle that will affect the next segment.

Step 3. To close the shape, drag near the first point in the path, as demonstrated in Figure 5-38. As in the previous path-closing steps, do *not* release the mouse button. You have created a new curve point that is linked to the most recent corner point by a curved segment.

Step 4. With the mouse button still down, press the Command key and move the curve point onto the first corner point in the path. FreeHand closes the shape and fuses the two points into a single corner point with a single Bézier control handle. The result is shown in Figure 5-39.

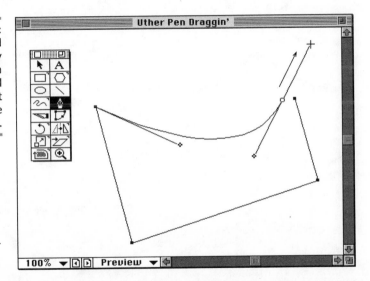

Figure 5-38: Create a curved segment by dragging with the pen tool near the first point in the path.

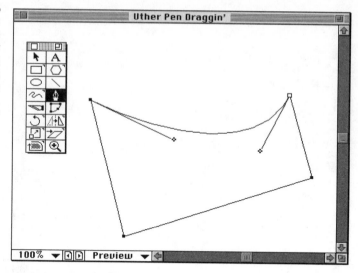

Figure 5-39:
Press the
Command key
and drop the
new curve point
onto the path's
first point.

Why the pen tool is so great

In time, you'll probably find that the pen tool is the tool of choice for creating complex paths, as opposed to tinkering with the bézigon tool. The reason is control. Take the fish shapes shown in Figures 5-40 and 5-41, for example. The top fish in each figure is the product of five corner points and five curve points, all created with the pen tool. By clicking, dragging, and Option-dragging, I manually specified the placement of each point and every Bézier control handle in the shape.

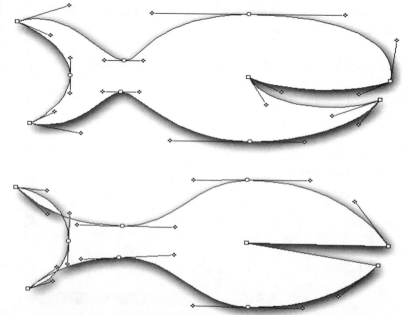

Figure 5-40:
The points in
a fish created
with the pen
tool (top) and
the bézigon
tool (bottom).

Figure 5-41:
The same fish as
they appear
when printed.

The bottom example in each figure shows the same shape drawn with the bézigon tool. Though each and every point is positioned identically to its pen-tool counterpart, the result is a rather malformed specimen, thanks to the repositioning and removing of key Bézier control handles. The culprit is FreeHand's built-in automatic curvature routine, which governs the placement of all control handles created with the bézigon tool. Automatic curvature encompasses a set of rules that guide the placement of Bézier control handles. The two simplest rules are as follows:

- Each point that neighbors a curve point gets one Bézier control handle pointing toward the curve point. The segment between the curve point and its neighbor is formed according to the definition of a circle and according to the locations of other neighboring points.

- If a corner point neighbors another corner point, the segment between the two points gets no Bézier control handle whatsoever and is therefore absolutely straight.

The first rule results in the distortion of the tail by exaggerating the curvature of its segments so that they appear like arcs in a circle. The second rule straightens out the mouth because the mouth is defined using corner points only.

I am not suggesting that by using the bézigon tool, you limit yourself to producing ugly results. In fact, automatic curvature has some real benefits, as discussed in Chapter 7. However, the results may not exactly suit your needs. The second example in each figure is, after all, a fish, but the first example shows the fish I wanted to create. The pen tool is the only tool among FreeHand's arsenal that is proficient enough to get the job done right the first time.

Summary

- Option-drag to draw a geometric shape from the center outward. Shift-drag to draw perfect squares and circles.

- Double-click on the polygon icon in the toolbox to change the number of sides in a polygon or adjust the angle of the points in a star.

- Rotating the constraint axes affects the angle at which rectangles, ellipses, and shapes created by Shift-dragging with the polygon tool are oriented.

- Press Command while dragging with the freehand tool to erase a line in progress. Option-drag to draw straight segments.

- Using the freehand tool, drag from the endpoint of an existing open path to extend the path or close it.

- While drawing variable weight paths with the freehand tool, press 1 or the left-arrow key to decrease the width of the path. Press 2 or the right-arrow key to fatten up the path.

- Press the Command key while dragging with the pen tool to move the point instead of its control handles.

- Press Option while dragging with the pen tool to break the symmetry of the curve point control handles, which converts the point to a cusp.

- Draw the last point in a path independently of the first and then Command-drag the last point onto the first to automatically close the path without upsetting the curvature of the neighboring segments.

Tracing an Imported Template

In This Chapter

- ➥ The benefits of tracing bitmapped sketches and scans

- ➥ Bitmapped image file formats

- ➥ How to place, position, and lock a tracing template

- ➥ Techniques for using the automated trace tool

- ➥ How FreeHand's tracing tool compares with Adobe Streamline, the stand-alone tracing program

- ➥ A slick method for tracing grayscale images

It Pays to Cheat

I know, that's not what your elementary school teacher taught you, but it's one of life's lessons that everyone must eventually learn. Simply put, starting from scratch is for losers. The folks who reap the big rewards in the shortest period of time are those who give themselves a boost up. They're looking out for number one. All that malarkey about a level playing field is a conspiracy cooked up years ago by a Communist fifth-column. The fact is, if you lift from a known quantity, you can't go wrong. It's the American way.

I'm speaking, of course, of cheating in FreeHand by introducing a tracing template. Wait, you thought I meant . . . and you were sitting there nodding your head in agreement? Oh, you *are* sick! You and your kind are exactly what's wrong with this great country.

Where'd I put that soapbox? (Ahem.) I am *not* condoning that you go around stealing artwork from your friends and neighbors. Okay, sure, 2 Live Crew showed us all that you can steal a Roy Orbison song and call it a parody. But don't be scanning copyrighted artwork, converting it in FreeHand, and calling it your own. That's absolutely verboten. Well, more or less verboten, anyway. I mean, there's the old criticism-and-commentary loophole. And artists have been seeking "inspiration" from other artists since the beginning of time.

On second thought, you look to me like you need a good lawyer.

A trace of tradition

What I really have in mind is tracing from noncopyrighted material as well as original sketches and compositions. It's a cheat, I grant you, but it's the kind of cheat that artists have been relying on for years. You think that Edouard Manet just started slapping paint on the canvas when he created his revolutionary *Le Déjeuner sur l'Herbe*? No way. First, he sketched a bunch of folks enjoying a picnic. Then he thought, "You know, what this picture really needs is a naked woman." Manet was a big believer that a naked woman spiced up any environment. So he dug through his vast collection of bordello sketches and found an appropriate subject, one who looked like she could go for some KFC and coleslaw. Doubtless, he combined a few other sketches and maybe even tried out an egg tempura treatment or two. Finally, after he had successfully assembled all his elements, he embarked on the final painting.

I'm guessing that's how it went, anyway. I wasn't there, so I have to rely on the testimony of the few witnesses who are still available. Considering that this all happened in 1863, the number of reliable witnesses is kind of limited. And they all spoke French.

But that's not the point. The point is that although few of us can live up to Manet's artistic prowess, we can all mimic his approach. Not the naked woman part, necessarily — misogyny is best left to experts like 2 Live Crew — but the tradition of preliminary sketch followed by final execution.

FreeHand enables you to trace scanned images and artwork created in painting programs. It also automates the conversion process by providing a trace tool. Even skilled computer artists are well advised to sketch their ideas on paper or in a painting program before executing them in FreeHand. The following section explains why.

Why trace a bitmap?

It's not easy to draw from scratch in FreeHand. Even if you draw exclusively with the freehand tool, you frequently have to edit your lines and shapes, point by point (as I discuss in the next chapter, "Reshaping and Combining Paths").

Also, to build an image in FreeHand, you have to do just that: *build.* You have to combine heaps of mathematically-defined lines and shapes and layer them much like girders at a construction site. (Don't you just love these analogies? I've got tons more where these came from.)

In fact, you'll probably have the most luck with FreeHand if you're part artist and part engineer. But for those of us who aren't engineers and can't even *imagine* how engineers think, a painting application such as Photoshop or Painter provides a more artist-friendly environment.

Painting programs provide straightforward tools such as pencils and erasers, which work just like their real-life counterparts. Your screen displays the results of your mouse movements instantaneously. You can draw, see what you've drawn, and make alterations in the time it takes the appropriate neurons to fire in your brain.

But despite the many advantages of painting programs, their single failing — grainy output — can be glaringly obvious, so much so that people who have never used a computer can recognize a bitmapped image as computer-produced artwork. Object-oriented drawings, on the other hand, are always smooth.

The jagged nature of images produced with painting programs is particularly noticeable in the case of black-and-white artwork. For example, the bitmapped fish in Figure 6-1 was fairly easy to create. The fish is well executed, but its jagged edges are far too obvious for it to be considered professional-quality artwork. By introducing a few shades of gray to the image, I softened much of its jaggedness, as illustrated in Figure 6-2. However, the fish now looks muddy and out of focus. Continuous-tone bitmaps are better suited to representing photographs than line art.

Figure 6-1:
A typically jagged black-and-white bitmapped image.

Figure 6-2:
Gray pixels soften the edges but also obscure details.

Only in a drawing application such as FreeHand can you create pristine line art. The fish in Figure 6-3, for example, required more time and effort to produce, but the result is a smooth, highly focused, professional-quality image.

Figure 6-3: By tracing the bitmapped fish image in FreeHand, I was able to create this smooth, exemplary drawing.

Importing Tracing Templates _____

Whether you sketch your idea on a sheet of paper and then scan it into your computer or sketch it directly in a painting application, you can import the sketch as a *tracing template* into FreeHand. FreeHand can import any bitmapped image that is saved in one of the following standardized graphic formats:

- **MacPaint:** MacPaint documents may originate not only from MacPaint itself but also from other low-end painting programs (such as DeskPaint and SuperPaint) and from scanning applications such as ThunderWare. The MacPaint format is one of the most widely supported graphics formats for the Mac. Unfortunately, it is also the most limited. The MacPaint format accommodates *monochrome* (black-and-white) images on vertically-oriented, 7 1/2 × 10 1/2-inch pages containing a maximum of 72 dots per inch.

- **PICT (QuickDraw picture):** The PICT format, commonly associated with moderately powerful drawing applications such as MacDraw and Canvas, is much more flexible. PICT is the original file-swapping format developed by Apple for transferring bitmapped and object-oriented pictures from one graphics application to another. PICT can accommodate any size graphic, resolutions exceeding 300 dots per inch, and over 16 million colors. For this reason, nearly all scanning and image-editing applications support this format.

Don't be surprised if you encounter an out-of-memory error when you import a color bitmap saved in the PICT format. Because FreeHand provides much more reliable support for the TIFF format, you may avoid most memory problems by saving your color scans and paintings as TIFF documents.

↪ **TIFF (Tag Image File Format):** Like MacPaint, the TIFF format is exclusively a bitmapped format. But, like PICT, it is otherwise unrestricted, accommodating graphics of any size, resolutions exceeding 300 dots per inch, and over 16 million colors. Aldus developed TIFF in an attempt to standardize images created by various scanners. Nearly all scanning and image-editing programs support the TIFF format.

↪ **EPS (Encapsulated PostScript):** The EPS format combines a pure PostScript-language description of a graphic with a PICT-format screen representation. Altsys (the developers of FreeHand) created the EPS format in cooperation with Aldus and Adobe. It's designed for swapping high-resolution images from one PostScript-compatible application to another. It is not, however, an efficient format for saving bitmaps. A color EPS bitmap, for example, is typically two to three times as large as the same bitmap saved in the TIFF format.

The PICT and TIFF formats offer compression options to save space on disk. If QuickTime is running on your computer, many applications can apply JPEG compression to PICT files. Regardless of QuickTime, you can compress TIFF files using the LZW protocol. FreeHand does not support the PICT format with JPEG compression but it does support the TIFF format with LZW compression.

Due to the poor performance of the PICT and EPS formats, I heartily recommend that you save all images in the TIFF format (with LZW compression, if available) before importing them for tracing.

Kinds of tracing templates

Tracing templates fall into three broad categories:

↪ **Scans:** Scans are electronic images of photographs, prints, or drawings. Old black-and-white scans lying on dusty, forgotten disks are commonly saved as MacPaint documents. Grayscale and color scans are typically saved in the PICT and TIFF formats. Scans offer exceptionally accurate tracing backgrounds, especially when taken from photographs. They are useful for detail work such as producing schematic drawings, medical illustrations, and other documents that require the utmost accuracy. Scans are also useful for people who want to draw but don't consider themselves very skilled at it. Scans can be the perfect bridge between an amateur effort and a professional product.

ᴄᴏ **Sketches:** Sketching is deeply embedded in the artistic tradition. If you were creating an oil painting, for example, you might make several sketches before deciding how the finished piece should look. Like oil paint, FreeHand is ill suited to sketching. Sketches are best created in painting applications, which provide environments conducive to spontaneity. You can scribble, erase, and create much as you do when you use a pencil — quickly and freely.

ᴄᴏ **Drafts:** Drafts include CAD (*computer-aided design*), schematic, or structured drawings created in MacDraw, MacDraft, Claris CAD, and similar applications. Such drafting programs rarely provide the array of free-form illustration tools and sophisticated transformation and special-effects capabilities available in FreeHand. Draft templates are typically transported via the PICT format.

Placing a template file

To import a template — whatever its format — into an open FreeHand illustration, follow these steps:

STEPS: Placing a Template Image

Step 1. Choose File ➪ Place or press Command-Shift-D. FreeHand displays the Place Document dialog box, as shown in Figure 6-4.

Figure 6-4:
Select the tracing template you want to import in the Place Document dialog box.

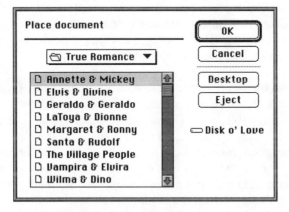

Step 2. Select a template file from the scrolling list and press Return. FreeHand reads the file from disk and displays the place cursor, as shown in the first example of Figure 6-5.

Figure 6-5:
Click with the
place cursor
(left) to
position the
upper left
corner of an
imported
template
(right).

Place cursor

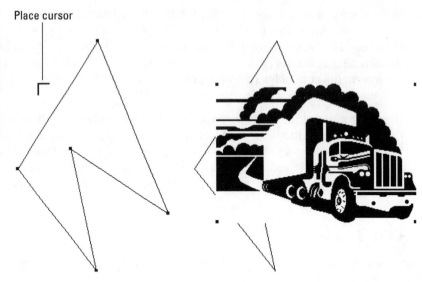

Step 3.   Click with the place cursor to specify the location of the upper left corner
of the template. FreeHand displays the selected template image in the
illustration window at actual size. All previously selected objects become
deselected, as shown in Figure 6-5.

By dragging with the place cursor, you can place a graphic and scale it at the same time.
When you release the mouse button, FreeHand scales the imported graphic to fill the
area surrounded by your drag. The resizing is always proportional, so that the horizontal and vertical dimensions of the imported graphic are equally affected.

For best results, send the template image to a background layer. To do this, just click on
the Background option in the Layers palette while the template is selected. (If the
Layers palette is not available, press Command-6.) The template then appears grayed,
as shown in Figure 6-6, which makes it easier to distinguish from paths and other
objects in your illustration. Also, you can display imported artwork on a background
layer in both the preview and keyline modes, while you can display imported artwork
that's on a foreground layer only in the preview mode. And background artwork does
not print, so you can isolate it from the actual illustration.

After you send the template to the background layer, be sure to press the Tab key and
click on Foreground in the Layers palette. Otherwise, you will end up tracing your
object-oriented paths on the background layer along with the template.

Lock icon

Figure 6-6:
A tracing template
appears grayed
when placed on a
background layer,
making it easier to
trace.

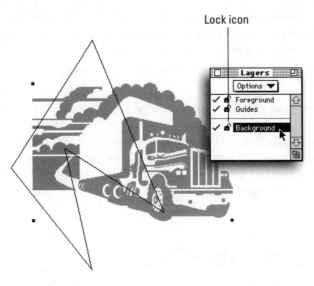

 To protect the template so that you don't accidentally move or otherwise alter it, click on the lock icon in front of the Background option in the Layers palette. The lock icon changes from unlocked (open) to locked (closed). With the template locked, you'll also have fewer problems selecting and manipulating objects in your illustration.

Pasting a template file

You can also import a template via the Macintosh Clipboard. You just use the Cut, Copy, and Paste commands common to the Edit menus of all Mac applications. The following steps explain how.

STEPS: Copying and Pasting a Template Image

Step 1. While inside a painting program (such as Photoshop), select the portion of the picture you want to use as a template and choose Edit ➪ Copy (Command-C).

Step 2. Switch to the FreeHand application. If FreeHand is currently running, choose the FreeHand icon from the list of running applications in the Applications menu. If FreeHand is not currently running, double-click on the FreeHand icon at the Finder level to launch the program.

Step 3. After FreeHand is running, choose Edit ⇨ Paste (Command-V). FreeHand displays the copied template image in the center of the illustration window (not necessarily in the center of the page).

As is the case when placing a graphic, you may encounter an out-of-memory error when pasting a color bitmap from the Clipboard, thanks to FreeHand's less reliable handling of the PICT format. So my earlier recommendation still stands: The most successful method for importing a grayscale or color template is to save it as a TIFF document and import it into FreeHand using the Place command in the File menu.

Automated Tracing

You can use any of the drawing tools I discussed in Chapter 5 to trace a bitmapped image. Just follow the outline of the bitmap using the tools as directed in that chapter. However, if the process seems too complicated, or if you just want to speed things up, FreeHand provides an additional drawing tool that automates the tracing process: the trace tool. The remainder of this chapter tells you everything you need to know to use this amazing device.

The trace tool

You can use the trace tool — the last tool on the left side of the toolbox — to trace the borders of a template image. To operate the trace tool, just drag to create a rectangular marquee around the portion of the template that you want to trace. FreeHand does the rest.

Using the trace tool is certainly easier than tracing a template image by hand. Unfortunately — you knew there had to be a catch, didn't you? — the results are less precise and require more adjustments than paths you create with the pen tool or even the freehand tool.

Take a look at the hornet in Figure 6-7. The following steps explain how to use the trace tool to convert a low-resolution, jagged-as-all-get-out image like this one to a mathematically precise, object-oriented one.

Figure 6-7:
The fuzzy nature of this low-resolution image is no doubt making this fellow mad as a hornet.

STEPS: Operating the Trace Tool

Step 1. Import your bitmap image using either the Place or Paste command, as explained earlier in this chapter.

Step 2. With the imported image selected, click on the Background option in the Layers palette to send the template to the background layer. The image then appears grayed in the illustration window. You're now ready to convert the image with the trace tool.

Step 3. Press the Tab key to deselect the template. Then click on the Foreground option in the Layers palette to make sure that FreeHand doesn't send your traced paths to the background layer.

Step 4. Drag with the trace tool as if you were drawing a rectangle around the template image. A marquee tracks the movements of your cursor, as shown in Figure 6-8. After the marquee entirely surrounds the template, release the mouse button. Several seconds later — or, if the template is very detailed, several lifetimes later — FreeHand produces a collection of selected closed paths that trace the various outlines of the template, as shown in Figure 6-9.

Trace tool

Figure 6-8:
Drag with the
trace tool to
marquee the
entire template
image.

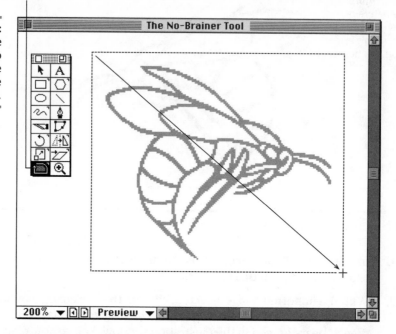

Figure 6-9:
FreeHand
automatically
produces
several closed
paths that
trace the
outline of the
marqueed
image.

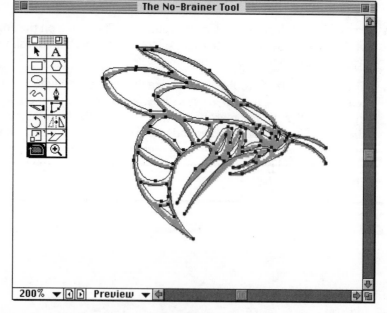

The trace tool always produces closed paths. Even if you drag the marquee around the template image of a line, FreeHand traces entirely around the line to create a long and very thin shape.

Trace curve fit

FreeHand lets you control the sensitivity of the trace tool by using the Tight check box in the Tracing Tool dialog box. To access this option, double-click on the trace tool icon in the toolbox.

Selecting the Tight check box results in a tight curve fit — just as it does when you use the freehand tool. A tight curve fit causes FreeHand to trace every single pixel of a bitmapped template. If you deselect the option, the software ignores jags in the outline of a template image and smooths out excessively imprecise forms.

Figure 6-10 shows how FreeHand interprets the hornet image differently depending on the selection of the Tight option. I created the path on left with Tight selected; I created the path on right with the option deselected. The two circled areas in each hornet highlight major differences between the two images.

Figure 6-10:
The results of selecting (left) and deselecting (right) the Tight check box in the Tracing Tool dialog box. Circled areas highlight major differences.

If you compare these images to those back in Figure 5-12, you can see that the Tight option affects the performance of the trace tool and freehand tool very similarly. However, with the trace tool, you adjust the curve fit to compensate for inaccuracies in the image you are tracing. With the freehand tool, you adjust for inaccuracies in your drawing ability.

All paths that you create with the trace tool are filled and stroked with the default attributes. So to complete a traced image, you need to apply your desired fill and stroke to each path, as explained in Chapters 13 and 14. Figure 6-11 shows the hornet paths (created with the Tight option on) filled and stroked to match the template.

Figure 6-11:
I filled and stroked the hornet to match the template image.

Image size

More important than curve fit is the size of your tracing template. Your image should be as large as possible; that is, the more pixels the better. You probably guessed as much — after all, it only makes sense that FreeHand can trace an image containing a lot of detail better than one that contains very little detail. As of yet, FreeHand isn't smart enough to make up detail on its own, so it has to rely on the image to provide as much information as possible.

However, you can also get better results from an image simply by scaling it. FreeHand is most successful at tracing when each and every pixel of the template image is visible at the 100 percent view size. The best way to accomplish this is to save the image to disk — whether from Photoshop or some other application — at a resolution of *exactly* 72 dots per inch, which is the resolution of a standard Macintosh monitor. (Even if your screen's resolution is slightly different, 72 will work just fine.) Regardless of what you've heard about images looking better at higher resolutions, they trace better in FreeHand at low resolutions.

To prove my point, I traced the image in Figure 6-11 at 72 dots per inch. To create the awful mess shown in Figure 6-12, I scaled the image to 50 percent of its original size — thereby increasing the resolution of the image to 144 dots per inch — and again marqueed the image with the trace tool. (The number of pixels in an image remains fixed inside FreeHand; therefore, reducing the size of an image squishes its pixels together and increases the resolution.) FreeHand is tracing the exact same image in both cases, so you might expect it to produce the exact same result. But in fact, the trace tool can only see half as much detail in the second image.

Figure 6-12:
The image from Figure
6-7 traced at a
resolution of 144 dots
per inch.

When in doubt, use the scale tool or Transform palette to increase the size of the image. For complete information on tool and palette, see Chapter 15.

Tracing layer control

The two last options in the Tracing Tool dialog box enable you to tell FreeHand which elements within a trace tool marquee should be evaluated. The options are incredibly straightforward, but here's an explanation just in case: Select the Trace Background check box to trace any marqueed images on a background layer; select the Trace Foreground check box to trace any marqueed images on the foreground layer. Phew, glad I was there to help.

Here's an example. Suppose that your illustration involves two bitmapped images, one directly in front of another. If one image is positioned on a background layer and the other is on some foreground layer, you can use the options in the Tracing Tool dialog box to trace one image without tracing the other. For more information about layering, read the section "Layering Objects" in Chapter 8.

Note that FreeHand traces *everything* surrounded by a marquee — not just the imported image but objects created directly inside FreeHand as well. When you're working inside a complicated illustration, play it safe: Keep the tracing template on the background layer and turn off the Trace Foreground check box.

Tracing Comparisons

The trace tool's greatest strengths are that it traces images automatically and can create more than one path at a time — a talent that no other drawing tool can claim. However, don't mistake it for a precise drawing tool. More often than not, you will have to spend a lot of time reshaping your traced paths, as described in the next chapter.

Sadly, the FreeHand trace tool offers fewer sensitivity controls than it did two versions ago. Very likely, the programmers thought that the old controls were too difficult for users to understand. The good news, however, is that the trace tool produces more reliable results than it did in the old days. Fewer options, better results — for many users, this is a perfect match. But try to see it from my point of view: Who's going to buy my books if there aren't a few complicated options to explain?

If you have a few hundred bucks to spare, you can buy software that's better equipped than FreeHand to convert bitmaps into object-oriented drawings. Adobe Streamline 3.0, which will set you back about $199, can automatically convert multiple paintings at a time — and at a level of quality that neither FreeHand nor Illustrator can match.

Just in case you're interested in how well FreeHand 4.0's trace tool works in comparison to the tracing capabilities of FreeHand 2.0 and Streamline 3.0, I set up a little experiment. Figure 6-13 shows another in my series of low-resolution, black-and-white images that seem to be coming into vogue in this chapter. The challenge is that the painting features a lot of loose pixels, which are very difficult for any application to trace.

Figure 6-13:
A mono-
chrome
painting
composed
largely of loose
shading pixels.

Figure 6-14 shows the results of marqueeing the eagle template with the trace tools supplied by FreeHand Versions 2.0 and 4.0. Tight curve-fit settings were in force when I created both illustrations. The results are similar, but Version 4.0 does a better job of catching the lines along the back of the eagle's head and the contours of its mouth. FreeHand 2.0, however, better handles the stars by more accurately translating the sides of the shapes as straight edges. The reason for this is that back in FreeHand 2.0, you had control over the sharpness of corners drawn with the trace tool, a setting that was sacrificed — I think wrongly — in FreeHand 3.0.

Figure 6-14:
The eagle template traced inside FreeHand 2.0 (top) and 4.0 (bottom).

Figure 6-15 shows the image interpreted by Streamline. Thanks to Streamline's more precise controls, you can see — even under brief scrutiny — that the conversion in Figure 6-15 is more accurate and more elegant than those in the preceding figure. Notice, for example, that the line defining the back of the eagle's head is unbroken. Streamline also catches more detail inside and around the eye and underneath the beak.

Figure 6-15:
The eagle
according to
Adobe
Streamline.

In all fairness, when you consider that I'm comparing a single FreeHand feature to an entire stand-alone utility, the trace tool performs quite admirably. In fact, if FreeHand provided a few more controls and automatically filled its paths (as does Streamline), I would find it very difficult to justify the purchase of Streamline to any but the most affluent user. Of course, judging by the fact that I first wrote that last sentence four years ago, I don't think that you should hold your breath.

Tracing Grayscale Images

Although you can import color images saved in the PICT, TIFF, or EPS format, FreeHand's trace tool will not necessarily interpret color images accurately. The trace tool treats *all* images as if they were monochrome, seeing only two color levels. It sees all colors that are lighter than medium gray as white; it sees all colors that are darker than medium gray as black. Figures 6-16 and 6-17 demonstrate how the trace tool interprets a typical grayscale scan.

Figure 6-16:
A color template is displayed accurately in the FreeHand illustration window (top), but the trace tool can only identify its black and white components (bottom).

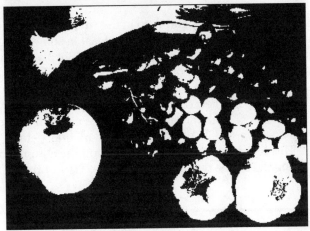

In other words, regardless of whether you trace the color image or the monochrome image shown in Figure 6-16, you get the result shown in Figure 6-17, because the trace tool sees them the same way. The color image takes longer to trace, however, because FreeHand has to spend more time computing the boundaries between the light and dark portions of the image.

 To trace a color scan, first marquee the image with the trace tool. After FreeHand finishes its automated tracing, use the freehand, bézigon, and/or pen tools (described in Chapter 5) to manually trace any details that the trace tool ignored.

Figure 6-17:
The still life image
as converted by
the trace tool.

Okay, okay, so that's not the most insightful tip in the world. Actually, I have a much better tip for you, but it's harder to describe and, at least in some respects, messier to execute. And unfortunately, it only works on grayscale scans. But it's still one heck of a tip.

Because FreeHand is capable of seeing 16 levels of gray in a grayscale scan, you can isolate and trace each of those levels one at a time. Then, you can apply a different fill to each set of traced objects. For example, after tracing the medium gray details in an image, you apply a medium gray fill. After tracing the dark gray details, you apply a dark gray fill, and so on. This technique enables you to exploit the automation of the trace tool without sacrificing the subtle details in your image. Try out the following steps to see how it works.

STEPS: Tracing a Grayscale Image One Level at a Time

Step 1.   Before importing a color image into FreeHand, convert the image from color to grayscale in your painting or image-editing software. Most of the detail will be retained, but FreeHand will be better able to interpret the image. Save the grayscale image as a TIFF document.

Step 2.   Import the template and send it to the Background layer. Be sure to press the Tab key and select the Foreground layer to make that layer active again.

Step 3.   Click on the bitmap to select it again and Command-Option-B to display the Object panel of the Inspector palette. (If the Inspector palette is not available, first press Command-I.) Then click on the Edit Image button to display the Image dialog box, shown in Figure 6-18.

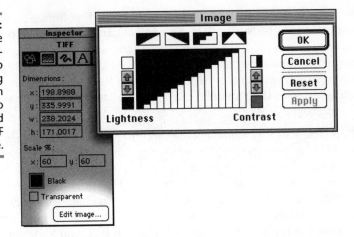

Figure 6-18:
The Edit Image button (spotlighted) brings up the Image dialog box, which enables you to edit an imported grayscale TIFF image.

Described in depth in Chapter 18, "Importing and Exporting Graphics," the Image dialog box enables you to edit each of the 16 gray values that exist in an imported bitmap. You do your editing by dragging up and down on the 16 vertical bars that form a stair-step pattern in the center of the dialog box. Dragging up on a bar lightens the corresponding gray value; dragging down darkens the value. Because the trace tool can only discern one color at a time (as in black against a white background), you can use the Image dialog box to isolate each of the 16 gray values, one by one.

Step 4. Click on the Cancel button in the Image dialog box. (You'll do your editing in a later step; for the moment, I just wanted you to see exactly what you'll be dealing with.)

Step 5. Now click on the Transparent check box at the bottom of the Object panel in the Inspector palette. FreeHand converts the template to a black-and-white image. That's FreeHand's way of telling you that all the dark grays have become black and all the light grays have become white. The image, which previously appeared as shown in the first example of Figure 6-16, has now been *polarized* so that it looks like the second example in that figure.

Step 6. Marquee the image with the trace tool. FreeHand automatically traces the bitmap, just as it would have if you hadn't checked the Transparent option. But it does the job faster because you clearly identified the blacks and whites for the trace tool. Human being aids machine. Flesh and plastic working in perfect harmony. It's truly beautiful, babe.

Step 7. FreeHand has just traced everything that is darker than medium gray. Fill all these objects with medium gray (50 percent gray). You segregate and fill areas that are darker than medium gray in later steps.

Step 8.   Again, with the template selected, click on the Edit Image button in the Inspector palette. Notice that the vertical bars have shifted to form a new pattern. Half of the bars have moved all the way down so that you can no longer see them; the other half have moved all the way up. By selecting Transparent, you isolated all values lighter than medium gray from those that are darker than medium gray. Now you must isolate the very darkest values from the others.

To isolate any gray value, just change all the other gray values to white. Try clicking near the top of the box containing the vertical bars, inside the black area. One of the vertical bars will jump to the top of the box, as shown in the first example in Figure 6-19. That gray value is now converted to white. Now drag along the top of the box to change all gray values except the very darkest shade (represented by the leftmost bar) to white, as shown in the second example of Figure 6-19. If you accidentally display the leftmost bar, click at the base of the bar to hide it.

Figure 6-19: Click above a single bar (top) to make a single gray value white. Drag across the top of the box (bottom) to change multiple gray values to white.

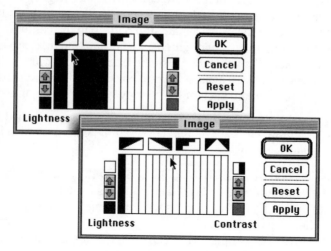

Step 9.   Press Return to implement your changes to the selected image. Only the darkest pixels in the template image remain visible, as shown in Figure 6-20. For the sake of comparison, the figure also shows the paths created in Step 6 with the trace tool. These paths represent the previous boundaries of the image.

Step 10.   Again marquee the image with the trace tool. If you have not deselected the Trace Foreground check box in the Tracing Tool dialog box — as I specifically told you to do back in the "Tracing layer control" section — an alert box appears, informing you that you are trying to trace items of different resolutions. In other words, you are trying to trace both a

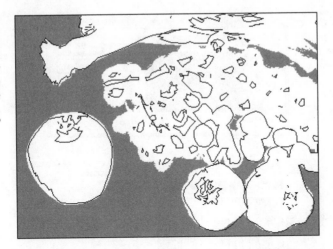

Figure 6-20:
The background template as it appears after changing all but the darkest gray value to white.

bitmapped image and object-oriented paths. The bitmapped image is the template. The object-oriented paths are the ones you created when you used the trace tool back in Step 6. There's no reason to retrace the paths, so click on the Cancel button or press Command-period. (If this alert box does not appear, skip to Step 12.)

Step 11. Double-click on the trace tool icon in the toolbox to display the Tracing Tool dialog box. Assuming that the tracing template is on a background layer and the object-oriented paths are on a foreground layer, you can isolate the template image by deselecting the Trace Foreground check box. Press Return to implement your change.

Step 12. Again marquee the image with the trace tool. FreeHand traces the template, this time isolating the dark grays, to create a new set of paths. Fill these new objects with dark gray and send them to the back of the drawing (Command-B).

Step 13. Continue isolating and filling each of the remaining gray levels. Put the darkest grays at the back of the drawing and the lightest at the front. For example, to trace all but the very lightest value, drag along the bottom of the bars in the Image dialog box to hide all except the rightmost bar, as in Figure 6-21. Depending on how accurate you want your converted image to be (and how much time you want to spend on this project), you won't necessarily want to isolate every one of the 16 gray values. However, you probably will want to isolate the medium-dark and medium-light gray values, as shown in Figure 6-22. Marquee the image with the trace tool between each alteration in the Image dialog box. The completed illustration should look something like the one in Figure 6-23.

Figure 6-21:
Drag along the bottom of the bars to blacken all but the lightest gray value.

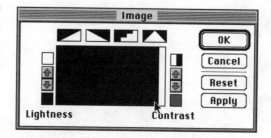

Figure 6-22:
You'll also probably want to isolate the medium dark gray values (top) and medium light gray values (bottom).

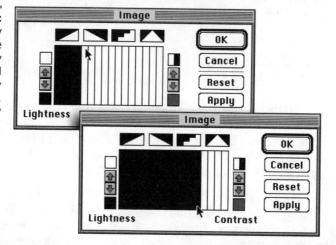

Figure 6-23:
The still life created by isolating and tracing each of five gray values.

For more information on filling paths, see Chapter 13. For an explanation of how layers work in a drawing, read Chapter 8.

To simplify the process of filling and stroking traced paths, press the Tab key to deselect all objects. Then change the colors in the Fill and Stroke panels of the Inspector palette before each application of the trace tool. In this way, you can determine the fill and stroke of traced paths *before* you create them. This technique helps distinguish one round of traced paths from the next. (See Chapters 13 and 14 for the full story.) You may also want to choose Arrange ⇨ Group after each application of the trace tool to group each round of traced paths.

There's no denying that this technique is complicated and time-consuming, but until FreeHand automates the process of tracing gray values, this is the most efficient means available. And, if you compare Figure 6-23 to Figure 6-17, you can see that your additional effort is well rewarded.

■ ■

Summary

- ➡ It's much easier to draw in a painting program or image editor than it is to construct paths in FreeHand.

- ➡ TIFF is the best format for storing bitmapped images that you want to use as tracing templates in FreeHand.

- ➡ After moving the template to the Background layer, click on the lock icon in the Layers palette to lock that layer. This way, you won't accidentally move the template while tracing it.

- ➡ Make sure that you can see every pixel in your imported image at actual view size. This ensures the highest degree of accuracy from the trace tool.

- ➡ FreeHand's trace tool isn't as capable as Adobe Streamline, but it doesn't cost an extra $200, either.

- ➡ Use the Image dialog box to isolate gray levels in an image so that you can trace them.

■ ■

Reshaping and Combining Paths

In This Chapter

➻ Selecting objects and elements inside objects with the arrow tool

➻ Resizing and reshaping geometric shapes

➻ Moving, constraining, and snapping points

➻ Changing the curvature of segments by dragging Bézier control handles

➻ Adding points to a path and adding control handles to points

➻ Deleting points and retracting control handles

➻ Changing the identity of a point between corner, curve, and connector

➻ Closing an open path and joining two open paths into one

➻ Combining paths using FreeHand's Intersect, Punch, and Union commands

➻ Slicing through selected paths with the knife tools

➻ Using the Undo, Redo, and Revert commands

The Forgiving Medium

Sometimes I think that Michelangelo made a mistake when he decided to take up marble sculpting. It's got to be the world's least forgiving medium. The integrity of the stone is inconsistent — one moment impervious, the next moment fragile. You have to swing the hammer like a pick ax to shave away small details from the body of the piece, while all it takes is a misplaced tap to knock off a delicate extremity. *Chink*. Oops, there goes the nose. *Pang*. Uh oh, there goes a finger. *Fwack*. Oh, *David*, buddy, that's got to hurt. Then again, maybe I can use it in my next piece, *Josephine and What's Left of Napoleon*. Okay, to keep things proportional, I'd have to make Josephine over 200 feet tall, but hey, waste not, want not.

Meanwhile, getting back to Michelangelo, I just don't think that he had the temperament for the whole sculpting scene. The city of Florence is teeming with his half-finished masterpieces, works that he either abandoned in disgust or willfully attacked in fits of rage. It wouldn't surprise me to find out that the guy who whacked off *David's* toe in the Galleria dell' Accademia a couple of years back was the reincarnation of Michelangelo intent on wreaking further damage on his work.

Okay, I guess that might surprise me. But if Michelangelo were to come to me today, I'd certainly feel compelled to put my hand on his shoulder and gently counsel him to stick with pencil and paper. "You can erase a pencil mark," I'd tell him. "No need to hack the paper to bits or burn it or anything. Just *rub, rub, rub,* and the mistake vanishes like a bad dream.

"Better yet, Michel . . . can I call you Mike? *You* should try out FreeHand. Really, it's a great program. You got a Mac, Mike? Windows? Well, then, you're set. You see, after you create a graphic object in FreeHand, the object is by no means permanent. You can *reshape* any path. Obviously, if you do most of your drawing with the freehand and trace tools, your paths are going to *need* some reshaping. But even if you're a pen tool master, you'll probably end up adjusting most of the paths you create. Reshaping in FreeHand is like painting over the same area on a canvas . . . . Well, then, it's like painting on a fresco, Mike. The point is, it's a fine-tuning process."

You never know. Michelangelo might not have listened to me. By the time the guy was my age, he had polished off two of the world's great masterpieces and was getting ready to start on the Sistine Chapel. So fine, if the guy wants to waste his life on marble, that's his funeral. I just think that maybe he could have really amounted to something if he had given FreeHand half a chance.

But enough about Michelangelo. What you're really interested in is developing *your* artistic talents, not those of some long-gone Italian. To that end, this chapter shows you how to fine-tune your FreeHand masterpieces by reshaping and combining paths.

Selecting and Deselecting

Before you can reshape a path, you have to *select* it. Selecting a path in FreeHand is not unlike selecting an element in some other object-oriented program on the Macintosh. You just position your arrow tool cursor over part of an object and click. Points or corner handles appear on the selected object to indicate that the next action you perform will affect it.

Selecting paths

Like most manipulations covered in this chapter, selecting is performed with the arrow tool (which some folks call the *selection* or *pointer tool*), the first tool in the toolbox. Clicking on a point or segment with the arrow tool selects the path that contains the element.

 You can access the arrow tool when any drawing tool is selected by pressing and holding the Command key. As soon as you release the Command key, FreeHand returns control to the selected tool. To permanently access the arrow tool, press Shift-F10.

Different kinds of paths have different ways of showing that they're selected. For example, if you click on a rectangle or ellipse, four small, black *corner handles* surround the shape, as illustrated in Figure 7-1. These handles signify that the selection comprises *grouped objects* that may be subject to special manipulations, as described in the "Reshaping Rectangles and Ellipses" section later in this chapter.

When you click on a polygon, straight line, or other free-form path, FreeHand displays all points in the path as small black squares, as shown in Figure 7-2. This indicates that the path is selected but the individual *points* in the path are deselected. Any manipulation you perform affects all portions of the path equally.

To select multiple paths, click on the first path you want to select and then Shift-click on each of the others. Or drag a marquee around portions of several paths and press the grave key (`). I discuss this second method in slightly more depth in the next section.

Figure 7-1:
A rectangle and ellipse, each shown as it appears when deselected (left) and after being selected with the arrow tool (right).

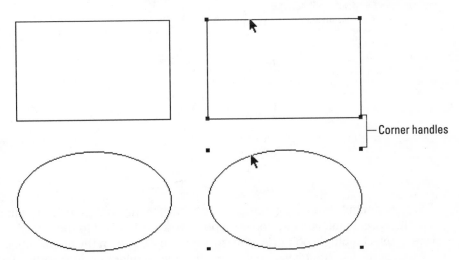

Corner handles

Figure 7-2:
Normally invisible
(left), the points in
a free-form path
display when you
select the path
with the arrow
tool (right).

Deselected path

Selected path

Selecting points

To select a specific point in a path, first select the path and then click directly on the desired point with the arrow tool. A selected point appears hollow, as shown in Figure 7-3. A selected corner point is a hollow square; a selected curve point is a hollow circle; and a selected connector point is a hollow triangle. All Bézier control handles associated with the selected point and the two neighboring segments also display. Deselected points in the path appear as small black squares.

Figure 7-3:
After selecting a free-form path,
you can select a specific point in
the path by clicking on it.

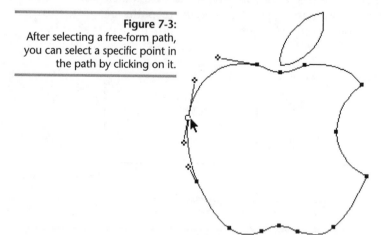

To select multiple points in a selected path, click on the first point you want to select and then press Shift and click on each point you want to add to the selection. Another way to select multiple points is to marquee them. Drag with the arrow tool in an empty portion of the illustration window to create a rectangular marquee with a dotted outline, as shown in the first example of Figure 7-4.

FreeHand positions one corner of the marquee at the spot where you begin to drag. The opposite corner of the marquee follows the movements of your cursor as you drag. All points within the marquee that belong to free-form paths become selected when you release your mouse button, as illustrated in the second example of the figure.

To select a grouped object, such as a rectangle or ellipse, you must surround the entire group with your marquee. Notice in the second example of Figure 7-4 that the square is selected, but the circle is not. The square fit entirely inside the marquee; the circle was only partially marqueed.

Marqueeing is possibly the most convenient means for selecting multiple objects. However, marqueeing selects not only paths, but also their points. If you drag a path in which specific points are selected, you end up stretching the shape rather than moving it (as explained in the "Moving Elements" section later in this chapter). If you want to manipulate whole paths and speed up the screen display, press the grave key (upper left key on the keyboard) to deselect all points while leaving their paths selected.

Figure 7-5 shows the result of pressing grave (pronounced *grahv* — like the accent, not the tomb) after marqueeing the points shown in the second example of Figure 7-4. Notice that all hollow points turn solid and all Bézier control handles disappear. Now you can drag these shapes without stretching them.

You can combine marqueeing with Shift-clicking to select multiple paths and points. You can also marquee while pressing the Shift key, which adds the marqueed points and paths to the existing selection.

Figure 7-4:
All points surrounded by a marquee (left) become selected (right). A rectangle or ellipse must be entirely surrounded to be selected.

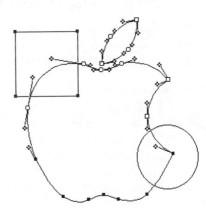

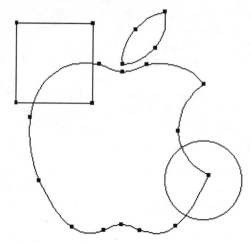

Figure 7-5:
The paths from the previous figure after I pressed the grave key.

Selecting everything

The only remaining selection method to talk about is the Select All command in the Edit menu (Command-A). When you choose this command, FreeHand selects every path, group, and other object in the current illustration (as long as the objects reside on unlocked layers, discussed in Chapter 8). The one exception is when a text block is active, in which case Edit ⇨ Select All highlights all text inside the text block. This command selects paths and other objects only; it does not select points.

Deselecting objects

If you don't want an object to be affected by a command or mouse operation, you need to *deselect* it. To deselect all objects, simply click with the arrow tool on an empty portion of the illustration window.

If the entire window is filled with objects and you can't find an empty portion to click on, press the Tab key. Tab deselects all objects in an illustration except when a text block is active. In fact, you'll probably want to get in the habit of pressing Tab even when an empty portion of the window is available; it's much faster than using the arrow tool.

FreeHand also deselects all currently selected objects when you do any of the following:

⮑ Select an object that was not previously selected by clicking on it with the arrow tool.

⮑ Click or drag with the rectangle, oval, polygon, line, or trace tool.

- ☞ Click or drag with the freehand, bézigon, or pen tool on an empty portion of the illustration window.

- ☞ Click or drag with the text tool.

- ☞ Choose File ⇨ Place (Command-Shift-D).

- ☞ Choose Paste (Command-V), Paste Behind, Duplicate (Command-D), or Clone (Command-equal) from the Edit menu.

Deselecting specific points and paths

You don't have to deselect every object in an illustration; you can deselect specific paths and points without affecting other selected objects. To deselect a single selected point, for example, Shift-click on it with the arrow tool. To deselect an entire path, Shift-click on any of its segments.

You can also deselect points and grouped objects by Shift-marqueeing. If you press the Shift key and then marquee a portion of your illustration, all selected points and grouped objects within the marquee become deselected. At the same time, all deselected points and grouped objects in the marquee become selected. It's a role reversal kind of thing.

 Shift-marqueeing deselects points and grouped objects only. The method does not work for deselecting entire free-form paths. To deselect a path, you have to Shift-click on one of its segments.

Reshaping Rectangles and Ellipses

Try this little experiment: Draw a rectangle with the rectangle tool. The shape and size don't matter. Now select the arrow tool and try to select a specific point in the shape.

Can't do it, huh? When you click on a point, is doesn't become hollow, as it would in a free-form path. If you Shift-click on a point, the entire rectangle becomes deselected. That's because rectangles and ellipses are created as *grouped objects,* or simply *groups*. FreeHand fuses all elements in a group into a single object, locking points into relative alignment so that the path cannot be reshaped.

Using handles

Grouped objects are not entirely immutable, however. The easiest way to alter a geometric shape is to *scale* it — change its size — by dragging one of its four corner handles. As shown in the first example of Figure 7-6, FreeHand displays the group's original size and shape during your drag for reference. The center point of the shape updates throughout the operation so that you can more precisely align the shape with other objects in the illustration window.

If you Option-drag a corner handle, you scale the path with respect to its center point, as illustrated in the second example of Figure 7-6. Press Shift while dragging to constrain a rectangle to a square or an ellipse to a circle.

 To scale a rectangle or oval exclusively horizontally or vertically, press the Control key while Shift-dragging. Press Control while Shift-Option-dragging to scale the path about its center point.

To scale a rectangle or ellipse *proportionally* — that is, to maintain a constant ratio between height and width — Shift-drag with the scale tool as described in the "Constrained scaling" section in Chapter 15.

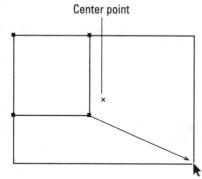 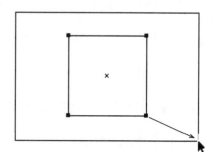

Center point

Figure 7-6:
Scale a geometric shape by dragging (left) or Option-dragging (right) one of its corner handles with the arrow tool.

Handle coordinates

One of the most basic ways to manipulate any object in FreeHand is to adjust the options in the Object panel of the Inspector palette. Press Command-Option-I to access the Object panel. If the Inspector palette is not available, first press Command-I.

Figure 7-7 shows the Object panel as it appears when a rectangle or ellipse is selected. The Dimensions option boxes control the size and location of the selected shape. The X and Y options list the coordinates of the shape's upper left corner handle in relation to the *ruler origin*, which is the point at which the horizontal and vertical coordinates equal zero (as described in the "Using the rulers" section of Chapter 8).

By default, the ruler origin is located in the lower left corner of the page. Positive X values are to the right of the origin; negative X values are to the left. Positive Y values are above the origin; negative Y values are below.

The W and H options control the width and height of the selected shape. All values are measured in the unit of measure specified in the Document Setup panel of the Inspector palette. The default unit is points.

When a rectangle is selected, the Object panel displays an additional option box, Corner Radius. This option controls the extent to which the corners of the selected shape are rounded. The radius of a rectangle with perpendicular corners is 0. As you increase the corner radius values, the rounded corner consumes a larger portion of the rectangle. For more information, read the "Drawing a rectangle with rounded corners" section of Chapter 5.

After changing any of the values in the Object panel, press the Return key to implement your changes. (The panel really ought to have an Apply button.)

 If two or more objects are selected, the Object panel appears blank. This happens because FreeHand can't communicate size and location information for more than one object at a time.

Figure 7-7:
The Object panel as it appears when a rectangle (left) or ellipse (right) is selected.

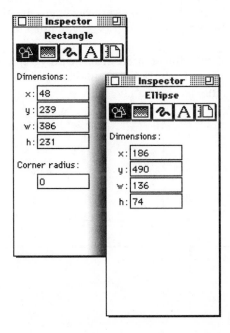

Ungrouping geometric shapes

As I described in the preceding pages, FreeHand gives you a number of ways to modify rectangles and ellipses. But none of these methods allows you to move one point in a path independently of its neighbors. The only way to truly reshape a geometric shape is to ungroup it by selecting it and choosing Arrange ⇨ Ungroup (Command-U). Ungrouping frees the points in a geometric path so that you can manipulate them independently, just like you can manipulate points in a free-form path. Figure 7-8 shows the effect of ungrouping three geometric shapes.

When you ungroup a geometric shape, its corner handles and center point disappear, and you gain access to points, segments, and Bézier control handles. So that you can see all these items, I took the liberty of selecting all points in the ungrouped paths. Notice that the selected points in the two rectangles are corner points (hollow squares), while those in the circle are curve points (hollow circles). This gives you maximum flexibility in reshaping the paths, as you'll discover in later sections.

 After you ungroup a rectangle, you can never again access the Corner Radius option shown in Figure 7-7 — not even if you regroup the path by choosing the Group command — unless you choose Edit ⇨ Undo Ungroup (Command-Z) immediately after ungrouping the path. To change the curvature of the corners of an ungrouped rectangle, you have to reshape the path manually, just as if it were created with one of the free-form drawing tools. Also, you can't scale an ungrouped path by dragging at its corner; you must instead use the scale tool.

It's not necessary to ungroup paths created with the polygon or line tool. Like paths created with free-form drawing tools, polygons and lines are created as ungrouped objects. You can reshape them immediately.

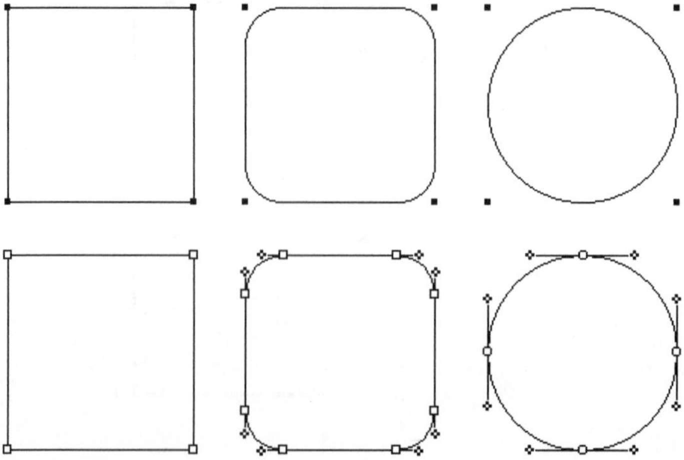

Figure 7-8:
Three geometric shapes before (top) and after (bottom) choosing the Ungroup command.

Moving Elements

The most common method for reshaping a path is to move some *element* — whether it be a point, segment, or Bézier control handle — in the path. Moving selected points independently of deselected points stretches the segments that connect the points. You can also stretch curved segments by moving a Bézier control handle, which changes the curvature of the path. And in FreeHand 4.0, you can Option-drag segments to stretch them directly.

 The following sections explain how to reshape paths by moving elements in the path. For information on moving entire paths, including a full-blown description of the Move panel in the Transform palette, read Chapter 15, "The Five Transformations," which is based on the escapades of a Motown group that never quite got off the ground.

Moving points

To move one or more points in a path, select the points you want to move and then drag any one of them. FreeHand moves all selected points the same distance and direction. When you move a point while a neighboring point remains stationary, the segment between the two points shrinks or stretches to accommodate the change in distance, as illustrated in Figure 7-9. If a point has any Bézier control handles, the handles move with the point, unless the point is governed by automatic curvature — as is the case with points created with the bézigon tool. When automatic curvature is in effect, the handles move independently according to how FreeHand thinks the path should look. Either way, the curved segment not only shrinks or stretches, but also bends to accommodate the movement of a point.

Figure 7-9:
Dragging the selected point (left) stretches the segments between the point and its deselected, stationary neighbors (right).

When you move multiple points, any segment located between two deselected points or between two selected points remains unchanged during the move, as illustrated in Figure 7-10. FreeHand allows you to move multiple points within a single path, as in Figures 7-9 and 7-10, or in separate paths, as in Figure 7-11. This means that you can reshape more than one path at a time.

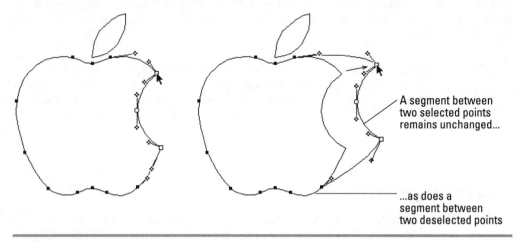

A segment between two selected points remains unchanged...

...as does a segment between two deselected points

Figure 7-10: Dragging at any selected point in a shape (left) moves all selected points an identical distance and direction (right).

As you can see from the figures, FreeHand displays both the previous and current locations of points and segments as you drag them. This useful feature lets you gauge the full effect of a move as it progresses.

Figure 7-11:
You can even move multiple points when selected points reside in different paths.

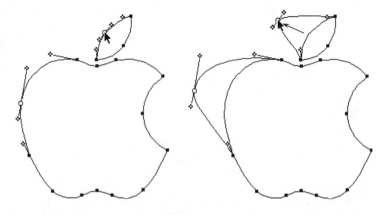

Constrained movements

You can constrain the movement of selected points to any angle that is a multiple of 45 degrees. Just press the Shift key *after* you begin your drag and hold the key down until after you release the mouse button. (If you press and hold Shift before beginning your drag, you run the risk of deselecting the point on which you click.) You can alter the effects of pressing the Shift key by rotating the *constraint axes*. You do this by entering a value into the Constrain option box in the Document Setup panel of the Inspector panel. (Sadly, there is no keyboard equivalent to navigate to this panel; you have to manually click on the icons along the top of the palette.) Figure 7-12, for example, shows the result of entering a value of 15 into the Constrain option box and Shift-dragging a few selected points.

Figure 7-12:
By entering a new value into the Constrain option box, you can change the angle of a Shift-drag.

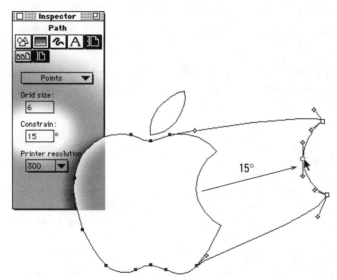

The constraint axes specify the eight directions in which you can move an element by Shift-dragging. By default, these directions are:

- ∞ **0 degrees:** Directly to the right
- ∞ **45 degrees:** Diagonally up and to the right
- ∞ **90 degrees:** Straight up
- ∞ **135 degrees:** Diagonally up and to the left
- ∞ **180 degrees:** Directly to the left
- ∞ **225 degrees:** Diagonally down and to the left (same as –135 degrees)
- ∞ **270 degrees:** Straight down (same as –90 degrees)
- ∞ **315 degrees:** Diagonally down and to the right (same as –45 degrees)

Each direction differs from its neighbor by an angle of 45 degrees. By entering a number between −360 and 360 in the Constrain option box, you rotate the constraint axes. The second example in Figure 7-13 illustrates the effect of rotating the axes 15 degrees. If you were to Shift-drag an element under these conditions, your movements would be constrained to the directions labeled in the figure. You wouldn't be able to Shift-drag in a horizontal or vertical direction until you changed the Constrain value back to 0.

The Constrain value also affects the following:

> ⌘ Rectangles and ellipses (as explained in the "Geometric shapes at an angle" section of Chapter 5). The angle of the constraint axes affects these shapes whether you press the Shift key or not.

> ⌘ Polygons and straight lines created by Shift-dragging

> ⌘ The angle of straight segments that you draw by Shift-clicking with the pen or bézigon tool or Shift-Option-dragging with the freehand tool

Unlike rotated constraint axes in Illustrator, rotated constraint axes in FreeHand do not affect the performance of transformation tools or the angle at which text blocks are drawn.

Snapping

While dragging an element, you may find that it has a tendency to move sharply toward another element. Called *snapping*, this effect is one of FreeHand's ways of ensuring that elements belonging together are positioned flush against each other to form a perfect fit.

When you drag an element within 1 to 5 pixels of any point on your illustration window — you specify the exact distance in the Snap Distance option box — your cursor snaps to the point. Both point and cursor then occupy an identical horizontal and vertical location.

One of the most useful applications for snapping is to align a point in one path with a point in another, as shown in Figure 7-14. However, if you drag a point in a selected free-form path, you end up moving only that point, which reshapes the path instead of moving it.

To move the entire path by dragging at a single point, you must either select all points in the path prior to dragging, or — and here comes the tip, folks — Control-drag the point. The Control key tells Freehand to move the entire path instead of just the selected points. Note that this technique results in the movement of only one path, even if more than one path is selected.

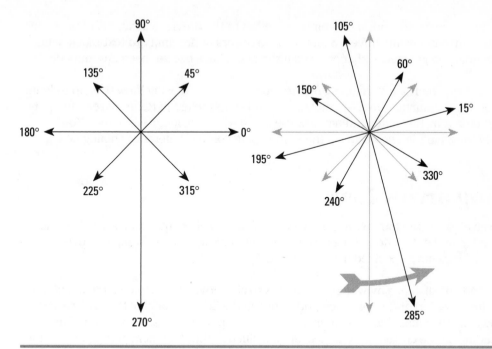

Figure 7-13: The default constraint axes (left) and the axes as they appear when rotated 15 degrees (right).

Figure 7-14:
Press the Control key to drag an entire path by one of its points.

Your cursor snaps to stationary points as well as to the previous locations of points that are currently being moved. Snapping also occurs in proximity to text block handles and to points in geometric shapes, even if the paths have not yet been ungrouped.

You can turn FreeHand's snapping feature on and off by choosing View ⇨ Snap to Point or pressing Command-quote — you know, that key to the left of Return. FreeHand puts a check mark by the command name in the menu when the feature is active. You specify the Snap Distance value in the Editing panel of the Preferences dialog box.

Using arrow keys

You can also use the four arrow keys to move selected elements. Each arrow key moves a selection in the direction of the arrow. The right arrow key, for example, moves all selected elements a specified increment to the right.

To specify the distance by which a single keystroke moves a selected element, enter a value into the Cursor Key Distance option box in the Editing panel of the Preferences dialog box. The value that you enter is measured in points, picas, inches, or millimeters, depending on the current unit of measure specified in the Document Setup panel of the Inspector palette.

You can use arrow keys to move selected points and whole paths. However, you cannot use arrow keys to move a selected Bézier control handle independently of its point. You can only move segments and Bézier control handles by dragging them, as described in the next sections.

Stretching segments

 You can also reshape a path by Option-dragging one of its segments. When you Option-drag a segment, you stretch it as shown in Figure 7-15. You can Option-drag curved and straight segments alike. When reshaping a straight segment, FreeHand automatically adds Bézier control handles to the neighboring points.

When you Option-drag a curved segment, the Bézier control handles extend and retract with your cursor movements. However, they do so along established lines, constant with their original inclination. In other words, although the length of a control handle lever changes as you Option-drag a curved segment, the angle of the lever remains fixed. As Figure 7-16 illustrates, the lever can flip in the opposite direction, but never, no never, will it sway back and forth. This guarantees that the segment moves in alignment with neighboring stationary segments.

Figure 7-15:
Option-dragging a curved
segment (top) and a straight
segment (bottom).

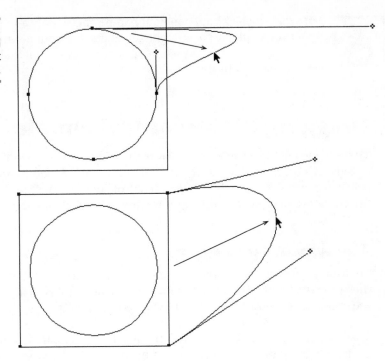

Figure 7-16:
When you drag
a curved
segment, each
control handle
extends and
retracts, but its
angle remains
fixed.

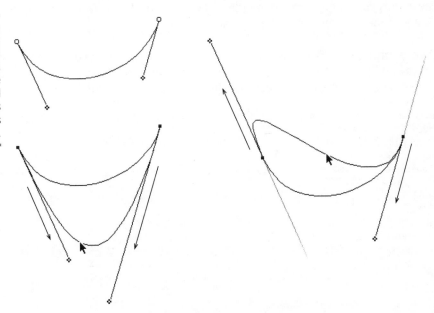

Note that the bit about constant handle angles only applies to curved segments. When you Option-drag straight segments, the handles are free to fly about willy-nilly. It makes the results a little less predictable, but it also makes for a more flexible editing atmosphere.

Dragging Bézier control handles

The only element I've neglected so far is the Bézier control handle. I saved it until last because it's the most difficult element to manipulate. So far, I've only introduced and briefly discussed the qualities of Bézier control handles, those pesky elements that control the curvature of segments as they enter and exit points. It's time we went all the way.

The way of the Bézier

To display a Bézier control handle, select the point to which the handle belongs and then drag the handle you want to move. That's all there is to it. But learning to predict the outcome of your drags can be a little more difficult.

That's where Figures 7-17 through 7-21 come in. Each figure features four curve points. Each point is located in the exact same position in each figure; from one figure to the next, only the labeled control handles have moved. However, these simple adjustments have a dramatic impact on the appearance of each path.

I've lettered the active handles to show the exact manner in which a handle is relocated from one figure to the next. For the record, handle A controls the left segment, handles B and C control the middle segment, and handle D controls the right segment.

Figure 7-17: A path composed of four curve points, two of which are selected to display their Bézier control handles.

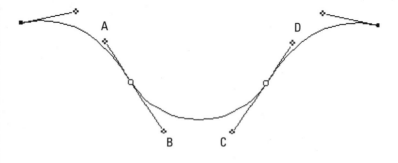

When you move one Bézier control handle for a curve point, the other handle for that point moves in the opposite direction. Hence, the two handles of a curve point form a constant lever. Compare Figure 7-18 with Figure 7-17. In Figure 7-18, handles C and D have been moved only slightly, while handles A and B have been moved dramatically. I dragged handle A in a clockwise sweep, sending handle B upward. Figure 7-19 shows the path as it appears during the drag. The arrow shows the motion of my drag. You can see how the control handle stretches the segment like taffy on a pull.

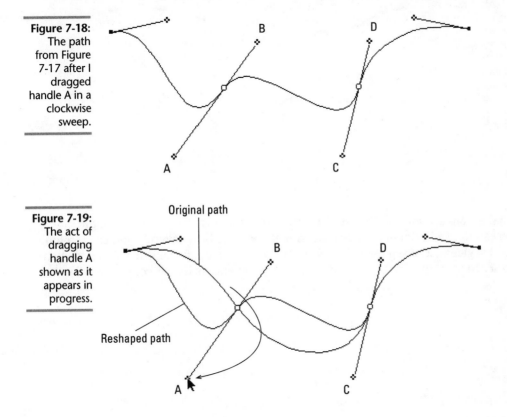

Figure 7-18:
The path
from Figure
7-17 after I
dragged
handle A in a
clockwise
sweep.

Figure 7-19:
The act of
dragging
handle A
shown as it
appears in
progress.

In Figure 7-18, handle B forces the center segment to ascend as it exits the left curve point. But because of handle C, the segment also ascends as it enters the right curve point. So somewhere between the two points, the segment has to change direction. Hence, the segment slopes up, then down, and then up again.

The farther I moved the two opposite handles away from each other, the more desperately the segment between them stretched to keep up. In Figure 7-20, I've moved handles B and C a few inches from each other. Now the segment proceeds leftward both as it exits point B and as it enters point C. Somewhere in between, it has to go rightward. (After all, what goes left must go right, right?) The result is a segment that bulges out in three directions — left, right, and downward.

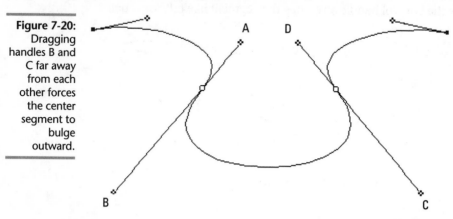

Figure 7-20: Dragging handles B and C far away from each other forces the center segment to bulge outward.

The final example, shown in Figure 7-21, shows that there is absolutely no limit to how far you can drag a Bézier control handle from its point or how severely you can stretch a curved segment. The segment always stretches to keep up, turning around only when necessary to meet the demands of the opposite point and its Bézier control handle.

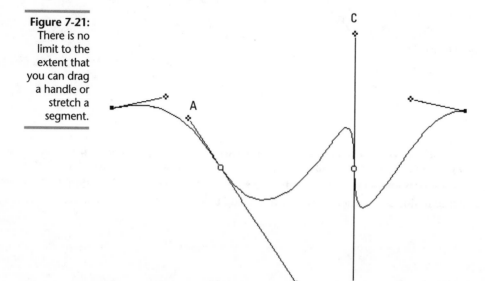

Figure 7-21: There is no limit to the extent that you can drag a handle or stretch a segment.

Certainly, I could come up with all kinds of analogies at this point. Segments stretch like taffy attached to rubber bands between two nails mounted on a medieval rack in a dark dungeon lifted off a comics page onto a piece of Silly Putty fortified with pieces of well-chewed gum spit out onto blacktops where they were thoroughly warmed just in time for you to step on them and mush them into the treads of your silicon sneakers . . . but I think that you already get the idea. These things are so flexible that they make Mr. Fantastic look like he was made out of plywood. And you can stretch them to your heart's content using Bézier's Believe-It-Or-Not control handles.

Rules of the Bézier road

Although you *can* stretch segments from here to the Pleistocene era, there's little reason you'd want to (unless you'd like to check out the origins of primitive man). As in all of life's pursuits, segment-stretching is best done in moderation. The art of dragging Bézier control handles is not so much a question of what can you do as when you should do it and to what extent.

One of the most common problems people have when learning to use FreeHand is trying to determine the placement of Bézier control handles. Several rules have been developed over the years, but the best are the *all-or-nothing rule* and the *30-percent rule*.

The all-or-nothing rule states that every segment in your path should be associated with either two Bézier control handles or none at all. In other words, no segment should rely on only one control handle to determine its curvature. The 30-percent rule says that the length of any control handle lever should be approximately 30 percent of the length of the segment it controls.

Figures 7-22 and 7-23 feature a pair of Gufus and Gallants of our Bézier curve rules. The top path in Figure 7-22 violates the all-or-nothing rule. Its two curved segments are controlled by only one handle apiece, resulting in weak, shallow arcs. In the case of both segments, you have no control over the way the segments attach to the base of the path. So one segment begins flat, and the other flattens out at the end. Flat curves are like flat tires; they don't fulfill their intended purpose.

The second example in the figure, however, obeys the all-or-nothing rule. As the rule states, its straight segment is associated with no handle and both curved segments have two handles apiece. The result is a full-figured, properly pumped-up dome, a credit to any illustration.

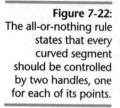

Figure 7-22:
The all-or-nothing rule states that every curved segment should be controlled by two handles, one for each of its points.

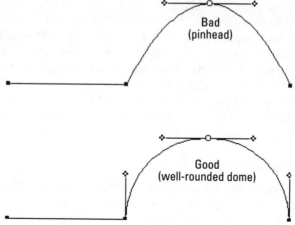

The first path in Figure 7-23 violates the 30-percent rule. The control handle levers for the central point are much too long, about 60 percent of the length of their segments, and the two outer levers are too short, about 15 percent of the length of their segments. The result, quite frankly, is an ugly, misshapen mess. In the second example, the two levers belonging to the left segment each measure about 30 percent of the length of the segment. The right segment is shorter, so its levers are shorter as well. The curvature of this path is smooth and consistent, giving the path an organic appearance.

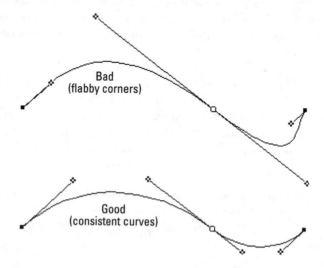

Figure 7-23:
The 30-percent rule states that every Bézier lever should extend about a third of the length of its segment.

Adding, Deleting, and Converting

Moving points and adjusting control handles are fundamental ways to change the shape of a path. But sometimes, no matter how much time you spend adjusting the placement of its points or the curvature of its segments, a path fails to meet the requirements of your illustration. When that happens, you may want to expand the path by adding points or to simplify the path by deleting points.

The number and identity of points and segments in a path is forever subject to change. Whether the path is closed or open, you can reshape it by adding, deleting, and converting points. Adding or deleting a point forces the addition or deletion of a segment. And the conversion of a point — whether from corner to curve or from curve to corner — frequently converts a segment from curved to straight or from straight to curved. The following pages describe how you can apply all these reshaping techniques to any existing path.

Adding points and other elements

Adding elements to a path is sort of like finishing a basement or adding a room above the garage, except that it's free and you don't need a building permit. It's a great way to expand upon a geometric shape or extend something you've drawn with the freehand or trace tool.

In the upcoming "Adding points inside a path" section, for example, I walk you through the process of converting a simple circle into something a little more meaningful by merely throwing in a few additional points. First, however, I need to show you how to add points to the end of an open path.

Appending endpoints

As discussed in Chapter 5, a point associated with less than two segments is an *endpoint,* because it represents one end or the other of a path. An open path always has two endpoints. A closed path contains no endpoint; each point is connected to another by a segment.

An active endpoint is waiting for a segment to be drawn from it. To *activate* an endpoint in a passive path so that you can draw a new segment from it, select the point with the arrow tool. Then you can click or drag anywhere else on your screen with either the bézigon or pen tool to create a segment between the selected endpoint and the newly created point. After you do this, the one-time endpoint is bound by segments on both sides — meaning that it's no longer an endpoint. It relinquishes its endpoint title to the newest point in the line.

You can use the same technique to close an existing path. Just select one endpoint and then click or drag on the other endpoint with the bézigon or pen tool. FreeHand draws a segment between the two endpoints, closing the path to form a shape. Both endpoints are eliminated and converted to interior points.

This brings up an interesting question: What happens to an endpoint when you close the path using a different method than you used to create the point? For example, if you Option-click on a corner point with the bézigon tool, does the point remain a corner point or convert to a curve point? In this case, it remains a corner point. A closing point retains its original identity any time you close the path with the bézigon tool. But when using the pen tool, you can convert an endpoint in the course of closing a path, as described below:

- ↪ Click on the closing point to make it a corner point.

- ↪ Drag on the closing point to change it to a curve point.

- ↪ Drag on the closing point and press Option before completing the drag to change the point to a cusp point with two independent control handles.

- ↪ Press Option and then drag on the closing point to change it to a corner point with only one Bézier control handle.

- ↪ Control-drag on the closing point to change it to a connector point with a single control handle.

The moral of the story is this: If you don't want to run the risk of changing the identity of the closing point, use the bézigon tool to close the path (or simply select the Closed check box in the Object panel of the Inspector palette). If you'd rather have full control over the final endpoint as you close the shape, use the pen tool. And finally, you can define a new point in the path and Command-drag it onto the first point to automatically join the points as described in the "Three cusp point vignettes" section of Chapter 5.

 As if you didn't already have enough options, you can also lengthen an open path by drawing from one of its endpoints with the freehand tool. To close a path, drag from one endpoint to the other. To close it with a straight segment, Option-drag from one endpoint to the other.

Adding points inside a path

Endpoints aren't the only kinds of points you can add to an existing path. You can also add an interior point to open and closed paths by clicking on existing segments with the bézigon tool.

First, select the path to which you want to add a point. Then click, Option-click, or Control-click with the bézigon tool on some segment in the path. A new corner, curve, or connector point appears at that location, depending on the method you used. What was once one segment becomes two.

You can use the pen tool to insert points in a path as well. Click on an existing segment to insert a corner point; drag on a segment to insert a curve point; and Control-drag to insert a connector point. Dragging with the pen tool allows you to determine the precise placement of Bézier control handles.

Suppose that you want to change an ordinary, ungrouped circle that's composed of four curve points into a crescent. You can get the job done by adding points within the path. The following steps describe one way to perform this task.

STEPS: Changing a Circle into a Crescent

Step 1.   Draw a circle by Shift-dragging with the oval tool. Then choose Arrange ⇨ Ungroup (Command-U) to ungroup the shape.

Step 2.   Select the path. Press the 8 key to select the bézigon tool and then Option-click in the middle of each of the right-hand segments. Each Option-click inserts a curve point, as illustrated in Figure 7-24.

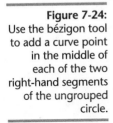

Figure 7-24:
Use the bézigon tool to add a curve point in the middle of each of the two right-hand segments of the ungrouped circle.

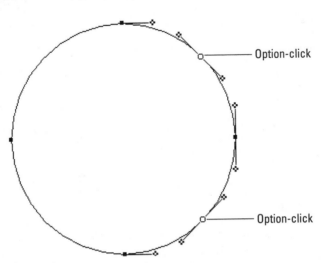

Option-click

Option-click

Step 3. Press and hold the Command key to access the arrow tool. While pressing the key, drag the rightmost point toward the center of the shape, as shown in Figure 7-25.

Figure 7-25:
Drag the rightmost point toward the center of the shape.

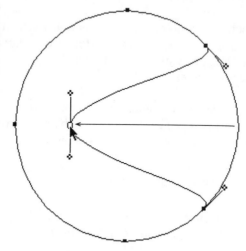

Step 4. Release the Command key to restore the bézigon cursor. Option-click in the middle of each of the two segments between the crescent tips and the dragged point, as indicated by the two selected curve points in Figure 7-26.

Figure 7-26:
Add a point to the middle of each of the segments that form the mouth of the shape.

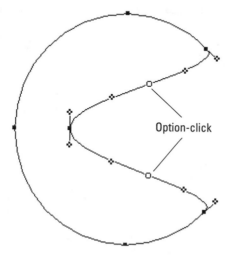

Option-click

Step 5. Finally, move the most recently created points outward from the center of the shape, in the direction indicated by the arrow in Figure 7-27. The Bézier control handles of the point at the center of the mouth will require some adjustment as well. Figure 7-28 shows the completed path as it appears when printed from FreeHand.

Figure 7-27:
Drag the most recent points into position.

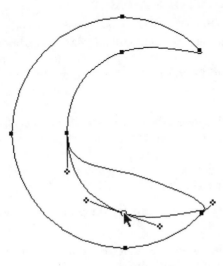

Figure 7-28:
The finished path as it appears when printed from FreeHand.

Although it is possible to click with the bézigon or pen tool directly on a point in a selected path, I recommend that you avoid doing so. FreeHand will add a new point to the path and position it directly in front of the previous point. It's unlikely that you will want two points in the same path to be positioned in such close proximity that you will probably have to zoom in to separate them.

Adding Bézier control handles

If you want to bend an existing straight segment, or if a curved segment doesn't curve sufficiently, you need to add a Bézier control handle to a neighboring point. In FreeHand, you can add control handles to a corner point or connector point long after the point was created. You cannot add a control handle to an existing curve point or to any other point that already has two control handles — such points are already at full capacity.

To add a control handle, first select the desired point and then Option-drag from the point with the arrow tool. The effect of your Option-drag depends on the following criteria:

- ☞ If no control handle yet exists for the point, the new control handle affects the more recent of the two neighboring segments.

- ☞ If one control handle already exists for the point, the new control handle affects the opposite segment.

- ☞ If two control handles already exist for the current point, Option-dragging simply moves the point to a new position.

You can't always predict which of two neighboring segments will be affected when you add a Bézier control handle, because you can't simply look at a path and recognize its direction. As a result, you just have to adopt a trial-and-error attitude when Option-dragging a point.

If the first control handle does not affect the desired segment, Option-drag the point again to produce another control handle. This second handle will by necessity be the one you want, because no more than two control handles can exist for a point. Delete the unwanted handle by dragging it back to the point until it snaps into place or by clicking on the second of the two Curve Handle icons in the Object panel of the Inspector palette. (Both techniques are described in "Retracting Bézier control handles" section later in this chapter.)

Better yet, use the Reverse Direction command, which changes the direction in which the path travels. After Option-dragging the unwanted Bézier control handle, choose Edit ➪ Undo Move (Command-Z) to put it away. Then choose Arrange ➪ Path Operations ➪ Reverse Direction. Now click on the point again to select it, Option-drag from the selected point, and — lo and behold — there's the control handle you were looking for.

To make things a little more predictable, choose Arrange ➪ Path Operations ➪ Correct Direction. This command makes all selected paths progress in a clockwise direction, regardless of how you drew them.

Deleting points and other elements

The simplest way to delete points is to select them and press the Delete key. The selected points disappear, as do the segments associated with the points. To prevent gaps in the outline of the paths to which the points belonged, FreeHand connects the points that neighbored the deleted points with new segments.

The first example in Figure 7-29 shows the familiar ungrouped circle path with the right point selected. The second example shows how the path changed after I pressed the Delete key. FreeHand fused the two segments surrounding the deleted point into a single segment. The segment's curvature is determined by the remaining points in the path. The result is a path that remains closed and selected, although all points are deselected.

If you delete an endpoint from an open path, you delete the single segment associated with the point. FreeHand doesn't draw a new segment in its place. Also, the new end-point in the path becomes selected, enabling you to extend the path using the freehand, bézigon, or pen tool or further shorten the path by pressing the Delete key again.

Avoid deleting a point from a line that consists of only two points. You'll end up with a single-point path, which is almost completely useless unless you intend to build on it immediately. Lone points tend to clutter up the illustration window and needlessly increase the size of your document when it's saved to disk.

Figure 7-29:
Selecting an interior point (left) and pressing the Delete key removes the point but retains a segment (right).

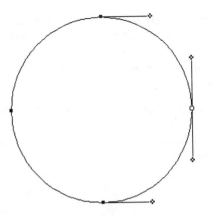
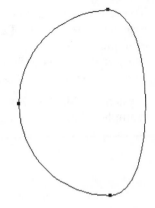

Removing a segment

FreeHand prevents breaks in the outline of a path by drawing new segments in place of deleted ones. If you want to delete a segment *and* create a break in the path — whether to open a closed path or to split an open path in two — you have to do a little additional work. Although FreeHand provides no direct means for deleting a segment, you can get the job done by following these steps.

STEPS: Creating a Break in a Path with the Knife Tool

Step 1.   Select the path that you want to open or split.

Step 2.   Press the 7 key to select the knife tool. Then click on the segment that you want to delete, as shown in the first example of Figure 7-30. You have now split the segment and inserted two endpoints into the path.

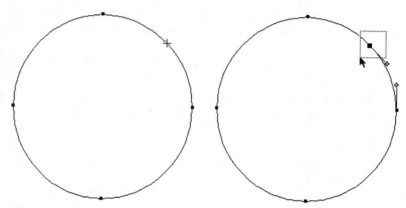

Figure 7-30:
Click on a segment with the knife tool (left) to split the segment and insert two endpoints (right).

Step 3.   To ensure that both new endpoints are selected, press the Command key to access the arrow tool and marquee the points, as shown in the second example of Figure 7-30. Because the selected points overlap, they disappear, as shown in the first example of Figure 7-31. This is FreeHand's way of showing that overlapping points are selected.

Step 4.   Press the Delete key. Both points disappear, as shown in the second example in Figure 7-31, leaving a break in the outline of the path.

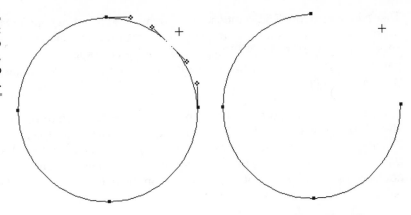

Figure 7-31:
After selecting the two coincident points (left), press the Delete key to open the path.

For a complete discussion of the knife tool, see the "Splitting and slicing" section later in this chapter.

Deleting a whole path

As shown in Figure 7-29, deleting a point from a closed path causes the remaining path to become selected. If you press the Delete key a second time, you delete the entire path. This means that if a closed path — in the course of its creation — ends up deviating so drastically from your original intention that there is no sense in attempting a salvage, you can delete the entire object by selecting any point in the path and pressing Delete twice in a row.

You can also delete any path, whether it's open or closed, by selecting the entire path and pressing Delete. Or, if you prefer, choose the Clear command from the Edit menu.

The Clear command deletes entire selected paths, whether or not one or more points in the path are also selected. To perform the same operation from the keyboard, press the grave key to deselect all points while leaving their paths selected and then press the Delete key.

Retracting Bézier control handles

To put away, or *retract*, a Bézier control handle, drag the control handle back to its point and release. If the Snap to Point command is active in the View menu, the control handle snaps to its point as you retract it. If you want to retract the corresponding control handles for multiple selected points at the same time, click on the Curve Handles icon in the Object panel of the Inspector palette.

Take a look at Figure 7-32. Suppose that you wanted to retract each of the control handles associated with the leftmost point in the crescent shape. In each case, you can either drag the handle back to its point or click on the spotlighted icon in the Object panel. How do you know which icon goes with which handle? Again, it's a function of the direction of the path.

The crescent in the figure was based on a circle created with the oval tool, which always travels in a clockwise direction. So the segment below the leftmost point enters it, and the segment above the point exits it. If you clicked on the right icon in the palette (labeled *Retract exit handle* in the figure), you would delete the upper handle, which controls the exiting segment. If you clicked on the left icon, you would delete the entrance — or in this case, lower — handle.

To make any path behave like the crescent in Figure 7-32 — that is, so that all segments travel in a clockwise direction — select the path and choose Arrange⇨ Path Operations ⇨ Correct Direction. The left Curve Handles icon then retracts the Bézier control handle pointing in the counterclockwise direction, and the right icon retracts the handle pointing clockwise. Complicated paths can be tricky because they can loop all over the place, but you'll eventually get the hang of it.

Generally, you'll only want to retract control handles belonging to corner and connector points. But as illustrated in the figures, it is possible to retract a curve point handle. Doing so ruins the purpose of the point by eliminating the seesaw lever. If you delete a handle from a curve point, I suggest that you convert the point to a corner point by clicking on the corner point icon in the Inspector palette (as described in the next section). If you leave the points as is, you're likely to confuse yourself in later editing stages because you may end up with curve points at obvious corners in the path.

Converting points

FreeHand lets you change the identity of an interior point; that is, to convert any point within an existing path to a curve, corner, or connector point. You convert a point by using the Point Type icons in the Object panel of the Inspector palette, as shown in Figure 7-33. Instead of choosing commands as in previous versions of FreeHand, you just select the point that you want to change and click on the appropriate icon in the palette.

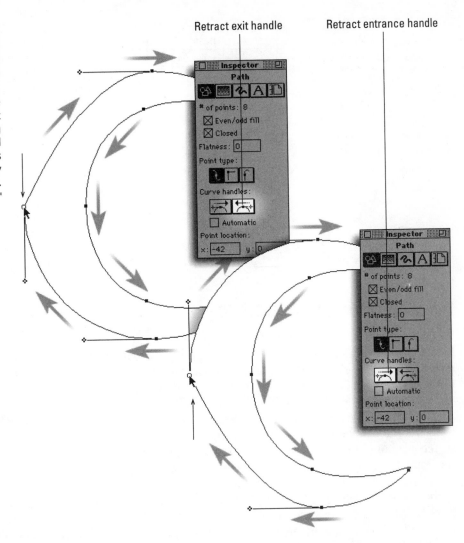

Figure 7-32:
In each example, the spotlighted icon performs the same effect as dragging the control handle, as indicated by the arrow.

Retract exit handle

Retract entrance handle

When a single point is selected, or when two or more points of the same type are selected, a Point Type icon appears highlighted to identify the points. If you select two or more dissimilar points, no icon appears highlighted. However, you can make the selected points similar by clicking on an icon.

Figure 7-33:
The three Point Type icons let you
change the identity of a point.

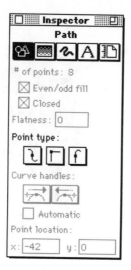

Automatic curvature

When you create a point with the bézigon tool, FreeHand automatically determines the location of any Bézier control handle for the point — a feature called *automatic curvature*. FreeHand bases its decision on the identity and location of the point with respect to the identities and locations of its immediate neighbors.

Any time you move, add, or retract a Bézier control handle, the affected point deviates from FreeHand's perception of automatic curvature. To restore the control handles of a selected point to their predetermined locations, select the Automatic check box below the Point Type icons in the Object panel of the Inspector palette.

Perhaps the best way to understand automatic curvature is to think of a line made up of three points — a corner, a curve, and another corner. Suppose that you drew this line with the pen tool, manually positioning the control handles of the points to create a path like the one shown in the first example of Figure 7-34.

Now imagine that there is a center spot equidistant from all three points. This center spot is shown in the figure as a small ×. If you select the three points and select the Automatic option, FreeHand moves the control handles so that the path curves symmetrically about the imaginary center spot, as shown in the second example of Figure 7-34. In other words, the automatic curvature function moves the control handles of selected curve points and their neighbors to mimic the arc of a circle.

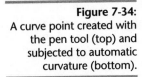

Figure 7-34:
A curve point created with the pen tool (top) and subjected to automatic curvature (bottom).

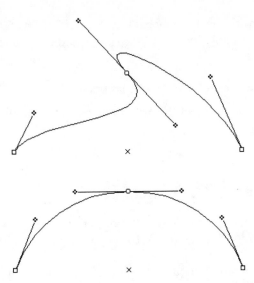

After you turn on the Automatic option, the rules of automatic curvature guide the manipulation of a point. In the first example in Figure 7-35, I selected the curve point in my path. When I moved the point to the left, as shown in the second example, FreeHand automatically repositioned the control handles belonging to the dragged point as well as both of its neighbors. With the automatic curvature function in force, you can move a point and reshape its segments in a single operation.

Figure 7-35:
Dragging a point when automatic curvature is active simultaneously moves the point and reshapes its segments.

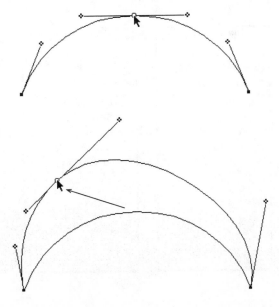

But as I demonstrated with the fish way back in Figures 5-40 and 5-41, automatic curvature is not always the best solution. You can remove automatic curvature from a selected point in two ways:

☞ Move at least one control handle for that point.

☞ Select the point and deselect the Automatic check box in the Object panel of the Inspector palette.

Free-Form Path Info

If you want to make several changes to a point or path at once, FreeHand provides a one-stop path manipulation headquarters: the Object panel in the Inspector palette.

After selecting an ungrouped path, press Command-Option-I (or, if the Inspector palette is not available, Command-I followed by Command-Option-I) to display the Object panel shown in Figure 7-36. The options in the panel apply to any free-form path, whether you created it with the polygon, line, freehand, bézigon, pen, or trace tool. They also affect any ungrouped rectangle or ellipse.

 If more than one path is selected, the Object panel is blank. You'll have to deselect all but one path to adjust the options described in the next few paragraphs.

Figure 7-36:
The Object panel as it appears when a path (left), multiple points (middle), and a single point (right) are selected.

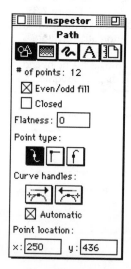

Assuming that a free-form path is selected, the Object panel always lists how many points make up the path. This information is particularly useful if the selected path is complicated or contains tightly packed points, which is often the case with paths created with the freehand or trace tool. The other items in the Object panel include the following:

- ↷ **Even/Odd Fill:** The Even/Odd Fill option controls the manner in which overlapping portions of a selected closed path are filled. Generally speaking, selecting this option makes overlapping areas transparent; deselecting the option fills overlapping areas according to the specifications in the fill panel of the Inspector palette.

- ↷ **Closed:** If you select the Closed check box, FreeHand inserts a segment between the two endpoints of the selected path. The identities of the endpoints dictate the curvature of the new segment. Deselecting the Closed option opens the selected path by eliminating the segment between the first and last points, which is a function of the order in which the points were created.

- ↷ **Flatness:** The Flatness option controls the manner in which the selected path is printed to a PostScript output device such as a LaserWriter or imagesetter. PostScript printers imitate curves as a collection of hundreds or even thousands of tiny, straight lines. The Flatness option determines the greatest distance, in device pixels, that any of these lines can stray from the mathematical definition of the curve. Enter any number between 0 and 100 for this option. Higher values permit fewer straight lines and therefore result in more jagged curves. Leave this option set to 0 unless you experience problems printing the current illustration. For complete information on this option, read the "Splitting long paths" section in Chapter 20.

- ↷ **Point Type:** These icons only appear when one or more points are selected. Click on an icon to change the identity of the points. Read the "Converting points" section a couple of pages back if this doesn't make sense.

- ↷ **Curve Handles:** Again, these icons only appear when at least one point is selected. Click on the left icon to retract the Bézier control handle associated with the segment that enters a selected point; click on the right icon to retract the handle that controls the segment that exits the point. Then read the "Retracting Bézier control handles" section earlier in this chapter to figure out what I'm talking about.

- ↷ **Automatic:** Select this check box and your life becomes fully functioning, just like you always dreamed it would. Your dishes will wash themselves, your roof will stop leaking, and your spouse and loved ones will behave themselves.

Oh, wait, wrong Automatic option. I was thinking of that one I saw advertised on QVC. (You mean *you* don't have one?) The Automatic option included with FreeHand subjects a selected point to the rules of automatic curvature, as described in the "Automatic curvature" section earlier in this chapter. Sadly, your roof will still leak.

↝ **Point Location:** When a single point is selected, two Point Location option boxes appear at the bottom of the panel, listing the horizontal (X) and vertical (Y) coordinates of the point as measured from the ruler origin. These values are very useful for aligning points. Say, for example, that you want to align point A horizontally with point B. Click on point A and note the coordinate in the X option box. Then click on point B, replace the value in the X option box with the coordinate for point A, and press Return. Bingo, the points are perfectly aligned.

Combining and Splitting Paths ____

Many of the reshaping techniques I've described so far are available in some form or another in just about every drawing software on earth. MacDraw Pro, for example — which Claris keeps threatening to replace with a revamped and improved ClarisDraw — allows you to move elements, add and delete points, play around with control handles, and convert straight segments to curved segments. Yet MacDraw is commonly considered too remedial for tackling a complex illustration.

This section discusses two areas in which FreeHand stands well above the common drawing crowd: the combining and splitting of points and segments in one or more paths. These features make it possible to break up portions of a path like pieces in a tailor-made puzzle and then assemble them in any way you see fit.

Joining open paths

The Join Objects command in the Arrange menu (Command-J) enables you to combine both closed and open paths. It combines multiple closed paths into a special kind of object called a *composite path,* as described in Chapter 17, "Blends, Masks, and Composite Paths." But first and foremost, this command joins endpoints from two different open paths to form a single free-form line.

Just for the record, the Join Objects command no longer joins text to a path. This function is now served by Type ⇨ Bind to Path (Command-Shift-Y, as in, "Y did they change this keyboard equivalent?").

Fusing endpoints from separate paths

If two endpoints from two separate paths are *coincident* — that is, if one point is positioned exactly on top of the other in the illustration window — issuing the Join Objects command fuses the two into a single interior point. The following steps show how this works, should you be inclined to try it out.

STEPS: Joining Two Open Paths

Step 1. Select an endpoint in the first path and drag it onto an endpoint in the second path using the arrow tool, as illustrated in Figure 7-37. The points snap together if the Snap to Point command in the View menu is active.

Figure 7-37:
Drag the endpoint of one path so that it snaps to the endpoint of another.

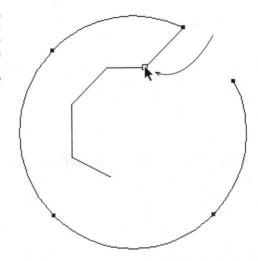

Step 2. Currently, only one path is selected. To use the Join Objects commands, both paths must be selected. So Shift-click with the arrow tool on the second path to add it to the selection, as illustrated in Figure 7-38.

Step 3. Choose Arrange ⇨ Join Objects (Command-J). FreeHand fuses the two endpoints into a single interior point inside a longer open path.

Figure 7-38:
Shift-click on the second path before choosing the Join Objects command.

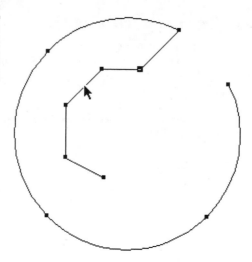

In the previous version of FreeHand, you had to select both endpoints by marqueeing them before pressing Command-J. This is no longer necessary. In Version 4.0, as long as you select the two paths that you want to join, FreeHand is smart enough to figure out which endpoints — if any — are coincident.

Joining two lines with a straight segment

Here's another bit of newness found in FreeHand 4.0. If none of the endpoints in two open paths are coincident when you choose the Join Objects command, Freehand joins the closest pair of endpoints — one point from each path — with a straight segment. In the first example of Figure 7-39, I selected two open paths. None of the endpoints overlapped. The two endpoints on the left side of the example are closer together than the endpoints on the right. So when I chose Arrange ➪ Join Objects, Freehand joined the left endpoints with a straight segment, as shown in the second example in the figure.

In order for this feature to work, the endpoints must be at least five pixels apart. (Actually, the exact minimum distance is determined by the value in the Snap Distance option box in the Editing panel of the Preferences dialog box.) If the points are closer, FreeHand moves them together and fuses them into a single interior point. Also, the Join Non-Touching Paths check box in the Editing panel of the Preferences dialog box must be turned on. If this option is off, and the endpoints are separated by more than five pixels, FreeHand ignores you when you choose Join Objects. (What an uppity program.)

Figure 7-39:
After you select
two open paths
(top) and choose
Join Objects,
Freehand draws a
straight segment
between the
nearest endpoints
(bottom).

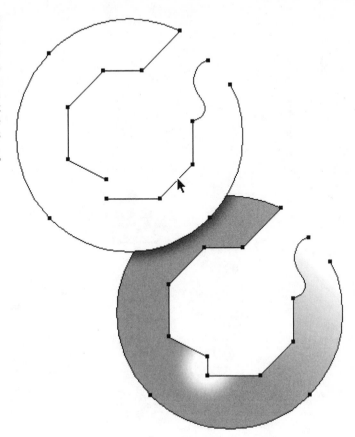

Auto joining

You don't need to use the Join Objects command when you're joining two endpoints in a single path. Endpoints in an open path will *auto join* when made coincident. Simply select one endpoint and drag it in front of the other endpoint in the same path, as shown in the first example of Figure 7-40. The two points automatically bond to form a selected interior point, as illustrated in the second example. If you turn to the object panel of the Inspector palette, you'll find the Closed check box selected, confirming that the path is closed.

Regardless of their original identities, endpoints auto join to form a corner point. The original Bézier control handles are retained.

Figure 7-40:
Drag one
endpoint in
front of the
other endpoint
in the same
path (top) to
automatically
fuse the two
points into one
(bottom).

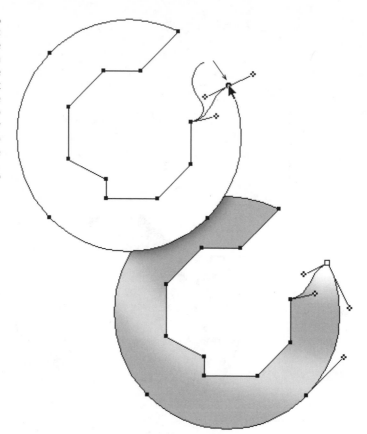

Combining path outlines

FreeHand provides several new commands under the Arrange ⇨ Path Operations submenu. Three of these — Intersect, Punch, and Union — enable you to combine paths in ways that the Join Objects command can't even begin to match, poor thing. All three commands make it easier to draw complex paths by combining more rudimentary shapes.

In the PowerPC-optimized version of FreeHand, the Intersect, Union, and Punch commands have been rewritten to take advantage of decimal-point calculations. This means that the commands can exploit the speed advantages of the PowerPC's FPU. Although most commands in FreeHand run twice as fast on the PowerPC as they do on a top-of-the-line Quadra, the Intersect, Union, and Punch commands run six to ten times as fast.

The Intersect, Punch, and Union commands share the following characteristics and parameters:

- ↷ To use any of these commands, you must select two or more closed paths. None of the commands are applicable to open paths.

- ↷ You can apply all the commands to rectangles and ellipses without first ungrouping the shapes, as well as to free-form paths.

- ↷ Each command deletes the selected paths and replaces them with a new path. If you want to retain the original paths for some reason, be sure to first clone the selection by choosing Edit ⇨ Clone (Command-equal) before applying Intersect, Punch, or Union.

- ↷ The Punch command can create multiple paths. Punch and Union can result in a composite path.

- ↷ The new paths move to the front of the current layer.

- ↷ When you choose the Intersect or Union command, FreeHand fills and strokes the new shape according to the attributes of the rearmost path in the selection.

- ↷ When you choose the Punch command, FreeHand fills and strokes each path according to the path's original attributes; only the frontmost shape is deleted.

With these little morsels of information in mind, read on for details about each command.

Intersect

The Intersect command retains the area in which all selected paths overlap. Consider, for example, Figure 7-41. In the first example, I selected two overlapping paths, a not-yet-ungrouped ellipse and a free-form path drawn with the pen tool. When I chose Arrange ⇨ Path Operations ⇨ Intersect, FreeHand deleted all portions of the path that did not overlap and drew a new path around the overlapping area. The result is a hand shape, the outside of which curves in a perfect oval. Drawing this shape from scratch would require considerable toil and Bézier tinkering, but building it by combining paths is easy.

Intersections abound in real life. The intersection of your body and your shoe is your foot; the intersection of Israel and Syria is the Golan Heights; the intersection of a box of Arm & Hammer and a spilled jar of vinegar is a childhood volcano; the intersection of a cowboy and a bucking bronco is a bruised behind; and the intersection of LaToya Jackson and a tenuous grasp on reality is nil.

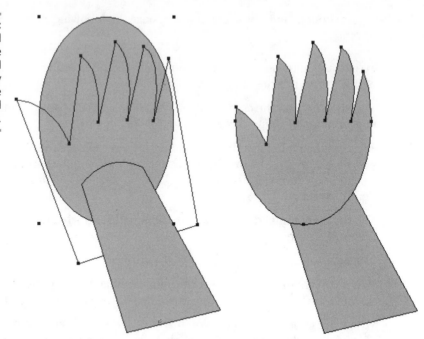

Figure 7-41:
Two selected closed
paths (left) and the
single combined
path formed by
choosing the
Intersect command
(right).

It is very important that *all* selected paths overlap when you choose Arrange ⇨ Path Operations ⇨ Intersect. If any two paths in the selection do not overlap, the Intersect command merely deletes the paths. Suppose that you select three shapes, a circle, a square, and a triangle. The circle and square overlap, the square and triangle overlap, but the triangle and circle do not overlap. When you choose the Intersect command, FreeHand looks at the paths and determines that the three paths don't share any common space. The Intersect command turns up empty-handed, and rather than delivering an error message, FreeHand simply deletes the selection.

The Intersect command is the only command capable of retaining your original shapes in the course of creating new ones. However, you have to press a special key to access this function. If you press the Option key when choosing Arrange ⇨ Path Operations ⇨ Intersect, FreeHand displays the Transparency dialog box shown in Figure 7-42. Not only will you retain your original shapes, you can also mix the fills of the shapes. If you want to use the fill of the rearmost object, change the Opacity value to 0 percent. To lift the fill from the frontmost object, change the Opacity to 100 percent. (Note that this is exactly opposite of the way a sane person would expect the option to work.) To mix the colors, enter a value in between. After you press Return, FreeHand creates a new shape and leaves the originals intact.

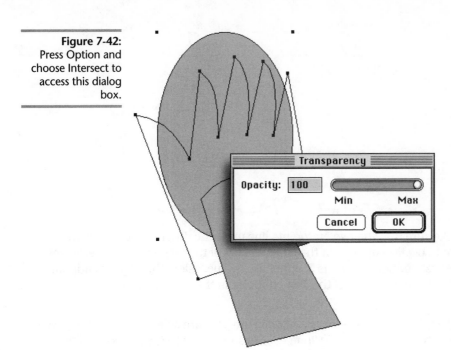

Figure 7-42:
Press Option and choose Intersect to access this dialog box.

When you Option-choose Intersect, the resulting shape lacks a stroke. Furthermore, the command can't mix gradations.

Punch

When using the Punch command, try to keep in mind that it has no bearing whatsoever to funny-looking, big-nosed, bat-wielding, psychotic puppets who speak in falsetto. Instead, this command takes one selected path and uses its outline to punch a hole in any and all selected paths behind it.

The following steps explain how to create the familiar Apple logo by using Control-dragging, the Join Objects and Punch commands, and a few techniques I have yet to properly introduce.

STEPS: Taking a Bite Out of the Apple

Step 1. Begin the graphic by drawing half of the apple as an open path using the freehand or pen tool — whichever makes you most comfortable. This is the only step that takes any talent. If you can draw even a rude approximation of half an apple, as shown in the first example of Figure 7-43, you'll breeze through the remaining steps.

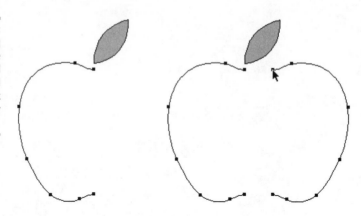

Figure 7-43:
After drawing half of the apple (left), I cloned the path and flipped it horizontally (right).

Step 2. Make sure that the two endpoints line up vertically. To do this, use the Point Location options in the Object panel of the Inspector palette. Select the first endpoint, note its X option box value, select the second endpoint, enter the coordinate of the first endpoint in the X option box, and press Return.

Step 3. Select the arrow tool. If any points in the path are selected, press the grave key. Then choose Edit ⇨ Clone (Command-Equal) to make a copy of the selected line.

Step 4. Flip the path horizontally. The best way to accomplish this is to display the Transform palette (Command-M), click on the Reflect icon in the palette (far right), enter 90 into the Reflect Axis option box, and press the Return key.

Step 5. The flipped clone no doubt overlaps the original. Drag it off to the side a bit so that you can better see what you're doing. Then Control-drag the path by one of its endpoints (see the second example of Figure 7-43) so that it snaps onto the corresponding endpoint in the original path.

Step 6. The result should look like an apple, but the path isn't closed yet. To do the honors, Shift-click on the original path so that both halves are selected. Then choose Arrange ⇨ Join Objects (Command-J). FreeHand joins one pair of coincident endpoints. Then, because the other two endpoints are also coincident, FreeHand auto joins them to form a closed path. (This is why it was so important to align the endpoints vertically in Step 2.)

Step 7. Shift-drag with the oval tool to draw a circle, which will represent the bite out of the apple. Then use the arrow tool to drag the bite into position, as shown in the first example of Figure 7-44.

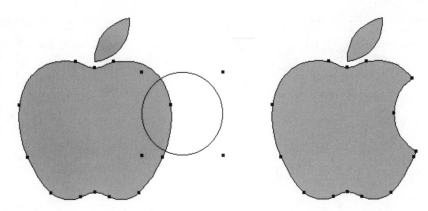

Figure 7-44:
Draw a circle to represent the bite (left) and then select both shapes and choose the Punch command (right).

Step 8. Shift-click on the apple shape so that both apple and bite are selected. Then choose Arrange ⇨ Path Operations ⇨ Punch. Because the circle is in front, FreeHand punches the circle out of the apple, as shown in the second example of Figure 7-44.

 When two or more paths are selected, FreeHand punches the frontmost selected path out of each of the other paths. If a rear shape entirely surrounds the front shape, FreeHand combines them into a composite path. For more information, check out Chapter 17, "Blends, Masks, and Composite Paths."

Union

The Union command traces an outline around all selected shapes. Like a silhouette or a chalk line around a corpse, the Union command eliminates overlapping details and retains only the overall outline. The first example in Figure 7-45 shows three simple shapes I created using the rectangle, ellipse, and pen tools. (Can you see how I created the gray shape by overlapping a rectangle and ellipse and applying the Intersect command?) I selected all three shapes and chose Arrange ⇨ Path Operations ⇨ Union to fuse the outlines of the path into a single shape. The result is shown in the second example of Figure 7-45.

 Notice how the shape in the second example of the figure contains two outlines, one around the cup — or whatever it is — and one inside the handle. The outline inside the handle is transparent. Only one kind of path can accommodate a transparent outline inside a filled shape, and that's a composite path. Again, for more information on these wonders of FreeHand drawing, read Chapter 17.

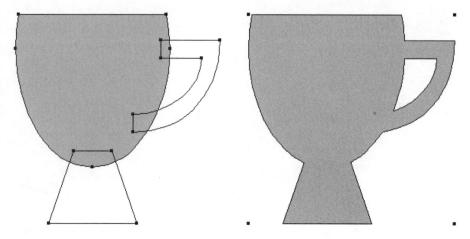

Figure 7-45:
Three select shapes (left) brought together using the Union command (right).

Just for fun, Figure 7-46 shows the paths created in the last three sections as they appear when printed from FreeHand.

Figure 7-46:
The paths from Figures 7-41, 7-44, and 7-45 as they appear when printed from FreeHand.

Splitting and slicing

The knife tool, the fifth tool on the left side of the toolbox, is used to split a point or segment. By selecting the knife tool and clicking at some location on a selected segment, you insert two endpoints into the segment — each associated with one segment — which splits the segment in two. If you click with the knife tool on an interior point, you split the point into two endpoints. Either way, using the knife tool opens a closed path or splits an open path into two lines.

In FreeHand 4.0, you can drag with the knife tool to slice through multiple segments at a time. Imagine — the knife tool actually behaves like a knife instead of a pair of scissors (Illustrator's equivalent and less capable tool).

Suppose that you want to split an ordinary circle into the three shapes shown in Figure 7-47. The following steps describe how you can accomplished this feat using the knife and pen tools.

Figure 7-47:
The completed tennis ball-looking thing printed from FreeHand.

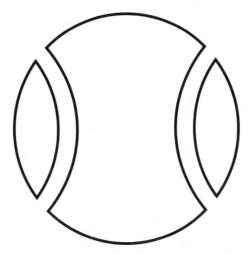

STEPS: Splitting a Circle into Three Paths

Step 1. Draw a circle with the oval tool. Then select the knife tool and Shift-drag to create a vertical slice through the right side of the circle, as shown in Figure 7-48. Shift-drag again to create a second vertical slice a quarter inch or so to the left of the first one. This adds two sets of points to each of the right-hand segments, which appear as selected in Figure 7-49. The circle is now split into four separate lines.

Step 2. Press the Tab key to deselect all elements. Then select the arrow tool and click on the topmost of the tiny single-segment lines created with the knife tool. Shift-click on the lower single-segment line to add it to the selection.

Step 3. Drag both lines away from the remaining paths of the circle, as shown in Figure 7-50. Neither line is a part of the prospective final image, so press the Delete key to remove them both. You are now left with two open paths.

Figure 7-48:
Shift-drag with the knife tool as indicated by the arrow to slice through the right side of the circle.

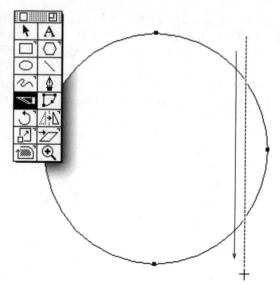

Figure 7-49:
The points created by Shift-dragging twice with the knife tool.

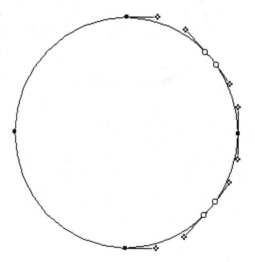

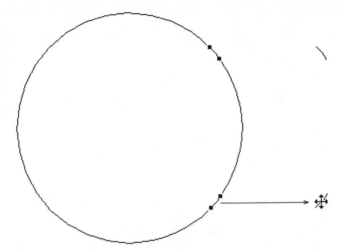

Figure 7-50:
Drag the two single-segment lines away from the rest of the circle and delete them.

Step 4. Select the right-hand path and then click on the top point in the path to select it. Press the Option key and drag down and to the left from the selected point to add a Bézier control handle to the corner point, making it a cusp.

Step 5. Press the 6 key to select the pen tool. Drag at a location that mirrors the center curve point of the right-hand path. A curved segment connects the new curve point to the previous cusp point.

Step 6. Drag at the bottom point in the right-hand path, closing the path. In the middle of the drag, press Option to convert the curve point to another cusp. Finish the drag up and to the right, forming a leaf-shaped path, like the one that appears in Figure 7-51.

Step 7. Close the second, larger path in a similar manner, adding two segments that are parallel to those you used to close the right-hand shape. The result is shown in Figure 7-51.

Step 8. Repeat Steps 1 through 7 on the left side of the circle to complete the tennis ball effect.

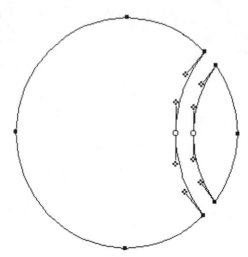

Figure 7-51:
Draw segments closing the
two remaining paths.

You can use the knife tool on a point or segment in any selected, ungrouped path. You can also split elements in a grouped or composite path, provided that you selected one or more individual paths by Option-clicking on the path with the arrow tool (as described in the "Selecting elements within groups" section of next chapter). Watch out, though — the cut paths are removed from the group. The knife tool produces no effect if no path is selected or if you click or drag in an empty portion of the window.

 Pressing the 7 key — either in the standard key set or on the keypad — selects the knife tool. If a text block or option box is active, press Shift-F7 instead.

You can also split an interior point into two endpoints by selecting the point and choosing the Split Object command from the Arrange menu (Command-Shift-J). The only advantage this command has over the knife tool is that you can use it to split multiple points simultaneously. Otherwise, the knife tool is typically more convenient.

Reneging the past

Because we all make mistakes, especially when drawing and tracing complicated paths, FreeHand provides you with the ability to nullify the results of previous operations. In fact, FreeHand offers a greater capacity to nullify past actions than the overwhelming majority of applications running on the Mac and Windows. So, when drawing anxiety sets in, remember this simple credo: *Undo, redo, revert.* That's Latin for "Chill, it's just a computer, not a crazed brain-sucking creature from another planet (much as it might resemble one)."

Undo

If you are familiar with other Mac or Windows programs such as PageMaker or CorelDraw, you are no doubt familiar with the Undo command in the Edit menu (Command-Z). This command allows you to negate the last action you performed. Suppose that you add a point to a path and then decide that you don't like how it looks. Choose the Undo command, and the new point disappears. You will, in fact, be returned to the moment before you added the point. Any previous selections are selected again, and so on. It's like a miniature time machine.

You can even undo such minor alterations as changing an option in a dialog box — which is a level of precision unmatched by most other applications. And you can *always* undo the last action, even if you have since clicked on-screen or performed some minor action that the Undo command does not recognize. FreeHand is truly amazing in this respect.

 Get this: FreeHand goes so far as to allow you to undo an operation that you performed before the most recent Save operation (although you cannot undo the Save command itself). You can delete an element, save the illustration, and then choose Undo to make the element reappear. It's an absolutely phenomenal, life-saving capability.

The Undo command, however, does have it limits. You cannot undo an operation that you performed in a previous FreeHand session. FreeHand displays the name of the operation that you're about to undo in the Edit menu, following the word Undo. Examples include *Undo Freehand* and *Undo Move Elements*. If you're not sure what action you're about to undo, check the menu first.

Multiple undos

In a typical application, after you undo an operation, the Undo command changes to a Redo command, providing a brief opportunity to reperform an operation — just in case you decide that you didn't want to undo it after all. In FreeHand, the Undo command remains available so that you can undo the second-to-last operation, and the one before that, and so on. In fact, you can undo up to 99 consecutive operations. This power-user feature takes a great deal of the worry out of using FreeHand. Even major blunders can be whisked away.

You adjust the number of possible consecutive undos by entering any value from 1 to 100 for the Number of Undo's option in the Editing panel of the Preferences dialog box (accessed by choosing File ➪ Preferences). The default value is 10. To make a new value take effect, you must quit FreeHand and relaunch the application. This gives FreeHand the opportunity to create an adequately sized undo buffer in the application RAM.

Conventional wisdom suggests that your machine must assign at least 8MB of application RAM to FreeHand to support the maximum 100 consecutive undos. If FreeHand cannot build a buffer large enough when launching, you may be presented with an out-of-memory error and returned to the Finder. In this worst-case scenario, you can reset the preference settings by throwing away the FreeHand Preferences file, found in the Aldus folder inside System Folder. Then relaunch FreeHand.

After you undo the maximum number of operations, the Undo command appears dimmed in the Edit menu. Pressing Command-Z produces no effect until a new operation is performed.

Redo

Just as you can undo as many as 100 consecutive actions, you can redo up to 100 consecutive undos by using the Redo command in the Edit menu (Command-Y). You can choose Edit ⇨ Redo only if the last command you issued was the Undo command. Otherwise, the Redo command appears dimmed. Also, if you undo a series of actions, perform a new series of actions, and then undo the new series to the point where you had stopped undoing previously — are you following me here? — you can't go back and redo the first series of undos. Instead, you can simply continue to undo from where you left off.

Revert

Suppose that you revise your illustration by performing a series of actions. After making these changes, you decide that the illustration looked better before you started. You may be able to use the Undo command to reverse all your changes one operation at a time. However, not only would that take a lot of time, there's no guarantee that you have enough undos at your disposal.

A better solution is to use the Revert command in the File menu. The Revert command returns your illustration to the state it was in immediately following the last save operation. This command is useful when you have made major changes in your illustration that you now regret, such as deleting important elements or editing text.

To revert to the version of the current illustration saved to disk, choose File ⇨ Revert. FreeHand displays an alert box to make sure that you haven't lost your mind and you really do want to dispose of all changes made since the last Save command.

After you revert to the last version of the illustration saved to disk, you cannot return to the previous version. If you want to go ahead and revert to the last saved version, click the OK button or press Return; if not, click Cancel or press Command-period.

 If you have not saved your illustration since opening it or if you are working on a new illustration that has never been saved to disk, the Revert command is dimmed.

 If you're not sure what the last saved version of your file looks like — or whether it's any better than the mess you just created — choose File ⇨ Save As and save the new file under a different name than the last saved version. Then open the old file and compare the two versions.

Summary

- Press and hold the Command key to access the arrow tool at any time.

- Draw a marquee with the arrow tool to select multiple points at a time. Shift-marquee to add to or subtract from the current selection.

- Press Command-A to select everything. Press Tab to deselect everything. Press the grave key to deselect points but leave their paths selected.

- Press the Control key while Shift-dragging the corner handle of a rectangle or ellipse to scale it exclusively horizontally or vertically.

- To reshape a rectangle or ellipse, you first have to ungroup it by pressing Command-U.

- Use the arrow keys to move selected points and objects in 1-point increments.

- Option-drag a segment to adjust its curvature on the fly. You can even Option-drag straight segments to add curvature.

- Bézier control handles act as levers that bend and stretch segments. There is no limit to how far you can drag a handle or stretch a segment.

- To add a point to a path, click on the path with the bézigon or pen tool. You can also Option-click or Control-click with the bézigon tool or drag or Control-drag with the pen tool.

- Option-drag from a point with the arrow tool to add a control handle; click on one of the Curve Handle icons in the Object panel of the Inspector palette to retract a handle.

- If you drag one endpoint in a path onto the other endpoint in the same path, FreeHand automatically fuses the two into a single point and closes the path.

- Choose the Intersect command to retain the intersecting area of multiple selected paths. Choose Union to draw an outline around selected overlapping paths. Choose Punch to use one selected path to take a bite out of another.

- FreeHand's path operations have been upgraded to take advantage of the PowerPC's super-fast FPU capabilities. As a result, these are among FreeHand's fastest operations, despite their relative complexity.

- Drag with the knife tool to slice through multiple selected paths at once. The tool does not affect deselected paths.

- The Undo command can even undo an operation that you performed before saving or printing a document.

The Regimental Approach

In This Chapter

- ➥ Tracking the movements of your cursor in the horizontal and vertical rulers
- ➥ Using grids and guidelines to create precise drawings
- ➥ Interpreting items displayed in the information bar
- ➥ Automatically aligning and distributing objects
- ➥ Using the Group and Lock commands to protect objects from accidental or unwanted editing
- ➥ Organizing and negotiating drawing layers

FreeHand Eliminates Drafting Nightmares

Are you ready for a tiresome personal story? If not, skip to the next section, where I finally manage to impart some information that might actually help you use FreeHand.

In my junior high school — you are ready for this, aren't you? In my junior high school, the boys — that's right, only the boys — had to take wood shop one semester and drafting another. (I forget what the girls had to take. Mending or "Learning to Love Baking Soda" or something like that. Oh, and the obligatory "How to Act Dumber than Your Prospective Husband," which I hear was actually a very challenging course.)

In seventh grade, I started off with shop class and came to hate it almost immediately. I was so awful at working with power saws and sanders that I finally just molded my spice rack out of putty. But all the eighth graders assured me that although shop was admittedly terrible, drafting was worse. You just sat there and drew boring geometric stuff, and nobody could talk except the teacher, who nagged you about your uneven lines and sloppy corners, like maybe someone was really going to build something based on your retardo drawing. Only a total nerd could tolerate it.

Being an avid nerd myself, I naturally took to drafting like a fish takes to chowing down on flies. I got an A on every project, easily earned an A in the class, and was generally the envy of those with poor fine-motor skills. It was a very successful experience. For me, anyway.

But I was, after all, a scrub. I may have been better than most of the other kids in the class, but I'm relatively certain that I wasn't perfect. (If I was, I'd like to know where I went wrong, because I've sure as heck managed to wander several figurative miles from the mark since.) Later in life, I had the opportunity to test out what a spaz I really was. I was hired to create a series of precision drawings for this so-called professional directory. It was really just a cheap magazine composed exclusively of paid advertisements from doctors, lawyers, and a host of Boulder's stereotypical new-age companies, including a few out-and-out charlatans who have since gone under, much to my general amusement. (Oh, man, that felt good. If you're a free-lance artist, I heartily recommend that you write a book someday and openly ridicule some old client. Truly cathartic.)

The point is, the drawings were a constant source of irritation. Every undesirable burp of ink from my Rapidiograph required an application of some white ink, which was supposed to cover up the mistake. But the white ink, of course, created a bump in the paper surface over which it was nearly impossible to draw a straight line or adhere that sticky halftone-dot transparency stuff without forming a slight shadow. I eventually created pieces that I was happy with, but the process was exasperating and incredibly time-consuming.

Don't you just love these personal stories? They allow us to bond. I mean, I *really* feel close to you right now.

So where was I? Yeah, okay, so the problem was, I was trying to draw like a machine. Like arithmetic and automobile assembly, drafting is one of those tasks that machines can accomplish quickly, efficiently, and accurately. The machine needs a human to guide it; I'm not trying to imply that you're out of the loop. But the machine greatly improves your chances of a timely success.

In the case of drafting, FreeHand (yes, it all comes back to that) combined with a Mac or PC is the machine of choice. Though it lacks a couple of useful features offered by Illustrator — a tool for measuring the distance between objects, custom guidelines for aligning points to circles and irregular paths — FreeHand also provides a couple of tricks of its own, including grids, better ruler tracking, automatic object distribution, and improved locking capabilities. But more importantly, FreeHand makes a mockery of drafting with conventional tools. Every corner is sharp, every line weight is absolutely consistent, every angle is accurate, and, if you make a mistake, absolution is no farther away than the Undo command or Delete key.

And don't think that you have to be an architect or engineer to take advantage of FreeHand's precision controls. These functions are designed with illustrators and designers in mind. If you've ever hoped to align two objects exactly, lock a path to prevent it from being altered, or organize objects onto separate layers, this chapter is essential reading.

Controlling Movements _____

Now that we've gotten my sordid history out of the way — really, (sniff), thanks for listening — I have a chapter of information just itching to be conveyed. If you read the last chapter, you've already had a taste of some of the precision techniques that FreeHand offers. Shift-dragging, rotating the constraint axes, snapping, and nudging points via the arrow keys all qualify as means for making controlled adjustments to an illustration. The following sections explain additional drawing and editing functions that enable you to make precise changes to your illustration.

Using the rulers

FreeHand provides access to one vertical and one horizontal ruler. These rulers track the movement of your cursor or, if you're dragging an object, the movement of the object. Choose View ⇨ Rulers (Command-R) to display the rulers, which appear at the top and left-hand edges of the illustration window, as shown in Figure 8-1. When the rulers are visible, a check mark precedes the Rulers command in the View menu. Choose the command again to hide the rulers.

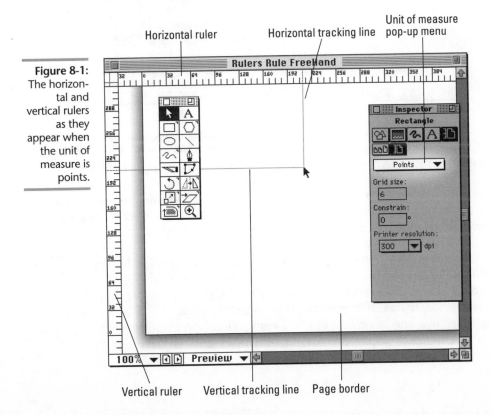

Figure 8-1: The horizontal and vertical rulers as they appear when the unit of measure is points.

Changing the unit of measure

The units displayed on both rulers can be points, picas, inches, or millimeters. For the record, a *pica* is almost exactly 1/6 of an inch, and there are 12 *points* in every pica (so, about 72 points in an inch). To change the unit of measure, select a new option from the pop-up menu at the top of the Document Setup panel in the Inspector palette. Figure 8-2 shows the result of changing the unit of measure to picas.

Figure 8-2:
Changing the unit of measure to picas makes the rulers look like this.

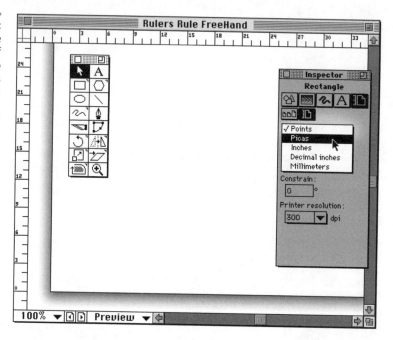

Whole picas, inches, or millimeters are indicated by long tick marks; fractions are indicated by short tick marks. As you magnify the view size, the units on the rulers become larger and more detailed. As you zoom out, units become smaller and less detailed. Numbers on each ruler indicate the distance from the *ruler origin*, the location in the illustration window at which the horizontal and vertical coordinates are zero. By default, the ruler origin is located in the bottom left corner of the page, as Figures 8-1 and 8-2 illustrate. All ruler measurements are made relative to this origin.

Notice in Figure 8-2 that the unit of measure pop-up menu offers two inches options, Inches and Decimal Inches. If you select Inches, FreeHand divides each inch using a series of differently sized tick marks, placing the longest tick mark at the half inch, two shorter marks at the quarter inches, four still shorter at eighth inches, and so on, just like on a conventional drugstore ruler. Select Decimal Inches to display a maximum of 10 tick marks, all sized equally, per inch. It's purely a matter of preference.

As I alluded to in previous chapters, the unit of measure you select in the Document Setup panel affects the way values in several of FreeHand's option boxes are measured. These option boxes include the following:

- Cursor Key Distance in the Editing panel of the Preferences dialog box
- Grid Size in the Document Setup panel of the Inspector palette
- Bleed Size in the Document Pages panel (Command-Option-D) of the Inspector palette
- Baseline Shift in the Text Character panel (Command-Option-T) of the Inspector palette
- All Paragraph Spacing and Indents option boxes in the Text Paragraph panel (Command-Option-P) of the Inspector palette
- Width in the Stroke panel (Command-Option-L) of the Inspector palette
- All Dimensions option boxes in the Object panel (Command-Option-I) of the Inspector palette
- All option boxes in the Dimensions & Inset panel (Command-Option-B) of the Inspector palette
- All option boxes in the Column & Row panel (Command-Option-R) of the Inspector palette

 You can override the unit of measure in any of these option boxes by adding the following abbreviations after the value that you enter: *i* for inch, *m* for millimeter, and *p* for pica, with any value following *p* indicating points. For example, *1.125i* means 1 1/8 inches; *40m* means 40 millimeters; and *12p6* means 12 picas, six points (12 1/2 picas).

Tracking lines

As long as the cursor is inside the illustration window, FreeHand tracks its movement on the horizontal and vertical rulers. It displays small dotted *tracking lines* to indicate the precise location of your cursor, as shown in Figure 8-1. For example, the cursor in Figure 8-1 is 212 points above and to the right of the ruler origin. (Each tick mark equals eight points, and each tracking line in the figure is two and a half tick marks past the 192 mark, hence 212.)

 Don't worry, you don't have to make these kinds of computations in your head. You can view the coordinates in the information bar, displayed by choosing View ➪ Info Bar (Command-Shift-R), as explained in the "Using the information bar" section later in this chapter.

When you drag a path or text block, FreeHand highlights portions of the horizontal and vertical rulers to show the size of the dragged object, as illustrated in Figure 8-3. This function is especially useful if you are trying to move an object to a specific location on the page. Too bad it's not in force during other transformations as well, such as scalings and rotations.

Figure 8-3:
When you
drag one or
more objects,
FreeHand
highlights
portions of
the horizon-
tal and
vertical rulers
to show the
size of the
selection.

Changing the ruler origin

As I mentioned a moment ago, the ruler origin is located at the bottom left corner of the page by default. What I didn't mention was that you can relocate the ruler origin by dragging from the *ruler origin box*, which is the square created by the intersection of the horizontal and vertical rulers. Figure 8-4 illustrates the process of relocating the ruler origin. The black lines that extend from the arrow cursor indicate the prospective position of the new origin. If you drag very near to a point (as in Figure 8-4), the ruler origin snaps to the point, enabling you to make all measurements from a specific portion of an object (in the case of the figure, the base of the leaf of the apple). Notice that the movement of the ruler origin is tracked by the rulers.

Ruler origin box

Figure 8-4:
Drag from the
ruler origin box
(top) to relocate
the point at
which the
horizontal and
vertical
coordinates are
zero (bottom).

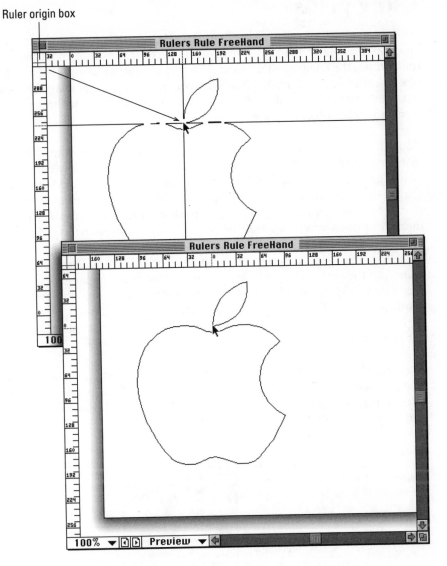

At the end of the drag, the ruler origin moves to the location occupied by the cursor. All ruler measurements are then made from the new ruler origin.

Using grids

In addition to rulers and tracking lines, FreeHand provides a *grid*, which is a network of imaginary, regularly spaced horizontal and vertical lines that constrain the operation of tools within the illustration window. The grid affects the creation of points and the placement of control handles. The segments themselves can snake along as they please, but points align to grid intersections. This feature helps you to line up objects and elements inside objects as you draw.

You can display the grid by choosing the Grid command from the View menu. However, just because the grid is visible doesn't mean that it will have any effect on your cursor — and just because it's invisible doesn't mean it won't. To make your cursor snap to grid intersections, choose View ⇨ Snap to Grid (Command-semicolon). When either of these commands is active, you'll see a check mark by the command name; the check mark disappears when you hide the grid or turn off the Snap to Grid command.

To specify the space between the imaginary horizontal and vertical grid lines, enter a value into the Grid Size option box in the Document Setup panel of the Inspector palette (see Figure 8-5). By default, the value is 6 points, or 1/12 inch. When you make the grid visible, however, FreeHand always spaces the lines about one inch apart, regardless of view size. This helps to avoid screen clutter. As Figure 8-6 illustrates, the window would get pretty busy if FreeHand displayed each and every grid line.

The individual dots in the grid lines represent the amount of space between the actual grid intersections. For example, if FreeHand displays 11 dots between visible grid lines — which is the default setting — then there are 11 actual grid lines between one inch and the next, for a total of 12 grid increments per inch.

Figure 8-5:
Change the Grid Size value to adjust the amount of space between imaginary grid lines.

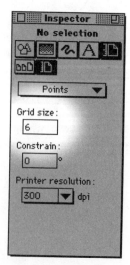

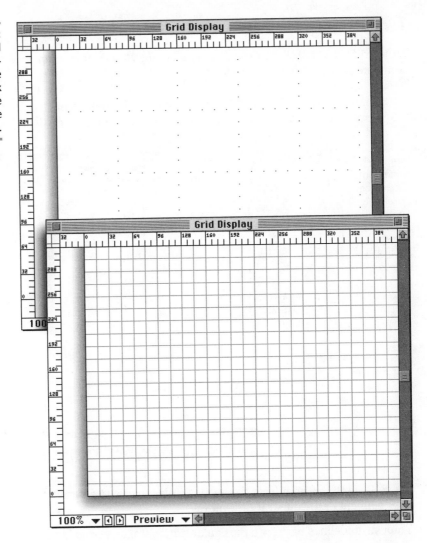

Figure 8-6:
How FreeHand
displays the grid on-
screen (top) and the
actual grid network
that controls the
movement of the
cursor (bottom).

When you turn on the Snap to Grid feature, FreeHand snaps your cursor or any object or element that you drag to the nearest grid intersection. This affects the creation and manipulation of all points and handles in a path, whether you're working with a free-form or geometric path. Suppose that the grid is turned on and set to 1/2 inch. Any time you drag with any tool, the cursor jumps in 1/2-inch increments. As a result, you can't create a rectangle that is, say, 3/4-inch wide; it must measure 1/2 inch or 1 inch.

FreeHand 3.0 allowed you to specify separate sizes for the visible and snap-to grids. This is no longer the case. Now your only control over the visible grid is the Grid Color option in the Display panel of the Preferences dialog box. Furthermore, FreeHand 4.0 provides no means for automatically aligning objects to the grid. You now have to drag objects manually.

Creating guidelines

If the grid is too regular for you, you can create your own custom *guidelines* by dragging from one of the rulers:

↪ Drag downward from the horizontal ruler to create a horizontal guideline that spans the width of the illustration window, as illustrated in Figure 8-7.

Figure 8-7:
Drag from
one of the
rulers to
position a
horizontal or
vertical
guideline.

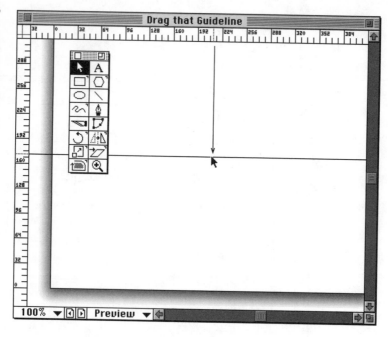

↪ Drag to the right from the vertical ruler to create a vertical guideline that is the height of the illustration window.

You use guidelines to mark a particular horizontal or vertical location inside the illustration window. You can then align points or segments in an object to the guideline and create perfect rows or columns of objects. When the Snap to Guides command is active in the View menu (Command-backslash), as it is by default, your cursor snaps to a guideline. When the command is active, FreeHand puts a check mark by the command name.

To move an existing guideline, use the arrow tool to drag it to a new location in the illustration window. To delete a guideline, drag it back to the horizontal or vertical ruler. This can be a frustrating task because FreeHand has the tendency to scroll as you drag beyond the confines of the illustration window. But if you drag and release quickly, it won't scroll very far. Hopefully, this problem will be remedied in a future version. Alternatively, you can drag the guideline off the page, assuming that you can see the edge of the page, of course.

Choose View ➪ Lock Guides to protect existing guidelines from being moved or deleted. To hide or display the guidelines, choose View ➪ Guides. When the guidelines are hidden, you can't create new guidelines. Also, hidden guidelines do not affect the creation or manipulation of objects. A check mark precedes Lock Guides or Guides when the command is active.

You can more conveniently control guidelines from the Layers palette. Click on the little lock icon that precedes the Guides layer name to lock and unlock the guidelines. Click on the check mark to hide and display the guidelines. Best of all, you can move the guidelines so that they're positioned in front of objects on a certain layer. Just drag the Guides option to a different location in the list included with the Layers palette. For more information on the Guides layer, read the "Layering Objects" section later in this chapter.

You can alter the interval at which a dragged element snaps toward a guideline. Just enter a new value in the Snap Distance option in the Editing panel of the Preferences dialog box. You can enter any value from 1 to 5; values are measured in screen pixels. The default value is 3.

Using the information bar

When you choose View ➪ Info Bar (Command-Shift-R), FreeHand displays the *information bar* directly below the menu bar. This thin horizontal strip provides all kinds of interesting and useful data about the current operation. The information bar constantly tracks the movement of your cursor in the illustration window and analyzes all changes that occur as a result of your clicks and drags.

For example, Figure 8-8 shows the information bar as it appears when you drag an object with the arrow tool. The first item in the information bar tells you what unit of measure is currently in force. The second and third items (X and Y) represent the horizontal and vertical coordinates of the cursor with respect to the ruler origin.

The fourth and fifth items (DX and DY) list the horizontal and vertical components — better known as the width and height — of the move. The sixth and seventh items (Dist and Angle) tell the distance and direction of the move. The latter is measured in degrees, relative to the 0-degree mark in a 360-degree circle. If the circle were a clock, the 0-degree mark would be 3 o'clock. (Refer back to lucky Figure 7-13, which shows the constraint axes and the directions associated with several common degree readings.)

Information bar

Figure 8-8: The information bar as it appears when you move an object.

The information bar also displays valuable information when you are creating geometric and free-form paths and when you are transforming selections with the arrow, scale, reflect, rotate, or skew tool. All position and distance items are listed in the unit of measure specified in the Document Setup panel of the Inspector palette. Table 8-1 lists all the items that you may see in the information bar and describes their meanings. I've listed the items in the order that they appear in the information bar.

Table 8-1	A Guide to the Information Bar	
Item	*Current Action*	*Meaning*
Lock icon	Any	Any and all selected objects are locked
Units	Any	Unit of measure specified in the Document Setup panel

Table 8-1 (continued)

Item	Current Action	Meaning
Tab position	Dragging a tab stop or indent marker in the tab ruler	Horizontal distance from left edge of text block to position of tab stop or insertion marker
X	Using any tool other than a transformation tool	Horizontal distance from the cursor to the ruler origin
Y	Using any tool other than a transformation tool	Vertical distance from the cursor to the ruler origin
CX	Scaling, reflecting, rotating, or skewing a selection	Horizontal distance from transformation origin to the ruler origin
CY	Scaling, reflecting, rotating, or skewing a selection	Vertical distance from transformation origin to the ruler origin
Width	Dragging with the rectangle, ellipse, trace, or zoom tool	Width of drag
Height	Dragging with the rectangle, ellipse, trace, or zoom tool	Height of drag
DX	Dragging a selection with the arrow tool or dragging with the line or pen tool	Width of drag
DY	Moving a selection with the arrow tool or dragging with the line or pen tool	Height of drag
Dist	Moving a selection with the arrow tool or with the line or pen tool	Direct measurement of distance dragged
Angle	Moving a selection with the arrow tool or dragging with the polygon, line, or pen tool	Direction of drag
	Reflecting a selection	Angle of reflection axis
	Rotating a selection	Angle of rotation
Radius	Dragging with the polygon tool of distance dragged	Direct measurement
Sides	Dragging with the polygon tool	Number of sides in the shape
SH	Scaling or skewing a selection	Horizontal extent of transformation expressed as a ratio (e.g., 1.0 equals 100%)
SV	Scaling or skewing a selection	Vertical extent of transformation expressed as a ratio (e.g., 1.0 equals 100%)

FreeHand 4.0 dropped the items that tracked changes to type size, leading, letterspacing, word spacing, and kerning. You now have no way to monitor changes that you make to these attributes by dragging text block handles. You can monitor keyboard kerning adjustments from the Text Character panel of the Inspector palette.

Alignment and Distribution

The capabilities I've discussed so far in this chapter are either no better or not quite as good as their counterparts in the previous version of FreeHand. Luckily, this sad-but-true trend comes to a screeching halt now, for FreeHand 4.0's alignment capabilities are superb. Oh, sure, you can no longer automatically align an object to the grid, but Version 3.0 didn't do such a hot job of implementing that feature anyway. The way they *should* have done it is to offer you the option to align every point in a selected object to the nearest grid intersection, and then . . . ah, but who cares? Really, what's done is done. Repeat after me, "I forgive FreeHand."

Now that I've healed that potential rift, let me continue with the good news. FreeHand's alignment and distribution functions enable you to adjust the locations of two or more selected objects with respect to one another. These functions are most useful when you're creating schematic drawings and want to line up objects in rows, columns, or other visual patterns.

To align or distribute (adjust the spacing between) two or more objects, select the objects and display the Align palette — shown in Figure 8-9 — by choosing Arrange ⇨ Align (Command-Shift-A). Then select the desired options from the Horizontal and Vertical pop-up menus and click on the Apply button or press Return. (If the Apply button is dimmed, it's because you haven't selected enough objects — "enough" being two.)

Aligning selected objects to each other

Each of the pop-up menus in the Align palette offers three alignment options and four distribution options. The alignment options line up selected objects according to their left or right edges, their tops or bottoms, or horizontally or vertically by their centers.

Here's an example. Suppose that you've drawn a series of silhouetted soldiers marching down a road. But you were naturally so busy concentrating on making the shapes look like soldiers against an eerie twilight sky that you entirely neglected to line them up properly. So rather than marching on a flat road, they bob up and down. To align their feet along a perfectly horizontal surface, you select all the soldier shapes, select the Align Bottom option from the Vertical pop-up menu, and press the Return key.

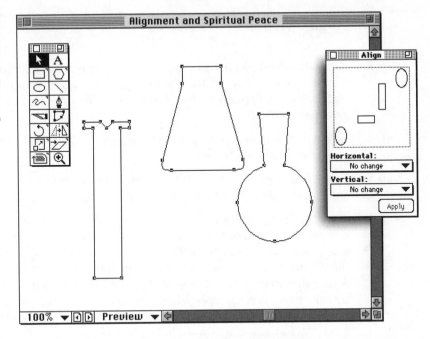

Figure 8-9:
The Align palette enables you to align and distribute selected objects with respect to each other.

 You don't have to select options from both the Horizontal and Vertical pop-up menus. When aligning the soldiers along the road, for example, you would leave the Horizontal pop-up menu set to No Change. In fact, you will more often than not select an option from only one pop-up menu. Otherwise, the shapes bunch up on each other.

Rather than run through every possible alignment permutation, I've included the following exercise, which begins with the three paths shown in Figure 8-10. The steps will only take you two or three minutes to complete — this is pretty easy stuff — so give them a whirl.

Figure 8-10:
Three beakers that want desperately to be aligned.

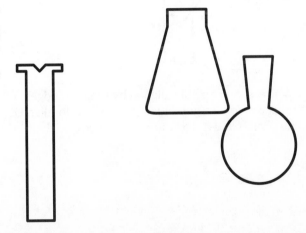

STEPS: Aligning a Bunch of Beakers

Step 1.   Draw three beaker shapes. Spend hours on this step and make your beakers look exactly like the ones in Figure 8-10. Or just draw three rectangles. It doesn't really matter; FreeHand is capable of dealing with nonbeaker shapes.

Step 2.   Select all three objects and choose Arrange ⇨ Align (Command-Shift-A) to bring the Align palette forward.

Step 3.   Select the Align Left option from the Horizontal pop-up menu. Just to be safe, make sure that the Vertical pop-up menu is set to No Change.

Step 4.   Click the Apply button in the lower right corner of the palette or just press Return. FreeHand then performs a two-step operation. First, it determines the leftmost point within each of the three selected shapes. For the sake of discussion, I'll call these key points A, B, and C. FreeHand notes that point A is farther to the left than B or C. The shape to which point A belongs therefore remains stationary. In the second step, FreeHand moves the shapes containing points B and C until all points — A, B, and C — line up in a vertical formation, as shown in Figure 8-11.

Figure 8-11:
The eager beakers horizontally aligned by
their left edges.

Step 5.   Ick, the beakers look terrible aligned by their left edges. Who in the world thought this would be a good idea? Choose Undo Align Objects from the Edit menu (Command-Z) to restore the objects to their original locations.

Step 6. Back inside the Align palette, select No Change from the Horizontal pop-up menu. Notice how the palette remembers your last setting? Then select Align Top from the Vertical pop-up menu.

Step 7. Press Return to produce the result shown in Figure 8-12. FreeHand finds the topmost point in each shape, makes the tippy-top shape stationary, and moves the others into position so that the tops of the shapes are aligned in horizontal formation. This configuration produces a better effect than Figure 8-11 because the beakers were positioned in a vaguely horizontal formation to begin with.

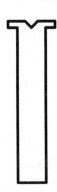
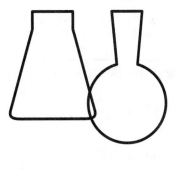

Figure 8-12:
The beaker boys aligned vertically by their tops.

In case you're wondering why FreeHand's Horizontal alignment options don't result in horizontal formations, as the option name might suggest, here's the reason. The Horizontal options align objects by their left or right edges, which results in a vertical column of objects. Likewise, the Vertical options align objects by their top and bottom edges, which creates a neatly aligned horizontal formation.

As demonstrated in the exercise, the Align Left and Align Top options work by moving key points in the selected paths into alignment with a model key point that remains stationary. The same is also true for the Align Right and Align Bottom options. However, the two Align Center options work a little differently. Each option first examines the equations that define all the selected paths. After plotting a few points along the outlines of the paths, the option averages the locations of these points to find a central horizontal and vertical coordinate. Finally, the option moves each path so that its center is located at the average coordinate.

Objects that are aligned horizontally fall into a linear column; objects that are aligned vertically fall into a straight row. If you want to align two objects by their exact centers, so that the smaller object is inset inside the larger one, select the Align Center options from both the Horizontal and Vertical pop-up menus.

Spacing objects evenly

To *distribute* objects is to place them so that the distance between object A and its neighbor, object B, is equal to the distance between object B and its neighbor, object C. For example, if a series of objects is distributed to the left, the leftmost point in each object is an equal distance from the leftmost point in each of its neighbors.

To use FreeHand's distribution options, you have to select at least three objects. FreeHand allows you to apply distribution options to two objects, but the options have no effect — FreeHand can't compare the space between one pair of objects to the space between another pair.

The following steps give you a quick introduction to the distribution options. Again, the steps involve the three beakers from Figure 8-10.

STEPS: Giving the Beakers Some Room to Maneuver

Step 1.   Select all three objects and press Command-Shift-A to bring up the Align palette.

Step 2.   Select the Align Bottom option from the Vertical pop-up menu. As you know — you *were* paying attention earlier, weren't you? — this option repositions the bottoms of two of the paths to align with the bottom of the lowest path.

Step 3.   Select the Distribute Widths option from the Horizontal pop-up menu, as shown in Figure 8-13. The Distribute Widths option instructs FreeHand to put an equal amount of horizontal space between each object. You see a preview of the option's effect in the top half of the palette.

Figure 8-13:
Select Distribute Widths from the
Horizontal pop-up menu.

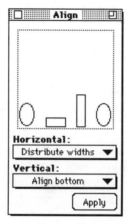

Step 4. Press Return. As shown in Figure 8-14, FreeHand's distribution feature automatically spreads the paths in an aesthetically pleasing formation. FreeHand's distribution options are a guaranteed hit.

Figure 8-14:
The bleak beakers aligned by their bottom edges and distributed horizontally according to width.

If you're not sure what results your alignment or distribution settings will produce, refer to the small icons inside the dotted rectangle at the top of the Align palette, as shown in Figure 8-13. These icons move to represent the effects of your selections. Keep in mind, however, that the icons may not bear a whole lot of resemblance to the selected objects in the illustration window, so you have to use a little bit of imagination. Or just apply a few options and undo the operation if you don't like it.

 To gain additional control when aligning objects, try locking one — and only one — of the objects by choosing Arrange ⇨ Lock (Command-L) before you apply options from the Align palette. The locked object remains stationary, while other selected objects are aligned to it. (For more information on the Lock command, keep reading.)

Grouping and Protecting Objects __

With the Group and Lock commands, you can protect objects from editing danger. Both commands make it difficult to access individual points in a path. And the Lock command goes as far as preventing you from moving or otherwise transforming whole objects.

Both commands build on FreeHand's assortment of precision functions by enabling you to put some objects off-limits. It's as if you could tell a bottle of ink, "No matter what I do — whack you, elbow you, or fling you across the room — don't spill all over this one drawing." To rope off entire collections of objects, check out the "Protecting layers" section later in this chapter.

Making many objects into one

A section or two ago, I asked you to imagine drawing silhouetted soldiers. You probably thought that I was just trying to stimulate your interest by setting a mood. But there was actually a modicum of method behind my madness.

You see, you can create a silhouette using a single shape. If, however, each of your soldiers comprised *multiple* shapes, the Align options would present a problem: They would align each and every object individually. Figure 8-15, for example, shows a soldier made up of 15 shapes. When I align the shapes along the bottom, the soldier falls apart, as in the second example. This is because FreeHand aligns the bottom of each and every shape.

Figure 8-15:
A soldier before
(left) and after
(right) I aligned its
various paths by
their bottoms.

To prevent this from happening, you need to make FreeHand think of all 15 shapes as a single object — which you can do by *grouping* the shapes. To do this, select the shapes and choose Arrange ➪ Group (Command-G). All shapes in the group then behave as a single, collective object. To align your platoon of soldiers, you would group the shapes in each soldier independently and then apply the desired options from the Align palette.

General grouping facts

When you choose the Group command, you achieve the same results whether you select only a single point or segment or an entire path. All objects that are even partially selected become grouped in their entirety.

You can apply the Group command to a single path to safeguard the relationship between points and segments. You can even group multiple groups and groups of groups. (But you can't group a grouper; you have to catch it with a rod and reel like everyone else.) In fact, you can apply the Group command to any type or graphic object that you can create or import into FreeHand.

After you group one or more objects, all points within the group disappear. When the group is selected, four corner handles define the perimeter of the group, much like those associated with a geometric shape. Using the arrow tool, you can drag any of these corner handles to scale a group, as discussed in the "Using handles" section of Chapter 7. Shift-drag a handle to scale the group proportionally.

 Hey, FreeHand 4.0 addressed one of the problems I complained about in the previous edition of my book! You can now scale a group with respect to its center by pressing the Option key. And you can scale a group horizontally or vertically by Shift-dragging and then pressing and holding the Control key midway into the operation.

Transforming as a unit

When a group is selected, the Object panel of the Inspector palette appears as shown in Figure 8-16. The first two Dimensions option boxes display the location of the lower left corner handle of the group in relation to the ruler origin. The second pair of options control the width and height of the group.

Figure 8-16:
The Object panel as it appears when a single group is selected.

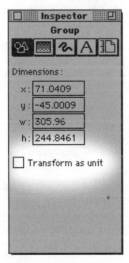

Below the option boxes is the Transform as Unit check box, which enables you to predetermine how a transformation will affect the attributes of the selected group. If you want certain aspects of a group — such as type orientation, fill, and stroke — to remain constant throughout a transformation, leave this option deselected. Although this is the default setting, it is generally not the setting you'll want to use.

Take a look at Figure 8-17, for example. To create the image on the right, I grouped the objects in the Slug-Man Clothiers logo on the left and then skewed the entire group. Because Transform as Unit was deselected, the stroke remained constant and the type simply rotated around its transformed ellipse. The relationship between paths in the cartoon has become hopelessly jumbled. I fixed the problem by transforming attributes along with the group, as shown in Figure 8-18. To do this, select the Transform as Unit check box before performing the transformation.

Figure 8-17:
After grouping several objects (left), I skewed the group (right), completely destroying every relationship the original group possessed.

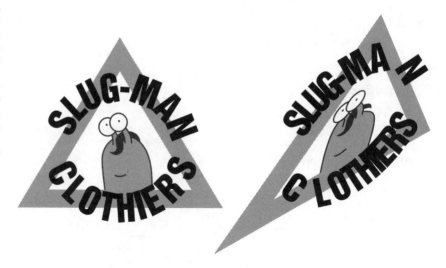

 Fans of Bill Amend's hilarious syndicated comic strip *FoxTrot* will recognize young Jason Fox's inspiring creation, the awesomely powerful Slug-Man, in these two figures. I'm certain that if this astonishingly gifted superhero had a line of baggy Slug-Pants, his logo would look exactly like this.

 For more information on transformations, including the skewing operation demonstrated here, read Chapter 15, "The Five Transformations." For more information on Slug-Man, buy every *FoxTrot* collection you can get your hands on.

Selecting elements within groups

To select a whole group, click on any path in the group with the arrow tool. You can also select an individual object in a group by Option-clicking on it with the arrow tool. Option-clicking with the arrow tool displays individual points in the path, allowing you to fill, stroke, reshape, or transform a single path within a group without affecting other objects in the group.

To select multiple paths in a group, Shift-Option-click on each path. Or press the Option key while marqueeing with the arrow tool and then press the grave key (`) to deselect the points and leave just the paths selected.

After selecting a single path in a group, you can select groups within groups by pressing the grave key (our friend in the upper left corner of the keyboard). Each time you press grave, you select the group that includes the previously selected group. The following steps demonstrate how this works.

STEPS: Ascending the Grouping Ladder

Step 1. Draw four separate paths with the freehand tool. After drawing each path, choose Arrange ➪ Group (Command-G) to group that single path.

Step 2. Select two of the grouped paths and again choose Arrange ➪ Group. Select the other pair of paths and group them as well.

Step 3. Select both grouped pairs and choose Arrange ➪ Group. The result is four groups (the original free-form paths) within two groups (the pairs) within a single group.

Step 4. Using the arrow tool, Option-click on any one of the paths. This selects the entire path and displays its points. Then click on a single point in the selected path to select the point.

Step 5. Press the grave key. FreeHand deselects the point but leaves the path selected. (I first introduced this technique in the "Selecting points" section of Chapter 7.)

Step 6. Press the grave key a second time. The points disappear, and four corner handles appear around the selected path, indicating that you have now selected the grouped object that contains this lone path.

Step 7. Press the grave key a third time. The larger group, containing two grouped paths, becomes selected.

Step 8. Press grave a fourth time. The highest-level group becomes selected, which includes all four free-form paths.

Although Option-clicking enables you to select elements inside objects that you combined with the Group command, you cannot Option-click to access segments or points inside a rectangle or ellipse. To select a point in a geometric shape, you must first ungroup the shape, as described in the next section.

Ungrouping

You can ungroup any group by choosing Arrange ➪ Ungroup (Command-U). Okay, that's obvious. But here are a few less obvious facts you may want to know about ungrouping:

- ✐ You can ungroup multiple groups simultaneously, but only one level at a time. In other words, if a group contains groups, you must ungroup the most recently created group first. You can then ungroup the member groups by choosing Arrange ➪ Ungroup again while all groups are still selected.

- ✐ If a selection contains both grouped and ungrouped objects when you choose the Ungroup command, FreeHand deselects the ungrouped paths and leaves only those objects that were previously grouped selected.

- ✐ You cannot ungroup a member of a group that you selected by Option-clicking. You must always ungroup objects sequentially.

- ✐ You can also ungroup a geometric path created with the rectangle or oval tool.

Ungrouping is sometimes an essential part of the reshaping process. Most notably, before you can join two elements that are contained in different groups, you have to ungroup the paths that contain the two elements. For example, if one endpoint in an open path is part of a group and an endpoint from another path belongs to a different group, you can't join the two endpoints. (In fact, if you choose Arrange ⇨ Join Objects, FreeHand ignores you.) You must ungroup the paths before choosing the Join Objects command.

Distinguishing groups from composite paths

What if ungrouping a path doesn't produce the desired effect? Then perhaps the object wasn't a group in the first place. Instead, it may be a composite path that was created using Arrange ⇨ Join Objects or Type ⇨ Convert to Paths.

To determine whether a combined object is a group or a composite path, display the Object panel of the Inspector palette (Command-Option-I). If the words *Composite Path* appear below the Inspector title bar, the selection is a composite path (like you needed me to tell you that). You can break apart a composite path by choosing Arrange ⇨ Split Object (Command-Shift-J). If the word *Group*, *Rectangle*, *Ellipse*, or *Blend* appears below the title bar, the selection is a group and can be ungrouped.

Avoiding accidental alterations

While working on a complicated illustration, you will probably create several objects that overlap. In the process of reshaping and transforming some of these objects, you may inadvertently select and alter an overlapping object that was positioned exactly where you wanted it to be. Fixing an object that was correct to begin with can be exceedingly frustrating. Unfortunately, the more complicated your drawing becomes, the greater the likelihood that you will disturb one or more perfectly positioned objects.

Luckily, FreeHand gives you a way to make sure that you don't ruin an object that you've spent hours slaving to create and position. By using the Lock and Unlock commands in the Arrange menu, you can protect text blocks and graphic objects from being upset or altered. These two commands are the subjects of the following pages.

Locking objects

Locking a path prevents the path or any of its points from being moved. You can't drag or transform a locked object in any way. A locked object, however, is not entirely unalterable. You can still select it and change its fill or stroke attributes.

To lock an object, select it and choose the Lock command from the Arrange menu. You cannot lock a single point independently of other points in a path. If you specifically select one point in a path and choose the Lock command, FreeHand locks the entire path.

The first example in Figure 8-19 displays two paths, one of which is selected. The following exercise demonstrates how you can use the Lock command to protect the selected path.

STEPS: A Locked Path Never Moves

Step 1.   Draw a couple of free-form paths. Make them pathetically simple. You don't want to waste too much time on this exercise.

Step 2.   Select one of the paths, as shown in the first example of Figure 8-19. Choose Arrange ⇨ Lock (Command-L) to lock the selection.

Figure 8-19:
After locking the selected path (left), I marqueed both paths and poised my arrow cursor to drag a segment in the locked path (right).

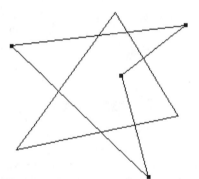 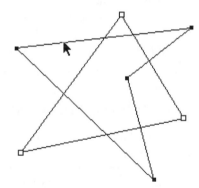

Step 3.   Drag a marquee around both shapes with the arrow tool. FreeHand selects all points in the unlocked path but selects none of the points in the locked one, as in the second example of Figure 8-19.

Step 4.   Drag a segment in the locked path. As you drag, only the unlocked shape moves, as shown in Figure 8-20, despite the fact that your cursor is not positioned over any part of that path. When an object in the current selection is locked, FreeHand treats the manipulation just as it would normally, except that it does not allow any point in the locked object to move.

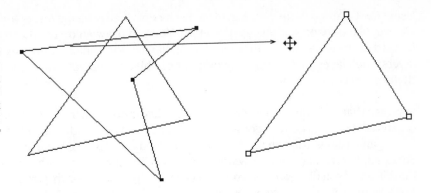

Figure 8-20:
If you try to drag a locked object, all unlocked objects in the current selection move and the locked object remains stationary.

If all objects in the current selection are locked, FreeHand displays a small lock icon in the information bar. If any object in the selection is unlocked, the lock icon does not appear.

Though you can't delete locked objects by pressing the Delete key, you *can* delete them by removing the layer on which the objects appear. For more information on this function, read the upcoming "Deleting an existing layer" section.

Unlocking objects

To unlock an object, select the object and choose Arrange ⇨ Unlock (Command-Shift-L). If the selected object is not locked, the Unlock command is dimmed.

FreeHand saves an object's locked status with the document. Therefore, when you open an existing file, all objects that were locked during the previous session will still be locked.

Layering Objects

When you preview or print an illustration, FreeHand describes it one object at a time, starting with the first object in the illustration window and working up to the last. The order in which the objects are described is called the *stacking order*. The first object described lies behind all other objects in the illustration window. The last object sits in front of its cohorts. All other objects exist on some unique tier between the first object and the last.

Left to its own devices, layering would be a function of the order in which you draw. The oldest object would be in back; the most recent object would be in front. But FreeHand provides a number of commands that enable you to adjust the stacking order of existing graphic objects and text blocks.

Using the Layers palette, you can create self-contained *drawing layers* (or simply *layers*) that act like transparent pieces of acetate. You can draw an object on any layer and see it clearly through all layers in front of it. An illustration can contain any number of layers; each layer can contain any number of objects; and you can name layers and alter their order as you see fit.

Suppose that you want to create a complex illustration of a frog, complete with internal organs, skeleton structure, googly eyes, and so on. To keep the objects that make up the organs from getting all jumbled together, you could isolate them on separate layers. For example, you might put the heart on one layer, the spleen on another, and the lungs on a third. Then, if you discover that you've accidentally gone and drawn a rat's heart instead of a frog's heart, you can replace or refine the heart without endangering the perfect little froggy spleen and lungs you created. You can even print all the layers to different pages, which is ideal for publishing your own visible frog inserts for encyclopedias.

Working with drawing layers

To display the Layers palette, choose Window ➪ Layers (Command-6). FreeHand displays all existing drawing layers in the foreground document as options in a scrolling list inside the Layers palette. You can define and manipulate the layers using the options in the Options pop-up menu, which appears in the second example of Figure 8-21.

Figure 8-21:
The Layers palette (left) and the contents of the Options pop-up menu (right).

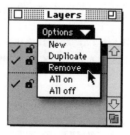

Three layers are included by default in all FreeHand documents:

- **Foreground:** This layer contains the objects that will print. The other two layers are reserved for nonprinting objects.

- **Guides:** This layer contains the nonprinting guidelines that you drag from the horizontal and vertical rulers, as described earlier, in the "Creating guidelines" section. By default, the Guides layer is located in back of the Foreground layer. You cannot send free-form objects to this layer; only guidelines can reside here.

- **Background:** The last layer is separated from its predecessors by a dotted line, which shows that it will not print. This is a good layer for positioning tracing templates and other visual guides. The Background layer is located in back of all layers above it in the list.

You can create as many foreground or background layers as you want. Any objects on foreground layers will print; objects on the background layers won't.

 If you want to create additional default layers that FreeHand will include with every new document, create the new layers and rename and reposition them as desired, as described in the upcoming sections. Then save your document as the new Aldus FreeHand Defaults file, as described in "The Aldus FreeHand Defaults file" section of Chapter 3.

When you select an object in the illustration window, FreeHand highlights the name of the object's drawing layer in the scrolling list. If you select multiple objects from different layers, no layer name appears highlighted. If no object is selected, the highlighted layer name is the default drawing layer, on which all future objects will be created.

Assigning objects to layers

To send one or more selected objects to a different layer, simply click on a layer name in the scrolling list. You can send only whole objects to a different layer. If a path is only partially selected when you click on a layer name, FreeHand moves the entire path to the selected layer. You cannot send objects to the Guides layer, and you cannot move locked objects. Objects that you send to the Background layer appear screened and do not print.

 You'll probably find that every time you send an object to a different layer, you also change the default layer. This happens when the Changing Objects Changes Defaults check box in the Editing panel of the Preferences dialog box is selected. To send a selection to a layer without affecting the default layer, you must deselect this option. (However, by doing so, you also prevent FreeHand from changing other default settings — such as the fill or stroke of an object — in keeping with your last operation.)

The following sections explain the various ways you can adjust layers from the Layers palette. Note that all these changes apply to the foreground document only; they do not affect all open documents, for example. The only way to make changes that affect multiple documents is to alter the Aldus FreeHand Defaults file, which changes all future documents created in FreeHand but does not affect existing documents.

Creating and naming a new layer

To introduce a new drawing layer to the foreground document, select the New option from the Options pop-up menu. (I recommend that you press the Tab key before selecting this option to prevent any objects in the document from being sent to the new layer.) FreeHand creates a new foreground layer in front of all other layers in the document and names it something meaningless like *Layer-5*. To rename the layer, double-click on its name in the list. Then enter the new name and press Return to accept it. (You must press the Return key. If you simply click on a different layer or perform some other operation, FreeHand assumes that you want to cancel the renaming and restores the original name.)

You can rename any layer in the layers palette except the Guides layer. FreeHand is very possessive of this layer and hates to see you do much of anything with it except move it around.

Another method for creating a new layer is to clone an existing one. Select the layer that you want to clone and then select the Duplicate option from the Options pop-up menu. FreeHand clones all objects on the existing layer and sends the clones to a new layer. FreeHand names the new layer something stupid like *Copy of Layer-5,* so it's up to you to rename it. Why clone an existing layer instead of creating a brand new one? Primarily because it enables you to experiment with reshaping and otherwise editing a collection of objects without risking permanent damage to your drawing.

To transfer a new layer from document A to document B, send an object to the new layer in document A and then copy it to the Clipboard. Next, switch to document B and paste. FreeHand pastes not only the object, but also its layering information. This technique assumes that you selected the Remember Layer Info check box in the Editing panel of the Preferences dialog box.

Reordering layers

The order in which layer names appear in the Layers palette determines the stacking order of your document. The first name in the list represents the foremost layer; the last name is the rearmost layer.

To change the order of layers in the foreground document, simply drag a layer name to a different position inside the scrolling list of the Layers palette. FreeHand takes objects assigned to that layer and repositions them behind or in front of objects on other layers, according to your drag. Drag a layer name below the dotted line in the Layers palette to make the layer a nonprinting background layer. All objects on that layer then appear grayed. Drag a layer above the dotted line to make it a printing foreground layer.

You can even drag a dotted line up or down in the Layers palette. This enables you to change multiple layers to background or foreground layers at a time.

By default, the Guides layer is in front of all background layers but in back of all foreground layers. You can reorder it in any way you see fit. However, whether foreground or background, guidelines never print.

Showing and hiding layers

A check mark in front of a layer name indicates that all objects on that layer will be displayed on-screen. Objects on foreground layers that are checked will print. Click on the check mark to hide it and, by so doing, hide all objects on that layer in the illustration window. This technique enables you to isolate a detail on another layer so that you can examine it more closely or make corrections to it. To display objects on a hidden layer, click in front of the layer name to redisplay the check mark.

To specify whether objects on hidden layers print or not, choose File ⇨ Output Options to display the Output Options dialog box, shown in Figure 8-22. Then select or deselect the Include Invisible Layers. This option is selected by default, so that hidden layers print — as long as they are foreground layers. For more information on printing, read Chapter 20, "Printing from FreeHand."

Figure 8-22:
Hidden foreground layers like White Fang and Luminous Fish print as long as the Include Invisible Layers check box in the Output Options dialog box is selected.

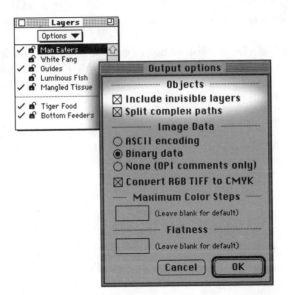

To hide all layers in the foreground document, select the All Off option from the Options pop-up menu or Option-click on any check mark in the Layers palette. Then click in front of specific layer names that you want to display. To display all layers, select the All On option or Option-click in front of a layer name that is hidden.

Protecting layers

Just as you can protect a selected object from being altered (by choosing Arrange ⇨ Lock), you can protect entire layers of objects. One way to protect a layer is to hide it as described in the preceding section. You cannot manipulate objects on a hidden layer, because you have no way to get to them.

You can also protect objects on a layer by locking the layer. To do so, click on the tiny lock icon in front of the layer name in the Layers palette. When the lock appears to be open, the layer is unlocked; when the lock appears closed, all objects on the corresponding layer are off-limits. To unlock a layer, click on its icon again.

To lock all layers in a document, Option-click on any open lock icon. To unlock all layers, Option-click on any closed lock icon.

Deleting an existing layer

You can delete any existing drawing layer — even if it's chock-full of objects, including locked objects — by selecting the layer name in the Layers palette and choosing the Remove option from the pop-up menu. If the layer is indeed filled with objects, FreeHand displays an alert box and warns you that all objects on the layer will be deleted from your illustration. If the layer is absolutely empty, no alert box appears.

 Before deleting a layer, hide all layers except the layer you want to delete and then choose the View ⇨ Magnification ⇨ Fit All. From this vantage point, you can view all objects that you intend to delete, including those in the area outside the boundaries of the page.

If you delete a layer by mistake, choose the Undo Remove Layer command from the Edit menu (Command-Z) to restore the layer and all its objects. Note that the Guides layer cannot be deleted.

Changing the stacking order within layers

You also can reorder objects on a single layer. Among the commands that FreeHand provides for this purpose are the common Bring to Front (Command-F) and Send to Back (Command-B) commands, which reside at the top of the Arrange menu.

If you select an object and choose Bring to Front, FreeHand moves the object to the front of its layer and then treats the object exactly as if it were the most recently created path in the layer. Therefore, the object is the last in the layer to be described when you preview or print the drawing. If you choose Send to Back, FreeHand treats the selected object as if it were the first path in the layer, describing it first when you preview or print.

You can apply both commands to whole objects only. If a path is only partially selected when you choose either command, FreeHand moves the entire path to the front or back of its layer. If you select more than one object when choosing Bring to Front or Send to

Back, the relative stacking order of each selected object is retained. For example, if you select two objects and choose Arrange ⇨ Bring to Front, the forward of the two objects becomes the frontmost object on its layer. The rearward of the two objects becomes the second-to-frontmost object.

Forward and backward

When you're creating complicated illustrations, it's not enough to be able to send objects to the absolute front or back of a layer. Even a simple illustration can contain over a hundred objects. Changing the layering of a single object from, say, 14th-to-front to 46th-to-front would take days using Bring to Front and Send to Back.

Fortunately, FreeHand provides two commands that make relative layering manipulations possible: Bring Forward (Command-left bracket) and Send Backward (Command-right bracket), also under the Arrange menu. Each command scoots a selected object one step forward or one step backward within its layer.

Figure 8-23 demonstrates the Bring Forward command. The first example shows four layered shapes. If you select the black shape and choose Arrange ⇨ Bring Forward, the selected path moves one step forward, as shown in the second example. The third example shows the results of choosing Bring Forward a second time.

Figure 8-23:
The effects of selecting the rearmost path (left) and choosing Bring Forward twice (center and right).

Regardless of stacking order, you can select the object directly behind the current selection by Control-clicking on it with the arrow tool. If you Control-click a second time, you select the next object back, and so on. Eventually, you will cycle through all overlapping objects and again select the frontmost object in the bunch.

Paste in back

FreeHand also enables you to send one object, call it A, directly in back of another, which — though I'd like to name it "Smelly Elephant" — I'll call B purely for the sake of consistency. To accomplish this, select object A, choose Edit ⇨ Cut (Command-X), select object B, and choose Edit ⇨ Paste Behind. FreeHand places object A at the exact horizontal and vertical location from which it was cut, directly in back of object B.

If multiple objects are selected when you choose the Paste Behind command, FreeHand places the contents of the Clipboard in back of the rearmost selected object. If no object is selected, the Paste Behind command is dimmed.

The effect of grouping and joining on layering

Because they combine selected objects, the Group and Join Objects commands also affect the layering of objects in an illustration. All elements in a group or joined path are fused into a single object. Therefore, they can't have any objects stacked between them. FreeHand handles this issue by automatically moving the elements you group to the front of a layer, as follows:

- ⊂➔ If all selected paths are on the same layer, FreeHand sends them to the front of their layer when you choose Arrange ⇨ Group or Arrange ⇨ Join Objects.

- ⊂➔ If the selected paths are on different layers, FreeHand sends them to the front of the active layer, even if none of the paths were on that layer before you chose the command.

- ⊂➔ Provided that the Remember Layer Info check box in the Display panel of the Preferences dialog box is selected, choosing Arrange ⇨ Ungroup or Arrange ⇨ Split Object restores the original paths to their original layers. This function is new to FreeHand 4.0.

But although you basically have to fork over control when using the Group and Join Objects commands, you can adjust the relative layering of objects inside groups and composite paths. Press the Option key and click on an object with the arrow tool. Then choose any of the four stacking order commands at the top of the Arrange menu.

Summary

- ➔ Change the unit of measure used throughout FreeHand by selecting a different option from the pop-up menu at the top of the Document Setup panel in the Inspector palette.

- ➔ There are almost exactly 72 points in an inch and absolutely exactly 12 points in a pica, which translates to nearly exactly 6 picas per inch. That's why they invented the decimal system — to get us away from these sorts of random measuring systems.

- ➔ Drag from the ruler origin box at the meeting of the rulers to change the location of the 0,0 coordinate.

- ➔ Drag from a vertical or horizontal ruler to create a vertical or horizontal guide-line. Drag the guideline off the page to delete it.

- ➔ FreeHand's Horizontal alignment options arrange objects along their left and right edges, and therefore result in vertical formations. Likewise, the Vertical alignment options result in horizontal formations.

- ➔ The distribution options adjust and equalize the amount of space between selected objects.

- ➔ Option-click on a path inside a group to select the path independently. You can then click on point to select it and drag points to reshape the path, even though it is grouped.

- ➔ Press the grave key (`) to select the group that contains the selected path or group.

- ➔ Layers work like transparent layers of acetate; you can see through each layer to the layer below.

- ➔ After you send an object to a different layer, it's a good idea to press Tab and click on your original layer. Otherwise, FreeHand changes the default layer as well.

Adding Text

PART III

Chapter 9:
Entering and Editing Text

Chapter 10:
Formatting and Copyfitting

Chapter 11:
Special Text Effects

Entering and Editing Text

In This Chapter

- ◆ Defining text blocks using the text tool
- ◆ Accessing special characters and moving the insertion marker inside a text block
- ◆ Flowing text inside a geometric or free-form path
- ◆ Importing text created in a word processor
- ◆ Dragging text block handles
- ◆ Reshaping free-form text objects
- ◆ Linking text objects to form a continuous chain
- ◆ Selecting characters and words

Text Is a Drawing's Best Friend_____

Some guy that was hoping to get his name in one of those books of pithy quotes once ventured that a picture is worth a thousand words. Judging by the relative earnings of artists and writers, I'd say that a picture is worth more like 2,500 words. But regardless of the current rate of exchange, a picture *doesn't* take the place of a thousand words. Otherwise, I wouldn't have to write these endless pages of text; I'd just show you a few choice pictures and call it a day.

Text explains pictures; pictures accompany text; and in the best of documents, pictures and text suggest complementary but unique information. That's why type and graphics are such bosom buddies in FreeHand. In fact, FreeHand 4.0 has more than bolstered its text-handling capabilities; it's completely revamped them. Nearly all of FreeHand's text functions either rival or surpass their counterparts in dedicated text wranglers such as PageMaker and QuarkXPress.

Isn't this a job for PageMaker?

I've heard some users of earlier versions of FreeHand making comments to the effect of, "What's with all the new text stuff? Isn't this supposed to be a *drawing* program? If I want to create a newsletter, I'll use a page-layout program."

Well, if that sums up your opinion, you and I have a bone to pick. Page-layout and drawing programs are twins separated at birth. Both rely on discreet objects to represent page elements. Both hinge on the capabilities of the PostScript page-description language. And both enable you to combine text and graphic objects.

The differences between page-layout and drawing programs are entirely a matter of emphasis. Page-layout programs provide only the most basic drawing tools and include a large supply of functions for manipulating text and importing artwork. Drawing programs generally emphasize drawing functions and downplay text editing and importing.

FreeHand, meanwhile, has a proud history of blurring the lines between page layout and drawing. It has long provided top-notch importing capabilities and respectable text handling. With Version 4.0, it merely went a step farther by introducing column pouring, table making, copyfitting, and a host of other functions that may sound like Greek to you now but will eventually be music to your ears.

Furthermore, FreeHand is alone in providing a sufficient number of capabilities to create professional-quality text and graphics within the same program. There's no need to switch out of the program to draw some complex graphic and then switch back to surround the graphic with text. You can see how the graphic looks on the page as you draw and edit it. FreeHand eliminates the guesswork and broadens your design options by supplying everything you need within easy reach. If you've ever heard yourself say, "Gee whiz, I'd like to add a special design element here, but it's too much effort," the new FreeHand is for you.

Come on, FreeHand can't do everything

You're right, FreeHand hasn't lifted *every* option from PageMaker and QuarkXPress. When creating a small document in FreeHand, you have to live without the following features:

- ⇨ **Spell-checker:** FreeHand currently can't check your spelling. But rumor has it that such a feature is on its way. In the meantime, you'll have to spell-check your text inside a word processor and then import it into FreeHand. For the record, FreeHand also lacks a thesaurus and a search-and-replace function.

- **Style sheets:** If you know what these are, you'll miss them in FreeHand. Style sheets allow you to store a variety of character and paragraph formatting attributes and apply them *en masse* to a selected paragraph. Hopefully, FreeHand will add styles in a future version.

- **Master pages:** That's right, you can't use master pages for positioning repeating elements such as page numbers and logos. But you can duplicate pages very easily by selecting the Duplicate option from the Options pop-up menu in the Document Pages panel of the Inspector palette. (See, wasn't that easy?) For more information, read Chapter 19, "Setting Up Documents."

- **Automatic page numbering:** Okay, so you're not going to be able to format the *Encyclopaedia Britannica* in FreeHand. But you can lay out an eight-page newsletter and number the pages manually.

- **Automatic indexing and table of contents generation:** Get serious — even QuarkXPress doesn't offer these features.

- **Kerning tables:** Yeah, yeah, this ultra high-end function and several others are missing from FreeHand. But it's taken PageMaker and QuarkXPress several years to hone these functions, so you can't expect FreeHand to master them overnight.

Introducing Text Objects

Rather than floating freely on your page, type in FreeHand is housed inside boundaries called *text objects*, which can be rectangles, ellipses, polygons, or free-form paths. These text objects define the shape formed by your type, as illustrated by the three examples in Figure 9-1. Many of FreeHand's general functions, including the transformation and duplication techniques described in Chapters 15 and 16, are as applicable to text objects as they are to graphic objects. For example, after creating a text object in the shape of a star, you can rotate it to any angle you please. However, FreeHand also offers a world of functions that apply exclusively to type, as explained throughout this chapter and the two that follow.

Creating a text block

The most common variety of text object is the rectangular *text block*, which you create with the text tool. Text blocks are the most formal as well as the most capable kinds of text objects. Most importantly, text blocks are equipped with special editing handles that other text objects lack. These handles allow you to experiment with formatting attributes, as explained in the "Manipulating text block handles" section later in this chapter.

Figure 9-1:
Three differently
shaped text objects,
with a lot of wacky
triangles to keep
them company.

We, the people of the United Nations, determined to save succeedinggenerationsfrom the scourge of war, which twice in our lifetime has brought untold sorrow to mankind,andtoreaffirmfaith infundamentalhumanrights, inthedignityandworthofthe human person, in the equal right of men and women and of nations large and small, and to establish conditions under which justice and respect for the obligations arising from treaties and othersourcesofinternational law can be maintained, and

to promote social progress and better standards of life in larger freedom, and for these ends to practice tolerance and live toge ther in peace with one another as good neighbors, and to unite our stre ngth to maintain international peace and security, and to ensure, by the acceptance of principles and the institution of methods, that armed force shall not be used, save in the com mon interest, and to

em
ploy
inter
national
machinery
for the promo
tion of the economic and social advancement
of all people, have resolved to combine
oureffortstoaccomplishtheseaims.
Accordingly,ourrespectivegov
ernments, through repre
sentatives assembled in
the city of San Francisco,
whohaveexhibitedtheirfull
powers to   be in good
& due   form,
ha   ve

After selecting the text tool — upper right in the toolbox — you can use it to create a new text block in the following ways:

- ∞ Click anywhere on the page to indicate the placement of the upper left corner of the text block. FreeHand automatically sizes the text block to three inches wide and two inches tall, as shown in Figure 9-2.

- ∞ Drag with the text tool to specify the dimensions of the text block manually. The width of your drag defines the width of the text block; the length of the drag defines the height.

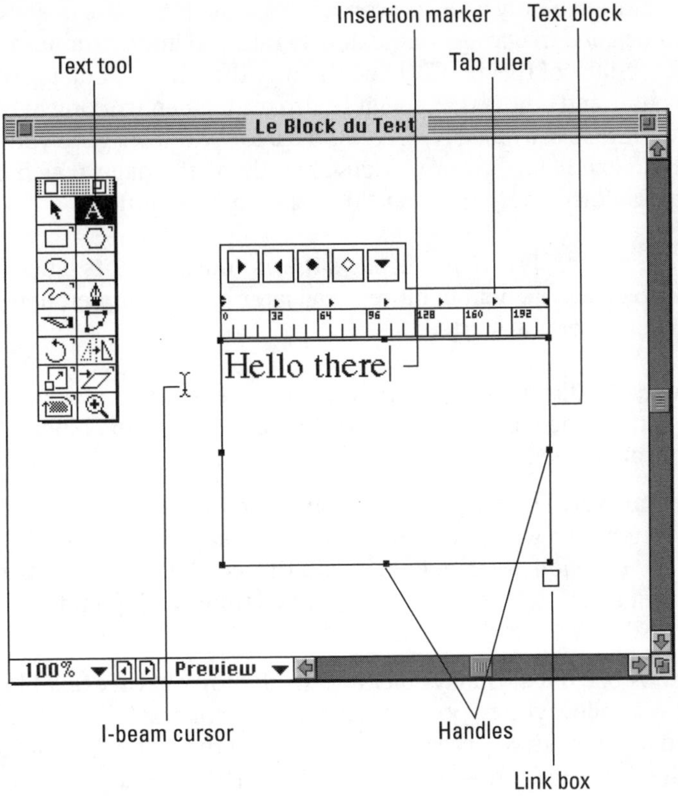

Figure 9-2:
A default text
block created by
clicking with the
text tool.

Text tool

Insertion marker   Text block

Tab ruler

Le Block du Text

Hello there

100% ▼ Preview ▼

I-beam cursor

Handles

Link box

⤷ To create a text block that is a specific numerical size, move the ruler origin to the point at which you want to position the upper left corner of the text block. Then begin dragging with the text tool at the ruler origin and monitor the movement of your cursor using the horizontal and vertical rulers.

⤷ Shift-drag with the text tool to draw a perfectly square text block.

⤷ Option-drag to draw the text block from the center outward.

Pressing the A key selects the text tool at any time *except* when a text block or option box is active. To access the text tool under those circumstances, press Shift-F9.

The mysteries of the text block

In case you haven't already noticed, the Text dialog box included with FreeHand 3.1 and earlier is a thing of the past. Nowadays, you enter and edit text directly on the page, just as in every other drawing program on earth. The disappearance of the Text dialog box is another of Version 4.0's harsh transitions — although only a few power users are likely to miss it. For example, Arne Hurty, *Macworld* magazine's ridiculously talented informational artist (and technical editor of this book), liked the way that the Text dialog box enabled him to enter and edit text at a legible size even when working in the fit-in-window view size. Ironically, FreeHand 3.0 for Windows gave you the option of using the Text dialog box or working directly on the page, which is the ideal solution. Unfortunately, Version 4.0 took away that option.

After you draw a text block, FreeHand displays the various elements labeled in Figure 9-2. Although I describe each element in more detail later in this chapter, here are a few brief introductions to get you started:

⊸ **I-beam cursor:** This cursor appears any time the text tool is selected or a text block is active. You can use the cursor to create a new text block or highlight text inside an active text block.

⊸ **Insertion marker:** The blinking insertion marker indicates the location at which text you enter from the keyboard will appear inside the text block. Some folks call this the *insertion point*, but what with the word *points* meaning everything from dots in a path to 1/72-inch increments, I think it's high time we gave that word a break.

⊸ **Tab ruler:** A big, huge, clunky ruler adorns the top of every text block. Its sole purpose is to allow you to position tabs and indent text. Never mind that nine out of ten text blocks you create won't include tabs and only a small percentage more will require indents — the tab ruler is standard equipment on every text block.

⊸ **Handles:** These guys let you stretch and squish text blocks and change some formatting attributes while you're at it.

⊸ **Link box:** Click on this box and learn about the origins of primitive man. No, wait, it's just a joke. You folks who believe in creationism, take a deep breath and count to ten before you try to get the book banned. The real purpose of the link box is to enable you to send excess text to another text object. You just drag from the link box to another text block and, zip, the excess text flows into place. If you have no idea what I'm talking about, skip to the "Flowing text from one block to another" section later in this chapter.

Pressing keys to enter text

Enter text from the keyboard to fill the text block with letters. As you type, the insertion marker moves rightward. When a word threatens to extend beyond the right side of the text block, FreeHand wraps the word and insertion marker down to the next line.

When you're entering text, most keys fulfill the same purpose as they do in a typical word processor such as Microsoft Word. Each letter and number key inserts the character that appears on the key. The Caps Lock key, Shift key and spacebar also work just like they do in a word processor. The following keys perform special functions:

- **Option:** Accesses special characters when pressed with letter and number keys. You can press the Shift and Option keys together to access still more special characters.

- **Delete:** Removes the character to the left of the insertion marker.

- **Tab:** Inserts a tab character, which creates a large, user-definable space between two words.

- **Return:** Inserts a *carriage return*, which moves the insertion marker, along with any text to the right of the marker, to the next line of type. (Also separates type along the top of an ellipse from type along the bottom of an ellipse, as explained in Chapter 11.)

- **Arrow keys:** Arrow keys move the insertion marker inside the text block.

Special characters and keyboard options

Did I just hear you say, "Duh," like maybe this isn't the most amazing information you've ever learned? Well, then, here are a few keyboard options you might *not* know about.

- **Option-spacebar:** This key combination inserts a nonbreaking space that prevents two words from wrapping to separate lines. You can also get this character by pressing — of all things — the Enter or Esc key. Bizarre.

- **Forward Delete:** Labeled *Del* on a Macintosh keyboard, this key removes the character to the right of the insertion marker. (I bet you thought that the Forward Delete key only worked in a word processor.)

- **Shift-Return:** When you press the Return key by itself, you finish off one paragraph and begin a new one. But when you press Shift-Return (or choose Type⇨ Special Characters ⇨ End of Line), you create a *line break* inside the paragraph. The text after the line break appears on the next line but remains part of the same paragraph as the line above it, which means that it isn't subject to new indents and paragraph spacing. Use a line return when you want to knock a word down to the next line without creating a new paragraph.

- **Shift-Enter:** Press this key combination or choose Type ⇨ Special Characters ⇨ End of Column to insert a *column break*. A column break moves all text to the right of the insertion marker to the top of the next column or to the next text block in a story. Like a carriage return, a column break results in a new paragraph.

- **Command-hyphen:** This key combination creates a *discretionary hyphen*, which is a hyphen that only appears when FreeHand needs to break the word at the end of a line. When the hyphen is not required, FreeHand does not display it. For more information, read the "Hyphenating words" section in the next chapter.

- **Shift-Option-hyphen:** The *em dash* — like the two dashes that surround this little remark you're reading now — is a standard part of the Macintosh character set. But for the sake of Windows users, FreeHand makes the character available from the Type ⇨ Special Characters submenu. You can also create an *en dash*, usually used to represent minus signs, by pressing Option-hyphen.

- **Command-arrow key:** If you press Command with the left- or right-arrow key, you move the insertion marker to the beginning of the previous word or the beginning of the next word, respectively.

- **Home:** Pressing the Home key moves the insertion marker to the beginning of the text block. If the block is part of a chain of linked text objects, Home moves the insertion marker back to the beginning of the very first block in the chain.

- **End:** Pressing End moves the insertion marker to the end of the text block unless the block is part of a chain. If the text block is part of a chain, pressing End moves the insertion marker to the beginning of the next text block. Note that Home and End are not exact opposites. In a chain, Home moves the insertion marker all the way to the beginning, but End moves it forward one block at a time.

- **Command-Tab:** Pressing this key combination deactivates the text block. Memorize this keyboard equivalent and be prepared to use it often.

Fixed spaces

This information doesn't deserve its own section, but I couldn't figure out for the life of me where else to put it, so here it is. Both the spacebar and Option-spacebar create *variable-width* space characters, meaning that FreeHand can automatically vary their widths depending on word spacing and justification settings. To create a *fixed-width* space whose width is dependent solely on type size, choose one of the Space commands from the Type ⇨ Special Character submenu. Or press one of the following key combinations:

- **Command-Shift-M:** This key combo creates a fixed space the width of the letter *M.* Called an *em space*, it is as wide as the type size is tall. For example, a 12-point em space is 12 points wide.

- **Command-Shift-N:** This combination creates an *en space,* which is half the width of the type size. In other words, a 12-point en space is 6 points wide or roughly as wide as a standard lowercase letter such as *n.*

↪ **Command-Shift-T:** Use this key combination to create a *thin space*, which is 1/10 of the width of the type size — even thinner than the letter *i*. We're talking super, ultra thin.

All these characters are *breaking spaces,* which means that FreeHand can break two words separated by one of these characters across two lines.

Creating a free-form text object

If a rectangular text block is too conventional for your purposes, FreeHand 4.0 allows you to enter type inside any closed path, whether it was drawn with one of the geometric shape tools or a free-form path tool. To do this, select the path and choose the Flow Inside Path command from the Type menu (Command-Shift-U). FreeHand creates a blinking insertion marker inside the path and even displays a tab ruler above the path. Enter text from the keyboard to fill the path with type, as shown in Figure 9-3. (I know, the cadence of the poem is way off, but it fits inside the star, which is more than I can say for most poems.)

Figure 9-3:
Choose
Type⇨Flow
Inside Path to
convert a path
into a text
object
complete with
tab ruler.

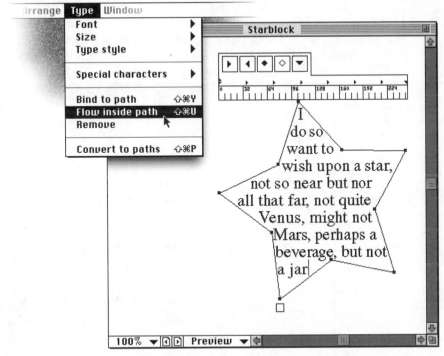

Alternatively, you can create your text inside a standard text block before assigning it to a free-form text object. If your text will require a fair amount of editing, you may want to try out this technique, because FreeHand can redraw text inside a standard text block faster than it can flow the text inside the nooks and crannies of a complex object. When you finish editing, select both text block and path and choose Type ⇨ Flow Inside Path.

Hiding the path outline

If you fill and stroke your path before you choose Type ⇨ Flow inside Path, FreeHand retains the fill and stroke attributes when it converts the path to a text object. You can remove both fill and stroke using the options in the Fill and Stroke panels of the Inspector palette, as described in Chapters 13 and 14. But if the stroke is your only problem, you can quickly remove it without changing any stroke settings by deselecting a single option. Switch to the Object Dimensions & Inset panel of the Inspector palette (Command-Option-B, for *border*), and deselect the Display Border check box. The outline disappears, as shown in Figure 9-4.

To display the rectangular border around a standard text block, first select the Display Border check box. Then assign the desired stroke attributes using the options in the Stroke panel of the Inspector palette (Command-Option-L). If either the Display Border check box is turned off *or* the pop-up menu in the Stroke panel is set to None, the border will be invisible (except in the keyline mode).

Figure 9-4:
Use the Display Border check box to show and hide the outlines around text objects, whether you're working with rectangular or free-form objects.

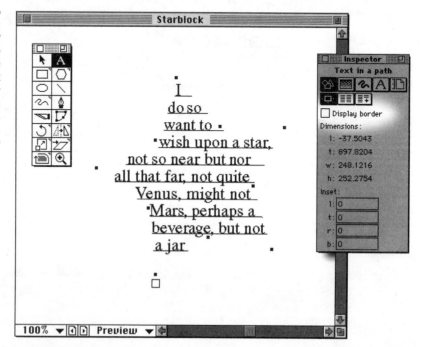

Separating text and path

To separate text from a path, select the free-form text object and choose the Remove From Path command from the Type menu. FreeHand creates a new text block for the type and converts the text object back to a geometric shape or free-form path, as illustrated in Figure 9-5.

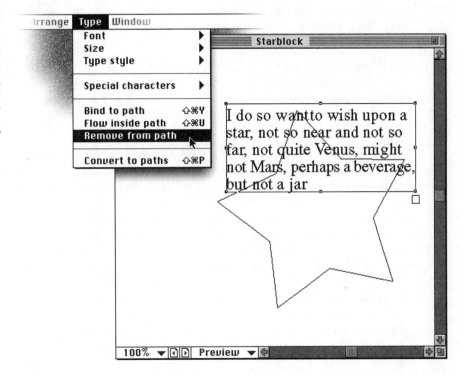

Figure 9-5: Choose Type⇨Remove From Path to convert text and path into separate objects.

The rectangular text block is the lowest form of container available to type in FreeHand. Therefore, you cannot apply the Remove From Path command to a lowly text block.

Importing Stories

Much — if not most — of the text you'll use in FreeHand will be entered directly in FreeHand. But there may be times when you want to create complete pages or mix graphics with large amounts of text, particularly now that the program accommodates multipage layouts. When long documents (called *stories*) are required, FreeHand enables you to import text documents created in a word processor. After all, word processors are faster for text entry and allow luxuries such as spell-checking. Also, it's easier to edit text and apply formatting attributes in a word processor.

Preparing text

When importing text, FreeHand reads the file from disk and copies it to the foreground illustration. Version 4.0 can import text stored in two formats:

- **Plain text:** If you save a word processing document in the plain text or *ASCII* (pronounced *ask-ee*) format, no formatting is retained. Font, type size, style, and all other attributes are thrown by the wayside during the saving process. All you get are the actual characters of text.

- **RTF (*Rich Text Format*):** If you want to retain formatting, save your document in the RTF format. Designed by Microsoft, RTF is basically plain text with a bunch of formatting codes thrown in. It's not the most efficient or reliable format in the world, but it is common and it works with FreeHand.

If your word processor does not support RTF, you may be able to convert the file using a file-conversion utility such as Apple File Exchange or MacLink from DataViz. Short of that, save the file as a plain text file, which sacrifices all formatting. You can then reformat the text in FreeHand, as described in Chapter 10, "Formatting and Copyfitting."

Some formatting attributes may get confused in the process of exporting the file to the RTF format and importing the file into FreeHand. The following list describes how FreeHand handles the most common formatting attributes. Formatting options not included in this list are most likely not supported by FreeHand and are therefore ignored.

- **Typefaces:** All text retains the font specified in the word processor. If one or more fonts are not available to the system software, FreeHand displays a list of the missing fonts in a dialog box, as shown in the first example of Figure 9-6. FreeHand suggests changing all fonts to Courier, the notoriously ugly IBM typewriter font. To specify your own replacements, click on the Replace button. The dialog box shown on the right side of Figure 9-6 appears once for every font that's missing. Select a substitute font from the pop-up menu and click on the Change button to replace the font. Click on the Don't Change button to skip a single missing font and let FreeHand change it to Courier. Click on the Cancel button to change all remaining missing fonts to Courier.

- **Type size and leading:** FreeHand retains the type size and leading (line spacing) specified in the word processor. The only exception is so-called "automatic" leading, which converts to some fixed value that may not match the leading of the original document.

- **Type styles:** FreeHand converts bold and italic type to their equivalent stylized screen fonts. If no stylized screen font is available for a particular style, FreeHand substitutes the plain style. Styles that are ignored include underline, strikethru, small caps, and hidden. Outline text is assigned a hairline stroke and a transparent fill. Shadow is converted to FreeHand shadow effect. Superscript and subscript styles remain intact.

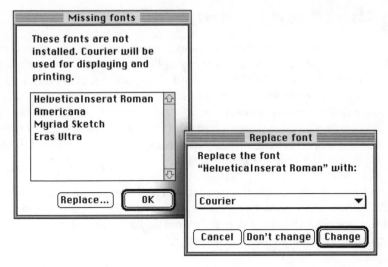

- **Colors:** In my tests, FreeHand usually handled colors accurately. The only exception occurred when the first line of type was assigned a different color from the rest of the text, in which case FreeHand carried the first-line color throughout the rest of the imported story.

- **Line and column breaks:** Although FreeHand correctly recognizes carriage returns and line breaks, it misinterprets column and page breaks as carriage returns.

- **Alignment:** FreeHand recognizes paragraphs that are aligned left, center, and right, as well as justified.

- **Paragraph spacing:** FreeHand can handle paragraph spacing accurately, whether you assign spacing before or after a paragraph, or both.

- **Indents:** FreeHand correctly transfers all indents, including first-line indents, left indents, right indents, and hanging indents. Margin settings that you establish in a Page Setup dialog box don't transfer. Your indents, therefore, are relative to the margins you set in FreeHand.

- **Tabs and tab leaders:** Tabs characters convert correctly; FreeHand even retains the locations of tab stops. However, tab leaders such as dot or dashes do not transfer successfully.

- **Special characters:** Word processors provide access to special characters not included in the standard Apple-defined character set. These include em spaces, nonbreaking hyphens, automatic page numbers, and so on. Of these, only discretionary hyphens and nonbreaking spaces transfer successfully.

- **Headers, footers, and footnotes:** FreeHand ignores weird extraneous items such as these in imported text.

Using the Place command

To import a story, choose File ⇨ Place or press Command-Shift-D. FreeHand displays the Place Document dialog box, which works just like the Open Document dialog box described in Chapter 2. Locate the file you want to import and press the Return key. After waiting a few moments for FreeHand to load the file into memory — or, if it's a long story, after waiting several minutes — you will be rewarded with a place cursor. Click with the cursor to import the text into a text block that is as wide as the original word-processing document. Drag with the tool as demonstrated in Figure 9-7 to define the width and height of the new text block.

If the story is too long to fit inside the text block, FreeHand puts a black circle inside the link box off the lower right corner of the block. To display the rest of the story, you can enlarge the path or pour the story into additional paths as described in the upcoming section "Flowing text from one block to another."

Figure 9-7:
Drag with the place cursor to define the size of the new text block into which FreeHand will pour the imported text.

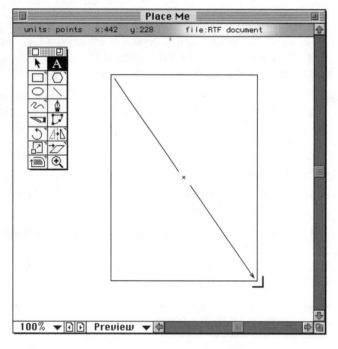

To cancel a place operation before clicking or dragging with the place cursor, select any tool from the toolbox or press its function key equivalent. For example, you could select the arrow tool or simply press Shift-F10.

Adjusting Text Objects

Text objects are very much like paths in that you can reshape them to make them fit your needs. You can drag a text block handle, adjust the points in a free-form text object, and flow excess text from one text object into another. The following sections describe all these techniques.

Manipulating text block handles

Unlike other kinds of text objects, text blocks drawn with the text tool are bordered by eight handles, one at each corner and one centered along each side. By dragging these handles, you can change the dimensions of a text block to permit more or fewer words per line; change the amount of vertical space between lines of text; and change the horizontal space between letters and words.

Enlarging or reducing a text block

When creating a text block, you don't have to accept the default dimensions provided by FreeHand or even the dimensions you specified by dragging with the type tool. At any time, you can change the size of an existing text block by selecting the block and dragging one of its four corner handles with the arrow tool.

Suppose that a text block is too narrow to hold one of your words on a single line. Even though the word is not hyphenated, FreeHand is forced to break it onto two lines, as it did with the word *determined* in Figure 9-8. This problem generally occurs only if the path is very narrow or the type is very big. To remedy the problem, you can:

- Reduce the size of the type (as described in the "Changing the type size" section of the following chapter).

- Hyphenate the word by inserting a discretionary hyphen (Command-hyphen), as in *deter-mined*.

- Increase the width of the text block as demonstrated in Figure 9-9.

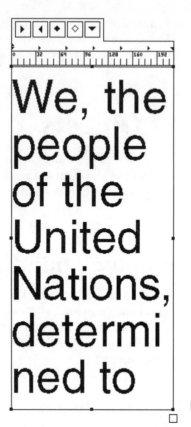

Figure 9-8:
If a single word is too long to fit on a single line, FreeHand arbitrarily breaks it onto two lines.

By changing the size of a text block, you can fit long words on a single line, include more or less text on each line, or display more or fewer lines of text inside the text block. To make the transition from Figure 9-8 to Figure 9-9, I just selected the arrow tool and dragged one of the corner handles in the text block. When you change a text block size, a dotted rectangle representing the size of the altered text block tracks the movements of your cursor. When you release the mouse button, FreeHand rewraps the text to fit the new dimensions.

If you're familiar with other drawing or desktop publishing applications, you may be tempted to adjust the size of the text block by dragging the top or bottom handle or one of the side handles. Avoid this urge, no matter how strong it may be. In FreeHand, dragging one of these handles changes both the size of the block and the formatting of the text inside. Only drag *corner* handles to adjust the dimensions of the text block and rewrap text.

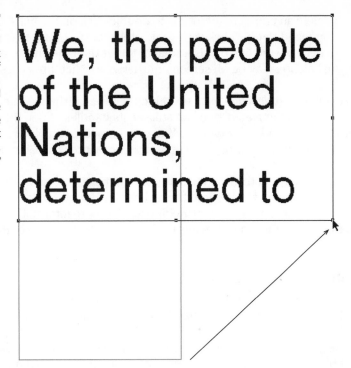

Figure 9-9:
After I dragged the lower right corner handle of the text block, FreeHand rewrapped the text to fit inside the new text block dimensions.

The deactivated text block

There's something interesting going on here that you may have missed. While you're entering or editing text inside any text object, the tab ruler hovers over the object like a thundercloud. The tab ruler and the blinking insertion marker are your visual cues that the text block is active. When you select the arrow tool, the tab ruler and insertion marker remain visible, meaning that the text block is still active. You can continue entering text just as before. However, if you click or drag with the arrow tool, you deactivate the text block. As long as you click or drag on the text block, the corner handles remain available, but the tab ruler and insertion marker immediately go into hiding.

This information is especially good to know when you want to delete a text block. When a text block is active, pressing the Delete key removes one or more characters of type. But if you press and hold the Command key (to access the arrow tool), click on the text block to deactivate it, and then press Delete, you delete the entire text block.

This may seem like a strange little trick, but believe me, you'll end up creating a lot of text blocks you don't need when working in FreeHand. A single click of the text tool can result in a new text block, and unlike most programs, FreeHand doesn't automatically delete empty text blocks. So remember, if you accidentally click with the text tool, Command-click on the offending text block and press Delete to eliminate it.

Another way to delete an empty text block is to double-click on the link box with the arrow tool (or Command-double click with some other tool). I prefer to Command-click and press Delete because the link box is a smaller target than the entire text block. Furthermore, the link box may be off-screen or otherwise difficult to access.

Keep in mind that *deactivating* a text block is different than *deselecting* it. When a text block is deactivated, you can still see its handles. When the text block is deselected, the handles disappear. (You can deselect a text block clicking outside the block with the arrow or some other tool or by pressing Command-Tab.)

Now, no doubt, somebody out there is wondering how to reactivate an inactive text block. Easy. Just click inside the text block with the text tool or double-click in the text block with the arrow tool. You can then enter or edit text. For more information on this topic, skip ahead to the "Selecting and Replacing Text" section near the end of this chapter.

Spacing out your text

Earlier I warned you against dragging the top, bottom, and side handles of a text block. In FreeHand, dragging these noncorner handles doesn't change the size of the text block so that more or less text will fit inside the block. Instead, your drag changes the space between the lines, letters, and words that are already visible. FreeHand also adjusts the size of the text block to accommodate the new spacing. The top, bottom, and side handles work as follows:

- **Drag the top or bottom handle:** Drag either the top or bottom handle to change the amount of vertical space — called *leading* — between lines of type. If you drag down on the top handle or up on the bottom handle, you reduce the leading. If you drag up on the top handle or down on the bottom handle, you increase the leading, as shown in Figure 9-10.

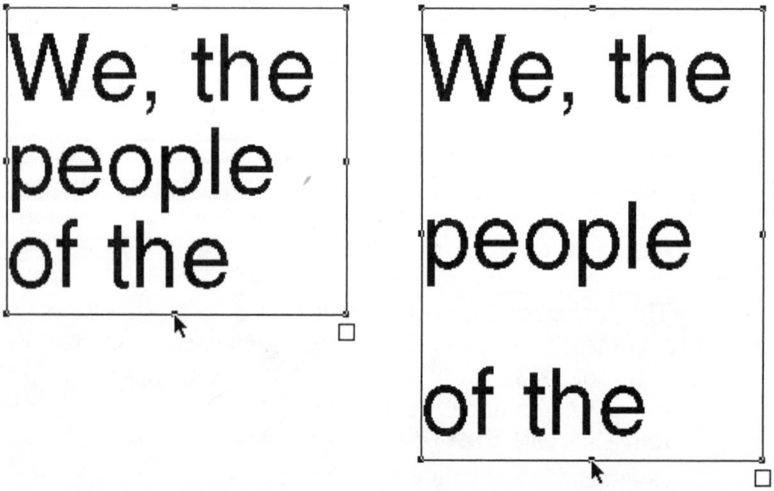

Figure 9-10: Drag the bottom handle of a text block (left) to change the amount of vertical space between lines (right).

We, the people of the

We, the people of the

✑ **Drag a side handle:** Drag the handle on the left or right side of a text block to change the amount of space between characters of text, called *letterspacing*. Drag the left handle farther to the left or the right handle to the right to increase the letterspacing (see Figure 9-11); drag the left handle to the right or the right handle leftward to decrease letterspacing.

Figure 9-11:
Drag the side handle of a text block (top) to change the amount of horizontal space between letters (middle). Option-drag the handle to change the width of space characters between words.

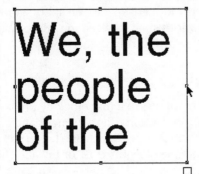

- ☞ **Option-drag a side handle:** If you press the Option key while dragging a side handle, you change the amount of space between words, which is called — you guessed it — *word spacing*. The space between characters within each word remains unchanged. In FreeHand, the space between two words depends on the width of the space character between them. When you Option-drag a side handle, only variable-width space characters are affected. FreeHand doesn't change the size of any fixed-width em spaces, en spaces, or thin spaces. If your text includes a lot of fixed-width spaces mixed in with variable-width spaces, Option-dragging can result in awkwardly spaced text.

Scaling text on the fly

You can also change the size of characters in a text block by pressing modifier keys while dragging a corner handle. If you Option-drag a corner handle, FreeHand scales the characters inside the text block relative to the block itself. You can make characters short and fat, as in the second example of Figure 9-12, or tall and thin, as in the last example. If you want to scale the text proportionally — so that horizontal and vertical proportions are affected uniformly — Shift-Option-drag a corner handle.

Reshaping geometric and free-form text objects

If you created a text block by choosing Type ⇨ Flow Inside Path instead of dragging with the text tool, you can reshape the path just as if it were a standard graphic object. For example, if you created the path with the rectangle or oval tool, drag one of its corner handles to enlarge or reduce the path. FreeHand rewraps the text inside the path, just as it does when you drag the corner handle of a standard text block.

 If you want to be able to drag the points in a geometric text object independently of each other, you must first ungroup the path. Using the arrow tool, Option-click on the outline of the path. Then choose Arrange ⇨ Ungroup and drag the points. The following steps explain the process in more detail.

STEPS: Ungrouping a Geometric Text Object

Step 1.   Draw a text block with the text tool and enter some completely random text.

Step 2.   Draw an ellipse with the oval tool.

Step 3.   Shift-click on the text block with the arrow tool to select both ellipse and text block. Then press Command-Shift-U or choose Type ⇨ Flow Inside Path. The first example in Figure 9-13 shows one possible result.

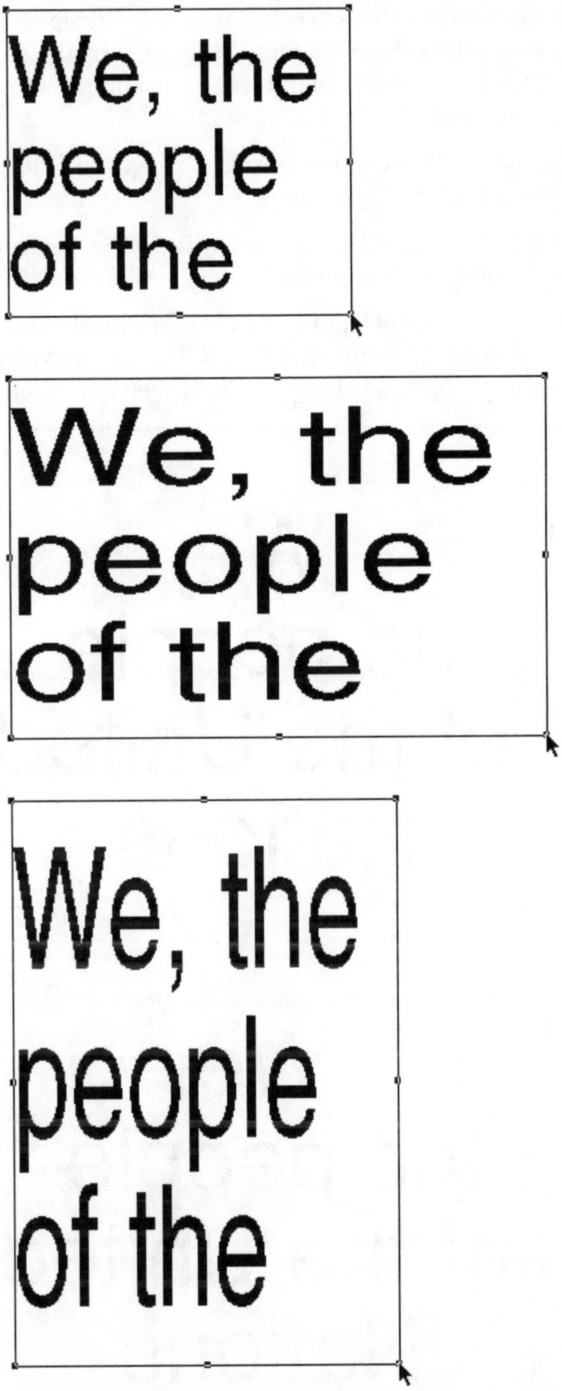

We, the
people
of the
We, the
people
of the
We, the
people
of the

Figure 9-12: Option-drag the corner handle of a text block (top) to scale the characters inside the text block (middle and bottom).

Step 4.   Option-click on the ellipse to select the shape independently of the text. As you can see in the second example in Figure 9-13, the *baselines* — those horizontal lines below the characters — disappear, showing that the text is no longer selected.

Step 5.   Press Command-U or choose Arrange ⇨ Ungroup. The individual points in the free-form path are now visible.

Step 6.   Click on a point to select it and display its Bézier control handles, as shown in the first example of Figure 9-14.

Step 7.   Drag one of the control handles associated with the point to reshape the path. You can also drag the point itself. The text moves with the new curvature of the path, as illustrated in the second example of Figure 9-14.

Figure 9-13:
After combining text block and ellipse into a single text object (top), I Option-clicked on the ellipse to select the shape and deselect the text (bottom).

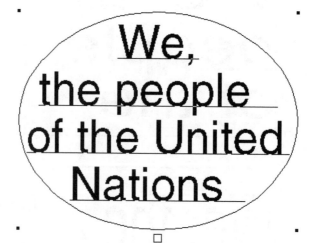

Figure 9-14:
Ungroup the path to
display its points (top)
and drag a Bézier
control handle to
reshape the path
(bottom).

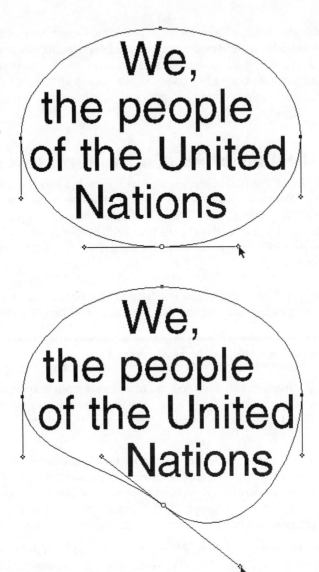

If you construct a text object using a free-form path drawn with the polygon, freehand, trace, bézigon, or pen tool, you can reshape the path by dragging points and Bézier control handles without first ungrouping the path. In fact, you don't even have to Option-click on the path to select it independently of its text. Just start right in — with a few exceptions, you can use any of the techniques discussed back in Chapter 7 that are applicable to closed paths. The only reshaping commands that you *can't* apply to a text object are those under the Type ⇨ Path Operations submenu.

Otherwise, you can do as you please. Move points, drag Bézier control handles, Option-drag segments to bend them, add points and control handles, delete points and retract control handles, and convert points from curve to corner, corner to connector, and so on. You can even open a text object or use the knife tool to split it into two separate paths. Doing so, however, permanently removes all text from inside the object (unless you choose Edit ➪ Undo, that is).

Changing the dimensions of a free-form text object

The problem with free-form text objects is that when you scale them, you scale the text inside them as well. You can't scale the whole object and force the text to rewrap inside the new boundaries. For example, try this: Select a free-form text object and group it by pressing Command-G. Then drag the corner handle. Whether or not the Transform as Unit check box in the Object panel of the Inspector palette is selected, FreeHand scales text and object together.

There is a solution, but it's a bit circuitous. You have to join the text object to another closed path to create a composite path. The following steps explain how this technique works.

STEPS: Creating a Composite Text Object

Step 1.   If you already created a free-form text object, split it apart by selecting the object and choosing Type ➪ Remove from Path. If you haven't created a free-form text object yet, draw a free-form path and then create a separate text block.

Step 2.   Draw a very slim rectangle — skinnier than a single character of text — with the rectangle tool. (It's not absolutely essential that you draw a rectangle, but a rectangle is about the easiest shape to draw. And why work any harder than you have to?) The rectangle should be in close proximity to the free-form path, but it should not overlap the path.

Step 3.   Select the arrow tool and Shift-click on the free-form path to select it and the already selected rectangle. Then press Command-J or choose Arrange ➪ Join Objects to combine the two paths into a composite path, complete with four corner handles.

Step 4.   Now Shift-click on the text block to add it to the selection and press Command-Shift-U (Type ➪ Flow Inside Path). FreeHand fuses the text block and composite path into a single free-form text object, as illustrated in the first example of Figure 9-15.

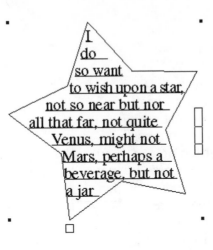

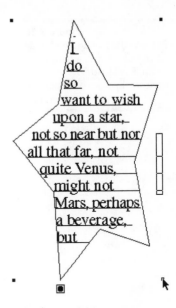

Figure 9-15:
After combining text block and composite path (left), you can drag the corner handle of the text object to scale the text object independently of the characters inside it (right).

Step 5.   Now drag one of the corner handles of the text object. The text object grows or shrinks according to your drag. But this time, rather than scaling the characters inside the path, FreeHand leaves the size of the letters unchanged and rewraps the words onto new lines, as illustrated in the second example of Figure 9-15.

For complete information on composite paths, read Chapter 17, "Blends, Masks, and Composite Paths."

See how the baselines of the text object in Figure 9-15 extend from the star into the rectangle? This is because FreeHand thinks of star and rectangle as isolated portions of the same path. When I widen the rectangle by Option-clicking on it with the arrow tool, selecting the two points on the right side of the path, and dragging outward, words appear inside the path, as shown in Figure 9-16. Notice that these aren't words from the end of my marvelous little poem, but rather from the middle. The words actually extend from the star out into the rectangle. This is why I instructed you to draw a slim rectangle in Step 2 — to prevent the rectangle from filling with type.

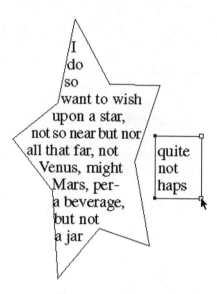

Figure 9-16
Because the star and rectangle
are combined into a composite
path, FreeHand flows the text
horizontally from one shape to
the other.

Of course, there's one problem with the technique that I described in these five steps: You're left with this extra rectangular path. If you want to display the border around the free-form text object, the border around the rectangle is also visible. Ah, but I have a solution in the form of Top Secret Step 6!

Step 6. Press the Option key and marquee around the rectangle, *without enclosing any other paths*, including the free-form text object. If it's impossible to avoid other paths, Option-click on the rectangle, click on one of its points, and Shift-click on each of the three remaining points. Either way, you will have selected all points in the rectangle. Then press the Delete key. This deletes the rectangle and leaves the free-form text object as a composite path that you can enlarge or reduce independently of the type inside.

I know it sounds weird, but it works every time. And believe it or not, there's presently no better solution. If you try to delete the rectangle without first selecting its points, you delete the text object as well. You can't make a single object into a composite path, so you have to join text object and rectangle and then turn around and delete the rectangle.

Using Inset values

One of the major difficulties in filling complex objects with type is getting the characters to accurately fill the little nooks and crannies. Multisyllabic phrases like *nationwide gubernatorial bipartisanship* always seem to coincide with the tiniest corners in your objects.

Rather than wasting huge amounts of time reshaping your path so that the text fits, experiment with the Inset values inside the Object Dimensions & Inset panel of the

Inspector palette (Command-Option-B). The Inset option boxes are labeled *L, T, R,* and *B,* for left, top, right, and bottom. Positive values create margins between the free-form path and the text — which is generally only useful if you plan on displaying the path outline and want the margins for aesthetic purposes.

If you want to squish more text into the path, negative values are the ticket. Negative values allow the text to extend beyond the boundaries of the free-form path. For example, if you can't seem to get a string of text to fit on a line — even though it looks like there's tons of room to spare — enter a negative value into the R option box. FreeHand then lets the text extend beyond the right edge of the text object.

Flowing text from one block to another

If a story contains more than a couple of paragraphs, you'll probably want to do more than simply reshape the text object to make the entire story visible in the illustration window. You can *flow* long stories across text objects to create multiple columns or even multiple pages of text. Figure 9-17 shows a story flowed into three paths. A story like this is called a *chain* because each text block in the story is *linked* to another.

Figure 9-17:
A Single sotry
flowed into three
text blocks

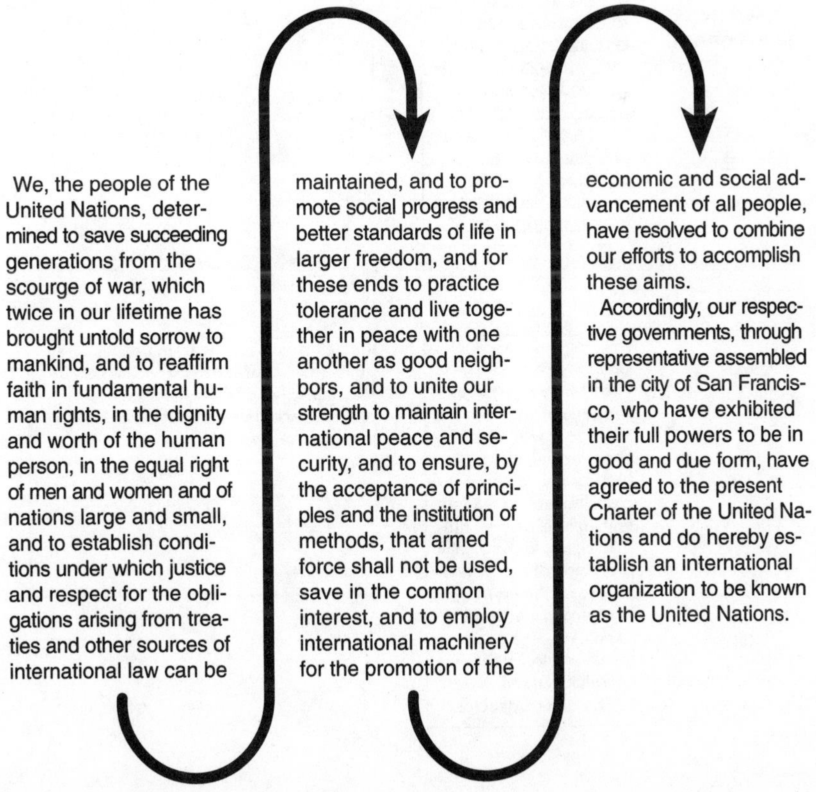

We, the people of the United Nations, determined to save succeeding generations from the scourge of war, which twice in our lifetime has brought untold sorrow to mankind, and to reaffirm faith in fundamental human rights, in the dignity and worth of the human person, in the equal right of men and women and of nations large and small, and to establish conditions under which justice and respect for the obligations arising from treaties and other sources of international law can be

maintained, and to promote social progress and better standards of life in larger freedom, and for these ends to practice tolerance and live together in peace with one another as good neighbors, and to unite our strength to maintain international peace and security, and to ensure, by the acceptance of principles and the institution of methods, that armed force shall not be used, save in the common interest, and to employ international machinery for the promotion of the

economic and social advancement of all people, have resolved to combine our efforts to accomplish these aims.

Accordingly, our respective governments, through representative assembled in the city of San Francisco, who have exhibited their full powers to be in good and due form, have agreed to the present Charter of the United Nations and do hereby establish an international organization to be known as the United Nations.

If you enter or import too much text to fit inside a single text object, the link box just outside the lower right corner of a text block contains a black circle. You can display the excess text — also called *overflow* text — in two ways.

- ↪ If the text appears inside a standard text block, drag a corner handle to enlarge the block. If you're working with a free-form text object, reshape the object as described earlier in this chapter.

- ↪ Send the overflow text to another text object by creating a link.

To use the second method, you must first create a new container for the overflow text. Click or drag with the text tool to create a new text block or use the drawing tools to create a new closed path. Then drag from the link box that contains the black circle into your new text object, as shown in Figure 9-18. The next time you select the original text block, you'll see that the link box symbol has changed from a black circle to a double-headed arrow (as in the second example in the figure), showing that a link has been established.

Figure 9-18:
Drag from a link box into a new text block (top) to link the two blocks and flow text between them (bottom).

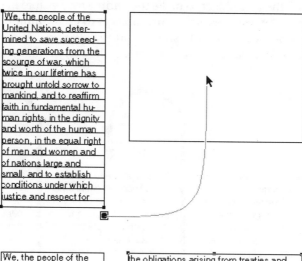

When linking text blocks, you'll generally want to work in the keyline mode. This way, you'll be sure to see the outlines of the text blocks. In the preview mode, any deselected text blocks that are not stroked — which is the default setting — are invisible.

You can even flow type into a text object that already contains type. As shown in Figure 9-19, FreeHand simply shoves the existing type in the receiving text object forward to make room for the type being flowed from the other text object. Flowed type and existing type are fused into a single story.

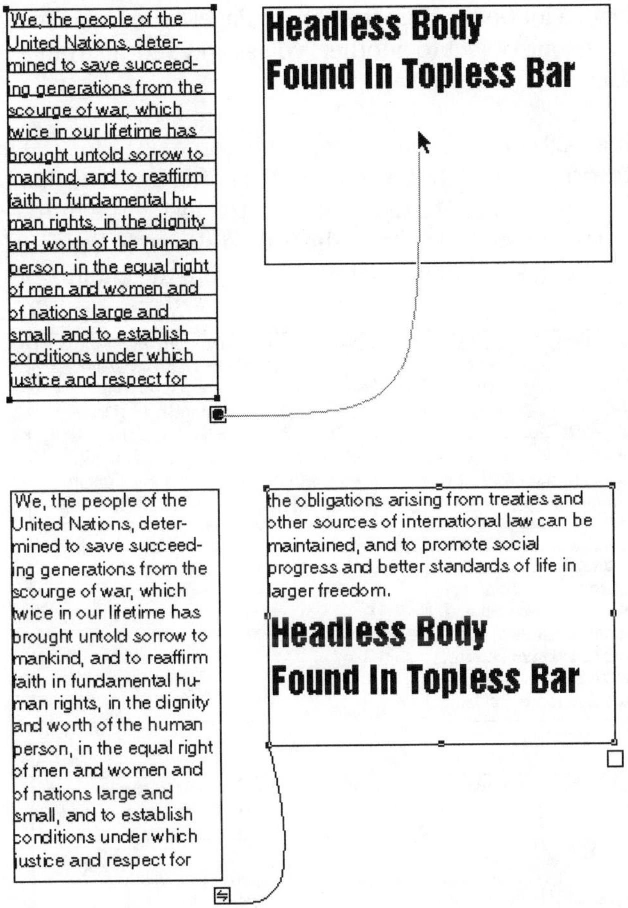

Figure 9-19: If you drag into a text block that already contains type (top), FreeHand flows the incoming type into the beginning of the text block and pushes the existing type to the end (bottom).

We, the people of the United Nations, determined to save succeeding generations from the scourge of war, which twice in our lifetime has brought untold sorrow to mankind, and to reaffirm faith in fundamental human rights, in the dignity and worth of the human person, in the equal right of men and women and of nations large and small, and to establish conditions under which justice and respect for

Headless Body Found In Topless Bar

We, the people of the United Nations, determined to save succeeding generations from the scourge of war, which twice in our lifetime has brought untold sorrow to mankind, and to reaffirm faith in fundamental human rights, in the dignity and worth of the human person, in the equal right of men and women and of nations large and small, and to establish conditions under which justice and respect for

the obligations arising from treaties and other sources of international law can be maintained, and to promote social progress and better standards of life in larger freedom.

Headless Body Found In Topless Bar

To create evenly sized, evenly spaced columns of type, you may want to establish a series of guidelines, as described in the "Creating guidelines" section of Chapter 8. You can also use the Align palette to even up the tops or bottoms of the text objects and distribute them evenly by selecting the Distribute Widths option from the Horizontal pop-up menu. See the "Alignment and Distribution" section of Chapter 8 for more information.

Reflowing a story

Chains of text objects in FreeHand are as flexible as they are in QuarkXPress (meaning that they're a heck of a lot better than they are in PageMaker). To change the order in which text flows from one object to another, you simply redrag from a link box that contains a double-arrow symbol.

For example, Figure 9-20 shows a chain comprising three text blocks. I numbered the blocks to show the order in which the text flows. If I drag from the link box associated with the first text block and release the mouse button inside the third text block, as illustrated in the figure, FreeHand reflows the text as shown in Figure 9-21. What was once the second text block has now been removed from the chain.

Figure 9-20:
By dragging from the link box for text block #1 into text block #3, . . .

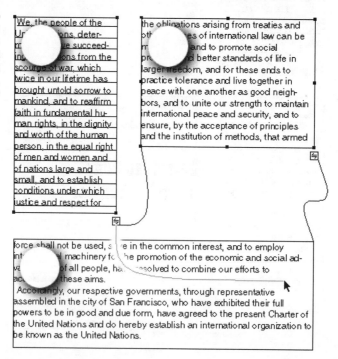

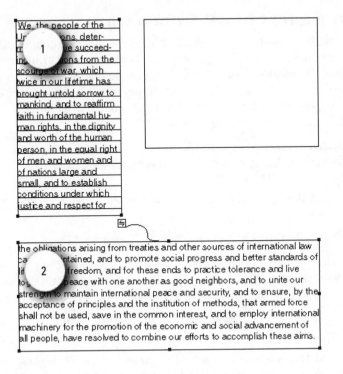

Figure 9-21:
. . . I instruct
FreeHand to reflow
the text and bypass
the block in the
upper right corner.

Other ways to reflow text inside a chain include:

- Select a text block in the chain and delete it or cut it to the Clipboard. Removing a text block leaves the text itself intact. The text reflows around the missing text block. For example, if you deleted the second block from Figure 9-20, the text would automatically flow between the first and third blocks, as shown in Figure 9-21.

- If you reduce the size of a text block by dragging its corner handle, text flows out of that block and into the next block in the chain.

- If you enlarge a text block — again by dragging a corner handle — text flows into that block and out of the next block in the chain. This may have the effect of sucking up the entire contents of the last text object in a chain. However, FreeHand doesn't delete the text object or remove it from the chain. If you want to delete the last text object, you have to do the job manually (by clicking on the object with the arrow tool and pressing the Delete key).

Separating a text block from a story

Separating a text block and the type inside it from the rest of a chain is a cumbersome operation in FreeHand, on par with extracting Estonia, Latvia, Lithuania, and Belarus from the Russian Federation. You can't simply cut the text block and paste it, as in Illustrator, for example. If you try, FreeHand simply removes and pastes the block without affecting any of the type inside it (as I explained a brief moment ago). So what's the solution? Read the following steps to find out.

STEPS: Forming Your Own Breakaway Chain Republic

Step 1. Select the text object that you want to separate. We'll call this object *Azerbaijan*.

Step 2. Copy it to the Clipboard by pressing Command-C.

Step 3. Select the text tool and double-click on the very first word inside Azerbaijan. We'll call this word *Baku*. (Actually, I'm getting a little carried away here. You can call the word *Tbilisi* if you want to, even if it is in Georgia.)

Step 4. Press Shift-End to select all remaining words in the text object. Words like *Sungait* and *Gyandzha*.

Step 5. Press the Delete key to get rid of them. Unless it's the last text object in the chain, Azerbaijan fills with all new words. (Don't worry, Azerbaijan's in the Clipboard, so *Baku, Sungait,* and all the rest of them are safe and sound. Isn't geography fun?)

Step 6. Press Command-Tab to deselect the text block. Then press Shift-F10 to select the arrow tool.

Step 7. Select Azerbaijan and press Delete. The text object disappears and the words flow back into the original positions.

Step 8. Select one of the other text blocks in the chain — Kazakhstan, Tajikistan, Uzbekistan, or one of them other Stan's — and then choose Edit ➪ Paste Behind. FreeHand pastes Azerbaijan back into its original location. Finally, Azerbaijan is free of the chain!

Step 9. Shout "Hooray" and start a war with one of your neighbors. Armenia looks vulnerable.

Breaking the link between text blocks

To unlink text objects in a chain, drag from a link box into an empty portion of the illustration window. FreeHand empties the type out of all the later text blocks in the chain, but those text blocks remain linked to each other. For example, if I dragged from the link box associated with the first text block back in Figure 9-20, I would destroy the link between blocks #1 and #2. Meanwhile, blocks #2 and #3 — now empty — would remain linked. If I then dragged from block #1's link box into block #2, I would reestablish the entire chain and fill blocks #2 and #3 with text.

Selecting and Replacing Text

I mentioned this earlier, but just to recap, you can activate an existing text object by double-clicking on it with the arrow tool. FreeHand automatically selects the text tool and displays an insertion marker inside the text object and a tab ruler over it. After the text object is active, you can replace characters inside the object by selecting them and entering new characters from the keyboard.

You can use the text tool to select the contents of any text object as follows:

- ∞ **Drag over the characters that you want to select:** Drag to the left or to the right to select characters on the same line of type; drag upward or downward to select characters on multiple lines; and drag across columns in a chain to select large portions of a story. The selected text becomes highlighted.

- ∞ **Double-click on a word to select the word and the space after it:** Hold down the mouse button on the second click and drag to select several words at a time.

- ∞ **Triple-click inside a paragraph to select the paragraph:** Hold down the mouse button on the third click and drag to select additional paragraphs.

- ∞ **Click at one end and Shift-click at the other:** Click to set the insertion marker at the beginning of the text you want to select. Then Shift-click at the end of the desired selection. All text between the two clicks becomes highlighted.

- ∞ **Press Command-A to select everything:** Choose the Select All command from the Edit menu (Command-A) to select all text throughout the entire story, including any text objects linked to the active block.

You can also select text using the arrow keys. Click to set the insertion marker at one end of the text you want to select and extend the selection using the keyboard equivalents listed in Table 9-1.

Table 9-1	Extending a Selection with the Arrow Keys
To Extend the Selection	**Press These Keys**
One character to the left	Shift-left arrow
One character to the right	Shift-right arrow
One word to the left	Command-Shift-left arrow
One word to the right	Command-Shift-right arrow
One line up	Shift-up arrow
One line down	Shift-down arrow
To beginning of text block	Shift-Home
To end of text block	Shift-End

In addition to replacing highlighted text, you can:

- Apply formatting attributes to it, as discussed in the following chapter.

- Delete the text by pressing the Delete key.

- Send a copy of the text to the Clipboard by choosing Edit ⇨ Copy or pressing Command-C.

- Remove the text and send it to the Clipboard by choosing Edit ⇨ Cut (Command-X).

- Replace the selected text with text that you copied earlier by choosing Edit ⇨ Paste (Command-V).

Pasted text always retains its original character formatting, although it assumes the paragraph-level formatting of the paragraph into which it is pasted. You can even copy text from a different application and paste it into FreeHand, or vice versa.

Summary

- Drag with the text tool to specify the exact dimensions of a text block.

- Press Command-Tab to deselect a text block. Command-click on the text block to deactivate it without deselecting it.

- Press Command-Shift-U to enter type inside any closed path.

- If you don't want to preview or print the outline of a free-form text object, press Command-Option-B and deselect the Display Border check box.

- To transfer text created in a word processor to FreeHand and retain the formatting, save the document in the RTF format. But be sure to spell-check it first.

- Drag the corner handle to resize a text block and rewrap the text inside it. If you drag a top, bottom, or side handle, you change the spacing of lines and characters as you resize the block.

- Option-drag a corner handle with the arrow tool to scale both text block and characters.

- If you want to reshape a geometric text object, Option-click on the path outline to select it independently of the type. Then press Command-U to ungroup the path.

- When a link box contains a black circle, type exceeds the boundaries of the text object. Drag from the link box into another text block or path to display the overflow type.

- Double-click on a text block with the arrow tool to activate the text block and select the text tool. Then drag inside the text block to select characters. Press keys to replace or delete the selected text.

Formatting and Copyfitting

In This Chapter

- ➤ My take on today's newfangled Maxwell House products
- ➤ Introductions to formatting and copyfitting
- ➤ In-depth examinations of font, type size, and type style
- ➤ How to expand and condense type
- ➤ Definitions of *leading, kerning,* and *baseline shift,* as well as reasons for using them
- ➤ FreeHand's goofy stylistic effects
- ➤ The right and wrong ways to use tabs, tab stops, and paragraph indents
- ➤ A thorough examination of alignment, paragraph spacing, letterspacing, and word spacing
- ➤ Automatic and manual hyphenation techniques
- ➤ How to assign rules (thin lines) to paragraphs, columns, and rows
- ➤ Ways to create and copyfit columns and rows

My Newest Office Caper

You wouldn't believe what just happened. Just this minute. You know those little Cappio thingies? They're little bottles of iced cappuccino that are marketed to beatnik wannabes (like me). I love them and heartily recommend them; they're great for caffeine addicts trying to wean themselves off Mountain Dew.

Well, anyway, you have to shake them. To mix the contents, I mean. It says so right on the label: "Shake well." So there I was, engaging in some vigorous agitation — *shicka shaka* (a couple of sound effects for you) — when I notice this stuff squirting all over my desk.

Okay, so the lid was off. But can you believe these labels? If they mean "Shake well before removing lid," why don't they say so? This is a clear case of planned obsolescence. They want you to throw your cappuccino all over the room so that you have to buy more. I think I'll sue. I'm a member of the Don't Take Responsibility for Your Actions generation. I'll sue Maxwell House until their lawyers weep openly. Desk damage and related trauma, $6 million.

Meanwhile, I have quite the mess on my desk. Luckily, I didn't get the stuff on either of my computers. Talk about your minor miracles. There's always the chance I'll be canonized for it. Check out Saint Deke, he squirts liquid out of open bottles without hitting his computers. But I really soaked everything in between. Half my library is sitting here in puddles of sugary, coffee-y, milky goop, the perfect recipe to stick, stain, and stink. Really, I couldn't be happier.

This Will Help Me Use FreeHand, Will It?

There we go. All cleaned up. So, without further ado, back to FreeHand. Text in FreeHand, in fact. For you folks who like to learn without a bunch of true-life-stories nonsense, skip to here. I should have told you earlier, but now you know.

The thing is, the importance of text can't be understated. You have to make your message clear — "Shake well before removing lid, you taffy-brained ferret" — and you have to format it so that the taffy-brained ferrets of the world (I must count myself among them) read your words. I can't help you with the making-your-message clear part, but I can explain all the options that FreeHand gives you for sizing, spacing, and styling the words that you use.

As far as pure formatting power is concerned, you've hit the jackpot. FreeHand offers more formatting options than any other product on the market. FreeHand is the only program that lets you modify the distance between the first line of type and the top of a text block, the distance between the last word in a line and the right edge of a text block, the order in which text flows inside rows and columns, and a bunch of other stuff that probably won't make a whole lot of sense to you this early in the game.

What is formatting?

First, what is *formatting* and what is that other thing that I alluded to in the title of the chapter but haven't bothered to so much as mention yet, *copyfitting*? Well, formatting options determine how individual characters look, how big they are, how far apart they are, the distance between lines of type — in short, formatting defines the appearance of text. FreeHand breaks formatting attributes into three categories: those that affect individual characters; those that affect entire paragraphs; and those that affect entire text blocks.

- ∞ Character-level formatting attributes include font, type size, style, leading, horizontal scale, kerning, baseline shift, and a few special effects. To change the formatting of one or more characters, you first select the characters in the text object and then apply the desired options. FreeHand modifies the selected characters only.

- ∞ Paragraph-level formatting attributes include tabs and indents, letterspacing and word spacing, hyphenation settings, and alignment options. To change the formatting of an entire paragraph, you need only position the insertion marker inside that paragraph and then apply the desired paragraph-level formatting options. To change the formatting of several consecutive paragraphs, select at least one character from each of the paragraphs you want to modify.

- ∞ Block-level formatting includes a few options that I discussed in the last chapter, such as the physical dimensions of the text object and the Inset values, as well as the number of rows and columns in a text object. To change the formatting of an entire text object, select the object with the arrow tool or click inside it with the text tool. Then apply the desired block-level formatting options.

Figure 10-1 shows the palettes and panels that contain all the formatting attributes offered by FreeHand. Except for the handful of options in the Type palette and tab ruler, all of FreeHand's formatting options are found in one of the panels of the Inspector palette.

None of FreeHand's formatting palettes include Apply buttons (but they all should). In order to apply changes that you enter into option boxes, you have to press the Return key. If you want to cancel an option, simply click in the illustration window with the arrow tool.

You can also specify the formatting attributes for a new text block before typing it. After clicking or dragging with the text tool, specify the formatting options you want and then begin typing.

Figure 10-1:
FreeHand's
formatting
options at a
glance.

Character-level attributes

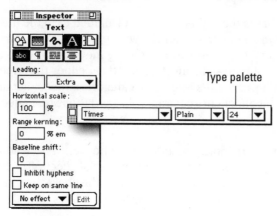

Paragraph-level attributes

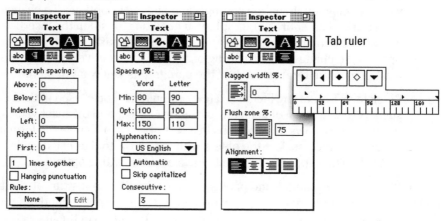

Block-level attributes

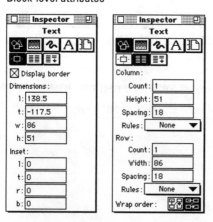

What is copyfitting?

Copyfitting refers to FreeHand's ability to change formatting attributes automatically so that a story exactly fits into an allotted space. You can balance the amount of text inside two columns, increase the leading in a column to fill the vertical space, and expand or reduce the type size and leading to fill several text objects in a chain. These options enable you to let FreeHand take some of the formatting responsibility instead of micromanaging the document all by yourself.

Character-Level Formatting_____

Some folks hate desktop publishing and design programs because they provide complete nincompoops with the power to create ugly type. I studied fine art in college and I learned a variety of techniques while serving a brief stint as an assistant art director for a local newspaper. But I've never taken a single design course in my life. For what it's worth, I learned my own personal brand of design on the job largely by trial and error. As a result, some of my early work met with disapproval. "Ugly, ugly, ugly," was one reviewer's reaction. Unfortunately, I can't say that the commentary was completely without merit. My first designs looked as if I was afraid that if I didn't use every typeface and shred of clip art at my disposal, I might hurt their feelings.

But so what? My early encounters with desktop publishing were a transitional learning phase just like any other. The fact that I was able to print my documents out didn't make my experimentation any less valid or any more odious than if I had created them using conventional tools. The same goes for you. You may be an expert designer or an absolute novice. But either way, I encourage you to experiment with FreeHand's formatting capabilities as much as possible. Only through experimentation can you grow as a designer. And FreeHand is about the most forgiving environment I can think of for developing a mastery of your craft.

All about fonts

In computer typography, the term *font* is frequently used as a synonym for *typeface*. But back in the days of hot metal type, a clear distinction existed. Because characters had to be printed from physical hunks of lead, you needed an entirely separate font of characters to express a change in typeface, style, or size.

Things have changed quite a bit since then. In FreeHand (or any other Mac or Windows program), you can access *scalable fonts,* which are mathematical definitions of character outlines. In its most fundamental form, each character is expressed as one or more paths, just like the ones you draw in FreeHand. You can scale these paths to any size, independent of the resolution of your screen or printer.

Type styles and families

Although a single font can satisfy any number of size requirements, it can convey only a single *type style*. The plain and bold styles of a typeface, in other words, are supplied as two separate fonts. So, in computer typesetting, every font carries with it both unique typeface and type style information.

Helvetica and Times, for example, can each be displayed in four type styles, as shown in Figure 10-2. Each type style is a separate font. Together, each set of four type styles makes up a *type family*.

Different type styles emphasize text in different ways. Plain text — sometimes called *Roman,* meaning upright with serifs — is by far the most common variety. It is used to display *body copy,* the large blocks or columns of text that represent the heart and soul of information contained on a page. The *italic* (cursive) or *oblique* (slanted) style may be used within body copy to highlight a foreign or unfamiliar phrase or simply to stress a word. The *bold* style is relegated to special text such as captions and headlines. You can even italicize bold text to create a *bold italic* style.

Applying typeface and type style

To assign a typeface to all selected characters, first display the Type palette by pressing Command-T. Then select an option from the font pop-up menu, labeled in Figure 10-3. To access the pop-up menu, be sure to click and hold on the down-pointing arrowhead rather than on the font name itself.

Figure 10-2:
Members of the
Helvetica and
Times type
families.

Helvetica
Helvetica Bold
Helvetica Oblique
Helvetica Bold Oblique

Times Roman
Times Bold
Times Italic
Times Bold Italic

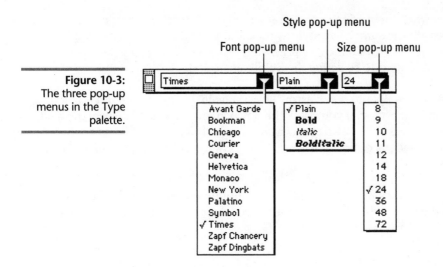

Style pop-up menu

Font pop-up menu   Size pop-up menu

Figure 10-3:
The three pop-up
menus in the Type
palette.

To change the type style, select an option from the style pop-up menu (also labeled in Figure 10-3). The style menu lists only those type styles that are applicable to the current font. For example, if you select Times from the font menu, all four style options — Plain, Bold, Italic, and BoldItalic — are available in the style menu because all four styles are part of the Times family. However, if you select Symbol, which supplies only one style, all options but Plain are dimmed in the menu.

Also, you can't apply a style to a stylized typeface. Suppose that you select the Adobe typeface I Times Italic from the font pop-up menu. This font is already italicized, so the Italic and BoldItalic options in the style pop-up menu are dimmed.

Typeface and style options are also available under the Type menu in the Font and Type Style submenus. But as long as the Type palette is available, there's no use in bothering with these menus.

Using the Type palette option boxes

An even better way to apply typefaces and styles is to enter text into the respective Type palette option boxes. You don't have to enter the full name of a typeface or style, just the first few letters. For example, if you click on the leftmost option box in the palette and enter a *B,* FreeHand automatically selects Bookman, because Bookman is the only typeface in the pop-up menu that begins with a *B* (see Figure 10-3). If more than one typeface begins with the same letter, as in the case of Chicago and Courier, pressing *C* selects the first typeface in alphabetical order. You would have to press *C* and *O* to select Courier. The same goes for selecting a style. After clicking or tabbing in the style option box, press *P* to select Plain, *B* for Bold, and so on.

But what happens when the first several characters in the names of two or more typefaces or styles are the same? The style options Bold and BoldItalic, for example, share many similar letters. You'd have to press five keys — *B, O, L, D,* and *I* — before FreeHand finally got around to selecting the BoldItalic option.

 That's where the up and down arrow keys come in. If you press *B,* FreeHand selects the bold option. If you press the down arrow, FreeHand selects the next option, Italic. Press the down arrow again to select BoldItalic. The up arrow selects the previous option in the list. This technique also works in the font option box.

After you change the values in the font and/or style option boxes, press the Return key to apply them to the selected text. If you want to cancel your selection, just click in the illustration window.

Enlarging and reducing type

After choosing a font to govern the fundamental appearance of your text, you can further enhance and distinguish individual characters and words by changing their size. But to enlarge or reduce type, you first need to understand how it's measured. To begin with, there are four basic kinds of characters. The horizontal guidelines that serve as boundaries for these characters are labeled in Figure 10-4.

☞ *Capital letters* extend from the *baseline* upward to the *cap height* line. Examples include *A, B,* and *C.* Numerals (*0123456789*) also qualify as capitals because they typically stay within the same boundaries as caps.

Figure 10-4: Type is measured using a series of horizontal guidelines.

- ☞ *Medials* fit entirely within the space between the *baseline* and the *x-height* line. Examples include *a, c,* and *e.*

- ☞ *Ascenders* are lowercase characters that extend above the cap height line. Examples include *b, d,* and *k.*

- ☞ *Descenders* are lowercase characters that extend below the baseline. Examples include *g, j,* and *p.*

Not every character fits snugly into one of these categories. For example, the lowercase characters *i* and *t* violate the x-height line but are nonetheless considered medials. This is because the dot of the *i* is not viewed as an integral part of the character, and the *t* does not usually extend to the cap height line. Other times, a letter qualifies as both an ascender and a descender, as is the case for the italic *f* in a serif font. Nonletters — such as %, #, and & — are generally considered capitals. But there are several exceptions, such as $, , and many forms of punctuation, including parentheses.

Changing the type size

Hot stuff, huh? Well, for those of you who are worried that we're delving too deeply into the territory of typo-dweebology, let me get straight to the point, which is this: The *type size* of a character is measured from the topmost point of the tallest ascender to the very lowest point of the deepest descender. Type size is always measured in points, regardless of the current unit of measure, which is why you frequently see type size called *point size.*

You can change the type size by selecting an option from the size pop-up menu in the Type palette (refer back to Figure 10-3) or by entering a value into the size option box. FreeHand accepts any value between 1 and 4,068 points (nearly 5 feet!) in 0.001-point increments. If you enter a value in the option box, make sure to press the Return key to implement it.

 If you're not sure what type size to use, you can enlarge and reduce selected characters incrementally from the keyboard. Press Command-Shift-comma (a.k.a. Command-<) to reduce the type size by 1 point; press Command-Shift-period (>) to make the selected type 1 point larger.

Horizontal scale

When you change the type size, you scale the width and height of each character by equal amounts. But you can also scale the width of a character independently of its height. Just enter a value into the Horizontal Scale option box in the Text Character panel of the Inspector palette (Command-Option-T). As illustrated in Figure 10-5, any value below 100 percent puts the characters on a weight-loss program; any value over 100 percent fattens them up. Fashion models probably like compressed type, but sumo wrestlers prefer expanded type.

If you're familiar with the range of commercial fonts available on the market, you probably know that you can purchase typefaces that are already compressed or expanded. And you may wonder why you would want to do that if you can simply compress or expand the font in FreeHand. The truth is that using the Horizontal Scale option can make your text look pretty weird.

Figure 10-6 shows two characters that are identical in height and width. The left character was set in Helvetica and compressed in FreeHand. The right character was set in Helvetica Condensed, a specially designed font. Notice that the vertical stems in the left

Figure 10-5: The same type size compressed (top) and expanded (bottom) by changing the Horizontal Scale value.

48-point Helvetica compressed to 60%

The same font & size expanded to 140%

character are much skinnier than the arches that join the stems, which is exactly the opposite of the way it's supposed to be. By compressing the letter, I reduced the width of the stems without changing the thickness of the arches one iota. In the condensed character on the right, the designers of the font resolved this problem. They also squared off the arches slightly to make the font more legible.

The moral is, don't squish your characters too much. As a general rule of thumb, stick to Horizontal Scale values between 80 and 125 percent. Anything beyond this range really upsets the design of the characters.

Figure 10-6: Two characters, one compressed inside FreeHand (left) and the other set in a condensed typeface (right).

Expanding the width of characters also expands the spaces between characters — so much so that the text can have as many gaps as David Letterman's dental work. To offset this effect, you can reduce the spacing by entering a negative Range Kerning value in the Text Character panel. As a general rule of thumb, enter one negative percentage point of Range Kerning for every 10 percent added to the Horizontal Scale value. For example, to create the 140-percent expansion shown in Figure 10-5, I entered a Range Kerning value of −4 percent. If only braces worked this quickly.

Vertical and horizontal spacing

Like the Horizontal Scale value, the remainder of the character-level formatting options are located in the Text Character panel of the Inspector palette, which appears in Figure 10-7. Assuming that the Inspector palette is available, you can access the panel by pressing Command-Option-T. If the Inspector palette is missing, press Command-I.

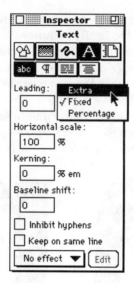

Figure 10-7:
The Leading and Kerning options are
located in the Text Character panel of
the Inspector palette.

Three character-level formatting attributes control the amount of space between selected characters:

- *Leading* is the amount of vertical space between one line of text and the next (as illustrated back in Figure 10-4).

- *Kerning* controls the amount of horizontal space between neighboring characters of text.

- *Baseline shift* raises or lowers selected characters with respect to the baseline, bringing them closer to neighboring lines of type. The primary purpose for this option is to create superscript and subscript type.

Increasing and decreasing leading

Back in the old days, printers actually shoved little pieces of lead between lines of type to increase the vertical spacing. Then they presumably licked their fingers and went crazy from lead poisoning, which is how they came up with term leading (pronounced *ledd-ing*, not *lee-ding*), a word no sane person would invent. A few recent typographers have tried to rename it *line spacing,* but *leading* has managed to stick it out as the preferred term of the trade.

FreeHand 4.0 now permits you to measure leading in one of three ways, each of which is represented by an option in the pop-up menu to the right of the Leading option box (displayed in Figure 10-7). In previous versions of the program, leading was always measured as the distance from the baseline of one

line of type to the baseline of the next. To measure leading this way now, you have to select the Fixed option.

The two new options measure leading relative to the type size of the selected characters. These options are most useful when the type size varies from one line to the next and you want to make sure that FreeHand compensates for this fact. Also, whereas a Fixed leading remains unchanged when you enlarge or reduce the type size, the other two options allow the leading to grow and shrink with type size adjustments. The two new options work as follows:

- **Extra:** By default, the leading value is identical to the type size. To insert a few additional points of leading, select the Extra option.

- **Percentage:** To measure leading as a percentage of the type size, select this option. This option improves on the old "automatic" leading setting, which was always 120 percent.

Regardless of which pop-up menu option you select, you change the leading by entering a value into the option box and pressing the Return key. Like type size, leading is always measured in points, regardless of the current unit of measure.

Generally, you should select entire lines of type when changing the leading. If a single line contains characters with two different leading specifications, the larger leading value prevails. When making a large initial capital letter, for example, you might have a 24-point character on the same line as several 12-point characters. If the leading for all characters is sent to 120 percent, the entire line is set at 29-point leading, which is 120 percent of the 24-point type size.

Pair and range kerning

The title of the third option box in the Text Character panel of the Inspector palette is either *Kerning* or *Range Kerning*. The former title appears when the insertion marker is positioned between two characters of type; the latter appears when one or more characters are selected. Both kerning and range kerning control the amount of space between each pair of selected characters.

Normally, FreeHand accepts the dimensions of each character stored in the font definition and places the character flush against its neighbors. The font defines the width of the character as well as the amount of space that is placed before the character and after it. This "flank space" is called *side bearing,* as illustrated in Figure 10-8. FreeHand arrives at its normal letterspacing by adding the right side bearing of the first character to the left side bearing of the second.

Left side bearing   Right side bearing

Figure 10-8:
A kerning pair is a
set of two letters
that look better
when spaced close
to each other than
when set shoulder
to shoulder as
prescribed by the
default side
bearings.

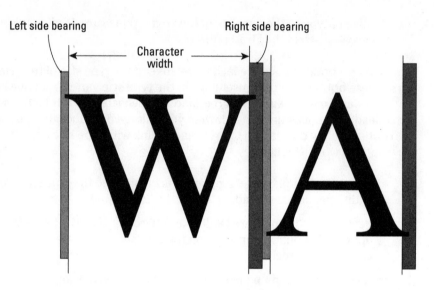

Character
width

Pair kerning compensation

However, font designers can specify that certain pairs of letters, called *kerning pairs,* should be positioned more closely together than the standard letter normally allows. Whenever the two characters of a kerning pair appear next to each other, as in the case of the *W* and *A* shown in the second example of Figure 10-8, they are spaced according to special kerning information contained in the font.

If you don't like the default amount of kerning between two characters of type, you can adjust the space. Position the insertion marker between the characters and enter a new value into the Kerning option box in the Text Character panel. If you want to change the kerning between multiple characters, select those characters and enter a value into the Range Kerning option box. Then press the Return key.

Both the Kerning and Range Kerning values are measured in 1/100ths of an em space (an em space, introduced in Chapter 9, is a character that's as wide as the type size is tall). A value of 25 is roughly equivalent to a standard space character. Enter any number between –200 and 1,000, in 0.01 increments, for this option. A negative value squeezes letters together; a positive value spreads them apart.

 If you don't know what kerning value to use, you can adjust the kerning from the keyboard. Press Option-left arrow to squeeze letters together by 1/100 (1 percent) em space; press Option-right arrow to spread them apart by the same increment. To adjust letters by 1/10 (10 percent) em space, press Shift-Option-left arrow or Shift-Option-right arrow. The Kerning value in the Text Character panel tracks your changes.

When kerning small type, you may not be able to see any difference as you add or delete space, because the display is not accurate enough. If that happens, use the zoom tool to magnify the drawing area while kerning or tracking characters from the keyboard. (If you're using PostScript fonts, you must have ATM installed to see any difference when you zoom.)

Baseline shift

The value in the Baseline Shift option box determines the distance between the selected type and its baseline. You can use this option to create superscripts and subscripts or to adjust the vertical alignment of text on a path (as discussed in the following chapter). Enter any value between negative and positive 1,000 points (nearly 14 inches) or the equivalent in another unit of measurement. Unlike type size and leading, the Baseline Shift value is measured in the unit specified in the Document Setup panel. A positive value shifts the text upward; a negative value shifts it downward. Press Return to apply the value to the selected text.

One of the most popular uses for the Baseline Shift option is to create fractions. You don't have to put up with pseudo-fractions like 1/2, where the numerator and denominator sit clumsily on either side of a slash. In FreeHand, you can create *real* fractions — the kind that would make your old math teacher proud. The following steps explain how.

STEPS: Creating the Perfect Fraction in FreeHand

Step 1.   Enter the fraction from the keyboard. Rather than dividing numerator (top value) and denominator (bottom value) with a slash, use the special fraction symbol, accessed by pressing Shift-Option-1.

Step 2.   Select the numerator. Change the size value in the Type palette to half its current size. If the type size is 12 points, for example, make it 6.

Step 3.   Enter a Baseline Shift value equal to about one-third the original type size. In the 12-point example, the Baseline Shift value would be 4.

Step 4.   Select the denominator and match its type size to that of the numerator, but do not change the baseline shift.

That's all there is to it. Amazingly easy, huh? The result will be a fraction like the one shown in Figure 10-9. This fraction was originally set in 120-point type. I changed the numerator (35) to 60-point type and shifted it 40 points upward. I changed the denominator (38) to 60-point type as well but did not shift it.

Figure 10-9:
A fraction created by varying the type size of all numbers and the baseline shift of the numerator.

35/38

 You can adjust the baseline shift from the keyboard in one-point increments. Press Option-up arrow to raise the selected text; press Option-down arrow to lower it.

Stylistic effects

Even since Version 1.0, FreeHand has provided a series of predefined special type effects that have little or no value in the real world. The effects have never been upgraded; as a matter of fact, Version 4.0 dumped several in an attempt to streamline things a bit. But, for better or worse, a few effects continue to hang on.

The most useful stylistic effect from previous versions, Fill and Stroke, has been dropped from Version 4.0. This is good news, though, because the most recent FreeHand makes it even more convenient to apply fill and stroke attributes to text. You now control these functions by selecting characters with the text tool and specifying attributes from the Fill and Stroke panels of the Inspector palette. For more information, read the first few pages of Chapters 13 and 14.

To apply an effect to a few selected words, select an option from the Effect pop-up menu at the bottom of the Text Character panel of the Inspector palette. In all likelihood, the current option shown in the pop-up menu is No Effect. You can customize two of the effects by clicking on the Edit button to the right of the pop-up menu.

For best results, apply these effects only to very large text — say, 48-point text or larger. You must select the Display Text Effects check box in the Display panel of the Preferences dialog box to view the effects in the preview mode. Needless to say, the effects don't display correctly in the keyline mode.

You can apply only one Effect option to a character at a time. However, you can combine stylized effects with type styles. For example, the bold type style and the inline effect can coexist quite happily.

And now, without further ado, the following sections explain FreeHand's stylistic effects.

The inline effect

Select the Inline Effect option to assign multiple outlines to selected type. An example of inline type appears in Figure 10-10.

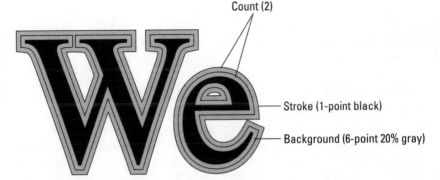

Figure 10-10:
A block of large text subjected to the inline effect.

Count (2)

Stroke (1-point black)

Background (6-point 20% gray)

To customize the effect, click on the Edit button in the Text Character panel, which displays the Inline Effect dialog box shown in Figure 10-11. The options in this dialog box work as follows:

- **Count:** This number tells FreeHand how many outlines to draw around each selected character.

- **Stroke:** Under Stroke, enter a line weight value into the Width option box. This value defines the thickness of each outline drawn around the selected characters. To change the color of the outlines as well as the color of the selected characters, drag a color from the Color List, Color Mixer, or Tints palette and drop it on the color box below the Width option.

- **Background:** The Background options specify the thickness and color of the areas between the outlines. In Figure 10-10, I used a 6-point, 20 percent gray Background.

Figure 10-11:
Drag a swatch from one of the color palettes to change the color of the outlines or the spaces between outlines in the inline effect.

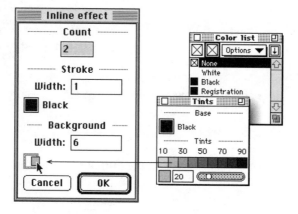

 For complete information on defining and dragging colors, read Chapter 12. Chapter 14 explains line weight and other stroke attributes.

The shadow effect

Drop shadows are immensely popular, though indisputably overused. Unfortunately, you don't have any way to control this effect in FreeHand. To apply a drop shadow to selected type, select the Shadow Effect option from the Effect pop-up menu. That's it. The Edit button is dimmed, so you can't change the color or position of the drop shadow — it's always gray and offset slightly down and to the right.

The zoom effect

Select the Zoom Effect option to create a continuous gradation that trails away from the text, as illustrated in Figure 10-12. After applying the effect, click on the Edit button to display the Zoom Effect dialog box shown in Figure 10-13. The options in this dialog box work as follows:

- ↪ **Zoom To:** The zoom effect works by creating several clones of the selected text, layering them one in front of another, and filling each with a slightly different color. The Zoom To value determines the type size of the rearmost clone, measured as a percentage of the type size of the selected type.

- ↪ **Offset:** Enter values into the Offset options to specify the distance between the selected text and the rearmost clone. The X value is measured from the center of the selected text. Positive is right, negative is left. The Y option is measured from the baseline. Positive is up, negative is down. Both values conform to the current unit of measure.

- ↪ **From:** Drag a color swatch from the Color list, Color Mixer, or Tints palette and drop it onto the From color box to define the color of the rearmost clone. This option also determines the color of the outline that surrounds the selected text.

- ↪ **To:** Drag a color onto the To color box to define the color of the selected text.

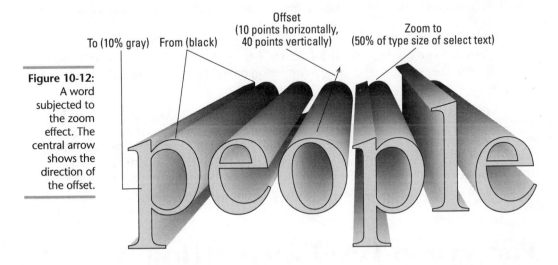

To (10% gray)　From (black)

Offset
(10 points horizontally,
40 points vertically)

Zoom to
(50% of type size of select text)

Figure 10-12:
A word subjected to the zoom effect. The central arrow shows the direction of the offset.

FreeHand automatically assigns an intermediate size, position, and color to each of the clones between the selected text and the rearmost clone, creating a smooth gradation. The result is an effect that takes forever to display on-screen and even longer to print.

Figure 10-13:
The Zoom Effect dialog box lets you size and position the rear portion of the gradation.

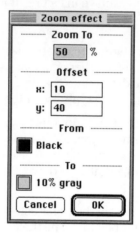

And lest we forget . . .

The Text Character panel provides two check boxes that I skipped in my overwhelming enthusiasm to discuss the Effects pop-up menu. These check boxes work as follows:

- ↪ **Inhibit Hyphens:** If you don't want FreeHand to automatically hyphenate a word, select the word and check the Inhibit Hyphens option. FreeHand drops the word down to the next line. For more information on hyphenation, read the "Hyphenating words" section later in this chapter.

- ↪ **Keep On Same Line:** Select this option to keep all selected text on the same line. FreeHand treats the selected text as if it were a single long word, dropping it down to the next line if so much as a single character doesn't fit. Use this option on two- or three-word phrases or unusual character combinations that look strange or don't make sense when broken onto different lines. For example, I might use this option to keep the phrase *Figure 10-8* from breaking.

Paragraph-Level Formatting _____

Nearly all of FreeHand's paragraph-level formatting options are located in three panels of the Inspector palette. These panels are Text Paragraph, Text Spacing & Hyphenation, and Text Alignment, accessed by pressing Command-Option-P, K (you know, for Spakink & Kyphenakun), and A, respectively. Refer back to Figure 10-1 if you forgot what these panels look like.

A few options in these panels bear more than a passing resemblance to those I've discussed already:

- ↝ The Paragraph Spacing options in the Text Paragraph panel add vertical space between paragraphs, much as the Leading option adds space between lines.

- ↝ In the Text Spacing & Hyphenation panel, the Spacing values add horizontal space between characters and words, much like the Kerning and Range Kerning values.

- ↝ The Lines Together option box near the bottom of the Text Paragraph panel — pay attention, because this is the only place I discuss this option — specifies the minimum number of lines that must appear in each half of a paragraph that's broken between two columns or linked text blocks. Just as the Keep on Same Line option prevents lines from breaking between certain words (as discussed in the previous section), the Lines Together value prevents paragraphs from breaking between certain lines. It's just the thing for eliminating those single-line orphans that have a habit of popping up so mournfully at the tops of columns. "If you plaise, sa', I'd lak to be wit the rest of me pa'graph." Gosh, this topic always brings a tear to my eye.

Tabs and indents

Although FreeHand devotes an unprecedented three panels to paragraph formatting, its most essential formatting options are found in the tab ruler that hovers above the active text object. With the tab ruler, you can control tabs and paragraph indents. You can also modify paragraph indents inside the Text Paragraph panel.

Why tabs are so great

For folks who grew up using a typewriter, tabs and tab stops can be the single most difficult typesetting concept to understand. It's not that typewriters don't provide these features but that few folks feel any need to use them. Most conventional typewriters provide movable *tab stops* for indenting text and creating tables. After moving a tab stop to a point along the carriage, you press the Tab key to advance the carriage so that the next character you enter begins at the tab stop. Although simple in structure, tab stops require a degree of planning that most occasional typists aren't willing to expend. As a result, they don't change the tab settings on their machines to fit the document they're trying to create; instead, they use the same tab stops for everything. If they need to create columns of text, they hit the Tab key, see where that takes them, and if they need to move farther across the page, they press the spacebar.

Suppose that you're working on a typewriter that has tab stops set at half-inch intervals — a typical default setting — and you want to create the three-column table shown in Figure 10-14. Ideally, you would reset your tab stops so that you could type the entry description, press Tab, enter the dollar value in the second column, press Tab again, and enter the dollar value in the third column. But you're short on time and energy, so you decide not to set the proper tab stops for the table and use the default settings instead. Although the values are roughly the same width, ranging between $2.99 and $200.00, the descriptions run as long as *Top Grain Italian Leather Attache* and as short as *Steno Notebook*. So to account for a short description, you have to press the Tab key two or more times in a row to advance even with the first column of dollar values.

Furthermore, to match the figure, you need to align the right sides of the dollar values so that ones, tens, and hundreds line up regardless of the number of digits in each number. You determine that you can accomplish this feat by taking a few whacks at the spacebar. For example, to properly align the value 4.99 with 129.99 above it, you press the spacebar twice in a row before entering 4.99 to account for the two-digit difference in the values.

Produced on an ordinary typewriter, your table looks fine. No one but you knows that you didn't set up the ideal tab stops for the document. But suppose that you make the mistake of using this same approach in creating a table inside FreeHand, which also provides you with default tab stops spaced 1/2 inch apart. You use multiple tabs to

Figure 10-14:
A typical
table created
on a
typewriter
using
multiple tabs
and spaces.

Item	List Price	Our Price
Business Credit Card Case	4.00	2.99
Card File Binder	28.50	21.99
Business Card File	5.50	3.99
Leather Card Case	27.00	19.99
Attache Case	43.00	18.99
Dome Top Attache	120.00	69.99
Executive Leather Attache	109.00	59.99
Expandable Leather Attache	130.00	79.99
Top Grain Italian Leather Attache	200.00	129.99
Business Clip Folder	7.00	4.49
Steno Notebook	16.00	11.99

align values after descriptions and you use spaces to align digits within the second and third columns. Everything looks fine on-screen. And although the numbers tend to weave slightly when printed, as illustrated in the first example of Figure 10-15, you figure that the table is good enough (especially after an attempt to remedy the alignment by adding and deleting spaces only worsens the situation).

In fact, everything's smooth sailing until you decide to subject the table to a different font or a larger type size. That's when the table goes haywire. As shown in the second example of Figure 10-15, entries that belong in the second column start nudging toward the third, forcing third-column entries onto their own lines. Your previously aligned digits now weave back and forth dramatically, making a mess of your fastidious spacing efforts. You're faced with the unpleasant alternative of going through your text and manually removing tabs and spaces.

Why does a change in font or size wreak so much havoc? The reason is that FreeHand treats tabs and spaces as *modifiable characters*. A *tab character* — created by pressing the Tab key — is constantly on the prowl for a tab stop. If a new font or size enlarges the first-column entry to the extent that it overlaps the second column, the next tab character abandons the second-column tab stop — which it can no longer reach — and makes a beeline for the third-column tab stop. Like a domino, the third-column tab character is sent looking for a fourth-column tab stop; finding none, it instead knocks the last entry onto a new line of type.

Spaces are even more problematic, because you can't depend on a space character to adhere to a constant width. On a typewriter, all characters, including spaces, are the same width. By contrast, most Macintosh and Windows fonts — with the exception of Courier, Monaco, and a few others — are *variable-width* fonts, meaning that different characters have different widths. An *i*, for example, is narrower than an *M*. Depending on the font, a space character may be as narrow as an *i* or as wide as a *t*. So when you change selected spaces to a new font, you are likely to increase or reduce the width of each space, thereby upsetting the alignment of any letters or numbers that follow space characters.

Suffice it to say that using spaces is absolutely forbidden when you're aligning table entries. Never *ever* use them for this purpose. As far as tabs are concerned, you are well advised to conserve tab *characters* and instead rely on tab *stops* to align columns. When creating table entries, press the Tab key no more than once in a row. After you finish entering a few lines, select what you've written so far and add, subtract, and move the tab stops in the tab ruler as explained in the next section.

Figure 10-15:
A tabbed and
spaced table set in
Times (top) reveals
its unstable
construction when
changed to
Helvetica (bottom).

Item	List Price	Our Price
Business Credit Card Case	4.00	2.99
Card File Binder	28.50	21.99
Business Card File	5.50	3.99
Leather Card Case	27.00	19.99
Attache Case	43.00	18.99
Dome Top Attache	120.00	69.99
Executive Leather Attache	109.00	59.99
Expandable Leather Attache	130.00	79.99
Top Grain Italian Leather Attache	200.00	129.99
Business Clip Folder	7.00	4.49
Steno Notebook	16.00	11.99

Item	List Price	
Our Price		
Business Credit Card Case	4.00	
2.99		
Card File Binder	28.50	21.99
Business Card File	5.50	3.99
Leather Card Case	27.00	19.99
Attache Case		43.00
18.99		
Dome Top Attache	120.00	69.99
Executive Leather Attache	109.00	59.99
Expandable Leather Attache		130.00
79.99		
Top Grain Italian Leather Attache	200.00	129.99
Business Clip Folder		7.00
4.49		
Steno Notebook		16.00
11.99		

Positioning tab stops

The tab ruler enables you to set tab stops in one or more selected paragraphs. As shown in Figure 10-16, the tab ruler is divided into three strips: the *icon strip,* the *marker strip,* and a horizontal ruler.

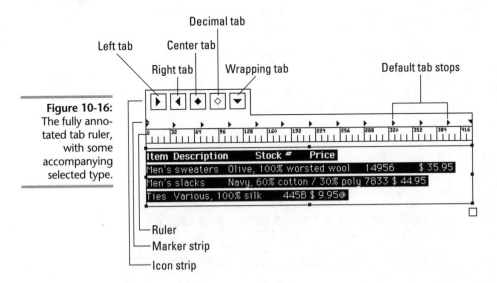

Figure 10-16: The fully annotated tab ruler, with some accompanying selected type.

The icon strip includes five tab icons, each of which produces a different kind of tab stop. Every tab stop controls the alignment of a clump of text between two tab characters or between a tab character and a carriage return. Several of these clumps result in a column. The icons are described below in the order they appear in the tab ruler:

- **Left tab:** The left edge of a selected clump of text aligns to this tab stop.

- **Right tab:** The right edge of a selected clump aligns to this tab stop.

- **Center tab:** The middle of a selected clump aligns to this tab stop.

- **Decimal tab:** The decimal points in numbers (such as $25.95) in a selected clump align to this tab stop.

- **Wrapping tab:** This one's a little different. Wrapping tab stops are always used in pairs. The left edge of a selected clump aligns to the first wrapping tab stop. If the right edge of the clump extends beyond the second wrapping tab stop, the text wraps down to a second line of type. (For an example of this tab stop in action, keep an eye out for Figure 10-18, which I explain momentarily.)

As I mentioned earlier, FreeHand supplies every new text block you create with a series of default tab stops: left tab stops spaced 1/2 inch (36 points) apart. To assign tab stops to a paragraph of text, select the paragraph with the text tool — FreeHand does not provide you with access to the tab ruler when you select a block with the arrow tool — and drag from one of the five tab icons into the marker strip. Any default tab stops to the left of the new tab stop disappear. You can track the movement of tab stops in the information bar (displayed by pressing Command-Shift-R).

In Figure 10-17, I dragged a center tab stop from the icon strip into the marker strip. This centers the text that follows the first tab character in each selected line. The figure also shows the effects of right and decimal tab stops, which align text following the second and third tab characters. I've included gray lines and gradations so that you can see the alignment more clearly.

Figure 10-17:
Examples of
how center,
right, and
decimal tab
stops affect a
tabbed
paragraph.

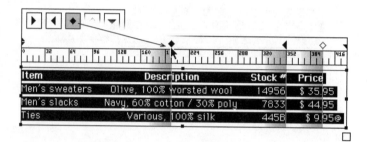

Wrapping tab stops are a little more difficult to use. You begin by positioning a wrapping tab stop on the left side of the column of text you want to align. You then position a second wrapping tab stop on the right side of the text. As shown in Figure 10-18, the column of text between the corresponding tab characters stays inside the boundaries represented by the two tab stops. In the figure, I lengthened the third row of text so that it no longer fits inside these boundaries. The wrapping tab stops send the leftover text to a fourth line. If it weren't for the wrapping tab stops, the extended clump of text would nudge its neighbors to the right, forcing them to search for new tab stops.

Figure 10-18:
Text wraps
between two
wrapping tab
stops.

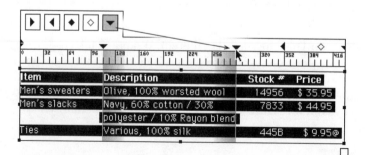

Any time you add a tab stop, as in the case of the second wrapping tab stop, you have to add a corresponding tab character to each line of type. Therefore, to align the text as shown in Figure 10-18, I needed two tab characters to separate each clump in the Description column from its neighbor in the Stock # column. This is the only circumstance in which you should enter two tab characters in a row.

To move a tab stop, simply drag it inside the marker strip. Unlike word processors, FreeHand doesn't give you an option box for entering a numerical value for a tab stop; you can only set tabs in the marker strip. To delete an existing tab stop, drag it off the marker strip. The tab stop disappears and ceases to affect the selected paragraph. Depending on which stop you delete, some default tab stops may reappear. You can adjust tab stops only after selecting text with the type tool.

Paragraph indents

In addition to the many tab icons, the tab ruler offers three *indent markers* that control the left and right boundaries of lines inside a text block. These markers, labeled in Figure 10-19, work as follows:

- ↬ First-line indent specifies the indentation of the first line of type in each selected paragraph.

- ↬ Left indent positions the left edges of all lines except the first one in each se-lected paragraph.

Figure 10-19:
The three indent markers (left) and their correspond-ing options in the Text Paragraph panel (right).

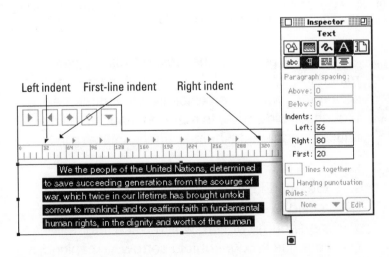

☞ Right indent positions the right edges of all lines — including the first one — in each selected paragraph.

To access the indent markers, you have to select your paragraphs with the text tool; otherwise, the tab ruler is not available. When you drag the first-line indent marker, it moves independently of the other indent markers. But when you drag the left indent marker, you move both it and the first-line marker simultaneously. The two are so frequently together that you may at first mistake them for one marker.

FreeHand also provides three Indents options in the Text Paragraph panel of the Inspector palette (Command-Option-P), as shown in Figure 10-19. The beauty of these options is that you can access them even when you use the arrow tool to select the text block. Each option performs the same function as one of the indent markers. The value in the Left option box is measured from the left edge of the selected text block. The Right value is measured from the right edge. But the First value is measured from the position of the left indent marker. So if the first-line indent marker is to the right of the left indent marker, the First value is positive; if the first-line marker is left of the left indent marker, the First value is negative.

Types of indents

If you drag the first-line indent marker to the right of the left indent marker (as in Figure 10-19) or enter a positive value into the First option box, you create a standard paragraph indent, as shown in the first example of Figure 10-20. To make your paragraphs more flexible, use this technique to create indents rather than pressing Tab at the beginning of every paragraph. If you later want to get rid of your indents, you can do it globally rather than deleting a bunch of tabs one by one.

Figure 10-20:
Two paragraphs, one formatted with a standard indent (top) and the other formatted with a hanging indent (bottom).

We the people of the United Nations, determined to save succeeding generations from the scourge of war, which twice in our lifetime has brought untold sorrow to mankind, and to reaffirm faith in fundamental human rights, in the dignity

1.   We the people of the United Nations, determined to save succeeding generations from the scourge of war, which twice in our lifetime has brought untold sorrow to mankind, and to reaffirm faith in fundamental human

If you drag the left indent marker to the right and then drag the first-line indent back to the left edge of the tab ruler, you create a hanging indent, as shown in the second example of Figure 10-20. You can achieve the same effect by entering a positive value (say, 24) into the Left option box and the opposite of that value (–24) in the First option box.

Hanging indents are perfect for creating numbered lists, bulleted items, and other special text blocks. Be sure to enter a tab character after the bullet or number. For example, a tab separates the *1.* from *We* in second example of Figure 10-20. Then drag a left tab stop exactly onto the left indent marker to complete the effect. The tabbed text in the first line aligns with the indented text in the remaining lines of the paragraph.

Changing the alignment

I'm willing to bet a quarter that every computer program that supplies a text tool lets you change the alignment of a paragraph. (And I usually limit my gambling to a dime.) You can align a paragraph so that all the left edges line up (called *flush left, ragged right*); so that all the lines are centered; or so that all the right edges line up (*flush right, ragged left*). You can also *justify* a paragraph, which stretches the lines so that they entirely fill the width of the text object. Only the last line in a justified paragraph is allowed to remain flush left.

Examples of all four alignment settings are shown in Figure 10-21. To access any of these settings, switch to the Text Alignment panel of the Inspector palette (Command-Option-A) and select one of the Alignment icons. From left to right, the alignment icons are flush left, centered, flush right, and justified.

But FreeHand is unusual in that it goes a few steps father. For one thing, you can control the minimum width of any line in a nonjustified paragraph. This is an ideal solution if you don't want to use justified type, which can make text blocks look overly square. It also keeps your text from weaving in and out dramatically. The effect is like partially justifying a paragraph; it's a happy medium between ragged right and fully justified text.

To specify the minimum width, enter a value into the Ragged Width % option box in the Text Alignment panel. The value is measured as a percentage of the width of the text block. A value between 80 and 90 percent produces the most legible results while retaining the informal appearance of nonjustified text.

You can also instruct FreeHand to justify the last line in a fully justified paragraph. But you don't accomplish this by turning the function either on or off, as you do in a program such as Illustrator. Instead, you enter a relative value into the Flush Zone % option box. Again, this value is measured as a percentage of the width of the text block. If the last line exceeds this length, FreeHand justifies it. Otherwise, the line remains flush left. (Note that the Flush Zone % option only affects the last line in fully justified paragraphs.)

Flush left (ragged right)

We, the people of the United Nations, determined to save succeeding generations from the scourge of war, which twice in our lifetime has brought untold sorrow to mankind, and to reaffirm faith in fundamental human rights, in the dignity and worth of the human person, in the equal right of men and women and of nations large and small, and to establish conditions under which justice and respect for the obligations arising from treaties and other sources of law can be maintained.

Centered

We, the people of the United Nations, determined to save succeeding generations from the scourge of war, which twice in our lifetime has brought untold sorrow to mankind, and to reaffirm faith in fundamental human rights, in the dignity and worth of the human person, in the equal right of men and women and of nations large and small, and to establish conditions under which justice and respect for the obligations arising from treaties and other sources of law can be maintained.

Flush right (ragged left)

We, the people of the United Nations, determined to save succeeding generations from the scourge of war, which twice in our lifetime has brought untold sorrow to mankind, and to reaffirm faith in fundamental human rights, in the dignity and worth of the human person, in the equal right of men and women and of nations large and small, and to establish conditions under which justice and respect for the obligations arising from treaties and other sources of law can be maintained.

Fully justified

We, the people of the United Nations, determined to save succeeding genera-tions from the scourge of war, which twice in our lifetime has brought untold sorrow to mankind, and to reaffirm faith in fundamental human rights, in the dignity and worth of the human person, in the equal right of men and women and of nations large and small, and to establish conditions under which justice and respect for the obligations arising from treaties and other sources of law can be maintained.

The last option that affects alignment isn't found in the Text Alignment panel. FreeHand's programmers tucked the Hanging Punctuation check box away in the Text Paragraph panel (Command-Option-P). Select this check box to make punctuation such as commas, quotation marks, hyphens, and so on, hang outside the edge of a selected paragraph, as shown in Figure 10-22. If two adjacent punctuation symbols occur at the beginning or end of a line, only the first or final symbol hangs outside the paragraph, as illustrated by the period and closing quote in the second example of Figure 10-22. You can apply this option to flush left, flush right, or justified paragraphs.

Paragraph spacing

Just as you can change the vertical and horizontal spacing of characters, you can change the vertical and horizontal spacing of whole paragraphs. For vertical spacing,

Figure 10-22: The quotation mark hangs outside the flush left paragraph (top). The closing quotation mark and some commas hang outside the flush right paragraph (bottom).

"We, the people of the United Nations, are determined to save succeeding generations from the scourge of war, which twice in our lifetime has brought untold sorrow to mankind."

"We, the people of the United Nations, are determined to save succeeding generations from the scourge of war, which twice in our lifetime has brought untold sorrow to mankind."

use the two Paragraph Spacing option boxes in the Text Paragraph panel. The Above value determines the amount of space between the first line in each selected paragraph and the last line in the paragraph above it. The Below value determines the amount of space between the last line in each selected paragraph and the first line in the paragraph below it.

Together, these values make up the *paragraph spacing* of a document. The paragraphs in this book, for example, are typically separated by one pica of paragraph spacing. Like the popular first-line indent, paragraph spacing is a form of visually separating one topic from another. It loosens up the page and makes it more readable. Generally speaking, however, you should use *either* a first-line indent or paragraph spacing in your designs. Although I have been known to use both in a single paragraph — there's no law against it — many professional designers consider one or the other to be sufficient. Anything more may be construed in some circles as overkill.

At this point, you may be wondering why FreeHand provides both Above and Below options. Isn't one or other sufficient to space out paragraphs? In most cases, yes. Generally, the only reason to include both options is to accommodate style sheets, and as we all know from the introduction to Chapter 9, FreeHand is currently without style sheets. The reason FreeHand includes two options is to accommodate paragraph *rules* — those thin lines that are sometimes used as paragraph borders.

The Below value determines the space between the rule and the paragraph above it; the Above value determines the space between the rule and the paragraph below it. (I know that it sounds backward, but this is the way it works.) For more information on paragraph rules, read the upcoming "Creating paragraph rules" section.

Spacing letters and words

You can control the amount of space between all characters in a paragraph by adjusting the *letterspacing*. You can also control the amount of space between words in a text block by changing the *word spacing*. To access these spacing options, press Command-Option-K to display the Spacing & Hyphenation panel of the Inspector palette. The Spacing % options appear spotlighted in Figure 10-23.

Figure 10-23:
The spotlighted options control the amount of horizontal space between letters and words in a selected paragraph.

You may be thinking to yourself, "How is letterspacing, which controls the amount of space between individual characters, different from kerning, which controls the amount of space between individual characters? It sounds like the same thing to me." Well, you've brought up a good point. (Actually, *I* brought it up, but I thought I'd be generous and give you the credit.) The outcome of kerning and letterspacing is frequently the same. But kerning applies to selected characters, and letterspacing affects entire paragraphs. Also, the two are measured differently. Kerning is measured in fractions of an em space; letterspacing is measured as a percentage of the standard character spacing. But most importantly, kerning is fixed, while letterspacing is flexible. FreeHand is allowed to automatically vary letterspacing according to guidelines that you establish.

There are two primary reasons for manipulating letterspacing and word spacing:

   ♺ To give a paragraph a tighter or looser appearance. You control this general spacing using the Opt (for Optimum) options.

ᗚ To determine the range of spacing manipulations that FreeHand can use when trying to fit text on a line, especially inside a justified paragraph. FreeHand has to tighten up some lines to get them to fit exactly inside the column; it must loosen up other lines. You specify how much FreeHand can shrink or expand spacing by using the Min and Max options.

Letterspacing values are measured as percentages of standard character spacing; word spacing values are measured as percentages of a standard space character. The exact character spacing and space character width depend on the font you select.

The values for the Spacing % options can range as follows:

ᗚ The Min value must be 0 percent or greater. It can't be larger than the Max value.

ᗚ The Max value must be larger than the Min value but can't be greater than 1,000 percent, or 10 times standard spacing.

ᗚ The Opt value can be no less than the Min value and no more than the Max value.

Figure 10-24 shows a single justified paragraph under various word and letterspacing conditions. In the first column of paragraphs, only the word spacing changes; all letterspacing values are set to 100 percent. In the second column, only the letterspacing changes; all word spacing values are set to 100 percent. The headlines above each paragraph indicate what values were changed. The percentages represent the values entered in the Min, Opt, and Max options, respectively.

If you have trouble making the spacing of a paragraph look like you want it to, it's probably because you're giving FreeHand too much latitude. To gain absolute control over word or letterspacing, enter the same value in the Min, Opt, and Max option boxes. In other words, make all the word spacing values the same, or make all the letterspacing values the same, or both. This way, FreeHand has to exactly conform to the value you give it. The only exception arises when you're working inside a justified paragraph, in which case FreeHand overrides your settings and increases the spacing as required. For example, if you set all six Spacing % values to 100 percent and then justify the selected paragraph, you're asking FreeHand to do the impossible. It has to change the spacing somehow, and it does so without your consent.

Hyphenating words

With the release of Version 4.0, FreeHand went from no hyphenation capabilities whatsoever to full automatic hyphenation. Its automatic hyphenation functions are now similar to those provided by PageMaker and QuarkXPress. This is an unqualified improvement, especially considering that FreeHand 3.0 didn't even *recognize* manual hyphens. To hyphenate a word, you had to enter a hyphen followed by a space so that FreeHand knew to break the word to a new line. Ah, the bad old days.

Word: 75%, 100%, 150%

We, the people of the United Nations, determined to save succeed-
inggenerationsfromthescourgeof
war, which twice in our lifetime has
brought untold sorrow to mankind,
and to reaffirm faith in fundamental
human rights, in the dignity and

Letter: 95%, 100%, 110%

We, the people of the United Nations, determined to save succeeding generations from the scourge of
war, which twice in our lifetime has
brought untold sorrow to mankind,
and to reaffirm faith in fundamental
human rights, in the dignity and

Word: 25%, 50%, 100%

We,thepeopleoftheUnitedNations,
determined to save succeeding
generationsfromthescourgeofwar,
whichtwiceinourlifetimehasbrought
untold sorrow to mankind, and to
reaffirmfaithinfundamentalhuman
rights,inthedignityandworthofthe

Letter: 75%, 85%, 100%

We, the people of the United Nations,
determined to save succeeding generations from the scourge of war, which
twice in our lifetime has brought untold
sorrow to mankind, and to reaffirm faith
in fundamental human rights, in the
dignity and worth of the human person,

Word: 150%, 150%, 200%

We, the people of the United Nations, determined to save succeeding generations from the
scourge of war, which twice in our
lifetime has brought untold sorrow
to mankind, and to reaffirm faith
in fundamental human rights, in

Letter: 100%, 125%, 150%

We, the people of the United Nations, determined to save succeeding generations from the
scourge of war, which twice in our
lifetime has brought untold sorrow
to mankind, and to reaffirm faith
in fundamental human rights, in

Figure 10-24: Examples of different word and letterspacing values. In the left column, letterspacing is constant. In the right column, word spacing is constant.

Nowadays, FreeHand recognizes that it can break a word across two lines at a hyphen character. But that's only the beginning. You can also instruct FreeHand to automatically hyphenate words according to a dictionary that's installed along with the software. (FreeHand uses the same dictionary as other Aldus programs, including PageMaker.)

To activate the automatic hyphenation function, select the paragraph that you want to hyphenate, press Command-Option-K to display the Text Spacing & Hyphenation panel (shown in Figure 10-25), and select the Automatic check box. FreeHand then adds hyphens and break words across lines as it deems necessary.

Figure 10-25:
FreeHand's automatic hyphenation options share a panel with the word and letterspacing options.

Automatic hyphenation controls

In addition to Automatic hyphenation, FreeHand provides three other hyphenation options in the Text Spacing & Hyphenation panel:

- **Language:** If you own a non-English version of Freehand or you have access to non-English hyphenation dictionaries, you can select a different language from the Hyphenation pop-up menu.

- **Skip Capitalized.** Select this option to instruct FreeHand not to hyphenate words that include capitalized letters. This not only prevents the program from hyphenating special capitalized words such as *FreeHand,* but also everyday run-of-the-mill words that are capitalized because they appear at the beginning of sentences. I suggest that you leave this option off and manually turn off hyphenation for special words, as discussed in the next section.

- **Consecutive:** By default, FreeHand doesn't allow any more than three consecutive lines to end in hyphens. The reasoning behind this practice is that more than three hyphens can distract readers from your text and make them say, "Whoa, do you think they used enough hyphens in this paragraph, or what? It's like every single line has a hyphen in it. This document is really starting to make me grouchy," or words to that effect. In truth, hyphens do indeed make a paragraph more difficult to read, so the fewer hyphens you use, the better. I personally set the Consecutive value to 2. Then, if I think more hyphens are warranted for a specific paragraph, I add them by hand.

Manual hyphenation controls

Just like FreeHand's other automated functions — the freehand tool, the trace tool, automatic curvature, power steering, and antilock brakes — automatic hyphenation doesn't always deliver the way you want it to. This is where you — the manual hyphenation engine — come in. You can remove hyphens from words that you don't want to hyphenate and add hyphens to words that either are not hyphenated or are not hyphenated to your satisfaction.

To unhyphenate — or is it dehyphenate? — a word, select the offending word, switch to the Text Character panel (trusty Command-Option-T), and select the Inhibit Hyphens check box. From this point on, FreeHand will know that the selected word is hands-off in the hyphenation department. "Absolutum wordis non gratis," is the Latin phrase, I believe. "Et tu hyphenatum?"

To add a hyphen, you can simply enter a hyphen character. But doing so can turn around and bite you. If you edit the text, for example, you may end up with stray hyphens between words that no longer break at the ends of lines. A better idea is to insert a *discretionary hyphen,* which disappears any time it's not needed. You can access the discretionary hyphen by pressing Command-hyphen. If no hyphen appears when you enter this character, it simply means that the addition of the hyphen does not help FreeHand break the word. You can try inserting the character at a new location or tighten the word and letterspacing slightly to allow room for the word to break.

Creating paragraph rules

You can append a rule (horizontal line) to the end of a selected paragraph in FreeHand using the options in the Rules pop-up menu in the Text Paragraph panel. But the implementation involves so many steps that it's almost easier to add a rule by drawing it with the line tool. For the record, though, here's the four-step process required to create a paragraph rule:

STEPS: Adding a Paragraph Rule

Step 1.   Select the paragraph to which you want to apply the rule. FreeHand will place the rule under the last line in the paragraph. (There's no way to put the rule at the top or sides of the paragraph.)

Step 2.   Switch to the Text Paragraph panel (Command-Option-P) and select an option from the Rules pop-up menu at the bottom.

Step 3. If you're in the preview mode, you won't see any paragraph rule. Why not? Because you haven't assigned a stroke yet. Silly you. Switch to the Stroke panel (Command-Option-L) and assign a stroke as described in Chapter 14, or simply choose a line weight from the Arrange ➪ Stroke Widths submenu.

Step 4. Aaugh. Now you can see your paragraph rule, but you've also outlined the text block. Switch to the Object Dimensions & Inset panel of the Inspector palette (Command-Option-B) and deselect the Display Border check box.

But wait, there's more. You create a rule by selecting one of two options — Centered or Paragraph — from the Rules pop-up menu. The Center option centers the rule below the paragraph; the Paragraph option aligns the rule flush left, flush right, or whatever, depending on the alignment of the paragraph.

The trouble is, the first time you apply either option, you get the same effect — a rule stretched across the entire length of the last line. To change this, click on the Edit button to the right of the pop-up menu. A small dialog box appears, as shown in Figure 10-26, which allows you to specify the length of the line as a percentage value. Select an option from the pop-up menu to decide whether the percentage is measured relative to the length of the last line or the entire text block (the Column option). Then press Return. Figure 10-27 shows the results of applying several different settings to two paragraphs at a time. All examples feature a hairline rule.

Figure 10-26:
Click on the Edit button in the Text Paragraph panel to display this dialog box.

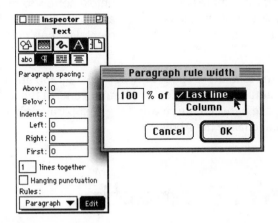

Centered, 75% of last line

*We, the people of the
United Nations,*

determined to save succeeding generations from the
scourge of war, which twice
in our lifetime has brought
untold sorrow to mankind,
and to reaffirm faith in fundamental human rights…

Paragraph, 75% of last line

*We, the people of the
United Nations,*

determined to save succeeding generations from the
scourge of war, which twice
in our lifetime has brought
untold sorrow to mankind,
and to reaffirm faith in fundamental human rights…

Centered, 75% of column

*We, the people of the
United Nations,*

determined to save succeeding generations from the
scourge of war, which twice
in our lifetime has brought
untold sorrow to mankind,
and to reaffirm faith in fundamental human rights…

Paragraph, 75% of column

*We, the people of the
United Nations,*

determined to save succeeding generations from the
scourge of war, which twice
in our lifetime has brought
untold sorrow to mankind,
and to reaffirm faith in fundamental human rights…

To increase the amount of space between a paragraph and its rule, enlarge the Below value at the top of the Text Paragraph panel of the Inspector palette. To adjust the space between the rule and the next paragraph, select the next paragraph and change the Above value.

Block-Level Formatting

The only formatting options that I haven't yet discussed are found in the Object Column & Row panel of the Inspector palette (Command-Option-R). With these options, you can subdivide a text block into vertical columns and horizontal rows and affect entire selected text blocks at a time. You can either click inside a text block with the text tool or select it with the arrow tool to prepare it for modification.

Columns and rows

As you can see in Figure 10-28, the Column & Row panel includes three sets of options — Column, Row, and Wrap Order. The Column and Row options work as follows:

- **Count:** In this option box, enter the number of columns or rows you want to create. You can enter any number between 1 and 100, though it's unlikely that you'll want to go quite that high.

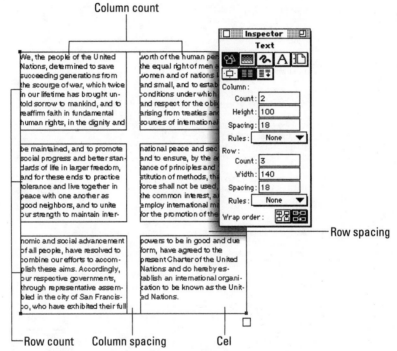

Figure 10-28: A single text block divided into two columns and three rows.

- **Height/Width:** Enter the height of a column or the width of a row into the option box. These options are only available when you're editing a standard text block. If one or more free-form text objects are selected, the Height and Width options are unavailable.

- **Spacing:** Enter the amount of space that separates one column or row from its neighbors into this option box. As with the Height and Width options, FreeHand interprets the value in the current unit of measure.

- **Rules:** You can select from two kinds of rules to separate columns and rows. Both Rules pop-up menus offer Inset options, which break the rule into several free-floating lines, one for each row or column of text. You can also select the Full Height or Full Width option, which extends the rule across the entire height or width of the text block. Figure 10-29 shows examples.

Figure 10-29:
The four kinds of rules
you can use to visually
separate columns and
rows.

Inset column rules

We, the people of the United Nations, determined to save succeeding generations from the scourge of war, which twice in our lifetime has brought untold sorrow to mankind, and to reaffirm faith in fundamental human rights, in the dignity and

worth of the human person, in the equal right of men and women and of nations large and small, and to establish conditions under which justice and respect for the obligations arising from treaties and other sources of international law can

Full width row rules

be maintained, and to promote social progress and better standards of life in larger freedom, and for these ends to practice tolerance and live together in peace with one another as good neighbors, and to unite our strength to maintain inter-

national peace and security, and to ensure, by the acceptance of principles and the institution of methods, that armed force shall not be used, save in the common interest, and to employ international machinery for the promotion of the eco-

nomic and social advancement of all people, have resolved to combine our efforts to accomplish these aims. Accordingly, our respective governments, through representative assembled in the city of San Francisco, who have exhibited their full

powers to be in good and due form, have agreed to the present Charter of the United Nations and do hereby establish an international organization to be known as the United Nations.

We, the people of the United Nations, determined to save succeeding generations from the scourge of war, which twice in our lifetime has brought untold sorrow to mankind, and to reaffirm faith in fundamental human rights, in the dignity and

worth of the human person, in the equal right of men and women and of nations large and small, and to establish conditions under which justice and respect for the obligations arising from treaties and other sources of international law can

Inset row rules

be maintained, and to promote social progress and better standards of life in larger freedom, and for these ends to practice tolerance and live together in peace with one another as good neighbors, and to unite our strength to maintain inter-

national peace and security, and to ensure, by the acceptance of principles and the institution of methods, that armed force shall not be used, save in the common interest, and to employ international machinery for the promotion of the eco-

nomic and social advancement of all people, have resolved to combine our efforts to accomplish these aims. Accordingly, our respective governments, through representative assembled in the city of San Francisco, who have exhibited their full

powers to be in good and due form, have agreed to the present Charter of the United Nations and do hereby establish an international organization to be known as the United Nations.

Full height column rules

When applying Rules options to a text block, you have to specify a stroke by choosing a command from the Arrange ⇨ Stroke Widths submenu — just as you do when applying Rules options to individual paragraphs. Also deselect the Display Border check box in the Object Dimensions & Inset panel (Command-Option-B) to hide the outline around the text block.

Press the Return key to apply your values to the selected text block. Figure 10-28 shows a few Columns and Rows settings as well as the results of applying them to a large text block. By creating two columns and three rows, I've partitioned the text block into six independent *cels* (one of which is labeled in the figure).

Columns, rows, and cels are great for creating tables, lists, and stories. For example, by partitioning a text block, you can create several columns of text without resorting to linking separate text objects into a chain. A chain is more flexible, because you can move and independently resize separate text blocks to your heart's content, but columns and rows are easier to create.

Wrapping order

Normally, FreeHand bumps text from one cel to the next in the same way it wraps a word to the next line. When the word exceeds the boundaries of one cel, off it goes to the next. If you don't like how FreeHand divides your text, you can insert a manual column break by pressing Shift-Enter. The text after the column break character goes to the next cel in the *wrapping order*.

The wrapping order determines whether excess text flows from the first cel in a text block to the cel in the next row or the cel in the next column. Select the first of the two Wrap Order icons at the bottom of the Column & Row panel to send text from one cel to the cel in the next row, as shown in the first example of Figure 10-30. When the text reaches the bottom of the column, it breaks to the first cel in the next column. Select the second wrapping icon to send text from one cel to the cel in the next column, as illustrated by the second example in the figure. When the text reaches the end of a row, it goes to the next row down.

Copyfitting

FreeHand's copyfitting controls are located in the Object Copyfitting panel of the Inspector palette (shown in Figure 10-31), which you can access by pressing Command-Option-C. This palette offers two varieties of copyfitting controls. The first controls — Balance and Modify Leading — are specifically designed to accommodate text blocks that include multiple columns. The second variety, represented by the Copyfit % option boxes, affect an entire story, even if the story flows between multiple linked text blocks.

Figure 10-30:
The effects of selecting each of the two Wrap Order icons.

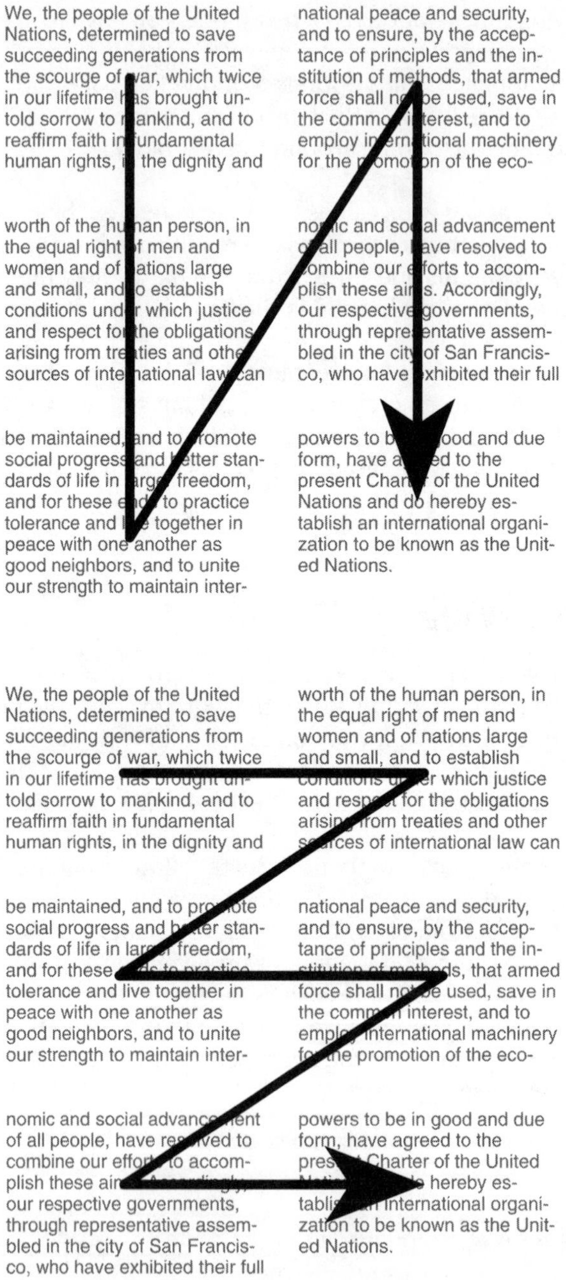

We, the people of the United Nations, determined to save succeeding generations from the scourge of war, which twice in our lifetime has brought untold sorrow to mankind, and to reaffirm faith in fundamental human rights, in the dignity and

worth of the human person, in the equal right of men and women and of nations large and small, and to establish conditions under which justice and respect for the obligations arising from treaties and other sources of international law can

be maintained, and to promote social progress and better standards of life in larger freedom, and for these ends to practice tolerance and live together in peace with one another as good neighbors, and to unite our strength to maintain inter-

national peace and security, and to ensure, by the acceptance of principles and the institution of methods, that armed force shall not be used, save in the common interest, and to employ international machinery for the promotion of the eco-

nomic and social advancement of all people, have resolved to combine our efforts to accomplish these aims. Accordingly, our respective governments, through representative assembled in the city of San Francisco, who have exhibited their full

powers to be in good and due form, have agreed to the present Charter of the United Nations and do hereby establish an international organization to be known as the United Nations.

We, the people of the United Nations, determined to save succeeding generations from the scourge of war, which twice in our lifetime has brought untold sorrow to mankind, and to reaffirm faith in fundamental human rights, in the dignity and

worth of the human person, in the equal right of men and women and of nations large and small, and to establish conditions under which justice and respect for the obligations arising from treaties and other sources of international law can

be maintained, and to promote social progress and better standards of life in larger freedom, and for these ends to practice tolerance and live together in peace with one another as good neighbors, and to unite our strength to maintain inter-

national peace and security, and to ensure, by the acceptance of principles and the institution of methods, that armed force shall not be used, save in the common interest, and to employ international machinery for the promotion of the eco-

nomic and social advancement of all people, have resolved to combine our efforts to accomplish these aims. Accordingly, our respective governments, through representative assembled in the city of San Francisco, who have exhibited their full

powers to be in good and due form, have agreed to the present Charter of the United Nations and do hereby establish an international organization to be known as the United Nations.

Figure 10-31:
In the Object Copyfitting panel, you can tell FreeHand to adjust the size and leading of selected type so that the text fits inside its text object.

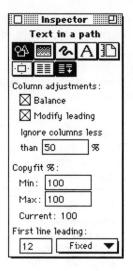

All these options instruct FreeHand to automatically adjust type size and/or leading to make type better fit inside its text object.

To approach the problem from the opposite angle — that is, to resize a text block so that it fits its text — select the text block and double-click inside the link box. This technique only works if the link box is empty, meaning that there is no overflow text. Also, you can only shrink a text block by double-clicking on the link box; you can't enlarge it. And finally, you can't use this method on free-form text objects or text blocks with more than one column or row.

Balancing columns

The two Column Adjustments options — Balance and Modify Leading — enable you to adjust the length of type in a text block with multiple-columns. You can only apply these options to one text block at a time.

Select the Balance option to equalize the number of lines of type in a multicolumn text block. For example, consider the three-column text block shown at the top of Figure 10-32. The first two columns contain 19 lines apiece, while the last contains only seven. If you select the Balance option, FreeHand adjusts all columns so that they each contain 15 lines, as in the second example in the figure. Of course, you could achieve the same effect by adding up the total number of lines, dividing them by 3, and dragging the corner handle of the text block until the columns balanced — but why go to all that trouble when you can just select an option? Save your energy for more important things.

Select the Modify Leading option to increase the leading of the type inside a text block so that the type exactly fits the height of the column. By default, FreeHand doesn't adjust columns that are less than 50 percent full. You can include or exclude columns by changing the value in the Ignore Column Less Than option box. If you enter large values, you prevent FreeHand from adjusting short columns; if you enter small values, FreeHand adjusts even short columns.

Figure 10-32:
A text block before (top) and after (bottom) selecting the Balance check box.

We, the people of the United Nations, determined to save succeeding generations from the scourge of war, which twice in our lifetime has brought untold sorrow to mankind, and to reaffirm faith in fundamental human rights, in the dignity and worth of the human person, in the equal right of men and women and of nations large and small, and to establish conditions under which justice and respect for the obligations arising from treaties and other sources of international law can be maintained, and to promote social progress and better standards of life in larger freedom, and for these ends to practice tolerance and live together in peace with one another as good neighbors, and to unite our strength to maintain international peace and security.

We, the people of the United Nations, determined to save succeeding generations from the scourge of war, which twice in our lifetime has brought untold sorrow to mankind, and to reaffirm faith in fundamental human rights, in the dignity and worth of the human person, in the equal right of men and women and of nations large and small, and to establish conditions under which justice and respect for the obligations arising from treaties and other sources of international law can be maintained, and to promote social progress and better standards of life in larger freedom, and for these ends to practice tolerance and live together in peace with one another as good neighbors, and to unite our strength to maintain international peace and security.

If you select both Balance and Modify Leading, FreeHand equalizes the number of lines and stretches them to fit the text block height. For example, Figure 10-33 shows two text blocks. In the first one, I selected the Modify Leading option, which slightly increased the leading of the first two columns and ignored the third because it is less than 50 percent full. If you compare the first example in Figure 10-32 to that in Figure 10-33, you'll see that the columns in the latter are a few points longer. FreeHand increased the leading to make the lines fit the column length, so the last line in Figure 10-33 is slightly lower than in Figure 10-32.

Figure 10-33:
The result of
selecting the
Modify Leading
check box (top)
and both the
Modify Leading and
Balance check
boxes (bottom).

We, the people of the United Nations, determined to save succeeding generations from the scourge of war, which twice in our lifetime has brought untold sorrow to mankind, and to reaffirm faith in fundamental human rights, in the dignity and worth of the human person, in the equal right of men and women and of nations large and small, and to establish conditions under which justice and respect for the obligations arising from treaties and other sources of international law can be maintained, and to promote social progress and better standards of life in larger freedom, and for these ends to practice tolerance and live together in peace with one another as good neighbors, and to unite our strength to maintain international peace and security.

We, the people of the United Nations, determined to save succeeding generations from the scourge of war, which twice in our lifetime has brought untold sorrow to mankind, and to reaffirm faith in fundamental human rights, in the dignity and worth of the human person, in the equal right of men and women and of nations large and small, and to establish conditions under which justice and respect for the obligations arising from treaties and other sources of international law can be maintained, and to promote social progress and better standards of life in larger freedom, and for these ends to practice tolerance and live together in peace with one another as good neighbors, and to unite our strength to maintain international peace and security.

The second example in the figure shows the result of selecting both the Modify Leading check box and the Balance check box. As in Figure 10-32, FreeHand pours 15 lines into each column. But this time, since every column is more than 50 percent filled with text, FreeHand loosens the leading to fill the text block completely.

Automatic size and leading adjustments

The Copyfit % options automatically adjust type size and leading values so that selected type exactly fits inside the text blocks you've provided for it. The Min and Max values provide FreeHand with a range of percentages by which to scale type size and leading. (The program always scales both size and leading by the same amount.) To use these options, select a single text block with the arrow tool or click inside a text block with the type tool. If the text is too small to fit inside its text blocks, as shown in the first example of Figure 10-34, increase the value in the Max option box. The Max value represents the largest percentage by which FreeHand can scale your text. In the case of Figure 10-34, I entered a value of 150 percent, but FreeHand only had to scale the type size and leading by 120 percent to achieve the second text block in the figure.

If your text is too large to fit inside a text object, reduce the Min value. In Figure 10-35, I filled a free-form path with text sized to 9 points and spaced with 10.8-point leading. The text is too large to fit inside the text object, so the link box contains a black circle. I selected the text object and changed the Min value in the Object Copyfitting panel to 50 percent. In the second example in Figure 10-35, FreeHand reduced the type size and leading to 70 percent of their original values, which was enough to get the text to fit entirely inside the path. As you can see, copyfitting is extremely useful for fitting text inside complex paths. When you enter a Min value, set it lower than you think may be necessary; that way, you give FreeHand an ample margin to work in.

First-line leading and initial caps

One option inside the Object Copyfitting panel that has nothing to do with copyfitting is First Line Leading, which affects the vertical placement of the very first line of type in a story. The value you enter is measured from the top of the text block to the baseline of the first line of type. You have access to the same options as when specifying standard leading; that is, you can enter a value into an option box and select one of three options — Extra, Fixed, and Percentage — from a pop-up menu.

The idea behind this option is that every line of type is spaced from another line of type according to the specified leading. But the first line of type has no preceding line from which to be measured. You can use this option to set up drop caps and prevent tightly leaded text from extending beyond the top of the block. You'll probably only use it once in a blue moon, but when that blue moon occurs, the option comes in pretty handy.

Figure 10-34:
To fill three text
blocks in a chain
(top), FreeHand
automatically
increases the type size
and leading values by
120 percent
(bottom).

Size: 7.5/ leading: 9

We, the people of the United Nations, determined to save succeeding generations from the scourge of war, which twice in our lifetime has brought untold sorrow to mankind, and to reaffirm faith in fundamental human rights, in the dignity and worth of the human person, in the equal right of men and women and of nations large and small, and to establish conditions under which justice and respect for the obligations arising from treaties and other sources of international law

can be maintained, and to promote social progress and better standards of life in larger freedom, and for these ends to practice tolerance and live together in peace with one another as good neighbors, and to unite our strength to maintain international peace and security, and to ensure, by the acceptance of principles and the institution of methods, that armed force shall not be used, save in the common interest, and to employ international machinery for the promotion of the economic and social advancement of all people, have resolved to combine our efforts to accomplish these aims. Accordingly, our respective governments, through representative assembled in the city of San Francisco, who have exhibited their full powers to be in good and due form, have agreed

to the present Charter of the United Nations and do hereby establish an international organization to be known as the United Nations.

Size: 9/ leading 10.8

We, the people of the United Nations, determined to save succeeding generations from the scourge of war, which twice in our lifetime has brought untold sorrow to mankind, and to reaffirm faith in fundamental human rights, in the dignity and worth of the human person, in the equal right of men and women and of nations large and small, and

to establish conditions under which justice and respect for the obligations arising from treaties and other sources of international law can be maintained, and to promote social progress and better standards of life in larger freedom, and for these ends to practice tolerance and live together in peace with one another as good neighbors, and to unite our strength to maintain international peace and security, and to ensure, by the acceptance of principles and the institution of methods, that armed force shall not be used, save in the common interest, and to

employ international machinery for the promotion of the economic and social advancement of all people, have resolved to combine our efforts to accomplish these aims. Accordingly, our respective governments, through representative assembled in the city of San Francisco, who have exhibited their full powers to be in good and due form, have agreed to the present Charter of the United Nations and do hereby establish an international organization to be known as the United Nations.

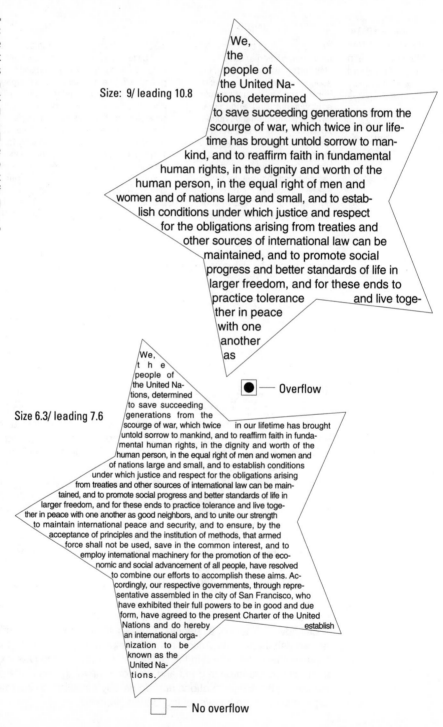

Size: 9/ leading 10.8

We,
the
people of
the United Na-
tions, determined
to save succeeding generations from the
scourge of war, which twice in our lifetime has brought untold sorrow to mankind, and to reaffirm faith in fundamental
human rights, in the dignity and worth of the
human person, in the equal right of men and
women and of nations large and small, and to establish conditions under which justice and respect
for the obligations arising from treaties and
other sources of international law can be
maintained, and to promote social
progress and better standards of life in
larger freedom, and for these ends to
practice tolerance   and live together in peace
with one
another
as

● — Overflow

Size 6.3/ leading 7.6

We,
t h e
people of
the United Na-
tions, determined
to save succeeding
generations from the
scourge of war, which twice   in our lifetime has brought
untold sorrow to mankind, and to reaffirm faith in fundamental human rights, in the dignity and worth of the
human person, in the equal right of men and women and
of nations large and small, and to establish conditions
under which justice and respect for the obligations arising
from treaties and other sources of international law can be maintained, and to promote social progress and better standards of life in
larger freedom, and for these ends to practice tolerance and live together in peace with one another as good neighbors, and to unite our strength
to maintain international peace and security, and to ensure, by the
acceptance of principles and the institution of methods, that armed
force shall not be used, save in the common interest, and to
employ international machinery for the promotion of the economic and social advancement of all people, have resolved
to combine our efforts to accomplish these aims. Accordingly, our respective governments, through representative assembled in the city of San Francisco, who
have exhibited their full powers to be in good and due
form, have agreed to the present Charter of the United
Nations and do hereby   establish
an international orga-
nization to be
known as the
United Na-
tions.

☐ — No overflow

Summary

- FreeHand only lets you apply type styles to fonts that include the corresponding style definitions.

- Enter the first few letters of a font name into the first option box in the Type palette to select that font. You can also scroll through fonts and styles by pressing the up and down arrow keys.

- Press Command-Shift-comma to reduce the type size of selected text; press Command-Shift-period to enlarge the text.

- Select the Extra or Percentage option to make the leading dependent on the type size. Select the Fixed option to keep the leading constant.

- Press Option-left arrow to tighten kerning between selected characters. Press Option-right arrow to loosen kerning.

- Use baseline shift to create superscripts, subscripts, and fractions. Remember that although you superscript the numerator in a fraction, you don't subscript the denominator.

- Never enter more than one tab character in a row. If a tab doesn't quite move a clump of text where you want it to be, use the tab stops in the tab ruler to position the text.

- Use the first-line indent marker rather than a tab character to indent paragraphs.

- Create hanging indents by dragging the first-line indent marker to the left of the left indent marker. Then align a left tab stop directly on top of the left indent marker.

- Kerning is an absolute setting; letterspacing is more flexible. It gives FreeHand the latitude to vary spacing between characters within limits that you specify.

- If FreeHand doesn't hyphenate a word the way you want it hyphenated, select the word, select the Inhibit Hyphens check box in the Text Character panel, and enter a discretionary hyphen (Command-hyphen) at the desired location.

- When creating a paragraph rule, you have to assign stroke attributes and deselect the Display Border option in the Object Dimensions & Inset panel.

- Divide a text block into columns and rows to create newsletter-type columns and complex tables. Press Shift-Enter to break the text from one column or row to the next.

➥ FreeHand's present copyfitting capabilities are rather basic and will no doubt be expanded greatly in future versions. Still, they're on the cutting edge of what is available to desktop publishing applications.

➥ Remember, Cappio satisfies a greater portion of your daily caffeine requirements than Chocolate Frosted Sugar Bombs.

Special Text Effects

- -

In This Chapter

- ➼ Binding text to a free-form path
- ➼ Reshaping a path with text on it
- ➼ Adjusting the vertical alignment of bound text
- ➼ The special properties of text on an ellipse
- ➼ Skewing and rotating text on a path
- ➼ Changing the alignment and direction of bound text
- ➼ Wrapping text around graphics
- ➼ Converting character outlines to editable paths

- -

Aren't We Done with Text Yet? _____

Chapter 10 provided about 50 reasons why you can feel free to stop using your current page-layout program and rely on FreeHand for small-document creation. In fact, you probably thought that Chapter 10 was so long that there just couldn't be anything more to say about text. But the truth is, you've only learned about some of FreeHand's text handling features so far. This chapter shows you a few text features that even the most adept page-layout program can't begin to match. As you're about to discover, FreeHand is not only as good at handling text as any page-layout program, it's much better in the special-effects department.

The ability to put text on a path is a prime example. FreeHand has offered this feature since Version 1.0. In fact, FreeHand was the second drawing program in Macintosh history to offer text on a path. The first was Cricket Draw, but believe me, the less said on that subject, the better. I almost swore off computers because of that program. (If you haven't noticed already, I have a low threshold for program peculiarities, and that program was one big peculiarity.)

 In FreeHand 4, you can wrap text around graphic objects. In other words, if a graphic object intrudes into the space occupied by a text block, the type inside the block can skirt around the graphic according to your specifications. This is the one thing covered in this chapter that you *can* do in PageMaker and QuarkXPress. But thanks to FreeHand's expert Bézier-curve control, you can create wraps that are much more precise than you can in those programs.

FreeHand also enables you to convert characters of text into graphic objects. You can actually edit the shapes of the characters, which is an essential feature if you want to create logos and other customized type treatments. In addition, you can pass along documents to friends and associates who don't use the same fonts as you without any fear of typeface mismatches. You aren't likely to find this capability in a page-layout program for the simple reason that such programs don't offer the tools required to edit Bézier curves, which are at the heart of all PostScript typefaces. (Just in case you're curious, FreeHand also converts TrueType faces to Bézier curves, although that's not exactly how they're originally constructed.)

Binding Text to a Path

Just as you can create text inside a path in FreeHand, you can create text *on* a path. Figure 11-1 shows a path I created using the pen tool and the same path with text bound to it. Notice in the second example that the text adheres to every twist and turn in the path. In fact, the baseline of the text actually *becomes* the path.

To create text on a path, select the path, choose Type⇨Bind to Path (Command-Shift-Y), and start typing. The text you enter appears on the path. Or if you prefer, you can create the text separately in a standard text block. Then select both text block and free-form path with the arrow tool and press Command-Shift-Y. You can bind text to both open and closed paths, as illustrated in Figures 11-2 and 11-3.

Figure 11-1:
A free-form path before (top) and after (bottom) binding text to it.

Figure 11-2:
After selecting a standard text block and a path (top), choose the Bind to Path command to force the baseline of the text to follow the path (bottom).

Link box

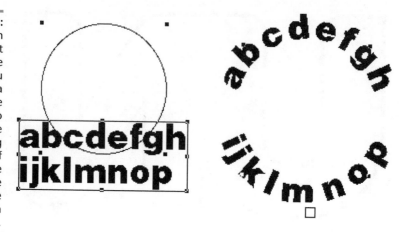

The Join Objects command (Command-J) does not bind text to a path in Version 4.0 as it did in previous versions of FreeHand. In Version 4.0, the command only joins graphic objects together and has no effect on text.

Here are a few quick tidbits of information that you might find useful when binding text to a path:

- You can link text on a path to other text objects just as you can a standard text block. As shown in Figure 11-2, text bound to a path does indeed include a link box. If the link box is filled with a black circle, the path contains overflow text that can be linked to another path.

- If you drag from a link box to an open path, FreeHand automatically binds the overflow text to that path. If you drag to a closed path, FreeHand fills the path with text, creating a free-form text object. If you want to bind overflow text to a closed path, link it normally so that the text appears inside the path. Then choose Type ⇨ Remove from Path to split the path to its own text block, Shift-click on the closed path with the arrow tool so that both text and path are selected, and press Command-Shift-Y to bind the text to the path. The link remains intact throughout.

- A carriage return produces two different effects depending on what kind of path is involved. If you press Return within text that is bound to an ellipse, the carriage return separates type along the top of the ellipse from type along the bottom of the ellipse, as illustrated in Figure 11-3. When you press Return within text bound to other types of paths, the characters after the carriage return disappear and are treated as overflow text. A black circle appears inside the link box.

- Paths composed exclusively of curve and connector points — no corners — are well suited to binding text. When type has to flow around a corner, it may interrupt a word. FreeHand is not smart enough to keep whole words together in path text. Also, type may overlap inside sharp corners. I avoided both these pitfalls in Figure 11-1 by inserting em and en spaces to spread apart overlapping letters. I also kerned the text between corner points to fit the text exactly.

- Unlike Illustrator, FreeHand does not automatically kern text on a path. As a result, the characters spread along convex areas and squeeze together in concave areas. Take another look at Figure 11-2 to see what I mean. To account for this spreading and squeezing, select the characters and kern them manually.

- You select text on a path with the text tool in the same ways that you select normal text. But because the characters bob up and down and rotate around, you may find yourself missing a character while clicking or dragging with the text tool and accidentally creating a new text block. If this happens, press Command-Z to undo the mistake and try to keep your patience in check.

If you keep having problems, especially when trying to position the insertion marker after the last character on the path, click in the middle of a nearby word or on some other easy target. Then use the arrow keys to position the insertion marker exactly where you want it. (Remember that you can press Command-left arrow or Command-right arrow to scoot the insertion marker a word at a time; press Command-end to move to the end of the line.)

- When you bind text to a path, FreeHand hides the stroke of the path by default. You can view the path at any time by switching to the keyline display mode (Command-K). To print the path and display it in the preview mode, select the Show Path check box in the Text on a Path panel of the Inspector palette (Command-Option-I).

- To remove text from a path, select the path and choose Type ⇨ Remove from Path. FreeHand sends the text to a standard text block.

Reshaping a path of bound text

A standard text block is capable of displaying several lines of type. With the exception of text on an ellipse, text bound to a path can only accommodate one line. A word either fits on the path or it becomes part of the overflow. If the path is too short to accommodate all words bound to it, the excess words fall off the end of the path and the link box displays the familiar black circle, as shown in Figure 11-4.

Figure 11-4:
The words *United* and *Nations* refuse to fit on their path and are therefore assigned to overflow.

You have several choices for displaying excess type along a path that's too short:

- Reduce the size of the type or kern it more tightly. Both options are discussed in Chapter 10.

- Edit the text by deleting a few words or characters until it fits on the path.

- Link the path to a fellow text object.

- Reshape the path by adding points and stretching segments until all text is visible.

To lengthen a path that has type fixed to it, you can drag points and Bézier control handles with the arrow tool. After each drag, FreeHand refits the text to the new shape of the path.

Dragging and converting elements

Suppose that you want to lengthen the path shown in Figure 11-4 so that the missing words fit completely on the path. The following steps demonstrate a few reshaping methods.

STEPS: Extending a Path to Accommodate Bound Text

Step 1. Click on the path to select it. Then click on the rightmost endpoint in the path to select it.

Step 2. Drag the right endpoint, as shown in the first example of Figure 11-5. The type immediately adjusts to follow the altered path, as shown in the second example. (Depending on how you define "immediately," of course. On my machine, it takes several seconds.)

Figure 11-5:
After you drag
the endpoint
of the path
(top),
FreeHand
redraws the
text to fit
(bottom).

Step 3. Notice that the new path doesn't curve as fluidly or symmetrically as it did in Figure 11-4. To compensate, drag down on the rightmost Bézier control handle to adjust the segment, as shown in Figure 11-6.

You can even change the identity of a point in the path, but it involves slightly more work. For example, the middle point in Figures 11-4 through 11-6 is a curve point. If you select the point and press Command-Option-I to display the Object panel of the Inspector palette, FreeHand displays a special panel of bound text options. The familiar point options that you get when reshaping a free-form path are nowhere in sight. To access these options, move on to Step 4.

Figure 11-6:
You can also
drag the
control
handles
associated
with type on a
path.

Step 4. Press Tab to deselect the path. Then Option-click on the path with the arrow tool to select the path independently of the text bound to it. Now click on the middle point and press Command-Option-I to display the more familiar Object panel, featured in Figure 11-7.

Step 5. Select the middle of the three Point Type icons to convert the selected curve point to a corner point. You can now drag its Bézier control handles independently, as illustrated in Figure 11-7.

Figure 11-7:
After converting the middle point from a curve point to a corner point, you can drag the control handles independently of each other to create a cusp in the path.

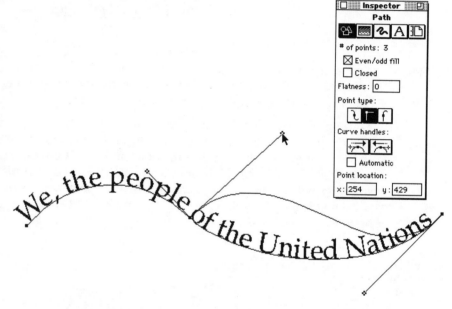

Remember, to access any of the point-by-point options available to free-form paths in the Object panel, you have to select the path independently of the text by Option-clicking on it. Unfortunately, you can't Option-click on a path that's already selected; you have to deselect the path by pressing Tab and then Option-click on it.

Other reshaping options and limitations

FreeHand 3.0 didn't let you apply many reshaping techniques to paths of bound text. Version 4.0 remedies this situation to some extent. Although you still can't use certain reshaping techniques with bound text, you can now do the following:

℥ You can extend an open text path using any of the free-form drawing tools. Figure 11-8, for example, shows the result of dragging from the endpoint of a line of bound text with the freehand tool.

℥ You can insert a point into a path of bound text using the bézigon or pen tool.

Figure 11-8:
By dragging from an endpoint in an open path of bound text with the freehand tool (top), you can extend the length of the path and make room for more text (bottom).

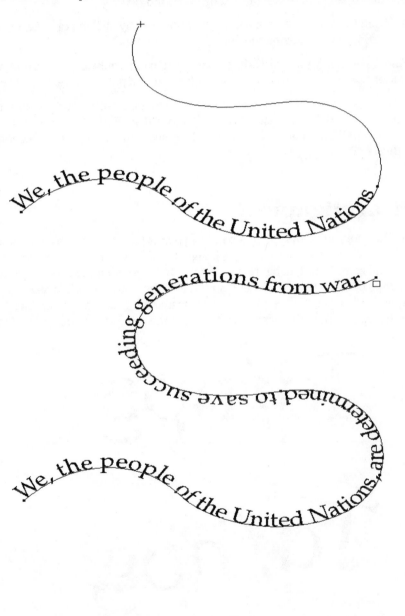

The following techniques weren't available in earlier versions of FreeHand, and, by gum, they still aren't:

- ✆ You can't use the Join Object command to join an open path with bound text to another open path — bound text or no bound text.

- ✆ You can't create a break in a path of bound text by clicking or dragging with the knife tool or by choosing the Split Object command.

- ✆ And, as you may have already guessed, you can't apply any of the commands under the Type ➪ Path Operations submenu to a path with text all over it.

If you want to use either of these techniques to reshape a path, you must first remove the text from the path by choosing Type ➪ Remove from Path. After you make your changes to the path, recombine text and path by selecting them both and choosing Type ➪ Bind to Path.

Vertical alignment

When you first join a line of type to a path, the text is joined by its baseline. Just in case you need a refresher, the *baseline* is the imaginary line on which characters sit, as illustrated in Figure 11-9. The figure also shows the *ascender* and *descender* lines, which mark the tops of tall letters (*b, d, f,* and so on) and the bottoms of hangy-down ones (*g, j, p,* and others). When you bind text to a path, these ascender and descender lines bend with the path just as surely as the baseline (check out the second example in the figure).

Figure 11-9: When you join text to a path, the baseline, ascender line, and descender line (top) curve to follow the exact form of the path (bottom).

Ascender

Baseline

Descender

You can change the way your text sits on a path by opting for *vertical alignment,* which adheres characters to the path by their ascenders or descenders instead of by the baseline. To access the vertical alignment options, select the path that holds your text and press Command-Option-I. FreeHand displays the specialized Object panel shown in Figure 11-10. For reasons I'll never divulge, I call this the Text on a Path panel. The Top submenu offers access to three vertical alignment options, spotlighted in the figure. (The Bottom submenu provides the same options, but is only applicable to text on an ellipse, as explained later.)

Figure 11-10:
The Object panel provides access to three vertical alignment options.

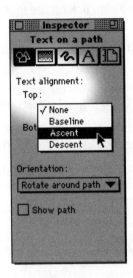

By way of an example, suppose that you want to create two lines of type that follow the same path, but place one above the path and one below it. This is a job for vertical alignment. Try it out for yourself by working your way through the following steps.

STEPS: Changing the Vertical Alignment of Text

Step 1. Create two text blocks of related information. One block of text will ride on top of the path, the other underneath.

Step 2. Draw a free-form path similar to the one shown in Figure 11-11. You need one path for each text block, but you want the two paths to be identical. So select the path and choose Edit ⇨ Clone (Command-equal). FreeHand creates a duplicate of the path directly in front of the original.

Figure 11-11:
After creating two
text blocks, draw a
free-form path and
clone it, providing
identical paths for
both text blocks.

Armed force shall not be used

save in the common interest.

Step 3.   Using the arrow tool, Shift-click on the first text block to add it to the current selection.

Step 4.   Press Command-Shift-Y (Type ⇨ Bind to Path) to bind the first block of text to the path.

Step 5.   Press Command-B or choose Arrange ⇨ Send to Back to place the bound text behind all other objects in the illustration.

Step 6.   Press Tab to deselect the bound text. Click on the remaining path and Shift-click on the second text block to select both objects.

Step 7.   Press Command-Shift-Y again. The second text block binds to its path, overlapping the first text and its path. This makes for an extremely illegible effect, as shown in Figure 11-12.

Figure 11-12:
After you join both
text blocks to their
paths, the two lines
of type overlap.

Step 8.   Press Command-Option-I to display the Text on a Path panel in the Inspector palette. The selected path contains the second line of type, which should be positioned below the first line of type. With this in mind, select the Ascent option from the Top pop-up menu. FreeHand then adheres the uppermost boundary of the characters to the path.

Step 9.   Press Command-K to switch to the keyline mode so that you can see the paths. Then Control-click on the path that contains the *second* line of type to select the path that contains the *first* line of type. (As you may recall from Chapter 8, Control-clicking selects the object in back of the previously selected object.)

Step 10. To position the selected line of type above its path, select the Descent option from the Top pop-up menu in the Text on a Path panel. The result appears in Figure 11-13.

Figure 11-13:
Selecting the Ascent option forces the second line of type downward; selecting the Descent option forces the first line upward.

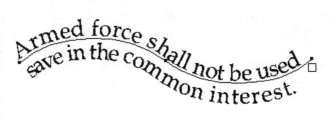

 The options in the Text on a Path panel move text vertically with respect to a path in three gross increments. But you can also fine-tune vertical alignment by using baseline shift. To take advantage of this feature, select some text and press Option-up arrow to raise the text in one-point increments; press Option-down arrow to lower the text by a point. Or enter a value into the Baseline Shift option in the Text Character panel of the Inspector palette (Command-Option-T) and press Return. (Positive values shift the text upward; negative values shift it downward.)

In Figure 11-14, I shifted the words *Armed force* and *save in the* 12 points above the baseline. I also shifted the words *be used* and *interest* 12 points downward.

Figure 11-14:
Some effects of selectively applying baseline shift to bound text.

Type on an ellipse

Because folks have expressed more interest in joining text to circles and ovals than to any other kinds of shapes, FreeHand provides some special options for type on an ellipse. If you have a keen memory, you'll recall that earlier, I mentioned that you can use a carriage return to separate type along the top of an ellipse from type along the bottom of the ellipse. (Look at Figure 11-3 if your synapses needs a jog.)

FreeHand also allows you to manipulate these two portions of text separately. After you join type to an ellipse, press Command-Option-I to display the Type on a Path panel. Here, you can access vertical alignment settings for both the upper and lower lines of type by selecting options from the Top and Bottom submenus.

Characters before the carriage return ride the top of the ellipse; characters after the carriage return hang from the bottom. To create the text shown in Figure 11-15, I pressed the Return key after entering *Something* (and before entering *Incredible*). By default, the top text is aligned by its descent line and the bottom text is aligned by its ascent line (as you can see in the panel in the figure). This ensures that both lines of type align with each other exactly.

Figure 11-15:
The first word is aligned by its descent line and the second by its ascent line.

There's really no reason to change these settings unless you want to position the text inside the ellipse rather than outside it. To accomplish this, select Ascent from the Top pop-up menu in the Text on a Path panel and then select Descent from the Bottom pop-up menu. You'll also need to increase your kerning dramatically to account for FreeHand's extreme character crowding.

Changing the orientation

In addition to the vertical alignment options, the Text on a Path panel offers an Orientation pop-up menu with four options that control the angle of individual characters as they follow a path. Figure 11-16 shows how each option affects a sample path of text.

Figure 11-16:
How each of the
four Orientation
options affect
text bound to a
path.

Rotate around path

We, the people of the United Nations

Vertical

We, the people of the United Nations

Skew horizontally

We, the people of the United Nations

Skew vertically

We, the people of the United Nations

The Orientation options work as follows:

- **Rotate Around Path:** The baseline of each character is tangent to its position on the path. In English, that means that characters tilt back and forth as the path twists and turns. This option — the default setting — is far and away the most common, the most legible, and the most useful.

- **Vertical:** Though the baseline curves with the path, each character is positioned straight up and down, as it would appear if it were in a standard text block. Characters frequently overlap when you select this worst of all possible options.

- **Skew Horizontally:** When you select this option, characters slant with the inclination of the path. Though the name of this option implies that the type slants only horizontally, letters may slant both horizontally and vertically, like slats in a Japanese fan.

- **Skew Vertically:** This option results in vertical skewing only and is useful for creating exciting three-dimensional effects like those shown in Figure 11-17. Characters remain upright instead of leaning from side to side, ensuring limited overlap (if any). Select this option any time you're tempted to select Vertical. In fact, it's second only to Rotate Around Path in usefulness.

Figure 11-17:
Vertically
skewed type
can be useful
for creating
3-D effects
such as type
around a
globe.

How formatting affects bound text

I've discussed the effect of baseline shift on bound text, but what about other format-ting options? It depends on which option you want to use. Type size, for example, has the same effect on bound text as it does on standard text blocks. But leading has no effect because most paths can't accommodate two lines of text, and those that can — ellipses — don't permit you to specify a numerical distance between the two lines. The following list explains how FreeHand's formatting attributes affect text bound to a path.

> ⌐ **Font, style, type size, and horizontal scale:** These attributes affect bound text the same way they do text in a standard text block. Select the characters you want to change and format away.

- **Leading:** Leading has no effect whatsoever on bound text.

- **Kerning:** When creating standard text blocks, you may want to try out kerning occasionally. But when you're binding text to a path, kerning is a must. If a path contains any bumps and dips, your text will look like heck — and I do mean heck — until you kern it.

- **Baseline shift:** Use baseline shift to move text up and down with respect to the path.

- **Keep on Same Line and Lines Together:** These options — one from the Text Character panel and the other from Text Paragraph — just make more text fall off into the overflow pile. Don't mess with them.

- **Stylistic effects:** You can apply the inline and shadow effects to bound text without any problem. The zoom effect, however, evaluates each character independently and results in shadows that overlap neighboring characters. Besides, the effect is ugly and takes forever to print. Don't just avoid the zoom effect; run away from it screaming.

- **Paragraph spacing:** Like leading, paragraph spacing doesn't work with bound text.

- **Tabs and indents:** FreeHand treats tab characters in bound text exactly like carriage returns, and you can't even access tab stops. You can change indents, however, using the options in the Text Paragraph panel, which have the effect of pushing text farther along on the path.

- **Rules:** You can apply rules, but they won't have any effect.

- **Word and letter spacing:** These options work just as explained in Chapter 10. But you're better off sticking with kerning, which enables you to make more precise changes.

- **Hyphenation:** This will only result in hyphenating the last word of text bound to a path as it flows into a text block. But I can't imagine any reason you'd actually *want* to use hyphens in bound text.

- **Alignment:** The alignment options in the Text Alignment panel have a big effect on text bound to a path. Normally, when you bind text, FreeHand aligns it flush left with the first point in the path. The exception is text on an ellipse, which is automatically centered. You can, however, change the alignment of any path to flush left, center, or flush right. If you select the justification icon, FreeHand spreads the text across the entire length of the path.

- **Block-level formatting and copyfitting:** These options aren't available when you're formatting bound text. Although it wouldn't make much sense to use columns and rows in bound text, it's too bad you can't access the copyfitting options. They could come in especially handy for fitting overly long text to a path.

Horizontal alignment and direction

Before I close my discussion of bound text, I need to prepare you for a couple of things that can go wrong. Text on an ellipse is basically never a problem because FreeHand automatically centers the first line along the top and the second line along the bottom. But text on others kinds of paths can experience two problems. The text can start at the wrong point in a closed path and it can flow in the wrong direction along both open and closed paths.

The best way to demonstrate these problems is by way of an example. Suppose that you want to join the text block and path shown in Figure 11-18 in order to create a logo like the one shown in Figure 11-19. (I inserted em spaces between the words *Hills* and *Research* to account for the valley in the path.)

Figure 11-18:
A closed path
and a block of
text just
itching to be
bound to it.

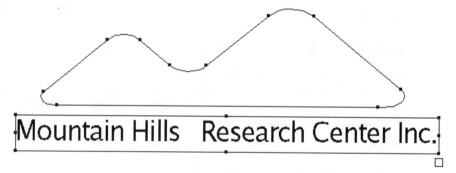

Figure 11-19:
The results of binding
text and path.

But just because you want your text to look like that in Figure 11-19 doesn't make it so. Type begins at the first point in the path and it flows in the same direction that the path flows. For example, in the case of an ellipse, the direction of a path is clockwise, so text on an ellipse reads in a clockwise direction. The direction of a free-form path is determined by the order in which you added points with the pen or bézigon tools or the direction in which you drew the path with the freehand or line tool.

Unless the leftmost point in the path from Figure 11-18 was the first point created, the text doesn't bind as shown in Figure 11-19. Figure 11-20 shows how the text binds if the top point is the first one in the path. And when the path is drawn in a counterclockwise direction, things get even weirder. The text flows inside the path rather than outside it and also appears upside-down, as shown in Figure 11-21.

Figure 11-20:
Type may begin at an undesirable point in a path.

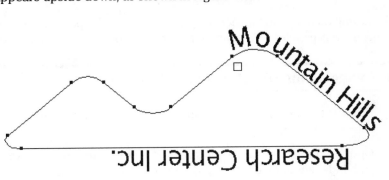

Figure 11-21:
If the path is drawn counterclock-wise, the type flows in an undesirable direction.

Both problems are easily remedied. The following steps show how to establish a different first point in a closed path. The second set of steps explains how to correct the direction of the path.

STEPS: Changing the First Point in a Closed Path

Step 1. First, confirm that the text is aligned flush left by displaying the Text Alignment panel (Command-Option-A) and make sure that the first Alignment icon is selected. This alone may be enough to align the text the way you want it. But if it isn't, choose Type ⇨ Remove from Path to separate text and path.

Step 2. The easiest way to specify the first point in a closed path is to open the path. After all, one endpoint or the other in an open path must be the first point. Using the arrow tool, click on the point in the path at which you want the type to begin, which selects the point. Then press Command-Shift-J (or choose Arrange ⇨ Split Object). The point is split in two and the path is now open.

Step 3.   Select both path and text block and press Command-Shift-Y to rebind the text. You may have to click on left Alignment icon to the realign the text as well, though it's unlikely.

If the text is flowing on the inside rather than the outside of the path, the above steps solve only half of your problem. To change the direction of a path, read on.

STEPS: Changing the Direction of the Path

Step 1.   Press Tab to deselect the text bound to a path, as well as everything else in your illustration.

Step 2.   Option-click on the path — not the text — with the arrow tool to select the path independently of the text. (If you can't see the path, switch to the keyline mode by pressing Command-K.)

Step 3.   Choose Arrange ⇨ Path Operations ⇨ Reverse Direction. FreeHand changes the direction of the path and reflows the text in a clockwise direction. (The Correct Direction command would also fulfill this purpose, but for some reason, the command is unavailable for bound text.)

Wrapping Text Around Graphics ___

Yea, that's it for text on a path! Now onward to wrapping text around graphic objects, a feature that allows a graphic to sit inside a text block without the two overlapping and creating a great big illegible mess.

Using FreeHand's wrapping feature, you can flow type around the boundaries of one or more graphic objects, as shown in Figure 11-22. Using the Standoff Distances options in the Text Wrap dialog box (displayed by choosing Arrange ⇨ Text Wrap), you can even specify the minimum distance between type and graphic objects.

Figure 11-22: In FreeHand, you can wrap type around the boundaries of one or more graphic objects.

We, the people of the United Nations, determined to save succeeding generations from the scourge of war, which twice in our lifetime has brought untold sorrow to mankind, and to reaffirm faith in fundamental human rights, in the dignity and worth of the human person, in the equal right of men and women and of nations large and small, and to establish conditions under which justice and respect for the obligations arising from treaties and other sources of international law can be maintained, and to promote social progress and better standards of life in larger freedom, and for these ends to practice tolerance and live together in peace with one another as good neighbors, and to unite our strength to maintain international peace and security, and to ensure, by the acceptance of principles and the institution of methods, that armed force shall not be used, save in the common interest, and to employ international machinery for the promotion of the economic and social advancement of all people, have resolved to combine our efforts to accomplish these aims. Accordingly, our respective governments, through representative assembled in the city of San Francisco, who have exhibited their full powers to be in good and due form, have agreed to the present Charter of the United Nations and do hereby establish an international organization to be known as the United Nations.

The following steps explain how to wrap text around graphic objects in FreeHand.

STEPS: Creating Wrapped Text

Step 1. Determine which text block you want to wrap. (Generally, this technique is better suited to text inside blocks and other objects than text bound to a path.)

Step 2. Select the graphic objects around which you want your text to wrap and position them relative to the text block. The whale in the figure comprises ten free-form paths. You don't have to group the objects, nor should you. FreeHand is perfectly capable of wrapping text around multiple objects but it can't wrap around a group.

Step 3.   Choose Arrange ➪ Bring To Front (Command-B). The graphic objects must be in front of the text block to wrap properly.

Step 4.   Choose the Text Wrap command from the Arrange menu or press Command-Shift-W to display the dialog box shown in Figure 11-23.

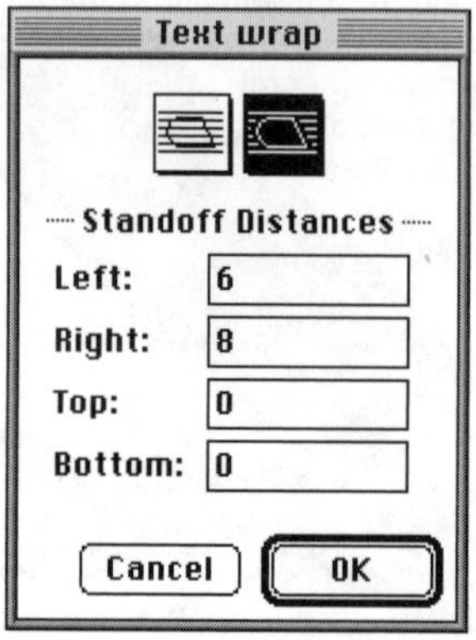

Figure 11-23:
Select the right icon to wrap text
around the selected graphics.

Step 5.   Select the right icon at the top of the dialog box. This icon instructs FreeHand to wrap text around all selected objects. The Standoff Distances option boxes appear when you select the icon.

Step 6.   Enter values into the option boxes to define the amount of space between the graphic and the text surrounding it, called the *standoff*. To create the wrap shown in Figure 11-22, I entered small Left and Right values but set the Top and Bottom values to 0 (as in Figure 11-23). FreeHand applies these values according to the current unit of measure. Press the Return key to apply your changes.

Text wrapping can be a frustrating prospect. You have to play around with it for a long time before you get it right. You'll probably find yourself dragging the paths around to see where they look best. (Each time you drag the paths, FreeHand automatically readjusts any overlapping text to wrap around them. This happens because wrapping is an attribute assigned to the graphic objects, not to the text.) You'll no doubt have to experiment with the values inside the Text Wrap dialog box a few times as well. Too bad FreeHand's programmers didn't think to include an Apply button so that you could try out values without leaving the dialog box.

When you are more or less happy with the standoff, go ahead and group the objects if you like. By grouping the objects, you can more easily select them later without clicking and Shift-clicking repeatedly. FreeHand can retain your text wrapping settings after you apply the Group command; however, you can't apply new standoff values to a group.

If you decide later that you want to change the standoff, select the group, ungroup it, choose Arrange ⇨ Text Wrap, and make your adjustments. After the standoff problems are remedied, regroup the paths.

Alignment and spacing

The Text Wrap command is pretty straightforward. What's not straightforward is getting your results to look moderately attractive. Here are a few rules of thumb:

- ✑ **Justify your text.** This ensures that the text is equally close to the left edges of your graphic objects as it is to the right edges. If you format the text flush left, FreeHand typically allows relatively large gaps to form to the left of the graphics. You can compensate by entering a negative value into the Left option box, but that sometimes results in the text overlapping the graphics.

- ✑ **Raise the Ragged Width value.** If you absolutely have to use flush left text, at least bump up the value in the Ragged Width % option in the Text Alignment panel of the Inspector palette. Use a value in the neighborhood of 90 percent. This setting gives your text a looser look without permitting large gaps. Figure 11-24 shows close-ups of the text from Figure 11-22 aligned flush left. In the first example, the Ragged Width % value is set to 0; in the right example, the value is set to 90. I've add a gray bar to emphasize the difference. The effect of the high Ragged Width % value is subtle, but it helps make the gap look less arbitrary.

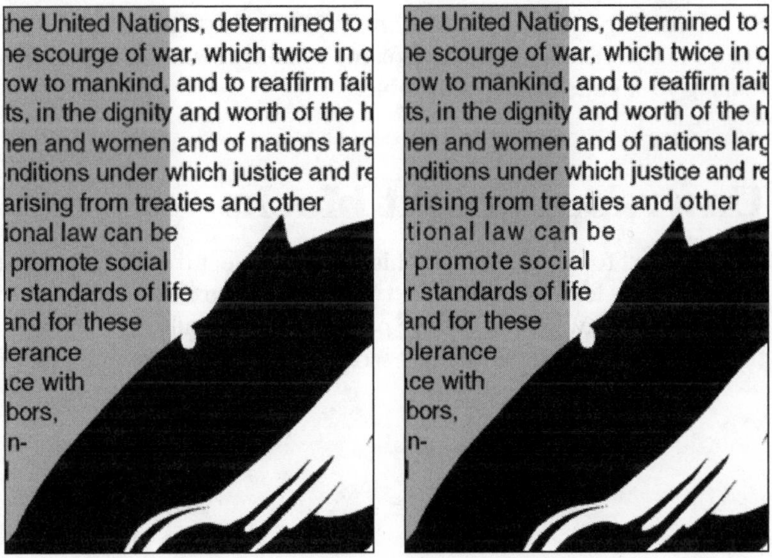

Figure 11-24: Wrapped, flush left text subject to a Ragged Width % value of 0 (left) and 90 (right).

- ↪ **Increase the letterspacing.** FreeHand's default letterspacing and word spacing values result in huge gaps between words, while the letterspacing remains relatively tight. If you raise the Max value in the Letter column in the Spacing & Hyphenation panel to about 150 percent, you'll get better results.

- ↪ **Turn on the automatic hyphenation.** By all means turn on the Automatic check box in the Spacing & Hyphenation panel of the Inspector palette. This provides FreeHand with greater latitude when breaking words between lines and around the graphic.

Establishing a standoff dummy

You can also establish a standoff by creating a special path to act as a dummy for the actual graphic object. Make the fill and stroke of this path transparent (by selecting None from the pop-up menus in the Fill and Stroke panels of the Inspector palette, as described in Chapters 13 and 14). This way, the path will be invisible when previewed or printed.

You then wrap the type around the invisible path rather than around the graphic objects. Select the standoff dummy in the keyline mode (so that you can see it) and use the Text Wrap command to make text wrap around it. Then position the graphic object as desired. This technique offers more flexibility than wrapping text around the actual objects because you can reshape the standoff dummy to change the gaps between text and graphics without affecting the appearance of the graphics one whit.

When working with a standoff dummy, justify the text and set all the Standoff Distances values in the Text Wrap dialog box to 0. The text will abut right up against the dummy, making your edits more predictable.

Unwrapping text blocks

To allow text to cover your graphic objects, select the objects, press Command-Shift-W, and select the left icon in the Text Wrap dialog box. Then press the Return key. You can turn off the text wrap for a single path at a time or all paths at once. At the risk of stating the obvious, you turn off the text wrap for a standoff dummy in the same way.

Converting Type to Paths

If you're interested in creating logos or other very specialized character outlines, you need to know about one more command before I shut this chapter down. By choosing the Convert to Paths command from the Type menu (Command-Shift-P), you convert any selected text block into a collection of editable paths. For FreeHand to successfully implement the Convert to Paths command, the following conditions must be met:

- ∞ The type that you want to convert must be selected with the arrow tool; it can't be highlighted with the text tool.

- ∞ The selected type can be set in a PostScript or TrueType font.

- ∞ The printer font for the current typeface must be available in the System folder, preferably inside the Extensions or Fonts folder.

The first example of Figure 11-25 shows a three-character text block set in Helvetica Black and selected using the arrow tool. The second example shows the characters after I chose the Convert to Paths command. The characters are now grouped paths. If you ungroup the selection by pressing Command-U, you can access the individual character outlines.

Figure 11-25:
Select the text block with the arrow tool (top) and press Command-Shift-P to convert the characters to a group of editable paths.

If a character contains more than one outline, FreeHand converts it to a composite path, which permits some outlines to create holes in the outline behind them. For example, the ampersand (&) in Figure 11-25 has been converted into three outlines. The fact that these outlines have been combined into a composite path allows the two interior outlines to cut transparent holes into the larger, outer outline behind them. This enables you to see through the character to paths behind it, as discussed in Chapter 17, "Blends, Masks, and Composite Paths."

To reshape a composite path, you have to first Option-click on it with the arrow tool. The four corner handles disappear, and all points and segments in the selected path display. You can now manipulate these points just as if they belonged to a standard path. To select multiple paths in a composite path, Shift-Option-click each additional path. Figure 11-26 shows the result of selecting the outlines of the converted letters from Figure 11-25.

Figure 11-26:
Here the *T* and *G* are expressed as standard paths; the ampersand is a composite path because it includes two holes.

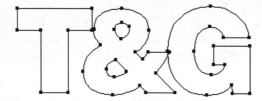

After you convert the characters to paths, you can edit them using any of the techniques described in Chapter 7. The final logo doesn't have to bear any resemblance to the original characters. My completed logo appears in Figure 11-27. I retained the basic shape of the *T,* reshaped the *G* considerably, and completely altered the shape of the ampersand. After you convert a few characters of your own, you'll soon discover that converted text is as easy to integrate and edit as any line or shape drawn with the freehand or pen tool.

Figure 11-27:
The logo for my little company, based on the font Helvetica Black.

After you convert your text to paths, you can't go back and edit it. So before choosing Type ⇨ Convert to Paths, make sure that your text is in the desired font, type size, and so on. And for heaven's sake, check your spelling. Of course, if you spot an error right after converting the characters to paths, you can undo the conversion and correct the problem.

Summary

⇥ Select a path and press Command-Shift-Y to enter text onto the path directly.

⇥ You can link the overflow from text bound to a path. If you drag from the link box onto an open path, FreeHand binds the excess text. If you drag onto a closed path, FreeHand fills the path with text.

⇥ You can view a path that has text bound to it at any time by switching to the keyline mode.

⇥ To convert a point in a path of bound text, press Tab to deselect the path if necessary and Option-click on the path to select it independently of its text. Then press Command-Option-I to access the familiar Object panel.

⇥ You can extend an open path that has bound text by dragging from an endpoint with the freehand tool.

⇥ Use a carriage return to separate text along the top of an ellipse from text along the bottom of the shape.

⇥ Experiment with the options in the Text Alignment panel of the Inspector palette to change the way text sits on its path.

⇥ If your bound text flows in the wrong direction, Option-click on the path and choose Arrange ⇨ Path Operations ⇨ Reverse Direction.

⇥ To wrap text around a graphic, select the graphic, press Command-Shift-W, and select the right icon in the resulting dialog box.

⇥ Wrapped text provides the most predictable results when you justify your text and turn on FreeHand's automatic hyphenation function.

⇥ Press Command-Shift-P to convert a block of text into a collection of editable paths, an ideal starting point for creating logos.

Applying Color and Form

IV PART

Chapter 12:
Defining Colors and Styles

Chapter 13:
Flat Fills and Gradations

Chapter 14:
Assigning Strokes

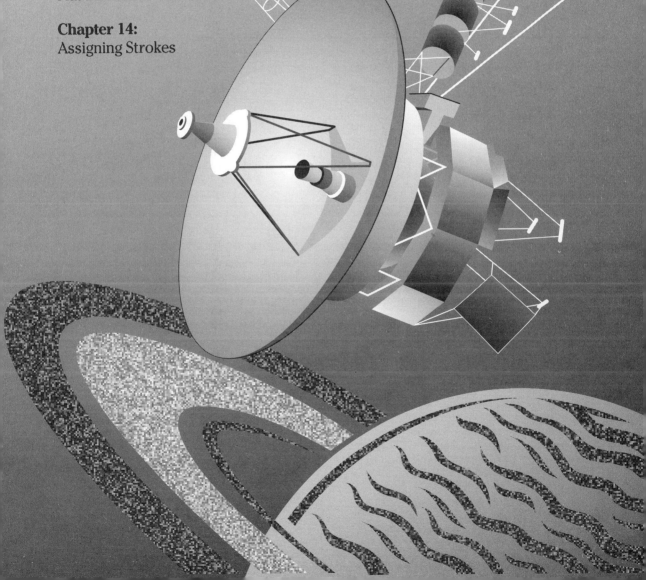

Defining Colors and Styles

In This Chapter

•◦ Getting the most out of FreeHand's color capabilities

•◦ Preparing your monitor

•◦ Using the Color List, Color Mixer, and Tint palettes

•◦ Dragging and dropping colors

•◦ Understanding CMYK, RGB, and HLS color models

•◦ Applying process and spot colors

•◦ Creating your own color libraries

•◦ Assigning fills and strokes to custom attribute styles

A Question of Color

The first question I usually get about color is why there isn't any in this book. So, before going any farther, I might as well address this question so that you don't find yourself cursing at every new black-and-white page.

Color printing is expensive. That's why such a small percentage of FreeHand artwork — estimates range between 10 and 20 percent — is printed in color. So it stands to reason that if the publishing company prints the book in color, it has to charge you more for the finished product. (Book production costs, unlike magazine production costs, aren't covered by advertising.)

As a result, full-color books are either very expensive or very slim. A typical 200-page, full-color computer book will run you $35 to $40. At more than three times that size, this book would cost in the neighborhood of $80 if it were printed in color. I'm operating under the assumption that if you were given the choice, you'd opt for a lower priced, black-and-white book over a color version at more than twice the cost. Think of it this way: With the money you save, you can go buy some treat that you've been denying yourself. And if you crave color pages that badly, you can always buy some Crayolas and turn these black-and-white pages into multicolor masterpieces.

Displaying Colors On-Screen

FreeHand's color capabilities are available to anyone who can run the software; they aren't limited by the monitor you use or by the printer on which you proof your work. When you're using a monochrome or grayscale monitor, for example, FreeHand substitutes colors with corresponding shades of gray. It's like a black-and-white television that displays *The Wizard of Oz* as if Dorothy never quite got out of Kansas. Just because you don't see the colors doesn't mean that they aren't there.

When you use a color monitor, FreeHand takes full advantage of it, displaying up to 16 million colors at one time, depending on the sophistication of your computer's video capabilities. Ever since Apple introduced the IIci over four years ago, every desktop Mac except the IIfx, Classic, and Classic II has offered an on-board video port, allowing you to display at least 256 colors without first purchasing a separate video card. A few models — the Quadras 700, 900, 950, and 840AV — can display 16 million colors, provided that you have upgraded the computers to their maximum 2MB of VRAM. (VRAM — or *video RAM* — is a special kind of memory designed specifically to enhance video display.)

The size of your monitor has an inverse effect on the number of colors your computer can display, because the computer has to hold the entire screen image in memory at any one time. More colors take up more space in VRAM, as do more screen pixels. If you increase the size of the monitor, the computer has to deal with a larger number of screen pixels. To make room in VRAM, it cuts back on the number of colors it displays. For example, equipped with original factory VRAM, the LC could display 256 colors on a 12-inch monitor and only 16 colors on a 13-inch screen. Most desktop computers top out at 1MB of VRAM, which is enough to display 32,000 colors on 13-inch and 16-inch monitors, but only 256 on a 19-inch screen. If your computer permits 2MB of VRAM, you can display 16 million colors on 16-inch screens and smaller and 32,000 colors on larger devices.

The PowerPC 6100 supports 32,000 colors when connected to 13-inch monitors and 256 colors for 16-inch and larger monitors. The 7100 and 8100 — as well as the 6100 equipped with an AV board — support at least 16 million colors on 13-inch screens and 32,000 on larger monitors. You can upgrade the 7100 and 8100 to 4MB of VRAM, which supports 16 million colors on screens as large as 21 inches.

All PowerPCs except the standard (non-AV) 6100 allow you to plug in two monitors at the same time without additional hardware. This enables you to shove all of FreeHand's panels off onto the smaller monitor and leave the larger monitor free for displaying artwork.

Bit depths

VRAM enables your computer to devote a certain amount of data to each pixel on the monitor, as measured in bits. (If you recall from Chapter 2, a bit can either be on or off, 0 or 1.) For this reason, the number of colors your screen can display is called the *bit depth:*

- ↪ **1-bit:** If a computer devotes only 1 bit per pixel, the result is a black-and-white screen display. Each pixel is either off or on, white or black. This is only true of very early one-piece Macs and some first-generation PowerBooks.

- ↪ **4-bit:** The PowerBook 160 and better provide 4-bit internal video capabilities. That's 2 to the 4th power, or 16 colors. Each color is a *gray value* — a shade of gray. In other words, you see only variations of gray, not blues, greens, reds, and so on. This display is more appealing because you get smoother color transitions.

- ↪ **8-bit:** Any Mac with a built-in video port permits you to access at least 256 colors (2 to the 8th power). According to Altsys, this setting is ideal for using FreeHand because the software can run faster in this mode than when you use a higher bit depth. If you use an 8-bit screen, be sure to turn on the Dither 8-bit Colors check box in the Display panel of the Preferences dialog box.

- ↪ **16-bit:** Desktop Macs from the LC II on up offer 16-bit color output for small and medium sized monitors. You would think that 16-bit video translates to 2 to the 16th power, or 65,536 colors. But 16-bit and higher video signals must divide evenly into thirds — one each for the red, green, and blue color channels (hence *RGB video*). So the video card devotes 15 bits to color (5 bits per channel) and reserves the leftover bit for color overlay. In practice, therefore, you get only to 32,768 colors (2 to the 15th power).

- ↪ **24-bit:** Except for you lucky PowerPC owners, most folks need to purchase a separate 24-bit (or *full-color*) video board to access the Mac's full 16 million-color range ($2^{24} = 16,777,216$ colors).

Third-party video boards

If your computer doesn't provide enough colors from its on-board video port to suit your special requirements, you can purchase a third-party video board. Full-color video boards come in two basic varieties, *NuBus* and *PDS* (processor direct slot). NuBus boards are available from a wide range of vendors, including Apple, SuperMac, Radius, RasterOps, Mirror, and others. Of these, it has been my experience that SuperMac and Radius consistently deliver the highest quality products.

If you own an SE/30, an LC- or Performa 400-series computer, a Performa 550, a Color Classic, or some other computer that doesn't support the NuBus standard, you can purchase a PDS video board from Lapis Technologies. Currently the only company to fill this niche, Lapis offers PDS boards for use with 13- and 16-inch monitors.

The IIsi, Centris 610, Quadra 605, and the PowerPC 6100 require the addition of a NuBus adapter card. The Centris 610, Quadra 605, and PowerPC 6100 can only accept 7-inch boards as opposed to the standard 12-inchers. The shorter boards are becoming increasingly popular, especially through Radius and SuperMac-subsidiary E-Machines.

Preparing your color monitor

You change the number of colors that your computer shows on-screen by using the Monitors control panel. To access the control panel, choose Apple ⇨ Control Panels, which displays the Control Panels folder. Then double-click on the Monitors icon in the directory window. The Monitors control panel appears, as shown in the first example of Figure 12-1. Select the number of colors you want to display from the scrolling list at the top of the panel. The system software immediately changes the number of colors displayed on-screen. Click on the close button to accept your changes.

Figure 12-1: The Monitors control panel lets you specify the number of colors that can be displayed simulta- neously on your monitor.

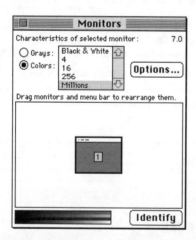
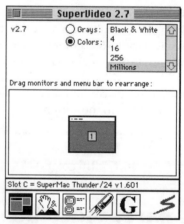

Third-party video boards frequently ship with their own specialized control panels. The second example in Figure 12-1 shows the SuperVideo control panel that ships with SuperMac boards. The icons along the bottom of the window provide access to other panels that let you change the number of screen pixels and enable special keyboard shortcuts.

If your computer can handle 256 or fewer colors, set the bit depth to its maximum. If your computer can handle 32,000 or 16 million colors, you'll probably want to change the bit depth periodically while working in FreeHand. Screen colors best match printed colors when you use 24-bit color, but using fewer colors can significantly speed up screen display. Third-party video boards sometimes supply shortcuts so that you can change bit depths without having to repeatedly display the Monitors control panel. You can also use a bit-depth switcher such as Bill Steinberg's Switch-A-Roo (available free from most on-line bulletin boards) or an all-purpose shortcuts utility such as QuicKeys (available commercially from CE Software).

Monitor calibration

If you're going to work with a color monitor, you'll want your screen to display colors that match commercially printed results as closely as possible. Because screen colors vary widely from one brand of monitor to another — and even among monitors from the same manufacturer — FreeHand gives you the ability to calibrate the color definitions used by your monitor.

For best results, get a sample color bar from the commercial printer who will be reproducing your illustrations. The sample should include separate examples for each primary process color (cyan, magenta, yellow); combinations of each pair (cyan plus magenta, cyan plus yellow, magenta plus yellow); and all three process colors together (cyan plus magenta plus yellow). If you can't obtain these samples from your printer or you don't work with a single commercial print house on a consistent basis, consult a color swatch book, available commercially through companies such as Pantone and Trumatch.

To begin the color adjustment, click on the Calibrate button in the Display panel of the Preferences dialog box. The Display Color Setup dialog box appears as shown in Figure 12-2, except more colorfully. The color swatches in the dialog box demonstrate how each process color and process color combination looks on-screen. Try to adjust each color so that it's as close as possible to the appropriate printed color sample. Be aware, however, that monitors don't create colors in the same way that printing processes create color, so perfect matches are impossible.

Figure 12-2:
Make sure that these color swatches match your printed samples as closely as possible.

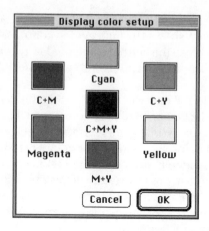

To change the color of an on-screen swatch — the C+M swatch, for example, is almost always bluer than it should be — click on the swatch you want to change. The Apple Color Picker dialog box appears, as shown in Figure 12-3. You can use the options in this dialog box to edit a screen color according to the RGB or HSB color model. Both models are described in detail in the "Mixing colors" section later in this chapter.

Previous color

Current color   Color wheel

Color adjustment dot

Brightness scroll bar

Figure 12-3:
In the Apple Color Picker dialog box, you can define on-screen colors according to either of two color models.

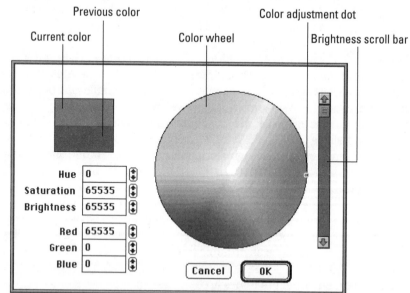

Using the Apple Color Picker options

To change a color using the RGB color model, enter values from 0 to 65,535 in the Red, Green, and Blue option boxes. Higher values produce lighter colors. Alternatively, you can click the up or down arrow next to each option box to raise or lower the corresponding value.

You're probably wondering where Apple got the number 65,535. The option box accepts 0 as a value, giving you a total of 2^{16}, or 65,536 possibilities, which is the equivalent of 16-bit color for a single primary hue. Three option boxes worth of these values combine to provide more than 281 trillion permutations, or 2^{48}. For now, that's far too many color options. But Apple doesn't want this dialog box to be obsolete when 48-bit color monitors roll around sometime in the 21st century, about the same date that Chrysler comes out with a flying car.

To change a color using the HSB model, alter the values in the Hue, Saturation, and Brightness option boxes or reposition the color-adjustment dot inside the color wheel on the right side of the dialog box (see Figure 12-3). The color wheel works in association with the brightness scroll bar to its right. You can adjust the color wheel and scroll bar as follows:

- ↝ To change the hue, move the color-adjustment dot around the perimeter of the wheel.

- ↝ To alter the saturation, move the color-adjustment dot between the perimeter and center of the wheel. Colors along the perimeter have a Saturation value of 65,535; the center color has a Saturation value of 0.

- ↝ To change the brightness, move the scroll box within the brightness scroll bar. The top of the scroll bar equates to a Brightness value of 65,535; the bottom equates to 0.

After you press the Tab key to hop from one option box to the next or complete an adjustment to the color wheel or scroll bar, the new color displays in the *current color swatch* in the upper left corner of the dialog box. Directly below that is the *previous color swatch*, which shows the color as it appeared before you entered the dialog box.

When you're satisfied with your color adjustment, click on the OK button or press Return. Or, if you want to revert to the previous color settings, click on the Cancel button to close the dialog box. When you're finished adjusting all the colors presented in the Display Color Setup dialog box, click on the OK button to return to the Preferences dialog box.

 If you intend to produce a lot of full-color artwork in FreeHand, I heartily recommend that you purchase a comprehensive process color guide from a local printer or art supplies dealer. My personal favorite is the Trumatch ColorFinder, which lists for $85. It shows over 2,000 achievable colors, all printed from a computer. With such a guide in hand, you'll know precisely what your artwork should look like when printed, regardless of the calibration of your screen.

Creating and Organizing Colors____

FreeHand's color capabilities have always been a little difficult to understand, but they've seen slow but steady improvement. The first drawing program to offer color, FreeHand 1.0 supplied an entire menu devoted exclusively to defining colors. The arrangement was needlessly complicated and involved a lot of to-ing and fro-ing between dialog boxes. FreeHand 3.0 simplified things greatly by introducing a Colors palette and integrating all color definition functions into a single dialog box. But the interface didn't always make sense when you applied colors, especially to gradations.

FreeHand 4.0 introduces drag-and-drop colors, which means that you can actually drag a color directly onto an object. This feature makes applying colors much easier. But it relies on three palettes — Color List, Color Mixer, and Tints — where a palette and a dialog box used to suffice. Hopefully, the next revision of FreeHand will sport a single palette with easy access to all color application and definition functions.

Using the Color List palette

The central headquarters for FreeHand's coloring options is the Color List palette, which appears labeled to the gills in Figure 12-4. To display this palette, press Command-9. From the palette, you can fill objects, stroke objects, name colors, and arrange colors created in the Color Mixer and Tints palettes.

The following items explain how to perform a few general operations from this palette. Later sections in this chapter explain many operations in greater detail.

- ∽ **Filling an object:** Select the object, click on the fill icon, and click on a color name in the scrolling color list. (You have to click on a name; clicking on the color swatch itself produces no effect.) Alternatively, you can drag a color swatch from the palette and drop it onto an object.

- ∽ **Stroking an object:** Again, you select the object, click on the stroke icon, and click on a color name in the scrolling list. You can also drag from a color swatch and drop it onto the outline of a path, though this can be a little tricky.

- ∽ **Creating a new color:** Select the New option from the Options pop-up menu to take the color defined in the Color Mixer palette and make it a new item in the scrolling list. FreeHand automatically assigns the color a name such as *Color-3*.

- ∽ **Cloning a color:** Click on a color name in the scrolling list and select the Duplicate option from the Options pop-up menu to clone a color. Or just drag a swatch from the scrolling list to the new color icon. You can then rename the color and edit it if desired.

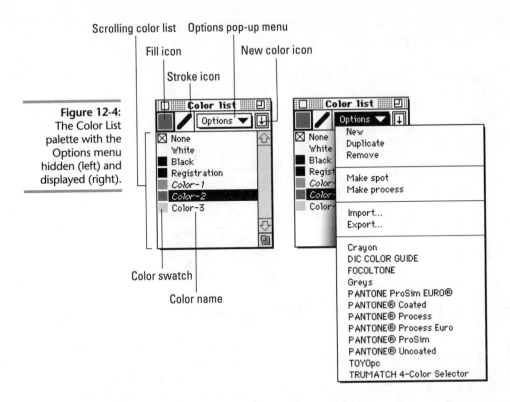

Scrolling color list   Options pop-up menu

Fill icon   New color icon

Stroke icon

Figure 12-4:
The Color List
palette with the
Options menu
hidden (left) and
displayed (right).

Color swatch

Color name

ↂ **Renaming a color:** Double-click on a color name to highlight it, enter the new name from the keyboard, and press the Return key. To cancel a name change, just click on a different color name. Press the Tab key (or Command-Tab) before double-clicking to avoid changing the color of a selected object. You cannot rename the White, Black, None, or Registration colors. (For more information on Registration, see Chapter 20, "Printing from FreeHand.")

ↂ **Editing a color:** To change a named color in the list — as well as all objects filled or stroked with that color — Option-click on the color swatch to transfer the color to the Color Mixer palette. (This assumes that the Color Mixer palette is available. If it's not, double-click on the color swatch.) Then edit the color as desired and drag it from the Color Mixer palette onto the color swatch in the scrolling color list, as demonstrated in Figure 12-5.

ↂ **Rearranging the order:** To change the order of names in the scrolling color list, drag a name up or down in the list.

ↂ **Deleting a color:** Press the Tab key (or Command-Tab) to deselect all objects. Then click on a color name in the scrolling list and select Remove from the Options pop-up menu to delete the color. If an object is filled or stroked with the color, or if the color is part of a tint or style (both defined later in this chapter), FreeHand doesn't let you delete the color.

⊷ **Get a color back:** You can retrieve a deleted color — or undo any other color operation — by pressing Command-Z.

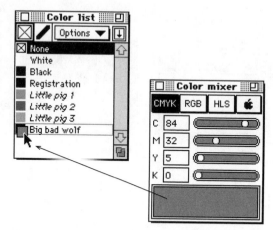

Dragging (and dropping) colors

In FreeHand 4.0, you can drag a color swatch from a palette and drop it onto an object or another color swatch in some other palette. To *drop* a color, incidentally, simply means to release the mouse button over a target. For example, if you were creating a flier for a dinner theater production of *Dumbo,* and your boss told you to drag the color pink and drop it onto a drawing of an elephant, you would drag the pink color swatch, position it over the elephant, and release the mouse button. It's like a little color bomb. *Feeeooo kaboom.* One pachyderm made psychedelic.

Dragging-and-dropping colors has two advantages. First, you can transfer colors between palettes quickly. Second, you can apply colors to objects without first selecting them. The limitation of dragging and dropping is that you can only color one object at a time. If you want to change multiple objects, select them, click on the fill or stroke icon, and click on a color name in the scrolling list.

Personally, I think that the term *drag and drop* is a waste of words. Why say "Drag A and drop it onto B" when you can say "Drag A onto B" and save a few words? With that in mind, here are a few ways to drag color swatches in FreeHand. Unless otherwise noted, these techniques work for dragging colors from any palette, including the Color List, Color Mixer, and Tints palettes as well as the Fill and Stroke panels of the Inspector palette.

☞ **Filling paths:** Drag a color from any palette into the middle of a closed path to fill the path with that color.

☞ **Filling type:** Drag a color swatch onto a character of type to fill the characters. If no type is selected, the color fills all characters in the text block. If one or more characters are selected with the text tool, only the selected characters are filled.

☞ **Filling a text block:** Drag a color swatch and drop it inside a text block — but not directly onto a character — to change the color of the interior of the text block.

☞ **Filling with a directional gradation:** Drag a color swatch and press the Control key before dropping the color to change a flat fill to a gradient fill. Use the same process to change the direction of an existing gradient fill. This technique does not work with characters of type, but it does work with text blocks. Also, the existing color of the object and the dragged color must both be process colors or tints of the same spot color.

☞ **Filling with a radial gradation:** Press the Option key before dropping the color to change the fill to a radial gradation or change the center of an existing radial gradation. The same limitations that apply to directional gradations govern radial ones.

☞ **Changing to a flat fill:** Press the Shift key before dropping a color to replace a gradation with a flat fill.

☞ **Stroking paths:** Drag a color onto the outline of a path to stroke the outline with the color. For some reason, this technique does not work with individual characters of type. But you can stroke a text block (provided that the Display Border check box in the Dimensions & Inset panel of the Inspector palette is selected).

☞ **Filling and stroking selections:** After selecting objects with the arrow tool or characters with the text tool, drag a color swatch onto the fill icon in the Color List palette to change the fill of all selected objects or characters. Drag a color onto the stroke icon to change the stroke of the selection or to add a 1-point stroke of that color if the object is strokeless.

☞ **Adding a color to the scrolling color list:** After defining a color in the Color Mixer palette, drag the color from the Color Mixer palette into an empty portion of the scrolling color list in the Color List palette. If the visible portion of the scrolling color list is full, drag the color onto the new color icon, as shown in Figure 12-6. (You can also drag from a color swatch in the Tints palette or from the swatch in the Fill or Stroke panel of the Inspector palette.)

Figure 12-6:
Drag from the color
area in the Color Mixer
palette onto the new
color icon in the Color
List palette (top) to add
a new color to the
scrolling list (bottom).

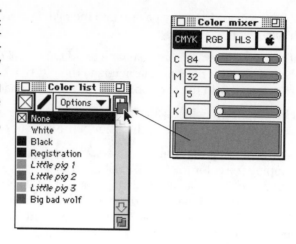

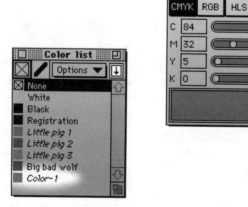

No doubt I'm overlooking some variation on the drag-and-drop motif, but you get the idea. You can replace any color inside or around an object or in a palette by simply dragging some other color around the screen.

Mixing colors

The Color Mixer palette lets you define colors by mixing primary hues in various quantities. It's like accidentally spilling some yellow paint and some blue paint on your kitchen floor, only to discover the perfect shade of avocado for painting your fridge and other major appliances. Except, of course, that you mix the colors on purpose and they aren't nearly so messy. Oh, and I suppose that FreeHand is more of an enamel than a semigloss.

 You can show and hide the Color Mixer palette by pressing Command-Shift-C. But perhaps more useful, you can show the Color Mixer and transfer a color to the palette by double-clicking on any color swatch in another palette. If the first double-click hides the palette, just double-click on the color swatch again to display the palette. (Hey, kids, it's a double-double-click!)

Double-clicking on a color swatch in the Tints or Inspector palette, incidentally, hides and shows both the Color Mixer and Color List palettes. I'm not sure how useful this is, but it's certainly worth a "Gee whiz."

 An even quicker and less click-intensive method of transferring a color into the Color Mixer palette is to Option-click on a color swatch. This technique works from inside the Color list and Tints palettes as well as from the Fill and Stroke panels.

You can access different *color models* by clicking on the first three icons along the top of the palette. (The last icon — the one with the Apple logo on it — is a button that brings up the Apple Color Picker dialog box, shown back in Figure 12-3.) Color models are different ways to define colors both on-screen and on the printed page. Figure 12-7 shows how each of the three color models defines a medium blue.

Figure 12-7:
The Color Mixer as it appears when each of the three color model icons is selected.

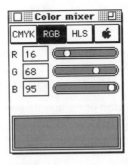

The following sections explain each color model in detail.

Using the CMYK color model

In nature, our eyes perceive pigments according to the *subtractive color model*. Sunlight contains every visible color found on earth. When sunlight is projected on an object, the object absorbs (subtracts) some of the light and reflects the rest. The reflected light is the color that you see. For example, a fire engine is bright red because it absorbs all non-red colors from the white-light spectrum.

Pigments on a sheet of paper work the same way. You can even mix pigments to create other colors. You might recall from second grade or thereabouts that you can mix red and yellow to make orange, yellow and blue to make green, and red and blue to make purple.

But what you learned in elementary school is only a rude approximation of the truth. Did you ever mix a vivid red with a canary yellow, only to produce a disappointingly drab orange, completely unrelated to the vibrant orange that your teacher had displayed? Talk about false advertising. The reason that you didn't achieve the vibrant orange you were hoping for is obvious if you stop and think about it. The fact that red starts out darker than bright orange means that you have to add a heck of a lot of yellow before you arrive at orange. And even then, you had better use an incredibly bright, lemon yellow, not some deep canary yellow that already has a lot of red in it.

The real subtractive primary colors used by commercial printers — cyan, magenta, and yellow — are for the most part very light. Cyan is a light blue; magenta is only a shade or two darker than pink; and yellow, well, you're probably familiar with yellow. Unfortunately, on their own, these colors don't do a very good job of producing dark colors. In fact, at full intensities, cyan, magenta, and yellow all mixed together don't get much beyond a muddy brown. That's where the nonlight color, black, comes in. Black helps to accentuate shadows, deepen dark colors, and, of course, print real blacks.

The colors in the CMYK (cyan, magenta, yellow, black) model mix as follows:

- ✑ **Cyan and magenta:** Full-intensity cyan and magenta mix to form a deep blue that tends toward violet. Subtract some cyan to make purple; subtract some magenta to make a dull medium blue. All of these colors assume a complete lack of yellow.

- ✑ **Magenta and yellow:** Full-intensity magenta and yellow mix to form a brilliant red. Subtract some magenta to make vivid orange; subtract some yellow to make rose. All of these colors assume a complete lack of cyan.

- **Yellow and cyan:** Full-intensity yellow and cyan mix to form a medium green with a surprising amount of blue in it. Subtract some yellow to make a deep teal; subtract some cyan to make chartreuse. All of these colors assume a complete lack of magenta.

- **Cyan, magenta, and yellow:** Full-intensity cyan, magenta, and yellow mix to form a muddy brown.

- **Black:** Black pigmentation added to any other pigment darkens the color.

- **No pigment:** No pigmentation results in white (assuming that white is the color of the paper).

When the CMYK icon is selected in the Color Mixer palette, FreeHand provides one option box and one slider bar each for cyan, magenta, yellow, and black ink. The values represent percentages from 0 for no color (or white) to 100 for full-intensity color.

Using the RGB color model

RGB is the color model of light. It comprises three primary colors — red, green, and blue — each of which can vary in *intensity* from 0 (no hue) to 65,535 (full intensity). The RGB model is also called the *additive primary model* because a color becomes lighter as you add higher levels of red, green, and blue light. All monitors, projection devices, and other items that transmit or filter light — including televisions, movie projectors, colored stage lights, even stained glass — rely on the additive primary model.

Red, green, and blue light mix as follows:

- **Red and green:** Full-intensity red and green mix to form yellow. Subtract some red to make chartreuse; subtract some green to make orange. All of these colors assume a complete lack of blue.

- **Green and blue:** Full-intensity green and blue with no red mix to form cyan. If you try hard enough, you can come up with 65,000 colors in the turquoise/jade/ sky blue/sea green range.

- **Blue and red:** Full-intensity blue and red mix to form magenta. Subtract some blue to make rose; subtract some red to make purple. All of these colors assume a complete lack of green.

- **Red, green, and blue:** Full-intensity red, green, and blue mix to form white, the absolute brightest color in the visible spectrum.

- **No light:** Low intensities of red, green, and blue plunges a color into blackness.

When you select the RGB icon in the Color Mixer palette, FreeHand provides option boxes and slider bars for red, green, and blue light. The values represent percentages from 0 for no light (or black) to 100 for full-intensity color. If you look closely at Figure 12-7, you'll notice that the values in the C, M, and Y option boxes are the opposite of their values in the R, G, and B options. For example, 100 percent minus 84 percent, the cyan value, equals 16 percent, the red value. This relationship exists because each of the primary pigments has an exact opposite in the primary lights. The only difference is that pigments are less pure and therefore tend to produce less dependable colors than lights.

Using the HLS color model

As I explained earlier, the Apple Color Wheel dialog box allows you to edit colors according to the HSB — hue, saturation, brightness — color model. If you click on the HLS icon in the Color Mixer palette, FreeHand provides access to the similar HLS color model, which stands for hue, luminosity, and saturation.

In either case, *hue* is pure color — the stuff rainbows are made of — measured on a 360-degree circle. Red is located at 0 degrees, yellow at 60 degrees, green at 120 degrees, cyan at 180 degrees (midway around the circle), blue at 240 degrees, and magenta at 300 degrees. It's basically a pie-shaped version of the RGB model at full-intensity.

Saturation represents the purity of the color. A zero saturation value equals gray. White, black, and other shades of gray have no saturation. Full saturation produces the purest version of a hue.

Brightness is the lightness or darkness of a color. A brightness value of zero equals black. Full brightness combined with full saturation results in the most vivid version of any hue. *Luminosity* (also called *lightness*) — the *L* in *HLS* — is slightly but significantly different than brightness. Zero luminosity still equals black, but full luminosity turns any hue or saturation value to white. Therefore, medium luminosity is required to produce the most vivid version of any hue.

When you select the HLS icon in the Color Mixer palette, FreeHand provides three options boxes — one each for hue, luminosity, and saturation — along with a wheel and a slider bar. Like the wheel in the Apple Color Picker, the perimeter of the wheel measures hue, and the interior portions control saturation. The slider bar adjusts luminosity.

Process colors, spot colors, and tints

Normally, every color that you define in the Color Mixer dialog box is a *process color*. This means that Freehand ends up separating the color into its cyan, magenta, yellow, and black components during the printing process even if you defined the color using the RGB or HLS color model. After all, colors on paper must use pigments.

Process-color printing is a very economical solution because it permits you to create a rainbow of colors using only cyan, magenta, yellow, and black ink. But it's not sufficient for all jobs. Suppose that you can only afford two inks — black and some other color. You don't want to use cyan, magenta, or yellow; in fact, you were thinking of forest green. It doesn't make sense to pay for cyan, magenta, and yellow just to mix one shade of green, especially when your printer can supply the precise shade of forest green ink that you want already mixed and ready to go. These premixed inks are called *spot colors*.

Although process inks provide access to a wide range of colors, there's an equal number of colors that they can't produce. Some people are very picky and refuse to settle for a process-color approximation of the color they want to use. For example, if you turn over a six-pack of Miller Genuine Draft beer — not that I've ever swilled the stuff, of course — you'll see five color marks, one each for our friends cyan, magenta, yellow, and black, plus a fifth for a spot color, goldenrod. A casual glance suggests that this goldenrod is hardly different than the process yellow. Surely if you threw in a smidgen of magenta and a pinch of cyan, you could get a similar color. But Miller Brewing Company apparently thought differently. Hence, the specialized goldenrod ink.

Using pre-mixed spot colors

You can access spot colors in FreeHand in two ways. The first and most popular option is to load one or more spot colors from the libraries included with FreeHand. Pantone is the primary supplier of spot-color inks in the United States; Dianippon Ink and Chemicals (DIC) serves this same function in Japan.

If you're not familiar with either of these organizations, you're probably thinking, "There are companies out there that sell *colors*?" It's true, Pantone and DIC are in the business of providing professional spot-color inks. They've designed standardized collections of colors that any printer with access to their custom primary inks can mix using a list of recipes. This ensures standardization, so that whether you print a document in Milwaukee, Wisconsin or Golden, Colorado (home of Miller and Coors, respectively), your beer boxes come out the same.

To add a spot color to the scrolling list in the Color List palette, select one of the options from the bottom portion of the Options pop-up menu in the Color List palette. The options that bring up spot-color libraries are DIC Color Guide, Pantone ProSim Euro, Pantone Coated, Pantone ProSim, and Pantone Uncoated. (All the Pantone options bring up the same basic colors designed for different paper stocks.)

After you select a library option, a dialog box filled with colors appears, as shown in Figure 12-8. You can scroll through the library by clicking in the scroll bar at the bottom of the dialog box. Click and Shift-click on the colors you want to add to the scrolling list in the Color List palette. After you select all the colors you expect to use, press Return.

Figure 12-8:
All colors you select from a color library appear in the scrolling list in the Color List palette.

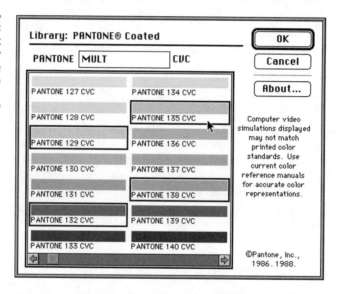

The second method for selecting a spot color is to create one yourself. This assumes that you know that your commercial printer can match the color with a premixed ink. Generally, you'll only use this option when working for clients who have had a few spot colors specially designed for their companies, as in the case of Miller's goldenrod.

To create your own spot color, first create a color normally in the Color Mixer palette. Drag the completed color onto the new color icon in the Color List palette, click on the color name, and select the Make Spot option from the Options pop-up menu. FreeHand changes the formatting of the color name from italic type, which indicates a process color, to upright type, which indicates a spot color.

For complete information on process- and spot-color printing, read Chapter 20, "Printing from FreeHand."

Creating tints

In FreeHand, a spot color isn't just one color, it's as many as 99 colors, each varying slightly in tint from 100 percent intensity down to 1 percent, so-light-it-probably-won't-print intensity. Tints can be especially useful for establishing shadows and highlights without having to purchase another color.

 When creating black-and-white artwork, tints are your means for creating shades of gray. Simply use black as the base color, as shown in Figure 12-9. You can also create tints of process colors. These tints are separated into their CMYK components when printed from FreeHand, just like any other process colors.

To create a tint, start by dragging the color on which you want to base the tint into the Base box in the Tints palette. In Figure 12-9, this color is Black, as it is by default. The Tints palette automatically creates nine variations on the color, ranging from 10 to 90 percent in 10 percent increments. You can specify some other tint by entering a value into the option box at the bottom of the palette or by using the slider bar.

Figure 12-9:
The Tints palette lets you create a
shade of an existing color.

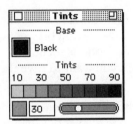

To add a tint to the scrolling color list, drag the color from any of the ten swatches at the bottom of the Tints palette and drop it onto the new color icon in the Color List palette. FreeHand is incapable of automatically naming the color something sensible like *30% Black*, so you have to rename the color manually.

Using color libraries

Because the process of defining colors is time consuming, and because you may want to use the same colors in many documents, FreeHand enables you to organize colors into libraries that you can load into any illustration.

To give you a few examples, FreeHand includes 12 libraries in the Color folder inside the Aldus folder, which is in the System folder. Five are the spot-color libraries from DIC and Pantone. Five are process-color libraries from other color companies such as Trumatch, Focoltone, and Toyo. (Pantone also includes two sets of process-color versions of its spot colors.) And the last two are just for fun. The Crayon library contains 64 colors such as Aquamarine, Cornflower, Mulberry, and Seafoam. And Greys includes every possible tint of black expressed both as process and spot colors.

To open a library, select the desired option from the bottom portion of the Options pop-up menu in the Color List palette. A dialog box filled with a scrolling list of colors appears, as shown back in Figure 12-8. The Options pop-up menu lists every library inside the Color folder in the Aldus folder. If a library is located elsewhere on disk, select the Import option and locate the library file using the controls in the Open Color Library dialog box.

The following steps explain how to create your own library:

STEPS: Creating a Color Library

Step 1. Select Export from the Options pop-up menu.

Step 2. A dialog box appears, asking you to select the colors from the Color List palette that you want to save to the library. Click and Shift-click on the colors as desired. To select several colors at a time, drag across the color names in the palette. Then press Return.

Step 3. FreeHand displays a dialog box like the one shown at the top of Figure 12-10. In the Library Name option box, enter name of the library as you want it to appear in the Options menu. In the File Name option box, enter the name under which you want to save the file.

Step 4. The Preference values control the number of columns and rows that appear in the dialog box when you open the library. For example, the Pantone library shown in Figure 12-8 was created by changing the Colors per Column value to 7 and the Colors per Row value to 2.

Step 5. If you like, enter some general information into the Notes field. You can access this information later by clicking on the About button in the Library dialog box, as illustrated in the second example in Figure 12-10.

Step 6. To save the library with the other libraries in the Color folder, click on the Save button. FreeHand adds the library to the bottom of the Options submenu. If you'd rather save the file elsewhere, click on the Save As button.

After you finish saving the library, try selecting its option from the Options pop-up menu in the Color List palette. The contents of the library appear in a dialog box, as shown at the bottom of Figure 12-10. You can now import colors from this library into other documents.

Figure 12-10:
After saving a
library file (top),
you can later
open it and
access the Notes
information by
clicking on the
About button
(bottom).

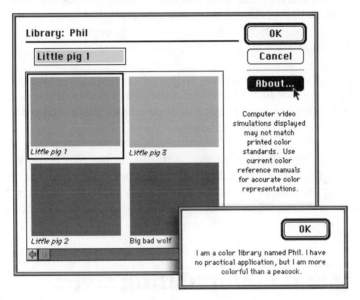

Using Attribute Styles

FreeHand's Styles palette, shown in Figure 12-11, is a time-saving feature that many
people overlook. You can display this palette by pressing Command-3. The Styles
palette contains a list of named *attribute styles* that you can use to control all aspects of
the fills and strokes of paths. By creating a style, you can apply a complex set of attributes with a single click of the mouse button. If you later decide that you want to
change the attributes, you just edit the style. FreeHand automatically applies the new
attributes to all objects (in the current illustration) to which you had applied the
original style.

Figure 12-11:
The Styles palette as it appears normally (left) and with pop-up menu displayed (right).

Attribute styles automate the process of filling and stroking graphic objects. They make it possible to define a set of fill and stroke attributes only once and then use those attributes an unlimited number of times — a major time- and energy-saver. Without styles, you must assign attributes again and again during the creation of a drawing, meaning several trips to FreeHand's many color palettes, not to mention the Fill and Stroke panels. Using styles also ensures consistency throughout an illustration; every object to which a single style is applied is colored identically.

 Alas, you cannot apply a style to characters of text. This would be extremely useful, not only for fill and stroke, but also for typeface, style, size, and so on. If you want to apply a style to type, you must first convert the type to paths by choosing Type ➪ Convert to Paths.

 Attribute styles also store custom halftone settings, which you specify in the Halftone palette. Because halftone settings specifically affect printing, they're covered in the "Halftone screens" section of Chapter 20. You may have also noticed that I have yet to discuss most fill and stroke options; these are the subjects of Chapters 13 and 14, respectively.

Creating and manipulating styles

To create a new style, apply the desired fill and stroke attributes to a graphic object. Then select the object and select New from the Options pop-up menu in the Styles palette. FreeHand adds a new style name, which it calls *Style-1* or something along those lines, to the scrolling list in the palette. You can rename the style by double-clicking on it, entering a new name, and pressing Return.

If no object is selected when you select the New option, the Styles palette grabs the default fill and stroke attributes. You can use this technique to capture fill and stroke settings that you want to use later but that aren't applicable to the objects you've created so far.

To apply your new style — or any other style — to another object in the document, select the object and click on the style name in the palette. Not only does the object immediately gain all fill and stroke attributes assigned to the style, it becomes *tagged* to the style. From now on, any changes you make to the style affect the tagged object as well. The next section explains how this process works.

Redefining styles

Editing styles is slightly more involved than creating them. Here are the steps:

STEPS: Editing an Attribute Style

Step 1. Press Tab to deselect all objects.

Step 2. Click on the style you want to edit. FreeHand makes the fill and stroke attributes the default attributes. (If the style was already selected but it has a plus sign next to it, click on some other style and then click on the desired style. I explain the significance of the plus sign in the next section.) This provides you with a starting point.

Step 3. Edit the settings in the Fill and Stroke panels of the Inspector palette as desired.

Step 4. Select the Redefine option in the Options pop-up menu of the Styles palette. A dialog box appears, asking you which style you want to redefine. Click on the style name and press the Return key. The style is now redefined.

Alternatively, you can edit the fill and stroke attributes of an object to which the style is already applied and then select the Redefine option. However, this strategy can lead to some weirdness on FreeHand's part. Suppose that you select an object that is tagged to Style A and use it as a jumping off point for redefining another style, Style B. After you define Style B, FreeHand reapplies Style A to the object, which upsets the edits you've made to the object's attributes. You then have to apply Style B to the object to restore the edits. It's not the end of the world, but it can be disconcerting, which is why I prefer to redefine styles while no object is selected.

The effect of style changes on tagged objects

Editing a style has the added effect of refilling and stroking every object tagged to that style, which is a great way to make global changes. Let's say that you drew several Norwegians sunbathing on a beach. The objects that make up their faces, arms, legs, belly buttons, and other exposed bits are tagged to a style called Sickly Pale. If you change the fill of the style from greenish peach to golden brown, you give the sunbathers automatic tans. Change the fill to brick red, and you give them a nasty burn, all without so much as selecting a single object.

This brings up an interesting phenomenon: *Every* object you create in FreeHand is tagged to some style or other. When you draw an object, FreeHand tags it to the default style, which is generally the last style used. If you've never touched the Styles palette, all your objects are tagged to the factory-default style, Normal. The original settings for Normal are a transparent fill and a 1-point black stroke. You'll notice that as you assign other fill and stroke attributes to objects, FreeHand displays a plus sign to the left of the word Normal, showing that the object is still tagged to the style but does not subscribe to all of the style's attributes.

If the tagged object matches the style in some respects and not others, what happens when you redefine the style? The answer is that the similar attributes change and the different ones don't. Suppose that an object tagged to the Normal style has a transparent fill with a 1-point red stroke. The only difference between the object and the style is the color of the stroke. If you edit the Normal style to include a yellow fill and a 13-point purple stroke, the object updates to include a yellow fill and a 13-point line weight, but the color of the stroke remains red.

Duplicating attribute styles

You can duplicate styles in two ways:

- ☞ Click on a style name and select the Duplicate option from the Options pop-up menu in the Styles palette.
- ☞ Click on a style name and select New from the Options pop-up menu.

That's right — both techniques produce identical results. In either case, you create a new style based on an existing one. What's more, the new style — I'll call it *Bubba Junior* — is tagged to the style you duplicated — *Bubba Senior.* What we've got here is a classic parent/child relationship.

The connection between a parent style and its child is the same as that between a style and a tagged object. When you change the parent style, all child style attributes that match the parent style attributes — blue fill, 4-point line weight, hairy arms — change as well. If you want to break the bond between parent and child — you heartless home-wrecker — click on the child in the Styles palette and select the Set Parent option from the pop-up menu. A dialog box asks you to select a new adoptive parent, such as Charles H. Maudlin III. When you press Return, FreeHand juggles the family structure and replaces Bubba Senior with Charles III. FreeHand also changes any attributes that Bubba Junior shared with Bubba Senior so that they match Chaz. For example, if both Bubbas had blue fills, and Chaz is filled with a mallard green to walnut brown gradation, Bubba Junior's fill changes to the gradation as well.

It's really sad, actually. When Bubba Junior visits the old homestead these days, the family hardly recognizes him. He doesn't even watch football anymore.

Cutting and copying

You can transfer styles from one document to another by cutting or copying objects. Just select one or more objects that are tagged to one or more styles, cut or copy the objects (Command-C or Command-X), switch to another open document, and paste the objects (Command-V).

To delete a style without sending it to the Clipboard, click on the style and select Remove from the options pop-up menu in the Styles palette. All objects tagged to the style are then tagged to the parent style.

Summary

- ⇢ You can create a color document in FreeHand even if your computer is equipped with a black-and-white monitor. You just have to use a little more imagination.

- ⇢ If the colors in your printed documents look markedly different than their on-screen counterparts, use the Display Color Setup dialog box to customize the appearance of cyan, magenta, and yellow color combinations.

- ⇢ Drag a color swatch onto the new color icon in the Color List panel to add a new color name to the scrolling list.

- ⇢ You can drag color swatches onto objects to fill and stroke them.

- ⇢ Option-click on a color swatch to transfer the color to the Color Mixer palette, where you can edit it.

- ⇢ Double-click on a color swatch in any palette to hide or show the Color List and/or Color Mixer palettes.

- ⇢ Cyan, magenta, yellow, and black inks mix to create a wide range of pigments. You can use spot colors to augment these pigments.

- ⇢ Generally speaking, red light is the opposite of cyan pigment; green light is the opposite of magenta pigment; and blue light is the opposite of yellow pigment. Black ink helps make up for the lightness of cyan, magenta, and yellow.

➥ Use tints to create lightened shades of a spot color. (You can also create tints of process colors.)

➥ All color libraries in the Color folder inside the Aldus folder appear in the Options pop-up menu in the Color List palette.

➥ After you tag one or more objects to an attribute style (from the Styles palette), you can change all objects at once without selecting them by editing the style.

➥ For a color version of this book, please mail this coupon with one dollar to, "Send Me a Crayon! Box 64, Greenland." Please wait 30 years to life for delivery.

Flat Fills and Gradations

▪▪

In This Chapter

➤ Applying transparent and flat fills

➤ Overprinting colors from different separations

➤ Creating directional and radial gradations

➤ Managing and modifying bitmapped and object-oriented patterns

➤ Transforming tile patterns

➤ Using FreeHand's predefined PostScript fill routines

▪▪

The Benefits of Fill

If FreeHand didn't give you the ability to fill objects, your paths and character outlines would be without substance and form. *Fill* — the colors, textures, and patterns that you assign to the interior of your paths — is like the skin wrapped around the skeleton of a path. Without an opaque fill, no object could cover another. You could see through the bones of one object to the bones of the objects behind it. This is why the best drawing programs — including FreeHand — invest heavily in the core functions of path drawing, filling, and printing. If FreeHand were less capable in any one of these categories, the power of the program would be greatly diminished; functions beyond these qualify either as convenience features or special effects.

Why all this hoopla over assigning a color to the interior of a path? Think about it. Together, fill and stroke are all that separate the Etch-A-Sketch keyline mode from the preview mode. If push came to shove, you could do without stroke by drawing thin shapes — like those produced by the freehand tool when the Variable Stroke option is active — and filling them. But there's no getting around fill. It enables you to shade objects, create shadows and highlights, or simply add color to a document. Fill is what fools your viewer into perceiving your abstract objects as representations of real life.

How fill affects objects

In FreeHand, you can fill any path or text block. When a closed path is filled, its entire interior is affected. Figure 13-1 shows a closed path as it appears in the keyline and preview modes. The shape acts like a kind of malleable water balloon — the fill seeps into every nook and cranny of the outline.

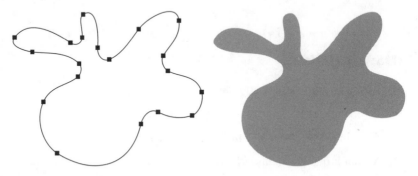

Figure 13-1:
A filled shape shown in the keyline (left) and preview (right) mode.

Although you can assign a fill to an open path, the fill doesn't preview nor print. I filled the open path in the first example in Figure 13-2 with gray. However, the fill didn't display until I closed the path, as shown in the second example in the figure.

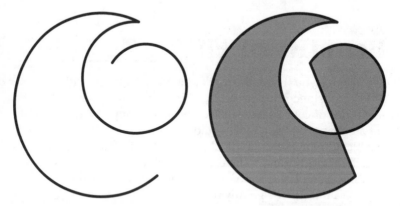

Figure 13-2:
The fill of an open path (left) doesn't preview or print until you close the path.

It's too bad that FreeHand can't display or print the fill of an open path, because filled paths with unstroked edges can be useful for establishing indefinite boundaries between shapes — boundaries that are implied by the surrounding shapes rather than spelled out with stroke. However, you can get around the deficiency. Notice in Figure 13-3 that the forward and rear wings on the port side of the plane (the side facing the viewer) look like they're open paths. If either path were closed, after all, you'd see a closing segment at the junction of the wing and the plane. And yet the wings are obviously filled, because they cover the portions of the plane behind them.

Figure 13-3:
Each of the port
wings comprises
two paths: one
closed and filled;
and one open
and stroked.

How do you create such a drawing? Well, here's how I did it — and how I recommend that you go about it, too. First, I created the port wings as two closed paths and assigned a white fill and a transparent stroke to each path. Then I cloned both paths, deleted the closing segment from each of the clones, removed the fills, and applied black strokes. So each of the wings is actually two paths, one closed and filled and one open and stroked.

Figure 13-4 shows a blow-out view of the plane that reveals some additional applications of this technique. I combined pairs of identically shaped paths — one filled and the other stroked — to create the body of the plane and the starboard wing.

Figure 13-4:
A blow-out view
of the plane from
Figure 13-3.

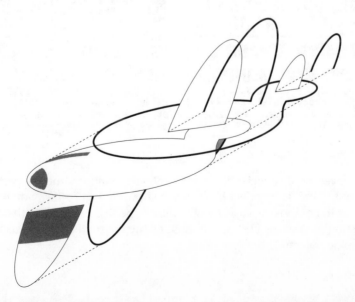

How fill affects text

You can also fill text objects. If you select a text object with the arrow tool and apply a fill, the fill affects the text object independently of the characters of type inside the object, as illustrated in Figure 13-5.

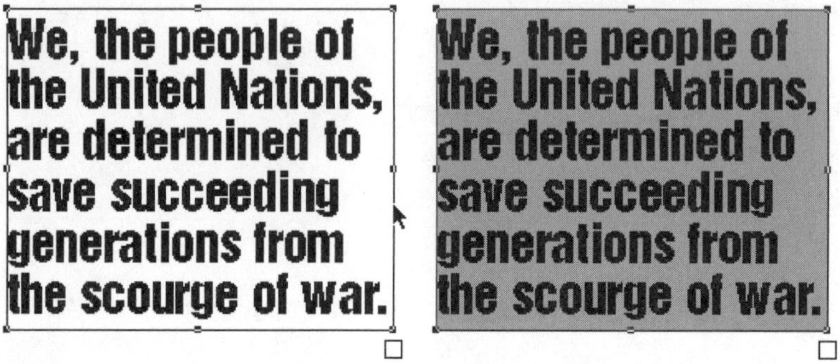

Figure 13-5:
If you apply a fill to a text block that was selected with the arrow tool (left), the fill affects the block and not the text (right).

To fill one or more characters of text without affecting the text block, select the characters with the text tool and then apply the fill. Figure 13-6 shows the result of applying a white fill to a few characters after filling the block with gray.

Figure 13-6:
If you select characters with the text tool (left), you can fill them without affecting other characters.

You can't, however, apply special fill effects such as gradations and tile patterns to type. If you want to create an effect like the one shown in Figure 13-7, you have to first convert the text to composite paths by choosing Type ⇨ Convert to Paths, as discussed in the last section of Chapter 11. You can then fill the character outlines as if they were any other graphic objects.

Assigning Flat Fills

To fill an object, you can drag a color onto it as described in the last chapter. You can even use modifier keys such as Control and Option to create gradations. But to access textures, tiles, and other special fill patterns as well as gain full control over gradations, there's no substitute for the Fill panel inside the Inspector palette.

To access this panel, press Command-Option-F. As shown in Figure 13-8, the panel sports a pop-up menu that lets you access different kinds of fills, all of which are covered in this chapter. When you select any of these menu options, FreeHand displays a new set of options that you use to design the particular fill.

Figure 13-8:
Click on the pop-up menu in the Fill panel to access various fill patterns and gradations.

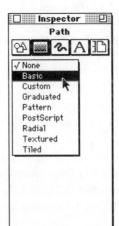

Transparent fills

The first two options in the pop-up menu enable you to accomplish basically the same thing as dragging and dropping color swatches from the Color List palette. They apply a single flat fill, which can either be transparent or an opaque color. For example, to make the interior of a selected object transparent, you can use any of the following techniques with absolutely identical degrees of success:

- ↪ Select the object and then select the None option from the pop-up menu in the Fill palette.
- ↪ Select the object, click on the fill icon in the Color List palette, and click on the None color name in the scrolling list.
- ↪ Select the object and drag the None color swatch — the one that looks like a box with an inset X — onto the fill icon in the Color List palette.
- ↪ Whether the object is selected or not, drag the None color swatch from the Color List palette onto the object.

Now, I don't know about you, but the last technique sounds the easiest to me. No selecting involved, no extra steps, just drag and drop. In fact, the only reason to use any of the other techniques is if you want to make multiple objects transparent. In that case, it's generally easier to select all the objects and apply the None option inside a palette.

Making the fill transparent is useful when you want to see only the stroke as well as see through the path to the objects behind it. You can even apply both a transparent stroke and a transparent fill to create an entirely transparent path that is visible in the keyline mode only. You can use such a path for alignment purposes or to surround an image that you intend to export as an EPS file, as described in the "Exporting an Illustration" section of Chapter 18.

 You can't make characters of type completely transparent. They either have to have a fill or stroke. By default, the stroke is already transparent, so you can't make the fill transparent as well. If you apply the None option to type selected with the text tool, FreeHand ignores you. You have to convert the characters to paths before you can make them completely transparent.

Single-color fills

The second option in the Fill panel pop-up menu is Basic, which applies a single color to the interior of an object. When you select Basic, a color swatch and an Overprint check box appear in the Fill panel of the Inspector palette. As shown in Figure 13-9, the only way to change the color swatch is to drag a swatch from the Color List, Color Mixer, or

Tints palette onto it. So why not simply drag the color directly onto the object and remove the middleman? The answer is, there is no reason. Even if you want to apply colors to multiple objects, it's quicker to select the objects and drag the color swatch to the fill icon in the Color List panel than to deal with the Basic option.

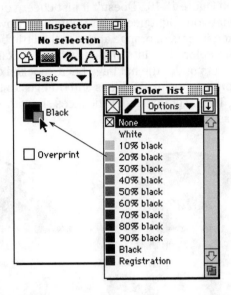

Figure 13-9:
To change the color of a flat fill, drag a color swatch from some other palette onto the color swatch in the fill panel.

If an object is filled with a gradation or pattern, and you want to change it to a flat fill, drag a color swatch over the object, press and hold the Shift key, and drop the color. (Be sure to release the Shift key *after* releasing your mouse button.)

Overprinting colors

The only reason to so much as display the Fill panel when an object is filled with a uniform color is to access the Overprint check box. This option controls whether the color inside the selected object mixes with the colors of the objects behind it — known as *overprinting*. When this option is selected, an object is allowed to overprint the object behind it, provided that the colors of the overlapping objects are printed to different separations.

For more information on color separations, see Chapters 12 and 20.

Suppose that your drawing consists of three spot colors: black, orange, and blue. Orange can overprint blue, blue can overprint orange, and either can overprint or be overprinted by black, because orange, blue, and black print to their own separations. However, a 30 percent tint of blue cannot overprint a 70 percent tint of blue, because all blue objects print to the same separation.

If the Overprint check box is deselected, as it is by default, portions of an object covered by another object are *knocked out*; that is, they don't print when the two objects are output to different separations.

Take a look at the faces in Figure 13-10. (Doesn't it just cheer you right up to see these happy faces? I thought that you might need a lift right about now.) Imagine that the faces are filled and stroked in tints of orange and that the little berets — these are French smiley faces — are colored in tints of blue. In the left example in the figure, the portion of the orange objects under the hat have been knocked out. In the right example, the objects overprint, allowing the blues and oranges to blend, giving the hat a translucent appearance. The diagrams under the faces show the hat and faces as they appear when printed to separate pages.

Figure 13-10: An orange face with a blue hat as it appears when the Overprint option is deselected (left) and selected (right).

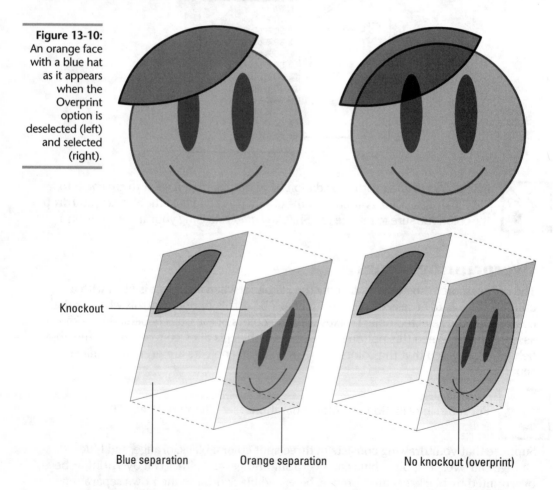

Knockout

Blue separation   Orange separation   No knockout (overprint)

The Overprint option makes no difference in grayscale or black-and-white illustrations that don't require separations. If the selected object is filled with one or more process colors, only those colors on different separations overprint. For example, if you apply the Overprint option to Object A, which is filled with 100 percent cyan and 20 percent magenta, and the object behind it, Object B, is filled with 50 percent magenta and 100 percent yellow, the intersection of the two objects will be filled with 100 percent cyan, *20 percent magenta*, and 100 percent yellow. The magenta value from Object A wins out — even though it's lighter than the magenta value in Object B — because overprinting doesn't affect colors on the same separation.

The problem with the Overprint option is that is doesn't display correctly on-screen, nor does it proof correctly to color printers. There's no way to tell by looking at an object on-screen whether it overprints or not.

 If you want to mix the colors in overlapping objects and see the results, select the two objects and press the Option key while choosing Arrange ➪ Path Operations ➪ Intersect. FreeHand displays the Transparency dialog box, described in the "Intersect" section of Chapter 7.

Option-choosing the Intersect command gives you added flexibility because it doesn't rely on color separations. For example, if you applied this technique to Objects A and B from a couple of paragraphs back, the new path created by the command would be filled with 100 percent cyan, *50 percent magenta*, and 100 percent yellow.

The result is heck of a lot more logical, and you can see it on-screen. The only downside is that you have to apply strokes to the new path manually because Option-choosing Intersect always produces a path with no stroke.

Lifting the color of a fill

Actually, the Basic option in the Fill panel has one additional use. If you work like I do, you rarely name colors and put them into the Color List palette like you're supposed to. It's just too much work. It's so much simpler to mix a color and drag it directly onto an object from the Color Mixer palette.

But this kind of flagrant laziness can get you into a bind. For example, what do you do if you want to modify the color of an object slightly or take the color of one object and apply it to another? It's highly unlikely that you will be able to remember the ingredients of the color, even if it's only a gray value. And unlike most other graphics programs, FreeHand doesn't provide an eyedropper tool for lifting a color from an object.

The solution is simple. Select the object, display the Fill panel of the Inspector palette, and Option-click on the color swatch in the panel. The color is immediately transferred to the Color Mixer. You can then edit the color or drag it onto the new color icon in the Color List palette for future use.

I know that I already explained how Option-clicking transfers a color to the Color Mixer palette in the previous chapter. But this is a slightly different and sufficiently common way to use the technique that I figured it warranted another mention.

Applying Gradient Fills

A *gradient fill* (also called a *gradation*) fades from one color to another inside an object. FreeHand provides two options in the Fill panel pop-up menu for creating gradations. The Graduated option creates gradations that fade in a constant direction, whether from top to bottom (as in the top example in Figure 13-11), side to side, or whatever. The Radial option creates gradations that flow outward in concentric circles, as in the second example in the figure.

Figure 13-11:
Gradations created by selecting the Graduated (top) and Radial (bottom) options.

Directional gradations

The Graduated option sounds as if it should give the selected object a high-school diploma or at least a certificate in VCR repair. But it really displays options for changing the colors and direction of a gradient fill. When you select Graduated from the Fill panel pop-up menu, as shown in Figure 13-12, FreeHand displays the following options:

⌐♦ **Color swatches:** Drag colors into the From and To color swatches to specify the first and last colors in a gradation. No more than two colors are permitted in a single gradation. You can use gray values, process colors, and tints of the same spot color in a single gradation. You can't use different spot colors or create a gradation from a spot color to a gray value or process color. (Keep in mind that default Black is a spot color.)

Figure 13-12:
Select Graduated from the Fill panel pop-up menu to display options for specifying the colors, speed, and direction of a gradation.

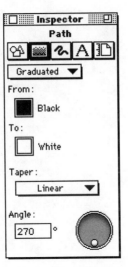

⌐♦ **Taper:** This pop-up menu provides two options that control the speed at which the first and last colors fade together. Select the Linear option to create a *linear gradation* in which every increment between the first and last colors is emphasized equally. Select the Logarithmic option to create a *logarithmic gradation*, which fades quickly at first and then more slowly as the gradation progresses. The result is a gradation that favors the last color over the first.

Figure 13-13 (the unluckiest figure on earth) shows two shapes filled with black-to-white gradations that flow in identical directions. The only difference is that the top gradation is linear and the bottom is logarithmic. Rectangles highlight the locations of medium gray, which is the middle color in either gradation. The medium gray is smack dab in the middle of the shape in the linear gradation, but it's scooted toward the From color of the shape in the second gradation. Less space is devoted to colors darker than medium gray than colors lighter than medium gray.

Figure 13-13:
A shape filled with a linear gradation (top) and another filled with a logarithmic gradation (bottom).

50% gray

50% gray

↦ **Angle:** This option controls the direction of the gradation. You can enter a value in degrees into the Angle option box or drag the knob around the perimeter of the wheel. The option box value and knob work dynamically with each other. If you enter 90 into the option box, the knob moves around to the 12 o'clock position, and so on. The default angle is 270 degrees, which is straight down. (Incidentally, if you liked being able to Shift-drag the knob in 5-degree increments in past versions of FreeHand, so sorry. This function was lost in the transition to Version 4.0.)

The top fill in Figure 13-14 shows the results of setting the Angle value to 45 degrees and using a From color of black and a To color of white. The lower path contains identical From and To colors, but the Angle value is changed to 225 degrees, forcing the gradation to progress in the opposite direction.

Figure 13-14:
Shapes filled with a 45-degree angle gradation (top) and a 225-degree angle gradation (bottom).

Together, the From, To, Taper, and Angle options can be used to create just about any directional gradation. The following steps explain how you can use all the options in combination to change a black-to-white gradation that favors white to one that favors black.

STEPS: Flipping the Colors and Direction of a Gradation

Step 1. Select a closed path and press Command-Option-F to display the Fill panel of the Inspector palette. (If the Inspector palette is missing, press Command-I and then Command-Option-F.) Select Graduated from pop-up option at the top of the panel.

Step 2. Drag the black color swatch from the Color List palette onto the From swatch in the Fill panel. Drag the white swatch from the Color List palette onto the To swatch. (This step may not be necessary because black and white are the Default To and From colors.)

Step 3.   Select Logarithmic from the Taper pop-up option.

Step 4.   Change the Angle value to 225 degrees and press Return. The result is a fill that fades from right to left, quickly at first and slowly toward the end, as seen in the first example of Figure 13-15. Suppose, however, that this effect isn't what you want. You're happy with the direction and the colors, but you want to emphasize black and play down white. Unfortunately, the Logarithmic option *always* stresses the To color. So you're stuck, right? Not at all. You just have to flip the colors and flip the direction while leaving the Logarithmic option alone.

Figure 13-15: Two shapes filled with logarithmic gradations, each of which uses different first and last colors and flows in the opposite direction of the other.

Step 5.   Inside the Fill panel, change the Angle value to 45 degrees, the exact opposite of 225 degrees.

Step 6.   Swap the From and To colors. Here's a fun way to do it: Option-click on the black From swatch to transfer it to the Color Mixer. Now drag the white To swatch onto the From swatch to make the From color white. Finally, drag the black from the Color Mixer palette onto the To swatch.

Your path now contains a gradation that appears to flow in the same direction as before and between the same colors. However, black now receives more emphasis than white because black is now the To color.

 To change the colors of a gradation without fussing with the From and To options, just drag a color swatch and drop it onto the desired end of an object. If you drop the swatch onto the side of the shape favored by the first color, you replace the first color; if you drop it onto the neighborhood occupied by the last color, you replace the last color.

To change the direction of a gradation, press and hold the Control key while dropping the color. Control-dropping always replaces the To color in the Fill panel (so be sure not to Control-drop the color that appears in the From swatch or you'll create what looks like a solid fill).

 Although FreeHand can't automate the gradation of more than two colors, you can create more complex gradations by using the Blend command, as described in the "Creating custom gradations" section of Chapter 17. The process requires some extra effort but also affords more control and a wider range of color options.

Radial gradations

To create a radial gradation, select the Radial option from the Fill panel pop-up menu. FreeHand displays the options shown in Figure 13-16.

Figure 13-16:
Select Radial from the Fill panel pop-up menu to display options for selecting the colors and locating the center point in a gradation.

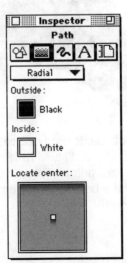

The options work as follows:

↝ **Color swatches:** Drag a color into the Outside color swatch to specify the color around the perimeter of the gradation. Drag a color into the Inside swatch to specify the center color. As with a directional gradation, you can use gray values, process colors, and tints of the same spot color within a single gradation.

Figure 13-17 shows two objects filled with radial gradations. In the first fish, the Outside color was set to black and the Inside color to white. A white Inside color usually creates a highlighting effect. In the second fish, the Inside and Outside colors are reversed. This results in the black-vortex-of-despair effect that is all the rage these days, particularly inside fish shapes.

Figure 13-17:
A radial gradation
from black to white
(top) and another
from white to black
(bottom).

↝ **Locate Center:** Drag the knob inside the Locate Center box to reposition the Inside color within the filled object. Figure 13-18 shows two black-to-white radial gradations with different center points. To create the first fish, I moved the knob to the upper right region of the Locate Center box. To achieve the second fish, I moved the knob down and to the left.

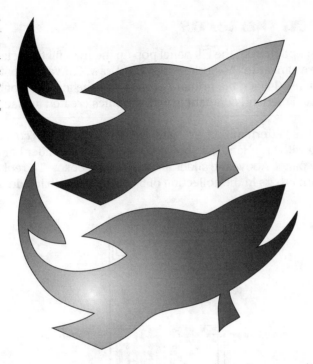

Figure 13-18:
The results of moving the center point — represented by the white spot — to different locations.

 If you can remember a few shortcuts, you won't ever need to select the Radial option in the Fill panel pop-up menu. To establish a radial gradation — or change the location of the center point — Option-drop a color onto an object. Option-dropping always determines the location of the Inside color, and it's a heck of a lot easier and more precise than messing around with the Locate Center knob. To replace the Outside color, simply drop a new color somewhere near the perimeter of the shape (but be sure not to get too close to the perimeter or you'll replace the stroke).

Applying and Editing Patterns

FreeHand provides two methods for applying patterns to shapes. You can either define simple and not particularly useful bitmapped patterns or you can draw complex patterns using graphic objects. In either case, you create the pattern as a *tile*, sort of like a bathroom tile. Bitmapped tiles are always square; object-oriented tiles can be square or rectangular. FreeHand repeats the tile over and over again inside the filled shape.

Bitmapped patterns

Select the Pattern option from the Fill panel pop-up menu to fill the selected path with a bitmapped pattern similar to those offered by MacDraw, Canvas, and other entry-level drawing applications. (In fact, the primary purpose for the inclusion of bitmapped patterns is to make FreeHand compatible with graphics created in MacDraw.)

When you select the Pattern option, you gain access to a scrolling collection of 64 patterns included with FreeHand. As shown in Figure 13-19, a slider bar appears along the bottom of the panel. Above the slider are six pattern boxes. To replace the patterns in these boxes with others in the collection of 64, drag the knob inside the slider.

Figure 13-19:
Select the Pattern option from the pop-up menu to select and edit bitmapped patterns.

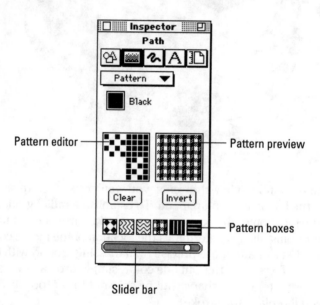

Pattern editor —

— Pattern preview

— Pattern boxes

Slider bar

Select a pattern by clicking on one of the six pattern boxes. The selected pattern appears inside the larger boxes in the middle of the panel. The left box is the pattern editor. It contains an enlarged version of the pattern, which you can edit by clicking pixels on and off. The right box is the pattern preview. It shows the pattern repeated many times at actual size. (Clicking in this box produces no effect — though it brings up the watch cursor and makes FreeHand think about things for a moment.)

Two buttons are also provided to enhance your editing abilities. The Invert button changes all black pixels in a pattern to white and all white pixels to black — in other words, you create a negative version of the current pattern. If you decide that you want to get a clean start and create an entirely new pattern, you can erase all pixels in a pattern by clicking on the Clear button.

The white pixels in a bitmap pattern are always white and opaque. But you can change the color of the black pixels by dragging a color swatch from the Color List palette onto the swatch below the pop-up menu in the Fill panel. You can't apply the None swatch to bitmapped patterns.

Although you can apply any color that you want to a bitmapped pattern, a color that requires a screen value may not print correctly, depending on whether your printer is equipped with PostScript Level 1 or Level 2. Older model Level 1 printers — like my LaserWriter IINTX — can't print tints (including gray values) or process colors unless they are composed of 100 percent CMYK combinations. Level 2 printers handle tints and process colors just fine.

Also, regardless of whether you enlarge or reduce a path, the bitmapped fill pattern always prints at 72 dots per inch, the same resolution as the venerable old MacPaint. The resolution doesn't even enlarge on-screen when you magnify the view size.

In other words, don't use bitmapped patterns. They are provided strictly to aid in the conversion of PICT graphics originally created in MacDraw or a similar program. If you find a bitmapped pattern, replace it.

Object-oriented tile patterns

The Tiled option in the Fill panel pop-up menu allows you to define a *tile* pattern, which is a repeating rectangular design composed of other filled and stroked objects. Using the Tiled option is one of two techniques that you can use to fill an object with one or more additional objects. The other and more versatile technique is *masking,* which is discussed in Chapter 17, "Blends, Masks, and Composite Paths."

Figure 13-20 shows the Fill panel as it appears when you select the Tiled option. The following list explains the function of each option in the panel. (Later sections examine the options in greater detail and show you how to use them to create a tile pattern.)

Figure 13-20:
Select the Tiled
option from the
pop-up menu to
define and
transform object-
oriented tile
patterns.

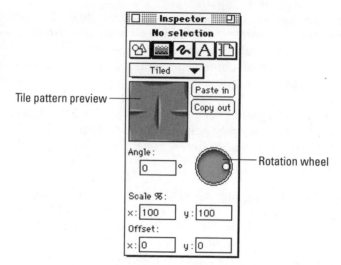

Tile pattern preview —

Rotation wheel

- ⤳ **Paste In:** After selecting and copying the objects that make up your prospective tile pattern, click on the Paste In button to paste the contents of the Clipboard into the tile pattern preview box (just left of the button).

- ⤳ **Copy Out:** Click on this button to transfer the contents of the tile pattern preview box to the Clipboard. You can then paste the objects into your illustration and edit them as desired.

The remaining options transform the repeating tiles inside the filled object. None of them affects the size of the object itself.

- ⤳ **Angle:** Enter a value into the Angle option box or drag the knob inside the rotation wheel to rotate the tiles. Rotating can help eliminate the rectangular appearance of the tiles.

- ⤳ **Scale %:** Enter values into the X and Y option boxes to scale the tiles horizontally and vertically, respectively. Values lower than 100 percent reduce the size of the tiles; values above 100 percent enlarge them.

- ⤳ **Offset:** Enter values into these X and Y option boxes to move the tiles inside the object horizontally and vertically, respectively. Negative values move the tiles to the left or down. Positive values move them to the right or up.

Creating and assigning a tile pattern

In FreeHand, all tile patterns are rectangular. Even if you select a completely nonrectangular object to serve as a tile pattern, FreeHand spaces the tile from each of its neighbors as if it were sitting on an invisible rectangle. For example, Figure 13-21 shows a series of stars. The first star is filled with a gradation; the star below that appears inside its implied rectangular boundary. I defined the star as a tile pattern and used it to fill an enlarged version of itself. (I've also reduced the tile pattern to 30 percent of its former size so that you can see many repetitions of it.) No star tile overlaps another star, nor does it intrude inside its neighbors' rectangular space.

Figure 13-21:
Even a nonrectangular shape like a star (left) is spaced as if it were sitting on an invisible rectangle when expressed as a tile pattern (right).

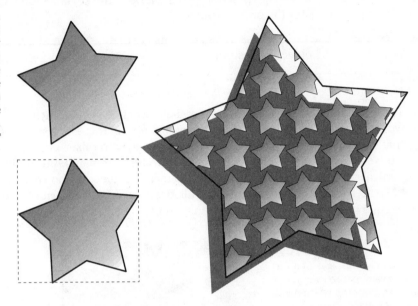

An interesting side note about Figure 13-21: Notice that because the star is the lone element in the tile, you can see through the cracks between the tiled stars to the drop shadow behind them. The only way to avoid this effect is to draw a rectangle without a stroke behind your object before making the object into a tile pattern.

All right, enough tidbits. Time to see how this tile stuff really works. The following steps explain how to define a tile and use it to fill a graphic object.

STEPS: Making and Using a Tile

Step 1. Begin by drawing, filling, and stroking all objects that you want to appear inside the tile. Then select the objects and send them to the Clipboard by pressing Command-C or Command-X (depending on whether or not you want the objects to remain available inside the illustration window).

Step 2. Select the graphic object that you want to fill with the tile pattern.

Step 3. Select the Tiled option from the pop-up menu in the Fill panel of the Inspector palette. The options shown in Figure 13-20 appear.

Step 4. Click on the Paste In button to paste the contents of the Clipboard into the tile pattern preview box. This box shows you how a single tile will look. Meanwhile, you can see your tile pattern in all its splendor inside the selected object. (If not, you must be in the keyline mode. Press Command-K to enter the preview mode.)

Step 5. Use the transformation options to rotate, scale, and move the tiles inside the object as desired.

Those are the basic steps. For some real-life practice in creating and using an actual tile, work your way through the following set of steps. In this exercise, you create a pattern that looks like a metal, nonslip surface, complete with raised edges. (You know, like on a fire-engine bumper. Didn't you ever want to be a fireman?) Alternating horizontal and vertical ridges appear to stand up from a metal surface, as shown in Figure 13-22. The tile pattern includes a square behind all its other objects to ensure that the pattern is opaque (rather than periodically transparent, as in Figure 13-21).

Figure 13-22:
A single tile (top) and an object filled with reduced versions of the tiles (bottom), which mimic the metal ridges on a fire-engine bumper.

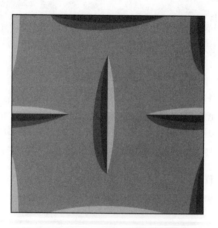

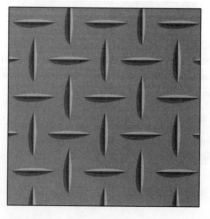

I haven't yet covered a few of the operations included in the following steps. For more information on the Duplicate command, see Chapter 16. For more information on reflecting objects, read Chapter 15. And for complete information on masking, see Chapter 17. You don't need to study up on these techniques to complete the steps, however; they're used in only the most straightforward ways here.

STEPS: Creating an Opaque Tile Pattern

Step 1. Draw the first ridge as a combination of three paths, as shown on the left side of Figure 13-23. Each path comprises only two corner points, one at the top and one at the bottom. Each corner handle has a single control handle, extending toward the curved side.

Figure 13-23:
The three paths that make up the ridge (left), and the ridge as it appears when the three paths are combined (right).

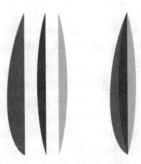

Step 2. Fill the paths with different shades of gray to impart a sense of depth and shadow. Fill the first path with 45 percent gray, the second with 60 percent gray, and the third with 15 percent gray.

Step 3. After you draw the paths, bring them together as shown in the right half of Figure 13-23. The middle shape covers the left one. (You can use the Align palette to align the right edges of the two shapes.) The straight side of the right shape meets flush with the straight sides of the other two shapes.

Step 4. Select the three paths and press Command-G to group them.

Step 5. Choose the Clone command from the Edit menu (Command-equal) to create a clone of the group directly in front of the original.

Step 6. Drag the cloned group while pressing Shift to move it an inch or so to the left.

Step 7. Choose the Duplicate command from the Edit menu (Command-D), which creates a second clone of the group that's spaced the same distance from the first clone as the first clone is from the original.

Step 8. Now select the middle group. This ridge needs to be reflected so that it lies horizontally. Display the Transform palette by pressing Command-M. Click on the Reflect icon, which is the farthest icon to the right. Then enter 45 into the Reflect Axis option box and press Return. FreeHand flips the object about a 45-degree axis, which has the added effect of laying it on its side, as shown in Figure 13-24.

Figure 13-24:
Clone two additional ridges and flip the middle one about a 45-degree axis.

Step 9. The first row of ridges is now complete. Now, create the second row. First, select the two left ridges and press Command-equal to clone them.

Step 10. Click on the Move icon in the Transform palette, which is the icon farthest to the left. There are two Move Distance option boxes. The X option box should contain a value; the Y value is 0. These values reflect your last move, which was entirely horizontal. To move the two clones to the second row, you want to match your last move to keep the spacing even. Leave the X value as is and enter that same value into the Y option box, but with a negative sign in front of it. These settings move the cloned groups to the right and down by the same distance as your previous moves. Press Return to implement the transformation.

Step 11. Now select only the horizontal ridge in the second row and press Command-equal yet again to clone it. This time you want to move the ridge far to the left, twice the distance of the previous moves, to clear the vertical ridge. To do this, double the X value in the Move panel of the Transform palette and enter a negative sign in front of it. For example, my previous X value was 75 (points), so I changed it to –150. Then change the Y value to 0 and press Return. You should now have the ridges shown in Figure 13-25.

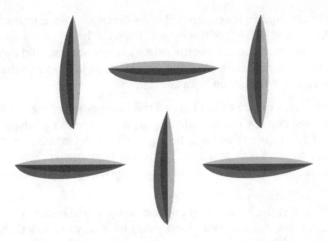

Figure 13-25:
The completed second row, with all ridges evenly spaced horizontally and vertically.

Step 12. To create a third row of ridges, select the three grouped objects in the top row and press Command-equal for the bazillionth time. This time, you want to move the clones far enough down to clear the second row. So enter the same value in the Y option box of the Move panel that's currently in the X option box, negative sign and all. In my case, I entered –150. Then change the X value to 0 and press Return. The third row is now in place.

Step 13. Beware Step 13 of the 13th chapter!

Step 14. Draw a square surrounding the portions of the ridge objects that you want to repeat in the pattern. This square should intersect the top- and bottom-row ridges along their straight sides, as shown in Figure 13-26. The square represents the boundaries of the tile.

Figure 13-26:
Draw a square to determine the boundaries of the tile.

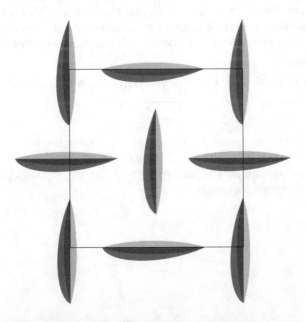

Step 15. While the square is selected, choose Arrange ➪ Send to Back (Command-B) to move it in back of the ridges. Then fill the square with 30 percent gray to act as a background for the ridges. The square should have no stroke. This is very important: A stroke would result in a border that would interrupt the transition between tiles.

Step 16. The pattern objects can't exceed the boundaries of the square. Therefore, you must clip the excess ridges away before defining the pattern. You could accomplish this by applying the Intersect command 27 times, but an easier solution is to mask the ridges with the square. Select all nine ridge groups and choose Edit ➪ Cut (Command-X) to send them to the Clipboard.

Step 17. Next, select the square and choose Edit ➪ Paste Inside (Command-Shift-V). All portions of the ridge objects that previously exceeded the boundary of the square are now clipped away, as shown back in the first example of Figure 13-22. (The one difference is that your path should *not* have a stroke surrounding the shape.)

Step 18. While the square is still selected, press Command-X, sending the square and its contents to the Clipboard.

Step 19. With nothing selected, press Command-Option-F to display the Fill panel of the Inspector palette. Then select the Tiled option from the pop-up menu and click on the Paste In button. The palette appears exactly as shown back in Figure 13-20.

Step 20. To make sure that you don't somehow lose this fill pattern — particularly since you haven't applied it to anything yet — make it into a style. Press Command-6 (if necessary) to display the Styles palette. Then select the New option from the Options pop-up menu. After FreeHand creates the new style, double-click on the style name, rename it *Metal Ridges*, and press the Return key.

Step 21. Save your document so that you don't lose all your hard work.

Congratulations, you have just created a tile pattern, one of the hardest things to do in FreeHand. I didn't tell you that at the beginning of the project because I didn't want you to wimp out on me. You can now fill any shape with the pattern using the Styles palette, as described in the previous chapter.

Transforming a tile pattern independently of a path

After applying a tile pattern, you can scale, rotate, or move the pattern inside the object it fills. Figure 13-27, for example, shows the results of transforming the metal ridges pattern inside a rectangle. The first example in the figure shows the pattern as it appears before any transformation. The second example on the left shows the pattern scaled to 200 percent. The first example on the right shows the pattern rotated 45 degrees. In the final example, both scaling and rotating have been applied to the pattern.

Figure 13-27:
The metal ridges
pattern subject
to various
internal
transformations.

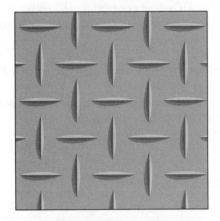

Normal (not transformed)

Rotated 45°

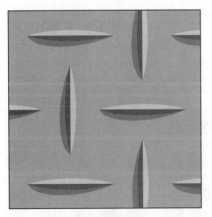

Scaled 200%

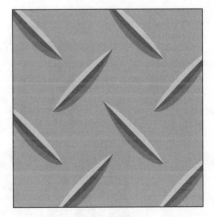

Rotated & scaled

Notice that transformations applied from inside the Fill panel do not transform the filled object itself, only the tiles within the object. Also, a pattern is transformed only within the selected object. Transforming a pattern within one object does not transform that pattern within other objects filled with the same pattern.

Incidentally, when you fill an object with a pattern, the relative location of each tile is based on its distance from lower left corner of the page. This location acts as the origin point for all tile patterns, even if an object filled with a pattern appears far from this origin. All manipulations performed in the Fill panel are performed with respect to this location. For example, when you rotate a pattern 45 degrees, you rotate it around the lower left corner of the page.

 You can also transform a tile pattern along with a filled object when you move the object or apply one of the four transformation tools. To transform tiles and object alike, make sure that the Fills check box in any one of the panels in the Transform palette is selected before applying the transformation. For more information, read Chapter 15, "The Five Transformations."

Tile pattern considerations

A few final notes: You can't apply tile patterns to type, as shown in Figure 13-28, unless you first convert the text block using the Convert to Paths command (Command-Option-P). Generally, large sans serif type is best suited to this purpose.

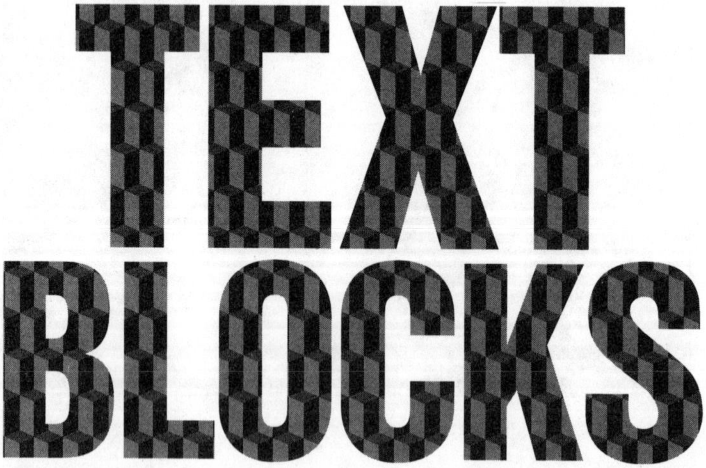

Figure 13-28:
A tile pattern can only be applied to text that is converted to paths.

TEXT BLOCKS

Also, you should know that although patterns may be beautiful to look at, they take a lot of effort to create and eat up disk space and printer memory like you wouldn't believe. For a more efficient filling technique that doesn't restrict you to using repeating images, create a mask as described in the "Using Clipping Paths" section of Chapter 17. Or use FreeHand's collection of custom PostScript fills. They're easy to use, they print quickly, and they're introduced in the following section.

PostScript Fill Effects

FreeHand has long been the only drawing program on the Mac to offer special PostScript fill effects. (At least one program, CorelDraw, offers an even wider variety of PostScript fill effects for Windows users.) A good many FreeHand users don't take advantage of these effects, but in my opinion, they're definitely worth the old once-over.

 PostScript fill effects only print from PostScript printers. If you own a QuickDraw printer such as the StyleWriter or LaserWriter SC, you won't be able to print any of the effects covered throughout the remainder of this chapter.

You can apply FreeHand's special PostScript fill effects in three ways:

- **Select Custom from the Fill panel pop-up menu:** This option provides access to a bunch of weird fill patterns, most of which you can edit using additional options. Except for the Noise effects, these patterns aren't particularly useful, but they're kind of fun.

- **Select Textured from the Fill panel pop-up menu:** FreeHand 4.0 split off half its custom fill effects and put them under a new heading. The so-called Textures effects resemble real-life fabric, gravel, paper patterns, and so forth. They're more useful than the Custom effects, but you don't have any control over the size or spacing of the texture tiles.

- **Select PostScript from the Fill panel pop-up menu:** If you know how to program in PostScript, you can select the PostScript option from the Fill panel pop-up menu. Then enter your routine in the PostScript Code field. Use spaces to separate code commands; don't use carriage returns.

Just as PostScript fill effects don't print on QuickDraw printers, they don't display correctly on QuickDraw devices such as your monitor. Instead, FreeHand demonstrates that an object is filled with a PostScript pattern by displaying a bunch of *C*s or — if you select the PostScript option — *PS*s inside the object. You won't see what the effect really looks like until you print your illustration.

Call me a philistine, but I think that one of the reasons for using FreeHand is to *avoid* PostScript programming. Granted, you can create some interesting effects, but you have to be clever enough to master a computer language, figure out some interesting way to apply it, tear out your hair debugging code, and for what? So that you can create a bunch of little curlicues, differently sized circles, or whatever. Meanwhile, you could have drawn the curlicues and circles by hand and saved about three years of research.

Like I said, call me a philistine, but I like to see my wife and engage in some noncomputer activities every once in a while, so PostScript programming is out.

The Custom fill effects

When you select Custom from the Fill panel pop-up menu, FreeHand displays a second pop-up menu filled with ten PostScript fill routines, as shown in Figure 13-29. Many of the options display additional options that enable you to customize the effect. A few effects, though, can only be applied as is. The following sections explain the effects in the order they appear in the pop-up menu.

Figure 13-29:
When you select Custom, FreeHand displays a second pop-up menu containing a list of ten PostScript fill routines.

 A word about how the following sections are organized: When an effect offers lots of options — as in the case of Bricks, Circles, Hatch, Squares, and Tiger Teeth — the section that explains the effect includes two figures. (For an example, see Figures 13-31 and 13-32.) The first figure in the section shows two versions of the palette. The left palette contains the default settings (except for the colors, which depend on the last colors you used to fill other objects); the right palette contains my custom settings. The second figure in the section shows the default and custom settings applied to two shapes. I created the top shape using the settings from the left palette (default settings); the bottom shape is the result of the right palette (custom) settings.

Now that I've laid out this general format, I won't repeat it within each and every individual section. Believe me, this will make the text more readable. Not only that, you'll be able to flip through the pages without reading the text and still know what's going on.

Black & White Noise

The Black & White Noise effect fills an object with a random pattern of black and white single-point pixels. FreeHand doesn't let you manipulate this effect, so no additional options display when you select Black & White Noise from the pop-up menu. An example of the Black & White Noise effect is shown in Figure 13-30.

Figure 13-30:
You can't edit the Black & White Noise effect.

Bricks

The Bricks effect fills an object with rows of offset rectangles that produce a brick pattern. Selecting Bricks from the pop-up menu displays the options shown in Figure 13-31.

Figure 13-31:
Selecting the Bricks effect displays the options shown in these palettes. The left palette contains the default settings; the right palette shows my custom settings.

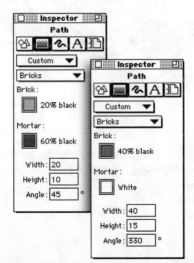

The options work as follows:

- ↪ **Brick:** Drag a color onto this swatch to specify the color of the background bricks.

- ↪ **Mortar:** This swatch controls the color of the 1-point lines between bricks. (The lines are always 1-point thick.)

- ↪ **Width:** Enter a value into this option box to specify the width of each rectangle in points.

- ↪ **Height:** This value determines the height of each rectangle, again measured in points.

- ↪ **Angle:** The value in this option box controls the angle of each row of rectangles in degrees.

Figure 13-32:
Two variations on the Bricks effect created using the options from the palettes in Figure 13-31.

Circles

The Circles effect fills an object with rows and columns of evenly spaced circles. Selecting Circles from the pop-up menu displays the options shown in Figure 13-33. These options work as follows:

⌘ **Color:** Drag a color onto this swatch to specify the color of the outline of each circle. The interiors of the circles are always transparent.

⌘ **Radius:** Enter a value into this option box to determine the radius of each circle, measured in points.

⌘ **Spacing:** The value in this option box controls the distance between the center of a circle and the center of each of its neighbors, again measured in points.

 To prevent circles from overlapping, make the Spacing value at least twice as large as the Radius value. If the Spacing value is exactly twice the Radius value, the circles touch, as in the top example in Figure 13-34.

⌘ **Angle:** This value controls the angle of each row of circles in degrees.

⌘ **Stroke Width.** Enter a value into this option box to determine the thickness of the outline of each circle in points.

Figure 13-33:
Selecting the Circles effect displays the options shown in these palettes. The left palette contains the default settings.

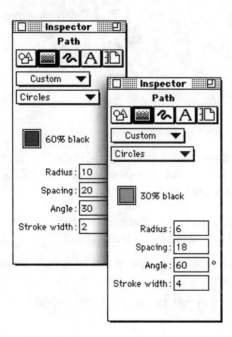

Figure 13-34:
Two variations on the
Circles effect, created
using the options from
the palettes in Figure
13-33.

Hatch

The Hatch effect fills an object with hatch marks created by overlapping two sets of parallel lines. Selecting Hatch from the pop-up menu displays the options shown in Figure 13-35. These options work as follows:

- **Color:** Drag a color onto this swatch to specify the color of the hatch lines. The areas between the lines are always transparent.

- **Angle 1:** Enter a value into this option box to specify the angle of the first set of parallel lines in degrees.

- **Angle 2:** This value controls the angle of the second set of parallel lines, again in degrees.

- **Spacing:** The value in this option box controls the distance, in points, between parallel lines in each set.

- **Stroke Width:** Enter a value into this option box to determine the line weight of all lines in points.

- **Dashed Lines:** Select this check box to create dashed hatch lines, as in the bottom example of Figure 13-36. Deselect the option to create solid lines, as in the top example.

Figure 13-35:
Selecting the Hatch effect displays the options shown in these palettes. The left palette contains the default settings.

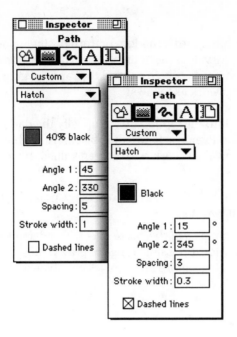

Figure 13-36:
Two variations on the Hatch effect created using the options from the palettes in Figure 13-35.

Noise

The Noise effect fills an object with a random pattern of single-point pixels, randomly colored with a range of gray values. Selecting Noise from the pop-up menu displays two Whiteness Value % option boxes, which control the range of gray values permitted in the pattern. These options work as follows:

- ➣ **Min:** Enter a value into this option box to specify the darkest gray value assigned to a pixel. The default value is 0, which is black. (Note that this is the opposite of how normal screen values work; with screen values, 100 percent indicates a solid color such as black.)

- ➣ **Max:** This value controls the lightest gray value assigned to a pixel. The default value is 100, which is white.

Figure 13-37 shows two examples of the Noise effect. The default effect, shown in the top example, permits the widest possible range of gray values. In the second example, I condensed the range, creating a more uniform, less grainy effect.

Figure 13-37:
Two variations on the Noise effect, one using Min and Max values of 0 and 100 (top) and the other using Min and Max values of 50 and 80 (bottom).

Random Grass

The Random Grass effect fills an object with a specified number of randomly placed, black-stroked curves. As shown in Figure 13-38, this effect is perhaps the least interesting of FreeHand's PostScript fill routines.

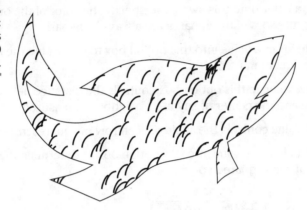

Figure 13-38:
The Random Grass effect filled with 200 blades.

When you select Random Grass from the pop-up menu, FreeHand displays the Number of Blades option box. Enter any value from 0 to 1,000 to specify the number of curved lines spread over the selected area. An example containing 200 curves is shown in Figure 13-38. Note that the lines are always black and 1-point thick.

Random leaves

The Random Leaves effect fills an object with a specified number of leaf shapes, which are randomly sized and positioned. The leaves are always filled with white and stroked with 1-point black outlines. Selecting Random Leaves from the pop-up menu displays the Number of Leaves option box. Enter any value from 0 to 1,000 into this option box to specify the number of leaf shapes spread over the selected area. An example containing 150 leaves is shown in Figure 13-39.

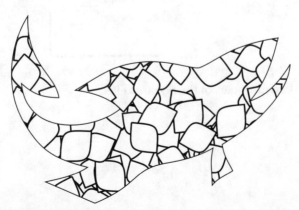

Figure 13-39:
The Random Leaves effect filled with 150 leaves.

Squares

The Squares effect fills an object with rows and columns of evenly spaced squares. Selecting Squares from the pop-up menu displays the options shown in Figure 13-40. These options work as follows:

- ⌖ **Color:** Drag a color onto this swatch to specify the color of the outline of each square. The interiors of the squares are always transparent.

- ⌖ **Side Length:** Enter a value into this option box to determine the length of every side of each square in points.

- ⌖ **Spacing:** The value in this option box controls the distance between the center of each square and the center of any of its neighbors, measured in points.

- ⌖ **Angle:** This value controls the angle of each row of squares in degrees.

- ⌖ **Stroke Width:** Enter a value into this option box to determine the thickness of the outline of each square in points.

Figure 13-40:
Selecting the Squares effect displays the options shown in these palettes. The left palette contains the default settings.

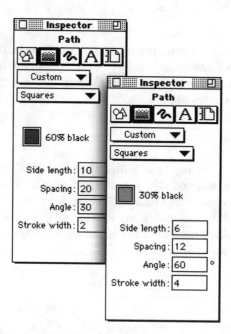

Figure 13-41 shows two examples of the Squares effect.

Figure 13-41:
Two variations on the
Squares effect created
using the options from
the palettes in Figure
13-40.

Tiger teeth

The Tiger Teeth effect fills an object with two sets of dovetailed triangles that resemble a closed mouth of sharp teeth. Selecting Tiger Teeth from the pop-up menu displays the options shown in Figure 13-42. These options work as follows:

- ∽ **Tooth:** Drag a color onto this swatch to specify the color of half the triangles. When the Angle value is set to 0 degrees, the Tooth swatch controls the color of the left teeth.

- ∽ **Background:** This swatch controls the color of the remaining triangles. When the Angle is 0, this swatch colors the right teeth.

- ∽ **Number of Teeth:** The value in this option box controls the number of Tooth-colored triangles that fill the selection.

- ∽ **Angle:** The value in this option box controls the angle of the triangles in degrees.

See Figure 13-43 for two examples of this effect.

Figure 13-42:
Selecting the Tiger Teeth effect displays the options shown in these palettes. The left palette contains the default settings.

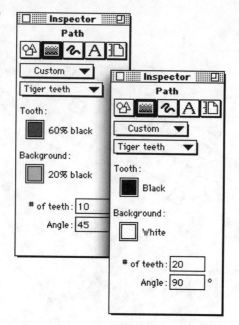

Figure 13-43:
Two variations on the Tiger Teeth effect created using the options from the palettes in Figure 13-42.

Top Noise

The Top Noise effect fills the selection with a random pattern of single-point pixels, colored according to your specifications and set against a transparent background. Selecting Top Noise from the pop-up menu displays a Gray Value option box, which controls the gray value assigned to the pixels. A value of 100 equals white; 0 equals black. An example of the Top Noise effect colored with 50-percent gray is shown in Figure 13-44.

Figure 13-44:
The Top Noise effect with a gray value of 50 percent.

Transparent Fill Routines

Five Custom fill routines have transparent backgrounds. These include Circles, Hatch, Random Grass, Squares, and Top Noise. A sixth pattern, Random Leaves, is partially transparent, because the leaves themselves are filled with white. Any of these PostScript routines can be stacked in front of an object, allowing the background object to partially show through.

The top fish in Figure 13-45 comprises three shapes stacked on top of one another. The rear shape is filled with flat 50 percent gray, the middle shape is filled with the Top Noise effect set to 80 percent (which is the same as 20 percent gray), and the front shape is filled with the Random Leaves effect set to 100. The bottom of the figure shows the three shapes as they appear when separated.

Now, you may think that you can make other routines, such as Bricks and Tiger Teeth, transparent by dragging the None swatch onto one of the colors in the Fill panel. But this strategy doesn't work. The color swatches included with Custom routines accept process color, spot colors, and tints, but you can't apply the None option.

Figure 13-45:
Three shapes
— two of
which
contain
Custom
routines —
stacked in
front of one
another (top)
and offset
slightly
(bottom).

PostScript textures

Selecting the Textured option from the pop-up menu at the top of the Fill panel provides access to FreeHand's nine PostScript texture routines. Regardless of which routine you select from the pop-up menu in the middle of the palette, FreeHand displays the same options, shown in Figure 13-46. A color swatch lets you change the color applied to the texture, but the background is always white and opaque. A preview box shows an enlarged version of the texture. This preview is designed to help you predict what the texture will look like when applied to an object, because PostScript textures don't preview in the illustration window. You should keep in mind, however, that the textures appear about three times larger in the preview box than they do when applied to objects. Figure 13-47 shows every one of the textures applied to my familiar fish shape.

Figure 13-46:
When you select the Textured option, a second pop-up menu contains a list of ten PostScript fill routines (right).

Texture preview

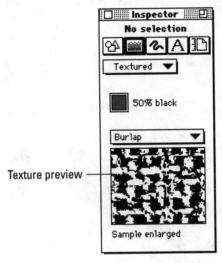

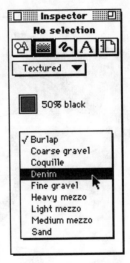

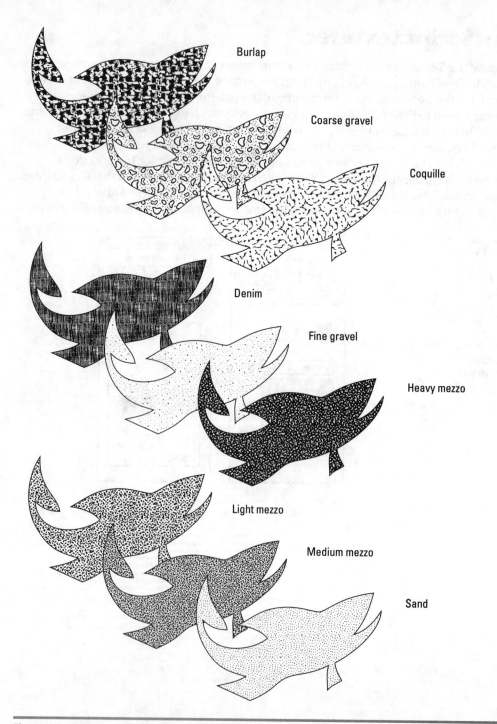

Burlap

Coarse gravel

Coquille

Denim

Fine gravel

Heavy mezzo

Light mezzo

Medium mezzo

Sand

Figure 13-47: The nine PostScript textures included with FreeHand 4.0.

■ ■

Summary

- To create the effect of filling an open path, stack an open, stroked version of the path in front of a closed, filled version of the path.

- Characters of type can only be filled with flat fills. To apply gradations, patterns, and PostScript effects, you must first convert the character outlines to paths.

- Press Command-Option-F to access the Fill panel in the Inspector palette.

- To create a better overprint that previews on-screen, select the two overlapping objects and Option-choose Arrange ⇨ Path Operations ⇨ Intersect.

- Option-click a color swatch in the Fill panel to send the color to the Color Mixer palette, where you can edit it or drag it to the Color List for future use.

- When you apply the Logarithmic option to a directional gradation, FreeHand fades the color quickly at first and then more slowly toward the end.

- To change the angle of an existing directional gradation manually (rather than numerically), Control-drop a color onto an object. The dropped color is always the last color in the gradation.

- To specify the center of a radial gradation, Option-drop a color onto an object.

- To create an object-oriented pattern, select the objects that make up the tile, select Tiled from the pop-up menu in the Fill panel, and click on the Paste In button. Make the pattern an attribute style to save it for future use.

- Both tile patterns and Custom PostScript routines have a habit of greatly slowing down the printing of an illustration.

■ ■

Assigning Strokes

In This Chapter

- ➥ Applying color and line weight to a stroke
- ➥ Selecting line caps and line joins to define the appearance of endpoints and corners
- ➥ Creating custom dash patterns
- ➥ Working inside the Arrowhead Editor
- ➥ Using FreeHand's predefined PostScript stroke routines
- ➥ Stacking stroked paths to create inline and depth effects
- ➥ Designing round dashes and dotted lines
- ➥ Converting a stroke into a closed path to take advantage of fill options

---

Every Good Object Deserves Strokes

Stroke is the PostScript-language term for the attribute that controls the appearance of the outline of a path. In early versions of FreeHand, however, this attribute was called *line*. Even though lots of computer artists were already familiar with *stroke* from Adobe Illustrator, I suppose that FreeHand's designers thought *line* sounded a little bit friendlier.

In Version 3.0, FreeHand's terminology was in a state of flux. The attribute was called *line* when it applied to a graphic object and *stroke* when it applied to text. (You used to have to use separate dialog boxes to stroke paths and text, a foible that the most recent product remedied.)

With Version 4.0, FreeHand embraced the industry standard *stroke* and completely abandoned *line*. Almost completely, anyway. Want to know the one remnant of old terminology left in the program? Make sure that the Inspector palette is available. Now press Command-Option-L — *L* for *line* — which brings up the Stroke panel.

What's weird about this feature is that Command-Option-L is a new shortcut. This particular keyboard combination didn't do anything in FreeHand 3.0. Meanwhile, what do you suppose is the function of Command-Option-S — you know, *S* for *stroke*? Absolutely nothing. Command-Option-L was a deliberate attempt to bring FreeHand 3.0 users into the fold. So all you long-time FreeHand users who are baffled by Version 4.0's array of minute but inexplicable interface alterations, take heart. You can now use a keyboard equivalent that never before existed but might somehow occur to you if you couldn't manage to get the term *line* out of your head.

How stroke affects objects

Deciding whether to stroke an object is one of the most painless choices you can make in FreeHand. If you want to see a path's outline, apply a stroke. Otherwise, don't.

The principle behind stroking is equally straightforward. The stroke is centered on the path. Half the stroke resides on the inside of the path, the other half resides on the outside. Figure 14-1 shows an identical stroke applied to an open path and to a closed path. In both cases, I've displayed the path in white to show how the stroke is centered.

Figure 14-1: An open path (left) and a closed path (right), each stroked with a heavy line. The actual paths appear in white.

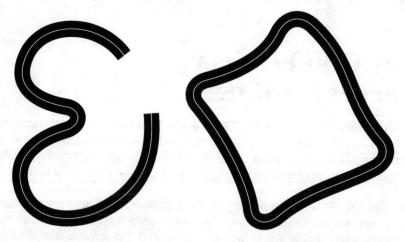

It's important to keep this centering in mind when you're trying to determine the amount of space the stroke will occupy when you print your artwork. You can also exploit this feature to create interesting effects, as described in the "Mixing Stroke Attributes" section later in this chapter.

How stroke affects text

Stroking text is slightly more complicated than stroking an ordinary path. If you select a text block or text bound to a path with the arrow tool and apply a stroke, the stroke affects the path, not the text itself, as shown in Figure 14-2.

Figure 14-2:
When you apply a stroke to a text object selected with the arrow tool, FreeHand strokes the path, not the text.

If the stroke does not appear in the preview mode after you apply it, it's because you haven't told FreeHand to display the path. If the text is inside a text object, press Command-Option-B to display the Dimensions & Inset panel of the Inspector palette. Then select the Display Border check box. If the text is bound to a path, press Command-Option-I to display the Object panel and then select the Show Path check box.

To stroke characters of type, select the characters with the text tool and then apply the stroke. The stroke has the effect of thickening the characters. In Figure 14-3, for example, I selected and stroked the words *the people*. Stroking is a great way to make text bolder if the font doesn't offer a sufficiently bold style.

Figure 14-3:
You can stroke text separately from its path when the Show Path check box is selected.

To see only the stroke, apply a transparent fill by dragging the None color swatch onto the characters. Because the characters are stroked, FreeHand allows you to make the interior of the characters transparent. (For some reason, FreeHand prevents you from making both the fill and stroke of text transparent at the same time.) In Figure 14-4, you can see through the characters to the bound path behind them.

Figure 14-4:
After you stroke the characters, you can make their fills transparent.

Just as FreeHand doesn't allow you to apply certain kinds of fills to text objects, it won't let you apply two stroking attributes — line caps and arrowheads — to type. If you want to create an effect like the one shown in Figure 14-5, you must first convert the text to composite paths by choosing Type ⇨ Convert to Paths (as described at the end of Chapter 11). You can then stroke the character outlines just like any other graphic object.

Figure 14-5:
After converting character outlines to paths, you can assign round line joins, dash patterns, and arrowheads, all shown here.

Assigning a Stroke

Just as you can assign colors to the interiors of paths by dragging color swatches from the Color List and other palettes, you can assign color to the outline of paths by dragging and dropping. The problem is, the target is typically much smaller. Although the interior of a path may be vast and expansive, the stroke might be a slim hairline. It's like trying to hit the side of a barn with a snowball one minute and then shooting for a tin can resting on the weather vane the next.

Luckily, FreeHand helps you out a little. As long as you drop the color within three or so pixels of the stroke — you specify the exact number of pixels using the Snap Distance option box in the Editing panel of the Preferences dialog box — FreeHand changes the stroke and not the fill.

This is not the case when you're stroking characters of text. In fact, FreeHand simply does not allow you to stroke characters by dragging and dropping. You have to use the stroke icon in the Color List palette or rely on the options in the Stroke panel of the Inspector palette.

Furthermore, dragging and dropping only changes the color of a stroke. And as you'll soon learn, there's much more to stroke than just color. In fact, FreeHand's stroking options rival its filling options in terms of variety and quantity.

To access these additional stroking options, bring up the Stroke panel by pressing Command-Option-L, which stands for *loopy*. You can select the variety of stroke by selecting an option from the pop-up menu at the top of the panel, as shown in Figure 14-6. Three of the options — None, Pattern, and PostScript — are very similar to their counterparts in the Fill panel. They work as follows:

- **None:** Select the None option to make the stroke transparent. You can also select the None color swatch from the Color List palette and drag it onto an object.

- **Pattern:** Select this option to apply a bitmapped pattern. If you've lost your sanity, that is. Otherwise, select a different option.

- **PostScript:** If you're a card-carrying propeller head, select this option and enter your own PostScript code. Better yet, define your illustration entirely by entering PostScript code into a word processor. That way, you won't have to spend any money on FreeHand and you can amaze all your friends in Mensa.

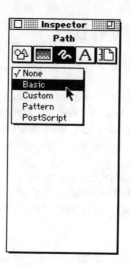

Figure 14-6:
Select an option from the pop-up
menu in the Stroke panel to determine
the variety of stroke applied to an
object.

Upcoming sections explain two other options, Basic and Custom, in a little more detail. Basic is far and away the most common variety of stroke you'll use in your illustrations. Custom provides access to predefined PostScript routines that are sufficiently different from their Fill panel counterparts to warrant further explanation in the "Custom PostScript strokes" section of this chapter.

Single-color strokes

Selecting Basic from the pop-up menu in the Stroke panel displays the options shown in Figure 14-7. These options allow you to stroke a selected path or character outline with a uniform color and thickness. You can also specify how the ends and corners of the stroked path will look, select dash patterns, and assign arrowheads.

Figure 14-7:
The Basic options control the color, thickness, cap, join, dash pattern, and arrowheads applied to the selected object.

The first two options in Figure 14-7 work exactly like their identical twins in the Fill panel:

- ☞ **Color swatch:** Change the color of a stroke by dragging a color swatch from the Color List, Color Mixer, or Tints palette onto the swatch in the Stroke panel.

- ☞ **Overprint:** You can print the stroke from one separation on top of the fills and strokes in another separation by selecting the Overprint check box. For the full story (and accompanying intrigue), see the "Overprinting colors" section of Chapter 13.

Nothing out of the ordinary; you've done it a billion times. But everything else in this panel may look a little foreign. The following sections explain how these options work.

Line weight

Directly below the Overprint check box is the Width option box, which controls the thickness, or *line weight*, of a stroke. Line weight in FreeHand is specified in points, picas, inches, or millimeters, depending on the unit of measure set in the Document Setup panel of the Inspector palette.

You can enter a line weight value into the Width option box and press Return to apply it to the selected object. Any value between 0 and 4,068 points (56 1/2 inches) is permitted, in 1/10,000-point increments. Alternatively, you can choose a command from the Arrange ➪ Stroke Widths submenu. These commands change the line weight only; other options, such as stroke color, line caps, dash pattern, and so on are not affected.

Figure 14-8 shows the nine line weights included in the Arrange ➪ Stroke Width submenu by default. Keep in mind that you can change these line weights by editing the FreeHand Preference file, as discussed in the "Editing hidden preferences" section of Chapter 3.

 The great thing about the Arrange ➪ Stroke Width submenu is that you can select options from it even when selected paths include different stroking attributes. For example, if two selected paths have differently colored strokes, the Stroke panel appears empty. You could change the line weights of both paths by selecting the Basic option and entering a value in the Width option box, but this would change the colors of the selected strokes as well. To leave the colors intact, simply select a command from the Arrange ➪ Stroke Width submenu.

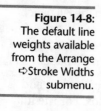

Figure 14-8:
The default line
weights available
from the Arrange
⇨Stroke Widths
submenu.

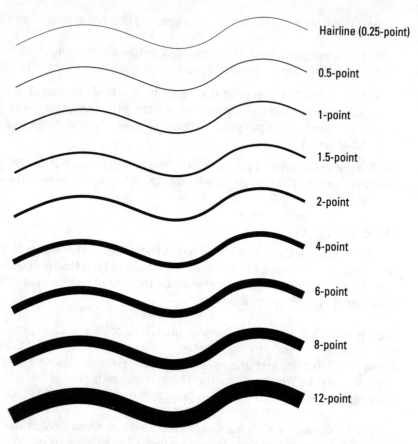

Hairline (0.25-point)

0.5-point

1-point

1.5-point

2-point

4-point

6-point

8-point

12-point

Generally, I advise against specifying a line weight value smaller than 0.15 point. FreeHand defines a hairline — the thinnest line weight traditionally available — as 0.25 point. So a 0.15-point line is just over half the weight of a hairline. As an example, suppose that you specify a 0-point line weight. This setting instructs FreeHand to print the thinnest line available from the current output device. The thinnest line printable by 300-dpi laser printer is 0.24-point thick (1/300 inch), approximately equal to a hairline. But higher-resolution printers, such as Linotronic and Compugraphic imagesetters, easily print lines as thin as 0.03 point, or eight times thinner than a hairline. Because any line thinner than 0.15-point is almost invisible to the naked eye, such a line will probably drop out when reproduced commercially.

Line caps

The next option in the Stroke panel is the Cap option. Using this option, you can select a *line cap*, which determines the appearance of a stroke at an endpoint. Line caps are generally useful only when you're stroking an open path. The only exception is when you use line caps in combination with dash patterns, as described in the "Dash patterns and line caps" section later in this chapter.

From left to right, the three Cap icons represent the *butt cap*, *round cap*, and *square cap*:

↪ **Butt cap:** Notice the black line that runs through the center of each of the Cap icons. This line denotes the position of the path relative to the stroke. When the butt cap icon is selected, the stroke ends immediately at either endpoint and is perpendicular to the final course of the path.

↪ **Round cap:** Giving a stroke a round cap is like attaching a circle to the end of a path. The endpoint acts as the center of this circle, and its radius is half the line weight, as illustrated in Figure 14-9. For example, if you have a 4-point line weight with round caps that follows a horizontal path, a 2-point portion of the stroke is on top of the path and the other 2-point portion is underneath. (Because the path is itself invisible, the two halves of the stroke meet with no break between them.) Upon reaching the end of the path, the top half of the stroke wraps around the endpoint in a circular manner and continues on to form the bottom half of the stroke. The end of the path, then, is a semicircle with a 2-point radius.

Figure 14-9:
When the round cap icon is selected, the stroke wraps around each endpoint in a path to form a semicircle.

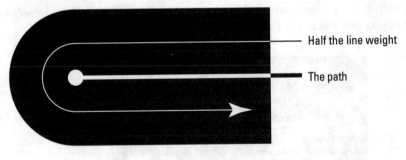

Half the line weight

The path

 Butt caps sometimes look like they were abruptly cut short, especially when combined with thick line weights. Round caps give exposed endpoints a more finished appearance. Figure 14-10 shows several open paths. The first set of paths is stroked with butt caps, and the second is stroked with round caps. (The actual paths appear inset with thin white strokes.) Round caps are like childproof corners — the other objects can run into them without hurting themselves.

Figure 14-10:
A set of five open paths stroked with butt caps (left) and round caps (right).

↪ **Square cap:** When you select the third icon, FreeHand attaches a square to the end of a line. The endpoint is the center of the square. As with the round cap, the size of the square depends on the line weight. The width and height of the square are equal to the current line weight, so that the square projects from the end-point a distance equal to one-half the line weight, as illustrated in Figure 14-11. If a path has a 4-point line weight, for example, the end of the stroke would extend 2 points beyond the endpoint.

Figure 14-11:
When the square cap icon is selected, the stroke extends half the line weight beyond the endpoint.

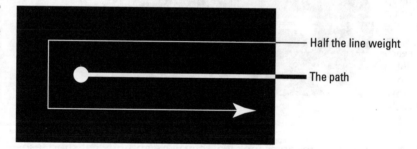

Half the line weight

The path

Line joins

Below the Cap radio buttons are the three Join radio buttons. Using these options, you can select a *line join*, which determines the appearance of a stroke at corners in a path. (Assuming that you followed my recommendations in Chapters 5 and 7, corners should occur exclusively at corner points, not at curve or connector points.)

From left to right, the Join icons represent the *miter join*, *round join*, and *bevel join* options, which work as follows:

- ☞ **Miter join:** If a corner has a miter join, the outside edges of a stroke extend until they meet, as shown in the top star in Figure 14-12. An uninterrupted miter join always forms a crisp corner. You can, however, cut a Miter join short by using the Miter Limit option, as explained in the next section.

Figure 14-12: Three stars, each stroked with a different kind of line join. Notice the appearance of the inward-pointing corners as well as the outward-pointing corners in each path.

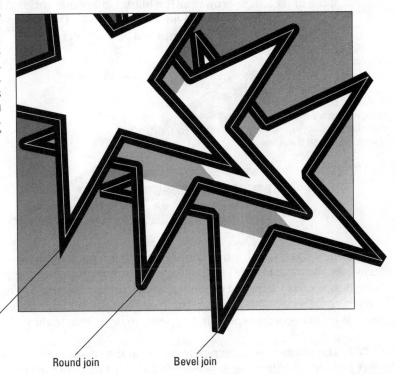

Miter join   Round join   Bevel join

- ☞ **Round join:** When this icon is selected, half the line weight wraps around the corner point to form a rounded edge, as in the middle star in the figure. Round joins and round caps are so closely related that they are almost always paired together. I recommend that you don't use round joins in combination with butt caps. This goes doubly if any dash pattern is involved, because round joins actually form complete circles around corner points.

- ☞ **Bevel join:** The bevel join is very similar to a butt cap. Instead of allowing the outer edges of a stroke to meet to form a crisp corner, as in the case of a miter join, the stroke is sheared off at the corner point, as in the lower right star in Figure 14-12. The result appears to be two very closely situated corners on either side of each corner point.

Cutting short overly long miter joins

Below the Join icons is the Miter Limit option box, which enables you to bevel excessively long miter joins on a corner-by-corner basis. In Version 3.0, the Miter Limit was measured as an angle in degrees. In Version 4.0, this value now represents the largest allowed ratio between the miter length and the line weight, both labeled in Figure 14-13. As long as the miter length divided by the line weight is less than the Miter Limit value, FreeHand creates a miter join. But if the miter length grows (or the Miter Limit value shrinks) to the point that the miter length divided by the line weight is more than the Miter Limit value, FreeHand lops off the miter and makes it a bevel join.

Figure 14-13:
If the miter length divided by the line weight is more than the Miter Limit value, FreeHand bevels the join.

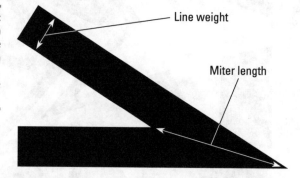

The primary use for this option is to hack off miter joins associated with curved segments. As shown in Figure 14-14, miter joins can become extremely long when a corner point is associated with one or more inward-curving segments. What's worse, the join doesn't curve along with the segment; it straightens out after the corner point. The result is an unbecoming spike that appears to have little to do with the rest of the path.

The solution — clipping the join as in the second example in Figure 14-14 — is a harsh compromise, however. In fact, it's not a compromise at all. FreeHand either gives you a ridiculously long miter or it bevels it completely. If you want to preserve the attractive quality of a miter join without allowing it to take over too large a portion of your drawing, manually adjust your path to increase the angle between a pair of segments, thus decreasing the miter length. If that fails, experiment with the round join to see if it looks better. Consider the Miter Limit option a last resort.

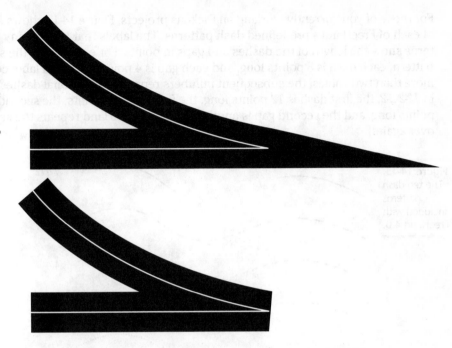

Figure 14-14:
A miter join
associated with
a curved
segment (top)
and the same
join beveled
(bottom).

The Miter Limit value can range from 0 to — of all numbers — 57. Though it's never dimmed, the Miter Limit option is applicable only to miter joins. If either the round join or bevel join icon is selected, the Miter Limit value has no effect.

Dash patterns

The pop-up menu below the Miter Limit option box enables you to select from ten *dash patterns*, which are repetitive interruptions in a stroke. For example, a standard coupon border in an advertisement is a dash pattern.

The first dash pattern offered in the pop-up menu is No Dash, which results in a solid stroke. The default setting, No Dash ensures that the stroke remains uninterrupted throughout the length of the path.

All the remaining patterns are dashed strokes. The most popular use of dashed strokes is to indicate cut-out lines for items that are meant to be clipped from a page: coupons, paper dolls, and so on. Dash patterns are also used to indicate a ghostly or translucent shape. If you were illustrating the scene from *A Christmas Carol* in which Marley comes back and scares the pants off Scrooge, for example, you might want to apply dash patterns to Marley. Or to the door nail, which, according to Dickens, "Marley was as dead as." Or to Scrooge's dead cat, Phil, who was edited out of the story at the last minute. (Few people know just how many dead characters there are in *A Christmas Carol*. Makes *The Dirty Dozen* look pretty peaceful.)

For those of you currently working on Dickens projects, Figure 14-15 shows an example of each of FreeHand's predefined dash patterns. The labels that accompany the patterns show the length of the dashes and gaps in points. For example, in the second pattern, each dash is 8 points long, and each gap is 4 points wide. If a label contains more than two values, the subsequent numbers represent additional dashes and gaps. In *12-2-2-2*, the first dash is 12 points long, the first gap is 2 points, the second dash is 2 points long, and the second gap is another 2 points. FreeHand repeats the sequence over again.

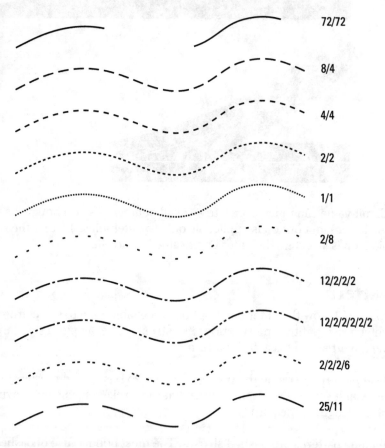

Figure 14-15:
The ten dash patterns included with FreeHand 4.0.

72/72

8/4

4/4

2/2

1/1

2/8

12/2/2/2

12/2/2/2/2/2

2/2/2/6

25/11

 Press the Option key while selecting any option from the pop-up menu except No Dash to display the Dash Editor dialog box shown in Figure 14-16. This dialog box displays the length of each dash and gap in the current dash pattern. Change the values to create a new dash pattern based on the existing one.

Figure 14-16:
Press Option when selecting a pattern to display this dialog box, which lets you design your own custom dash pattern.

Each option box in the Dash Editor dialog box represents the interval — measured in the current unit of measure — during which a dash will be On or Off in the course of stroking a path. On values determine the length of dashes; Off values determine the length of the gaps between the dashes. All values can range from 1 to 200 points; decimal values and zeros are ignored (even though FreeHand shows a bunch of zeros in the dialog box).

Suppose that you want to create a dashed line composed of a series of 6-point dashes followed by 3-point gaps. After displaying the Dash Editor dialog box, enter 6 in the first On option box and 3 in the first Off option box. Leave the remaining six option boxes set to 0. If a series of consecutive On and Off options are 0, FreeHand simply ignores them. Therefore, after FreeHand creates the first 6-point dash and following 3-point gap, it repeats the sequence over and over throughout the length of the selected path.

You can establish the same dash pattern in several different ways. For example, instead of leaving the last six options blank, you could fill them with 6-3-6-3-6-3. Many other variations produce the same effect.

When you press Return or click on the OK button, FreeHand adds the new dash pattern to the end of the pop-up menu. Therefore, you don't endanger an existing dash pattern when you Option-select it; FreeHand always applies your changes to a new pattern. All custom dash patterns are saved with the foreground document. They are transferred from one illustration to the next if you cut a line stroked with the pattern and paste it into another document.

Arrowheads

FreeHand 4.0 offers editable arrowheads, a new feature. You can either select from the predefined arrowheads included with the product or design your own. Arrowheads affect open paths only.

Apply an arrowhead by selecting an option from one of the two Arrowheads pop-up menus, shown in Figure 14-17. The first pop-up menu appends an arrowhead to the first endpoint in the path; the second menu appends an arrowhead to the last endpoint. (Remember that which endpoint is first and which is last depends on the order in which you drew the path.)

Figure 14-17:
Select an option from one of the Arrowheads pop-up menus to assign an arrowhead to an open path.

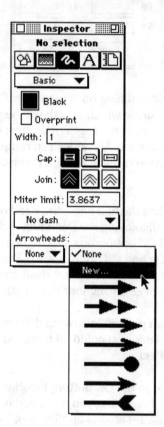

Arrowheads grow and shrink according to the line weight that you apply to the path. Figure 14-18 shows every one of FreeHand 4.0's predefined arrowheads applied to a column of 8-point lines and a column of 2-point lines. The arrowheads themselves are the same. But because FreeHand sizes the arrowheads according to the line weight, they appear four times larger on the left side of the figure than they do on right.

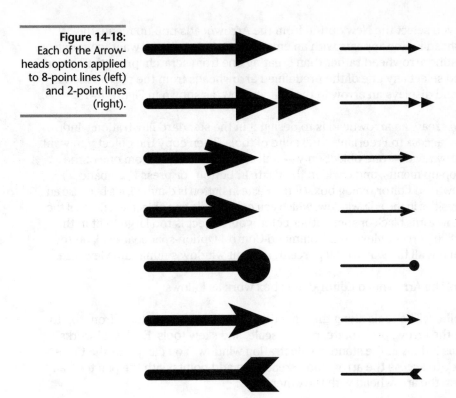

Figure 14-18:
Each of the Arrow-
heads options applied
to 8-point lines (left)
and 2-point lines
(right).

To create your own custom arrowhead, select the New option from either of the Arrowheads pop-up menus. FreeHand displays the Arrowhead Editor dialog box shown in Figure 14-19. The dialog box provides you with a little illustration window (which I call the *edit window*), a set of drawing and transformation tools, and a bunch of buttons and other options. This arrowhead designer is without a doubt the best I've seen in any drawing program.

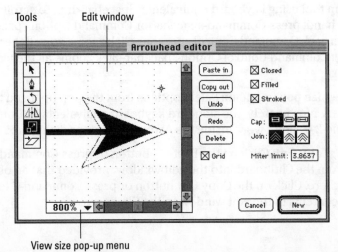

Tools   Edit window

Figure 14-19:
The Arrowhead
Editor is its own
little mini-
program. Here,
I'm enlarging the
arrowhead with
the scale tool.

View size pop-up menu

When you select the New option from the Arrowheads pop-up menu, the Arrowhead Editor appears with an empty edit window. If you want to work from an existing arrowhead rather than creating one from scratch, press the Option key and select any one of the predefined arrowheads from the pop-up menu. FreeHand displays an arrow in the edit window, as shown in Figure 14-19.

Another way to create an arrowhead is to design it in the standard illustration window, where you have access to FreeHand's full suite of tools. Then copy the object you want to use as an arrowhead — one object only — select the New option from one of the Arrowheads pop-up menus, and click on the Paste In button (or press Command-V) inside the Arrowhead Editor dialog box. (If the Paste In button is dimmed, it's because an object already resides in the edit window, which can only handle one object at a time.) If the entire edit window turns black or some other color, your object is too large to fit in the window at the 800 percent view size. Command-Control-Option-spacebar-click on the screen to zoom out all the way to 100 percent, the edit window's minimum view size.

The elements of the Arrowhead Editor dialog box work as follows:

- **The toolbox:** The tools along the left side of the dialog box include, from top to bottom: the arrow, pen, rotate, reflect, scale, and skew tools. Each tool works exactly as it does in the standard illustration window. You can press the Command key to access the arrow tool, create and add points with the pen tool, and transform the arrowhead with the other tools.

If you're editing one of FreeHand's predefined arrowheads and you merely want to enlarge the arrowhead for use with thin line weights, don't edit the path with the arrow tool; use the scale tool instead. As shown in Figure 14-19, begin dragging at the center of the arrowhead and drag up and to the right to enlarge the shape.

- **Hidden tools:** They're not in the toolbox, but you can access the grabber hand and zoom tool using keyboard equivalents. Spacebar-drag to scroll with the grabber hand; press Command-spacebar or Command-Option-spacebar to get the zoom tool. Command-Control-spacebar-click zooms you all the way in (800 percent); Command-Control-Option-spacebar-click zooms all the way out (100 percent).

- **The view-size pop-up menu:** Select options from the pop-up menu to change the view size. Unfortunately, the standard keyboard equivalents — Command-1, Command-2 — don't work inside the Arrowhead Editor dialog box.

- **Paste In, Copy Out:** Click on the Paste In button or press Command-V to paste an object from the Clipboard into the edit window, provided that an object is not already there. Click on the Copy Out button or press Command-C to copy the current contents of the edit window to the Clipboard.

- ↪ **Undo, Redo:** What would an edit window be without these two buttons? You can undo and redo the same amount of consecutive operations that you can throughout the rest of FreeHand. You can also use the familiar keyboard equivalents, Command-Z and Command-Y.

- ↪ **Delete:** Just press the Delete key to delete the contents of the edit window.

- ↪ **Grid:** If you want to constrain your edits using the grid, select the Grid check box.

- ↪ **Closed:** This check box ensures that the arrowhead is a closed path. Be sure that this check box is selected if you want your arrowhead to be filled rather than hollow.

- ↪ **Filled:** When this option is checked, FreeHand fills the arrowhead with the color applied to the stroke (not the fill) in the Inspector palette. To create a hollow arrowhead, deselect this option.

- ↪ **Stroked:** This option is certainly an unexpected one — it enables you to apply a stroke to a stroke attribute. When you select Stroked, FreeHand applies the same color and line weight to the arrowhead that you apply to the rest of the stroke. However, you can specify an independent line cap and line join using the Cap and Join icons and the Miter Limit option box.

When you finish creating or editing the arrowhead, press Return or click on the New button. FreeHand adds the new arrowhead to the end of both Arrowheads pop-up menus in the Stroke panel of the Inspector palette. To transfer the arrowhead to another illustration, copy a path stroked with the arrowhead and paste it into the other document.

Custom PostScript strokes

All right, that's it for the Basic options. If you select Custom from the pop-up menu in the Stroke panel, FreeHand lets you select from 23 special PostScript routines, as shown in Figure 14-20. Unlike the Custom fill effects covered in Chapter 13, 22 of the 23 Custom stroke effects are remarkably similar, so much so, in fact, that if you know how to use one, you know how to use them all. The only exception is the Neon effect, which is described at the end of this section.

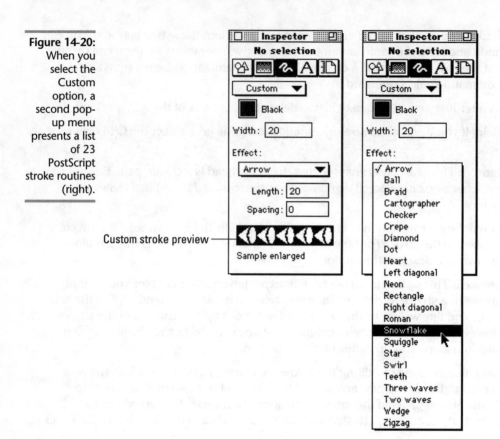

Figure 14-20:
When you select the Custom option, a second pop-up menu presents a list of 23 PostScript stroke routines (right).

Custom stroke preview

To explain all stroking effects except Neon, I'll use the Arrow effect as an example. Like the others, the Arrow effect repeats a series of objects — in this case, a stylized arrow-head motif — along the length of a selected path. Choosing Arrow from the Effect pop-up menu displays the options shown on the left side of Figure 14-20. Here's how they work:

- **Color:** Drag a color onto this swatch to specify the color of the outlines of the arrowheads. The interior of each arrowhead is transparent.

- **Width:** Enter a value into this option box to specify the thickness of the custom stroke in points.

- **Length:** This value controls the length of each arrowhead, measured in points.

- **Spacing:** This value determines the distance between the end of one arrowhead and the beginning of another, again measured in points.

Figure 14-21 shows the Arrow pattern and the other 21 custom patterns that use these options. In each case, I set the color to black, the width and length to 20, and the spacing to 0, all of which are default settings. The only exception is the Rectangle effect (lower left corner), which uses a Spacing value of 2 to keep the rectangles from butting up against each other. All the Custom strokes look fine on a straight line, but as you can see in the figure, some lend themselves to curved lines better than others.

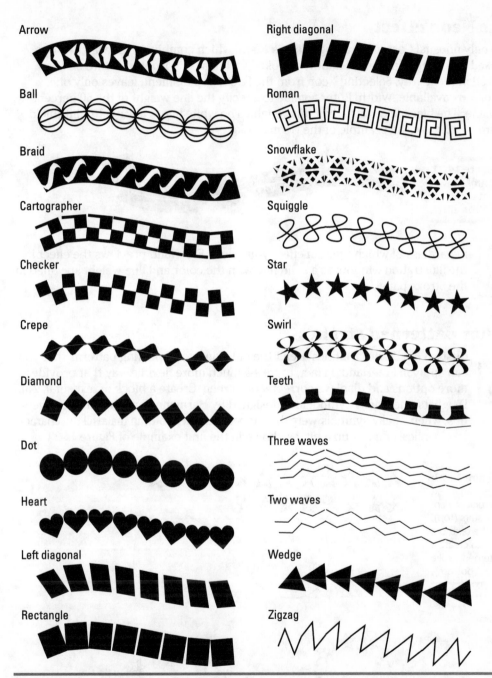

Figure 14-21: You can access these custom stroke patterns from the Custom pop-up menu in the Stroke panel.

The Neon effect

The only unusual Custom stroking effect is Neon, which combines three lines — one stroked with white, in front of another stroked with black, in front of a third stroked with 50 percent gray. Selecting Neon from the Effect pop-up menu leaves only one option box available, Width. Enter a value to specify the line weight of the 50 percent gray line. The black line will be half this weight. The white line is always 1 point thick. Figure 14-22 shows an example of the Neon stroke.

Figure 14-22:
A path stroked with a 20-point version of the Neon effect.

 Regardless of which Custom effect you select, FreeHand previews the effect in the illustration window as a solid line with the color and line weight specified in the Stroke panel.

Other patterned strokes

 Custom PostScript routines aren't the only kinds of repeating patterns that you can apply in FreeHand. In fact, there's a much more flexible way that provides more options and displays correctly on-screen. Create a block of text set in Zapf Dingbats, the wacky symbol font designed by Hermann Zapf back in the seventies, when wacky symbols were the happenin' scene. You can make all the characters identical or mix it up a bit, as shown in the first example of Figure 14-23.

Figure 14-23:
After creating a text block of Zapf Dingbats stars (top), bind the text to a path to create a patterned stroke (bottom).

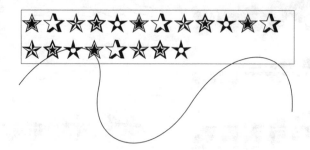

After you create your text, draw a path, select both text and path, and combine the two by choosing Type ⇨ Bind to Path. The text becomes a stroke, as shown in the second example of Figure 14-23. Color the text by selecting the characters with the text tool and applying a fill color. The type size serves as the line weight. You can even kern the text if you don't like the spacing. Try doing *that* with the Custom effects!

Mixing Stroke Attributes

You can create interesting effects by mixing dash patterns with caps, joins, and line weights. You can also stack clones of an object, one in front of another, and stroke each with a slightly different line weight and color. Provided that the weight of each stroke is thinner than the weight of the stroke behind it, portions of each stroke show through, an effect that's ideally suited for creating hollow or gradient outlines.

Stacking strokes

I'll start things off by showing a few ways to stack strokes. The following steps demonstrate how to apply an inline effect to some converted text. If you read Chapter 10, you're probably thinking, "Inline? Isn't that the wimpy little effect you access from the Text Character panel?" Yes, it is. The problem isn't really with the inline effect itself, but rather with the way that FreeHand's automated Inline option implements it. If you're willing to spend some time experimenting with stacked strokes, you can create some pretty cool inline effects that are well beyond anything the Inline option can do. If you take a peek at Figures 14-25 and 14-26, you'll see what lies in store for you.

STEPS: Creating Inline Paths with Depth

Step 1. Convert some text to paths or draw simple shapes. Figure 14-24 shows a combination of the two. The *X* is a Zapf Dingbats character; I drew the *O* to match. For the best results, make sure that the paths are large — say, a few inches tall.

Step 2. Apply a thick stroke and no fill to the paths. In the case of Figure 14-24, I applied a 12-point line weight with round joins. You can use any color you want (except white).

Step 3. Select the paths and clone them (Command-equal). This creates duplicates of the paths right in front of the originals.

Figure 14-24:
Two paths
stroked with
12-point
outlines.

Step 4.   Change the stroke to a slightly thinner white outline. I used a 9-point line weight. You now have a standard inline effect, in which a white outline is bordered on either side by colored outlines peeking out from the rear stroke.

Step 5.   To give the effect a three-dimensional feel, offset the clones slightly. With the cloned paths selected, press the up-arrow key once and the left-arrow key once. Assuming that the Cursor Key Distance value in the Editing panel of the Preferences dialog box is set to 1, you have nudged the clones one point up and on point left, resulting in the effect shown in Figure 14-25. The offset clones make the paths look like they have engraved edges.

Figure 14-25:
Clone the
paths, apply a
9-point white
stroke, and
offset them
one point up
and one point
left.

Step 6. You can keep cloning, applying thinner strokes, and offsetting till you're blue in the face. To create the characters shown in Figure 14-26, I cloned the paths, applied 5-point black strokes, and offset the clones another one point up and one point left. I then cloned them a third time, stroked them with 2-point white outlines, and offset them again. Finally, I selected the original paths way in back — it helps to switch to the keyline mode and zoom in — and filled the originals with gradations.

Figure 14-26: The result of two more sets of offset clones, one with 5-point black strokes and the top with 2-point white strokes. I also filled the original paths with a gradation.

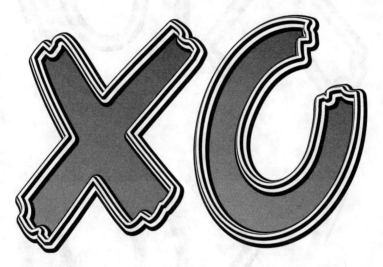

You can create other stroking effects by stacking clones with progressively thinner line weights and lighter tints. By lightening the color of a stroke each time you reduce the line weight, you can create neon type. In Figure 14-27, for example, the rearmost paths are stroked with a 100 percent black, 12-point line weight. I then cloned the paths and changed the line weight to 11-point and the tint to 90 percent. I cloned again, changed the line weight to 10-point and the tint to 80 percent, and so on. The tenth clone is stroked with a white, 2-point outline. All paths were given round joins to emulate the curves associated with neon tubes.

If you want to add some depth to the effect, offset each set of paths immediately after you clone it, as in the previous set of steps. To create Figure 14-27, I offset each clone 1/2 point up and to the left. The result looks less like neon lights and more like letters sculpted in relief.

Figure 14-27:
You can create neon strokes by repeatedly cloning paths and stroking each clone with a thinner, lighter outline than the path behind it.

Figure 14-28:
The paths from Figure 14-27 offset from each other 1/2 point vertically and horizontally.

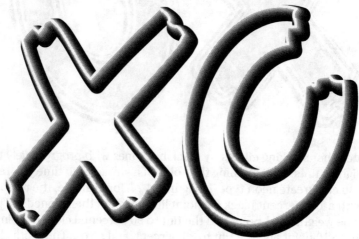

 Actually, there's a quicker way to achieve the neon effect: Use the Blend command, described in Chapter 17. For example, to make a neon *X,* stroke the original path with a 12-point black line weight, clone the path, offset the clone if necessary, and apply a 2-point white stroke. Then select one point in each path — if the paths are coincident (right on top of each other), marquee the points with the arrow tool — and choose Arrange ⇨ Path Operations ⇨ Blend or just press Command-Shift-E.

Dash patterns and line caps

You can combine dash patterns with line caps to create effects like the one shown in Figure 14-29. Because FreeHand treats the beginning and ending of each dash in a pattern as the beginning and ending of a stroke, both ends of a dash are affected by the selected line cap. This allows you to create round dashes as well as rectangular ones.

To produce the pattern shown in Figure 14-29, you create a black stroke with round caps and a 12-point line weight. You then Option-select an option from the dash pattern pop-up menu in the Stroke panel. When the Dash Editor dialog box appears, enter 1 for the On value (the smallest value permitted for a dash) and 18 for Off. Then press Return.

Figure 14-29:
A dash pattern with a 1-point dash, 18-point gap, 12-point line weight, and round caps.

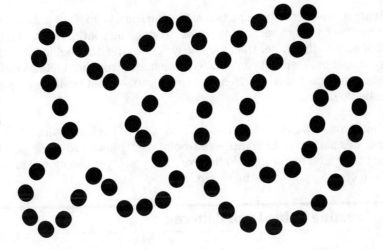

The diagram in Figure 14-30 shows how each dash is constructed. By setting the length of each at 1, you instruct FreeHand to allow only one point between the center of the round cap at the beginning of the dash and the center of the round cap at the end of the dash, which results in an oval. (The endpoints of the dashes appear as small white circles in Figure 14-30.) The cap of each oval has a 6-point radius, so the complete oval measures 13 points wide. Because 13 points of each 19-point sequence (1-point dash plus 18-point gap) is consumed by a round cap oval, a distance of only six points separates each oval.

The moral of the story is that when you're creating round dashes, the Off value in the Dash Editor dialog box must be greater than the line weight to prevent the dashes from overlapping. The On value must be 1 to achieve near-circular dashes.

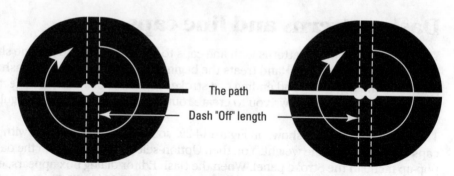

Figure 14-30:
Round caps
wrap around
the ends of
each dash in a
dash pattern.
Small dashes
result in near-
perfect circles.

The path

Dash "Off" length

Stacking dash patterns and line caps

You can create more interesting effects by stacking round-cap dash patterns in front of other dash patterns. Using a technique similar to stacking solid strokes, you make the line weight of each path thinner than the line weight of the path behind it. Although you can vary the line caps, keep the dash pattern constant throughout all layered paths; that is, the length of each dash and length of each gap — what I call the *periodicity* of the pattern — should not vary.

The following steps begin with the stroke pattern shown back in Figure 14-29. The periodicity of this pattern is 19 points — a 1-point dash plus an 18-point gap. The stroke also includes a 12-point line weight. In the exercise, you layer two clones in front of these paths to create a pattern of inline circles.

STEPS: Creating Inline Dash Patterns

Step 1.   Follow the process described in the preceding section to create the dash patterns shown in Figure 14-29. Then clone the paths by pressing Command-equal.

Step 2.   Change the stroke color to white with a 9-point line weight.

Step 3.   Offset the paths one point left and one point up by pressing the left-arrow key and then the up-arrow key. The result is shown in Figure 14-31.

Step 4.   Clone, stroke, and offset some more, as desired. I created Figure 14-32 by creating two more clones, each offset one point left and one point up from its predecessor. I applied a black 5-point stroke to the second clone and a white 2-point stroke to the third clone. The effect is rather like a string of shimmering jewels. Or perhaps they're a bunch of disembodied eyeballs, staring at something stage left. Now if we could only make them blink, that'd be really cool. (Insert a Beavis and Butt-head laugh here.)

Figure 14-31:
Clone the
paths from
Figure 14-29,
apply a 9-point
white stroke,
and offset the
paths one
point up and
one point left.

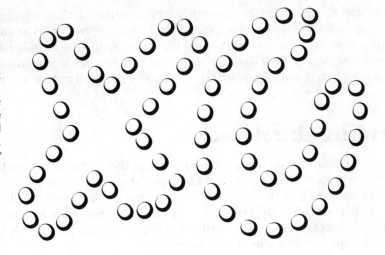

Figure 14-32:
The result of
two more sets
of offset clones
with 5-point
black and 2-
point white
strokes,
respectively.

Converting a Stroked Line to a Filled Shape

The last features to cover in this chapter convert strokes into paths, in much the same way that Type ⇨ Convert to Paths converts character outlines to paths. By converting your strokes to paths, you can reshape each edge along a stroke — inside and outside — and apply fill effects such as gradations and patterns that you can't apply to strokes.

FreeHand 4.0 provides two commands for converting strokes to paths. Choose Arrange ⇨ Path Operations ⇨ Expand Stroke to trace two paths around a stroke, one along the inside edge and the other around the outside edge. Choose Arrange ⇨ Path Operations ⇨ Inset Path to trace around the inside *or* outside edges of a stroke, which results in only one path instead of two.

Expanding the stroke

Neither of these commands pays any attention to the existing stroke applied to a path. You specify the stroke inside a dialog box after you choose the command. For example, when you choose Arrange ⇨ Path Operations ⇨ Expand Stroke, FreeHand displays the Expand Stroke dialog box shown in Figure 14-33. Enter the line weight for the traced stroke in the Width option box or drag inside the slider. You can also specify line cap and line join, complete with a Miter Limit value.

Figure 14-33:
Use this dialog box to specify the thickness of the stroke that FreeHand converts to a composite path.

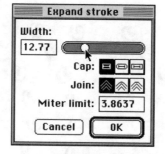

After you press Return, FreeHand creates two paths along the inside and outside edges of the stroke. (This assumes that you're converting a stroke associated with a closed path, which is the more complex scenario. The command traces a single closed path around strokes associated with open paths.) The two paths are combined into a composite path so that the smaller path knocks a hole into the larger path. FreeHand also converts the old stroke color to the fill color. This means that you can apply a different fill to create a special stroking effect.

Figure 14-34 shows examples of the different effects you can achieve. Both sets of paths were created using the Width value shown in Figure 14-33. To create the first star graphic, I applied the Burlap textured PostScript fill routine to get what appears to be a textured stroke. This isn't necessarily an amazing effect, but it is one that you can't get without first converting the strokes to paths.

Figure 14-34:
Two graphics
created by first
converting the
strokes to
composite paths
and filling and
stroking the
paths.

The second example in Figure 14-34 is a little more exciting. To create this effect, I Option-clicked on the inside shape with the arrow tool to select it independently from the outside shape. I then offset the shape by dragging it up and to the left, resulting in what appears to be a variable-weight stroke. I also applied real 0.5-point black strokes to each shape to add definition.

To create the thick black stripes, I resorted to masking (discussed in detail in Chapter 17). First I drew a squiggly line with the freehand tool and stroked it with a 24-point black line weight. I cut the path (Command-X), Option-clicked with the arrow tool on the larger of the two star shapes to select it, and chose Edit ⇨ Paste Inside (Command-Shift-V) to mask the freehand line with the star. For now, just let it wash over you. As you'll see in Chapter 17, there's absolutely no end to the fill patterns you can achieve using masking.

 You can retrieve your original path by using the Blend command, discussed in Chapter 17. Select the composite path that you created with the Expand Stroke command. Choose Arrange ⇨ Path Operations ⇨ Blend or press Command-Shift-E. FreeHand creates a slew of intermediate paths between the two shapes in the composite path. Press Command-Option-I to display the Blend panel in the Inspector palette. Then enter 1 into the Number of Steps option box. Voilà — there's your original path.

Creating an inset path

The Expand Stroke command traces new paths around either side of your selected path. The expanded stroke is centered on the original path, just like a standard stroke. The distance between the new paths and the original equals half the Width value in the Expand Stroke dialog box. So, if the Width value is 12, FreeHand traces one path six points inside the selected path and another six points outside the selected path.

The Inset Path command works differently. When you choose Arrange ⇨ Path Operations ⇨ Inset Path, FreeHand displays a dialog box identical to the one in Figure 14-33 except for the title bar. However, the Width value represents the total distance between the selected path and the single traced path. If you enter a Width value of 12, the command traces a new path 12 points inside the selected one.

Furthermore, you can enter either a negative or positive value into the Width option box. A positive value traces inside the path; a negative value traces outside the path.

Generally, you'll want to apply the Inset Path command to clones of a path. With both clone and original to work with, you can create inline effects and variable weight strokes. You can also use fills to emulate fancy strokes, as in Figure 14-34.

Summary

- ➡ Press Command-Option-L to access the Stroke panel in the Inspector palette.

- ➡ Drop a color within three pixels of the outline of a path to change the color of its stroke.

- ➡ To change the line weight of two differently stroked paths at once — without upsetting any other stroking attributes — select a command from the Arrange ⇨ Stroke Width pop-up menu.

- ➡ Don't assign line weights thinner than 0.15 point unless you want the stroke to be invisible when printed. Such strokes are too thin to reproduce reliably.

- ➡ Round caps and square caps extend beyond the endpoint of a path a distance equal to half the line weight.

- ➡ Instead of simply beveling off overly long miter joins with the Miter Limit option, edit the path to make the miter join shorter. Or apply a round join to the entire path.

- ➡ Press the Option key when selecting a dash pattern option to bring up the Dash Editor dialog box, which enables you to create your own dash patterns.

- ➡ The size of an arrowhead depends on the line weight applied to the path. To enlarge the arrowhead independently of the stroke, press Option while selecting an arrowhead option and scale the arrowhead in the Arrowhead Editor dialog box.

- ➡ Inside the Arrowhead Editor, you can access the grabber hand and zoom tools from the keyboard by pressing spacebar and Command-spacebar, respectively.

- ➡ You can create a custom patterned stroke by binding text formatted in Zapf Dingbats or some other symbol font to a path.

- ➡ Clone a path and apply a thinner line weight to its stroke to create inline effects, neon paths, and strokes that appear to have depth.

- ➡ Line caps applied to dash patterns result in rounded dashes. You can clone and stack such patterns to created beaded strokes.

- ➡ After applying the Expand Stroke command to a path, you can apply fill effects — including gradations — to the converted outlines. You can also offset the converted paths to create variable-weight outlines.

Special Effects

Chapter 15:
The Five Transformations

Chapter 16:
Duplicating Objects and Effects

Chapter 17:
Blends, Masks, and Composite Paths

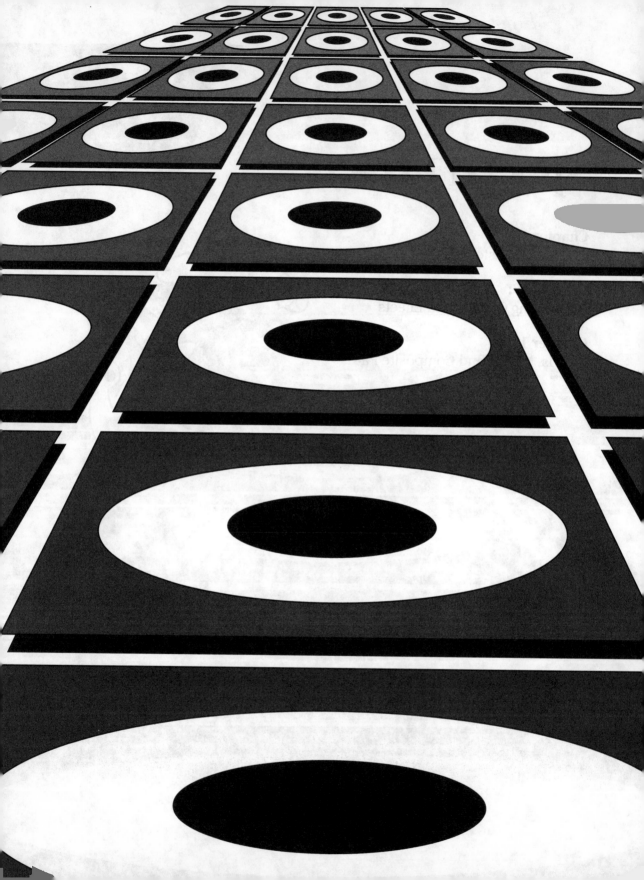

The Five Transformations

■ ■

In This Chapter

→ Working productively with the new Transform palette

→ Using different techniques to move an object

→ Calculating direct distances in the Move panel

→ Using the scale tool to enlarge and reduce objects

→ Scaling selected points independently of their deselected neighbors

→ Flipping objects with the scale and reflect tools

→ Defining the reflection axis

→ Getting the most out of the rotate tool

→ Slanting objects with the skew tool

■ ■

The Miracle of FreeHand's Transformations _____

Emcee:	Ladies and gentlemen, tonight's guests are those kings of object manipulation, those movers and shakers, twisters and quakers, benders and breakers: Please welcome Move, Scale, Reflect, Rotate, and Skew — *The Five Transformations!*
Viewer 1:	(*Claps once, hesitantly.*) Who?
Viewer 2:	(*Sleepily.*) Wake me up for the Kingston Trio.
Viewer 1:	Who?
Viewer 2:	(*Snores loudly.*)

All right, I suppose that you might be able to find more miraculous transformations than those you can accomplish in FreeHand. The transformations from water to wine, demons into swine, Dan Quayle to Al Gore, eight tracks to CDs, The Brady Bunch to The Simpsons, Andrew Dice Clay to a complete absence of Andrew Dice Clay . . . all these qualify as more miraculous, in fact. But the ability to take an object and stretch it, spin it, and slant it in various directions is not to be scoffed at. These transformations are at the root of FreeHand's special effects capabilities and are absolutely essential to creating digital illustrations.

The transformations themselves aren't likely to elicit much in the way of screaming or fainting. You can move objects, enlarge or reduce them, flip them, rotate them, and slant them, all of which FreeHand has enabled folks to do since Version 1.0. But thanks to the precision, immediacy, and predictability of the controls, transformations double as practical solutions to everyday problems and inspirational ways to experiment with objects.

Transforming objects in Version 4.0

As shown on the left side of Figure 15-1, FreeHand 4.0 provides the four transformation tools that it has offered since the old days. To use any of these tools, you drag in the illustration window to transform one or more selected objects. The only transformation tool not labeled in the figure is the arrow tool, which — in addition to its seven million other functions — lets you move selected objects.

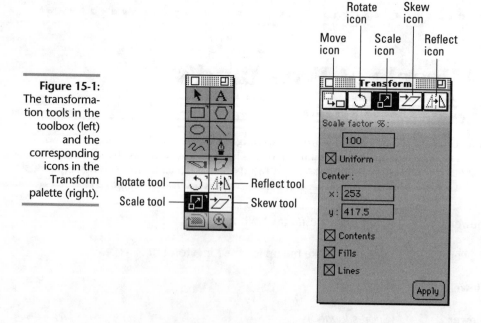

Figure 15-1: The transformation tools in the toolbox (left) and the corresponding icons in the Transform palette (right).

Version 4.0 also includes a Transform palette (shown on the right side of the figure), which you display by pressing Command-M. The palette contains five separate panels of options, one for each of the five transformations. You display the panels by clicking on the icons just below the title bar.

If you're familiar with previous versions of FreeHand and you've gotten in the habit of transforming objects in certain ways, you may be more frustrated with the new Transform panels than enamored of them. It used to be that if you wanted to move an object by a certain numerical distance, you pressed Command-M to display the Move Elements dialog box, entered the horizontal distance value, pressed Tab, entered the vertical distance value, and pressed Return. The process was implicit, the kind of thing you might do over and over without thinking. Now, due to FreeHand's internal transformation from dialog boxes to palettes, this task is more cumbersome. Pressing Command-M brings up the Transform palette. There's no keyboard equivalent for displaying the Move panel, so you have to click on the Move icon. Then you have to click inside an option box to activate the palette or press Command-grave who knows how many times to cycle to the palette. Only then can you enter values and press Return to move the selected object. Unlike the old way, the new way doesn't lend itself to quick repetition; it forces you to think about a process that used to be entirely automated.

Without a doubt, this is a step in the wrong direction. However, not all applications of the Transform palette are so ponderous. In fact, I'm happy to report that with the exception of moving objects, the palette typically makes numerical transformations more convenient, especially if you need to perform a certain kind of transformation several times in a row. Instead of having to Option-click with a tool over and over again to display and redisplay a specialized dialog box, you simply click inside an option box, enter a new value, press Return, examine the results, adjust the value, press Return again, and so on, until you get the desired results.

Here are a few things that both new and experienced users should know about working with the transformation tools and Transform palette:

- To transform an entire path, select the path but not its points. If any of the points are selected, FreeHand transforms the segments between those points independently of other points in the path.

- To transform a text object independently of the characters inside it (or bound to it), Option-click on the path with the arrow tool to select only the path. Then apply the desired transformation. The type rewraps to fit the transformed text object. (If you apply a transformation to a text block without first Option-clicking, FreeHand transforms text and object equally.)

✑ When you're dragging with a transformation tool, FreeHand allows you to drag outside of the illustration window (as long as you start dragging inside the window). This can be useful for enlarging and reducing an object dramatically with the scale tool or rotating an object with extreme precision using the rotate tool.

✑ Double-click on a transformation tool icon in the toolbox to switch to the corresponding panel in the Transform palette. Alternatively, you can Option-click with the tool in the illustration window. (Because there is no specific move tool, you can access the Move panel only by clicking on its icon in the Transform palette.)

✑ The point at which you begin dragging with any of the four transformation tools serves as the center of the transformation. For example, when you drag with the rotation tool, FreeHand rotates the object around the point at which you pressed the mouse button.

✑ Whether you double-click or Option-click, FreeHand records the coordinates for the center of the selection into the two Center option boxes in the Transform palette. These coordinates serve as the center of the transformation. To change the Center coordinates, you can enter new values or just click with the transformation tool in the illustration window. (This doesn't apply to using the Move panel because there is no center for a move.)

✑ All panels in the Transform palette include Contents and Fills check boxes. These options enable you to transform masked objects and tile patterns, respectively, along with an object. If you deselect the Contents check box, FreeHand transforms the selected object independently of the elements pasted inside it (if any such objects exist). If you deselect Fills, FreeHand transforms the object independently of its tile pattern (again, if the object is filled with such a pattern). For more information on masking, skip ahead to Chapter 17.

✑ You can click inside an option box to activate the Transform palette or press Command-grave one or more times to cycle through to the palette. When the palette is active — the title bar appears highlighted — you can press the Return key to apply your changes. If the palette is not active, you have to click on the Apply button.

✑ Both techniques have the added effect of deactivating the palette. So to apply a transformation a second time, you have to reactivate the palette by pressing Command-grave and then press Return. (Or you can leave the palette inactive and simply click on the Apply button.)

✑ Pressing Command-grave always takes you back to the palette you used last. So, if you're using the Transform palette several times in a row, a single press of Command-grave reactivates the palette. If you used some other palette last, you have to press the keyboard combination two or more times in a row.

✑ To bring the Transform palette forward so that no other palette is covering it, press Command-M.

That's good enough for now. Don't worry if a few of the finer points of these operations — such as "Why should I care?" — escape your understanding for the moment. All are covered in greater detail in later sections.

The pasteboard error

A weird thing sometimes happens when you're transforming text objects, especially if the document has been imported from a different format. You may get an error message that says, "Could not complete the Transform command because an object would be placed off the pasteboard." Officially, this error message occurs when you try to transform an object beyond FreeHand's 54 × 54-inch maximum page size. But a bug — one that will probably be remedied in a future release — causes the error to occasionally pop up when you're transforming complex text objects as well.

If you get this error when transforming objects that easily fit inside a 54 × 54-inch area, press the Return key to hide the message. Then follow these steps:

STEPS: Bypassing the Pasteboard Error Message

Step 1. Group the selected objects, even if only a single object is selected, by pressing Command-G.

Step 2. Switch to the Object panel of the Inspector palette by pressing Command-Option-I. Make sure that the Transform as Unit check box is selected.

Step 3. Reapply your transformation. This time, the operation should work without problem.

Step 4. If you want to edit the text or some object in the group, press Command-U to ungroup the selection.

Moving Whole Objects

The "Moving Elements" section of Chapter 7 described several techniques for moving points, segments, and Bézier control handles inside a path. However, it didn't say much about moving entire objects, because I was saving up this information for this chapter. Aren't you glad that you stuck it out?

In many ways, moving is the odd transformation out. If the five transformations really were a band, Move would be the guy who played the drums, never wrote any of the songs, got paid less than the other members, and was generally considered to be a no-talent jerk who got incredibly lucky. You know, sort of like Ringo Starr, or Oates in Hall and Oates. Then again, maybe Hall is the no-talent one. It's pretty hard to tell.

Anyway, moving is the odd transformation: FreeHand doesn't give you a special tool for doing the job; if you don't do things right, you can end up deselecting the object; there's no shortcut for accessing the Move panel; and the panel lacks a couple of options that would make it more useful. Some folks don't even think of moving as a transformation because it doesn't in any way alter the appearance of an object — it just changes its location.

Manual movements

On the other hand, you can use all kinds of techniques to move objects that aren't applicable to other kinds of transformations. It's as if — wait a second, maybe Ringo was the best Beatle after all. He had a great solo album. He got the most fan mail. He had the sense not to marry Yoko Ono, he didn't write an opera about Liverpool, he didn't join the Traveling Wilburys. By gum, it was those other guys that were no-talent jerks.

The following list explains all the ways that you can move selected objects in FreeHand. A few may be familiar to you from Chapter 7, but it never hurts to recap.

- **Drag with the arrow tool:** Drag on a selected object to move it. This information may sound ridiculously remedial, but if you don't drag on the object when moving it, you deselect the object. When you perform other transformations, you don't have to begin dragging on the object. Instead, you drag from the point that will serve as the center of the transformation, which can be literally anywhere in the illustration window.

  When moving an open or unfilled path, you have to begin dragging on a segment in the path. When moving a filled path in the preview mode or a text block in either display mode, you can begin dragging inside the object.

- **Press and hold to preview:** If you start right in dragging an object, FreeHand displays a rectangular dotted outline to show you the object's approximate location. This outline isn't very useful for gauging the position of an object during a move, but it doesn't take any time for FreeHand to draw, so the program can easily keep up with your movements. If you want to see an exact outline when working in the preview mode, click and hold for a moment before beginning your drag. This tells FreeHand that you want to preview the object with accurate outlines and proper fill and stroke colors throughout the move.

↪ **Press Option to preview:** Assuming that you haven't changed the Preview Drag value in the Editing panel of the Preferences dialog box, the above technique only works when a single object is selected. To preview multiple objects during a move or to preview objects in the keyline mode, simply press the Option key while dragging. You only need press Option long enough to draw the preview. After accurate fills, strokes, and path outlines appear, you can release the Option key.

You can bump up the Preview Drag value in the Preferences dialog box to accommodate the press-and-hold technique when more than one object is selected. However, I personally think that it's less trouble to press the Option key for a moment than to press and hold the mouse button while FreeHand generates a drag preview.

↪ **Control-drag a point:** You can drag a single object by one of its points by Control-dragging, as described in the "Snapping" section of Chapter 7. Although extremely useful, this technique is not without its problems. If an object resides in front or in back of the point on which you Control-drag, FreeHand selects that object. This is no surprise, because Control-clicking selects objects in a stack. If you run into this problem, you must first move the object away from other objects and then Control-drag on one of its points to move the object.

↪ **Snap to points:** Drag onto a point in a stationary path to snap to it. (For this to work, the Snap to Point command under the View menu must be active.)

↪ **Press Shift after you drag to constrain:** It's important that you press Shift after beginning your drag. If you press Shift before dragging — as you can when using any of the transformation tools — you deselect the object. To constrain the movement of an object along the constraint axes, start dragging, press and hold the Shift key, release the mouse button, and release Shift.

↪ **Press an arrow key:** This moves the selected objects by the amount specified in the Cursor Key Distance option box in the Editing panel of the Preferences dialog box.

Moving by the numbers

You can also specify the movement of a selected object numerically via the Move panel of the Transform palette, shown in Figure 15-2. As I mentioned earlier, you have to click on the Move icon, labeled in the figure, to access this panel.

Move icon

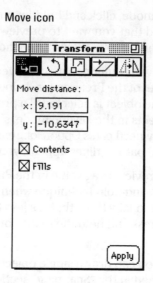

To use the Move panel, enter values into each of the Move Distance option boxes. The values are measured in the unit specified in the Document Setup panel of the Inspector palette and are accurate to 1/10,000 point.

- The X value moves the selection horizontally; the Y value moves it vertically.

- Positive values move the selection to the right or up; negative values move it to the left or down.

- If you want to move an object exclusively up or down, enter 0 for the X value. If you want to move it directly left or right, enter 0 into the Y option box.

After you enter the X and Y values, press Return or click on the Apply button to apply the transformation.

Moving in direct distances

What's missing are direct distance and angle options. For example, what if you want to move an object 20 points along a 30-degree axis? Rotating the constraint axes has no effect on the performance of options in the Move panel. So what do you do?

Well, there are two possible solutions. One is to drag the object manually while monitoring your progress in the information bar (which you display by pressing Command-Shift-R). If you really want to be precise, enter the angle of your drag into the Constrain option box in the Document Setup panel of the Inspector palette. Then press the Shift key while dragging the object to constrain the movement to the axes and monitor the distance (Dist) in the information bar.

The other and even more precise solution is to do the math. Don't be afraid; as long as you have a calculator with Cos, Sin, and π buttons (pronounced *co-sign, sign,* and *pie*), you can handle it. On the other hand, if your calculator is strictly the generic business variety, you're out of luck. There's no way to do these equations in your head.

What you need to do is convert a direct distance and angle to horizontal and vertical distance values. Together, these items make up a triangle, as illustrated in Figure 15-3. All it takes to compute the X and Y values for the Move panel is a little geometry.

 Figure 15-3 diagrams the movement of an object up and to the right. But it doesn't matter which direction you want to move. If you move down and to the right, flip the triangle vertically in your head. If you want to move up and to the left, flip it horizontally.

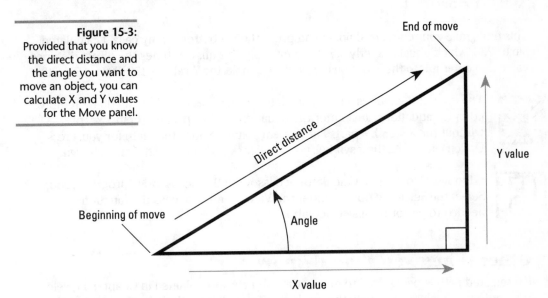

Figure 15-3:
Provided that you know the direct distance and the angle you want to move an object, you can calculate X and Y values for the Move panel.

The first step is to convert your angle from degrees to a fraction of π. It's sort of like converting a temperature from Fahrenheit to Celsius. To make the conversion, use this equation:

$$A \div 180 \times \pi$$

where *A* is the angle. For example, if the angle is 30 degrees, divide it by 180 to get 1/6, or 0.1667. Then multiply that times π, which gives you π/6, or 0.5236.

Now that you have the converted angle, which I'll call C, you can figure out the X and Y values. To calculate the X value, use this equation:

$$X = \text{Cos } C \times D$$

where D is the direct distance value. In other words, after calculating the converted angle C, press the Cos button on your calculator. In the case of my 30-degree example, Cos 0.5236 equals 0.8660. Then multiply the result times the direct distance. I wanted to move my object 300 points, so I multiplied 0.8660 by 300 to get approximately 260 points. Enter the final answer — in my case 260 — into the X option box.

To calculate the Y value, use this equation:

$$Y = \text{Sin } C \times D$$

This time, take your converted angle and press the Sin button. In my case, I calculated Sin 0.5236, which equals exactly 0.5. Then multiply this answer times the direct distance value and enter it into the Y option box. In the example, the Y value is 150 ($300 \times 0.5 = 150$).

 The PowerPC includes a new Calculator desk accessory that can do incredibly complex equations. Just enter the equations as I've printed them, except without the $X =$ or $Y =$ part. The system software does the math for you. Press Option-P to create the π symbol; use an asterisk (*) in place of the multiply sign.

 Windows also offers a Calculator accessory in the Accessories program group. Select the Scientific option under the View menu to access the functions needed to perform these calculations.

Other things you should know

If a selected path is being used to mask other objects, as explained in Chapter 17, select the Contents check box to move the masked objects along with the path. Deselect the option to move the selected path independently of the masked objects. This forces FreeHand to mask a different portion of the objects.

If a selected path is filled with a tile pattern, select Fills to move the pattern with the object. Deselect the option to move the path and leave the tile pattern in place. This has the effect of offsetting the pattern inside the path (much as if you entered values into the Offset options in the Fill panel of the Inspector palette).

The X and Y options in the Move panel record past moves. After you move an object by hand, the X and Y option boxes display the exact horizontal and vertical components of the move, accurate to 1/10,000 point. This information makes it possible for you to repeat or nullify all or part of the most recent move, regardless of how long ago the move was made. Simply take the values in the X and Y option boxes, enter their opposites, and press Return or click on the Apply button. (In other words, if there is a negative sign before the value, delete it; if there isn't a negative sign, add one.)

Suppose that you move one object until it snaps onto another object. In doing so, you move the object up and slightly to the right. But you didn't actually want to change the horizontal position; you *had* to change it because that was the only way to make the snap work. (Sometimes, Shift-dragging an object can interfere with snapping, so it's best to drag without the Shift key.) To nudge the object leftward to its previous horizontal position, you'd change the X value from plus to minus and enter 0 for the Y value.

The only kinds of moves that the X and Y options don't record are moves made with the arrow keys. This is a feature, not a bug. FreeHand rightly assumes that you can keep track of arrow key movements.

One more thing: The Move panel isn't only applicable to whole objects. You can also use the X and Y options to move selected points independently of other points in a path.

Scale, Reflect, Rotate, and Skew

Now for the *real* transformation tools, the tools with heart, soul, and spunk. Every one of these tools changes the appearance of an object, sometimes in addition to changing its placement. Okay, I know what you're thinking. "Hey, if Ringo is FreeHand's move functions, who are the other transformations? Aren't we short a Beatle?" Not at all. Let me explain:

- ⮑ The scale tool is Paul, because it's remarkably capable and possibly the most popular of the bunch. You'll find yourself using it more often than you hum "Yesterday."

- ⮑ The reflect tool is Stuart Sutcliffe — one of the early Beatles — because Paul can do everything he can do. And just as there's no point in having Stuart if you have Paul — you just don't need two bass players, after all — you don't need the reflect tool as long as the scale tool is around. Why? Because the scale tool can just as easily flip objects as resize them. On the other hand, the reflect tool is there if you need it, unlike Stu, who is, unfortunately, dead.

↝ The rotate tool is John because it's the hippest transformation tool, if not quite so popular with the teenyboppers as the scale tool. It's the musical equivalent of "Strawberry Fields Forever," sending objects spinning and reeling into trippy, far-out scenes. Also, the farther you drag the rotate tool away from its origin, the better it performs. John goes to the Middle East and comes up with the poetic "Dear Prudence"; he moves back to the Dakota and shouts "Mother" at the top of his lungs. The connection is so uncanny that it's scary.

↝ The skew tool is George because you hardly ever use the thing and it works more predictably when it's constrained. On his own, George sang a bunch of sappy stuff and droned away on his sitar as melodically as if he were playing a power mower. With a little help from Eric Clapton, he came up with "While My Guitar Gently Weeps." As we'll see, the skew tool needs the same kind of adult supervision, which you apply by pressing the Shift key.

I also have this thing about how the Transform and Inspector palettes are like Captain and Tennille, but I doubt that you want to hear it. It's a "Muskrat Love" kind of thing.

Enlarging and reducing objects

Use the scale tool, the second-to-last tool on the left side of the palette, to reduce and enlarge paths and text objects. It's not the only way to scale; you can group objects and scale them by dragging a corner handle with the arrow tool, for example. But the scale tool works more precisely than other techniques, and you can apply it to any number of objects whether they are grouped or not.

After selecting the objects you want to scale, drag with the scale tool to enlarge or reduce them. The direction in which you drag determines whether an enlargement or reduction takes place:

↝ Drag up to enlarge an object vertically.

↝ Drag to the right to enlarge an object horizontally.

↝ Drag down to reduce an object vertically.

↝ Drag to the left to reduce an object horizontally.

In both examples in Figure 15-4, I dragged up and to the right in order to enlarge the selected object both vertically and horizontally. You can track the extent of your scaling by keeping an eye on the SX and SY values in the information bar. The values are expressed as ratios of the new size over the previous size. Move the decimal point two digits to the right to make the conversion to percents. For example, the SX value in Figure 15-4 is 1.82, which is the same as 182 percent. The SY value, 1.95, is 195 percent. Any value over 1.00 indicates an enlargement; a smaller value indicates a reduction.

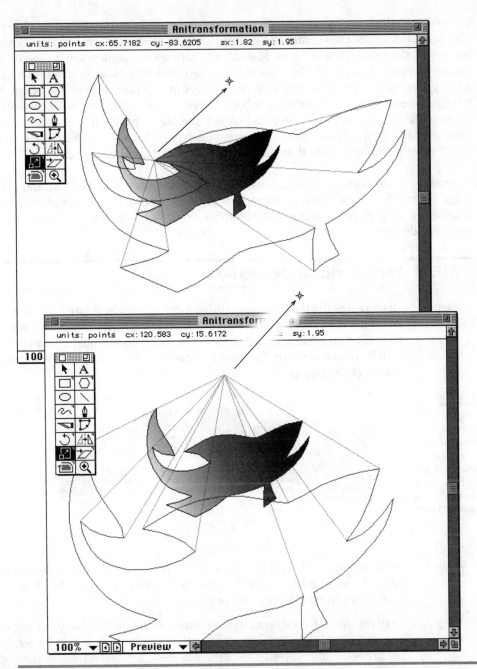

Figure 15-4: Enlarging an object by dragging with the scale tool.

The point at which you begin dragging also has an effect on the scaling of an object. This point determines the center of the enlargement or reduction, called the *transformation origin*. Both examples in Figure 15-4 show identical enlargements, but they begin at different origins. As a result, the objects in the two examples move to different locations as they increase in size. Enlarging an object always moves it away from the origin, as the figure demonstrates. Reducing an object moves it toward the origin. Because the origin in the first example is close to the object, the object hardly moves at all as in enlarges. Meanwhile, the origin in the second example is high above the object, so the object moves dramatically in the opposite direction as it increases in size.

The following steps give you a chance to experience the scale tool up-close and personal. Figure 15-5 displays two paths representing a telephone. The path of the receiver is selected; the path below it is not. In the steps, you enlarge the receiver, reduce it, and flip it upside down.

STEPS: Playing with the Scale Tool

Step 1.   Draw two paths that look something like the ones in Figure 15-5. Don't sweat it if they don't look exactly like my phone paths; you're not going to be graded on accuracy. Just draw some rough approximation and be done with it. Then save your document, because you use these paths three more times in this chapter.

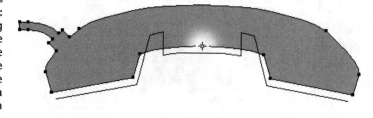

Figure 15-5:
Begin dragging with the scale tool near the middle of the selected shape to establish a transformation origin.

Step 2.   Select the top path with the arrow tool. Then switch to the scale tool and begin dragging at the location of the small cursor in Figure 15-5. This establishes the transformation origin.

Step 3.   Drag up and to the right, as demonstrated in Figure 15-6. As you drag away from the transformation origin, the path of the receiver grows larger. Both the previous and current size of the selected path are displayed throughout your drag, allowing you to gauge the effect of the enlargement. Release your mouse button to complete the scaling operation.

Figure 15-6:
Drag up and to the right from the transformation origin to enlarge the selected object.

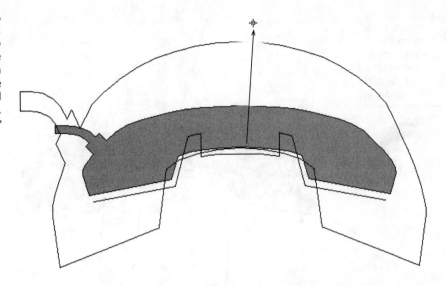

Step 4. Press Command-Z to undo the enlargement and return the path to its original size. We're just playing around here. No permanent progress made.

Step 5. Again, using the scale tool, drag from the same spot in the middle of the receiver to establish the transformation origin. But this time, drag down and to the left to reduce the selected object, as shown in Figure 15-7. As you drag, the selected path shrinks. Release the mouse button to complete the reduction.

Figure 15-7:
Drag down and to the left to reduce the selected object.

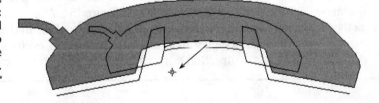

Step 6. Press Command-Z again. I hate to bore you with such recent history, but in the previous steps, you enlarged the receiver both horizontally and vertically. Then you reduced it both horizontally and vertically. This time, however, you'll enlarge the path one direction and reduce it the other.

Step 7. Starting at the same old transformation origin, drag with the scale tool up and to the left. FreeHand stretches the object vertically and squishes it horizontally, as shown in Figure 15-8.

Figure 15-8:
Drag up and to
the left to make
the receiver
taller and
narrower.

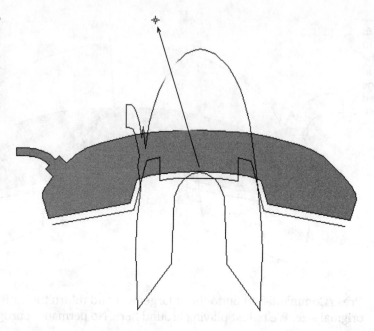

You can enlarge a selected object as much as you want, but it can't exceed FreeHand's maximum 54 × 54-inch page size. You can also reduce an object into virtual invisibility. If you drag *past* the point at which a selection is reduced into nothingness, you flip the selected object.

Step 8. Press Command-Z to undo the previous scaling. Then drag downward from the familiar origin, which reduces the size of the shape. Keep dragging downward until the receiver flips, as shown in Figure 15-9. After the shape flips, it stops shrinking and begins growing as you continue to drag. In the figure, for example, the receiver is bigger than it was when I started, even though I'm dragging downward, a direction normally associated with reductions.

This little known feature of the scale tool allows you to reflect and scale objects at the same time. However, you can only flip objects horizontally and vertically with the scale tool. To flip an object across an angled axis, you have to use the reflect tool, as described in the "Flipping objects" section later in this chapter. (I guess maybe Stu had something on Paul after all.)

Figure 15-9:
Drag very far down or very far to the left to flip the selected object and eventually enlarge it.

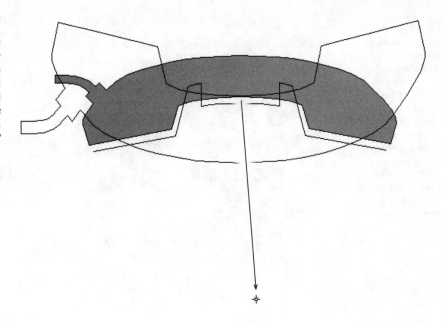

Constrained scaling

To constrain the scale tool so that it affects the height and width of a selected object equally, Shift-drag with the tool. Shift-drag up and/or to the right to enlarge an object proportionally. I say "and/or" because either action produces the same result when the Shift key is down. Shift-drag down and/or to the left to reduce the object proportionally.

 Although you can combine operationally opposite directions by Shift-dragging up and to the left or down and to the right, it isn't a particularly good idea. The scale tool can't both enlarge the width and reduce the height or vice versa when the Shift key is pressed, so it treats the 135-degree axis as a border between the worlds of proportional reductions and proportional enlargements (see Figure 15-10). If you drag in one of these directions, you may find yourself crossing these boundaries and switching from enlargement to reduction to reflection with disconcerting frequency.

 You can constrain an exclusively horizontal or vertical resizing, but you can't do it with the scale tool. Select an object, group it, and then drag a corner handle with the arrow tool. While dragging, press and hold the Shift and Control keys to make the resizing purely horizontal or vertical.

Figure 15-10:
Shift-dragging with the scale tool divides the illustration window in half. Drag in one half to enlarge the selection; drag in the other half to reduce it.

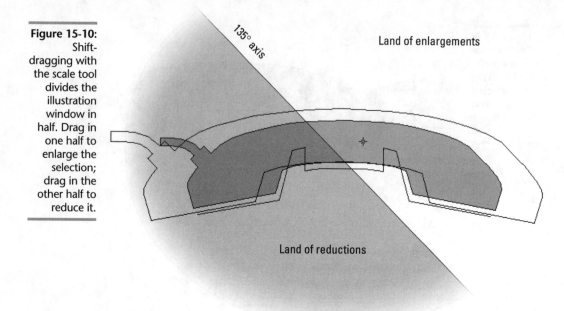

135° axis

Land of enlargements

Land of reductions

As for *why* FreeHand devotes more control to scaling groups with the arrow tool than performing the same task with the scale tool, I have no idea. But that's the way it is.

Scaling partial paths

In addition to scaling whole objects, you can scale selected elements inside a path independently of their deselected neighbors. Simply select the points that you want to enlarge or reduce and use the scale tool as directed in the previous sections.

For example, only six points are selected in the skyline path shown in Figure 15-11. The segments that border each of these points are the only segments that will be affected by the scale tool. In Figure 15-12, I dragged down and to the left with the scale tool to reduce the selected elements. This had the effect of shrinking the segments between selected points and stretching those between a selected point and a deselected point.

Figure 15-11:
An open path with six points selected.

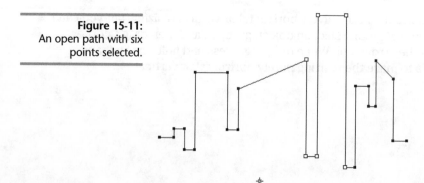

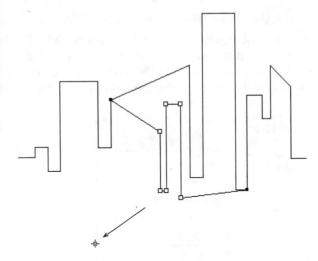

Figure 15-12:
Dragging down and to the left reduced the selected elements while leaving segments between the deselected points unchanged.

Dragging points with the scale tool can be very much like dragging them with the arrow tool. But when you use the scale tool, each selected point moves a different amount, depending on its proximity to the transformation origin. If you look closely at Figure 15-12, you'll notice that points close to the transformation origin move much less than those farther away. For example, the two selected points on the left side of the base of the tower move a few picas apiece, while the points at the top of the tower move a full inch.

 For this reason, the scale tool can prove very useful for moving specific points in ways that the arrow tool does not allow. For example, to move two selected segments equal distances in opposite directions about a central point, drag from the point with the scale tool. In the left example of Figure 15-13, I selected the points bounding each of two horizontal segments in a hexagonal shape. By positioning the scale cursor midway between the points and dragging upward, I moved the points in opposite directions, as illustrated in the right example.

Figure 15-13:
After selecting a few points (left), I dragged with the scale tool to move the points away from each other (right).

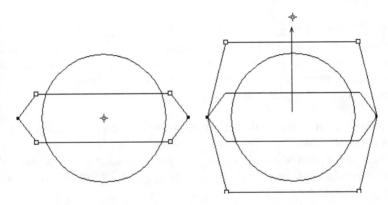

Using the Scale panel options

Double-click on the scale tool icon in the toolbox or Option-click with the scale tool in the illustration window to display the Scale panel of the Inspector palette, shown in Figure 15-14. (If worse comes to worst, you can always click on the scale icon in the Transform palette itself.) This panel allows you to scale selected objects with numerical precision.

Figure 15-14:
The Scale panel lets you specify percentages by which to enlarge or reduce selected objects.

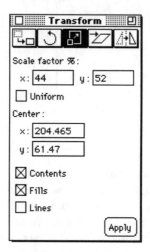

To scale the width and height of an object proportionally, select the Uniform check box and enter a value into the Scale Factor % option box. Values less than 100 percent reduce the size of a selected object; values greater than 100 percent enlarge the object; a 100 percent value leaves the object unaltered.

To scale the width and height of an object independently, deselect the Uniform check box, which splits the Scale Factor % option box into two option boxes, X and Y, as shown in Figure 15-14. The X value makes the object fatter or thinner; the Y option box makes it taller or shorter.

Below the Uniform check box are two Center option boxes, which determine the location of the transformation origin, as measured from the ruler origin. By default, FreeHand automatically stores the coordinate of the exact center of the selection. If you click on the Apply button without changing these values, FreeHand scales the selected objects with respect to their shared center.

FreeHand used to be a little more flexible. When you Option-clicked to bring up the old Scale dialog box, FreeHand recorded the location at which you clicked. This location then became the origin of your transformation. If you wanted to instead scale the selection about its center, you selected a Center button.

If you want FreeHand to record a click point now, you have to click — don't Option-click — with the scale tool (or some other transformation tool) in the illustration window. FreeHand immediately records the coordinates of the click point in the two Center option boxes. Then enter the desired percentages in the Scale Factor % option boxes and click on the Apply button as usual.

The Contents and Fills check boxes work as they do in other panels, scaling masked elements and tile patterns along with the selected objects when applicable. The Lines check box, however, is unique to the Scale panel. It enables you to choose whether or not to scale the line weights of selected objects. For example, if you reduce a path stroked with a 4-point line weight to 25 percent of its original size, and the Lines check box is selected, FreeHand reduces the stroke to a 1-point line weight.

If the scale is not proportional (Uniform is turned off), FreeHand runs through a strange and complicated procedure (that you may or may not care about). It divides the X and Y values by 100 percent, takes their square roots, and multiplies them times the line weight. Suppose that you scale the 4-point line weight 300 percent horizontally and 50 percent vertically. FreeHand divides both values by 100 to get 3 and 1/2. The square roots of these numbers are roughly 1.732 and 0.707, which, when multiplied by 4, yield a new line weight of 4.898 points.

Incredibly complex and deadly boring. That's the way computer books were meant to be, right?

Flipping objects

Flipping objects with the scale tool is a nifty parlor trick and even useful on rare occasions, but you can achieve better control if you flip with the reflect tool. The third-to-last tool on the right side of the toolbox — the one that looks like two triangles — the reflect tool flips an object around a reflection axis, which acts like a pivoting mirror. The selected object looks into this mirror; the result of the flip is the image that the mirror projects.

To use the reflect tool, drag in the illustration window to define the angle of the reflection axis. As you drag, FreeHand previews the effect of the transformation so that you can easily predict the results of different axis angles.

Suppose that you want to flip the receiver path from Figure 15-5 around an angled axis. The following exercise explains how to do this:

STEPS: Flipping with the Reflect Tool

Step 1. Select the reflect tool and begin dragging from the center of the receiver (at the spot indicated by the star cursor in Figure 15-5). This establishes the transformation origin, which is first point in the reflection axis.

Step 2. Drag with the tool to determine the angle of the reflection axis, which forms a straight line between the cursor and the origin.

Step 3. Drag above and to the left of the origin, as shown in Figure 15-15. FreeHand displays the reflection axis as a solid line across the illustration window. It also shows both original and current positions of the selected object on-screen. Release the mouse button when you've reflected the object as desired.

Figure 15-15:
Drag with the reflect tool to tilt the reflection axis and flip the select object accordingly.

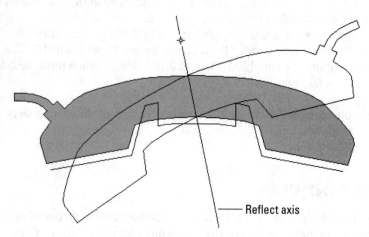

Reflect axis

You can monitor the angle of the reflection axis in the information bar by watching the Angle value. To constrain the reflection axis in 45-degree increments — so that the selection is flipped vertically, horizontally, or diagonally — Shift-drag with the reflect tool. (The performance of the tool is not in any way influenced by the angle of the constraint axes.)

Flipping partial paths

Just as you can scale selected elements independently of their deselected neighbors, you can also flip them. Simply select the points that you want to flip and use the reflect tool as usual.

Figure 15-16 shows the result of dragging with the reflect tool while the points from Figure 15-11 are selected. The effect is a little rough and tumble, but you can see that each selected point is flipped to the opposite side of the reflection axis. Segments between selected points are rotated but not stretched. Meanwhile, segments between selected and deselected points are stretched dramatically.

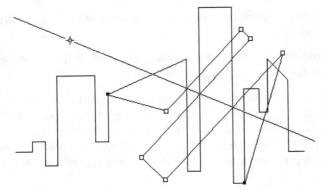

Figure 15-16:
Drag with the reflect tool to flip the selected points across to the other side of the angled reflection axis.

This technique generally produces the most satisfactory results when you Shift-drag with the reflect tool. The segments are less likely to overlap in the spider-web mess shown in Figure 15-16.

Using the Reflect panel options

Double-click on the reflect tool icon in the tool box, Option-click with the reflect tool in the illustration window, or click on the Reflect icon in the Transform palette to display the Reflect panel, shown in Figure 15-17. This panel allows you to flip one or more selected objects around a numerically angled axis.

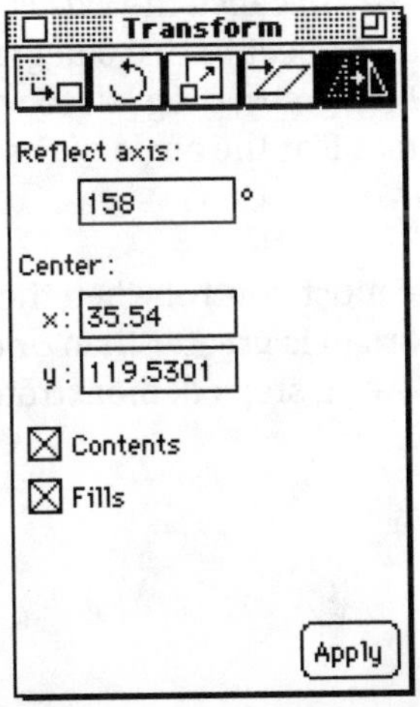

Figure 15-17:
Use the Reflect Axis option in the Reflect panel to specify the angle of the reflection axis with numerical accuracy.

The Reflect panel offers a Reflect Axis option box, which determines the angle of the reflection axis as measured from absolute horizontal. The Reflect Axis value works as follows:

- ☞ To flip an object upside-down, enter 0 into the Reflect Axis option box and press Return. This setting reflects the object around a horizontal axis.

- ☞ To flip an object horizontally, enter a value of 90, which reflects the object around a vertical axis.

- ☞ To flip an object around an angled axis, enter some other value between 0 and 180 degrees (all other values are repetitious).

All the other options — Center, Contents, and Fill — work just as they do in the Scale panel. The coordinates in the Center option boxes represent a point on the line of the reflection axis, although this point may not be smack dab in the middle of the axis. Generally, you should click inside the illustration window to locate the transformation origin before entering a value into the Reflect Axis option box and pressing Return.

Rotating objects

You operate the rotate tool, which is the third-to-last tool on left side of the palette (it looks like a circle with an arrowhead) by dragging relative to one or more selected objects. The point at which you begin dragging determines the location of the transformation origin, which determines the center of the rotation, as illustrated by the enhanced rotation-in-action scene in Figure 15-18.

Immediately after you begin dragging, FreeHand displays the *rotation axis,* which connects your cursor to the origin throughout your drag. Dragging directly to the right doesn't rotate the selection at all — regardless of the orientation or location of the object before you began dragging — because the axis is then resting at 0 degrees. Any other drag rotates the object with respect to this 0-degree position. For example, drag directly up to rotate the object 90 degrees, drag left to rotate it 180 degrees, and so on. Throughout your drag, you can monitor the angle of the rotation axis by peeking at the Angle item in the information bar.

 The rotate tool offers the most control when the distance between your cursor and the transformation origin is greater than or equal to the length of the selected object. The following steps demonstrate how this works.

Rotate tool

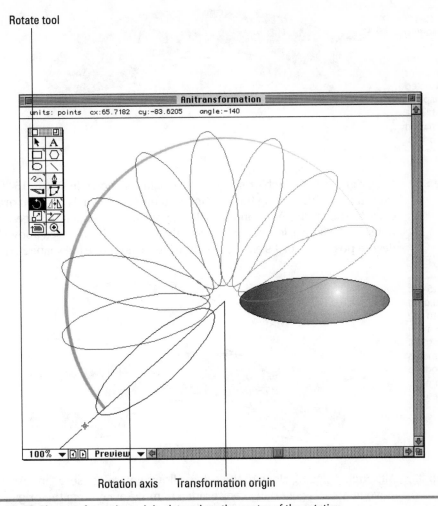

Rotation axis   Transformation origin

Figure 15-18: The transformation origin determines the center of the rotation.

STEPS: Dragging in Big Sweeps with the Rotate Tool

Step 1.   Start with the selected receiver shown back in Figure 15-5. But this time, rather than beginning your drag in the middle of the shape, drag from the lower left corner of the shape, as illustrated by the location of the star cursor in Figure 15-19.

Figure 15-19:
Begin dragging
with the rotate
tool at the
lower left point
in the selected
shape to
establish a
transformation
origin.

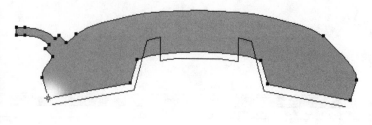

Step 2. Drag rightward an inch or so from the origin, as shown in Figure 15-20, and experiment with moving the rotation axis up and down. When you drag close to the origin, FreeHand translates your movements into huge rotations. In the figure, for example, I've only dragged about a pica above the 0-degree position, but it's enough to make FreeHand rotate the shape 20 degrees.

Figure 15-20:
When you drag
close to the
transformation
origin, small
movements
produce
dramatic
results.

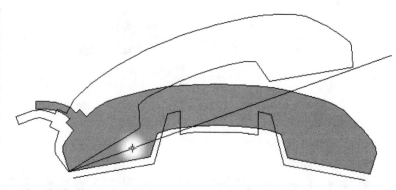

Step 3. Although dragging close to the origin allows you to conserve mouse movements, it's generally a better idea to move away from the origin, where you have more control. To test this out, continue dragging rightward until your cursor is outside the path, as shown in Figure 15-21. Here I've dragged about four times the distance from the origin as in the previous figure. My cursor is still only about a pica above the 0-degree position, but the rotation is about 5 degrees, roughly a quarter of what it was before. I'd have to drag nearly an inch above the 0-degree position to get the same rotation as shown in Figure 15-20.

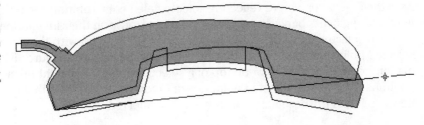

Figure 15-21:
Drag far away from the transformation origin to make more refined adjustments.

Step 4. Continue dragging farther and farther away from the origin. You can even drag far outside the illustration window along the perimeter of your screen if you want. In fact, the farther out you go, the more subtle and exact your rotations will be.

Of course, you can always constrain the performance of a transformation tool by pressing the Shift key. In the case of the rotate tool, Shift-dragging rotates a selected object by a multiple of 45 degrees from its original position.

Rotating partial paths

Figure 15-22 shows the effect of rotating selected points independently of deselected points in a free-form path. As you drag, all selected points maintain their original distances from the transformation origin — a feature that makes rotating perhaps the most predictable transformation you can apply to a partial path.

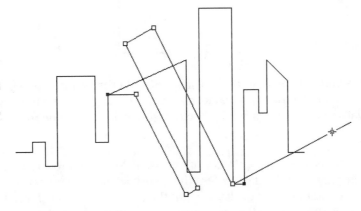

Figure 15-22:
Drag with the rotate tool to spin the selected points around the transformation origin.

As is the case when you're reflecting selected elements, rotating has no effect on the length of segments between two selected points, only on their inclination. Segments between selected and deselected points stretch to keep up with the movements of the selected points, depending on their proximity to the origin. In Figure 15-22, the transformation origin is located right on top of a selected point that neighbors a deselected point. As a result, the selected point doesn't move, which means that the segment between it and the deselected neighbor is not affected.

Using the Rotate panel options

Figure 15-23 shows the Rotate panel, which you access by double-clicking on the rotate tool in the toolbox, Option-clicking with the tool in the illustration window, or clicking on the Rotate icon at the top of the Transform palette. Using this panel, you can rotate selected objects numerically.

Figure 15-23:
The Rotate panel allows you to specify the number of degrees by which you want FreeHand to rotate a selected object.

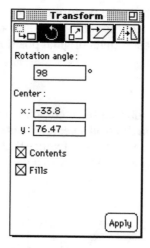

Enter any value between negative and positive 180 (all other values are repetitious) in the Rotation Angle option box. The value is measured in degrees and is accurate to 1/10 degree. A negative value rotates an object clockwise; a positive value rotates it counterclockwise.

The Center, Contents, and Fills options work as usual. You venerable old FreeHand users, remember that FreeHand 4.0 enters the coordinates of the center of the selected objects into the Center option box. If you want the center of the transformation to be at some other spot, either click in that spot inside the illustration window or enter new coordinates into the option boxes.

Slanting objects

Slanting — also called *skewing* — is perhaps the most difficult transformation to conceptualize. To skew an object is to slant its vertical and horizontal proportions independently of each other. For example, a standard kite shape is a skewed version of a perfect square. As shown in Figure 15-24, I first skewed the shape vertically and then skewed it horizontally, in two separate operations. The result is a perfect diamond shape.

Figure 15-24:
Transforming a
square into a kite
by skewing the
shape in two steps,
once vertically and
once horizontally.

Skew tool

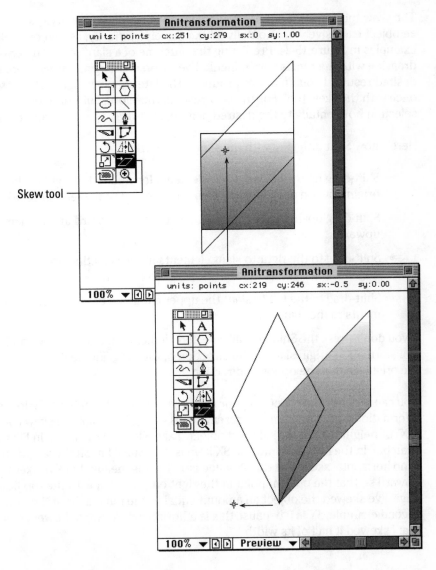

I transformed the kite in Figure 15-24 using the skew tool, the second-to-last tool on the right side of the palette. As usual, the point at which you begin dragging determines the transformation origin. The direction in which a selected object slants depends on the direction in which you drag and the side of the origin on which the object appears. Portions of the selection on opposite sides of the origin slant in opposite directions, as illustrated in the first example of Figure 15-24. The left side of the square slants downward, while the right side slants up.

The skew tool works more predictably when you Shift-drag with it, which either slants an object exclusively horizontally or exclusively vertically, as demonstrated in the two examples in Figure 15-24. Predicting the outcome of a slant that you perform by simply dragging with the tool is very difficult. Even worse, dragging rarely produces the desired results. I couldn't have produced the kite shape in Figure 15-24 by dragging once with the skew tool. For the best results, therefore, Shift-drag once to slant the selection horizontally to the desired degree; Shift-drag again to slant it vertically.

Here's how Shift-dragging with the skew tool works:

- ✆ Shift-drag up to slant selected elements located to the right of the transformation origin upward and slant any elements located to the left of the origin downward.

- ✆ Shift-drag down to slant the right elements downward and the left elements upward.

- ✆ Shift-drag to the right to slant elements in the selection above the transformation origin to the right and elements below to the left.

- ✆ Shift-drag to the left to slant the upper elements to the left and the lower elements to the right.

If you don't press the Shift key, all selected elements that are above and to right of the transformation origin slant in the direction of the drag. Elements below and to the left of the origin slant in the opposite direction.

You can monitor the effects of your skewing by noting the SX and SY items in the information bar. Both items represent ratios — the length of the skew over the width (SX) or height (SY) of the selected object. Take a look at the items in Figure 15-24, for example. In the first example, the SX item is 0 because I'm Shift-dragging upward; there is no horizontal skew. But the SY value is 1.00. This means that I've skewed the shape upward so that the bottom point in the right edge is even with the top point in the left edge. I've skewed the object an amount equal to the full height of the object. In the second example, SY is 0 because this is a horizontal skew. SX, however, is 0.5, showing that I skewed it half of its width.

It may take some experimenting with the skew tool before you're able to accurately predict the results of your actions. If you need some practice, give the following steps a try. As usual, we'll be abusing the receiver path from long-past Figure 15-5.

STEPS: Shift-Dragging and Just Plain Dragging with the Skew Tool

Step 1. Select the receiver with the arrow tool. Then Shift-drag upward with the skew tool from the center of the shape (the point indicated by the cursor in Figure 15-5). The right half of the phone shrugs upward with your drag because it is located on the right side of the transformation origin. The left half of the phone shrugs down, as shown in Figure 15-25. Release the mouse button once the SY item in the information bar reads 0.3.

Figure 15-25:
Shift-drag upward with the skew tool to slant the right half of the selected shape up and the left half down.

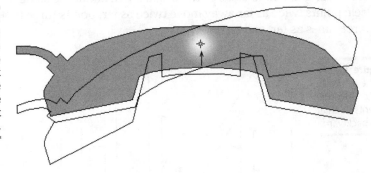

Step 2. Shift-drag again with the skew tool, but this time drag to the left. The top of the shape slants backward, and the bottom portion slants forward, as shown in Figure 15-26. Release mouse button and Shift key once the SX value reads –1.8. FreeHand skews the shape backward by an amount equal to nearly twice its former width.

Figure 15-26:
Shift-drag left to slant the top half of the receiver to the left and the bottom half to the right.

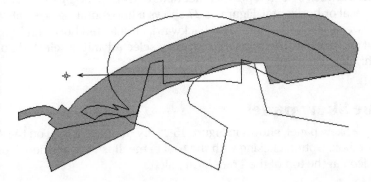

Step 3. Press Command-Z twice in a row to undo both the vertical and horizontal skewing. Now try dragging up and to the right with the tool — without pressing the Shift key — to get the same results shown in Figure 15-26. The truth is, you can't. It just proves the old adage: Two Shift-drags are better than one without a Shift.

Slanting partial paths

What good would the skew tool be if you couldn't slant selected elements independently of their deselected neighbors? In Figure 15-27, I Shift-dragged to the left with the skew tool. The selected points move with the star cursor based on their proximity to the transformation origin. Points close to the origin move about the same distance as the cursor itself; points twice as far away move twice as far, points three times as far away move three times as far, and so on.

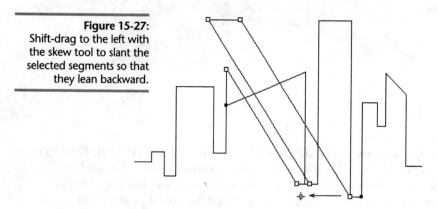

Figure 15-27:
Shift-drag to the left with the skew tool to slant the selected segments so that they lean backward.

The segments between selected points react differently depending on whether they are primarily vertical or horizontal. Figure 15-27 shows a horizontal skew, so all vertical segments between selected points slant backward; all selected horizontal segments don't slant at all. As usual, the segments between selected and deselected points just stretch or shrink to keep up.

Using the Skew panel

You access the Skew panel, shown in Figure 15-28, by double-clicking on the skew tool icon in the toolbox, Option-clicking with the tool in the illustration window, or clicking on the Skew icon at the top of the Transform palette.

Figure 15-28:
In the Skew panel, you can specify the horizontal and vertical components of a skew in degrees.

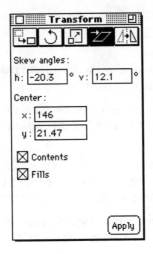

Enter the degree to which you want to skew a selected object in the two Skew Angles option boxes. The H option determines the horizontal slant; the V value determines the vertical slant. Both negative and positive values are accepted. Here's how they work:

- A negative H value slants a selected object backward, as if you dragged to the left with the skew tool.

- A positive H value slants the object forward — which is the opposite of the way this option worked in Version 3.0.

- A positive V value slants the right side of the object upward and the left side downward, as if you dragged up with the skew tool.

- A negative V value slants the right side of the object downward and the left side upward.

With one exception, these items work the same way in the information bar. Whereas FreeHand measures skews as ratios in the information bar, it measures them in degrees inside the skew panel. One (ratios) is a relative system, the other (degrees) is absolute.

To understand how degrees work, imagine that you are slanting a rectangle. If you enter 30 in the H option box, FreeHand slants the vertical sides from their normal 90-degree posture to 60 degrees (90 − 30 = 60). If you enter 30 in the V option box, the horizontal sides slant up from a 0-degree to a 30-degree incline. A value of 90 degrees in either the H or V option box flattens the selection to virtual nothingness, which is why FreeHand won't accept this value. The highest (or lowest) acceptable value is 89.9 (or −89.9). But values beyond negative or positive 45 degrees are rarely useful.

After you enter your values in the H and V option boxes, press Return to implement your changes. The Center option boxes and Contents and Fills check boxes work the same in the Skew panel as they do in the other transformation panels.

Summary

- Press Command-M to display the Transform palette and then click on an icon along the top of the palette to change panels.

- You can also display a panel by double-clicking on one of the transformation tool icons in the tool box or by Option-clicking with the tool in the illustration window.

- The Move panel records all moves that you make by dragging selected elements with the arrow tool. To revert the move later, make positive values negative, make negative values positive, and press Return.

- The point at which you begin dragging with any transformation tool serves as the center of the transformation. This point is called the transformation origin.

- Drag up and to the right with the scale tool to enlarge a selected object; drag down and to the left to reduce it.

- You can use the scale tool to move selected points in equal but opposite directions.

- Select the Lines check box to scale the stroke of a selected object as you scale the object itself.

- A vertical reflection axis flips a selected object horizontally. A horizontal axis flips it vertically.

- When using the rotate tool, drag far away from the transformation origin to gain the most control.

- To produce the most predictable transformations with the skew tool, Shift-drag with the tool to slant the selected object horizontally and then Shift-drag again to slant it vertically.

Duplicating Objects and Effects

. . . .

In This Chapter

➥ Primary uses for the Cut, Copy, and Paste commands

➥ How to clone objects with the Clone and Duplicate commands

➥ Ways to repeat recent transformations

➥ The wonders of series duplication

➥ How to achieve a perspective effect

. . . .

Clones to the Rescue

The older you get, the more precious your time becomes. It's not just that you sense you'll eventually run out of time or that the rate at which it disappears increases exponentially with each year that passes. On top of that, you have more to do. Make a living, clean the house, balance the checkbook, invest your savings, resolve conflicts, take care of family members, hobnob with associates — even getting together with friends can seem like a chore. These are the responsibilities that accompany the personal and financial freedoms of adulthood.

Now imagine for a moment that you can buy more time by cloning yourself. Certainly, there are some nagging details to consider before you jump into such a purchase. I mean, would your clones expect you to pitch in and work just as much as you do now? Would you have to manage them like other employees? Would they consume as much as you do, thereby nullifying the benefits of cloning? Would they all want their own bedrooms? Would you have to clone your spouse to keep your clones happy, so that they didn't tear around the countryside like demented Frankenstein's monsters? This is beginning to sound terrible!

Well, obviously it wouldn't be like *that*. Those kinds of clones would never sell. The clones that I'm asking you to imagine are the result of meticulous engineering and first-rate design. They can do what you do without supervision and have no ego to get in the way. You can go on one vacation after another as your clones slave away for the greater good of you. And for a limited time only, you can purchase a special adapter that allows you to eat all the Häagen-Dazs you want and have a clone exercise it off.

Send $100,000 now for your introductory starter kit. In the meantime, while I book my getaway to Brazil, I'll tell you about a means of cloning that is already at your disposal. FreeHand enables you to clone any object or text block as many times as you want. This feature is an amazing time-saver. No longer do you have to draw and redraw similar objects. Nor do you have to trace duplicates, as when drawing conventionally, or work from photocopies that take nearly as long to clean up as it takes to create an illustration from scratch.

Every clone in FreeHand is absolutely identical to the original; you don't lose any quality or functionality. Clones are fully editable, so you can modify them to fit special requirements (as demonstrated by the conversion of Groucho's eyebrow to a mustache back in Chapter 4). You can even repeat transformations or automatically reapply a transformation as you clone an object.

You have enough demands on your time without spending an inordinate amount of it inside FreeHand. If you draw something once, don't draw it again. This way, you can spend less time working on the computer and spend more time with other time-saving appliances such as your dishwasher, your food processor, your fax machine, your washer and dryer, your VCR, your car, your vacuum cleaner, your cellular phone, your lawn mower . . . .

Heck, by time you get done with those things, you'll be grateful to take a break and get back to FreeHand.

Duplicating Objects and Type

FreeHand provides several sets of commands for replicating objects. All are located under the Edit menu.

The foremost commands included with all Macintosh programs are Cut, Copy, and Paste. Although these commands aren't the most efficient means for duplicating objects inside a document — a job better suited to the Clone and Duplicate commands — they do serve a variety of purposes in FreeHand:

- **Swapping objects between illustrations:** Cut or copy an object and paste it into another document. This method is also useful for transferring attribute styles and other settings to another document.

- **Transferring objects to different applications:** After you cut or copy objects, you can paste them into other applications. You can even cut or copy items from other applications and paste them in FreeHand. The program's support for foreign Clipboard objects is excellent.

- **Duplicate or move some type inside a text block:** Select some characters with the text tool, choose the Copy command, and then paste the copied text into another position or into another text block. Use Cut and Paste to remove selected characters from one location and move them to another.

- **Stacking objects:** If you want to move an object several objects forward or backward within a layer, you can cut the object, select the object that's immediately in front of where you want to position the cut object, and choose Edit ⇨ Paste Behind.

- **Creating special effects:** Choosing Cut or Copy is the first step in creating tile patterns and masks, as discussed in Chapters 13 and 17, respectively.

- **Saving one object from reversion:** If you hate the changes you've made to an illustration — except those applied to one object — cut or copy that one object to the Clipboard. Then use the Revert command to get rid of all the other changes. When the illustration is back to its previous form, press Command-V to place the object from the Clipboard back into the illustration.

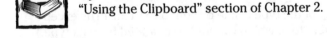 If you're unclear on how to use the Cut, Copy, and Paste commands, read the "Using the Clipboard" section of Chapter 2.

Cloning objects

Cloning functions much like the Copy command, with two important exceptions: First, cloning bypasses the Clipboard. It doesn't displace the current occupant of the Clipboard and it doesn't replace that object with the cloned object. Second, cloning acts like a combined Copy-and-Paste command. The cloned object appears immediately in your illustration, in front of all other objects in the current layer. If the originals are spread about onto more than one layer, each clone appears at the front of the layer that contains its original.

You can clone objects by using either of two commands, Edit ⇨ Clone (Command-equal) or Edit ⇨ Duplicate (Command-D). The Clone command creates a clone of the selected object directly in front of the original — which means that your document appears to be no different after you choose Clone than it did before, a fact that invariably confuses new users. To see the clone, you have to drag it away from the original.

(Only the cloned objects are selected immediately after you choose Clone, so dragging the selection moves only the clones.)

Like Clone, the Duplicate command creates a clone in front of all other objects in the layer. But it also offsets the clone 10 points down and 10 to the right from the original. The Duplicate command has the added ability to replicate series of transformations, as described later in this chapter.

Some experienced users rely exclusively on the Clone command to create clones and reserve the Duplicate command for use with transformations. But my suggestion is this: If you want to create an effect that relies on a clone being positioned directly in front of an original or offset only slightly — as in the case of the stroking effects covered in Chapter 14 — use the Clone command. If you want to use the clone elsewhere in the illustration or reshape it to serve an entirely different function in your artwork, use the Duplicate command. Then you'll know that the clone is there in case you decide to go off and do something else for a moment.

Sometimes, I find myself creating several clones directly on top of each other. If you ever need to check how many clones occupy the same space, marquee them with the arrow tool to select them all and take a look at the Inspector palette. Regardless of which panel is displayed, FreeHand tells you the number of selected objects just below the title bar.

Cloning partial objects

You can clone text objects separately of the type inside or bound to them. (The exception is a text block created with the text tool, which cannot be separated from its type.) Simply Option-click on the path with the arrow tool to select it independently of its type and then choose the Clone or Duplicate command. You can then use the object to hold more type, stroke or fill it to add an effect to the text, or use it for any of a thousand other purposes.

The same goes for cloning objects inside groups or composite paths. Option-click on the path and choose Edit ⇨ Clone or Edit ⇨ Duplicate. When you clone such an object, the original object remains part of the group or composite path, but FreeHand makes the clone entirely independent. If you want to bring the clone into the group or composite path, you have to ungroup (Command-U) or split (Command-Shift-J) the original objects, Shift-click on the clone with the arrow tool to add it to the selection, and regroup (Command-G) or join (Command-J) the objects back together.

The only chink in FreeHand's replicating capabilities is that you can't clone a partial path. Even if only a few points in a path are selected, FreeHand clones the entire thing. Compare this with Illustrator, which can copy and clone individual segments for integration into other objects. If you want to reuse just a segment or two in an existing path in FreeHand, you have to clone the whole path and use the knife tool to split off the portion of the path you want to retain.

Repeating Transformations

You can duplicate the effects of a recent transformation by choosing Arrange ⇨ Transform Again (Command-comma). This command applies the most recently used transformation to the selected object. It doesn't matter how long ago the transformation effect was applied, as long as it was during the current session.

I'll use Figure 16-1 as an example. After drawing the fish and ellipse at the top of the figure, I skewed the ellipse as shown in the second example to offset it at a different angle from the fish. Later, I decided that I wanted the fish to be skewed too. I'd drawn a few paths but hadn't applied any transformations — including moving — since I skewed the ellipse. I selected the fish and pressed Command-comma to apply the exact same skew percentages to the fish that I applied to the ellipse. The result appears at the bottom of figure 16-1.

 The Transform Again command only remembers the last transformation performed. But you can make it remember even older transformations by using the Undo command. Simply undo the results of any transformations performed since the transformation you want to repeat, select the object you want to transform, and press Command-comma.

The problem with this technique, of course, is that you have to undo a lot of operations that you may be perfectly happy with. So before you go to all that trouble, check the Transform palette. The panels in the palette record the last transformations performed in each of the five transformation categories (move, rotate, scale, skew, and reflect). If you're lucky, the transformation that you want to repeat will be one of the five. If so, just click on the Apply button.

Another use for the Transform Again command is to apply a slight transformation several times to the same object. By using this technique, you can experiment with a transformation until you get it just right. If you go one step too far with a transformation, just press Command-Z to return the object to its previous position, size, or angle.

Suppose that you've created a complicated object that's too small to match the size of another object in your illustration. Rather than going back and forth, scaling the object by guess and by golly, you can perform a slight enlargement — about a quarter of what you think is needed — and repeat the transformation several times by pressing Command-comma. With each application of the command, the selected object grows by the specified percentage. When it gets too big, just press Command-Z to take it down a notch.

Series Duplication

Using the Duplicate command simply to create offset clones is fine, but it doesn't take full advantage of the command's capabilities. When used on the heels of a transformation operation, Duplicate functions much like Transform Again. But Duplicate clones an object before transforming it and can repeat a series of transformations instead of just one. These features come in handy when you want to create a string of objects and place them in a consistent pattern.

To use the Duplicate command to repeat a series of transformations, follow these steps:

STEPS: Repeating a Series of Transformations

Step 1. Select the object that you want to clone and transform.

Step 2. Choose Edit ⇨ Clone or press Command-equal to clone the object. You can also clone the object using the Duplicate command, but the Clone command is usually the better choice because it doesn't include an automatic offset, which can interfere with aligning objects in a series.

Step 3. Transform the clone to your heart's content. You can move it twice, scale it once, rotate it once, whatever you want. However, if you're going to apply a certain kind of transformation twice — two moves, for example — be sure to apply them one right after the other, without some other transformation in between. Also, be sure not to deselect the clone or perform any operation other than a transformation.

Step 4. Choose Edit ⇨ Duplicate or press Command-D. FreeHand not only creates a new clone of the object, it also repeats every one of the transformations applied to it.

To create Figure 16-2, I started with the single fish shape at the top of the figure. I then selected the fish, cloned it, dragged it down to the location of the second fish, and used the Scale panel to enlarge the clone proportionally to 120 percent of its former size. To create the third and fourth fish, I merely pressed Command-D twice. FreeHand repeated the cloning, moving, and scaling operations automatically.

Figure 16-2:
After selecting the fish (top), I cloned it, moved it, and scaled it (second). I then pressed Command-D twice in a row to clone the fish twice more and repeat the transformations (third and bottom).

By duplicating both transformation and object, you can achieve perspective effects. The following steps demonstrate how to use Clone, Duplicate, and a few transformations to create a gridwork of objects. These steps make use of the three paths shown in Figure

16-3. The bottom segment of the outermost path is longer than the top segment, giving it an illusion of depth. The inner ellipses are positioned slightly closer to the top segment of the outer shape, enhancing the illusion.

Figure 16-3:
By using Clone, Duplicate, and a few transformations, you can turn these three paths into the illustration shown in Figure 16-9.

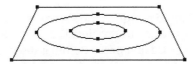

STEPS: Scaling and Duplicating in Perspective

Step 1.   Select the paths and press Command-equal to clone them. FreeHand positions the three cloned paths directly in front of the originals.

Step 2.   Select the skew tool. Begin dragging above the paths at the location indicated by the star cursor at the top of Figure 16-3. This establishes the transformation origin.

Step 3.   Continue dragging to the right. Press the Shift key while dragging to slant the cloned paths horizontally. After they reach the location of the selected paths in Figure 16-4, release the mouse button and Shift key. Notice that the cloned tile appears to lean into the original, extending back into the same visual horizon. This effect is a result of setting the transformation origin high above the paths.

Figure 16-4:
Shift-drag to the right with the skew tool to slant the cloned paths to the left.

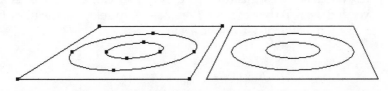

Step 4. Press Command-D to create another clone and repeat the horizontal skew operation. Figure 16-5 shows the result, which further enhances the illusion of perspective.

Figure 16-5:
Choose the
Duplicate
command to
repeat the skew
and clone
operations.

Step 5. Use the arrow tool to marquee the six paths that make up the two leftmost tiles. Press the grave key to deselect the points and leave only the paths themselves selected. Then press Command-equal to clone them.

Step 6. In this step, you flip the clones about the center of the original tile to make the series symmetrical. Double-click on the reflect tool icon in the toolbox to switch to the Reflect panel in the Transform palette. Click with the reflect tool in the center of the right tile to transfer the coordinates of the desired transformation origin to the Center option boxes in the Reflect panel. Then enter a value of 90 into the Reflect Axis option box and press Return. The result is shown in Figure 16-6: five symmetrical tiles emerging from the surface of the page.

Figure 16-6:
The result of
selecting the six
leftmost paths,
cloning them,
and flipping the
clones about the
center of the
deselected set of
paths.

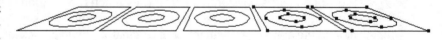

Step 7. You have now managed to impart a sense of perspective through the use of cloning, skewing, and flipping. But the illustration lacks . . . gee whiz, I don't know, call it "drama." What's needed are additional rows of slanting tiles, which are most easily created by scaling clones of the existing row over and over. To begin, press Command-A to select all the tiles. Then press Command-equal to clone again.

Step 8.   Double-click on the scale tool icon in the toolbox to switch to the Scale panel in the Transform palette. Click with the scale tool above the tiles at the location indicated by the star cursor at the top of Figure 16-7. This establishes a transformation origin at the same location as the origin used to skew the first clone back in Step 2.

Figure 16-7:
Clone the entire row of tiles and click with the scale tool to set the transforma-tion origin in the Scale panel.

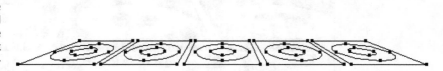

Step 9.   Select the Uniform check box in the Scale panel, enter 150 into the Scale Factor % option box, and press Return. Figure 16-8 shows how a second, larger row of tiles is created. Again, because of the placement of the transformation origin, the second row lines up perfectly with the first. By scaling the cloned shapes to 150 percent of their original size, you enlarge both the size of the shapes and the distance between the shapes and the transformation origin, thus pushing the shapes downward.

Figure 16-8:
Scale clones of the top row of tiles to 150 percent to create two perfectly aligned rows.

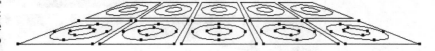

Step 10.   Press Command-D to create a third row of larger clones directly beneath the second row.

Step 11.   To create the illustration shown in Figure 16-9, press Command-D several more times. Each series of paths increases in size and distance from the paths above it, thereby creating an even and continuous sense of perspec-tive. Figure 16-9 is shown as it appears when printed. All shapes are filled and stroked. Foreground tiles are filled with darker shades of gray than background tiles, heightening the sense of depth. I also added a layer of shadows just for the sake of general coolness.

Figure 16-9:
The result of choosing Duplicate several times and filling and stroking the resulting paths.

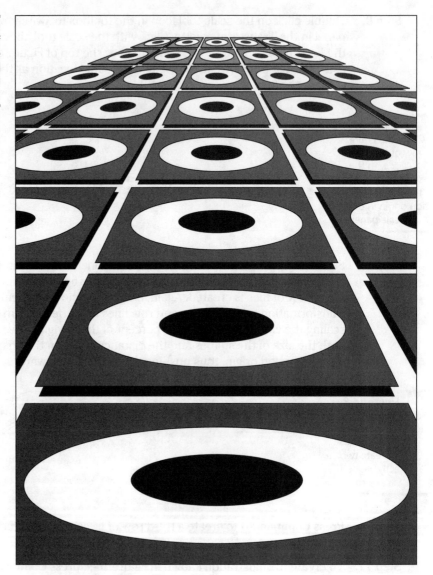

Summary

- Use the Clone and Duplicate commands to clone objects inside a single document.

- To clone a path independently of text or a group, Option-click on the path with the arrow tool and then press Command-equal.

- Press Command-comma to apply the most recent transformation to a selected object. You can also use the panels in the Transform panel to access and reapply other recent transformations.

- The Duplicate command repeats a clone operation and all transformations immediately following it.

- Create perspective effects by positioning the transformation origin a fair distance from the objects that you want to skew or scale. Experiment with the transformation origin to find the best spot.

- Do not really send me $100,000 for a cloning machine. It's an entirely fraudulent offer. I have my own cloning machine — how else could I write so many books? — but I'm not willing to sell it.

Blends, Masks, and Composite Paths

In This Chapter

- ➽ Using the options in the Blend panel
- ➽ Creating custom gradations and morphing effects
- ➽ Reshaping and recoloring paths in a blend
- ➽ Masking objects with clipping paths
- ➽ Poking transparent holes in filled paths
- ➽ Creating composite clipping paths
- ➽ Flowing a single fill over multiple shapes

The Most Special of Special Effects

This chapter is Chapter 13's older and more sophisticated brother. In Chapter 13, you learned how to apply automated fills, including gradations, tile patterns, and predefined PostScript routines. You have to love the fact that the fill patterns are fully automated, but they can be equally limiting. You can create only two kinds of gradations and you can't control them nearly to the extent that you can in FreeHand's arch-rival, Illustrator. And although repeating patterns are great for backgrounds and stylized drawings, both can appear simplistic and overly geometric when used inside more true-to-life illustrations.

That's where this chapter comes in. If you want to create a custom gradation, for example, you can create two paths, fill them with different colors, and then blend them to create a host of incremental color bands. To apply the blend to the interior of a shape, you can cut the blend and paste it inside the shape to create a mask. Blends aren't the only objects you can mask; in fact, any graphic object or text block you create in FreeHand can be pasted inside a path, allowing you to create organic fill patterns that never repeat. To top it all off, you can cut holes in a path to make portions of the path transparent or apply a single fill across multiple separate objects, both functions of composite paths.

None of these functions is new to FreeHand 4.0. Version 1.0 was the first drawing program to offer masking; blends were lifted from Illustrator in Version 2.0; and composite paths made a splash in Version 3.0. But all are as fresh, exciting, and teeming with untapped applications as they were the day they debuted. If you've just recently started using FreeHand, this chapter should make your eyes pop. If you're an old FreeHand hack, you may learn a few new tricks that have evaded you these many years. But regardless of your experience level, this chapter is mandatory reading if you're at all interested in creating professional-quality illustrations.

Blending Paths

Blending is part duplication, part distribution, and part transformation. It creates a series of intermediate paths — called *steps* — between two selected free-form paths. I say that it's part duplication because the Blend command creates as many clones of a path as you like. It's part distribution because the steps are evenly distributed between the two original objects. And it's part transformation because FreeHand automatically adjusts the shape of each step depending on where it lies. Steps near the first of the two original paths resemble the first path; steps near the second path more closely resemble the second path.

If blending had been introduced in the last year or so, it probably would have been called *morphing* because it creates a metamorphic transition between one shape and another. For example, suppose that you create two paths, one that represents a caterpillar and one that represents a butterfly. By blending these two paths, you create several steps that represent metamorphic stages between the two life forms, as shown in Figure 17-1. The first intermediate path is shaped much like the caterpillar. Each intermediate path after that becomes less like the caterpillar and more like the butterfly.

FreeHand also blends the colors or the fills and strokes between two paths. If one path is white and the other is black, the steps between the paths are filled with a fountain of transitional gray values. Though each step is filled with a solid color (assuming that you're blending objects with flat fills), the effect is that of a gradation. To create the steps shown in Figure 17-1, for example, I originally filled the caterpillar with black. That is why the steps get darker as they progress from the butterfly to the caterpillar. After creating the blend, I filled the caterpillar with white; I also applied heavier strokes to both the caterpillar and butterfly.

Figure 17-1:
Blending a caterpil-
lar and a butterfly
creates a series of
transformed and
distributed dupli-
cates between the
two objects.

Applying the Blend command

To create a blend, you must first select two free-form paths. You can't blend more than
two paths at a time. If you want to blend rectangles or ellipses, you must first ungroup
them. You can't blend paths that are part of groups, composite paths, or text objects
without first separating them. (Option-clicking on the paths to select them independently doesn't work.) Also, you can't blend an open path and a closed path. Both paths
must be either open or closed. And finally, both paths must be filled and stroked
similarly. For example, if one path is stroked with a 6-point line weight, you can't blend
it with a path that has a transparent stroke.

You can, however, blend between a path stroked with a 6-point line weight and
one stroked with a 0-point line weight. Because a 0-point line weight results in
the thinnest line that your printer can create, the stroke is practically transparent when printed to a high resolution imagesetter. (When you proof the stroke
to a laser printer or preview it on-screen, you'll be able to see the 0-point stroke
clearly.)

To blend two paths, select the paths and then select one (and only one) point in each path, as illustrated in the first example in Figure 17-2. If the paths are open, you must select an endpoint in each path. Then choose Arrange ⇨ Path Operations ⇨ Blend or press Command-Shift-E (*E* for *eh?* or perhaps *evolve*) to create a series of steps. FreeHand treats the frontmost path of the two originals as the first path in the blend and the rear path as the last path. For this reason, these paths are sometimes called the *source* and the *windup,* respectively. The steps are layered between the source and windup paths, descending in stacking order — one in back of another — as they approach the windup. FreeHand automatically combines original paths and steps into a grouped object that has special properties that are discussed in later sections. This object is called a *blend.*

Figure 17-2:
Select one point
in each of two
paths (left) and
then choose the
Blend command
to create a series
of intermediary
steps (right).

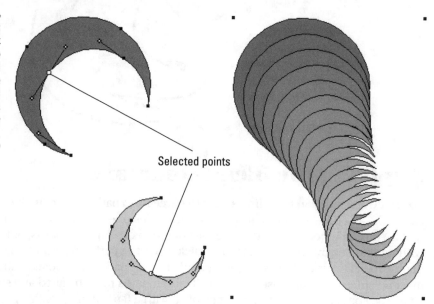

Selected points

Adjusting values in the Blend panel

When you chose the Blend command in previous versions of FreeHand, a dialog box appeared. In Version 4.0, you don't get the dialog box. Instead, FreeHand automatically creates a default quantity of steps depending on the colors applied to the source and windup paths. The maximum number of default steps is 25, which FreeHand applies to a blend between a white path and a black path. If one or both of the selected paths are filled with a tint or gray value, FreeHand creates fewer steps.

After FreeHand applies its default number of steps, you can edit the steps using the options in the Blend panel, a specialized Object panel of the Inspector palette (Command-Option-I). This panel, shown in Figure 17-3, contains three options that enable you to control the number of steps in a blend and the manner in which the steps are positioned and colored with respect to the originals.

Figure 17-3:
The Blend panel replaces the old Blend dialog box, allowing you to control the number of steps in a gradation.

The three option boxes in the Blend panel work as follows:

- **Number of Steps:** In this option box, enter the number of intermediate paths that you want FreeHand to create. Any value from 1 to 1,000 is acceptable. The First and Last values update automatically.

- **First:** The two Range % values allow you to adjust the color and placement of the first and last steps in the blend. The value in the First option box affects how the first step is colored as a percentage of the difference between the fills and strokes of the source and windup paths. This value also determines the location of the first step as a percentage of the total distance between the source and windup paths.

- **Last:** This option works just like the First option, but it controls the color and location of the last step. The location is measured from the source path, not the windup.

Press Return to apply changes made to the values in the Blend panel. By the way, if you don't quite understand how each of these options works — especially the Range % values, which are pretty cryptic — don't keep reading the preceding paragraphs over and over; your brain will just turn to mush. Instead, read the following section, which explains the Blend panel options in more detail.

Specifying steps and range

Suppose that you specify nine steps between your source and windup paths. FreeHand determines the positioning of each step as a percentage of the distance between both paths. The source — which is the front path — occupies the 0 percent position and the windup — the rear path — occupies the 100 percent position. To space the steps evenly, FreeHand automatically spaces the steps in 10 percent intervals. Therefore, the First option box contains the value 10 percent, and the Last option box contains 90 percent.

The two Range % values control the colors and placement of the steps. To understand how to modify these values, you need to understand how FreeHand assigns colors to blends. By way of an example, suppose that the source path is filled with white and stroked with a 50 percent black, 1-point line weight, as in the case of the lower crescent on the left side of Figure 17-4. Meanwhile, the windup path is filled with 50 percent black and stroked with a 100 percent black, 6-point line weight, as in the top crescent in the figure.

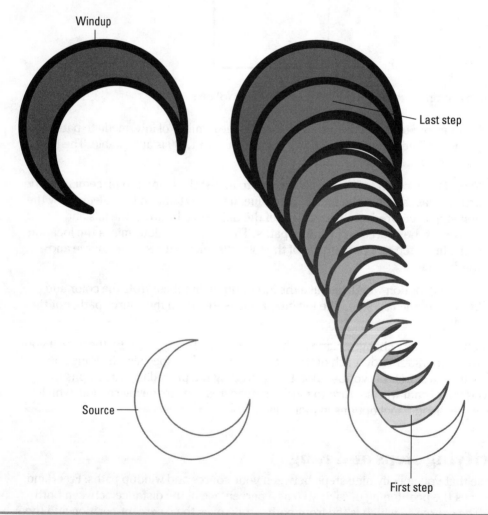

Figure 17-4: After filling and stroking two paths (left), I created a nine-step blend between them (right).

By default, the fill and stroke attributes of the steps are averaged incrementally as a function of the number of steps you specify. To calculate this average, FreeHand divides the difference for each attribute by the number of steps. In this case, the differences between source and windup paths are as follows:

- The difference in fill color = 50% black – 0% black (white) = 50%.

- The difference in stroke color = 100% black – 50% black = 50%.

- The difference in line weight = 6 points – 1 point = 5 points.

 The Blend command ignores other stroke attributes, such as line caps, joins, and dash patterns. It also ignores tile patterns and PostScript fill routines. However, FreeHand *can* blend shapes filled with gradations, as explained in the "Creating custom gradations" section later in this chapter.

With 9 steps, a First value of 10 percent, and a Last value of 90 percent, the blend appears as shown on the right side of Figure 17-4. Table 17-1 lists the fill and stroke of the source and windup paths as well as those FreeHand assigns to each and every step.

Table 17-1	A Sample 9-Step Blend			
Step	*Percent Change*	*Fill Color*	*Stroke Color*	*Line Weight*
Source		0% black	50% black	1 point
1st	10%	5% black	55% black	1.5 point
2nd	20%	10% black	60% black	2 point
3rd	30%	15% black	65% black	2.5 point
4th	40%	20% black	70% black	3 point
5th	50%	25% black	75% black	3.5 point
6th	60%	30% black	80% black	4 point
7th	70%	35% black	85% black	4.5 point
8th	80%	40% black	90% black	5 point
9th (last)	90%	45% black	95% black	5.5 point
Windup		50% black	100% black	6 point

You can change the two Range % values to alter both the color and placement of the first and last steps. In the case of Figure 17-4, FreeHand would then automatically space the second through eighth steps evenly between the first and last steps. If you change the First value to 30 percent and the Last value to 70 percent, for example, you compress the steps closer together while leaving some breathing room between the steps and the source and windup paths.

Figure 17-5 shows an example of changing the Range % values. The eye at the top of the figure is filled with black and stroked with a white hairline outline. The eye at the bottom of the page is filled with white and stroked with a 2-point black outline. (The eyebrow and lower eyelid shapes are not involved in the blend.) Insofar as stacking order is concerned, the top eye is in back of the bottom eye.

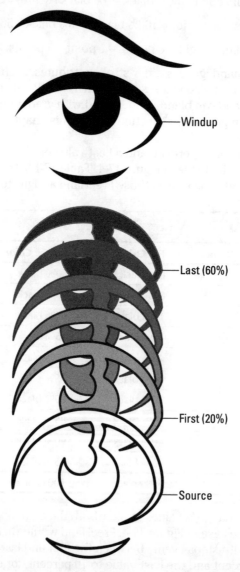

Figure 17-5:
The result of changing the First value to 20 percent and the Last value to 60 percent.

Windup

Last (60%)

First (20%)

Source

After blending the two shapes and displaying the Blend panel, I specified 5 steps and changed the First option to 20 percent. The distance between the two eye paths is roughly 24 picas, so a First value of 20 percent changed the distance between the source path and the first step to 20 percent of 24 picas, which is about 5 picas. This slightly exaggerated the gap between the source path and the first step. It also affected the color of the fill and stroke. The fill is slightly lighter than it would have been if I hadn't raised the First value; the stroke is slightly darker.

To create the gap between the windup path and the last step, I lowered the Last value to 60 percent. This changes the distance from the last step to the source path to 60 percent of 24 picas, or about 14 1/2 picas. It also lightens the fill of the last step and darkens the stroke.

Selecting points in a blend

The other factor that plays a crucial role in the appearance of blended paths is the placement of points inside the steps. The quantity and location of points in the steps, as well as the form of the segments between points, is based on two criteria:

- The number of points in the source and windup paths
- The specific point selected in each path when you choose the Blend command

The Blend command relies on points as guidelines. FreeHand tries to match each point in the source path with a point in the windup path. It then draws segments between each consecutive pair of points.

For the most predictable results, your source and windup paths should contain an identical number of points. This is extremely important. If the two paths contain different numbers of points, FreeHand has to periodically insert or remove points inside steps, which can results in some pretty strange looking transitions. When both paths contain an identical number of points, the Blend command produces a consistent series of steps that looks more or less like you thought it would.

The points that you select before choosing Blend also influence the appearance of the steps. FreeHand uses the selected points as origin points. It then progresses around the paths in the direction that each path was created, coupling a point from the source path with a point from the windup.

Try to select a similarly positioned point in each path. If possible, select a point that occupies a central position in its path (unless the paths are open, in which case FreeHand requires you to select an endpoint in each path).

If you select points that occupy different positions in the source and windup paths, FreeHand creates distorted steps. Figure 17-6 shows three examples. In each, I selected different pairs of points in the two source and windup triangles. Each point in one triangle blends toward a point in the other triangle based on its proximity to the selected point, as illustrated by the gray lines. The points are labeled according to the order in which FreeHand blends them, starting with the selected points.

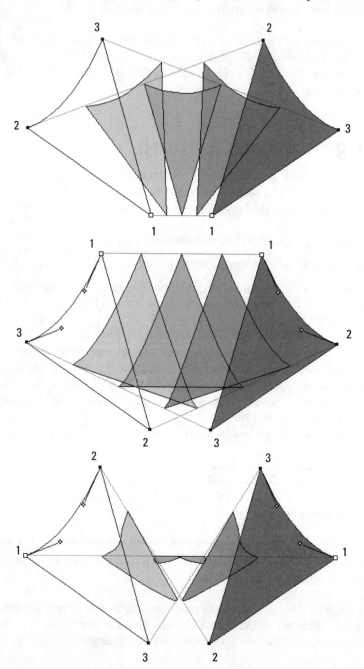

Figure 17-6: Selecting three different pairs of points affects the appearance of the steps, even though the source and windup paths are identical.

Both the source and windup paths in the examples in Figure 17-6 proceed in a clockwise direction. Had one path proceeded in a counterclockwise direction, the steps would look different. For example, the blend at the top of the figure would look like the last blend, because FreeHand would have paired points 2 and 3 in the left triangle with points 3 and 2, respectively, in the right triangle.

To confirm that your source and windup paths proceed in the same direction, select both of them by Option-clicking on one and Shift-Option-clicking on the other with the arrow tool. Then choose Arrange ⇨ Path Operations ⇨ Correct Direction, which makes both paths flow counterclockwise.

Blending multiple paths

Although you can blend only two paths at a time, you can blend as many pairs of paths as you desire within a single illustration. The faces in Figure 17-7 each contain five open paths. I drew only two of these sets of paths — the man in the upper left corner and the werewolf in the lower right corner. I designed each face to be parallel; for each path in the man's face, a path performs a similar function in the werewolf's face.

I carefully selected corresponding endpoints in each pair of corresponding paths and specified six steps between them. The final transitional paths appear exactly as FreeHand created them with the Blend command. The only difference is that I moved them into a formation that better fits on the page.

Keep in mind that when you're creating such a difficult series of blends, some of the intermediate paths will undoubtedly suffer from aesthetic imperfections, as do a few in the figure. You may need to reshape some paths after you complete the Blend.

 Blending is also a good way to create and distribute multiple clones between two sets of paths. For example, if you want to create a line of five soldiers, you can create a soldier, clone it, and move it away from the original. Then you can select and blend between each pair of identical paths in your two soldiers, specifying three steps in the blend. The advantage to this method is that you only have to create one clone rather than four. And if you select the cloned soldier (by Option-marqueeing it) and move it, all the steps adjust automatically between the clone and the stationary original. The disadvantage is that you have to blend between each pair of paths. So if the soldier you want to duplicate comprises many paths, it may be easier to group the paths, clone them four times, and then use a Distribute option in the Align palette.

Figure 17-7:
Blending five separate open paths to create a late-show metamorphosis.

Creating custom gradations

Despite the amazing morphing effects that you can produce using the techniques just described, you'll probably find the Blend command most helpful in creating custom gradations. The top example in Figure 17-8 shows two paths viewed in the keyline mode. The central path is filled with white and the V-shaped path is filled with 70-percent black. Neither path is stroked, because a repeating stroke would interrupt a continuous gradation. Also, the central path is in front, making it the source path.

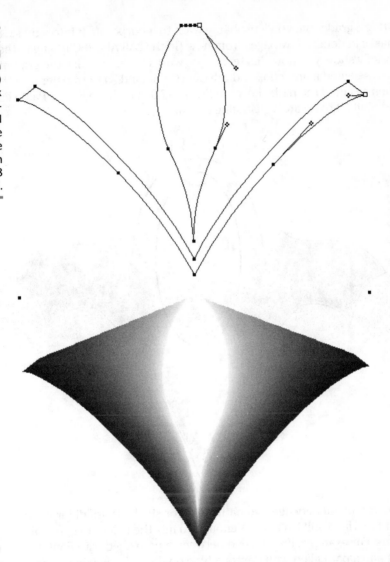

Figure 17-8:
After selecting a white path (top, central) and a black path (top, V-shaped), I blended the paths to create a gradation containing 68 steps (bottom).

If you look at the paths, you'll notice that even though they're shaped differently, they contain the same number of points. Each offers a cusp point at the bottom of the shape and two points along each side. The outside path contains three extra points that form the top of the V. Although I didn't need these points to create the central shape, I added them to the top of the path to even things out — which is why the top of the path sports a total of five points.

After selecting the two paths, I selected the upper right point in each path and pressed Command-Shift-E to blend them. Inside the Blend panel, I bumped up the Number of Steps value to 68. With this value, FreeHand made each step 1 percent darker than the step in front of it. The second example of Figure 17-8 shows the resulting blend, as seen in the preview mode.

After creating a gradation, you'll probably want to incorporate it into a mask. Although I discuss masks in detail a few pages from now (in the "All About Clipping Paths" section), I'll briefly show you how this technique works here. To mask the gradation from Figure 17-8, I selected it and chose Edit ⇨ Cut (Command-X) to transfer it to the Clipboard. I then selected the path shown in Figure 17-9 and chose Edit ⇨ Paste Inside (Command-Shift-V) to create a glistening charm.

Figure 17-9:
The result of cutting the gradation from the previous figure and pasting it into a clipping path.

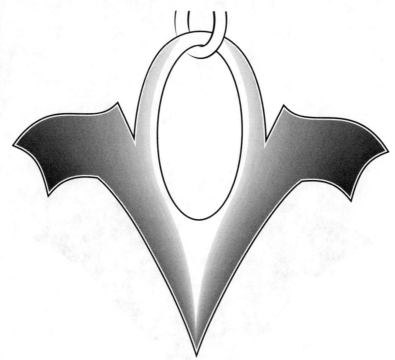

 You can blend between two paths filled or stroked with different spot colors, but FreeHand still isn't smart enough to mix the colors to spot-color separations. For example, if you blend between a path filled with Pantone red on the left and a path filled with Pantone blue on the right, you ideally want FreeHand to print a black to white gradation (reading left to right) on the red separation and a white to black gradation on the blue separation. This would produce the effect of one blending into the other without paying for extra inks. Unfortunately, FreeHand converts the colors of all steps to incremental process colors, which necessitates four additional inks — cyan, magenta, yellow, and black — if you want to print them. For the best results, blend only between tints of a single spot color. Or just stay away from spot colors and stick with process colors.

Blending between gradations

Have I mentioned that FreeHand's blending capability is the best around? No? Well, it is. If you don't believe me, here's proof: In FreeHand, you can blend between two paths filled with directional and radial gradations. That's right, the program can actually create gradations between gradations.

The top example in Figure 17-10 features two slim paths filled with logarithmic gradations. (I've outlined the paths so that you can see them.) Both gradations flow in the same direction, but one flows from 80 percent black to white, and the other flows from white to 80 percent black. Blending between them creates a four-point gradation that flows from 80 percent black in the upper left and lower right corners and from white in the lower left and upper right corners. The second example in the figure shows the blend masked inside a letter converted to paths.

Figure 17-10:
The result of blending two paths with gradient fills (top) and masking the blend inside a converted character outline (bottom).

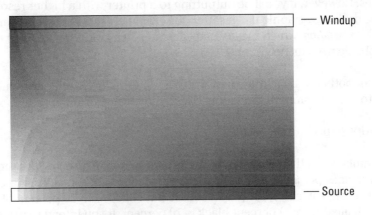

— Windup

— Source

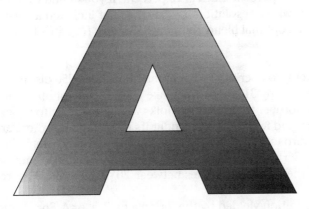

Blending gradations is a great way to create even more stupendous gradations — try it out in color! — but it can be a little tricky. For the best results, use only directional gradations. Radial gradations don't work nearly as well. Also, make sure that the gradations in both paths flow in the same direction. In other words, don't assign different Angle values in the Fill panel of the Inspector palette. And finally, assign different colors to both of the To and both of the From swatches for the two gradations. FreeHand blends these colors, so you get the most mileage out of the effect if all the colors are different.

Avoiding banding

If you'll be printing your final illustration to a 60 line-per-inch, 300 dot-per-inch laser printer, you won't need more than 24 steps, because such a device can print only 26 gray values. However, if you'll be outputting to a printer with a higher resolution — a Linotronic or Compugraphic imagesetter, for example — such a small number of steps may result in *banding*, which means that each step in a gradation appears clearly distinguishable from its neighbor.

If you're not bothered by a little math, you can determine the optimal number of steps required to create a smooth gradation. Use the following formula:

$$[(\text{dpi} \div \text{lpi})^2 + 1] \times \%C - 2$$

In this formula, *dpi* is the resolution of the printer in dots per inch; *lpi* is the screen frequency in lines per inch; and *%C* is the percentage change in color. For example, the percentage change in color between a source path filled with 20 percent black and a windup path filled with 90 percent black is 70 percent. If you intend to print this gradation to a Linotronic 300 with a resolution of 2,540 dots per inch and a default frequency of 120 lines per inch, the optimal blend contains 312 steps: $[(2,540 \div 120)^2 + 1] \times 0.7 - 2 = 312$.

The ringer is that Level 1 PostScript can't generate more than 256 distinct gray values — not to mention that having 312 steps will make your document huge and unwieldy, and the thing will take forever to print. Some folks will tell you just to knock down the number of steps to 256 and let PostScript render its maximum. But there are two problems with this approach. First, it still results in an incredibly complicated document. Second, the older PostScript can print 256 gray values between black and white, so it can handle only 70 percent as many values between 20 percent and 90 percent black.

I prefer to divide the solution yielded by the formula by 2, 3, or 4. For example, dividing 312 by 4 results in 78. That's a much more manageable number of blends and is unlikely to produce bands if your printer's equipment is properly calibrated.

But this is just a rule of thumb. I've read ten or so solutions to banding — including one from Adobe, the inventors of PostScript — and I've seen banded gradations created using every one of them. None of the solutions is perfect. My personal solution usually works for me; that's why I stick with it.

Editing a blend

Here's another reason why FreeHand's blend feature is so great: You can edit it. FreeHand treats a blend as a unique kind of grouped object — just like a rectangle or ellipse, except better. You can change the number of steps, assign different colors, or reshape the source and windup paths. FreeHand adjusts the steps to your new specifications automatically.

To change the number or location of steps in a blend, select the blend with the arrow tool and enter new values into the option boxes in the Blend panel. When you press the Return key, FreeHand implements your changes.

 To reshape or recolor a blend, Option-click with the arrow tool on the source or windup path to select that path separately from the rest of the blend. (You can't select an individual step in a blend; Option-clicking on a step selects the entire blend.) You can even select both the source and windup paths by Option-clicking on one and Shift-Option-clicking on the other.

After selecting the source or windup path, you can reshape it by dragging one or more points, adding or deleting points, dragging Bézier control handles, and so on. You can also apply a different fill, stroke, or attribute style to the path. FreeHand continuously updates the steps as you work, so you may find it easier to work in the keyline mode, which offers faster screen redraw.

Ungrouping a blend

If you want to adjust one or more of the steps manually or if you simply want to eliminate a blend, select the blend and press Command-U to ungroup it. Ungrouping frees the source and windup paths from the grouped steps. To separate the steps, press Command-U again.

After you ungroup a blend, you cannot access the Blend panel again except by undoing the Ungroup command or reblending the paths. Also, editing the source and windup paths no longer has an effect on the steps. However, you can now edit the steps independently, which can sometimes prove extremely useful.

All About Clipping Paths

Clipping path is the PostScript term for a path filled with other objects. A clipping path is also called a *masking object* or simply a *mask*, after the airbrushing technique in which masking tape (or some other masking tool, such as a frisket) is laid down to define the perimeter of a spray-painted illustration.

The basic concept behind the clipping path is simple: Instead of filling an object with a color, gradation, or repeating pattern, you fill it with other objects. The objects inside a mask are called *masked elements* or just *contents*.

You can use absolutely any graphic object created in FreeHand as a clipping path. You can even use text objects (including text blocks drawn with the text tool), paths inside groups, and composite paths. Any number of lines, shapes, and other objects — grouped or ungrouped — can appear inside a clipping path. You can even mask another clipping path.

Creating a clipping path

Since Version 1.0, creating clipping paths in FreeHand has been a straightforward process. After filling and stroking all objects, assemble the mask and contents in their desired locations. Then select all the prospective contents and choose Edit ⇨ Cut (Command-X) to transfer the selection to the Clipboard. Next, select the path you want to use as a mask and choose Edit ⇨ Paste Inside (Command-Shift-V). FreeHand pastes the contents of the Clipboard into the interior of the mask. Any portions of the contents that are too big to fit within the boundaries of the masking object are hidden.

Figure 17-11 shows a popsicle next to some stripes. The following exercise demonstrates how to set the stripes inside the body of the popsicle to create a bomb-pop — you know, one of those three-color frozen treats kids like to rub all over their faces. You set the stripes inside the bomb-pop body without affecting the drip, the stick, or the little shiny mark on the right side of the popsicle.

STEPS: Making the Perfect Bomb-Pop

Step 1.   Draw the shapes shown in Figure 17-11. Just rough them out. Feel free to come up with your own personal interpretations. The drip is filled with a radial gradation. The stripes are three rectangles filled with logarithmic gradations; the strokes are transparent. The other shapes get flat fills.

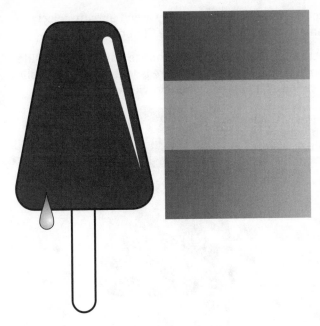

Figure 17-11:
You can combine the popsicle (left) and its stripes (right) using FreeHand's masking feature.

Step 2. In order to create the clipping path, you must first move the stripes into position relative to the popsicle. Figure 17-12 shows the proper location of masked elements and mask as viewed in the keyline mode. (If I were to show them in the preview mode, you couldn't see the popsicle beneath the stripes or vice versa.) If necessary, enlarge the stripes so that they completely cover the popsicle shape, as in the figure. This positioning determines the exact manner in which the contents fit inside the clipping path.

Figure 17-12:
Mask and contents assembled, as viewed in the keyline mode.

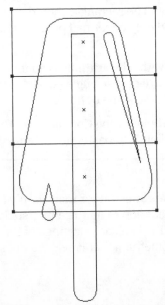

Step 3.   Select the three stripes — if they aren't already selected — and press Command-X to send them to the Clipboard.

Step 4.   Select the popsicle shape and choose Edit ⇨ Paste Inside or just press Command-Shift-V. That's all there is to it. Figure 17-13 shows the resulting illustration as it appears when previewed or printed.

Figure 17-13:
The finished bomb-pop as it appears with stripes inset.

Step 5.   For extra credit, add a shadow to the stick, also included in Figure 17-13. Draw a small rectangle around the stick at the point where it meets with the popsicle shape. The rectangle should cover the entire width of the stick, but it should only cover half of its height; leave the lower half of the stick uncovered.

Step 6.   Fill the rectangle with a logarithmic gradation progressing from 20 percent gray to white at a 270-degree angle (straight down). Make the stroke transparent (using the None option).

Step 7.   Cut the rectangle by pressing Command-X. Then select the stick shape and press Command-Shift-V to paste the rectangle inside the stick.

Why paste a gradation inside the stick rather than simply filling it with a gradation? Because we didn't want the gradation to fill the entire stick, just the upper portion of it. Masking is a great way to specify the exact locations of the beginning and ending colors of a gradation inside a path, something that FreeHand doesn't allow you to do from the Fill panel of the Inspector palette.

Provided that the stick was behind the popsicle shape and the drip and reflection were in front of it, you get the result shown in Figure 17-13, regardless of the stacking order of the stripes. The Paste Inside command leaves the stacking order of the mask unchanged.

 The contents of a clipping path display only when you preview or print the illustration. Masked elements are not visible in the keyline mode.

Adjusting masked elements

If you decide that you don't like the appearance of a clipping path, you can make adjustments in the following ways:

- **Transforming masked elements:** To transform all masked elements inside a clipping path en masse, display the Transform panel and deselect the Contents check box inside any one of the panels. You can then transform the path independently of its contents. Transform the path opposite to the way you want to transform the masked elements. For example, if you want to rotate the contents of the path 40 degrees, rotate the clipping path –40 degrees. The mask will rotate; the contents won't.

 Be sure to keep track of your transformations exactly. If you perform more than a few, write them down. When you're finished, select the Contents check box in the Transform panel and reapply all your transformations opposite to the way you applied them before. In the rotation example, you would now rotate the clipping path 40 degrees. This moves the contents along with the mask, achieving the effect you wanted in the first place.

- **Selectively editing masked elements:** To alter a few masked elements inside a clipping path without affecting others, select the clipping path and choose Edit ▷ Cut Contents (Command-Shift-X). FreeHand removes the contents of the path from the mask and places them at the front of the current layer. (Despite the word *Cut* in the command name, the contents are not sent to the Clipboard. The Clipboard's previous contents remain undisturbed.)

  After reshaping, transforming, deleting, and otherwise editing the masked elements, select them, press Command-X (*now* they're in the Clipboard), select the clipping path, and press Command-Shift-V to restore the mask.

- **Adding more masking elements:** To add elements to an existing clipping path, position the objects relative to the path, press Command-X, select the clipping path, and press Command-Shift-V, just as if you were creating a new mask. Both new and original masked elements appear inside the clipping path, with the new elements appearing in front of the original elements.

If you want to mix the stacking order of the new masking elements with that of the old ones or you want the new elements to appear in back of the old ones, you have to use the Cut Contents command to remove the old contents. Then stack all the objects as desired and recreate the mask using the Cut and Paste Inside commands.

Creating and Using Composite Paths

Another way to display objects inside objects is to create one or more holes in the middle of a path by using the Join Objects command in the Arrange menu. For example, consider the cartoon man in Figure 17-14. The first version of the cartoon shows the guy's gorgeous face. But suppose that you need to add a ski mask to the illustration. A real-life ski mask has eye holes that let you see where you're going while you hold up convenience stores. Therefore, your cartoon ski mask must also have holes for the eyes, as shown in the second example in the figure. The holes in the cartoon ski mask are actually paths that have been combined with the ski mask path using the Join Objects command.

Figure 17-14:
A cartoon face (left) and the same face dressed to apply for a non-qualifying, interest-free loan (right).

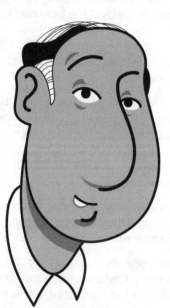

Eye holes and ski mask together are known as a *composite path* because in a few key respects, FreeHand treats the object as a single path. All objects included in the composite path must be filled and stroked identically. And, as it does with a group, selecting any part of a composite path with the arrow tool selects all objects in the composite path. To select and manipulate individual paths, you have to Option-click on the path with the arrow tool, just as you do with a group.

Poking holes

Like a clipping path, a composite path is easily to create in FreeHand:

STEPS: Creating a Composite Path

Step 1. First, assemble the objects that you want to combine in their desired relative positions. One path will act as the background path and one or more other paths will act as the holes. All holes should overlap some portion of the larger background path.

Step 2. Select the background path and choose Arrange ⇨ Send to Back or press Command-B to send the path to the back of the layer.

Step 3. Select all paths — background path and holes — and choose Arrange ⇨ Join Objects or press Command-J. Background and holes are now combined into a single composite path.

Figure 17-15 shows a doughnut on a checkered napkin. Unfortunately, it doesn't look much like a doughnut because the hole hasn't been removed. You can save this doughnut from a heartbreaking exile to the Island of Misfit Pastry — where neither Rudolf nor Julia Child dare venture — by completing the following steps. You will also create a shadow beneath the doughnut that is itself a composite path.

STEPS: Punching a Hole Through a Doughnut

Step 1. Draw the objects in Figure 17-15. The doughnut is merely two circles. The stylized shadows on the doughnut are both stroked lines. The napkin is a square rotated 60 degrees and filled with a tile pattern.

To create the tile pattern, just draw two squares and fill both with black. Position them so that the bottom right corner of one square is even with the upper left corner of the other. Then cut the two squares and paste them into the Fill panel in the Inspector palette as described in the "Object-oriented tile patterns" section of Chapter 13.

Figure 17-15:
This doughnut would look more like a doughnut if you could see through its center.

Step 2. To ensure that the larger circle in the doughnut acts as the background, select the shape and press Command-B to send it to the back of its layer. In this case, this step is not essential — smaller shapes automatically poke holes in larger shapes — but it's a good precaution and it may help you to better see the results of the next operation.

Step 3. The large circle now appears in back of the napkin, as shown in Figure 17-16. That's a little too far back, but the problem will take care of itself. Control-Shift-click on the front circle with the arrow tool to select both circles and then choose Arrange ⇨ Join Objects or press Command-J to combine them.

Step 4. The doughnut now has a hole in it, but it covers the stylized shadow lines, because the Join Objects command always moves all selected objects to the front of the layer. To nudge the doughnut to behind the shadow lines, choose Arrange ⇨ Send Backward or press Command-right bracket two or three times. The result appears in Figure 17-17.

Figure 17-16:
Send the large circle to the back of the illustrtation.

Figure 17-17:
Joining the circles makes a hole and moves the large cicle in front of the napkin.

Step 5. To create the shadow, clone the doughnut by pressing Command-D. This has the added effect of offsetting the clone 10 points down and another 10 points to the right, which will do for our purposes.

Step 6. Fill the clone with 50 percent black (by dragging the corresponding color swatch in the Tints palette and dropping it onto the clone). Set the stroke of the clone to None.

Step 7. Press Command-B to send the clone to the back of the layer, as shown in Figure 17-18.

Figure 17-18:
The completed
doughnut with shadow.

 In case you're wondering, the shadow appears to shade the napkin because the napkin is filled with a partially transparent tile pattern. As I instructed in Step 1, the pattern contains only black squares. The appearance of white squares is created by an absence of black squares. Therefore, you can see through the transparent squares to the shadow at the back of the illustration.

 You can also poke holes in objects by choosing Arrange ⇨ Path Operations ⇨ Punch. In fact, if you were to substitute choosing the Join Objects command in Step 3 with the Punch command, the result would be exactly the same. (Punch has no keyboard equivalent, so Join Objects is generally more convenient.)

Why does FreeHand have two commands that do the same thing? Actually, they perform different functions; their capabilities just happen to overlap in this one respect. If the selected paths do not entirely overlap — if they merely intersect slightly, for example — the Join Objects command makes a hole out of the intersection, but the

Punch command clips away the intersection and deletes the forward shape. If the selected paths don't overlap at all, Join Objects combines the paths into a single continuous path (see the upcoming "Filling across multiple shapes" section), while Punch deletes the frontmost path.

If, after creating a composite path, you decide that you don't like it and want to break it back up into its separate objects, select the composite path and choose Arrange ➪ Split Object (Command-Shift-J). FreeHand restores all paths to their previous independence. If the Remember Layer Info check box in the Editing panel of the Preferences dialog box is selected, FreeHand restores the independent shapes back to their previous layers.

Composite masking

A composite path can double as a clipping path, enabling you to create a path that is filled with objects *and* has holes punched out of it. After creating a composite path, position the masked elements in front of the path, cut all masked elements to the Clipboard, select the composite path, and choose the Paste Inside command.

In Figure 17-19, I added several stripes of icing in front of the doughnut. The following steps describe how to use the doughnut as a clipping path for the icing.

Figure 17-19:
Several stripes of icing created by drawing a single line and cloning it many times.

STEPS: Adding Icing to the Doughnut

Step 1. Draw the icing stripes using the freehand tool. Actually, you only need to draw one line. Stroke the line with a white, 3-point outline. Clone it by pressing Command-equal, and press the left- and down-arrow keys to offset it slightly. Change the color of this line to 70 percent black. Then select both lines, clone them, drag the clones down and to the left a pica or so, and press Command-D four times in a row to replicate the stripes.

Step 2. Select all the icing stripes and the two curved reflection lines with the arrow tool. These lines are packed so closely together that you'll probably need to press the Control key to access some lines — as in Control-Shift-click. You may find it easier to select the lines in the keyline mode.

Step 3. Press Command-X to transfer the paths to the Clipboard.

Step 4. Select the doughnut and press Command-Shift-V to paste the stripes inside the larger of the two circles. The small circle continues to form a hole in the path; the stripes are invisible inside the hole. The completed illustration appears in Figure 17-20.

Figure 17-20:
The finished doughnut
with icing.

Filling across multiple shapes

Shapes joined into a composite path don't have to overlap. When they do, FreeHand creates holes where the paths intersect. But if they don't, FreeHand simply treats all the shapes as if they were parts of a single continuous path. It's sort of like a country composed of multiple islands.

The first example in Figure 17-21 may give you a clearer idea of what I'm talking about. The example shows four shapes combined into a composite path. Because I joined them together, FreeHand fills them as a single unit. As a result, the radial gradation inside the composite path begins as white in the center of the third shape and proceeds outward to deep gray in the first and last shapes. In other words, all shapes share the same continuous gradation.

Shapes in a composite path also share masked elements. In the middle example of Figure 17-21, I drew a series of lines and shapes that I wanted to mask with the composite path. After cutting them to the Clipboard and pasting them inside the composite path, I achieved the effect shown in the last example in the figure. The masked elements start in the first shape, continue into the second, then into the third, and so on.

Composite paths and text

Many characters of type are automatically converted to composite paths when you choose Type ⇨ Convert to Paths. Characters with holes — *A, B, D, O,* and others — are actually defined as composite paths in the PostScript printer font definitions.

Each character, however, is its own independent composite path. The converted characters are automatically grouped, but grouping does not force them to share the same fill. Therefore, if you fill converted characters with a gradation, each character receives a separate gradient fill, as shown in the first example of Figure 17-22.

If you select the converted text and choose Arrange ⇨ Join Objects, FreeHand changes all outlines to a single composite path. The gradation now flows across the entire length of the converted type, as shown in the second example in the figure.

Figure 17-21: After filling a composite path with a radial gradation (top), I drew a bunch of lines and shapes (middle), cut them, and pasted them inside the composite path (bottom).

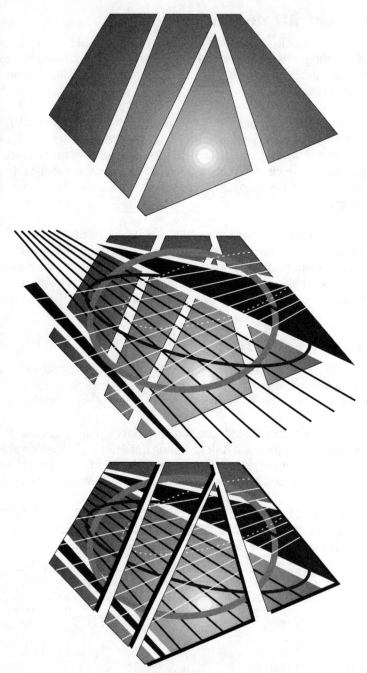

Figure 17-22:
Converted text filled with directional gradations (top) and the same text after choosing Arrange ➪ Join Objects (bottom).

Summary

➥ After blending two paths, press Command-Option-I to access the Blend panel in the Inspector palette, which lets you change the quantity and position of steps.

➥ For the best results, be sure that both your source and windup paths contain the same number of points. Also be sure that the paths proceed in the same direction.

➥ Not only can you create custom, two-color gradations by blending, you can also blend between shapes filled with gradations, which allows you to create four-color gradations.

➥ Option-click on the source or windup path in an existing blend to edit the path. FreeHand automatically updates the blend to keep up.

➥ To fill an object with other objects, create a mask (also known as a clipping path). Select the objects that you want to mask, press Command-X, select the path that you want to use as a clipping path, and press Command-Shift-V to paste the objects inside the path.

➥ You can paste additional objects stored in the Clipboard into an existing clipping path by selecting the clipping path and pressing Command-Shift-V.

➥ When you join multiple selected shapes into a composite path by pressing Command-J, FreeHand makes the overlapping areas of the paths transparent.

➥ You can edit a shape inside a composite path by Option-clicking on it with the arrow tool and reshaping it normally.

➥ Shapes in a composite path share the same fill, whether or not they overlap. Therefore, if you want a gradation or set of masking elements to extend across several shapes, simply join the shapes into a composite path.

Desktop Publishing

Chapter 18:
Importing and Exporting Graphics

Chapter 19:
Setting Up Documents

Chapter 20:
Printing from FreeHand

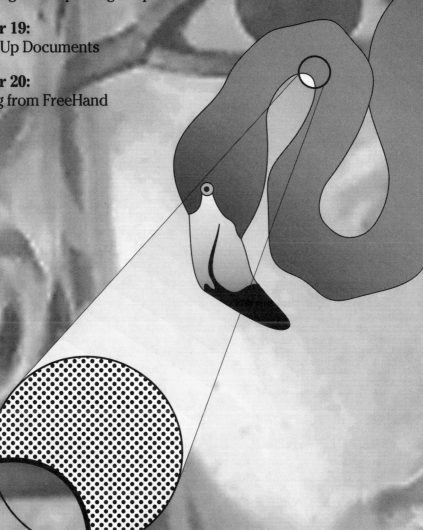

Importing and Exporting Graphics

In This Chapter

- ➡ Selecting a format for importing artwork into FreeHand
- ➡ Placing images and illustrations
- ➡ Transferring artwork via the Clipboard
- ➡ Resizing placed artwork
- ➡ Changing the brightness and contrast of an imported grayscale TIFF image
- ➡ Exporting an illustration for use in another program

FreeHand Publishes

Since PageMaker invented the category of desktop publishing in 1985 — which I like to call "The Year Nothing Worked" and which was followed by 1986, "The Second Year Nothing Worked" — desktop publishing programs have been brokers for type and graphics. They enable you to bring together elements that were created in different applications and mix them inside a single document. Desktop publishing programs such as PageMaker and QuarkXPress are the middlemen of computer graphics. They aren't so hot in the creation department, but they sure can sell information.

That's why programs such as FreeHand resent them. FreeHand is *very* hot in the creation department — it's one of the best creators around — and it's tired of being dependent on overstuffed kingpins like PageMaker and XPress to get the page to the printer. Granted, FreeHand isn't as adept at creating and editing text as a word processor and it lacks the image-editing capabilities of Photoshop, but it's otherwise able to create any page element you might desire.

With Version 4.0, FreeHand has learned to act as both creator and middleman. And with this new desktop publishing prowess — see the next chapter for details — comes improved importing capabilities. The program supports nearly twice as many graphic file formats as its competitor, Illustrator. It's capable of swapping artwork with Illustrator, Photoshop, Canvas, and half a dozen other popular programs. It can even edit imported object-oriented graphics. (Heck, about the only thing it can't do is open old FreeHand 1.0 files.)

FreeHand is also realistic. It knows that you aren't likely to throw away PageMaker or XPress just because some fly-by-night author keeps telling you how great FreeHand is at producing small documents. So it's fully capable of preparing illustrations for use in any program that supports the EPS format. It can even export drawings in the PICT and Illustrator formats and export text in Microsoft's RTF format. FreeHand 4.0 is a can-do program that knows its way around the complex world of file-format diplomacy.

In case you haven't guessed from the title, this chapter covers importing and exporting of graphics only. If you want to know how to import text, read the "Importing Stories" section of Chapter 9.

Importing Graphics

FreeHand can import bitmapped images stored in the MacPaint, PICT, TIFF, or EPS formats. It can also import object-oriented graphics stored as either PICT or EPS files. (MacPaint and TIFF formats can't accommodate objects.)

If you're not familiar with one or more of these formats, you'll find definitions in the "Importing Tracing Templates" section of Chapter 6.

Because of the way FreeHand works with different formats and the limitations of the formats themselves, I recommend that you save graphics that you intend to import into FreeHand according to the following rules:

- **Nix on MacPaint:** Don't save *anything* in the MacPaint format. If you have some old MacPaint images lying around, don't worry; FreeHand handles them just fine. But there's no point in using this format for future artwork.

- **Save grayscale images to TIFF:** Save your grayscale bitmapped images, including those you create in Photoshop, in the TIFF format. This is also an acceptable format for storing 8-bit (so-called "indexed") color images. PICT is acceptable, but FreeHand doesn't support PICT as well as TIFF. First of all, it takes longer to import a PICT image than a TIFF image. Second, FreeHand doesn't support JPEG image compression, which is made available to the PICT format when Apple's QuickTime system extension is running. If you import a JPEG-compressed PICT file into FreeHand, the QuickTime JPEG placeholder appears, as shown at the top of Figure 18-1. Such a graphic isn't usable in FreeHand.

Figure 18-1:
If an imported graphic looks like a big error message (top) instead of a continuous-tone image (bottom), open the image in Photoshop and save it in the TIFF format.

When saving images in the TIFF format in Photoshop or some other painting program, be sure to select the LZW compression option if one is available. Using this option will save space on your hard disk without diminishing the image quality one iota. (In computer jargon, LZW is a *lossless* compression format — which means that it doesn't lose any image details.) LZW is fully supported by FreeHand.

↪ **Save color images to EPS:** If you use a PostScript printer, you may want to consider saving 24-bit color images in the EPS format before importing them into FreeHand. Though the EPS format handles images less efficiently than TIFF and takes up 3 to 10 times as much disk space, FreeHand can print EPS files faster. This is because the pixel-to-PostScript conversion has already been done in an EPS file; FreeHand has to do it on the fly when printing a TIFF image.

I myself don't save images to the EPS format very often because I'm a selfish jerk. Think about it: Who are you helping by speeding up the printing process? Not yourself. Printing a black-and-white proof of an imported image on a laser printer isn't measurably faster for EPS images than TIFF images. The real savings occur when printing color separations to a high-resolution device such as an imagesetter. But then you're saving the service bureau's time, not your own. So you may just want to stick with TIFF and save disk space. And please, don't tell your service bureau that I gave you this recommendation.

↪ **Save objects to EPS:** Most object-oriented drawing programs on both the Mac and Windows platforms now support the EPS format. Assuming that you'll eventually be printing your artwork to a PostScript printer, this is the format of choice for objects. If you want to be able to edit the graphic in FreeHand, save the drawing in the Adobe Illustrator format (.AI on Windows), an editable and widely supported variation of EPS. Otherwise, FreeHand can import the file, and you'll be able to transform the entire graphic by scaling it, rotating it, and so on, but you won't be able to reshape or transform individual paths inside the graphic.

↪ **If no EPS, use PICT:** If your associates are using a low-end drawing program such as MacDraw 1.1, have them save their drawings to the PICT format. If you're lucky, FreeHand will allow you to edit the file after you import it. The problem with PICT is that it doesn't support a lot of PostScript drawing options, including a whole squad of fill and stroke routines.

You can import artwork saved in any of these file formats and integrate it into your FreeHand document. You can transform, layer, duplicate, mask, and print any imported artwork, whether it's bitmapped or object-oriented. However, you can edit the contents of an imported graphic only if it's object-oriented and saved in the PICT or Illustrator-type EPS format.

Placing a graphic file

You can access a graphic created in another application and stored on disk in two ways. You can either try to open the graphic directly using File ⇨ Open (Command-O), or you can import the graphic into an open FreeHand document by choosing File ⇨ Place (Command-Shift-D).

⚭ **Open:** If you use the Open command, FreeHand creates a new window for the document. If the graphic is an object-oriented drawing saved in the PICT or Illustrator-type EPS format, FreeHand tries to convert the objects so that you can edit them. Otherwise, the graphic appears in the lower left corner of the page, as shown in Figure 18-2.

Figure 18-2:
A TIFF image imported using the Open command appears in a new window.

⚭ **Place:** The Place command lets you import the graphic into the foreground document. You'll generally want to use this command when you've already created an illustration and you want to enhance it with imported artwork. After you choose File ⇨ Place, select the desired file in the Place Document dialog box, and press Return, FreeHand presents you with a place cursor. Click with the cursor to import the graphic without scaling it. Drag with the cursor to scale the graphic as you import it. FreeHand sizes the image to your marquee, as illustrated in Figure 18-3.

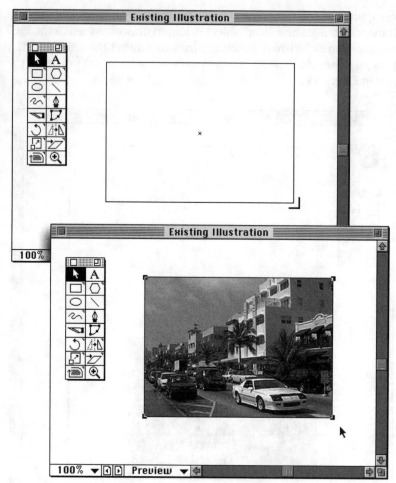

Figure 18-3:
Drag with the place cursor (top) to marquee the area into which you want FreeHand to import the graphic (bottom).

To cancel the Place command after exiting the Place Document dialog box, just click on a tool in the toolbox. This selects the tool and gets rid of the place cursor.

By default, FreeHand does not try to convert objects from PICT and Illustrator-type EPS files when you use the Place command (as it does when you use the Open command). This means that you can't edit the objects in the imported graphic.

However, you can change the default setting. If you modify the *CrackPlacedEPS* item in the FreeHand Preferences file to Yes instead of No, FreeHand tries to convert the objects when using the Place command as well. For more information, see the "Editing hidden preferences" section of Chapter 3.

In case you're wondering where FreeHand got Command-Shift-D for the Place command, it's from PageMaker. Aldus is always trying to guide the interfaces of the two programs so that they're more similar. The company has been largely unsuccessful in this regard, but they made the tiniest bit of progress with the Place command. In PageMaker, the keyboard equivalent for File ⇨ Place has long been Command-D. In FreeHand, Command-D is Edit ⇨ Duplicate (a standard among drawing programs), so the programmers threw in the Shift key. How PageMaker came up with Command-D, I have no idea. Maybe it's because you're duplicating a file on disk. Yeah, that's the ticket.

Pasting a graphic file

You can also import a graphic via the Macintosh Clipboard using the Cut, Copy, and Paste commands common to the Edit menus of all Macintosh and Windows applications. While inside a painting, drawing, or graphing program — such as Photoshop, Illustrator, or Microsoft Excel — select the portion of the picture that you want to import into FreeHand and press Command-C to copy it. Then switch to FreeHand and press Command-V to paste the graphic. That's all there is to it.

Although FreeHand is tops at converting graphics copied to the Clipboard — it always tries to convert copied objects so that you can edit them — it doesn't always get it right. If you encounter an out-of-memory error when pasting a color bitmap, or if bits and pieces of the graphic disappear, as sometimes happens when pasting objects, return to the originating program, save the graphic to disk in one of the formats listed earlier, and import the file into FreeHand using the Open or Place command.

Manipulating Imported Graphics __

If FreeHand is able to convert the objects in an imported drawing into editable paths and text blocks, you'll know immediately because the objects will be riddled with points and handles. If FreeHand can't convert the graphic, it will be surrounded by four corner handles. Every once in a while, however, FreeHand imports the drawing as a grouped object, which also shows four corner handles. If you think that this might be the case with your graphic, select it and display the Arrange menu. If the Ungroup command is available, choose it and see whether FreeHand separates the objects. If Arrange ⇨ Ungroup is dimmed, the graphic is not editable inside FreeHand.

Scaling the graphic

Even though a graphic is not editable, you can still transform it and duplicate it, as discussed in Chapters 15 and 16. You can also cut it and then paste it inside a clipping path, as discussed in Chapter 17.

Another way to manipulate an imported graphic is to drag one of its corner handles with the arrow tool. FreeHand scales the graphic just as it does when you drag the corner handle of a group. Shift-drag the corner handle to scale the graphic proportionally. Press the Control key while Shift-dragging to scale the graphic horizontally or vertically only.

All uneditable graphics, however, are not created equally. Because bitmapped images have a fixed resolution, FreeHand provides special means for scaling images to make them compatible with high-resolution output devices.

Suppose that you're printing a 72-pixel per inch bitmapped image to a 300-dot per inch laser printer. Each pixel in your image is a 1/72-inch square, while each pixel (or *dot*) in the laser printer is a 1/300-inch square. Therefore, each pixel in the image wants to take up 4/16 printer dots (1/72 ÷ 1/300 = 300 ÷ 72 = 4 1/6). But because pixels can't be divided into pieces, each image pixel must be represented by a whole number of printer dots. Unfortunately, your laser printer can't just round down each image pixel to four dots square; if it did, it would shrink the size of the image. To maintain the size of the graphic, five image pixels in a row are assigned four printer dots, while every sixth pixel is assigned five dots. These occasional larger pixels give your bitmapped image a throbbing appearance, known generically as a *moiré pattern*.

Phew, that was a tough one, eh? Don't sweat it too much; you can use the tip that I'm leading up to whether or not you understand exactly how this works.

To eliminate moiré patterns, scale the imported image so that the resolution of the image divides evenly into the resolution of the printer. For example, if you scale the image so that its resolution is 75 dots per inch, it divides evenly into the resolution of your printer — 300 ÷ 75 = 4 printer dots per pixel.

But you don't want to whip out your calculator every time you print an imported image. So make FreeHand do the calculations for you. Switch to the Document Setup panel of the Inspector palette and select the resolution of your *final* output device from the Printer Resolution pop-up menu, as shown in Figure 18-4. (If the desired resolution isn't listed, just enter the exact value into the Printer Resolution option box.)

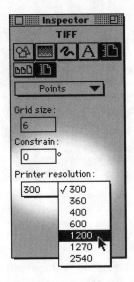

Figure 18-4:
Use the Printer Resolution pop-up menu in the Document Setup panel to specify the resolution of the final output device.

I say *final* output device because you should be concerned with the appearance of your completed artwork, not some proof along the way. For example, if you print proofs to a 300-dpi laser printer but you'll eventually have your commercial printer output the illustration to a 2540-dpi Linotronic, select the 2540 option. Who cares if some moirés show up in your laser printed proofs. The final printed piece is all that matters.

 Now for the tip: After you specify a target resolution, Option-drag a corner handle of the imported image with the arrow tool. You'll notice that FreeHand scales the image in increments; each increment represents a size that is exactly compatible with the resolution of your printer. To proportionally scale a bitmap to a compatible size, Shift-Option-drag a corner handle.

Editing a grayscale image

Scaling isn't the only special feature devoted to imported images. You can also adjust the brightness values of grayscale and monochrome images. (The techniques covered in this section are *not* applicable to color images.)

When the image is selected, switch to the Object panel of the Inspector palette (Command-Option-I) to see the options shown in Figure 18-5. Here you can control the location and scale of the image, colorize the image, and change the contrast and brightness of the image.

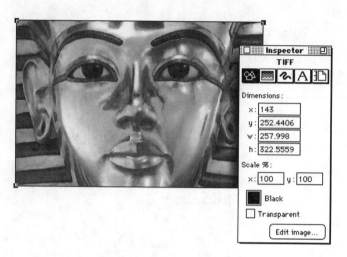

Figure 18-5:
When a grayscale image is selected, the Object panel of the Inspector palette contains special image-editing options.

As always, the Dimension option boxes show the location of the lower left corner of the selected image in relation to the ruler origin as well as the horizontal and vertical dimensions of the graphic. The two Scale % option boxes indicate any reduction or enlargement that you make to the image (by Option-dragging a corner handle, for example). Any value below 100 percent reduces the width or height; a value greater than 100 percent enlarges the image. These options are especially useful if you decide that you don't want to scale the image after all, in which case you just select the image and enter 100 percent for both options.

You can colorize a grayscale image by dragging a color from the Color List palette (or some other palette) onto the color swatch below the Scale % option boxes. Both process colors and spot colors are accepted. (You can also drag the color directly onto the image in the illustration window.)

Select the Transparent check box to convert the image to black and white and make all white pixels transparent. This option can be useful for establishing textural effects. For example, you can create a monochrome "noise" pattern in Photoshop, which is an image composed entirely of random grayscale pixels. You can then save it to the TIFF format and import it into FreeHand. By selecting the image and activating the Transparent option, you make the white pixels transparent. You can then drag a color onto the color swatch in the Object panel and, voilà, you have a color fill pattern. Just position it over a path, cut it, and paste it into the path to mask it. You can even mix the pattern with another fill by applying a flat fill, gradation, or tile pattern to the clipping path. Or leave the clipping path transparent and use it to partially cover other paths. It's a great way to create your own custom textures similar to the PostScript texture fills built into FreeHand.

Image mapping

To change the brightness and contrast of an imported grayscale image, click on the Edit Image button at the bottom of the Object panel to display the Image dialog box shown in Figure 18-6. The options in this dialog box allow you to convert — or *map* — the original gray values in the selected image to new gray values. The *brightness graph* in the center of the dialog box contains 16 bars, each of which represents a brightness value in the image. (Most grayscale images actually contain 256 gray values, but FreeHand simplifies things by only showing you 16 in the graph.)

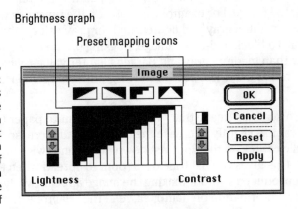

Figure 18-6: Using the bars inside the brightness graph (detailed at bottom), you can convert each of 16 gray values in a selected image to any level of brightness from black to white.

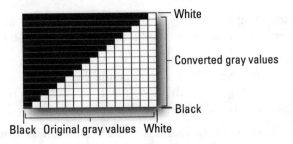

The horizontal position of each bar represents the original gray value, black being the leftmost bar and white being the rightmost bar, as illustrated in the second example in Figure 18-6. The height of each bar represents the converted appearance of the gray value, black being at the bottom and white being at the top. When an image is first selected, a *linear mapping* is in force, so that the height of each bar increases in even increments relative to the bar's position in the chart. A black pixel is mapped to black, a dark gray pixel is mapped to dark gray, and so on.

There are four different ways to control gray-value mapping in the Image dialog box. You can use any one or all of them:

- **Lightness:** Click on the Lightness scroll arrows to uniformly lighten or darken pixels in the selected image. Clicking on the up arrow lightens all values (except those already white); clicking on the down arrow darkens all values (except those already black). As these changes occur, they are reflected by the bars in the brightness graph.

- **Contrast:** Click on the Contrast scroll arrows to adjust the amount of contrast between pixels in the image. For example, clicking on the up arrow darkens values darker than medium gray and lightens lighter gray values, thus increasing the contrast toward a black-and-white image. Clicking on the down arrow lightens values darker than medium gray and darkens lighter values, which decreases the contrast toward flat gray. The bars in the brightness graph constantly reflect your changes.

 When adjusting a scanned image that you intend to print to paper (rather than film), you may want to slightly decrease the contrast and increase the lightness. (For example, click twice on the Contrast down arrow and twice on the Lightness up arrow.) This gives the halftone dots room to spread when the image is commercially reproduced without making the image appear overly dark or muddy. (For more information on halftones, read the "Halftone screens" section of Chapter 20.)

- **Preset mapping icons:** Select one of the *mapping icons* above the gray-value bars to perform one of four special graphic effects, explained in the next section.

- **Move a bar:** Drag an individual bar up or down to lighten or darken a single gray value. You can also click at a point inside the brightness graph to raise or lower the corresponding bar to that location. If you drag in a roughly horizontal direction inside the chart, several bars adjust to follow the path of your drag.

- **Apply:** To preview your changes in the illustration window, click on the Apply button.

You can use options in the Image dialog box to make slight changes or to create special effects. Figure 18-7 shows the result of dragging selective bars up and down in the brightness graph. In the first example of the figure, I dragged the first four bars all the way to the top of the graph, making the very darkest pixels in the image white. As a result, Tut gets white eyes. I also dragged the next four bars all the way to the bottom, making the corresponding pixels black. This creates exaggerated shadows along the eyebrows, nose, and lips.

Figure 18-7:
Two examples of special effects created by playing with the bars in the brightness graph.

In the second example in Figure 18-7, I lessened the severity of the exaggerated shadows by tapering the colors lighter than medium gray. I made medium gray black, the next lighter gray dark gray, and so on, all the way up to white. This mapping helped restore some of the details I lost in the first image in the figure.

Keep in mind that there are no rights or wrongs when you're raising and lowering bars in the brightness graph. The beauty of this dialog box is that it can't do any permanent damage to an image. In fact, that's the only reason to use it. These options have been around for years, more than long enough for a dedicated image editor such as Photoshop to trounce all over them. But whereas Photoshop makes permanent changes to an image, FreeHand makes temporary ones. If you ever want to return to your original, untainted image, just display the Image dialog box and click on the Reset button. Everything goes back to normal.

Preset mapping icons

If you want to try out some preset effects, click on one of the icons at the top of the Image dialog box and then click on the Apply button to see what they look like applied to your image. Each effect is shown in Figure 18-8. The effects work as follows:

↪ **Normal:** Normal isn't actually an effect; choosing it produces the same results as clicking on the Reset button. Click on the Normal icon to return the gray-value bars to their original linear configuration. This is the icon you click on when you're done fooling around with the other ones.

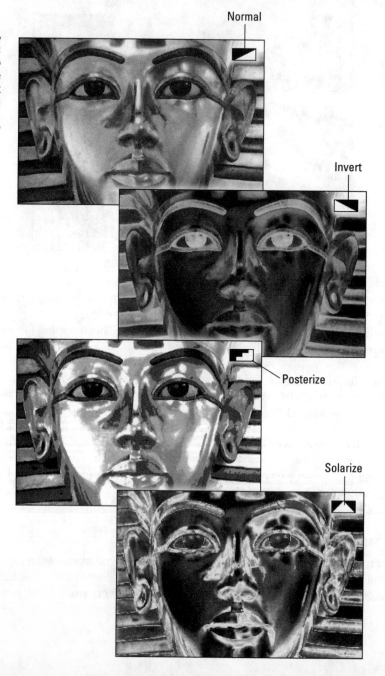

Figure 18-8: Tut subject to each of the preset mapping settings.

Normal

Invert

Posterize

Solarize

- ☞ **Invert:** Click on this icon to invert the light and dark gray values in a selected image. White pixels become black, black pixels become white, and so on. The effect is like a photographic negative.

- ☞ **Posterize:** Click on this icon to establish a stair-stepped map that groups a range of gray values into one of four clusters. Converted values jump from black to 66 percent black to 33 percent black to white. Transitions between gray values are abrupt rather than smooth, which is ideal for artwork that you intend to photocopy or submit to some other low-quality printing process.

- ☞ **Solarize:** Click on this icon to double the brightness of all gray values between black and medium gray and both invert and double the brightness of all values lighter than medium gray. Both white and black pixels become black; light and dark gray pixels become medium gray; and medium gray pixels become white. The result is a unique glowing effect, as shown at the bottom of Figure 18-8.

Cropping imported graphics

Normally, when an application allows you to import graphics, you expect some kind of *cropping* feature for deleting unwanted portions of the graphic. For example, after importing a scanned snapshot of your family, you might want to crop the photo tightly around their faces, as illustrated in Figure 18-9.

FreeHand provides no specific cropping feature. However, you can crop imported images by creating a mask. Draw a rectangle or other path to represent the outline of the cropped image. Then position the imported image relative to the path, transfer it to the Clipboard using the Cut command (Command-X), select the path, and choose Edit ⇨ Paste Inside (Command-Shift-V). The stroke of the path acts as the outline of the cropped graphic.

Linking graphic files

An illustration that contains a TIFF image or EPS drawing must always be able to reference its original TIFF or EPS file in order for FreeHand to preview or to print the placed image successfully. Therefore, when you save an illustration, FreeHand remembers where the original imported graphic file was located on disk. If you try to open an existing illustration after moving its imported TIFF or EPS graphic to a different disk or folder, FreeHand displays a standard Open dialog box requesting that you locate the original graphic file on disk. Select the original TIFF or EPS file in the scrolling list and press Return. If you click on the Cancel button, the illustration will not preview properly. If FreeHand can't reference the graphic file on disk during the printing process, neither an imported TIFF image nor EPS drawing will print at all.

Figure 18-9: Great family, but too much picture (top). By pasting the image inside a rectangle, I cropped out the background and honed in on those gorgeous faces (bottom).

Exporting an Illustration

Illustrations created in FreeHand can be used in any Macintosh or Windows application that supports the EPS format. Your illustration can become part of a larger document such as a book or catalog or part of a video or on-screen presentation.

Exporting an EPS or PICT file

To store an illustration in the EPS or PICT format, choose File ⇨ Export or press Command-E. The Export Document dialog box shown in Figure 18-10 appears. In this dialog box, you can name the file and select the file format in which you want FreeHand to store the file.

Figure 18-10:
The Export
Document dialog
box as it appears
normally (top)
and with the
Format pop-up
menu displayed
(bottom).

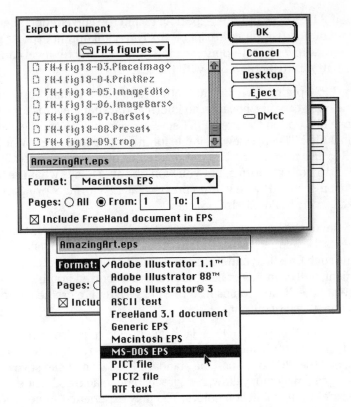

FreeHand can *export* (save your file) to a variety of file formats, including variations on the EPS, Illustrator, and PICT formats. The options in the Format pop-up menu include the following:

- **Adobe Illustrator:** FreeHand can save to three old Adobe Illustrator file formats. These formats are entirely editable and are widely supported by drawing programs on the Mac and Windows platforms. However, each format sacrifices some data from a FreeHand document. The Illustrator 3 format doesn't support layers, imported TIFF images, tabs, columns and rows, the orientation of text bound to a path, stylistic effects, and a few other text formatting options. The Illustrator 88 format ignores all those items as well as composite paths and text on a path. The Illustrator 1.1 format is the least capable, lacking support for masks, tile patterns, and color. Regardless of the format you select, FreeHand converts gradations to blends inside masks. FreeHand 4.0 does not support the Illustrator 5.0 or 5.5 format or the Illustrator 4.0 for Windows format.

◌◈ **ASCII and RTF:** These options export all text in the current document, whether it is selected or not. (Graphics are ignored.) The ASCII option exports plain text with no formatting; the RTF option exports most character-level and paragraph-level formatting attributes along with the text.

◌◈ **EPS:** The EPS options save the illustration to the EPS format. These options are by far the most capable, because no information whatsoever is lost. Select the Macintosh EPS option to save a PICT screen preview with the file. Select MS-DOS EPS to include a TIFF preview, suitable for importing into most Windows programs. Because the Generic EPS option creates no screen preview, it's equally applicable to both platforms, but you won't be able to see what the illustration looks like on-screen. Preview or no preview, all EPS formats print accurately and print exclusively to PostScript printers.

 All EPS documents created by FreeHand contain *Open Press Interface* (OPI) comments. Developed by Aldus for outputting to ultra-high-end prepress systems such Crosfield and Scitex, OPI specifications communicate the size, placement, and cropping of illustrations and imported graphics. You can then manipulate the illustration using a prepress system to create four-color, professional-quality output.

◌◈ **PICT:** If you want to export a FreeHand illustration to a format that prints to a non-PostScript printer, and you'll be importing it into a Macintosh application, select one of the PICT options. The standard PICT format can save only eight colors — cyan, magenta, yellow, red, green, blue, black, and white. The PICT2 format stores up to 16 million colors. You may experience some loss of information with this format — for example, masks and composite paths don't translate — but according to Altsys, the loss should be minimal.

When you select one of the EPS formats, the Export Document dialog box provides access to a few additional options. These options include the Pages radio buttons and the Include FreeHand Document in EPS check box. If your document includes multiple pages — the subject of the next chapter — you may want to export all of them or just one of them to the EPS format. Each page is exported to a separate file, cropped according to the page boundary. (To crop a very large illustration in one piece, you have to create a large custom page, as described in the next chapter.)

When the Include FreeHand Document in EPS check box is selected, the EPS file contains all information necessary to edit the document. For example, if you pass the EPS file along to an associate or client, another artist could open the file and edit it. Some artists aren't too keen on this idea. If you want to prevent people from monkeying around with your documents, turn this option off.

The downside of turning off the check box is that you have to save two versions of every file, one that you can edit — which you save normally using File ➪ Save — and one that you can pass along to clients or import into other applications yourself. I need the disk space, so I generally leave the option selected and save only one copy of my illustration via File ➪ Export. Of course, I don't mind it when people mess with my artwork. Really, go ahead. Draw mustaches on every face in this book. You paid for it, you can mess it up. Just don't expect a refund.

Drawing an export boundary

When FreeHand creates an EPS file, it automatically crops the document to the exact boundaries of the objects in the illustration. For example, suppose that you create a 3 × 4-inch illustration on a letter-sized page. When you save the illustration, FreeHand saves the page size information. But when you export the illustration for use in another application, FreeHand is interested only in the graphic itself. After all, you don't want to import an 8 1/2 × 11-inch drawing into PageMaker when the graphic consumes only one-quarter of the drawing area. Therefore, the exported document measures 3 × 4 inches, exactly matching the size of the objects inside the document.

More often than not, FreeHand determines the size of an EPS file correctly. Every once in a while, however, FreeHand may crop a graphic a bit too drastically. The casualties are usually strokes. The edges of heavy outlines may be sliced off or a mitered join may disappear.

 To prevent the loss of strokes around the edges of an exported illustration, or simply to create a margin around an illustration, draw a rectangle that completely surrounds your artwork. While the rectangle remains selected, drag the None color swatch onto both the fill and stroke icons in the Color List palette, making both fill and stroke transparent. The rectangle doesn't preview or print, but it does affect the size of the exported EPS file.

Summary

→ Save grayscale images in the TIFF format before importing them into FreeHand. For quicker printing, save full-color images in the EPS format.

→ Use the EPS format only when printing to a PostScript output device. If you use a non-PostScript printer, stick with the TIFF format for images and the PICT format for objects.

→ Change the *CrackPlacedEPS* item in the FreeHand Preferences file from No to Yes to convert objects imported using File ⇨ Place so that they're fully editable (whenever possible).

→ Option-drag the corner handle of an imported image to scale the image to incremental resolutions that are compatible with the value specified in the Printer Resolution option box in the Document Setup panel.

→ To create a custom fill pattern, import a black-and-white TIFF image, select the Transparent option in the Object panel, and paste the image inside an object filled with a color or gradation.

→ Use the bars in the Image dialog box to change the brightness and contrast of an imported grayscale image.

→ To crop an imported image, cut it and paste it inside a rectangle, ellipse, or other path.

→ Select the Include FreeHand Document in EPS option if you want to edit the exported illustration file in the future. To prevent folks from editing your artwork, deselect this option.

→ If an object extends outside the page boundary, FreeHand crops it when exporting the page. If the entire illustration fits inside the page boundary, FreeHand crops the file to the smallest size that will accommodate all objects.

→ If you have problems with an exported illustration being over-cropped when you import it into another application, draw a rectangle with no fill and no stroke around the illustration. Then export the illustration again.

Setting Up Documents

In This Chapter

➥ Using the pasteboard

➥ Adding pages to a document

➥ Dragging pages inside the Document Pages panel

➥ Moving from one page to the next

➥ Changing the size and orientation of a page

➥ Using the Bleed Size option

FreeHand Does Small Documents __

I think that I've mentioned FreeHand's prowess in the small-document department 10 or 12 times now, and no doubt this news was received with skepticism by long-time users who are heavily invested in the status quo. "FreeHand is a drawing program, dag-gum it," you might protest. "If I want to create documents, I'll use QuarkXPress, just like I've been doing for the last three years," or however long it's been. "Why do you keep making FreeHand out to be some kind of gift from the gods that's going to take care of all my publishing needs?"

Well, because it is. Okay, not *all* your publishing needs. I'm not suggesting that you lay out magazines and other text-intensive documents with FreeHand. And the program isn't particularly suited to documents that contain more than, say, eight pages. But for design-intensive documents, it just can't be beat. Honestly, it mops the floor with XPress, and the things that it does to PageMaker are too gruesome for words.

"What about my service bureau?" you might counter. "They darn near refuse to print anything that's not in XPress. A guy there even told me that XPress is the only program that prints the least bit reliably. I doubt they'll be very interested in printing my FreeHand documents." It's true — you may get hassled a little bit. And I've heard accounts of some legitimate printing limitations when using FreeHand with highly sophisticated Scitex and Crosfield systems. But these aren't small-document printing problems; I'm talking about special effects-laden graphics with half a dozen imported images inside complex masks and layered all over each other.

Having worked at a service bureau, I can assure you that print operators can be as lazy as folks in any other industry. It's easier to use a single program for printing and say that all the others have this problem or that than it is to keep up with five or six different applications, every one of which has its own little quirks. Commercial printers may seem like high-tech wizards — and many are — but there's always the chance that they're more interested in getting home to the family than learning a new piece of software, especially if a four-page job is the only incentive that you're offering.

It's always difficult to buck the system. And although it's hard to believe that using one of the most solid graphics programs on the market falls into this category, some service bureaus look down their noses at printing from any program but QuarkXPress. It's up to you to be a maverick and force them to print some FreeHand documents. Really, it's for their own good.

Having shared my two cents on that topic — just enough to infuriate a few print operators — let me encourage you not to accept my word or anyone else's on this subject. Instead, do your own test. Use FreeHand to put together the next small-document job you have, whether it's a newsletter, report, flier, whatever. Write the text in a word processor so that you have access to a spell-checker and use Photoshop or the equivalent to prepare the images, but otherwise rely entirely on FreeHand. You'll have to create the document from scratch; FreeHand can't open XPress or PageMaker templates. So do this project on a day that you have time to experiment a little.

I know — you don't have any time. No one does. But make some time. If you aren't convinced after a few hours that FreeHand provides an environment more conducive to professional-level small-document production than any other software you've worked with, so be it. Write me off as a screwball rabble-rouser, swear off my books for good, and go back to XPress or PageMaker.

But if you're like me, you'll discover a side to FreeHand that you hadn't considered before. No more switching back and forth between graphics program and layout program trying to decide how to reshape a drawing so that it better fits with your design. After all, every tool that you need to put together outrageously complex layouts is available in FreeHand. You can reshape paths and rewrap text on the fly, bind text to paths, automate the creation of columns and rows, copyfit text, access a nearly infinite range of fill and stroke options, and — as described in this chapter — create custom page layouts. Only in FreeHand can you assign every single page in your document a different size and orientation.

All right, that's enough. You're probably beginning to think that I get a cut off the software sales or something. I doubt that a FreeHand sales rep could be as long-winded on this subject. Aldus sold millions of dollars worth of FreeHand last year, and I'm making the program out to be some neglected little underdog. So I'll drop the subject now.

Really, I think if you'll just try it, though, you'll agree . . . no, no, I'm done. I said I'm done, so I'm done.

Examining the Printed Page

So far, I've spent hundreds of pages explaining how to create and manipulate type and graphics, but I've barely mentioned the page on which the objects sit. If you export most of your artwork to the EPS format and import it into a layout program — the standard desktop publishing route — you generally have no reason to even notice the page. As long as your artwork fits entirely inside the page boundary, FreeHand dutifully exports every detail and automatically crops the EPS file to fit.

But when you're printing final documents from FreeHand, the page becomes a primary concern. The page boundary in the illustration window represents the final page printed from the output device. Generally speaking, all objects print exactly as they appear relative to the page boundary in the illustration window.

 If this is the first object-oriented drawing program you've ever used, you may need some background information on how pages in FreeHand work. When you create a new FreeHand document, you're presented with an empty page smack in the middle of the illustration window (assuming that you haven't changed the Aldus FreeHand Defaults file). So when you draw an object, it's automatically sitting on a page. You can then take that object and drag it off the page or drag it onto another page. Each page is free-floating and independent of other elements.

The pasteboard

The area outside the page boundary is called the *pasteboard*. Labeled in Figure 19-1, the pasteboard is the electronic equivalent of a table top — a rather immense table top, in fact, measuring 54 × 54 inches. We're talking more than 20 square feet of working space, about the size of a Twister board, or tarp, or whatever that thing with big colored dots was called.

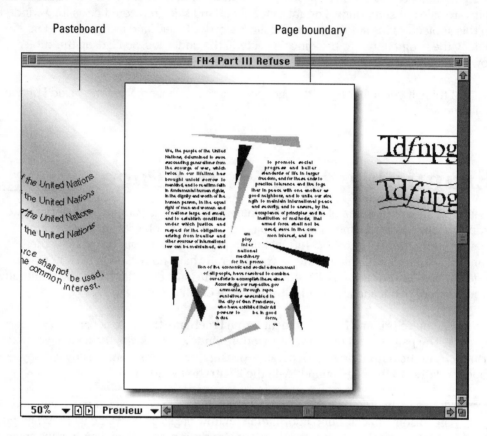

Figure 19-1: The pasteboard is an undefined work space that contains the pages in your document.

 You won't see eerie shadows falling on your pasteboard as you do in Figure 19-1. I added the shadows to this figure — and many of the figures that follow — to clearly distinguish page and the pasteboard. Besides, it looks so cool.

The pasteboard is a convenient holding area for items that you don't want to print or that you think you may integrate into the artwork later. Suppose that you want to make a change to a set of objects but you're not sure what your client will think of the revision. Before making your changes, clone the objects and drag them off into the pasteboard. You can easily retrieve them from the pasteboard if the client gets grumpy over your alterations.

You can move around the pasteboard using the scroll bars and grabber hand. To view more of the pasteboard, zoom out with the zoom tool. If you zoom out to the 12 percent view size, you may see a gray area around the pasteboard. This nether area is outer space as far as FreeHand is concerned. If you try to move something to this area, FreeHand presents you with an alert box telling you that it can't accommodate you. This may seem like a Stalinist tactic — "Hey, this is a free country, I'll move my objects into outer space if I want to!" — but the truth is that if FreeHand did let you move the objects to this area, you wouldn't be able to get them back.

Creating multipage documents

By default, FreeHand creates single-page illustrations. However, you can add pages any time you want. Press Command-Option-D to access the Document Pages panel of the Inspector palette, shown in Figure 19-2. The central portion of the palette is a miniature representation of the entire pasteboard with a single page inset. The page even has a number 1 on it so that you don't get confused.

Figure 19-2:
The Document Pages panel shows the entire 54 × 54-inch pasteboard reduced to about 2 1/2 percent of its actual size.

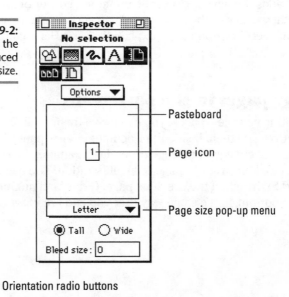

To create one or more new pages, select the Add Pages option from the Options pop-up menu in the panel, as illustrated in Figure 19-3. FreeHand displays the Add Pages dialog box. Enter the number of pages you want to add into the Number of Pages option box. You can also select a page size and orientation and enter a Bleed Size value, as described later in this chapter. If you're not sure what kind of page you need, just click on the OK button or press Return. You can always change the size, orientation, and bleed size later.

Figure 19-3:
Select the Add Pages option to insert new pages into a document.

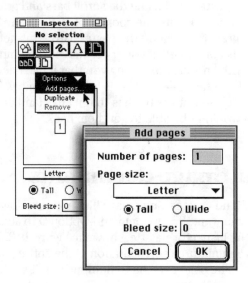

FreeHand adds the new pages to the upper left corner of the pasteboard. If you try to add too many pages — the pasteboard can accommodate a maximum of 30 letter-sized pages — an alert box appears to explain that FreeHand can't fulfill your excessive request.

Moving pages in the pasteboard

After creating your new pages, you can move them to different locations in the pasteboard by dragging them inside the Document Pages panel. Dragging pages may have the added effect of changing the page order. For example, the left panel in Figure 19-4 shows the result of adding a single page to an illustration. The page is numbered 1 because it is above and to the left of the previous page. (FreeHand numbers pages from left to right and top to bottom, in the same way that you and I read type.)

Figure 19-4:
The result of dragging the
new page to a different
location in the paste-
board.

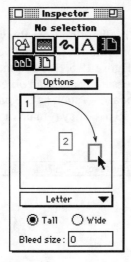 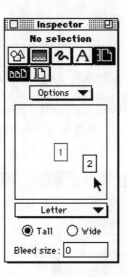

However, when you drag the new page below and to the right of the previous page — as indicated by the arrow in the figure — FreeHand renumbers the new page 2, as in the second panel in Figure 19-4. The previous page reverts to page 1. FreeHand updates the pages in the real pasteboard to keep up with your changes.

This feature brings up an interesting point: What happens to objects in your illustration when you drag a page? If the page already has objects on it, the objects move with the page, regardless of whether they reside entirely inside the page or barely overlap the page boundary. Objects that extend over two pages move with either page.

 If you move a page to a location on the pasteboard that contains objects, the objects remain in their previous positions but they automatically jump on board the page. If you move the page a second time, the objects move with the page. You can run into some real messes if you drag a page that already contains objects under a bunch of objects that previously resided on the pasteboard. The objects pile up quickly if you don't pay attention. That's why I recommend that you reduce the view size in the illustration window to 12 percent — the minimum zoom — to monitor the results of moving pages inside complicated illustrations. This way, if you accidentally disturb some objects, you can see the damage immediately and undo the move by pressing Command-Z.

Navigating between pages

To see all pages in an illustration, select the Fit All option from the view size pop-up menu in the lower left corner of the illustration window. (Alternatively, you can choose View ➪ Magnification ➪ Fit All.) As shown in Figure 19-5, this command reduces the view size to show all pages but it does not necessarily show all objects in your illustration. Objects in remote portions of the pasteboard — such as the partially-visible text bound to paths on the far right side of Figure 19-5 — may remain outside the illustration window.

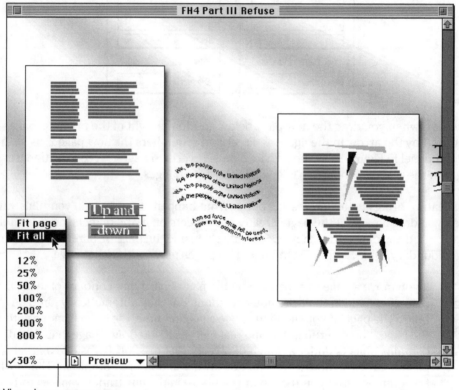

View size pop-up menu

Figure 19-5: Select the Fit All option to see all pages in the illustration window.

One of the hidden features of the Fit All option is that it allows you to reduce the view size to smaller than 12 percent, the minimum view size that you can access using the zoom tool.

Try this: Drag the current page of an illustration to the lower right corner of the miniature pasteboard in the Document Pages panel. Now create a new page using the Add
Page option. The new page is automatically placed in the upper left corner of the
pasteboard, so the two pages are on opposite ends of the earth, so to speak. Now
reduce the illustration window to its minimum size by dragging the size box (at the
intersection of the scroll bars). And finally, select the Fit All option from the view size
pop-up menu. The result is an unprecedented 2 percent view size, as shown in Figure
19-6. It's too small for you to be able to see individual objects in your illustration clearly,
but it's perfect for making sure that you don't mess up large groups of objects when
moving pages around.

Figure 19-6:
The smallest view size you can
achieve in FreeHand.

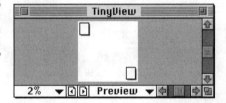

To view the active page at the fit-in-window view size, press Command-W. The active
page is the one that appears black in the miniature pasteboard in the Document Pages
panel. All other pages appear grayed.

You can activate a different page by clicking on its icon in the Document Pages panel. If
you double-click on the page icon, FreeHand displays that page at the fit-in-window
view size in the illustration window.

If you want to switch to a page and display it at some other view size, click on
the page icon and press the corresponding view size keyboard equivalent. For
example, if you're presently looking at page 1 and want to switch to page 2 at
actual size, click on the page 2 icon and press Command-1.

When working in documents with three or more pages, you may find it helpful to scroll
between the pages by clicking on the page-advance icons. These icons are located at
the bottom of the illustration window, just to the right of the view size pop-up menu, as
labeled in Figure 19-7. The left page-advance icon takes you to the previous page; the
right icon takes you to the next page. If you click on the left icon when viewing the first
page in a document, FreeHand takes you to the last page; clicking on the right icon
takes you from the last page to the first. But regardless of which icon you click on, the
page appears in the illustration window at the fit-in-window view size.

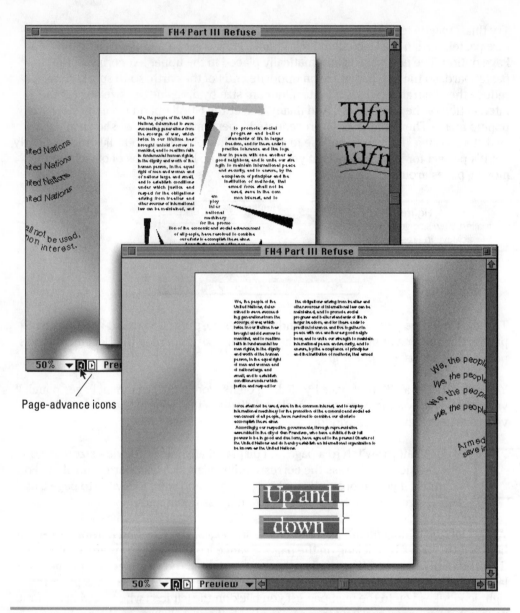

Page-advance icons

Figure 19-7: Clicking on the left page-advance icon takes you from the second page in the document (top) to the first page (bottom).

Editing pages

You can change the size and orientation of any page in a document long after you create it. You can also clone whole pages and delete them. These options are fairly obvious, so I'll burn through the most essential facts first:

cx **Page size:** To change the size of a page, click on its icon in the miniature pasteboard in the Document Pages panel. Then select a different option from the page size pop-up menu, as shown on the left side of Figure 19-8. Table 19-1 lists the measurements of the various size options. (The letter options, like A3 and B5, are common European sizes.)

Figure 19-8:
Select an option from the size pop-up menu to change the size of the active page (left). Select Custom to create your own page size (right).

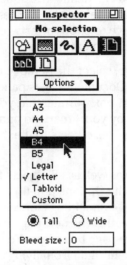 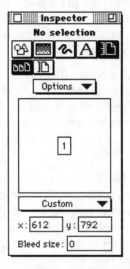

Table 19-1	FreeHand's Page Sizes		
Page Name	**Size in Inches**	**In Millimeters**	**In Points**
A5	5.83 × 8.27	148 × 210	420 × 595
B5	6.93 × 9.84	176 × 250	499 × 708
Letter	8.50 × 11.00	216 × 279	612 × 792
A4	8.27 × 11.69	210 × 297	595 × 842
Legal	8.50 × 14.00	216 × 356	612 × 1,008
B4	9.84 × 13.89	250 × 353	708 × 1,000
Tabloid	11.00 × 17.00	279 × 432	792 × 1,224
A3	11.69 × 16.53	297 × 420	842 × 1,190

↪ **Orientation:** Below the page size pop-up menu are two orientation radio buttons. Select Tall to position the page upright (known as *portrait* printing); select Wide to lay it on its side (known as *landscape* printing).

↪ **Custom page size:** If you select the Custom option from the page size pop-up menu, FreeHand replaces the orientation radio buttons with two option boxes (see the second example in Figure 19-8). By entering values into these options, you can define your own custom page size. Enter the width of the page in the X option box; enter the height in the Y option box; press Return to implement your changes. FreeHand interprets the values in the current unit of measure.

 Generally, you should only use the Custom option when printing to an imagesetter. After all, just because you can define a 20-square-foot page doesn't mean that you can feed it through your laser printer. To get large artwork to print from a consumer printer, you have to chop the artwork into pieces using a technique called *tiling,* as described in the next chapter.

↪ **Delete a page:** To delete the active page, select the Remove option from the Options pop-up menu at the top of the Document Pages panel. If the page has objects on it, FreeHand displays an alert box warning that you're about to delete the objects. Press Return if that's okay by you. FreeHand annihilates objects that are fully within the page boundary; it spares objects that extend out onto the pasteboard.

↪ **Clone a page:** To clone the active page as well as all objects that so much as touch that page, select Duplicate from the Options pop-up menu. Because FreeHand insists on locating new pages — including clones — in the upper left corner of the pasteboard, it balks at creating the new page if an object extends beyond the left or top edge of the active page boundary. You have to bring the objects into the page boundary to prevent them from flying off into outer space.

Printing differently sized pages

Sounds easy enough, right? Unfortunately, there's one problem: When you combine pages with different sizes and orientations within a single document, you confuse the computer. The Macintosh system software is set up to handle no more than one page size per print job. So it's up to you to print the pages correctly.

Say that you've created a two-page document. Both pages are letter sized (8 1/2 × 11 inches), but page 1 is oriented upright and page 2 is on its side. If you just print the pages normally, page 1 will print fine, but part of page 2 will be cut off because neither FreeHand nor the system software is capable of accounting for the horizontal page. As a small consolation, FreeHand warns you of this fact in advance by displaying another in its series of alert boxes.

When printing to a laser printer, you can solve the problem in only one way. You have to print each page independently. First print page 1 as a vertical page. Then tell FreeHand that you want to print a horizontal page (using options in the Print Options dialog box, as discussed in the next chapter), and print page 2.

This solution isn't too realistic when you're submitting a document to be printed at a service bureau. If you think that the folks at the service bureau might complain over a simple FreeHand document, wait till you tell them that they have to print each page independently and make special changes in between. It won't go over too well.

What you need to do is set up a printed page size that's big enough to accommodate both pages. Because typesetters print to long rolls of film — not individual pieces of paper as laser printers do — you have a lot more latitude when setting up custom pages. For example, you can ask your service bureau operator to select an 11 × 11-inch printed page size inside the Print Options dialog box. Such a printed page size can handle both your upright page and the one on its side.

 Actually, it's a little early to be talking about printing, but I just wanted to prepare you for what you're up against, particularly if you're an experienced FreeHand user. For more information on all printing issues, read the following chapter, "Printing from FreeHand."

Bleed size

The last option in the Document Pages panel is the Bleed Size option box, which enables you to print objects beyond the boundary of a page. Normally, objects that extend out into the pasteboard are cut off abruptly at the page boundary. Everything inside the page boundary prints; everything outside the boundary does not.

The *bleed* is an area outside the perimeter of a page that can be printed. It basically extends the page boundary by the amount that you enter in the Bleed Size option box.

If you're not familiar with bleeds, you're probably wondering why in the world you would want to extend the printable area. Why not just create a larger page if you want to print more stuff? The answer lies in the printing process. The pages of this book provide a case in point. This page, for example, has a nice, healthy border around it. No word or graphic comes within two picas of the physical edge of the page. This boundary ensures even and consistent printing.

Now check out the first page of the next chapter. The first page of every chapter features a gray bar that touches the right edge of the page. Any time a page element extends off the edge of the paper, it's called a bleed.

To create an effective bleed, you have to print more of the bleeding element than actually reproduces in the printing process. The gray bar at the front of the chapters, for example, extends 1/2 inch or so beyond the page cut. This gives the printer room to maneuver. If the page is slightly crooked during the printing process, as many pages are, the bleed ensures that no gap appears between the gray bar and the edge of the page.

Okay, now back to FreeHand. The bleed size enables you to print elements that extend off the page. For example, if you want to print an extra 1/2 inch of a graphic, enter 0.5i into the Bleed Size option box. (The *i* makes FreeHand interpret the value in inches.)

But this still doesn't answer the original question — why not just make the page size larger? As you'll learn in the next chapter, printers need *crop marks* to guide them. Crop marks tell the printer how to align the printed page with your artwork. The crop marks align to the page boundary, so the bleed extends beyond the crop marks. If you just made the page size larger, you would nudge the crop marks outward farther as well. As a result, the printer wouldn't be able to distinguish the elements you wanted to bleed from those that you wanted to appear fully inside the page.

Keep in mind that this information generally only applies to printing from professional-quality imagesetters. You can't create a bleed for a letter-size page on a laser printer because laser printers can't print all the way to the edge of the page. However, you can create bleeds for smaller jobs such as mailers and business cards.

Summary

➠ FreeHand is a great program for creating small documents.

➠ After adding a page to a document, be sure to drag it to the central portion of the pasteboard so that you can access it more easily.

➠ You can see pages inside the Document Pages panel but you can't see objects. So be careful that you don't upset objects on the pasteboard when dragging pages.

➠ Double-click on a page in the Document Pages panel to display that page in the illustration window at the fit-in-window view size. Or click on the page and press Command-1 to view the page at actual size.

➠ Each page in a document can be a different size and orientation. But if you take advantage of this feature, you need to tell FreeHand the size and orientation of each printed page using the options in the Page Setup or Print Options dialog box, as described in the next chapter.

➠ The Bleed Size option enables you to print objects that extend outside the page boundary. The purpose of this option is to print all the way to the edge of a page.

Printing from FreeHand

In This Chapter

- ➤ Exploiting the benefits of the new LaserWriter 8 printer driver
- ➤ Using PostScript printer definition files
- ➤ Tiling large artwork onto multiple pages
- ➤ Setting up the printed page inside the Print Options dialog box
- ➤ Creating crop marks, registration marks, and page labels
- ➤ Printing process- and spot-color separations
- ➤ Writing the PostScript-language definition of an illustration to disk
- ➤ Specifying custom halftones
- ➤ Downloading printer fonts
- ➤ Remedying limitcheck and out-of-memory errors

Getting Your Work on Paper

Who says the printed page is dead? I wish it were, frankly; it's a horrible waste of natural resources, and we would all benefit if someone put a tourniquet on the steady flow of paper products through our mail slots. But we still communicate heavily via the printed page. Whatever advantages CD-ROM and multimedia may offer, they don't have the immediacy of paper. You don't need a computer, a player, a television, or any other special equipment to read a page. Heck, you don't need electricity — if it's dark, light a candle. The only platform incompatibility you encounter is the one inside your head. And even if you don't read the language, you can look at the pictures.

At any rate, until the human race masters the art of communicating telepathically, you'll need to print your FreeHand creations, either on your own printer or on a disk that you give to someone else to print. Unfortunately, printing can be a real pain (in addition to wasting a lot of good lumber that could otherwise be turned into butcher-block sofas and end tables). Either you press Command-P and it works or you spend half your life trying to uncover some immeasurably minute problem that only a machine would have difficulty handling.

Could be, of course, that you're not taking the proper approach to solving your printer problems. Instead of searching for whatever's causing the machine to hang up, perhaps you need to sublimate yourself before the powerful and capricious printer gods. Recommended items for sacrifice include old modems, power cables, ribbons, empty cartridges, and ugly mouse pads that you were embarrassed to use anyway. Assemble these items in front of your printer, set them on fire, and pray, "Print my page right now or I'm going to torch you, too." That should get the printer's attention.

If this approach doesn't work, I'm afraid that you'll have to resort to reading this chapter. I can't promise that it will solve every one of your printing problems, but it will help you take advantage of FreeHand's huge and sometimes overwhelming supply of printing options. You learn how to print black-and-white proofs, create color separations, define custom halftone patterns, and solve a few problems along the way.

But, you know, I bet you're not giving it 100 percent. Maybe if you threw some old printouts into the fire and shouted, "Look at what I'm doing to your children!" Make sure to have a maniacal glint in your eye and laugh broadly. I really think it's worth a shot.

Outputting Pages

FreeHand can print to just about any output device you hook up to your computer. Assuming that your printer is turned on — "Oh, great, I burned down my office for nothing!" — properly attached, and in working order, printing from FreeHand is a five-step process, as outlined below.

STEPS: Printing an Illustration from FreeHand

Step 1.   Use the Chooser desk accessory to select the output device to which you want to print. Unless your computer is part of a network that includes multiple printers, you probably rely on a single output device, in which case you can skip this step.

Step 2.   Choose File ⇨ Page Setup to specify the size and orientation of the printed page. If you're using a PostScript printer, you can skip this step and specify the page size and orientation in the Print Options dialog box.

Step 3.   Choose File ⇨ Print (Command-P) to print the illustration to the selected output device.

Step 4.   If you are using a PostScript printer, adjust the page size, page orientation, and lots of other settings inside the Print Options dialog box. If you're using a QuickDraw printer, skip this step.

Step 5.   Return to the print dialog box and click on the OK button to initiate the printing operation.

The following sections describe each of these steps in detail.

Choosing the printer driver

Because FreeHand is designed primarily as a PostScript-language drawing application, it provides the most reliable results when printing to a PostScript-compatible output device. Although you can print an illustration to a QuickDraw printer such as the StyleWriter or other model, many elements — most notably halftone screens, text effects, and imported EPS graphics — print as low-resolution bitmaps, exactly as they appear on-screen. Custom PostScript fill and stroke routines do not output at all to a non-PostScript device.

To select a printer, choose the Chooser desk accessory from the list of desk accessories under the Apple menu. The Chooser dialog box appears, as shown in the top portion of Figure 20-1. The dialog box is split into two parts, with the left half devoted to a scrolling list of printer driver icons and the right half to specific printer options.

Select the printer driver icon that matches your model of printer. *Printer drivers* help the Macintosh hardware, system software, and FreeHand itself translate the contents of an illustration to the printer hardware and the page-description language it uses. Generally, if you intend to use a PostScript-compatible printer, select the LaserWriter 8 driver. (This driver is supplied inside the Extensions folder of Disk 3 inside your FreeHand 4.0 package.)

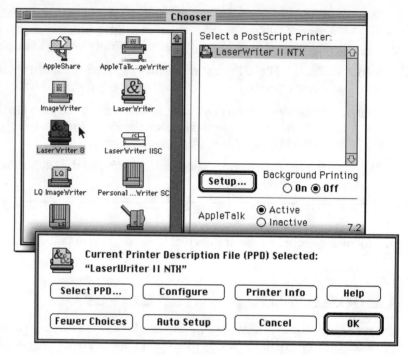

Figure 20-1:
The Chooser desk accessory as it appears when the LaserWriter 8 icon is selected (top). Click on the Setup button to select a PPD file (bottom).

Only use the old LaserWriter driver — Version 7.1.2 or earlier — if LaserWriter 8 poops out on you. For example, if the printer produces some bizarre PostScript error but you know that the illustration is fine, or if the printer simply stops reacting but never produces any error whatsoever, try switching to the old LaserWriter driver. If that doesn't work, you have a more serious problem.

If your computer is connected to one or more printers via AppleTalk or some other brand of network — as required when you print to a PostScript device — select the name of the printer from the scrolling list on the right side of the dialog box. For example, in Figure 20-1, the printer name is *LaserWriter II NTX*.

If your printer does not require AppleTalk cabling, as is generally the case with ImageWriters, StyleWriters, and other low-end devices, the right-hand scrolling list contains two icons, one for the printer port and the second for the modem port. Select the icon that corresponds to the serial port that connects your Mac to your printer (the port is located in the back of your computer).

When you select the LaserWriter 8 printer driver, the Chooser dialog box includes a Setup button. (If no printer is selected in the right-hand scrolling list, the button is dimmed.) Click on this button to display a second dialog box (see the bottom of Figure 20-1) that lets you select the *PostScript printer definition* (PPD) file that matches your specific brand of printer. The PPD includes special information about your model of printer that tells FreeHand how to print tints and gray values and ensures a smoother printing process in general.

Click on the Auto Setup button to instruct the system software to automatically select the correct PPD file for your brand of printer. For this function to succeed, you must have installed the correct PPD file on your computer when you installed FreeHand. If a matching PPD is not available, you need to install the required file from the Printer Descriptions folder inside the Extensions folder on Disk 3 of your FreeHand disks, as explained in the "Contents of the FreeHand disks" section of Chapter 3. This file should be installed in the Printer Descriptions folder inside the Extensions folder in your System Folder.

 You can get more PPD files from on-line services such as CompuServe and America Online. These services are also good places to find updated versions of the LaserWriter driver itself. For example, the driver included on the FreeHand disks is Version 8.0, but as I write this, Version 8.1.1 is available. Updated drivers are less likely to generate printer errors.

Click on the More Choices button to display all the buttons shown in the bottom example of Figure 20-1. These buttons allow you to select a PPD manually, set special configuration options supplied with a handful of PPDs, and display particular information about your printer. After you click on the More Choices button, it becomes the Fewer Choices button.

When you finish selecting options in the Chooser dialog box, click on the close box in the upper left corner of the title bar to return to the FreeHand desktop.

Setting up the page

If you use a PostScript printer and you installed the correct PPD for your brand of printer, you can skip this section and move on to the "Printing pages" section. If you use a non-PostScript printer or you simply can't get any PPD file to work, you need to specify the size and orientation of your printed pages by choosing File ⇨ Page Setup. Figure 20-2 shows two different kinds of dialog boxes that may display. One is for the StyleWriter and the other is for the Personal LaserWriter LS. Both are non-PostScript devices.

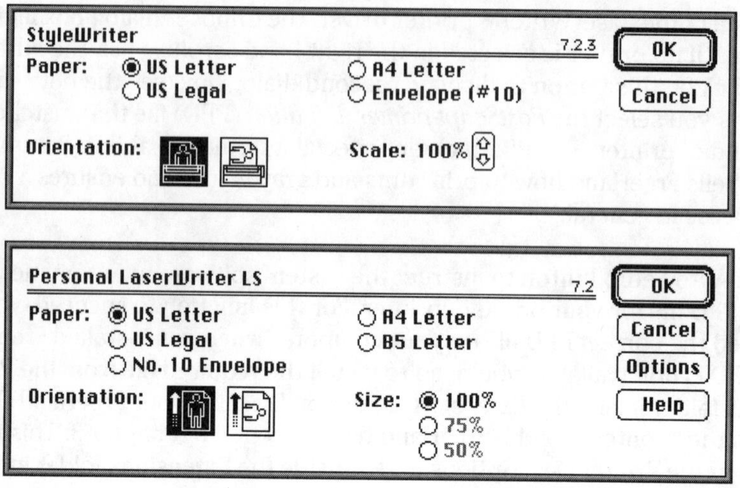

Figure 20-2:
Two page
setup dialog
boxes for
different
varieties of
non-
PostScript
printers.

```
┌─────────────────────────────────────────────────────────┐
│ StyleWriter                                    7.2.3  ┌──────────┐ │
│ Paper:    ⦿ US Letter        ○ A4 Letter            │   OK     │ │
│           ○ US Legal         ○ Envelope (#10)       └──────────┘ │
│                                                     ┌──────────┐ │
│ Orientation:  [🖶] [🖶]      Scale: 100% ⬍          │ Cancel   │ │
│                                                     └──────────┘ │
└─────────────────────────────────────────────────────────┘
```

```
┌─────────────────────────────────────────────────────────┐
│ Personal LaserWriter LS                         7.2  ┌──────────┐ │
│ Paper:    ⦿ US Letter        ○ A4 Letter            │   OK     │ │
│           ○ US Legal         ○ B5 Letter            └──────────┘ │
│           ○ No. 10 Envelope                         ┌──────────┐ │
│                                      Size: ⦿ 100%   │ Cancel   │ │
│ Orientation:  [🖶] [🖶]                   ○ 75%     └──────────┘ │
│                                            ○ 50%    ┌──────────┐ │
│                                                     │ Options  │ │
│                                                     └──────────┘ │
│                                                     ┌──────────┐ │
│                                                     │  Help    │ │
│                                                     └──────────┘ │
└─────────────────────────────────────────────────────────┘
```

Though the specific options that appear in the page setup dialog box vary from one model of printer to the next, the options fall into the basic categories discussed below:

- ↝ **Paper:** Select the radio button that corresponds to the size of the paper loaded into your printer's paper tray. Most U.S. laser printers are set up to handle letter- or legal-sized sheets. You have to manually feed other page sizes, including number 10 envelopes.

- ↝ **Orientation:** Select the portrait or landscape icon to specify whether FreeHand prints the artwork on the page upright or sideways. Select the icon that corresponds to the orientation of the page as it looks in the illustration window. (I know that it seems that FreeHand should be smart enough to print your wide pages in the illustration window to wide printed pages, but the truth is that the software needs your help.)

- ↝ **Scale or Size:** Some page setup dialog boxes let you scale the illustration to fit on a smaller page. For example, if you draw a tabloid-sized illustration and want to fit it onto a letter-sized page, you can shrink the illustration to fit by selecting the 50% option.

Other page setup dialog boxes provide even more options. Don't worry about them; in most cases, they don't work with FreeHand. When you finish specifying the page size and orientation, press Return to exit the dialog box and confirm your changes.

Printing pages

To initiate the printing process, press Command-P or choose File ⇨ Print. The specific dialog box that appears depends on the kind of printer you selected using the Chooser desk accessory. Figure 20-3 shows two of many possible examples for non-PostScript printers. Figure 20-4 shows the only possible examples when you're using a PostScript printer. If you selected the old LaserWriter driver 7.1.2 or earlier, the top dialog box appears. If you're using LaserWriter 8, the spotlighted dialog box comes up. In most respects, the two dialog boxes are identical; the spotlight highlights the only differences.

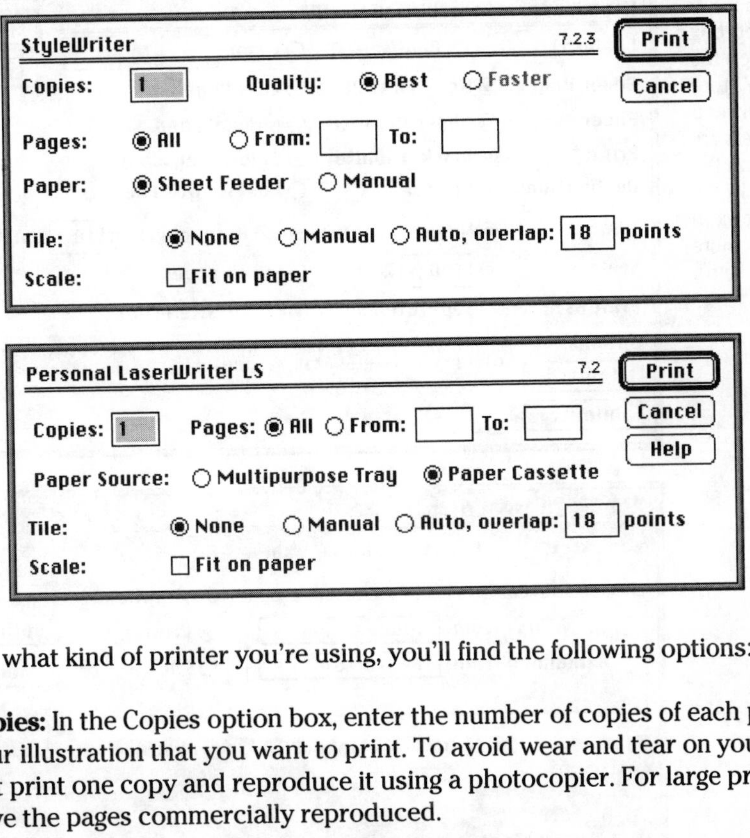

Figure 20-3: Two print dialog boxes for different varieties of non-PostScript printers.

No matter what kind of printer you're using, you'll find the following options:

- ✍ **Copies:** In the Copies option box, enter the number of copies of each page of your illustration that you want to print. To avoid wear and tear on your printer, just print one copy and reproduce it using a photocopier. For large print runs, have the pages commercially reproduced.

- ✍ **Pages:** Select the All radio button to print all pages in your illustration. If you only want to print a few of them — perhaps some pages are sized or oriented differently than others — enter the range of pages in the From option boxes. To print a single page, enter the same page number in both option boxes.

✯ **Paper Source:** If you want to print your illustration on a piece of letterhead stationery or other special paper, select the Manual Feed (or just plain Manual) radio button. The LaserWriter 8 dialog box lets you print the first page to different paper than other pages in the document by selecting options from pop-up menus. In Figure 20-4, for example, I specified that I wanted to manually feed the first page and print all other pages to paper loaded into the cassette. When the page is ready to print, your laser printer will display a manual feed light directing you to insert the special paper.

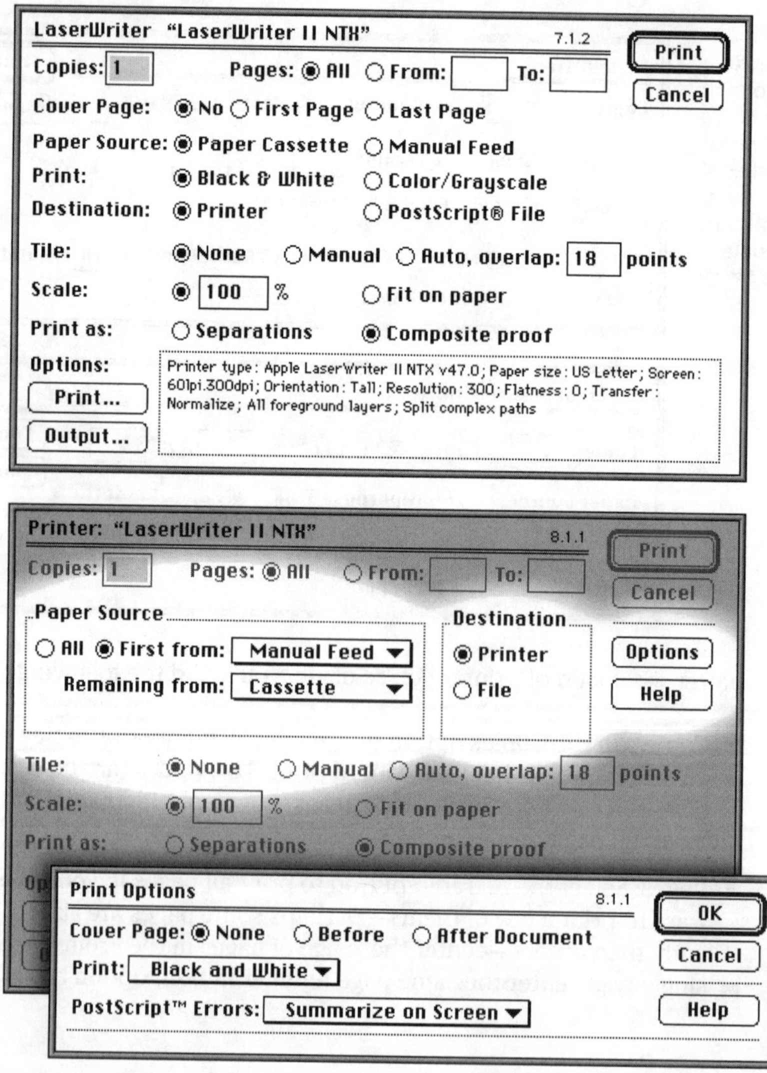

Figure 20-4:
The print dialog box as it appears when the LaserWriter 7 (top) and LaserWriter 8 (middle) drivers are selected. Click on the Options button in the latter dialog box to reveal a few more options (bottom).

The Paper Source options are ignored when you print to a color laser printer or to an imagesetter or other film-based output device. These printers don't permit manual paper feed because they use special types of paper and film.

- ☞ **Tile:** To proof large artwork to a laser printer, you can *tile* it. Tiling means to divide the artwork onto different pieces of paper that you later reassemble by hand using traditional paste-up techniques. If you select None, FreeHand prints only one page for each page in your document. It aligns the lower left corner of the printed page with the lower left corner of the on-screen page.

  If you want to tile your artwork, you can either select the Manual or Auto radio button. If you select the Manual option, FreeHand aligns the lower left corner of the printed page with the ruler origin. As with the None option, it only prints one page. But you can reposition the ruler origin between printouts to create additional tiles.

  Select the Auto radio button to instruct FreeHand to automatically tile the illustration. FreeHand prints as many pieces of paper as are required to output each page of the document. The first tile begins at the lower left corner of the page. Other tiles overlap the right and top edges of the first tile by the amount you specify in the Overlap option box.

- ☞ **Scale:** Enter a value into the Scale option box to enlarge or reduce the size at which the illustration prints. Reductions can be as small as 10 percent and enlargements as large as 1,000 percent. If you specify a percentage that expands the illustration beyond the current paper size, you have to tile the illustration, as described above.

  If your illustration is larger than the current paper size, select the Fit on Paper radio button to create a reduced version of your artwork. FreeHand automatically calculates the exact reduction necessary to fit the entire illustration on a single sheet of paper. However, don't expect to be able to blow up your printed illustration to a larger size — for example, by using a photocopier or stat camera. Doing so would increase the size of the printed pixels, which decreases resolution. Therefore, use this option only when creating proofs or thumbnails.

The following options are only available when you print to a PostScript output device. These options aren't any more advanced than the previous ones — sometimes, they don't even have any particular relationship to the PostScript language — but you won't find them when printing to your StyleWriter.

The first few options covered are available in the main body of the LaserWriter 7 dialog box. But when using LaserWriter 8, you have to click on the Options button to display the Print Options dialog box (shown at the bottom of Figure 20-4).

- **Cover Page:** This option allows you to print an extra page that lists the user name, application, document name, date, time, and printer for the current job. The cover page can precede or follow the rest of the illustration. It's designed to be used in an office setting where lots of folks use the same printer. The idea is that the artwork is more likely to get back to you if it has a cover on it. But of course, no one could mistake your unique style, right?

- **Print:** If you are using the LaserWriter 7 driver, two Print radio buttons appear in the middle of the dialog box. In the Print Options dialog box included with LaserWriter 8, you get three options in a pop-up menu. Either way, these options have no influence over printing illustrations from FreeHand. They are designed to translate color QuickDraw images to the PostScript language; FreeHand doesn't need the help.

- **PostScript Errors:** This option is only available if you're using the LaserWriter 8 driver, and again, it's an area in which FreeHand already has the bases covered. In some applications, you have to tell the system software to explain PostScript printing errors by selecting the Summarize On Screen option. But FreeHand explains printing errors whether you select this option or not.

The following two options are available in the main body of the print dialog box, regardless of which version of the LaserWriter driver you're using:

- **Destination:** This option enables you to generate a PostScript-language definition of the file on disk rather than printing it directly to your printer. Use this option when preparing an illustration to be printed on a remote PostScript printer. For more information on this option, read the "Printing to Disk" section later in this chapter.

- **Print As:** These options determine whether the colors in your illustration print separately — one color per page — or all on the same page. Selected by default, the Composite Proof option prints a *composite,* which shows the illustration in its entirety. A black-and-white composite printed from a standard laser printer or imagesetter translates all colors in the illustration to gray values. A color composite printed from a color printer or film recorder shows the colors as they actually appear. Composites are useful any time you want to proof an illustration and when you want to print a final grayscale illustration from an imagesetter, an overhead projection from a color printer, or a full-color slide from a film recorder.

Select Separations when you want to print each color on its own page. FreeHand can create a printout for each of the four process colors — cyan, magenta, yellow, and black — as well as each spot color used in the current illustration. Spot-color tints are printed on the same page as their parent color. The commercial printer then transfers each printout to a plate that's used in the actual reproduction process.

To specify exactly which color separations print and which do not, use the Separations options at the bottom of the Print Options dialog box, as discussed in the next section.

The dotted Options box at the bottom of the dialog box lists a printer abbreviation, the current paper size, the default screen frequency, the orientation of the page, the resolution of the output device, and so on. If any of these items are missing, or they're listed as *None* — as in *Printer type: None* — click on the Print button to display the Print Options dialog box shown in Figure 20-5. The following section describes the options in this dialog box.

Adjusting print options

Click on the Print button in the print dialog box to display the Print Options dialog box shown in Figure 20-5. (This dialog box appears the same regardless of which LaserWriter driver you use.) In the dialog box, you specify the paper size, the orientation of the page, the separations that you want to print, crop marks, and all kinds of other stuff.

Figure 20-5:
Click on the Print button to display this dialog box, in which you adjust various options that are unique to printing in FreeHand.

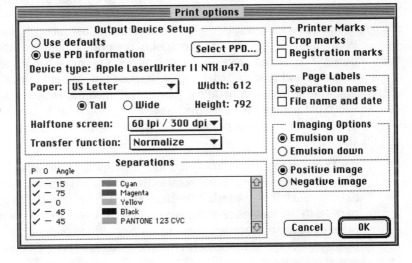

To permanently alter the default settings inside the Print Options dialog box, adjust the options as desired, click OK to return to the print dialog box, and then click on the Cancel button in the print dialog box to return to the illustration window. Save the illustration over the existing Aldus FreeHand Defaults file in the Aldus folder inside the System Folder, as described in the "The Aldus FreeHand Defaults file" section of Chapter 3.

Pages and margin notes

The following list explains every option in the Print Options dialog box except the scrolling Separations list in the bottom left corner. This latter item is sufficiently complex enough to deserve its own section.

↪ **Select PPD:** By default, the Use Defaults radio button is selected. This setting is tantamount to saying, "Use the settings in the page setup dialog box and ignore the PPD file." How irritating. To make FreeHand pay attention to the PPD file you select with the Chooser desk accessory, select the Use PPD Information radio button.

If you're using the old LaserWriter 7 driver, the Use PPD Information radio button may be dimmed. In this case, click on the Select PPD button to locate and select the PPD that corresponds to your brand of printer. These PPD files are located either in the PPDs folder in the Aldus folder or in the Printer Definitions folder in the Extensions folder. Both the Aldus and Extensions folders are inside the System Folder.

↪ **Paper:** Based on information contained in the selected PPD file, the Paper pop-up menu lists the page sizes that can be printed by your output device. If the selected printer allows you to set custom page sizes — as in the case of a professional-quality imagesetter — you can select a Custom option to change the Width and Height values to the right of the pop-up menu to editable option boxes. You can enter values as high as 3,888 points — or 54 inches — the size of the FreeHand pasteboard. But just because you can enter a value doesn't mean that your printer can handle it. The actual maximum size is determined by the width of the paper used by the imagesetter. Some PPDs provide a MaxMeasure option in the Paper pop-up menu that selects the maximum permissible page size.

If a Transverse suffix follows an option in the Paper pop-up menu (as in *Letter.Transverse*), FreeHand rotates the page size relative to the roll of paper or film on which it is printed. By default, FreeHand places the long edge of the page parallel to the long edge of the paper. In most cases this is correct, but when printing to an imagesetter, you can usually reduce paper or film waste by setting pages *transverse* — that is, with the short edges of the page parallel to the long edges of the paper.

An Extra suffix adds an inch to both the horizontal and vertical dimensions of the page size, allowing room for margin notes such as crop marks and page labels (discussed later in this immense list). For example, Letter.Extra measures $9\ 1/2 \times 12$ inches.

The Tall and Wide radio buttons below the Paper pop-up menu control the orientation of the page inside the specified paper size. Unless you specified a custom paper size large enough to accommodate both horizontal and vertical pages, as described in the "Printing differently sized pages" section of Chapter 19, you should select the option that matches the orientation of pages that you want to print.

✎ **Halftone Screen:** The options in this pop-up menu control the screen frequency and the resolution used by your printer. The *screen frequency* represents the number of halftone cells per linear inch and is measured in lines per inch, or *lpi. Halftone cells* are the dots used to represent gray values, process colors, and tints. Both are described in more detail in the "Halftone screens" section later in this chapter.

The *resolution* of the printer is the number of pixels printed per linear inch. Resolution is measured in dots per inch, or *dpi,* with *dots* being the common name for the printer's tiny pixels. When printing to a laser printer, you generally can't change the resolution. However, when printing to an imagesetter, you can speed up printing by reducing the resolution or increase the quality of the printout by increasing the value.

✎ **Transfer Function:** This pop-up menu provides access to three options — Default, Normalize, and Posterize — each of which controls the lightness and darkness of gray values and tints printed from FreeHand. Select the Default option to bypass special instructions included in the current PPD file and rely on the default screen settings used by your printer.

Unfortunately, different printers render screens differently. A light tint printed from a typical laser printer, for example, is darker than the same tint printed from an imagesetter. To help eliminate this inconsistency, select the Normalize option, which uses special instructions from the PPD file to make screens printed from a low-resolution laser printer more accurately match those printed from a high-end imagesetter.

Choose Posterize to remap tints to one of four screen values — 100 percent, 67 percent, 33 percent, or 0 percent (white). Transitions between tints are abrupt rather than smooth. (An example of a posterized image appears back in Figure 18-8.) Select this option when printing speed is more important than quality. It dramatically speeds up the printing of gradations, for example, because FreeHand only has to render four steps instead of the 26 steps that a laser printer outputs by default.

✎ **Printer Marks:** Select the Crop Marks check box to print eight hairline *crop marks,* which mark the four corners of an illustration. When you print to an imagesetter, for example, all illustrations are printed on paper one or two feet wide, regardless of their actual size. When you have the illustration commercially reproduced, the printer will want to know the dimensions of the final paper size and how the illustration should be positioned on the final page. Crop marks specify the boundaries of the reproduced page and the position of your artwork relative to these boundaries.

Select the Registration Marks check box to print five *registration marks,* one centered along the top of the illustration, one centered along the bottom, one centered along each side, and a fifth in the lower right corner of the page. Registration marks are used to align color separations. When you're printing a black-and-white or color composite, registration marks are not necessary. However, if you are printing separations, they're absolutely imperative because they provide the only reliable means for ensuring exact registration of different process and spot colors during the commercial printing process.

✏ **Page Labels:** Select the Separation Names check box to print the name of the separation color in the lower left corner of the page, just outside the crop marks. If you're printing a black-and-white or color composite, FreeHand prints the word *Composite.* When you print color separations, it prints *Cyan, Magenta,* or whatever is the name of the separation color. Again, be sure to select this option when printing color separations. Otherwise, your commercial printer won't know which separation is which.

Select the File Name and Date check box to print the file name and the date on which you last saved the current illustration in the upper left corner, just outside the crop marks. Use this option to avoid the which-version-is-which confusion that often accompanies the creation of electronic documents.

All margin notes — crop marks, registration marks, and page labels — print outside the area consumed by the page and bleed size, as specified in the Document Pages panel. Therefore, be sure to select a Paper option that's larger than the page size and bleed added together; otherwise, your margin notes will not print. The Extra paper sizes are especially useful for this purpose. For example, if the current illustration is set on a letter-sized page, choose Letter.Extra from the Paper pop-up menu to leave room for margin notes.

The commercial printer reproducing your illustration will use all margin notes, so be sure that they are not removed when excess paper or film is trimmed from your printed separation.

✏ **Imaging Options:** Select the Emulsion Down radio button to print a flipped version of the illustration. The resulting illustration is a mirror image of its former self. The option name refers to the orientation of an illustration relative to the emulsion side of a piece of film. When printing film negatives, you will probably want to select Emulsion Down; when printing on paper, select the Emulsion Up radio button. If you're unsure which option to use, consult with your commercial printer.

Select Negative Image to change all blacks to white and whites to black. For example, 100 percent black becomes white, 40 percent black becomes 60 percent black, and so on. As a general rule, select the Positive Image option when printing to paper; select Negative Image only when printing to film. Again, be sure to confirm your selection with your commercial printer.

Printing color separations

The only options in the Print Options dialog box that I haven't discussed so far are the Separations options in the scrolling list in the lower left corner. But before I can explain these options, I need to introduce a little color-separation theory.

A specific color can be professionally reproduced on a sheet of paper in two ways. In the first method, called *spot-color printing,* inks are premixed to create the desired color and then applied to the paper. One separation is printed for each spot color used in the illustration. Spot-color printing is usually used when the illustration includes only one or two colors (in addition to black). This printing method is neither exceedingly expensive nor technically demanding. Spot-color printing allows for precise colors to be selected and applied with perfect color consistency.

In the alternative printing method, *four-color process printing,* cyan, magenta, yellow, and black ink are blended in specific percentages to create a visual effect approximating a whole rainbow of colors. Four-color process printing is technically demanding and tends to be more expensive than spot-color printing, but it also results in more colors.

When printing a process-color illustration, FreeHand generates a separation for each of the four component inks. Every colored object in an illustration is broken down into its component colors according to their original definitions in the Color Mixer palette. For example, Figure 20-6 shows a monochrome composite followed by four color separations. The forward star is filled with a process color that is defined as 100 percent cyan, 40 percent magenta, 30 percent yellow, and 0 percent black. It therefore outputs as solid color on the cyan separation, a 40 percent screen on the magenta separation, a 30 percent screen on the yellow separation, and white on the black separation. When these colors are printed in these percentages, the placement of the halftoned dots visually simulates a grayish blue.

It's possible to combine four-color process printing with spot-color printing. This option is more expensive than process printing alone and is subject to the capabilities of your commercial printer. But it combines the benefits of the four-color process — which permits many colors with few inks — and spot-color printing — which ensures precise color matching — in one printed piece. Many magazines, for example, use four-color process printing for photos and artwork and spot-color printing for advertisements and logos.

Figure 20-6:
Four process-color separations and a monochrome composite of the same illustration.

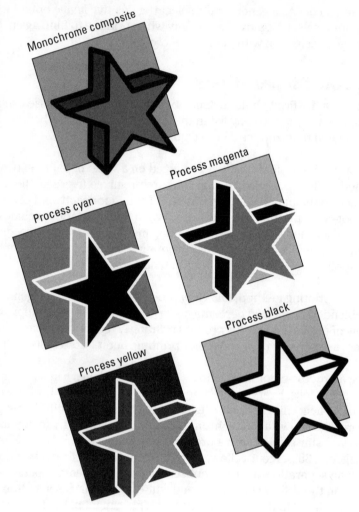

Monochrome composite

Process magenta

Process cyan

Process black

Process yellow

Now, on to the options offered by FreeHand 4.0, as shown in Figure 20-7. The scrolling list of Separations options in the lower left corner of the Print Options dialog box contains the name of every spot color defined in the current illustration, including black. If any process color has been defined, the three nonblack process colors — cyan, magenta, and yellow — are also displayed. No tints are shown in the scrolling list. Instead, each tint is printed to the same separation as its parent color: 10 percent black prints to the black separation, 40 percent Pantone 123 prints to the Pantone 123 separation, and so on.

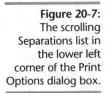

Figure 20-7:
The scrolling
Separations list in
the lower left
corner of the Print
Options dialog box.

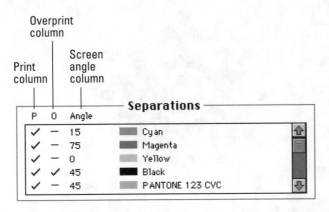

The left side of the scrolling list is divided into three columns. The print column, headed by a *P,* determines whether the corresponding color prints. A check mark means that the separation in that row will print when the Separations option in the print dialog box is selected. No check mark means that the color won't print. To hide or display a check mark, click inside the print column. For example, to proof only the cyan separation, click in front of the magenta, yellow, and black rows to hide their check marks and prevent these colors from printing. (The check marks stay hidden until the next time you revisit the Print Options dialog box.)

The second column, headed by an *O,* is the overprint column. When no check mark appears in this column, the corresponding color knocks out any colors behind it, as described in the "Overprinting colors" section of Chapter 13. If a check mark precedes a color name, that color overprints colors that it overlaps. To change the overprint setting, click in the overprint column to display or hide a check mark. Because this option applies to *all* objects filled or stroked with a color, it's generally a bit drastic unless you're trying to create a specific effect. The only color that you may want to overprint on a regular basis is black. In fact, black traditionally overprints other colors because it's so dark that you don't see the colors behind it. So by overprinting, you avoid gaps between other process colors and black.

The number in the third column controls the *screen angle,* which is the angle at which halftone screens in the corresponding separation print. When one of the LaserWriter PPDs is selected, FreeHand rotates process-color screens as shown in Figure 20-8. The following items explain how these angles work:

    ✏ Cyan screens are rotated 15 degrees counterclockwise from the mean horizontal.

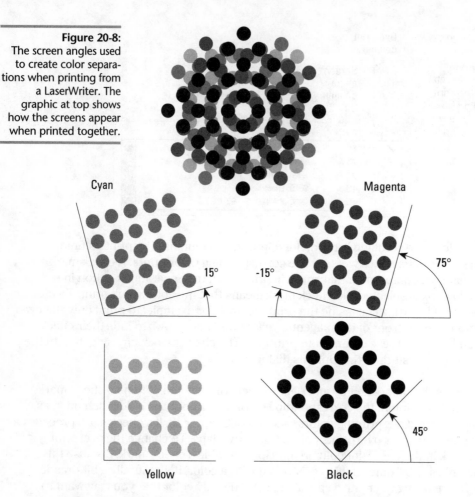

Figure 20-8:
The screen angles used to create color separations when printing from a LaserWriter. The graphic at top shows how the screens appear when printed together.

Cyan

Magenta

15°

−15°

75°

Yellow

Black

45°

⮑ Magenta screens are rotated 75 degrees, which produces the same effect as if they were rotated –15 degrees from the mean horizontal. So the magenta rotation is exactly the opposite of the cyan rotation.

⮑ Yellow screens aren't rotated at all.

⮑ Black screens are rotated 45 degrees, smack dab in the middle of the others.

Other PPDs may rotate the screens to different angles. Typically, the yellow and black screens remain at 0 and 45 degrees respectively, while the cyan and magenta screens are rotated slightly differently. For example, if you select the Agfa ProSet 9800, the cyan screen rotates to 18.43 and the magenta rotates to 71.57 degrees. Again, these values produce exactly opposite effects (90 – 18.43 = 71.57). This opposite relationship between cyan and magenta is one of the factors that ensures even printing of process colors.

Unless you know what you're doing, don't change the values associated with process colors. Spot colors, however, are a different matter. FreeHand rotates all spot colors to the same angle as black because they are not intended to overlap other colors. But if you overprint an object filled or stroked with a spot color or you overprint the entire spot color separation by displaying a check mark in the overprint column, change this angle. To do so, double-click on the value in the screen angle column and enter a new value in the tiny dialog box that appears. Then press Return.

 Generally speaking, set the screen angle of an overprinting spot color 45 degrees different than the process color that it overlaps most often. For example, if you combine the spot color and black — probably the most popular combination — change the screen angle to 0 degrees.

Initiating printing

When you're finished setting the options in the Print Options dialog box, click on the OK button or press Return to close the dialog box and return to the print dialog box. Press Return again to initiate the printing process. The standard dialog boxes that are presented during any PostScript printing process appear. During the printing process, you can press Command-period to cancel the Print command.

Printing to Disk

When you print a FreeHand illustration to a PostScript printer, FreeHand *downloads* a PostScript-language text file to the printer. The printer reads the file and creates your illustration according to its instructions. FreeHand also allows you to print an illustration to disk; that is, write the PostScript-language text file to your hard drive. If you're familiar with the PostScript language, you can edit the file using a word processor. Or you can copy the file to a floppy disk or other removable media to transfer to your service bureau.

After you print the illustration to disk, you can download it to the printer using a utility such as the Adobe Font Downloader, much as you would download a font file. This feature allows you to control the way in which an illustration is output even if you don't own or have direct access to a PostScript printing device.

Printing to disk is easy. Prepare your artwork for printing as discussed in the previous sections of this chapter, defining all settings in the print and Print Options dialog boxes as desired. Then, before pressing Return to initiate the Print command, select File from the Destination options in the print dialog box. (If you're using LaserWriter 7, the option is called PostScript File.)

After you click on the Save button — assuming that you're using the LaserWriter 8 driver — the system software produces the save dialog box shown in Figure 20-9. You can name the file and specify its destination, just as in any save dialog box. You can also select from a few other options:

∾ **Format:** This dialog box allows you to select the format that you want to use to save the illustration. The dialog box offers three EPS options, but don't select them. You can create an editable EPS file from inside FreeHand. To create a file you can download to a printer, select the PostScript option, which is the default setting.

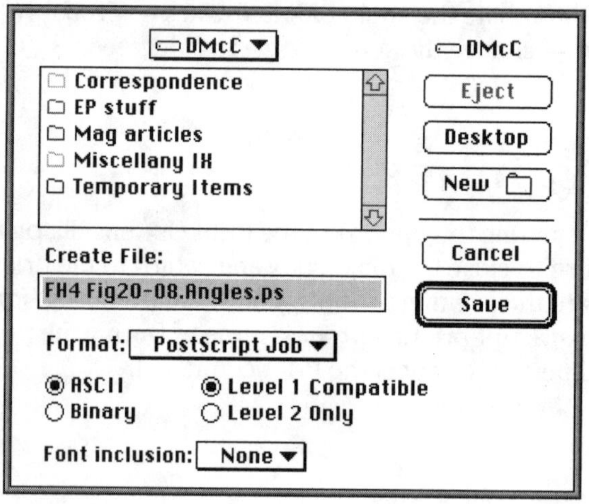

Figure 20-9:
Use this dialog box to print a file to disk.

∾ **ASCII or Binary:** If you'll be downloading the file from a Mac, select the Binary option. Binary encoding is much faster, much more efficient, and results in smaller files. Only select the ASCII option if you'll be doing something weird with the file, like giving it to a DOS user.

∾ **Level 1 or 2:** You'll have to consult with your service bureau on this one. If the service bureau uses an imagesetter equipped with Level 2 PostScript, by all means select the Level 2 Only option. Otherwise, select Level 1 Compatible.

∾ **Font Inclusion:** If you used any special fonts in your illustration — anything besides Times, Helvetica, Courier, and Symbol — select the All But Standard 13 option. This tells FreeHand to include printer font definitions for every font that you use except Times and the others. Including fonts greatly increases the size of the file on disk but it also prevents your text from printing incorrectly. If you know that your service bureau is already equipped with the fonts you're using, select the None option to keep the size of the file down.

Click on the Save button or press Return to save the file on disk.

Special Printing Considerations _____

All print jobs are not the same. Your illustration may require special treatment that the Print command options can't provide. Or you may encounter complications that prevent your document from printing properly even though the illustration itself seems fine. In either of these scenarios, the information in the following sections may be of help. It explains how to alter settings for halftone screens, use downloadable printer fonts, avoid limitcheck errors, and solve out-of-memory errors.

Halftone screens

In addition to altering halftone screen frequencies for an entire illustration from the Print Options dialog box, you can control halftones on an object-by-object basis. However, if you want to adjust the halftone settings for an object, it must be filled or stroked with a gray value, tint, or process color (all directional and radial gradations fall into this camp). Any 100 percent color — black, white, a solid spot color, or a mix of 100 percent process colors — is not affected because such colors print as solid ink; no halftoning is required.

To alter the halftone screen for a specific text block or graphic object, select the object that you want to change and then press Command-H to display the Halftone palette shown in Figure 20-10. You can use the options in this palette to create special effects or manipulate a document in preparation for some specific commercial printing process. Both the fill and stroke of the selected object are affected by your settings.

Manipulations performed in the Halftone palette affect only the printing of selected objects; they do _not_ in any way affect the manner in which objects display in the preview or keyline mode. Also, these options are applicable only for printing to PostScript printers.

Figure 20-10:
The Halftone palette as it appears when the default halftone setting is selected (left) and when the Screen pop-up menu is displayed (right).

But before I go any further, let me explain how halftones work. The whole idea behind printing is to use as few inks as possible to create the appearance of a wide variety of colors. For example, if you wanted to print a picture of a pink flamingo wearing a red bow tie, your printer could print the flamingos in one pass using pink ink, let that color dry, and then load the red ink and print all the bow ties. But why go to all that trouble? After all, pink is just a lighter shade of red. Why not imitate the pink by lightening the red ink? Unfortunately, offset printing presses don't do lighter shades of colors. They recognize only solid color and the absence of color.

So how do you print the 30 percent shade of red necessary to represent pink? The answer is *halftoning*. Hundreds of tiny dots of ink are laid down on a page. Because the dots are so small, your eyes cannot quite focus on them. Instead, the dots appear to blend with the white background of the page to create a lighter shade of a color. Figure 20-11 shows a detail of the flamingo enlarged to display the individual dots. He isn't wearing a bow tie — the one he ordered from Neiman Marcus didn't come in.

Figure 20-11: A tint or gray value is made up of hundreds of tiny dots called *halftone cells*, as illustrated by the enlarged detail on the right.

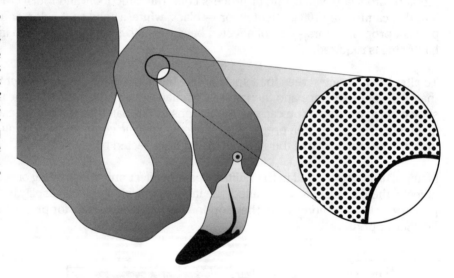

The dots in a tint are arranged into a grid of *halftone cells*, much like a checkerboard. The dots grow and shrink inside their cells to emulate different shades of color. Large dots create dark tints; small dots create light tints. Each pixel in your PostScript printer belongs to one of the halftone cells, and each halftone cell comprises some number of pixels.

As an example, consider the LaserWriter: By default, it prints 60 halftone cells per linear inch. Because the resolution of the LaserWriter is 300 pixels per linear inch, each halftone cell must measure 5 pixels wide by 5 pixels tall ($300 \div 60 = 5$), for a total of 25 pixels per cell. If all 25 pixels in a cell are turned off, the cell appears white. All pixels turned on produces solid ink; any number from 1 to 24 pixels turned on produces a particular gray value or tint. By turning on different numbers of pixels — from 0 up to 25 — the printer can create a total of 26 unique tints or gray values, as illustrated in Figure 20-12.

Figure 20-12:
A 5 × 5-pixel halftone cell with different numbers of pixels activated, ranging from 25 (top left) to 0 (bottom right). Each cell represents a unique gray value or tint from 100 to 0 percent.

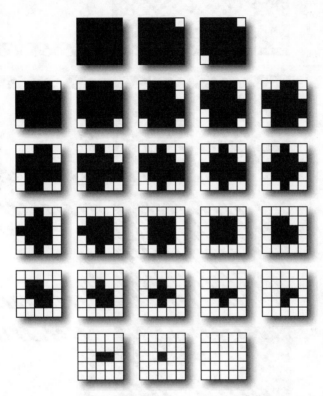

The options in the Halftone palette enable you to alter the shape, angle, and size of every halftone cell used to represent gray values, tints, and process colors in the fill and stroke of the selected object. The Screen pop-up menu determines the *screen function,* which is the pattern FreeHand uses to simulate gray values and tints. You can select from four options, each of which is shown applied to objects in Figure 20-13:

- **Default:** This option accepts the default screen function produced by the current output device. Some PostScript devices rely on round black dots against a white background inside light tints, white dots against a black background inside dark tints, and a squarish checkerboard pattern when simulating medium tints. On other printers, the Default option produces the same effect as the Round Dot option.

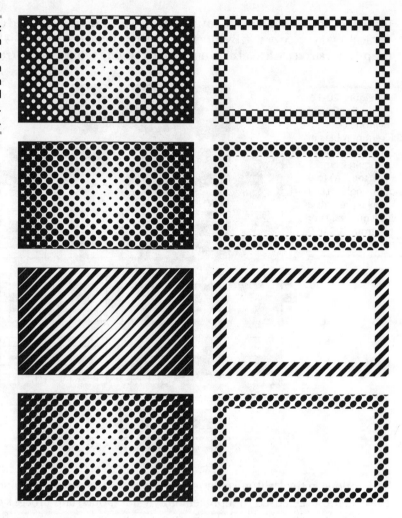

- ☞ **Round Dot:** This option represents gray values and tints using a pattern of perfectly circular black dots against a white background, even when representing light and medium tints.

- ☞ **Line:** The Line option represents gray values and tints using a series of parallel straight lines. When applied to a gradation, the lines gradually increase and decrease in thickness, resulting in spikes.

- ☞ **Ellipse:** This option creates a series of black ovals against a white background.

The value in the Angle option box determines the *screen angle,* which is the orientation of the halftone cells. By default, this grid is rotated 45 degrees with respect to the printed page. To rotate the halftone grid to some other angle, enter a value between 0 and 90 degrees (all other values create repeat effects) into the Angle option box. Examples are shown in Figure 20-14.

Figure 20-14:
Angle values of 0 (top), 30 (middle), and 60 (bottom) degrees applied to the fill and stroke of two objects.

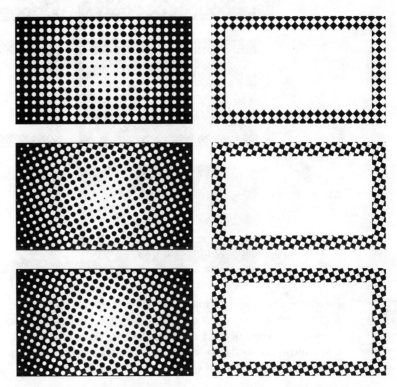

The value in the Frequency option box determines the *screen frequency,* which is the number of halftone cells that print per linear inch. Frequency is measured in lines per inch, or lpi. If no value appears in this option box, FreeHand accepts the default screen frequency for the current output device. Examples include 60 lpi for the LaserWriter and 120 lpi for the Linotronic 300. FreeHand accepts any value from 4 to 300 lpi.

As shown in Figure 20-15, higher Frequency values result in smoother-looking gray values and tints. However, raising the frequency also decreases the number of gray values a printer can render, because it decreases the size of each halftone cell, thus decreasing the number of pixels per cell. Therefore, when raising the Frequency value above the default setting, consider how your change affects the number of gray values printable by the current output device (as explained back in the "Avoiding banding" section of Chapter 17).

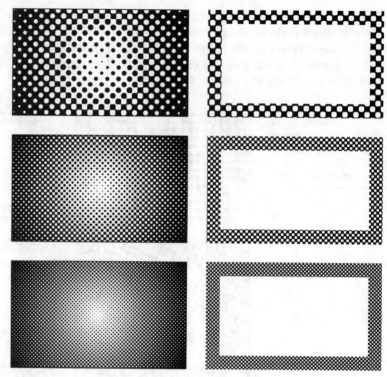

Figure 20-15:
Screen frequencies of 12
lpi (top), 24 lpi (middle),
and 36 lpi (bottom).

Be aware that changes made to halftone settings alter the default settings applied to new objects if the Changing Objects Changes Defaults check box in the Editing panel of the Preferences dialog box is selected. Because you can't see halftone screens on-screen, you can easily start applying them to every new object that you create if you aren't careful.

Using downloadable fonts

If your illustration uses fonts that aren't built into your printer's ROM or included on the printer's hard drive — known as *nonresident* fonts — you must make sure that those fonts either are downloaded manually to the printer's RAM or hard drive or are available for automatic downloading during printing. If you manually download a font to the printer's memory — which you accomplish by using a special utility such as the Adobe Font Downloader — it remains there until the next time you turn off or restart the printer. If you download the font to the printer's hard drive — only a handful of printers offer hard drives —

the font remains available until you remove it. If you don't download the font at all, the system software will automatically download it for you. Automatically downloaded fonts are always sent to the printer's RAM and are purged immediately after the printing process completes.

Storing fonts on the printer's hard drive speeds up the printing process because the printer can access them more quickly than it can downloaded fonts stored in your computer's hard drive. When using fonts from the Adobe Type Library, you can use the Adobe Font Downloader to install the fonts on your hard drive. The Font Downloader allows you to check which fonts are currently stored on the hard drive and to manually download fonts to RAM for temporary use.

If you're planning on using a font that isn't available on the printer's hard drive several times throughout the day, you may want to manually download the font into RAM. Although manual downloading takes time, you gain back every minute and then some if you use the downloaded fonts more than four or five times.

Available printer RAM, however, is a major constraint in deciding how many fonts can be downloaded manually. In general, printers that have only a 200K to 300K of available RAM, such as the LaserWriter Plus, can hold only two or three manually downloaded fonts at a time. Printers with 2MB of RAM, such as the LaserWriter II NTX, can hold six or more fonts, and printers with 3MB or more of RAM can hold a dozen or more fonts.

When a printer is holding its maximum number of downloaded fonts, it cannot accept any more fonts, whether downloaded manually or automatically. Also, you can't remove a single font from printer RAM; if you want to get rid of one font, you have to purge them all. Therefore, before downloading a font, consider not only how many times it will be used, but also how many other downloadable fonts you'll need to use in the same printing session.

Suppose that you plan to print a number of illustrations that contain different downloadable fonts within a few hours. You can save time by allowing the required fonts to download automatically rather than downloading the fonts manually and restarting the printer every time you print a different illustration. Of course, if your printer offers sufficient memory, you may be able to download all fonts at once.

When deciding on your strategy for using downloadable printer fonts, try not to forget the needs of the other users of your printer. In a networked situation, you shouldn't download fonts manually unless your printer has adequate memory; a reasonable amount of working memory should be kept available for other users to print documents with automatically downloaded fonts. If you don't have enough memory to manually download all the fonts that you expect to use, just download the one or two fonts that you will be using most often.

Use automatic downloading whenever it's impossible or impractical to download fonts manually to the printer's hard drive or RAM. Under System 7.0, printer fonts must reside in the Extensions folder inside the System Folder in order to downloaded automatically. Under System 7.1 and later, printer fonts can be located in the Extensions or Fonts folder inside the System Folder.

Splitting long paths

You may encounter several errors when printing an illustration. One of the most common is the *limitcheck error,* which results from a limitation in your printer's PostScript interpreter. If the number of points in the mathematical representation of a path exceeds this limitation, the illustration will not print successfully.

 Unfortunately, the points used in this mathematical representation are not the corner, curve, and connector points you used to define the objects. Instead, they are calculated by the PostScript interpreter during the printing process. When presented with a curve, the PostScript interpreter has to plot hundreds of tiny straight lines to create the most accurate rendering possible. So instead of drawing a perfect curve, your printer creates a many-sided polygon whose exact number of sides is determined by a device-dependent variable known as *flatness.* The default flatness for the LaserWriter is one pixel, or 1/300 inch. The center of any tiny side of the polygon rendering may be at most 1/300 inch from the farthest X,Y-coordinate of the actual mathematical curve, as demonstrated by Figure 20-16.

Figure 20-16:
The flatness of a curve is the greatest distance between any tiny straight line used to represent the curve and its true mathematical description.

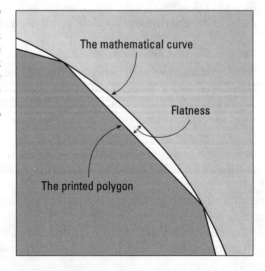

The mathematical curve

Flatness

The printed polygon

Each tiny line in the polygon rendering meets at a point. If the number of points exceeds your printer's built-in path limit, an alert box appears to inform you that the printer has encountered a limitcheck error, and the print job will be canceled. The path limit for the original LaserWriter was 1,500, seemingly enough straight lines to imitate any curve. But in practice, you can easily create a curve that proves too much for that limit. For example, a standard signature contains several complex loops that might tax the limitations of the most advanced output device.

There are two ways to avoid limitcheck errors. The most preferred method is to enter the resolution for the final output device in the Printer Resolution option box in the Document Setup panel of the Inspector palette. The next time you print or export the current illustration, FreeHand automatically breaks up every path that it considers to be at risk into several smaller paths. This doesn't affect the actual paths in your FreeHand document, just those in the EPS file and the PostScript description sent to the printer.

 If you don't want FreeHand to break up your paths, choose File ⇨ Output Options to display the Output Options dialog box, shown in Figure 20-17. Then deselect the Split Complex Paths check box. I can't imagine any reason why you'd want to do this — as far as I know, this option is utterly without negative side effects — but I figured that if I go and slap a name like *Bible* on this book, I have to tell you everything.

Figure 20-17:
The Output Options dialog box.

```
╔══════════ Output options ══════════╗
│ ·········· Objects ··········        │
│ ⊠ Include invisible layers          │
│ ⊠ Split complex paths               │
│ ·········· Image Data ··········     │
│ ○ ASCII encoding                    │
│ ◉ Binary data                       │
│ ○ None (OPI comments only)          │
│ ⊠ Convert RGB TIFF to CMYK          │
│ ······ Maximum Color Steps ······   │
│ ┌──────┐ (Leave blank for default)  │
│ └──────┘                            │
│ ·········· Flatness ··········       │
│ ┌──────┐ (Leave blank for default)  │
│ └──────┘                            │
│      ( Cancel )  (( OK ))           │
╚═════════════════════════════════════╝
```

Unfortunately, FH's automated path splitting feature accounts only for the complexity of the path. It doesn't account for whether a path is filled with a complex tile pattern, which is a common cause of the limitcheck error.

If the automatic splitting technique doesn't solve your printing problem, you can use the Flatness value, also found in the Output Options dialog box. Enter a value between 0 and 100 in the Flatness option box. This value increases the distance that a straight line can vary from the mathematical curve, thus reducing the risk of limitcheck errors. However, the affected path also appears less smooth.

 Another great use for the Flatness value — and for the Maximum Color Steps value that appears right above it — is to speed up the printing of proofs. If you lower the Maximum Color Steps value, which controls the number of steps used to print gradations (this value has no effect on steps in blends) and raise the Flatness value, FreeHand prints very quickly, as well as very roughly. When it comes time to print the final output, be sure to delete both values so that FreeHand relies on the printer's default settings.

Printing pattern tiles

As I mentioned a moment ago, tile patterns can cause limitcheck errors. But more often, they cause *out-of-memory errors,* especially if several patterns are used in a single illustration. To accelerate the printing process, FreeHand downloads tiles to your printer's memory, much as if they were nonresident fonts. The printer can then access tile definitions repeatedly throughout the printing of an illustration. However, if the illustration contains too many tile patterns, or if a single tile is too complex, the printer's memory may become full, in which case the print operation is canceled and an alert box informs you that an out-of-memory error has occurred.

It's been my experience that out-of-memory errors are about equally common when printing from new, high-resolution output devices as from old, low-memory printers. Imagesetters tend to include updated PostScript interpreters and have increased memory capacity, but they also need this additional memory to render the complex tile patterns at a higher resolution. But regardless of which kind of device you use, you can try any one of these techniques to remedy the problem:

- Change all typefaces in the current illustration to Times, Helvetica, or some other printer-resident font so that FreeHand doesn't have to download both patterns and printer fonts.

- Print objects painted with different tile patterns in separate illustrations. Then use traditional paste-up techniques to combine the pages into a composite proof.

☞ Send all objects filled with pattern tiles to a separate layer, hide the layer by clicking its check mark in the Layers palette, and then deselect the Include Invisible Layers radio button in the Output Options dialog box before printing. This technique allows you to proof all portions of your illustration except objects filled with tile patterns. If the illustration prints successfully, you know that the tile patterns are the culprit and can set about getting rid of some.

Some service bureaus charge extra for printing a complex document that ties up an imagesetter for a long period of time. Tile patterns almost always complicate an illustration and increase printing time. Therefore, use masks and composite paths instead of patterns whenever possible.

Summary

⇢ FreeHand 4.0 is designed to work with the LaserWriter 8 PostScript printer driver. But if you have printing problems, try switching back to LaserWriter 7.

⇢ Choose File ⇨ Page Setup to specify the size and orientation of a printed page only when proofing illustrations to non-PostScript printer. Otherwise, select a PPD file inside the Print Options dialog box and select from the accompanying options.

⇢ When you select a page size option with a Transverse suffix, FreeHand rotates the page with respect to the roll of film or paper output from the imagesetter. The Extra suffix adds an inch to both the vertical and horizontal dimensions of the page.

⇢ When printing color separations, be sure to select all Printer Marks and Page Labels options so that your printer knows which page is which and how the pages align.

⇢ When printing to film negatives, select the Emulsion Down and Negative Image options. When printing paper positives, select Emulsion Up and Positive Image.

⇢ To gain absolute control over the printing process without having access to an imagesetter — or even to a PostScript printer — set all the printing options as desired and print the illustration to disk by selecting File from the Destination options.

⇢ Use the options in the Halftone palette to set the function, angle, and frequency of the halftone screen assigned to a selected object. This is a great way to create custom printing effects.

Index

• Symbols •

1-bit depth, 425
3-D text effects, 408
4-bit depth, 425
8-bit depth, 425
16-bit depth, 425
24-bit depth, 425
` (grave key), 215, 291
  fourth time, 292
  second time, 292
  third time, 292

• A •

Add Pages dialog box, 638
  Bleed Size value, 638
additive primary model, 437
Adobe Font Downloader, 667, 674
Adobe Illustrator
  files
    formats for, 629
    opening, 18
  Freehand vs., 15-18
  top ten tasks, 15-16
Adobe Streamline 3.0, 202
  FreeHand vs., 203-204
Adobe Type Manager (ATM), 61
  versions, 62
airplane drawing, 451
Aldus folder, 70
Aldus Installer Main Window,
    68-69
  illustrated, 69
  options, 69
alias icon, 37
aliases, 37
Align palette, 80, 286, 334
  Apply button, 284
  displaying, 282
  icons, 287
  illustrated, 283
aligning, 282-287
  objects to each other, 282-285
    locking, 287
  paragraphs, 371
  steps for, 284-285
  text, 319

alignment
  bound text, 409
    horizontal, 410-412
  text, 319
    changing, 371-372
    vertical, 402-405
  wrapping text, 415-416
Altsys software manual, 2, 3
Apple Color Picker dialog box, 428
  accessing, 435
  Brightness option box, 429
  Hue option box, 429
  illustrated, 428
  options, 428-429
  Saturation option box, 429
Apple Color Wheel dialog box, 438
Apple logo, creating, 257-259
Apple menu, 35
  About FreeHand command, 71
  Chooser command, 54
  Control Panels command, 426
AppleTalk cabling, 652
application clipboards, 57
application icon, 37
  dragging document icon on, 46
Application menu, 36, 52
  Hide Others command, 55
  icons, dimmed, 55
  Show All command, 56
application RAM, 47
applications
  choosing, 52
  multiple, managing, 51-56
  RAM assignment, 47
  running, 37
    in background, 52
    in foreground, 52
    hiding/showing, 55-56
  starting, 45-46
  switching between, 52-53
  working with, 45-56
arcs, 118
Arrange menu
  Align command, 282, 284
  Bring to Front command, 300,
    301
  Group command, 288, 291, 302

Join Objects command, 108,
    250, 251, 258, 293, 302,
    330, 396, 602
Lock command, 287, 293, 294
Path Operations command, 27
  Blend command, 520, 526,
    582
  Correct Direction command,
    241, 244, 589
  Expand Stroke command,
    524
  Insert Path command, 524,
    526
  Intersect command,
    255-257, 457
  Punch command, 257-259,
    604-605
  Remove Overlap command,
    164
  Reverse Direction command,
    240, 412
  Simplify command, 158
  Union command, 259-260
Send to Back command, 300,
    301, 404, 474, 602
Split Object command, 264,
    293, 302, 411, 605
Strokes Width command, 379,
    383, 501
Text Wrap command, 412, 415
Transform Again command,
    569-570
Ungroup command, 222, 237,
    302
Unlock command, 293, 295,
    326
arrow cursor, 76
Arrow effect, 514-515
  illustrated, 515
  See also PostScript strokes
arrow keys, 228
  entering text and, 313
  extending selection with, 340
  for selecting text, 339
arrow tool, 74, 215
  dragging with, 536
  marqueeing with, 291
  selecting, 215, 238
  text objects and, 326

Arrowhead Editor dialog box, 511-513
  Closed check box, 513
  Copy Out button, 512
  Delete button, 513
  Filled check box, 513
  Grid box, 513
  hidden tools, 512
  illustrated, 511
  Paste In button, 512
  Redo button, 513
  Stroked check box, 513
  toolbox, 512
  Undo button, 513
  view-size pop-up menu, 512
arrowheads, 509-513
  applying, 510
  creating, 512
  designing, 16
  editable, 509
  illustrated, 511
  pop-up menus, 511
  predefined, 510
  sizing, 510
ascenders, 351
ASCII files, 630
attribute styles, 443
  copying, 447
  creating, 444-446
  cutting, 447
  deleting, 447
  duplicating, 446-447
  editing, 445
  function of, 444
  manipulating, 444-446
  redefining, 445
  tagged objects and, 445-446
  using, 443-447
  See also Styles palette
author, contacting, 10
auto joining, 253-254
  illustrated, 254
  See also joining
automatic curvature, 246-248
  Automatic option and, 250
  defined, 246
  illustrated, 247
  removing, 248
  using, 247
automatic hyphenation, 376
  controls, 377
  See also hyphenation
automatic page numbering, 309
axes
  constraint, 153
    changing, 154
    Constrain value, 226

directions, 225
  rotating, 225
  reflecting about, 126

• B •

background, 52
  hiding applications in, 55
  printing in, 53-54
  screen refresh, 54-55
  window, 52
balloon help, 35
banding, 594
  avoiding, 594-595
  defined, 594
baseline shift, 357-358
  defined, 354
  keyboard adjustment, 358
  steps for using, 358
  uses for, 357
  See also formatting
baselines, 328
  defined, 402
Basic options (Stroke panel), 500
  Arrowheads pop-up menus, 509-513
  Cap option, 502-504
  color swatch option, 501
  dash patterns, 507-509
  illustrated, 500
  Join buttons, 504-505
  Miter Limit option, 506-507
  Overprint option, 501
  Width option box, 501-502
bevel join, 505
Bézier control handles, 170, 174
  30-percent rule, 233
    illustrated, 234
  adding, 240-241
  all-or-nothing rule, 233
    illustrated, 234
  displaying, 230
  dragging, 230-234
  moving, 231
  placement of, 176, 233
  retracting, 243-244
  with selected points, 216
Bézier curves, 167
Bézier, Pierre, 166
bézigon cursor, 238
bézigon tool, 75, 237
  Alt-click with, 169
  clicking with, 240
  Option key and, 168
  Option-click and, 168
  Option-drag and, 168
  selecting, 170

  Shift key and, 173
  Shift-click and, 168, 173
  Tab key and, 169
  using, 167-169
    example, 170-172
binary counting system, 29
binding text, 394-412
  ascender/descender lines, 402
  baseline, 402
  baseline shift effect, 405
  break in, 402
  carriage return and, 396
  to ellipses, 405-406
  formatting and, 408-409
  horizontal alignment and direction, 410-412
  leading and, 408, 409
  lengthening, 398-400
  orientation, 406-408
  removing, 397
  reshaping path of, 397-402
  spacing and, 409
  stylistic effects and, 409
  tips for, 396-397
  vertical alignment, 402-405
bit depth, 425
bitmaps, 19
  tracing, 189-191
Black & White Noise effect, 479
bleeds, 645
  creating, 646
  size of, 645-646
Blend panel, 582
  adjusting values in, 582-583
  First option box, 583
  illustrated, 583
  Last option box, 583
  Number of Steps option box, 583
    raising value of, 591
  Range % values, 584
    changing, 585
    changing example, 586
blending
  between gradations, 593-594
  defined, 580
  five separate open paths, 590
  illustrated, 581
  multiple clones and, 589
  paths, 580-595
    multiple, 589-590
  rectangles/ellipses, 581
  shapes with gradations, 585
  two paths, 582
    filled/stroked, 592
    with gradient fills, 593
  See also blends

blends, 580
  creating, 581
  defined, 582
  editing, 595
  recolor, 595
  reshaping, 595
  sample 9-step, 585
  selecting points in, 587-589
  ungrouping, 595
  See also blending
block-level formatting, 380-383
  attributes, 346
  bound text and, 409
  defined, 345
  See also formatting
body copy, 348
borders, displaying, 316
breaking spaces, 315
Bricks effect, 479-480
  illustrated, 480
  options, 480
brightness, 438
buffered drawing, 104
butt caps, 503
buttons, 41
  navigation, 43-44
  radio, 40
  See also specific panel and
    dialog box buttons

• C •

CAD (computer-aided design),
    193
calligraphic lines, 162-165
Cancel button, 43
capital letters, 350
cartoon face, 600
cdevs, 33
CD-ROM, 28
center point, 147
character-level formatting,
    347-362
  attributes, 346
  defined, 345
  spacing, 354
  See also formatting
check boxes, 41
Chooser, 650
  extensions. *See* drivers
  illustrated, 652
  window, 54
Chooser dialog box, 651
  Auto Setup button, 653
  More Choices button, 653
  Setup button, 653

Circles effect, 480-482
  illustrated, 482
  options, 481
CISC (complex instruction set
    computer), 26
Clipboard, 34
  application, 57
  Edit menu commands and, 56
  transferring to Scrapbook, 58
  using, 56-58
clipping paths, 596-600
  adjusting, 599-600
  contents display, 599
  creating, 596-599
  defined, 596
clones, 565-566
  blending and, 589
  flipping, 574
  scaling, 575
cloning, 124
  Groucho Marx eyebrows, 128
  Groucho Marx eyes, 126-127
  objects, 566-569
    partial, 568-569
  ovals, 124
  pages, document, 644
  scaling and, 573-576
  series of transformations,
    571-576
  type, 566-569
close box, 38
closed paths, 118
  changing first point in, 411-412
  interior points and, 236
  stroking, 496
  trace tool and, 198
  See also open paths; paths
CMYK, 79
  color mix, 436-437
  color model, 436-437
Color folder, 442
color images, 204
  converting, to grayscale, 206
  trace tool and, 205
color libraries, 441
  creating, 442
  opening, 442
  spot-color, 441
  using, 441-443
Color List palette, 79, 430
  default settings, 101
  displaying, 430
  fill icon, 430
  illustrated, 431
  Options pop-up menu, 431
    Duplicate option, 430
    Export option, 442

    Make Spot option, 440
    New option, 430
  rearranging colors in, 431
  stroke icon, 430
  using, 430-432
Color Mixer dialog box, 439
Color Mixer palette, 79, 430
  color icons, 435
  dragging from, 434
  function of, 435
  showing/hiding, 435
  transferring colors to, 435
color models, 79, 435
  accessing, 435
  additive primary, 437
  CMYK, 436-437
  defined, 435
  HLS, 438
  RGB, 437-438
  See also Color Mixer palette
color monitor
  calibration, 427-428
  preparing, 426-429
Color Picker, 79, 106
color printing, 423-424
  See also printing
color separations, printing,
    663-667
  options, 664-665
ColorFinder, 429
coloring, shortcuts, 90
colors
  adding, to scrolling color list,
    433
  brightness, 438
  cloning, 430
  creating, 430-443
    new, 430
  deleting, 431
  display
    adjusting, 104-105
    brightness, 429
    hue, 429
    number of, 425
    saturation, 429
  displaying, on-screen, 424-429
  dragging/dropping, 432-434
    advantages, 432
  editing, 431
  gradation, 463
  gray values, 425
  hue, 438
  line, 118
  luminosity, 438
  mixing, 435-438
  organizing, 430-443
  overprinting, 455-456

process, 439, 667
renaming, 431
retrieving, 432
saturation, 438
spot, 439-440, 667
libraries, 441
stroke, 501
variation, 427
Column & Row panel, 273
Column option, 381
Count option, 381
Height/Width option, 381
Row option, 381
Rules option, 381-383
Spacing option, 381
Wrap Order option, 383
column breaks, 313, 319
columns, 381-383
balancing, 385-388
height of, 381
number of, 381
rules, 382-383
spacing, 381
See also rows
commands
arrow symbol and, 8
ellipse following, 39
in this book, 8
*See also specific menus and
commands*
composite masking, 605-609
composite paths, 250
combining text block with, 330
creating, 600-609
defined, 601
groups vs., 293
radial gradation in, 607
illustrated, 608
reshaping, 418
single, 607
text and, 607-609
using, 600-609
computers
anatomy of, 25-31
brains of, 25-29
powering up, 32
sensory organs of, 29-31
using, 23-24
connector points, 168
creating, 174
with pen tool, 177
handles, moving, 175
illustrated, 169
smooth transitions and, 175
uses, 176
using, 174-176
constraint axes, 153

changing angle of, 154
Constrain value, 226
directions, 225
rotating, 225
control handles, 166
associated with type on a
path, 399
Bézier, 170, 174, 176
30-percent rule, 233, 234
adding, 240-241
all-or-nothing rule, 233, 234
displaying, 230
dragging, 230-234
moving, 231
placement of, 176, 233
retracting, 243-244
with selected points, 216
curve point, 173
retracting, 181-182
dragging, independently, 400
moving, independently, 178-
181
restoring, 246
control panel devices, 33
control panels, 33
third-party video boards, 427
Control Panels folder, 426
Control-clicking, 404
converting
graphics, 619
points, 128-129, 244-246
stroked lines to filled shapes,
523-526
strokes, 525
type to paths, 417-419
cooperative multitasking, 45
copy protection, network, 70-71
copyfitting, 383-390
bound text and, 409
controls, 383
defined, 347
See also formatting; text
corner handles, 215
Option-drag, 220
Shift-Option-drag, 326
corner points, 168
corner points neighboring, 185
creating, with one handle,
182-184
illustrated, 169
corners, 118
radius of, 149
rounded, 148-149
Cowden.FH, 53
CPU (central processing unit), 25
crop marks, 646
printing, 661

cropping, imported graphics, 627
cursors, 76-77
bézigon, 238
I-beam, 312
key distance, 108
list of, 76-77
place, 194
curve fit, 157
tracing, 199-200
curve points, 168
changing to corner point, 178
changing to cusps, 179
control handle, 173
retracting, 181-182
creating, 178
illustrated, 169
points neighboring, 185
using, 174
See also points
curved segments, 168
creating, 183
drawing, 173-174
followed by straight, 168
illustrated, 169
Option-dragging, 228
illustrated, 229
See also segments
curves
automatic, 185, 186
Bézier, 167
cusp points, 168
creating, 177-178
defined, 177
examples, 178-183
illustrated, 169
in paths, 400
See also points
Custom option (Fill panel), 477
Black & White Noise option, 479
Bricks option, 479-480
Circles option, 480-482
Hatch option, 482-483
illustrated, 478
Noise option, 484
Random Grass option, 485
Random Leaves option, 485
Squares option, 486-487
Tiger Teeth option, 487-488
Top Noise option, 489
Custom option (Stoke panel),
514
Effect pop-up menu, 514
Arrow, 514
Neon, 516
illustrated, 514

• D •

DAs. *See* desk accessories
Dash Editor dialog box, 508-509
  illustrated, 509
  line caps and, 521
  Off value, 521
  On value, 521
  option boxes, 509
dash patterns, 507-509
  defined, 507
  illustrated, 508
  inline, creating, 522-523
  line caps and, 521-522
  periodicity, 522
  selecting, 508
  stacking, 522-523
  See also patterns; tile patterns
Defaults file, 100-102
  settings, 100-101
Delete key
  in deleting edit window
      contents, 513
  in deleting last text object, 336
  in deleting paths, 243
  in deleting points, 241
  in deleting segments, 242
  in deleting text blocks, 323
  entering text and, 313
deleting
  attribute styles, 447
  automatic curvature, 248
  Bézier control handles, 243-244
  colors, 431
  edit window, 513
  endpoints, 241
  guidelines, 279
  layers, 300
  locked objects and, 295
  pages, document, 644
  paths, 243
  points, 129-131, 241-244
  rectangles, 332
  segments, 242-243
  tab stops, 369
  text blocks, 323
      empty, 324
  text objects, 336
descenders, 351
deselecting, 218-219
  illustrated, 215
  objects, 211, 218-219
  paths, 219, 400
  points, 219
  Tab key and, 218
  text blocks, 324
  See also selecting

desk accessories, 33-34
  types of, 34
desktop. *See* Finder desktop;
      FreeHand desktop
Desktop button, 43
dialog boxes, 39-42
  button, 41
  check box, 41
  navigating, 42-44
  option box, 40
  options in, 40-41
      illustrated, 40
  page setup, 654
  pop-up menu, 41
  print, 655-659
  radio button, 40
  Shift-Tab in, 41
dialog boxes, list of
  Add Pages, 638
  Apple Color Picker, 428
  Apple Color Wheel, 438
  Arrowhead Editor, 511-513
  Chooser, 651
  Color Mixer, 439
  Dash Editor, 508-509
  Display Color Setup, 105, 427
  Expand Stroke, 524
  Export Document, 628-630
  Freehand Tool, 157-158, 162-163
  Image, 206-207, 623-624
  Info, 48-49
  Inline Effect, 360
  Open, 42
  Output Options, 100, 299,
      677-678
  Place Document, 193, 320, 617
  Polygon Tool, 152
  Preferences, 95
  Print Options, 657-659
  Printer, 100
  Rectangle Tool, 148
  Save, 44, 668
  Save Document, 102
  Scale, 550
  Text, 311
  Text Wrap, 412, 414
  Tracing Tool, 199, 201
  Transparency, 256-257, 457
  Zoom Effects, 361-362
digital space, 28-29
directional gradations, 459-463
  converted text filled with, 609
  linear, 459
      illustrated, 460
  logarithmic, 459
      illustrated, 460

  See also gradations; radial
      gradations
directory window, 37
discretionary hyphen, 314
  accessing, 378
  inserting, 321
disk
  ejecting, 43
  printing to, 667-668
disk icon, 36
disk space, 28
  memory vs., 28
Display Color Setup dialog box,
      105, 427
  color swatches, 427, 428
      changing, 428
  current color swatch, 429
  previous color swatch, 429
display modes, 85-86
  pop-up menu, 86
Display panel, 102-106
  Adjust Display Colors option,
      104-105
  Better (But Slower) Display
      option, 103
  Buffered Drawing option, 104
  Calibration button, 427
  Convert PICT Patterns to
      Grays option, 104
  Display Text Effects option,
      104
  Dither 8-bit Colors option,
      104, 425
  Greek Type Below Pixels
      option, 106
  Grid Color option, 277
  Guide Color/Grid Color
      option, 106
  High-Resolution TIFF Display
      option, 105
  illustrated, 103
  Redraw While Scrolling
      option, 104
  Remember Layer Info check
      box, 302
distributing, 282-287
  defined, 286
  objects, 286-287
  steps for, 286-287
  See also aligning
dithering, 104
  8-bit colors, 104
document formats, 36
  native, 36
document icon, 36
  dragging on application icon,
      46

Document Pages panel, 100, 637
  accessing, 637
  Bleed Size option, 273, 645-646
  Custom option, 644
  dragging pages in, 638
  illustrated, 637
  Options pop-up menu
    Add Pages option, 638, 641
    Duplicate option, 644
    Remove option, 644
  page size pop-up menu, 643
  Tall button, 644
  Wide button, 644
Document Setup panel, 100
  Baseline Shift option, 357
  Constrain option, 154, 155,
    173, 225, 538
  Grid Size option, 273, 276
  Printer Resolution pop-up
    menu, 620, 677
documents
  creating, 637-642
  defined, 36
  multipage, 17
    working in, 641
  page-advance icon, 642
  selecting, 43
  setting up, 633-647
  small, 633-635
  See also pages, document;
    pasteboard
donut drawing, 601-605
  finished, 606
  icing on, 606
downloadable fonts, 674-676
drafts, 193
drag preview, 107
dragging
  on application icon, 46
  colors, 432-434
  Command-dragging, 37
  with freehand tool, 155-156
  mouse, 30
  pages, 638-639
  past the point of nothingness,
    546
  with pen tool, 168, 176
  with reflect tool, 552
  with rotate tool, 554
    steps for, 555-557
  with scale tool, 543
    points, 549
  scroll box, 84
  Shift-dragging, 31
  with skew tool, 561-562

  with trace tool, 197
  with transformation tools, 534
  with zoom tool, 83
draw cursor, 77
drawing
  benefits of, 19-20
  buffered, 104
  disk space of, 20
  ellipses, 149-150
  freehand lines, 155-162
  geometric shapes at angles,
    153-154
  Groucho Marx caricature,
    120-143
  issues, fundamental, 2
  with objects, 116-120
  polygons, 150-151
    free-form, 159-161
    sides, 152-153
    straight-sided, 170-172
  rectangles, 146-148
    with rounded corners,
      148-149
  schematic, 17
  segments
    curved, 173-174
    perpendicular, 173
  shortcuts, 89
  stars, 152-153
  straight lines, 154-155
  theory, 18-22
drawing layers, 296
  working with, 296-300
  See also layers
drawing programs, page layout
  and, 308
drivers, 34
drop-launching, 46
duplicating. *See* cloning

• E •

Edit menu
  Clear command, 243
  Clone command, 219, 255, 403,
    471, 567-568
    Option click and, 568
  Copy command, 56, 58, 195, 340
  Cut command, 56, 58, 340, 474,
    592, 596
  Cut Contents command, 599
  Duplicate command, 219, 471,
    567
    Option-click and, 568
    several times, 576

  Paste Behind command, 219,
    302
  Paste command, 45, 56, 58,
    196, 219, 340, 596
  Paste Inside command, 526, 592
  Redo command, 266
  Select All command, 218, 339
  Undo Align Objects command,
    284
  Undo command, 265
  Undo Freehand command, 265
  Undo Move command, 240
  Undo Move Elements
    command, 265
  Undo Remove Layer
    command, 300
  Undo Ungroup command, 222
editing
  attribute styles, 445
  blends, 595
  colors, 431
  grayscale images, 621-627
  hidden preferences, 96-99
  imported graphics, 619
  masked elements, 599
  pages, document, 643-646
  patterns, 465-477
    bitmapped, 466
  Preferences file, 95
  selected objects, 90
  type to path conversion and,
    418
Editing panel, 106-109
  Changing Object Changes
    Defaults option, 108, 297,
    674
  Cursor Key Distance option,
    108, 228, 273, 518, 537
  Dynamic Scrollbar option, 109
  Groups Transform as Unit by
    Default option, 109
  illustrated, 106
  Join Non-Touching Paths
    option, 108, 252
  Number of Undo's option, 107,
    265
  Pick Distance option, 107
  Preview Drag option, 107
  Remember Layer Info option,
    108, 605
  Snap Distance option, 108,
    279, 499
  Snap Distance value, 228
edition file, 37
  icon, 37

effects, 358-362
  applying, 359
  inline, 359-360
  PostScript, 477-492
  shadow, 360
  zoom, 361-362
Eject button, 43
ellipse (...), 39
ellipses
  deselected, 215
  drawing, 149-150
  joining text to, 396
  reshaping, 219-222
  scaling, 220
em dash, 314
en dash, 314
Encapsulated PostScript. *See*
  EPS format
endpoints, 154
  activating, 235
  appending, 235-236
  automatically joining, 181
  defined, 235
  deleting, 241
  fusing, 251-252
  overlapping, 180
  See also points
EPS format, 192
  files, 109, 630
    correct size of, 631
    exporting, 628-631
    linking, 627
  if no EPS, 616
  saving images to, 616
  saving objects to, 616
Expand Stroke dialog box, 524
  Width value, 526
Export Document dialog box,
  628-630
  Format pop-up menu, 629
    Adobe Illustrator option, 629
    ASCII option, 630
    EPS option, 630
    PICT option, 630
    RTF option, 630
  illustrated, 629
  Include FreeHand Document
    in EPS check box, 630
exporting graphics, 628-631
  EPS/PICT files, 628-631
Exporting panel, 109-110
  Bitmap PICT Previews option,
    109
  illustrated, 110
  Include Fetch Preview option,
    110

• F •

Fetch preview, 110
File menu
  Export command, 628, 631
  Find Again command, 70
  Find command, 70
  Get Info command, 48
  Make Aliases command, 37
  New Folder command, 36
  Open command, 42, 46, 616
  Output Options command,
    100, 299, 677
  Page Setup command, 653
  Place command, 193, 219,
    320-321, 616
  Preferences command, 84, 95,
    102-111
  Print command, 655
  Put Away command, 36
  Revert command, 266
  Save As command, 44, 267
  Save command, 44
files
  ASCII, 630
  EPS, 109, 630, 631
  Finder, 33
  graphic
    linking, 628-629
    pasting, 619
    placing, 616-619
  PICT, 630
  RTF, 630
  suitcase, 60-61
  support, 34
  System, 33
  system software, 33-34
  template, 193-196
  TIFF, 192
  See also Preferences file
Fill panel, 316, 432
  accessing, 453
  Angle value, 462
  dragging color swatch from, 433
  illustrated, 453
  manipulations performed in,
    476
  offset options, 540
  Option-clicking on color
    swatch, 458
  Overprint check box, 455
  pop-up menu, 453
    Basic option, 454, 457
    Custom option, 477
    Graduated option, 458, 459
    None option, 454

    Pattern option, 466
    PostScript option, 477
    Radial option, 458, 463
    Textured option, 477, 490
    Tile option, 467, 474
  uses, 453
filling
  across multiple shapes, 607
  with directional gradation, 433
  objects, 430
  paths, 211, 433
  with radial gradation, 433
  selections, 433
  text blocks, 433
  type, 433
fills, 118
  benefits of, 449
  defined, 449
  flat, 433, 449-452
    assigning, 453-458
    changing color of, 455
  gradient, 458-465
    defined, 458
    illustrated, 458
  lifting color of, 457-458
  objects and, 450-451
  open paths and, 450
  PostScript, effects, 477-492
    applying, 477
    Black & White Noise, 479
    Bricks, 479-480
    Circles, 480-482
    custom, 478-490
    Hatch, 482-483
    Noise, 484
    Random Grass, 485
    Random Leaves, 485
    Squares, 486-487
    textures, 490-492
    Tiger Teeth, 487-488
    Top Noise, 489
    transparent routines,
      489-490
  single-color, 454-458
  text and, 452-453
  transparent, 454
  See also filling
Finder desktop, 33
  elements of, 34-37
  function, 34
  illustrated, 35
  running program from, 46
Finder file, 33
flat fills, 433, 449-452
  assigning, 453-458
  changing color of, 455

single-color, 454-458
transparent, 454
See also filling; fills
flatness, 676
flipping
clones, 574
objects, 551-554
Reflect Axis value and, 554
partial paths, 552-553
with reflect tool, 552
floating palettes, 73-74
collapse box, 73
contents of, 74
displaying, 80
explained, 78
navigating, 92-93
See also specific palettes
floating-point unit (FPU), 26
optimized operations for, 27
floppy disks, 28
mounted, 36
flowing
reflowing, 335-337
text from one block to
another, 333-339
type, 334
folder bar, 42
folder icon, 36
folders, 36
creating, 36
current, 42
exiting, 43
opening, 43
parent, 42
selecting, 43
See also specific folders
font metrics, 62
fonts, 59
compression of, 67
defined, 347
downloadable, 674-676
installation disk, 68
multiple master, 62
nonresident, 674
outline, 59
PostScript, 59-62
printer, 61-62
scalable, 347
screen, 59-61
storing, 675
SuperATM, 62
TrueType, 62-63
typefaces vs., 347
using, 59-63
variable-size, file, 62
variable-width, 365

See also type; type size; type
styles
Fonts folder, 60-61
footers, 319
footnotes, 319
formatting
block-level, 380-383
attributes, 346
bound text and, 409
defined, 345
bound text and, 408-409
character-level, 347-362
attributes, 346
defined, 345
spacing, 354
defined, 345
options, 346
paragraph-level, 362-380
attributes, 346
defined, 345
See also copyfitting; text
formatting attributes, 345
block-level, 346
character-level, 346
default, 101
paragraph-level, 346
four-color process printing, 663
illustrated, 664
free-form artwork, 121
FreeHand 1.0 documents, 66
FreeHand
Adobe Streamline vs., 204
defined, 14
disk contents, 66-68
features missing from, 308-309
getting started with, 65-66
hiding, 55
Illustrator files and, 18
Illustrator vs., 15-18
installing, 66-71
Photoshop vs., 18-19
as right program, 14-18
top ten tasks, 16-17
when to use, 21
FreeHand desktop, 72-80
elements of, 73-74
illustrated, 72
freehand tool, 75, 155
bound text and, 401
double-clicking on, 162
dragging, 155-156
erasing with, 159
extending open path with, 161
Option key and, 160-161
pressure-sensitive, 162
selecting, 157

sketching paths with, 161-162
straight segments with, 159
using, 155-157
Freehand Tool dialog box,
157-158
Angle option box, 165
Calligraphic Pen option, 162,
165
Draw Dotted Line option, 158
Fixed button, 165
illustrated, 162
Min and Max option boxes, 163
Tight Fit option, 157, 158
Variable button, 165
Variable Stroke button, 162
freehand
curve fit, 157-158
drawing, 155-162
mouse use and, 157
See also drawing

• G •

geometric shapes, 146-154
at angles, 153-154
ellipse, 149-150
polygon, 150-153
rectangle, 146-149
scaling, 220
ungrouping, 222
See also specific shapes
gigabyte, 29
grabber hand, 85
gradations, 118
angle, 460-461
illustrated, 461
blending between, 593-594
blending shapes with, 585
changing colors of, 463
custom, 463
creating, 590-595
directional, 433, 459-463
blending, 594
converted text filled with, 609
display control for, 103
flipping colors of, 461-462
formula for smooth, 594
linear, 459
illustrated, 460
logarithmic, 459
illustrated, 460
pasting, 598
radial, 433, 463-465
blending, 594
center point, 465
in composite paths, 607-608

creating, 463
illustrated, 464
options, 464
radial options for, 464
See also gradient fill
gradient fills, 458-465
defined, 458
illustrated, 458
See also fills; gradations
Graduated option (Fill panel), 459
Angle option, 460-461, 462
color swatches, 459
From/To swatches, 459
Taper pop-up menu, 459-460
Logarithmic option, 462
graphic files
linking, 627-628
pasting, 619
placing, 616-619
with Open command, 617
with Place command, 617
graphics
converting, 619
imported
cropping, 627
editing, 619
manipulating, 619-627
scaling, 619-620
importing, 614-619
scaling, 620-621
uneditable, 620
See also graphic files
grave key (`), 215, 291
fourth time, 292
second time, 292
third time, 292
gray value, 425
grayscale images
colorizing, 622
editing, 621-627
gray values, 209
illustrated, 210
saving to TIFF, 614-615
scanning, 206
selecting, 622
tracing, 204-211
one level at a time, 206-209
grids, 276
display, 277
sizes, 276
separate, 277
space between, 276
using, 276-277
See also guidelines
Groucho Marx caricature,
120-143

cigar, 129-132
deleting/adding points and,
129-131
layering shapes and, 131-132
pasting end of, 132
tracing end of, 130
cigar smoke, 142
collar, 140-142
completed, 143
complex shapes in, 138-139
ear, 138, 139, 140
eyebrows, 127-129
cloning, 128
left, 127
reflecting, 134
reshaping, 129
eyes, 122-127
cloning the oval, 124
cloning/transforming right
eye, 126-127
crescent-shaped wrinkle,
124-125
filling shapes, 125-126
first oval, 122-123
finishing the face, 137-140
keyline mode view, 137
lapels, 140-141
low-resolution sketch, 122
nose and mustache, 132-137
adding second nose,
136-137
changing eyebrow to
mustache, 133-135
rough sketch, 121-122
tie, 141
grouping
layering and, 302
objects, 287-293
defined, 288
facts of, 288-289
illustrated, 290, 291
steps for, 291-292
See also ungrouping
groups, 219
composite paths vs., 293
multiple paths in, 291
selecting, 291
individual objects in, 291
transforming as unit, 109,
289-291
ungrouping, 292-293
multiple, 292
wrapping text around, 413
guidelines, 278
controlling, 279
creating, 278-279
deleting, 279

locking, 279
moving, 279
type and, 334
See also grids

• **H** •

halftone cells, 661
5x5-pixel, 671
defined, 670
illustrated, 670
Halftone palette, 79, 444
Angle option box, 673
default settings, 101
Frequency option box, 673
illustrated, 669
Screen pop-up menu, 671
Default option, 671
Ellipse option, 672
Line option, 672
options illustrated, 672
Round Dot option, 672
halftone patterns, 79
printing, 16
halftone screens, 669-674
altering, 669
halftoning, 670
hand cursor, 76
handles
coordinates of, 220-221
side, 325
dragging, 325
Option-dragging, 326
text block, 312, 321-326
top/bottom, 324
using, 220
See also corner handles
hanging indents, 371
hard disk icon, 36
Hatch effect, 482-483
illustrated, 483
options, 482
headers, 319
help
balloon, 35
cursor, 77
Help menu, 35
hiding
applications, 55
Color Mixer palette, 435
layers, 299
path outline, 316
templates, 123
toolbox, 92
hierarchical submenus, 39
HLS, 79
color model, 438

holes, 601
  creating, 601-605
    with Punch command,
      604-605
    illustrated, 603-604
    shadow, 603
Horizontal pop-up menu
  Align Center option, 285
  Align Left option, 284
  Distribute Widths option, 286,
    334
  No Change, 285
hue, 438
hyphenation, 375-378
  automatic, 376
    controls for, 377
    wrapped text and, 416
  bound text and, 409
  discretionary, 314, 321, 378
  manual, controls, 378

• I •

I-beam cursor, 312
icons
  alias, 37
  Align palette, 287
  application, 37
  Application menu, 55
  Cap, 503
  Curve Handles, 181, 240, 243,
    249
  defined, 36
  disk, 36
  document, 36
  edition file, 37
  folder, 36
  hard disk, 36
  mapping, 624
    Invert, 627
    Normal, 626
    Posterize, 627
    preset, 625-627
    Solarize, 627
  Move, 472, 537
  page advance, 73
  panel, 78
  Point Type, 244-246, 249, 400
  Reflect, 258, 472
  RGB, 438
  System Folder, 36
  tab, 367
  in this book, 9-10
  tool, 73
  trash, 36
  Wrapping Order, 383

illustration window, 73
  setting defaults, 101
  view size, 81-82
  working in, 80-87
Illustrator. *See* Adobe Illustrator
Image dialog box, 206-207
  Apply button, 624
  brightness graph, 623
  Contrast scroll arrows, 624
  illustrated, 207
  Lightness scroll arrows, 624
  mapping icons, 624
  moving bars in, 624
  special effects created in, 625
image editors, 19
image mapping, 623-625
images
  color, 204
  tracing, 196-201
    grayscale, 204-211
    imported, 16
    size of, 200-201
  See also EPS format; imported
    images; PICT; TIFF
    images
imported graphics
  cropping, 627
  editing, 619
  manipulating, 619-627
  scaling, 620-621
imported images
  colorizing, 622
  editing, 621-627
  tracing, 16, 187-211
  See also images
importing
  graphics, 614-619
  stories, 317-321
  text, 317-321
  TIFF images, 17
  tracing templates, 191-196
indent markers, 369-370
  accessing, 370
  first-line, 369
  illustrated, 369
  left, 369
  right, 370
indents, 319
  bound text and, 409
  hanging, 371
  options, 370
  paragraph, 369-370
  types of, 370-371
Info dialog box, 48-49
  illustrated, 48
  Memory Requirements values,
    48-49

information bar, 73, 279
  displaying, 279
  guide to, 280-281
  illustrated, 280
  using, 279-281
INITs. *See* system extensions
Inline Effect dialog box, 360
  illustrated, 360
  options, 360
insertion marker, 312
  moving, 397
    to beginning of text, 314
    to end of text, 314
inset paths, creating, 526
inset values, 332-333
Inspector palette, 78-79
  Document Pages panel, 100
  Document Setup panel, 100
  illustrated, 78
  Object panel, 181
  panel icons, 78
  Text Alignment panel, 101
  Text Character panel, 101
  Text Paragraph panel, 101
  Text Spacing & Hyphenation
    panel, 101
  words below title bar, 293
  *See also specific Inspector
    palette panels*
installation
  advice, 68-70
  disks
    compression, 67
    contents, 66-68
  FreeHand, 66-71
Installer/Utility, 66, 68, 69
interior points, 171
Intersect command (Path
    Operations menu), 255-
    257
  characteristics, 255
  choosing, 255
  Option key and, 256
  using, 256
italicized words, 8

• J •

joining
  auto, 253-254
  layering and, 302
  open paths, 250-254
  two lines with straight
    segment, 252-253
JPEG image compression, 614-615

• K •

kerning, 355-357
  defined, 354
  function of, 355
  keyboard adjustments, 282, 357
  letterspacing vs., 374
  measurement of, 374
  range, 355
  tables, 309
  See also formatting
kerning pairs, 356
  illustrated, 356
keyboard
  extended, 38
  mouse and, 31
  techniques, 29
keyboard shortcuts
  Command-2, 82
  Command-3, 93
  Command-4, 82
  Command-5, 82
  Command-6, 93, 194, 296, 474
  Command-7, 92
  Command-9, 93, 430
  Command-/, 94
  Command-A, 218, 284, 339, 574
  Command-B, 209, 300, 404, 474
  Command-backslash, 278
  Command-C, 56, 58, 195, 340,
    447, 512
  Command-comma, 569, 570
  Command-Control-spacebar, 84
  Command-D, 43, 219, 471, 567,
    574, 575
  Command-dragging, 37
  Command-E, 43, 94, 628
  Command-equal, 219, 255, 403,
    471, 567, 574
  Command-F, 70, 300
  Command-G, 70, 288, 291, 330,
    471, 568
  Command-grave, 80, 93, 534
  Command-H, 93
  Command-hyphen, 321, 378
  Command-I, 48, 82, 92, 94, 206
  Command-J, 94, 108, 250, 251,
    258, 293, 330, 396, 568, 602
  Command-K, 86, 87, 397, 404,
    412
  Command-L, 287, 294
  Command-left arrow, 44, 94, 397
  Command-left bracket, 301
  Command-M, 93, 94, 258, 472,
    533

Command-N, 36
Command-O, 42, 43, 46, 616
Command-Option-A, 93, 371, 411
Command-Option-B, 92, 206,
  273, 316, 333, 497
Command-Option-C, 93, 94, 383
Command-Option-D, 93, 100,
  273, 637
Command-Option-Escape, 69
Command-Option-F, 93, 461, 474
Command-Option-I, 92, 181,
  220, 248
Command-Option-K, 93, 374
Command-Option-L, 93, 273,
  316, 379, 496
Command-Option-P, 93, 362,
  370, 372
Command-Option-R, 92, 273, 380
Command-Option-T, 93, 352, 378
Command-P, 650, 655
Command-period, 43, 56, 86,
  87, 209, 667
Command-quote, 228
Command-R, 271
Command-right arrow, 44, 94,
  397
Command-right bracket, 301
Command-S, 44
Command-semicolon, 276
Command-Shift-A, 93, 282
Command-Shift-C, 93, 435
Command-Shift-comma, 351
Command-Shift-D, 193, 219,
  320, 616, 619
Command-Shift-E, 520, 526,
  582, 591
Command-Shift-J, 264, 411,
  568, 605
Command-Shift-L, 295
Command-Shift-M, 314
Command-Shift-N, 314
Command-Shift-P, 417
Command-Shift-R, 273, 279,
  368, 538
Command-Shift-T, 315
Command-Shift-Tab, 93
Command-Shift-U, 315, 326, 330
Command-Shift-V, 94, 526, 592,
  598
Command-Shift-W, 414, 416
Command-Shift-X, 599
Command-Shift-Y, 250, 394,
  396, 404, 412
Command-Shift-Z, 93
Command-T, 93, 348

Command-Tab, 85
Command-U, 222, 237, 417,
  568, 595
Command-V, 56, 58, 196, 219,
  340, 447, 512, 567, 596
Command-W, 82
Command-X, 56, 58, 340, 447,
  474, 526, 592, 596
Command-Y, 36, 266
Command-Z, 222, 240, 265,
  284, 300, 432, 545
  defined, 29
  entering text and, 313-314
  Tab, 93
  See also shortcuts
keyline mode, 85, 397
  access to, 86
  Groucho Marx view in, 137
kilobytes (K), 29
knife tool, 75
  for creating break in paths, 242
  dragging, 261
  on points/segments, 264
  Shift-dragging with, 262
  for slicing, 261
  for splitting, 260-261

• L •

layering, 201
  grouping and, 302
  joining and, 302
  objects, 295-302
layers
  assigning objects to, 297
  Background, 296-297
  creating, 297-298
  default, 296-297
    creating, 297
  deleting, 300
  drawing, 296
    working with, 296-300
  Foreground, 296
  Guides, 296
  hiding, 299
  object, 108
  protecting, 299-300
  reordering, 298
  showing, 299
  stacking order, changing,
    300-302
  unlocking, 300
Layers palette, 79, 194
  Background option, 197
  default settings, 101

Foreground option, 194, 197
   illustrated, 296
   Options pop-up menu, 296
      All Off option, 299
      All On option, 299
      Duplicate option, 298
      New option, 297
   using, 296
leading, 324
   automatic, 388
   bound text and, 408, 409
   defined, 354
   first-line, 388
   increasing/decreasing, 354-355
   measurement, 354-355
letterspacing, 325, 374
   kerning vs., 374
   manipulating, 374-375
   values, 375
      examples of, 376
   wrapped text and, 416
   See also formatting
limitcheck errors, 676-677
   avoiding, 677
line breaks, 313, 319
line caps, 502-504
   butt, 503
   dash patterns and, 521-522
   defined, 502
   icons, 503
   round, 503
   square, 504
   stacking, 522-523
   uses, 503
line joins, 504-505
   bevel, 505
   defined, 504
   miter, 505
      cutting short, 506-507
   round, 505
line tool, 75
   selecting, 155
   Shift-drag with, 155
   using, 154-155
lines, 116
   color of, 118
   defined, 118
   drawing
      calligraphic, 162-165
      freehand, 155-162
      straight, 154-155
   examples of, 117
   extending, 161
   joining, with straight segment,
      252-253

path, 117-118
   points, 117
   properties of, 118
   shapes vs., 116-118
   stroked, converting, 523-526
   thickness of, 164
   weight of, 118
      stroke, 501-502
link box, 312
   dragging from, 396
   redragging, 335
locking, 293-295
   defined, 293
   layers, 299-300
   objects, 287, 293-295
   paths, 293
      steps for, 294
logic board, 25
luminosity, 438
LZW compression, 615

• **M** •

Mac icon, 32
MacPaint, 614
   format, 191, 614
Macworld FreeHand 4 Bible
   conventions, 7-10
   features, 2
   organization, 3-7
Magnification submenu, 82
mapping
   gray-value, 624
   icons, 624
      Invert, 627
      Normal, 626
      Posterize, 627
      preset, 625-627
      Solarize, 627
   image, 623-625
   linear, 623
   preset, icons, 625-627
marqueeing
   with arrow tool, 291
   for selecting multiple objects,
      217
   Shift key and, 219
   with Shift-clicking, 217
masked elements, 596
   adding, 599
   adjusting, 599-600
   editing, 599
   stacking order, 600
   transforming, 599
masking, 467, 471
   composite, 605-609

masking object. *See* clipping paths
masks, 596
   restoring, 599
   See also clipping paths
master pages, 309
math coprocessor. *See* floating-
      point unit (FPU)
medials, 351
megabytes (MB), 29
memory, 27
   disk space vs., 28
   fragmentation, 50-51
   hard-wired, 27
   requirement values, 48-49
   tile patterns and, 477
   uninterrupted, 50
   See also RAM (random access
      memory); ROM (read-
      only memory)
menu bar, 34
menus, 39
   pop-up, 41
   See also specific menus
miter join, 505
   cutting short, 506-507
Miter Limit value, 506
   range of, 507
modes, display, 85-86
Monitors control panel, 426
   illustrated, 426
monochrome images, 191
morphing, 580
motherboard, 25
mouse
   clicking, 30
   double-clicking, 30
   dragging, 30
   dust particles and, 157
   freehand drawing and, 157
   keyboard and, 31
   moving, 30
   press and hold, 30
   techniques, 30
move cursor, 77
Move panel, 472, 537
   illustrated, 538
   using, 538
   X and Y options, 541
moving, 223-234
   Bézier control handle, 231
   constraining, 225-226
   in direct distances, 538-540
   objects, 535-541
      Control-drag points, 537
      dragging-with arrow tool, 536

press and hold to preview, 536-537
press arrow key, 537
press Option to preview, 537
press Shift after drag to constrain, 537
snap to points, 537
pages in pasteboard, 638-639
points, 223-224
multiple, 224
tab stops, 369
multitasking, 45

• N •

navigation buttons, 43-44
Neon effect, 516
strokes with, 520
networks, copy protection, 70-71
Noise effect, 484
NuBus video boards, 425, 426

• O •

Object Column & Row panel, 380
Object Copyfitting panel, 383
Balance option, 383, 385
result of using, 387
Copyfit % option, 383, 388
Max value, 388
Min value, 388
First Line Leading option, 388
Ignore Column Less Than option box, 386
illustrated, 385
Modify Leading option, 383, 386
result of using, 387
Object Dimensions & Insert panel, 273, 316
Display Border check box, 316, 383, 433, 497
Inset values option, 333
Object panel, 181, 248-250
accessing, 220
Automatic check box, 246, 248
defined, 249-250
blank, 248
Closed check box, 249
Curve Handles icons, 181, 240, 243
defined, 249
Dimensions option boxes, 220, 289
Edit Image button, 206-207, 208, 623

Even/Odd Fill option, 249
Flatness option, 249
illustrated, 221, 248
Point Location option, 250
Point Type icons, 244-246, 400
defined, 249
Show Path check box, 497
with single group selected, 289-290
Transform as Unit check box, 290
Transparent check box, 207
vertical alignment options, 403
objects
aligning, 282-285
assigning, to layers, 297
blending, 17
cloning, 567-569
partial, 568-569
color assignment to, 17
coloring, shortcuts for, 90
copying, 57
deselecting, 211, 218-219
drawing with, 116-120
duplicating, 566-569
enlarging, 542-551
filling, 430
fills and, 450-451
flipping, 551-554
Reflect Axis value and, 554
grouped, 215
selecting, 217
selecting individual, 291
grouping, 287-293
defined, 288
facts for, 288-289
steps for, 291-292
layering, 295-302
layers of, 108
locked
deleting and, 295
dragging, 295
locking, 287, 293-295
moving, 535-541
Control-drag a point, 537
drag with arrow tool, 536
press and hold to preview, 536-537
press arrow key, 537
press Option to preview, 537
press Shift after drag to constrain, 537
snap to point, 537
pasting, 132

reducing, 542-551
reflecting, 471
rotating, 554-558
saving, from revision, 567
scaling, 542-551
selecting, 90
slanting, 559-563
spacing, 286-287
stacking, 567
stacking order of, 295
strokes and, 496-497
stroking, 430
swapping, between illustrations, 567
text, 309-317
adjusting, 321-339
composite, 330-332
defined, 309
deleting, 336
free-form, 315-317, 330-332
illustrated, 310
reshaping, 326-333
transforming, 533
ungrouping, 326-328
transferring, 567
ungrouping, 292-293
unlocking, 295
See also Object panel
OK button, 43
Open dialog box, 42
open paths, 118
blending, 590
extending, 161
fills and, 450
interior points and, 236
joining, 250-254
steps for, 251
stroking, 496
See also closed paths; paths
operating system. *See* system software
option boxes, 40
Option-clicking, 31
Option-dropping, 465
out-of-memory errors, 678
remedies for, 678-679
Output Options dialog box, 100
Flatness value, 678
illustrated, 299, 677
Include Invisible Layers option, 299, 679
Maximum Color Steps value, 678
Split Complex Paths check box, 677

oval
    cloning, 124
    points in, 123
    scaling, 124
    See also ellipses
oval tool, 75
    accessing, 150
    Option key and, 150
    Shift key and, 150
    Shift-dragging with, 237
    using, 149-150
overflow text, 333
overprinting, 455

• P •

page setup dialog boxes, 654
pages, document
    cloning, 644
    deleting, 644
    editing, 643-646
    moving, in pasteboard, 638-639
    navigating between, 640-642
    page-advance icon, 642
    printing different sized,
        644-645
    sizes of, 643
    viewing, 640-641
    See also documents
pages, outputting, 650-657
    printing, 655-659
    setting, 660-661
    setting up, 653-654
    transverse, 660
painting programs, 19
    advantages, 189
    drawbacks, 20-21, 189
    image examples of, 190
palettes. *See* floating palettes
Paper pop-up menu, 660
paragraph alignment, 371-372
paragraph indents, 369-370
paragraph rules, 373
    creating, 378-380
    spacing and, 380
paragraph spacing, 319, 372-373
    defined, 373
    vertical, 372-373
paragraph-level formatting, 362-
    380
    attributes, 346
    defined, 345
    See also formatting
pasteboard, 636-637
    defined, 636
    illustrated, 636

moving around, 637
moving between pages in,
    640-642
moving pages in, 638-639
uses, 637
view sizes, 640-641
viewing, 637
    active page, 641
    See also documents
pasteboard error, 535
    bypassing, 535
pasting
    behind, 302
    end of Groucho Marx cigar, 132
    gradations, 598
    graphic files, 619
    objects, 132
Path Operations submenu.
        See Arrange menu, Path
        Operations command
paths, 117
    adding points inside, 236-240
    adding points to, 172
    appearance, 118
    beginning, 172
    binding text to, 394-412
    blending, 580-595
        multiple, 589-590
    breaks, creating in, 242
    clipping, 596-600
        adjusting, 599-600
        contents display, 599
        creating, 596-599
        defined, 596
    closed, 118
        changing first point in,
            411-412
        interior points and, 236
        stroking, 496
        trace tool and, 198
    closing, 172
    coincident, 251
    combining, 250-267
        outlines, 254-260
    composite, 250
        combining text block with,
            330
        creating, 600-609
        defined, 601
        groups vs., 293
        radial gradation in, 607-608
        reshaping, 418
        single, 607
        text and, 607-609
        using, 600-609
    constructing, 145-186

converting type to, 417-419
cusp in, 400
deleting, 243
deselecting, 219, 400
determining, 119-120
direction of, 412
filling, 211, 433
free-form, 155-162
hiding, outline, 316
inline, 517-519
inset, 526
lengthening type, 398
locking, 293
    steps for, 294
multiple
    blending, 589-590
    in group, 291
open, 118
    blending, 590
    extending, 161
    fills and, 450
    interior points and, 236
    joining, 250-254
    stroking, 496
partial
    rotating, 557-558
    scaling, 548-549
    skewing, 562
reblending, 595
scaling, partial, 548-549
selecting, 215-216
    multiple, 215
sketching, 161-162
source, 582
    points and, 587
    selecting, 595
    windup differences, 585
splitting, 250-267, 676-678
straight, 154-155
stroking, 211, 433
text separation from, 317
transforming, 533
ungrouping, 329
windup, 582
    last step gap, 587
    points and, 587
    selecting, 595
    source differences, 585
    See also segments
Pattern option (Fill panel), 466
    Clear button, 467
    Invert button, 467
patterns
    applying, 465-477
    bitmapped, 466-467
    collection of, 466

dash, 507-509
  defined, 507
  illustrated, 508
  inline, creating, 522-523
  line caps and, 521-522
  periodicity, 522
  selecting, 508
  stacking, 522-523
  editing, 465-477
    bitmapped, 466
  stroke, 516-517
  tile, 467-477
    assigning, 468-474
    creating, 468-474
    defining, 467
    memory and, 477
    opaque, 471-474
    printing, 678-679
    type and, 476
  See also tiles
PDS (processor direct slot)
      video boards, 425-426
pen tool, 75, 176-186
  advantages, 184-186
  Alt-click and, 170
  clicking with, 240
  Command key and, 182
  for complex path creation, 184
  for connector point creation,
      177
  for creating cusps, 177-178
  dragging with, 168, 237
    illustrated, 176
  for inserting points, 237
  Option key and, 168, 179, 182
  Option-drag and, 168, 177
  selecting, 170
  Shift-click and, 168
  Tab key with, 170
  using, 167-169
periodicity, 522
Photoshop
  FreeHand vs., 18-19
  when to use, 21-22
  See also painting programs
PICT, 191-192
  bitmap previews, 109
  files, 630
    exporting, 628-631
  pattern conversion, 104
  saving to, 616
pixels, 19
place begin cursor, 77
Place command (File menu), 193,
      219, 320-321
  canceling, 321
  dragging with, 320

place cursor, 194
  dragging with, 321
Place Document dialog box, 193,
      320, 617
  exiting, 618
place end cursor, 77
point size, 351
pointer tool, 215
points, 117
  adding, 129-131, 172, 235-241
    inside paths, 236-240
    steps for, 237-239
  center, 147
  connector, 168, 169
    using, 174-176
  Control-dragging, 226
  converting, 128-129, 244-246
  corner, 168, 169
    corner points neighboring,
      185
    creating, with one handle,
      182-184
  curve, 168, 169
    changing to corner point, 178
    changing to cusps, 179
    control handle, 173, 181-182
    creating, 178
    points neighboring, 185
    using, 174
  cusp, 168, 169
    creating, 177-178
  deleting, 129-131, 241-244
  deselecting, 219
  endpoints, 154
    activating, 235
    appending, 235-236
    automatically joining, 181
    defined, 235
    deleting, 241
    fusing, 251-252
    overlapping, 180
  function of, 119
  inserting, 237
    in paths of bound text, 401
  interior, 171
  knife tool and, 264
  moving, 223-224
    as created, 170
    multiple, 224
  paths, 219
  segments and, 117, 118, 167
  selecting, 216-218
    in blends, 587-589
    multiple, 216
  splitting, 260-264
    interior, 264

  too many, 139
polygon tool, 75
  dialog box, 152
  selecting, 151
  Shift key and, 151
  using, 150-151
polygons
  center points and, 151
  drawing, 150-151
    free-form, 159-161
    straight-sided, 170-172
  equilateral, 150
popsicle, creating, 596-598
pop-up menus, 41
  display mode, 73
  view size, 73, 82
PostScript fill effects, 477-492
  applying, 477
  Black & White Noise, 479
  Bricks, 479-480
  Circles, 480-482
  custom, 478-490
  Hatch, 482-483
  Noise, 484
  Random Grass, 485
  Random Leaves, 485
  Squares, 486-487
  textures, 490-492
  Tiger Teeth, 487-488
  Top Noise, 489
  transparent routines, 489-490
PostScript fonts, 59-62
  installing, 59-62
  printer, 61-62
  screen, 59-61
  See also fonts
PostScript language, 667
PostScript printer definition
      (PPD), 653
  selecting, 660
PostScript printers, 653
  Flatness option and, 249
PostScript strokes, 513-517
  Arrow effect, 514-515
  illustrated, 515
  Neon effect, 516
PostScript textures, 490-492
  illustrated, 492
  previewing, 491
PowerPC 6100, 424
PowerPC, 26-27
  Calculator desk accessory, 540
  software, 27
  video display, 424-425
preference settings, 94-95
  factory default, 94

Preferences command (File
      menu), 84, 95, 102-111
   Display panel, 102-106
   Editing panel, 106-109
   Exporting panel, 109-110
   Sounds panel, 110-111
Preferences dialog box, 95
   Preview Drag value, 537
Preferences file, 70, 95-100
   AlwaysEmbedImports, 99
   contents, 96
   CrackPlacedEPS, 99
      modifying, 618
   editing, 95
   hidden preferences, 96-99
   NewDocumentTemplate, 99
   NewStylesTakeCurProps, 99
   RememberDocumentView, 98
   SaveWindowSizeNLoc, 97
   StockLineWeights, 98
   TiffModePrintOverride, 98
   update, 95
   UseQTCompression, 97
   UserPSIncludeFile, 97-98
   ViewingSetsActivePage, 97
Preferences submenu, Edit
      command, 84
preview mode, 85
   navigating in, 17
previewing
   multiple objects, 537
   press and hold for, 536
print dialog boxes, 655-659
   Copies option box, 655
   Destination option, 658, 667
   illustrated, 655
   LaserWriter 7/LaserWriter 8,
      656
   Pages buttons, 655
   Paper buttons, 656
   Print As option, 658
   Print button, 659
   Scale option, 657
   Tile buttons, 657
   See also Print Options dialog
      box; printing
Print Options dialog box, 657-659
   Cover Page option, 658
   displaying, 657
   Halftone Screen pop-up menu,
      661
   illustrated, 659
   Imaging Options option, 662-663
   Page Labels option, 662
   Paper pop-up menu, 660-661

PostScript Errors option, 658
Print option, 658
Printer Marks option, 661-662
Select PPD option, 660
Separations options, 659,
      664-665
   screen angle, 665-666
   Transfer Function pop-up
      menu, 661
printed page, 635-646, 649-650
Printer dialog box, 100
printer drivers, 651-653
   defined, 651
   LaserWriter 7, 658
   LaserWriter 8, 653
Printer Resolution pop-up menu,
      620
   illustrated, 621
printers
   downloading to, 667
   non-PostScript, 653-654
      setup dialog boxes, 654
   PostScript, 249, 653
   RAM, 675
   resolution, 661
   See also printer drivers
printing, 649-679
   in background, 53-54
   cancelling, 667
   color, 423-424
   color separations, 663-667
   crop marks, 661
   custom halftone patterns, 16
   differently sized pages,
      644-645
   to disk, 667-668
   four-color process, 663
      illustrated, 667
   illustrations, 650-651
   initiating, 667
   to laser printer, 645
   pages, 655-659
   pattern tiles, 678-679
   process-color, 439
   spot-color, 663
   strokes, 501
   See also print dialog box
programs. *See* applications
protected-mode multitasking, 45
Punch command (Path Opera-
      tions menu), 257-259
   characteristics, 255
   choosing, 255
   multiple paths and, 255
   using, 259

• Q •

QuickDraw picture, 191-192
QuicKeys, 56, 427
QuickTime, 69, 615

• R •

radial gradations, 103, 433,
      463-465
   center point, 465
   in composite paths, 607
      illustrated, 608
   creating, 463
   illustrated, 464
   options for, 464
   See also directional grada-
      tions; gradations
Radial option (Fill panel), 433,
      463-465
   color swatches, 464
   Locate Center box, 464
radio buttons, 40
radius, 149
   corner, 149
RAM (random access memory),
      27
   application, 47
   assigning, 47
   dividing up, 28
   erasing, 32
   printer, 675
   viewing, 49
   VRAM (video RAM), 424
      bit depth and, 425
   See also Memory
Random Grass effect, 485
Random Leaves effect, 485
rectangle tool, 74, 219
   dialog box, 148
   double-clicking on, 148
   operation, 147
   Option-drag with, 147-148
   selecting, 148
   Shift key and, 148
rectangles
   deleting, 332
   deselected, 215
   drawing, 146-148
   reshaping, 219-222
   with rounded corners, 148-149
   scaling, 220
   ungrouping, 222
redoing, 266
Reflect panel
   displaying, 553
   illustrated, 553

options, 553-554
Reflect Axis option, 553-554
reflect tool, 75, 541
dragging with, 552
flipping with, 552
icon, 553
Shift-drag with, 552
using, 551-554
reflecting, 134
about an axis, 126
objects, 471
reflection axis, 552
reshaping
blends, 595
composite paths, 418
options and limitations,
400-402
paths of bound text, 397-402
rectangles/ellipses, 219-222
text objects, 326-333
retracting, 181
reverting, 266-267
RGB, 79
color mix, 437
color model, 437-438
icon, 438
RISC (reduced instruction set
computer), 26
ROM (read-only memory), 27
See also Memory
Rotate panel
illustrated, 558
options, 558
rotate tool, 75, 542
dragging with, 554
steps for, 555-557
Option-clicking with, 558
using, 554-558
rotating
objects, 554-558
partial paths, 557-558
segment length and, 558
rotation axis, 554
illustrated, 555
transformation origin and,
554-555
round caps, 503
dashes and, 522
round join, 505
rows, 381-383
number of, 381
rules, 381-382
spacing, 381
width of, 381
See also Column & Row panel;
columns

RTF (Rich Text Format), 318
files, 630
ruler origin, 220
box, 274
illustrated, 275
rulers
hiding, 271
horizontal, 271
origin, changing, 274-275
tab, 312, 367
tracking lines and, 273-274
units of measure, 272-273
using, 271-275
vertical, 271
visible, 271

• **S** •

saturation, 438
Save Changes? alert box, 41
Save dialog box, 44, 668
Save Document dialog box, 102
scalable fonts, 347
Scale dialog box, 550
Scale panel
Center option boxes, 550
Contents check box, 551
displaying, 550
Fills check box, 551
illustrated, 550
Lines check box, 551
options, 550-551
Scale Factor % option box, 550
Uniform check box, 550
scale tool, 75, 201, 541
constraining, 547-548
dragging with, 543
points, 549
playing with, 544-546
reflecting/scaling simultaneously, 546
Shift-drag with, 220, 548
using, 542-549
scaling, 124
clones, 575
constraining, 547-548
duplicating and, 573-576
graphics, 620-621
objects, 542-551
ovals, 220
partial paths, 548-549
rectangles, 220
text, 326
See also Scale panel; scale tool
scans, 192

Scrapbook, 58
retrieving data from, 58
screen angles, 665, 673
illustrated, 666, 673
screen frequency, 661
defined, 673
Frequency values, 673-674
screen function, 671
screen refresh
background, 54-55
canceling, 86-87
reinitiating, 87
scroll bars, 38
dynamic, 109
scroll box, dragging, 84
scrolling list, 43
scrolling, redrawing while, 104
segments, 117, 167
arcs and, 118
corners and, 118
curved, 168, 169
creating, 183
drawing, 173-174
followed by straight, 168,
169
Option-dragging, 228, 229
deleting, 242-243
knife tool and, 264
perpendicular, 173
splitting, 260-264
straight, 168, 169
followed by curve, 168, 169
joining two lines with, 252-
253
Option-dragging, 229
stretching, 228-230
See also paths
selecting, 214-218
defined, 214
everything, 218
grayscale images, 622
grouped objects, 217
paths, 215-216
multiple, 215
points, 216-217
in blends, 587-589
multiple, 216
source/windup paths, 595
text, 339-340
on a path, 397
See also deselecting
shadows, 360
drop, 360
hole, 603
shapes
applying patterns to, 465
complex, 138-139

constraining, 148
defined, 118
filling, 125-126, 131
geometric, 146-154, 220, 222
layering, 131-132
lines vs., 116-118
multiple, 288
properties of, 118
skewing, 134
Shift-dragging, 31
shortcuts, 87-90
coloring objects, 90
drawing lines/shapes, 89
editing selected objects, 90
formatting text, 89
navigation tricks, 88
selecting objects, 90
special characters, 89
text tricks, 88
See also keyboard shortcuts
side bearing, 355
illustrated, 356
size box, 38
sketches, 193
Skew panel, 562-563
accessing, 562
Center option boxes, 563
illustrated, 563
Skew Angles option boxes, 563
skew tool, 75, 542
dragging with, 561-562
Shift-dragging with, 560, 573
example, 561-562
using, 560-563
skewing, 559
Groucho Marx eyebrows, 135
illustrated, 559
monitoring, 560
objects, 559-563
partial paths, 562
shapes, 134
See also Skew panel; skew tool
slicing, 260-264
snap distance, 108
snapping, 226-228
defined, 226
Distance value, 228
illustrated, 227
turning on/off, 228
uses, 226
sonic snapping, 110
Sound panel, 110-111
illustrated, 111
Play Sounds When Mouse Is
Up option, 111
Snap Sound Enabled option, 110

source path, 582
points and, 587
selecting, 595
windup differences, 585
spaces
breaking, 315
fixed-width, 314-315
variable-width, 314
spacing
bound text and, 409
character-level attributes, 354
columns/rows, 381
effects of, 380
letters, 374-375
paragraph, 319, 372-373
rule, between, 380
text, 353-358
words, 374-375
wrapped text and, 415-416
special characters
entering text and, 313-314
shortcuts for, 89
word processors and, 319
Special menu, Empty Trash
command, 36
splash screen, 71
Option-clicking on, 71
splitting, 260-264
long paths, 250-267, 676-678
steps for, 261-263
spot colors, 439-440
adding, 440
angles, 667
libraries, 441
selecting, 440
spot-color printing, 663
square caps, 504
Squares effect, 486-487
illustrated, 487
options, 486
stacking
dash patterns, 522-523
line caps, 522-523
objects, 567
strokes, 517-520
stacking order, 295
changing, 300-302
forward and backward, 301
paste in back, 302
stars
drawing, 152-153
illustrated, 153
starting, applications, 45-46
Startup Disk control panel, 32
steps, 580
See also blending

stories
chain, 333
defined, 317
importing, 317-321
reflowing, 335-337
separating text blocks from,
338
straight segments, 168
followed by curve, 168
illustrated, 169
illustrated, 169
joining two lines with, 252-253
Option-dragging, 229
Stroke panel, 316, 379, 432, 496
displaying, 496, 499
dragging color swatch from, 433
None option, 499
Pattern option, 499
pop-up menu
Basic option, 500
Custom option, 514
PostScript option, 499
Width option, 273
Stroke Width submenu, 501-502
default weights, 502
strokes
assigning, 495-526
attributes, mixing, 517-523
color of, 501
converting, 525
defined, 495
expanding, 524-526
industry standard, 496
line weight, 501-502
multiple, 498
neon, 520
objects and, 496-497
offset clones, 519
patterned, 516-517
PostScript, 513-517
illustrated, 515
printing, 501
single-color, 500-513
stacking, 517-520
text and, 497-498
viewing only, 498
stroking
characters of type, 497
dragging/dropping and, 499
objects, 430
paths, 211, 433
illustrated, 496
selections, 433
See also Stroke panel; strokes
StuffIt, 67
Expander, 69-70

style sheets, 309
Styles palette, 79, 443
    default settings, 101
    illustrated, 444
    Options pop-up menu
        Duplicate option, 446
        New option, 446, 474
        Redefine option, 445
        Remove option, 447
    See also attribute styles
submenus, 38
SuperATM, 62
SuperVideo control panel, 427
    illustrated, 427
support files, 34
Switch-A-Roo, 427
System 6
    printer fonts and, 61
    screen fonts and, 60
    TrueType fonts and, 63
System 7.0
    printer fonts and, 61
    screen fonts and, 60
    TrueType fonts and, 63
System 7.1
    printer fonts and, 61
    screen fonts and, 60
    TrueType fonts and, 63
system extensions, 33
System file, 33
System Folder, 32
    files, 33
    icon, 36
system software
    defined, 31
    elements, 39-44
    files, 33-34
    licensing and, 31
    organization, 31-34
    storage, 31
    using, 31-38

• **T** •

tab characters, 319, 365
    conserving, 365
tab icons, 367
Tab key
    for deselecting elements, 261
    entering text and, 313
tab ruler, 312
    horizontal ruler, 367
    icon strip, 367
    illustrated, 367
    marker strip, 367
    using, 367

tab stops, 363-369
    advantages of, 363-366
    assigning, 368
    bound text and, 409
    center, 367
    controlling, 363
    decimal, 367
    deleting, 369
    effect of, 368
    left, 367
    moving, 369
    positioning, 367-369
    right, 367
    wrapping, 367, 368
        illustrated, 368
        second, 369
tables, creating, 17
tabs. *See* tab stops
Tag Image File Format. *See* TIFF
    images
TeachText, 70
template files, 193-196
    pasting, 195-196
    placing, 193-195
templates, 122
    deselecting, 197
    gray, 122
    showing/hiding, 123
    subtle features in, 137
    tracing, 191
        copying, 195
        drafts, 193
        importing, 191-196
        kinds of, 192-193
        protecting, 195
        scans, 192
        size of, 200-201
        sketches, 193
text, 307
    alignment, 319
        changing, 371-372
    binding, to paths, 394-412
        ascender/descender lines,
            402
        baseline, 402
        baseline shift effect, 405
        break in, 402
        carriage return and, 396
        on ellipses, 405-406
        formatting and, 408-409
        horizontal alignment and
            direction, 410-412
        leading and, 408, 409
        lengthening, 398-400
        orientation, 406-408
        removing, 397

        reshaping, 397-402
        spacing and, 409
        stylistic effects and, 409
        tips, 396-397
        vertical alignment, 402-405
    colors, 319
    composite paths and, 607-609
    entering, 312-313
        key functions in, 313
        keyboard options, 313-314
        special characters and,
            313-314
    fill attribute and, 359
    fills and, 452-453
    flowing from one block to
        another, 333-339
    formatting, 89
    importing, 317-321
    indents, 319
    orientation, 406-408
    outline, 318
    overflow, 333
    plain, 318
    preparing, 318-319
    reflowing, 335-337
    replacing, 339-340
    scaling, 326
    selecting, 339-340
    separating from path, 317
    shortcuts, 88
    size and leading, 318
    spacing, 353-358
        letters, 374-375
        paragraphs, 372-373
        words, 374-375
    spacing out, 324-326
    special effects, 393-419
    stroke attribute and, 359
    styles, 318
    tabs and, 319
    typefaces, 318
    vertical alignment of, 402-405
    wrapping
        alignment and spacing,
            415-416
        around graphics, 412-416
        around objects, 394
        frustration of, 414
        settings, 414
        standoff dummy and, 416
    wrapping order, 383
    See also copyfitting; format-
        ting; text blocks; text
        objects; type
Text Alignment panel, 362
    accessing, 371

Alignment icons, 371, 411
alignment settings, 372
Flush Zone % option box, 371
Ragged Width % option box,
    371, 415
text blocks, 311-312
    adjusting size of, 322
    breaking into two lines, 322
    breaking link between, 339
    creating, 309-315
    deactivating, 314, 323-324
    default, 311
    defined, 309
    deleting, 323
        empty, 324
    deselecting, 324
    enlarging, 321-323, 336
    filling, 433
    flowing text from, 333-339
    handles, 312
        manipulating, 321-326
    increasing width of, 323
    linking, 333
    rectangular, 317
    reducing, 321-323
    separating from stories, 338
    unwrapping, 416
    See also text
Text Character panel
    Baseline Shift option, 273, 405
    Effect pop-up menu, 359
        Inline Effect option, 359
        Shadow Effect option, 360
        Zoom Effect option, 361
    Horizontal Scale option box,
        351-352
    illustrated, 354
    Inhibit Hyphens check box,
        362, 378
    Keep On Same Line check box,
        362
    Kerning option, 354, 355
    keyboard kerning adjustments
        and, 282
    Leading option, 354
    Range Kerning option, 353,
        355, 357
text cursor, 77
Text dialog box, 311
text effects, displaying, 104
text objects, 309-317
    adjusting, 321-339
    composite, 330-332
    defined, 309
    deleting, 336
    free-form, 315-317

changing dimensions of,
    330-332
illustrated, 310
reshaping, 326-333
ungrouping, 326-328
See also objects; text; text
    blocks
Text on a Path panel
    displaying, 404
    illustrated, 403
    options, 405
    Orientation pop-up menu, 406
        Rotate Around Path option,
            407
        Skew Horizontally option,
            407
        Skew Vertically option, 407
        Vertical option, 407
    Show Path check box, 397
    Top pop-up menu
        Ascent option, 404
        Descent option, 405
Text palettes, 101
Text Paragraph panel, 362
    All Paragraph Spacing option,
        273
    Edit button, 379
    Hanging Punctuation check
        box, 372
    Indent options, 370
    Indents option boxes, 273
    Left option box, 370
    Lines Together option, 363
    Paragraph Spacing options,
        363, 373
        Above value, 373
        Below value, 373
    Rules pop-up menu, 378
Text Spacing & Hyphenation
    panel, 362
    Automatic check box, 416
    Consecutive option, 377
    illustrated, 374
    Language option, 377
    Letter column Max value, 416
    Skip Capitalized option, 377
    Spacing % options, 374
        Max values, 375
        Min values, 375
        Opt values, 374-375
    Spacing values, 363, 375
text tool, 74
    selecting, 311
    for selecting text, 339
    Shift-drag with, 311
    using, 310-311

Text Wrap dialog box, 412
    displaying, 414
    illustrated, 414
    Standoff Distances values, 416
Textured option (Fill panel), 490
    illustrated, 491
textures, PostScript, 490-492
    illustrated, 492
    previewing, 491
TIFF format, 192
    with LZW compression, 192
TIFF images
    high-resolution, 105
    importing and manipulating, 17
    linking, 627-628
    saving, 614-615
Tiger Teeth effect, 487-488
    illustrated, 488
    options, 487
Tile option (Fill panel), 467
    Angle option, 468
    Copy Out option, 468
    illustrated, 468
    Offset option, 468
    Paste In option, 468, 470
    Scale option, 468
    selecting, 474
tile patterns, 467-477
    assigning, 468-474
    creating, 468-474
    defining, 467
    memory and, 477
    opaque, 471-474
    printing, 678-679
    transforming
        independent of path,
            475-476
        objects and, 476
    type and, 476
    See also dash patterns;
        patterns
tiles, 465, 467-477
    boundaries of, 473
    creating, 469-470
    illustrated, 470
    transforming, 470
    using, 469-470
    See also patterns; tile patterns
tiling, 644
tints, 441
    adding, 441
    creating, 441
    See also colors
Tints palette, 79, 430
    dragging color swatch from, 433
    illustrated, 441

title bar, 37
toolbox, 31, 73
  Arrowhead Editor, 512
  categories, 76
  hiding/showing, 92
  See also tools
tools, 74-76
  arrow, 74, 215, 238, 291, 326, 536
  Arrowhead Editor, 512
  bezigon, 75, 167-173, 240
  freehand, 75, 155-162, 401
  keyboard equivalent for, 91
  knife, 75, 242, 260-261
  line, 75, 154-155
  oval, 75, 149-150
  pen, 75, 176-186, 237, 240
  pointer, 215
  polygon, 75, 150-152
  rectangle, 74, 147-148, 219
  reflect, 75, 541, 551
  rotate, 75, 542, 554
  scale, 75, 220, 541, 542-549
  selecting, 91
  skew, 75, 542
  text, 74
  trace, 75, 196-198, 202, 205-208
  transformation, 532
  zoom, 75, 82-84
Top Noise effect, 489
trace tool, 75, 196-198
  advantages, 202
  closed paths and, 198
  color images and, 205
  disadvantages, 202
  double-clicking on, 209
  dragging with, 197
  grayscale images and, 205-206
  marqueeing with, 208
  using, 197
tracing
  automated, 196-201
  comparisons, 202-204
  contents included in, 201
  curve fit, 199-200
  example image, 191
  layer control, 201
  scanned images, 188-189
  templates, 191
    copying, 195
    drafts, 193
    importing, 191-196
    kinds of, 192-193
    protecting, 195
    scans, 192
    size of, 200-201
    sketches, 193
Tracing Tool dialog box

Tight check box, 199
Trace Background check
  box, 201
Trace Foreground check box,
  201, 208, 209
tracking lines, 273-274
transform cursor, 77
Transform palette, 80, 201
  cycle through, 534
  displaying, 258, 472, 533
  illustrated, 532
  Move icon, 472, 537
  panel icons, 78
  panels, 534
  Reflect tool, 532
  Rotate tool, 532
  Scale tool, 532
  Skew tool, 532
transformation origin, 544, 554
  center of rotation and, 555
transformation tools, 532
  dragging with, 534
  reflect, 541, 551
  rotate, 542, 554-558
  scale, 541, 542-549
  skew, 542, 560-563
transformations, 531-563
  moving, 535-541
  repeating, 569-570
  series of, 571
  *See also specific transfor-
    mations*
transforming
  objects, 532-535
    text, 533
  paths, 533
Transparency dialog box, 256,
  457
  illustrated, 257
Trash icon, 36
TrueType fonts, 62-63
type
  converting, to paths, 417-419
  duplicating, 566-569
  effects, 358-362
  on ellipses, 405-406
  enlarging, 350-353
  filling, 433
  flowing, 334
  guidelines and, 334
  measurement, 350
  point size, 351
  reducing, 350-353
  size and leading, 318
  tile patterns and, 476
  See also text; type size;
    type styles

Type menu
  Bind to Path command, 250,
    394, 402, 404, 517
  Convert to Paths command,
    293, 417, 452, 498, 523
  Flow Inside Path command,
    315, 326, 330
  Font submenu, 349
  Path Operations command, 402
  Remove From Path command,
    317, 330, 396, 397, 402
  Special Character command
    End of Column command,
      313
    End of Line command, 313
  Type Style submenu, 349
Type on a Path panel, 406
Type palette, 79
  Bold option, 350
  BoldItalic option, 350
  displaying, 348
  option boxes, 349-350
  pop-up menus, 349
  settings, 101
  size pop-up menu, 351
type size, 60
  automatic adjustment of, 388
    enlarging, 389
    reducing, 390
  bound text and, 408
  changing, 351
  horizontal scale and, 351-353
  See also fonts; type
type styles, 60, 318
  applying, 348-349
  bold, 348
  bold italic, 348
  changing, 349
  families and, 348
  italic, 348
  oblique, 348
  Roman, 348
  See also fonts
typefaces, 318
  applying, 348-349
  fonts vs., 347

• U •

undos, 265-266
  multiple, 265-266
  redoing and, 266
  reverting and, 266-267
ungrouping, 292-293
  blends, 595
  geometric shapes, 222, 292-293
  geometric text object, 326-328

multiple groups, 292
paths, 329
using, 293
See also grouping
Union command (Path Operations
    submenu), 259-260
  characteristics, 255
  choosing, 255
  function of, 259
unlocking
  layers, 300
  objects, 295
unwrapping, text blocks, 416

• V •

version numbers, 8-9
Vertical pop-up menu
  Align Bottom option, 286
  Align Center option, 285
  Align Top option, 285
  No Change option, 284
video boards
  full-color, 425
  third party, 425-426
    control panels, 427
View menu
  Grid command, 276
  Guides command, 279
  Info Bar command, 273, 279
  Lock Guides command, 279
  Magnification command, 82
    Fit All command, 300, 640
  Preview command, 86
  Rulers command, 271
  Scientific command, 540
  settings, 101
  Snap to Grid command, 276, 278
  Snap to Point command, 228,
    243, 251, 537
view sizes, 81-82, 640-641
  changing, 81
  commands for, 82
  fit-in-window, 81
  maximum, 84
vocabulary, this book, 7-8
VRAM (video RAM), 424
  bit depth and, 425

• W •

Wacom ArtZ, 163
watch cursor, 77
weight, 118

windows
  background, 52
  deactivating, 37
  directory, 37
  illustrated, 38
  illustration, 73, 80-87
  parts of, 37-38
Windows menu, Layers
    command, 296
windup path, 582
  last step gap, 587
  points and, 587
  selecting, 595
  source differences, 585
words
  hyphenating, 375-378
  spacing, 326, 374-375
    illustrated, 376
    manipulating, 374-375
  See also text
wrapping order, 383
  effects, 384
wrapping text
  alignment and spacing,
    415-416
  around graphics, 412-416
  around groups, 413
  around objects, 394
    multiple, 413
  frustration of, 414
  illustrated, 413
  settings, 414
  standoff dummy and, 416
  steps for, 413-414
  unwrapping and, 416

• Z •

zoom box, 38
zoom effects, 361-362
Zoom Effects dialog box, 361-362
  illustrated, 362
  options, 361-362
zoom in cursor, 76
zoom limit cursor, 76
zoom out cursor, 76
zoom tool, 75, 82-84
  accessing, 84
  dragging with, 83
  Option-click with, 82
  Option-drag with, 84
  using, 82-84

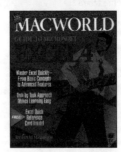

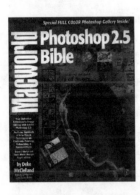

Order Form

Order Center: (800) 762-2974 (8 a.m.-5 p.m., PST, weekdays) or (415) 312-0650

For Fastest Service: Photocopy This Order Form and FAX it to: (415) 358-1260

Quantity	ISBN	Title	Price	Total

Shipping & Handling Charges

Subtotal	U.S.	Canada & International	International Air Mail
Up to $20.00	Add $3.00	Add $4.00	Add $10.00
$20.01-40.00	$4.00	$5.00	$20.00
$40.01-60.00	$5.00	$6.00	$25.00
$60.01-80.00	$6.00	$8.00	$35.00
Over $80.00	$7.00	$10.00	$50.00

In U.S. and Canada, shipping is UPS ground or equivalent.
For Rush shipping call (800) 762-2974.

Subtotal _____

CA residents add applicable sales tax _____

IN and MA residents add 5% sales tax _____

IL residents add 6.25% sales tax _____

RI residents add 7% sales tax _____

Shipping _____

Total _____

Ship to:

Name _____

Company _____

Address _____

City/State/Zip _____

Daytime Phone _____

Payment: ❏ Check to IDG Books (US Funds Only)   ❏ Visa   ❏ Mastercard   ❏ American Express

Card# _____ Exp._____ Signature_____

Please send this order form to: IDG Books, 155 Bovet Road, Suite 310, San Mateo, CA 94402.

Allow up to 3 weeks for delivery. Thank you!